THE ARCTIC
65

Greenland
65

Western Canada
and Alaska
36-37

CONTINENTAL MAP:
NORTH AMERICA
34-35

Aleutian Islands
36-37

Eastern Canada
38-39

C A N A D A

The Pacific
States
50-51

Central and
Mountain States
46-47

The Great
Lakes
44-45

Northeastern
United States
40-41

U N I T E D S T A T E S
O F A M E R I C A

The Southwestern
States
48-49

The Southern
States
42-43

THE ATLANTIC OCEAN
66-67

Hawaii
144-145

Mexico
52-53

Central America
and the Caribbean
56-57

THE PACIFIC OCEAN
144-145

Northern
South America
58-59

Brazil
60-61

CONTINENTAL MAP:
CENTRAL AND
SOUTH AMERICA
54-55

Fiji
144-145

CONTINENTAL MAP:
AUSTRALASIA AND OCEANIA
142-143

Southern
South America
62-63

ew Zealand
148

Falkland
Islands
66-67

THE ANTARCTIC
64

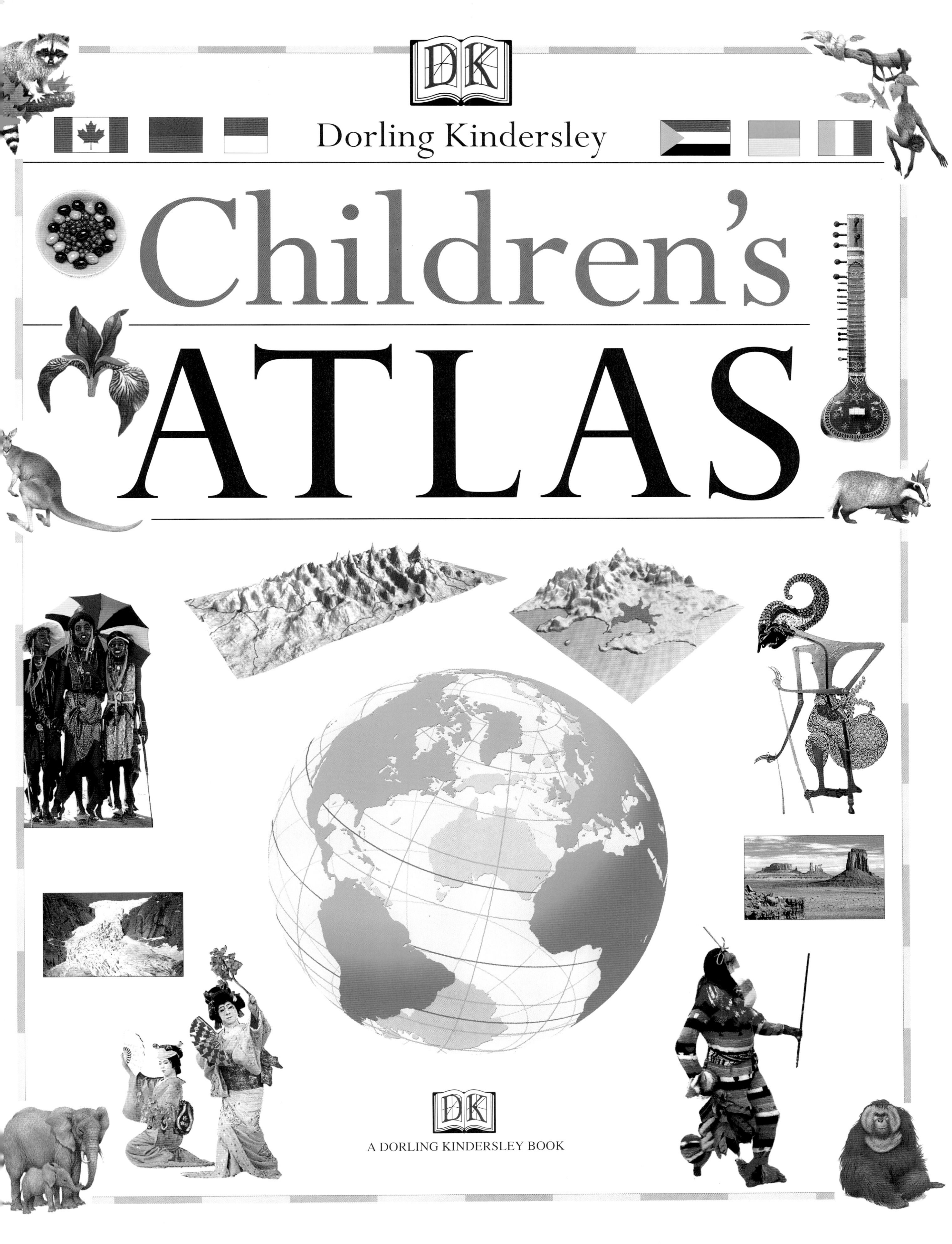

Dorling Kindersley

Children's ATLAS

A DORLING KINDERSLEY BOOK

DORLING KINDERSLEY
www.dk.com
LONDON • NEW YORK • SYDNEY •
DELHI • PARIS • MUNICH • JOHANNESBURG

NEW EDITION

Project Editor
Elizabeth Wyse

Editorial Assistance
Sam Atkinson

Index Gazetteer
Julia Lynch

Systems Coordinator
Phil Rowles

Cartographic Publisher
Andrew Heritage

Project Cartographers
James Anderson • Martin Darlison

Cartography
Ruth Hall • Christine Johnston
John Plumer • Jane Voss • Peter Winfield

Digital Maps Created in DK Cartopia by
Rob Stokes

Senior Cartographic Editor
Roger Bullen

Senior Managing Cartographer
David Roberts

Project Art Editors
Nicola Liddiard
Carol Ann Davis

Senior Managing Art Editor
Philip Lord

Picture Research
Deborah Pownall

Production
Shivani Pandey

FIRST EDITION

Project Editor
Elizabeth Wyse
Caroline Lucas

Editors
Jayne Parsons • Phillip Boys
Chris Whitwell • Donna Rispoli
Margaret Hynes • Ailsa Heritage
Sue Peach • Laura Porter

Project Cartographer
Julia Lunn

Cartography
Roger Bullen • Michael Martin
James Mills-Hicks • James Anderson
Yahya El-Droubie • Tony Chambers
Simon Lewis • Caroline Simpson

Project Art Editor
Nicola Liddiard

Design
Lesley Betts • Rhonda Fisher
Paul Blackburn • Jay Young

Illustrations
John Woodcock • Kathleen McDougall
Mick Gillah • David Wright

Photography
Andy Crawford • Tim Ridley • Steve Gorton

Picture Research
Clive Webster • Charlotte Bush • Frances Vargo
Sharon Southren • Caroline Brook

Art Director
Chez Picthall

Production
Susannah Straughan

CONSULTANTS

Consultant editor
Dr. David R. Green,
Department of Geography, King's College

Contributors
Peter Clark, Former Keeper,
Royal Geographical Society, London
Martin McCauley, Senior Lecturer in Politics,
School of Slavonic and East European Studies, University of London

Dorling Kindersley would also like to thank
Dr. Andrew Tatham, Keeper, and the Staff of the Royal Geographical Society, London, for their help and advice in preparing this Atlas

Professor Jan-Peter A. L. Muller,
Professor of Image Understanding and Remote Sensing,
Department of Photogrammetry and Surveying, University College London

Department of Photogrammetry and Surveying, University College London:
Philip Eales (Producer) • Kevin Tildsley • David Rees
James Pearson • Peter Booth • Tim Day • Planetary Visions Ltd

First published in Great Britain in 1994
by Dorling Kindersley Limited,
9 Henrietta Street, London WC2E 8PS

Reprinted in 1994
Second Edition 1996
Reprinted with revisions 1998
Fully revised and updated edition 2000

A CIP catalogue record for this book is available from the British Library.

ISBN 0-7513-6015-5

Color reproduction by Colourscan, Singapore
Printed and bound in Spain by Artes Gráficas Toledo, S.A.U.
D.L. TO: 657 - 2000

This Atlas was first published in 1994 as the DK Eyewitness Atlas of the World

Contents

The Earth in Space • 4-5
The Earth's Structure • 6-7
Shaping the Landscape • 8-9
Climate and Vegetation • 10-11
People and Planet • 12-13
The World Today • 14-15
How to use this Atlas • 16

The British Isles • 17-32
Physical British Isles • 17
Political British Isles • 18-19
Southern England • 20-21
Central England • 22-23
Northern England • 24-25
Wales • 26-27
Scotland • 28-29
Ireland • 30-31
The Environment • 32

The Atlas of the World

North America • 34-35
Western Canada and Alaska • 36-37
Eastern Canada • 38-39
Northeastern United States • 40-41
The Southern States • 42-43
The Great Lakes • 44-45
Central and Mountain States • 46-47
The Southwestern States • 48-49
The Pacific States • 50-51
Mexico • 52-53

Central and South America • 54-55
Central America and the Caribbean • 56-57
Northern South America • 58-59
Brazil • 60-61
Southern South America • 62-63
The Antarctic • 64
The Arctic • 65
The Atlantic Ocean • 66-67

Europe • 68-69
Scandinavia and Finland • 70-71
The British Isles • 72-73
Spain and Portugal • 74-75
France • 76-77
The Low Countries • 78-79
Germany • 80-81
The Alpine States • 82-83
Central Europe • 84-85
Italy and Malta • 86-87
Southeast Europe • 88-89
Romania and Bulgaria • 90-91
Greece • 92-93
The Baltic States and Belarus • 94-95
European Russia • 96-97
Ukraine, Moldova and the Caucasus Republics • 98-99

Africa • 100-101
Northwest Africa • 102-103
Northeast Africa • 104-105
West Africa • 106-107
Central Africa • 108-109
Central East Africa • 110-111
Southern Africa • 112-113
The Indian Ocean • 114-115

North and West Asia • 116-117
Turkey and Cyprus • 118-119
The Near East • 120-121
The Middle East • 122-123
Central Asia • 124-125
Russia and Kazakhstan • 126-127

South and East Asia • 128-129
The Indian Subcontinent • 130-131
China and Mongolia • 132-133
China and Korea • 134-135
Japan • 136-137
Mainland Southeast Asia • 138-139
Maritime Southeast Asia • 140-141

Australasia and Oceania • 142-143
The Pacific Ocean • 144-145
Australia and Papua New Guinea • 146-147
New Zealand • 148

Glossary and Picture Acknowledgements • 149-150

Index-Gazetteer • 151-176

The Earth in Space

The Earth is one of nine planets that orbit a large star – the Sun. Together they form the solar system. All life on Earth – plant, animal and human – depends on the Sun. Its energy warms our planet's surface, powers the wind and waves, drives the ocean currents and weather systems, and recycles water. Sunlight also gives plants the power to photosynthesize – to make the foods and oxygen on which organisms rely. The fact that the Earth is habitable at all is due to its precise position in the solar system, its daily spin, and an annual journey around the Sun at a constant tilt. Without these, and the breathable atmosphere that cloaks and protects the Earth, it would be as barren as our near-neighbours Venus and Mars.

Asteroid belt
Mars 687 days
Jupiter 12 years
Uranus 84 years
Mercury 88 days
Earth 365 days (1 year)
Venus 225 days
Neptune 165 years
Saturn 29 years
Pluto 248 years

THE SOLAR SYSTEM

Although the planets move at great speeds, they do not fly off in all directions into space because the Sun's gravity holds them in place. This keeps the planets circling the Sun. A planet's "year" is the time it takes to make one complete trip around the Sun. The diagram shows the length of the planet's year in Earth-days or Earth-years.

THE SUN

The Sun is 1,392,000 km (865,000 miles) across. It has a core temperature of 14 million°C and a surface temperature of 5,500°C.

Venus 465°C
Mars -23°C
Mercury Day: 430°C Night: -180°C
Earth 15°C
Jupiter -150°C
Saturn -180°C
Uranus -210°C
Neptune -220°C
Pluto -230°C

*You can use this sentence to remember the sequence of planets: **M**any **V**ery **E**ager **M**ountaineers **J**og **S**wiftly **U**p **N**ew **P**eaks.*

Above: The relative sizes of the Sun and planets, with their average temperature.

Mercury 57,910,000 km (36 ,000,000 miles)
Venus 108,200,000 km (67,200,000 miles)
Earth 149,500,000 km (92,900,000 miles)
Mars 227,940,000 km (141,600,000 miles)
Jupiter 778,330,000 km (483,000,000 miles)
Saturn 1,426,980,000 km (886,700,000 miles)
Uranus 2,870,990,000 km (1,783,000,000 miles)
Neptune 4,497,070,000 km (2,800,000,000 miles)
Pluto 5,913,520,000 km (3,670,000,000 miles)

Above: The planets and their distances from the Sun.

The Life Zone: The Earth seems to be the only habitable planet in our solar system. Mercury and Venus, which are closer to the Sun, are hotter than an oven. Mars, and planets still farther out, are colder than a deep freeze.

Huge solar flares, up to 200,000 km (125,000 miles) long, lick out into space

THE FOUR SEASONS

The Earth always tilts in the same direction on its 950 million-km (590 million-mile) journey around the Sun. This means that each hemisphere in turn leans toward the Sun, then leans away from it. This is what causes summer and winter.

MARCH 21ST (EQUINOX)

Spring in the northern hemisphere; autumn in the southern hemisphere. At noon, the Sun is overhead at the Equator. Everywhere on Earth has 12 hours of daylight, 12 hours of darkness.

DECEMBER 21ST (SOLSTICE)

Summer in the southern hemisphere; winter in the northern hemisphere. At noon, the Sun is overhead at the Tropic of Capricorn. The South Pole is in sunlight for 24 hours, and the North Pole is in darkness for 24 hours.

It takes 365 days 6 hours 9 minutes 9 seconds for the Earth to make one revolution around the Sun. This is the true length of an Earth "year"

To North Star

The Earth takes 23 hours 56 minutes 4 seconds to rotate once. This is the true length of an Earth "day"

Sun

The Earth travels around the Sun at 107,244 km per hour (66,600 miles per hour)

South Pole

JUNE 21ST (SOLSTICE)

Summer in the northern hemisphere; winter in the southern hemisphere. At noon, the Sun is overhead at the Tropic of Cancer. The North Pole is in sunlight for 24 hours, and the South Pole is in darkness for 24 hours.

SEPTEMBER 21ST (EQUINOX)

Autumn in the northern hemisphere; spring in the southern hemisphere. At noon, the Sun is overhead at the Equator. Everywhere on Earth has 12 hours of daylight, 12 hours of darkness.

24 HOURS IN THE LIFE OF PLANET EARTH

The Earth turns a complete circle (360°) in 24 hours, or 15° in one hour. Countries on a similar line of longitude (or "meridian") usually share the same time. They set their clocks in relation to "Greenwich Mean Time" (GMT). This is the time at Greenwich (London, UK), on longitude 0°. Countries east of Greenwich are ahead of GMT. Countries to the west are behind GMT.

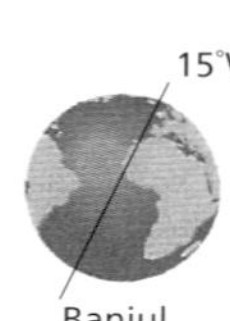
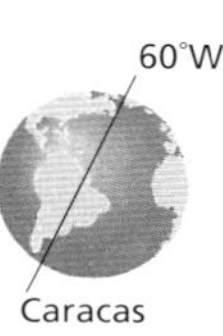
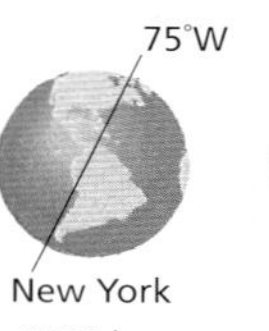
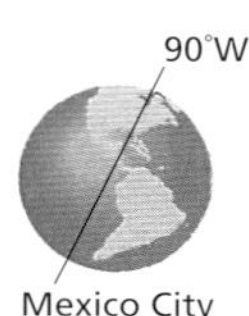
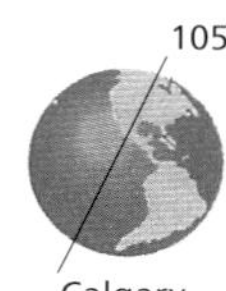
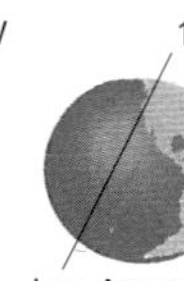
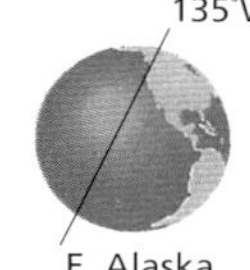
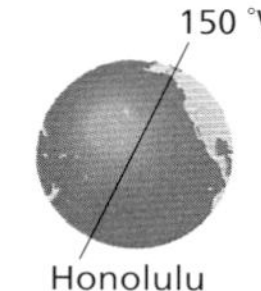

Noon on this meridian

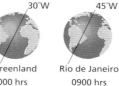

	0°	15°W	30°W	45°W	60°W	75°W	90°W	105°W	120°W	135°W	150°W	165°W
Noon at:	Greenwich	Banjul	E. Greenland	Rio de Janeiro	Caracas	New York	Mexico City	Calgary	Los Angeles	E. Alaska	Honolulu	(Pacific Ocean)
Greenwich time:	1200 hrs	1100 hrs	1000 hrs	0900 hrs	0800 hrs	0700 hrs	0600 hrs	0500 hrs	0400 hrs	0300 hrs	0200 hrs	0100 hrs

Craters made by collision with meteors

MOON AND EARTH

The Moon is a ball of barren rock 3,476 km (2,156 miles) across. It orbits the Earth every 27.3 days at an average distance of 384,400 km (238,700 miles). The Moon's gravity is only one-sixth that of Earth – too small to keep an atmosphere around itself, but strong enough to exert a powerful pull on the Earth. The Moon and Sun together create tides in the Earth's oceans. The period between successive high tides is 12 hours 25 minutes. The highest (or "spring") tides occur twice a month, when the Moon, Sun and Earth are in line.

The Moon's surface temperature falls from 105°C in sunlight to -155°C when it turns away from the Sun

MAGNET EARTH

The Earth acts like a gigantic bar magnet. As the Earth spins in space, swirling currents are set up within its molten core. These movements generate a powerful magnetic field.

The geographical North and South Poles are the two ends of the Earth's axis, the line around which the Earth spins.

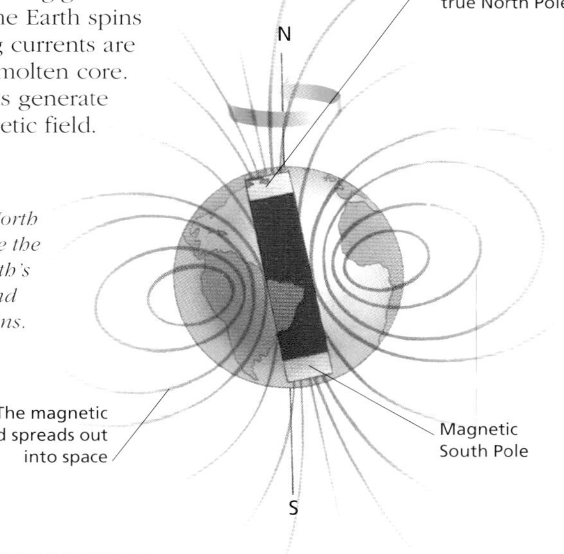
Magnetic North Pole, close to the true North Pole
N
The magnetic field spreads out into space
Magnetic South Pole
S

North Pole (90°N). The distance around the Earth through the poles is 40,008 km (24,860 miles)

Arctic Circle (66.5°N)

Tropic of Cancer (23.5°N)

Lines of latitude are parallel. They run east to west

Equator (0°) Length: 40,075 km (24,901 miles)

Tropic of Capricorn (23.5°S)

Lines of longitude run from north to south. They meet at the North and South Poles. They are widest apart at the Equator

LONGITUDE AND LATITUDE

These imaginary points and lines drawn on the Earth's surface help locate places on a map or globe. The Earth spins around an axis drawn between the North and South poles through the centre of the planet. Lines of longitude are vertical lines running through the poles. Lines of latitude are horizontal lines drawn parallel to the Equator, the line around the middle of the Earth.

Diameter of earth at equator: *12,756 km (7,927 miles).*
Diameter from pole to pole: *12,714 km (7,900 miles).*
Mass: *5,988 million, million million tonnes (tons).*

THE ATMOSPHERE

An envelope of gases such as nitrogen and oxygen surrounds our planet. It provides us with breathable air, filters the Sun's rays and retains heat at night.

Height in km (miles)

INTERPLANETARY SPACE
COMMUNICATIONS AND SOME ASTRONOMICAL SATELLITES
35,880 km
(22,295 miles)
EXOSPHERE
500–2,000 km
(300–1,240 miles)
Outer limit of atmosphere
40,000 (25,000)

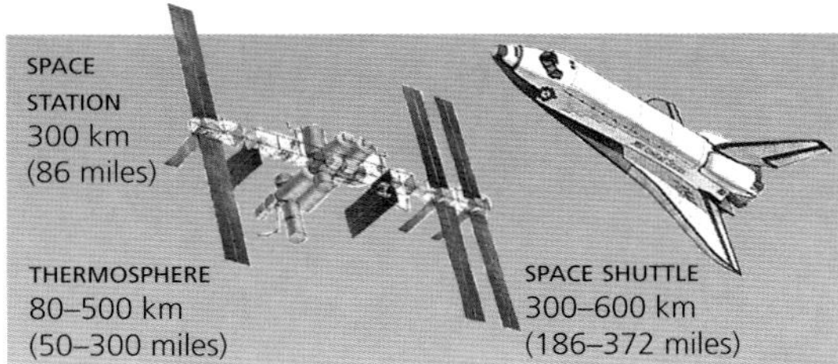
SPACE STATION
300 km
(86 miles)
THERMOSPHERE
80–500 km
(50–300 miles)
SPACE SHUTTLE
300–600 km
(186–372 miles)
500 (300)

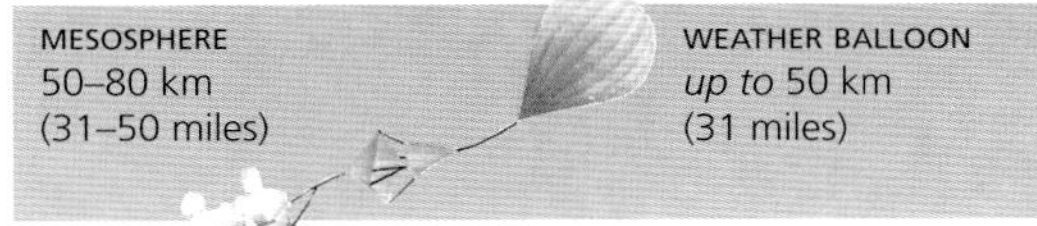
MESOSPHERE
50–80 km
(31–50 miles)
WEATHER BALLOON
up to 50 km
(31 miles)
80 (50)

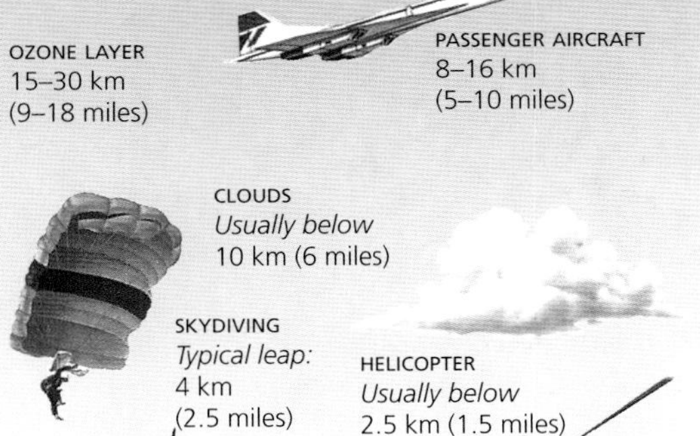
50 (31)
STRATOSPHERE
15–50 km
(9–31 miles)
OZONE LAYER
15–30 km
(9–18 miles)
PASSENGER AIRCRAFT
8–16 km
(5–10 miles)
CLOUDS
Usually below
10 km (6 miles)

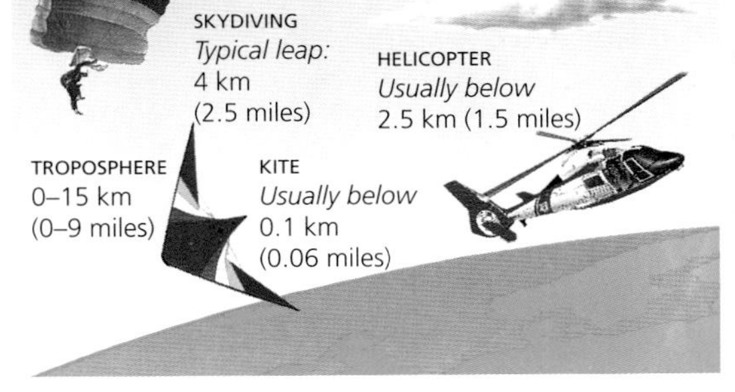
SKYDIVING
Typical leap:
4 km
(2.5 miles)
HELICOPTER
Usually below
2.5 km (1.5 miles)
TROPOSPHERE
0–15 km
(0–9 miles)
KITE
Usually below
0.1 km
(0.06 miles)
Sea level

Cold air descends from the poles toward the Equator

Warm air and water travel to the poles from the Equator

Air circulates between the poles and the Equator in stages called "cells"

Winds and currents do not move in straight lines because the Earth spins

WINDS AND CURRENTS

The world's winds and ocean currents are caused by the way the Sun heats the Earth's surface. More heat energy arrives at the Equator than at the poles because the Earth is curved and tilted. Warm air and warm water carry much of this energy toward the poles, heating up the higher latitudes. Meanwhile cool air and water moves back toward the Equator, lowering its temperature.

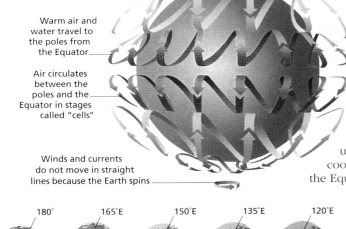

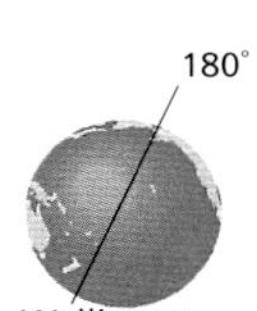
180°
Wellington
2400 hrs

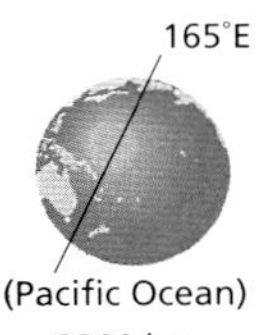
165°E
(Pacific Ocean)
2300 hrs

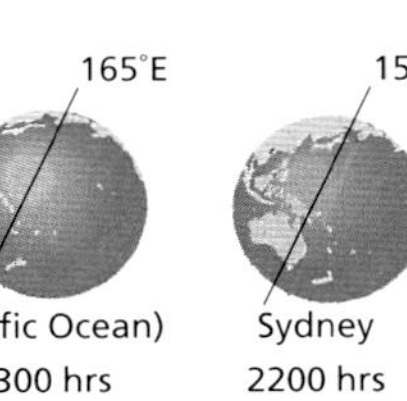
150°E
Sydney
2200 hrs

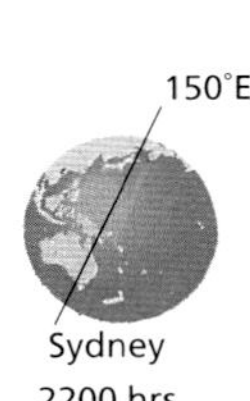
135°E
Tokyo
2100 hrs

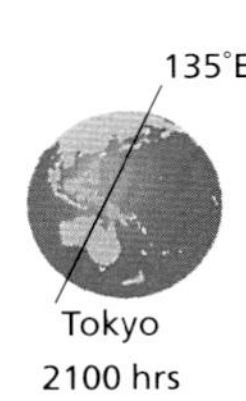
120°E
Manila
2000 hrs

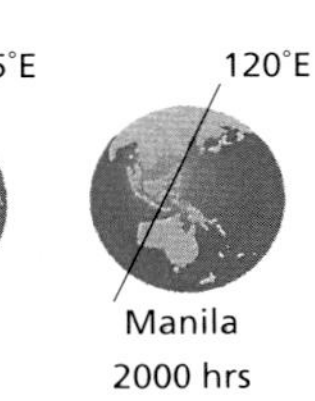
105°E
Jakarta
1900 hrs

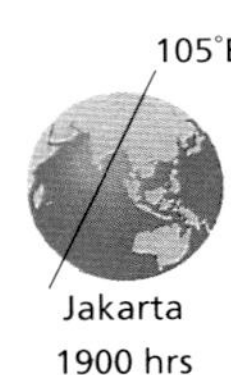
90°E
Dhaka
1800 hrs

75°E
Karachi
1700 hrs

60°E
Muscat
1600 hrs

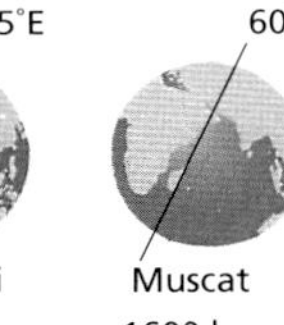
45°E
Baghdad
1500 hrs

30°E
Cairo
1400 hrs

15°E
Berlin
1300 hrs

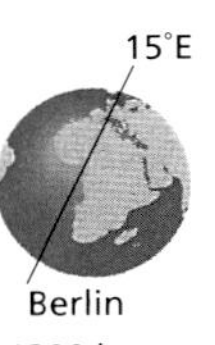
0°
Greenwich
1200 hrs

THE EARTH'S STRUCTURE

THE EARTH IS IN SOME WAYS like an egg, with a thin shell around a soft interior. Its hard, rocky outer layer – the crust – is up to 70 km (45 miles) thick under the continents, but less than 8 km (5 miles) thick under the oceans. This crust is broken into gigantic slabs, called "plates", in which the continents are embedded. Below the hard crust is the mantle, a layer of rocks so hot that some melt and flow in huge swirling currents. The Earth's plates do not stay in the same place. Instead, they move, carried along like rafts on the currents in the mantle. This motion is very slow – usually less than 5 cm (2 in) a year – but enormously powerful. Plate movement makes the Earth quake and volcanoes erupt, causes immense mountain ranges such as the Himalayas to grow where plates collide, and explains how over millions of years whole continents have drifted across the face of the planet.

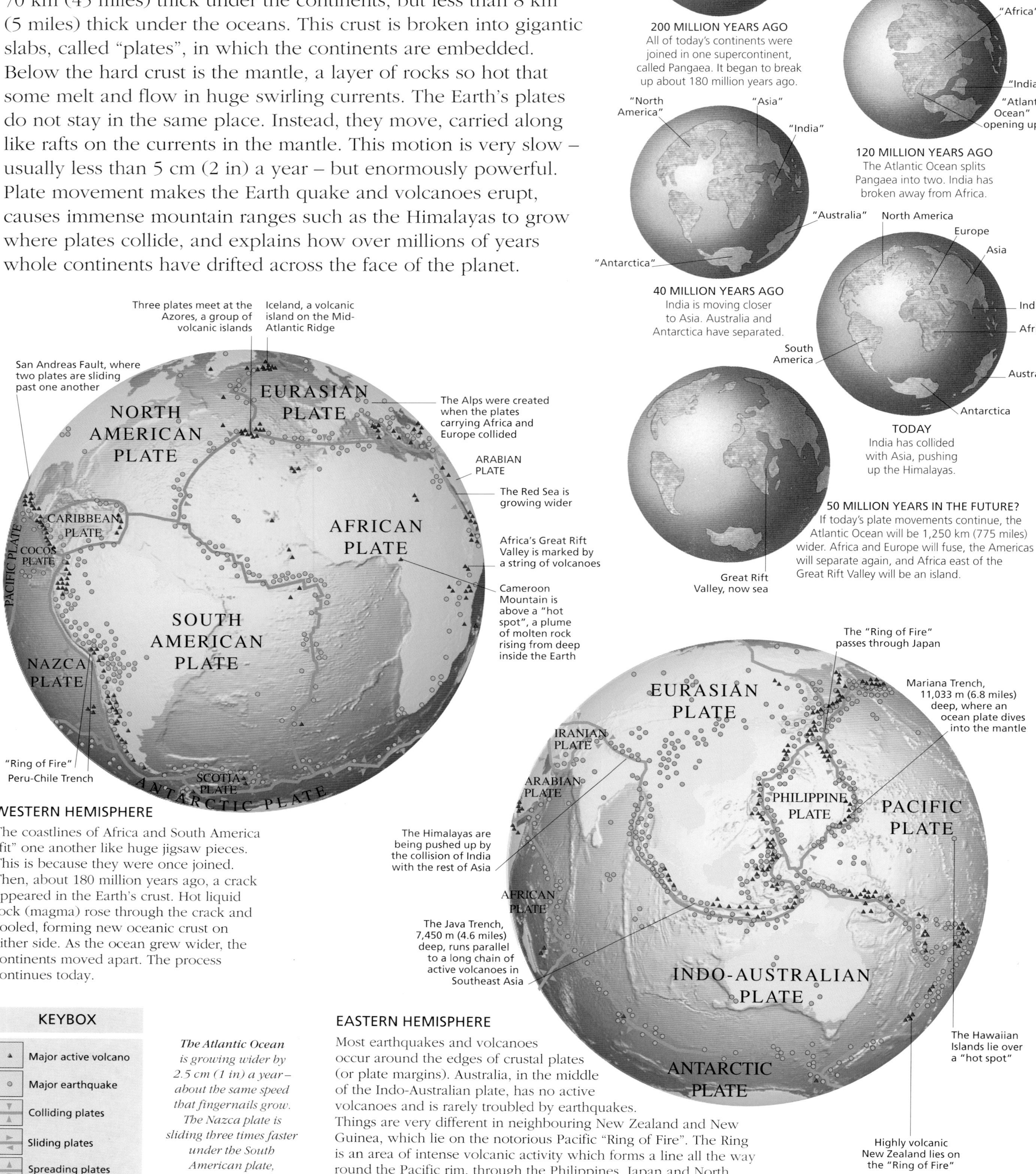
Pangaea
"Africa"
"India"
"Atlantic Ocean" opening up
"North America"
"Asia"
"India"
"Australia"
"Antarctica"
North America
Europe
Asia
India
Africa
South America
Australia
Antarctica
Great Rift Valley, now sea
Three plates meet at the Azores, a group of volcanic islands
Iceland, a volcanic island on the Mid-Atlantic Ridge
San Andreas Fault, where two plates are sliding past one another
NORTH AMERICAN PLATE
EURASIAN PLATE
The Alps were created when the plates carrying Africa and Europe collided
ARABIAN PLATE
The Red Sea is growing wider
CARIBBEAN PLATE
COCOS PLATE
PACIFIC PLATE
AFRICAN PLATE
Africa's Great Rift Valley is marked by a string of volcanoes
Cameroon Mountain is above a "hot spot", a plume of molten rock rising from deep inside the Earth
SOUTH AMERICAN PLATE
NAZCA PLATE
"Ring of Fire"
Peru-Chile Trench
SCOTIA PLATE
ANTARCTIC PLATE
The "Ring of Fire" passes through Japan
Mariana Trench, 11,033 m (6.8 miles) deep, where an ocean plate dives into the mantle
EURASIAN PLATE
IRANIAN PLATE
ARABIAN PLATE
PHILIPPINE PLATE
PACIFIC PLATE
The Himalayas are being pushed up by the collision of India with the rest of Asia
AFRICAN PLATE
The Java Trench, 7,450 m (4.6 miles) deep, runs parallel to a long chain of active volcanoes in Southeast Asia
INDO-AUSTRALIAN PLATE
ANTARCTIC PLATE
The Hawaiian Islands lie over a "hot spot"
Highly volcanic New Zealand lies on the "Ring of Fire"

DRIFTING CONTINENTS

Currents of molten rock deep within the mantle slowly move the continents. Over time, they appear to "drift" across the Earth's surface.

200 MILLION YEARS AGO
All of today's continents were joined in one supercontinent, called Pangaea. It began to break up about 180 million years ago.

120 MILLION YEARS AGO
The Atlantic Ocean splits Pangaea into two. India has broken away from Africa.

40 MILLION YEARS AGO
India is moving closer to Asia. Australia and Antarctica have separated.

TODAY
India has collided with Asia, pushing up the Himalayas.

50 MILLION YEARS IN THE FUTURE?
If today's plate movements continue, the Atlantic Ocean will be 1,250 km (775 miles) wider. Africa and Europe will fuse, the Americas will separate again, and Africa east of the Great Rift Valley will be an island.

WESTERN HEMISPHERE

The coastlines of Africa and South America "fit" one another like huge jigsaw pieces. This is because they were once joined. Then, about 180 million years ago, a crack appeared in the Earth's crust. Hot liquid rock (magma) rose through the crack and cooled, forming new oceanic crust on either side. As the ocean grew wider, the continents moved apart. The process continues today.

KEYBOX

- Major active volcano
- Major earthquake
- Colliding plates
- Sliding plates
- Spreading plates

The Atlantic Ocean is growing wider by 2.5 cm (1 in) a year – about the same speed that fingernails grow. The Nazca plate is sliding three times faster under the South American plate, pushing up the Andes.

EASTERN HEMISPHERE

Most earthquakes and volcanoes occur around the edges of crustal plates (or plate margins). Australia, in the middle of the Indo-Australian plate, has no active volcanoes and is rarely troubled by earthquakes. Things are very different in neighbouring New Zealand and New Guinea, which lie on the notorious Pacific "Ring of Fire". The Ring is an area of intense volcanic activity which forms a line all the way round the Pacific rim, through the Philippines, Japan and North America, and down the coast of South America to New Zealand.

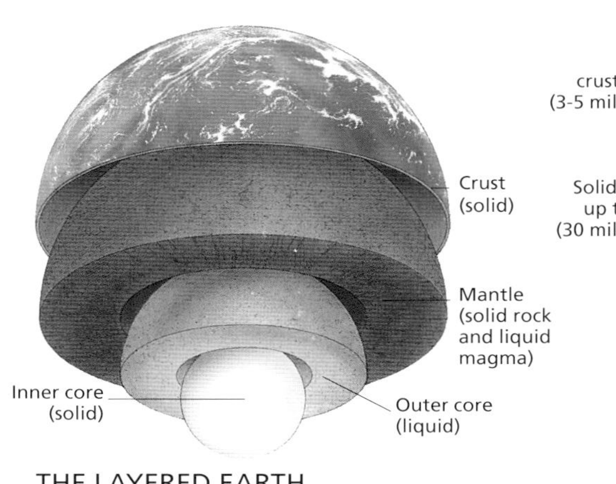
Crust
(solid)
Mantle
(solid rock
and liquid
magma)
Outer core
(liquid)
Inner core
(solid)

THE LAYERED EARTH

The Earth has layers, like an egg. The core is made of metals such as iron and nickel. This is surrounded by a rocky mantle and a thin crust.

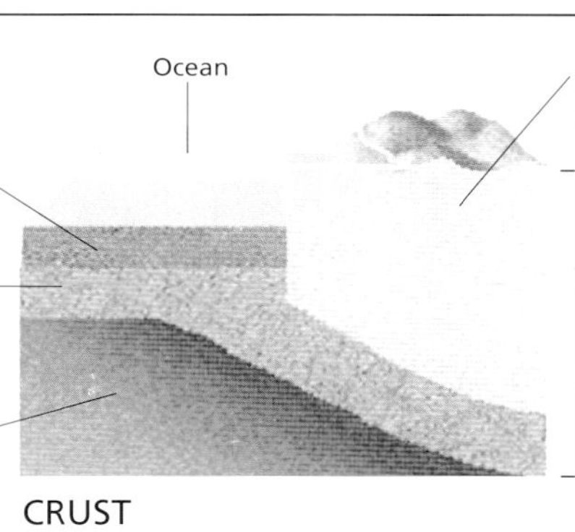
Ocean
Oceanic
crust, 5-8 km
(3-5 miles) thick
Continental
crust, up to 70 km
(45 miles) thick
Solid mantle,
up to 50 km
(30 miles) thick
Lithosphere
(all crust plus
solid layer of
mantle). Up
to 120 km
(75 miles) thick
Liquid
mantle

CRUST

Crust is of two kinds: continental and oceanic. Continental crust is older, thicker and less dense. Beneath the crust is a solid layer of mantle. Together, these form the lithosphere, which is broken into several plates. These float on the liquid mantle layer.

15°C (59°F)
3,000°C (5,400°F)
4,000°C (7,200°F)
4,500°C (8,100°F)
CRUST
MANTLE
OUTER CORE
INNER CORE
6,370 km (3,955 miles)
5,000 km (3,100 miles)
3,000 km (1,850 miles)
Sea level

TEMPERATURE AND DEPTH

Our planet is a nuclear-powered furnace, heated from within by the breakdown of radioactive minerals such as uranium. Temperature increases with depth: 100 km (60 miles) down it is 1,350°C (2,460°F), hot enough for rocks to melt.

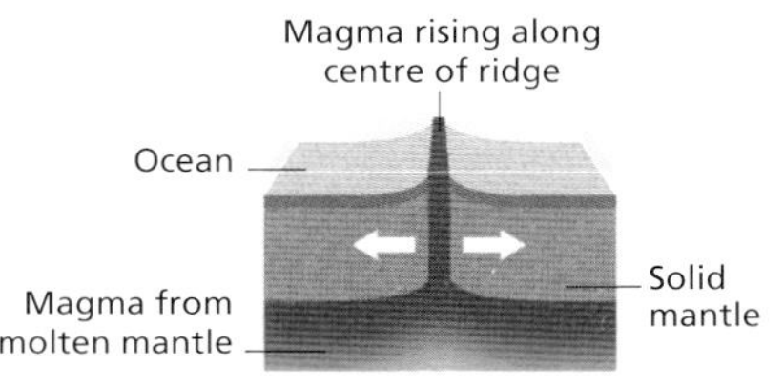
Magma rising along
centre of ridge
Ocean
Solid
mantle
Magma from
molten mantle

SPREADING PLATES

When two plates move apart, molten rock (magma) rises from the mantle and cools, forming new crust. This is called a constructive margin. Most are found in oceans.

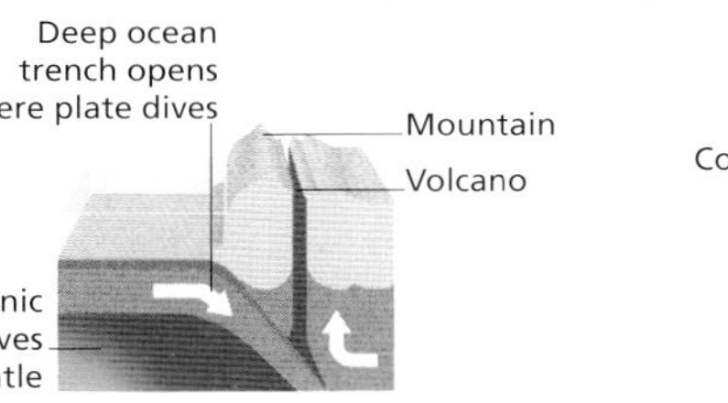
Deep ocean
trench opens
where plate dives
Mountain
Volcano
Oceanic
plate dives
into mantle

COLLIDING PLATES THAT DIVE

When two ocean plates or an ocean plate and a continent plate collide, the denser plate is forced under the other, diving down into the mantle. These are destructive margins.

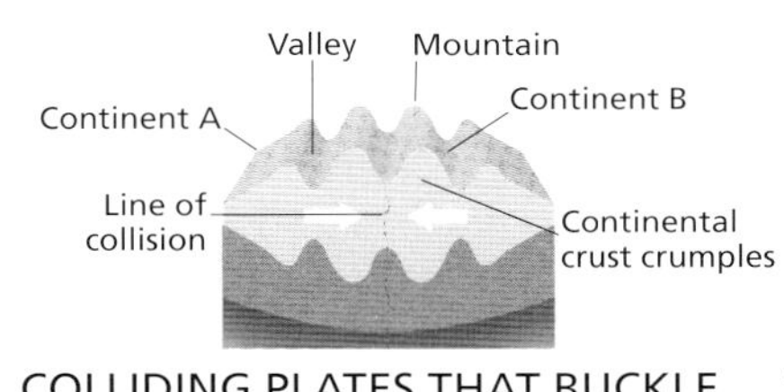
Valley
Mountain
Continent A
Continent B
Line of
collision
Continental
crust crumples

COLLIDING PLATES THAT BUCKLE

When two continents collide, their plates fuse, crumple and push upwards. Mountain ranges such as the Himalayas and the Urals have been formed in this way.

Fault
Plate
Plate

SLIDING PLATES

When two plates slide past one another, intense friction is created along the "fault line" between them, causing earthquakes. These are called conservative margins.

ICELAND, MID-ATLANTIC RIDGE

Most constructive margins are found beneath oceans, but here in volcanic Iceland one comes to the surface.

VOLCANO, JAVA

Diving plates often build volcanic islands and mountain chains. Deep ocean trenches form offshore.

FOLDING STRATA, ENGLAND

The clash of continental plates may cause the Earth to buckle and twist far from the collision zone.

SAN ANDREAS FAULT

A huge earthquake is expected soon somewhere along California's San Andreas Fault, seen here.

EXPLOSIVE VOLCANO

About 50 of the world's 600 or so active volcanoes erupt each year. Explosive pressure is created by the build-up of magma, gases, or super-heated steam.

Crater
Cloud of ash, gases and steam
Lava flows
Main vent (opening)
Cone of ash and lava from old eruptions

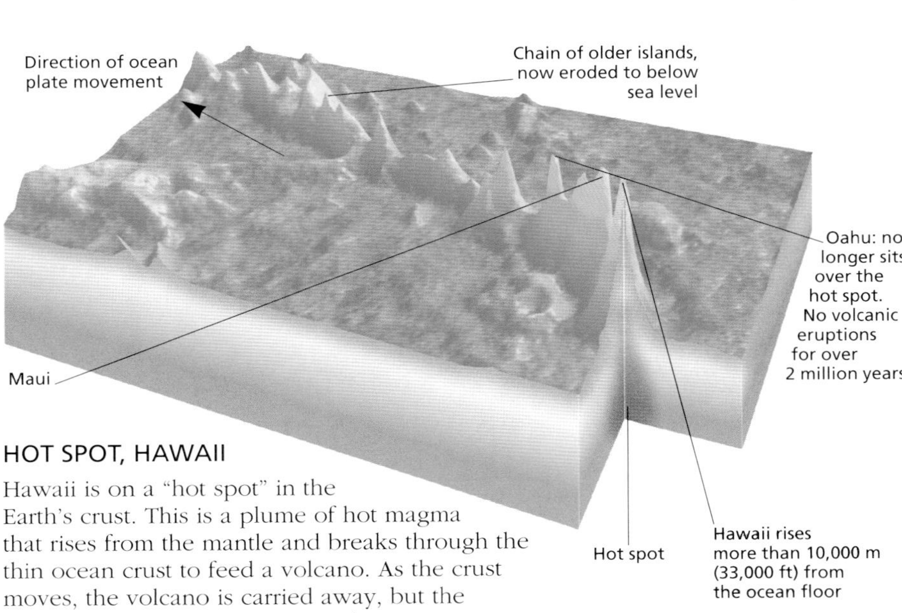
Direction of ocean
plate movement
Chain of older islands,
now eroded to below
sea level
Oahu: no
longer sits
over the
hot spot.
No volcanic
eruptions
for over
2 million years
Maui
Hot spot
Hawaii rises
more than 10,000 m
(33,000 ft) from
the ocean floor

HOT SPOT, HAWAII

Hawaii is on a "hot spot" in the Earth's crust. This is a plume of hot magma that rises from the mantle and breaks through the thin ocean crust to feed a volcano. As the crust moves, the volcano is carried away, but the hot spot stays, forming a new volcano.

SOME MAJOR QUAKES AND ERUPTIONS

This map shows some of the worst natural disasters in recorded history. Over one million earthquakes and about 50 volcanic eruptions are detected every year. Most are minor or occur where there are few people, so there is no loss of human life or great damage to property. But crowded cities and poorly-constructed buildings are putting ever-greater numbers at risk.

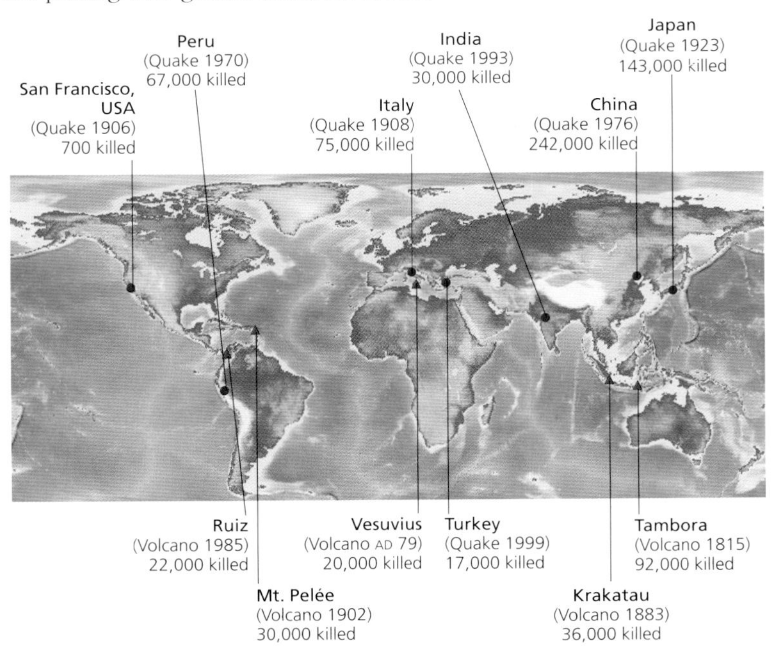
San Francisco, USA
(Quake 1906)
700 killed
Peru
(Quake 1970)
67,000 killed
Italy
(Quake 1908)
75,000 killed
India
(Quake 1993)
30,000 killed
China
(Quake 1976)
242,000 killed
Japan
(Quake 1923)
143,000 killed
Ruiz
(Volcano 1985)
22,000 killed
Mt. Pelée
(Volcano 1902)
30,000 killed
Vesuvius
(Volcano AD 79)
20,000 killed
Turkey
(Quake 1999)
17,000 killed
Krakatau
(Volcano 1883)
36,000 killed
Tambora
(Volcano 1815)
92,000 killed

Shaping the Landscape

Landscapes are created and changed – even destroyed – in a continuous cycle. Over millions of years, constant movements of the Earth's plates have built its continents, islands and mountains. But as soon as new land is formed, it is shaped (or "eroded") by the forces of wind, water, ice and heat. Sometimes change is quick, as when a river floods and cuts a new channel, or a landslide cascades down a mountain slope. But usually change is so slow that it is invisible to the human eye. Extremes of heat and cold crack open rocks and expose them to attack by wind and water. Rivers and glaciers scour out valleys, the wind piles up sand dunes, and the sea attacks shorelines and cliffs. Eroded materials are blown away or carried along by rivers, piling up as sediments on valley floors or the sea bed. Over millions of years these may be compressed into rock and pushed up to form new land. As soon as the land is exposed to the elements, the cycle of erosion begins again.

MAP FEATURES

Area covered in ice today	Area drained by major river
Ice and snow 18,000 years ago	Protected coastline
Desert	Coast affected by tidal swell
Wind direction (simplified)	Coast affected by storm waves

THE "ROOF OF NORTH AMERICA"

Steeply-sloping Mount McKinley (also called Denali), Alaska, is North America's highest mountain at 6,194 m (20,320 ft). It is a fairly "young" mountain, less than 70 million years old. The gently sloping Appalachians in the east of the continent are very much older. Once, they were probably higher than Mount McKinley is today. But more than 300 million years of ice, rain and wind have ground them down.

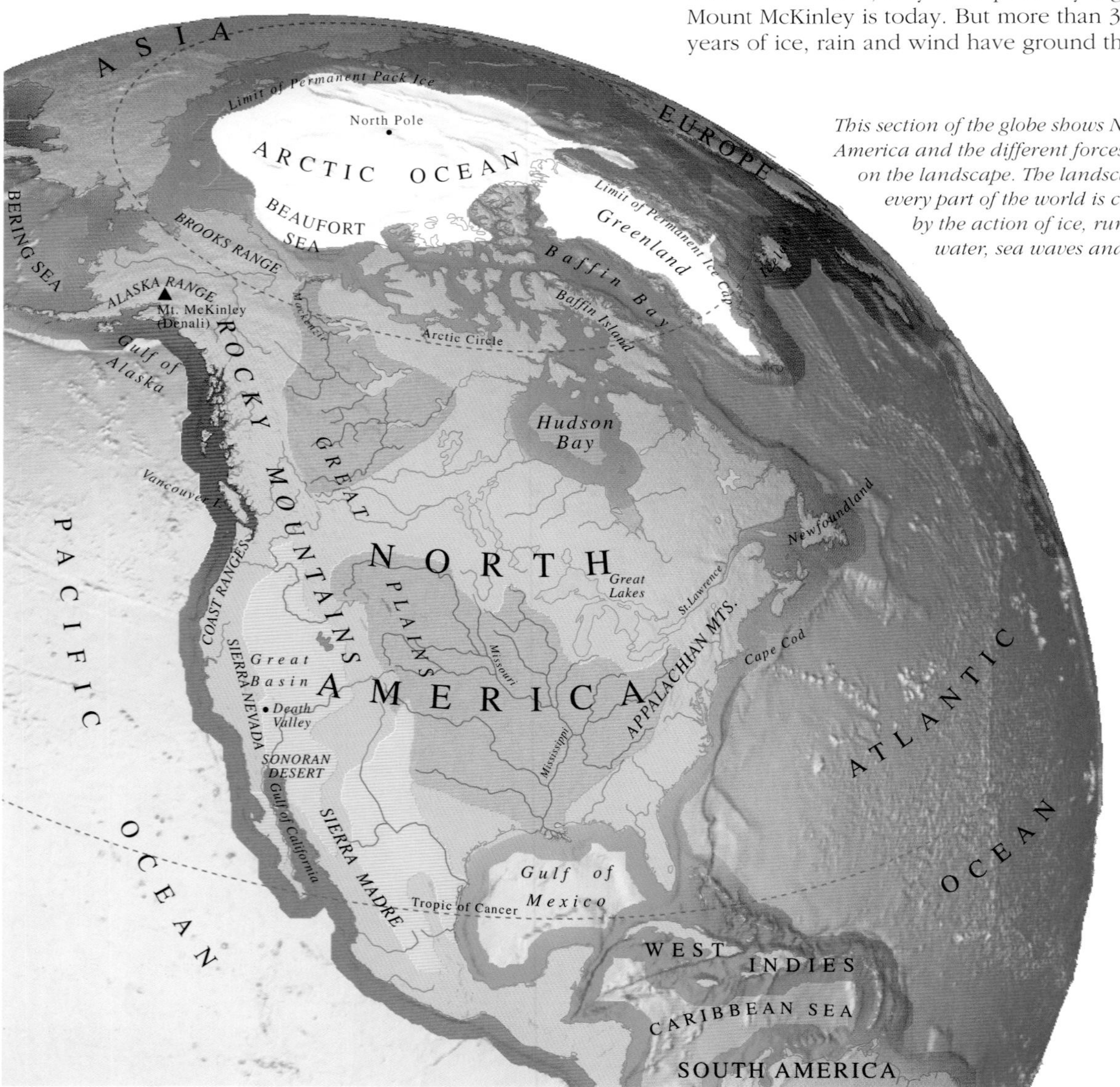
ASIA
EUROPE
Limit of Permanent Pack Ice
North Pole
ARCTIC OCEAN
BEAUFORT SEA
Greenland
Limit of Permanent Ice Cap
Baffin Bay
Baffin Island
BERING SEA
BROOKS RANGE
ALASKA RANGE
Mt. McKinley (Denali)
Gulf of Alaska
Arctic Circle
ROCKY MOUNTAINS
GREAT PLAINS
Hudson Bay
Vancouver I.
Newfoundland
NORTH AMERICA
Great Lakes
St. Lawrence
PACIFIC OCEAN
COAST RANGES
SIERRA NEVADA
Great Basin
Death Valley
Missouri
Mississippi
APPALACHIAN MTS.
Cape Cod
ATLANTIC OCEAN
SONORAN DESERT
Gulf of California
SIERRA MADRE
Gulf of Mexico
Tropic of Cancer
WEST INDIES
CARIBBEAN SEA
SOUTH AMERICA

This section of the globe shows North America and the different forces working on the landscape. The landscape in every part of the world is changed by the action of ice, running water, sea waves and wind.

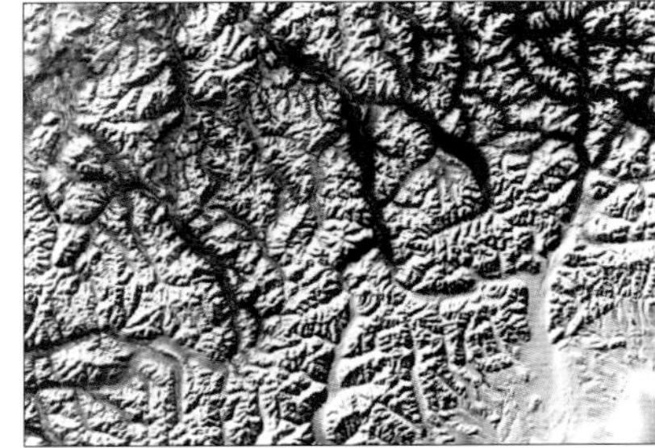

ICE ACTION, ALASKA

Areas close to the North Pole are permanently covered in snow and ice. Glaciers are rivers of ice that flow towards the sea, scouring the landscape as they cross it. Some glaciers are over 60 km (40 miles) long.

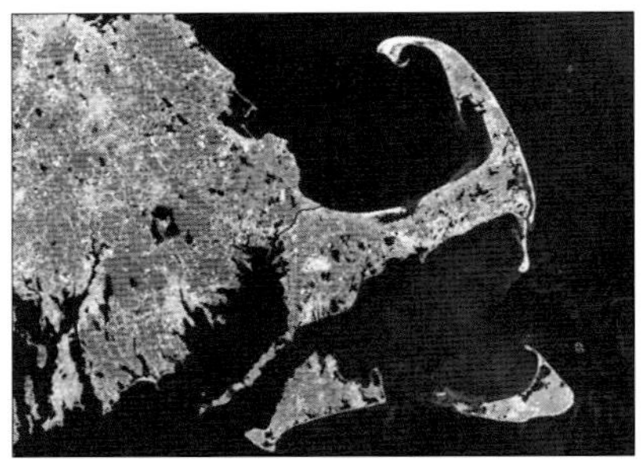

SEA ACTION, CAPE COD

Cape Cod, a sandy peninsula 105 km (65 miles) long, juts out like a beckoning finger into the Atlantic Ocean. Its strangely-curved coastline has been shaped by wave action.

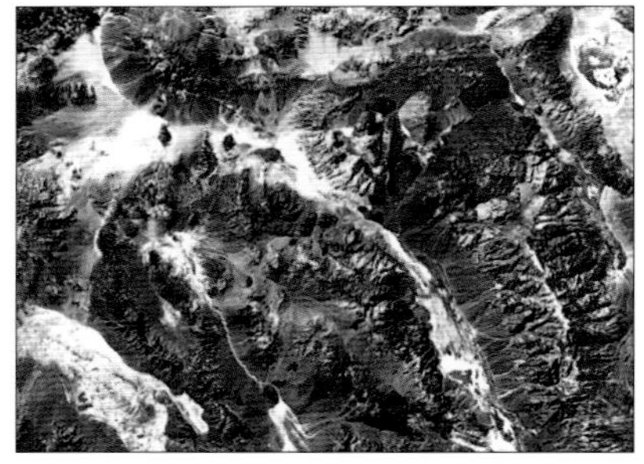

WIND ACTION, DEATH VALLEY

Death Valley is the hottest, driest place in North America. Its floor is covered in sand and salt. Winds sweeping across the valley endlessly reshape the loose surface.

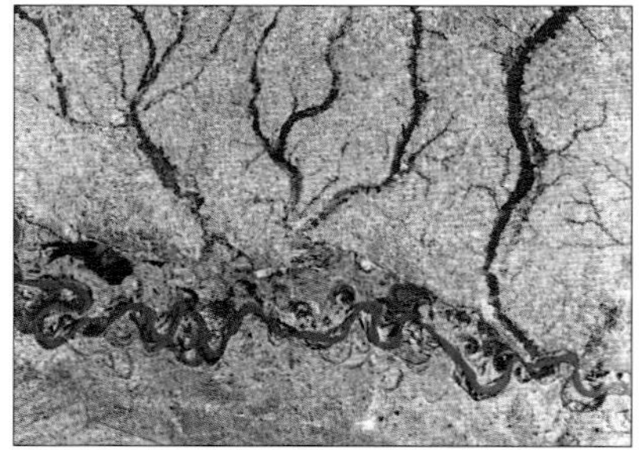

WATER ACTION, MISSISSIPPI

The Mississippi River and its many tributaries frequently change course. Where two loops are close together, the river may cut a new path between them, leaving an "ox-bow lake".

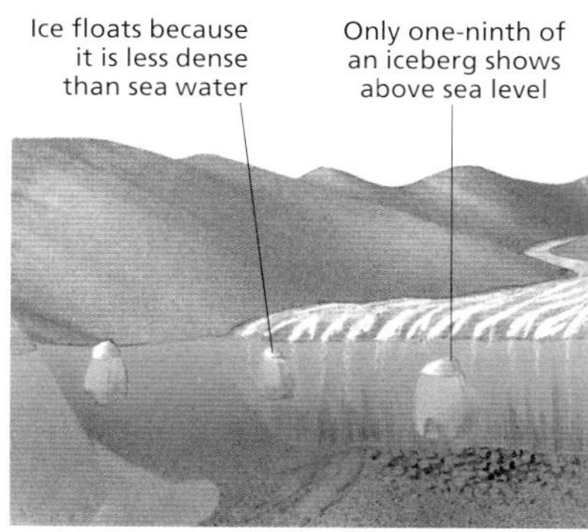
Ice floats because it is less dense than sea water
Only one-ninth of an iceberg shows above sea level

A GLACIER REACHES THE SEA

When a glacier enters the sea, its front edge or "snout" breaks up and forms icebergs – a process called calving. These "ice mountains" are then carried away by ocean currents.

ICE COVER

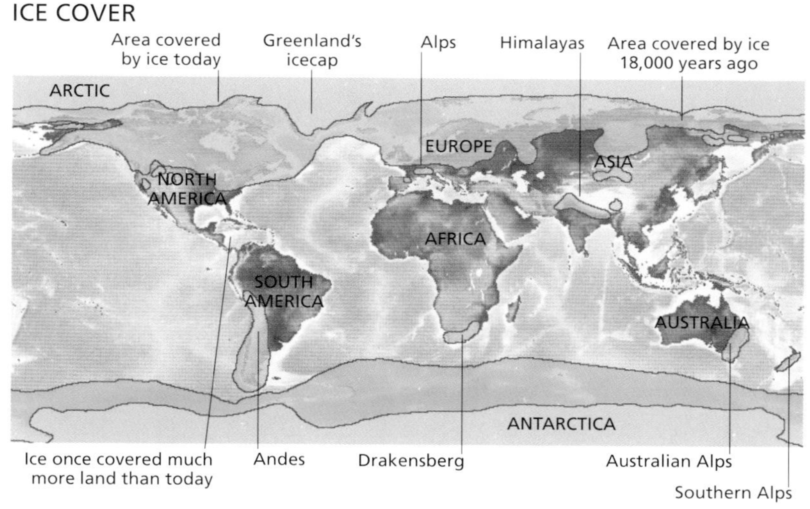
Area covered by ice today
Greenland's icecap
Alps
Himalayas
Area covered by ice 18,000 years ago
ARCTIC
EUROPE
ASIA
NORTH AMERICA
AFRICA
SOUTH AMERICA
AUSTRALIA
ANTARCTICA
Ice once covered much more land than today
Andes
Drakensberg
Australian Alps
Southern Alps

NORDFJORD, NORWAY

One sign of glacial action on the landscape is the fjord. These long, narrow, steep-sided inlets are found along the coasts of Norway, Alaska, Chile and New Zealand. They mark the points where glaciers once entered the sea.

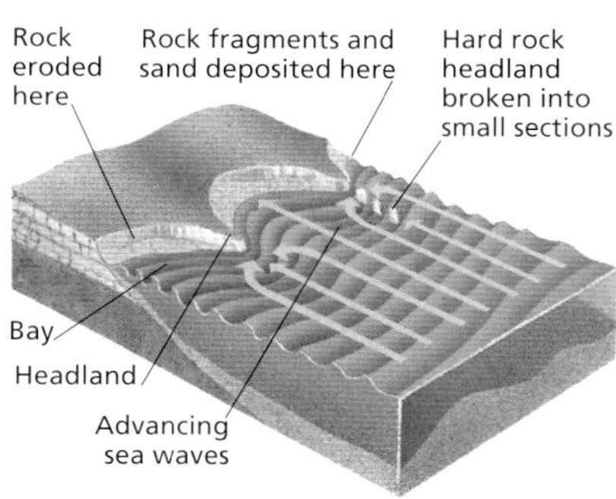
Rock eroded here
Rock fragments and sand deposited here
Hard rock headland broken into small sections
Bay
Headland
Advancing sea waves

COASTAL ATTACK

The ceaseless push and pull of waves on a shore can destroy even the hardest rocks. The softest rocks are eroded first, leaving headlands of hard rock that survive a little longer.

COASTAL EROSION

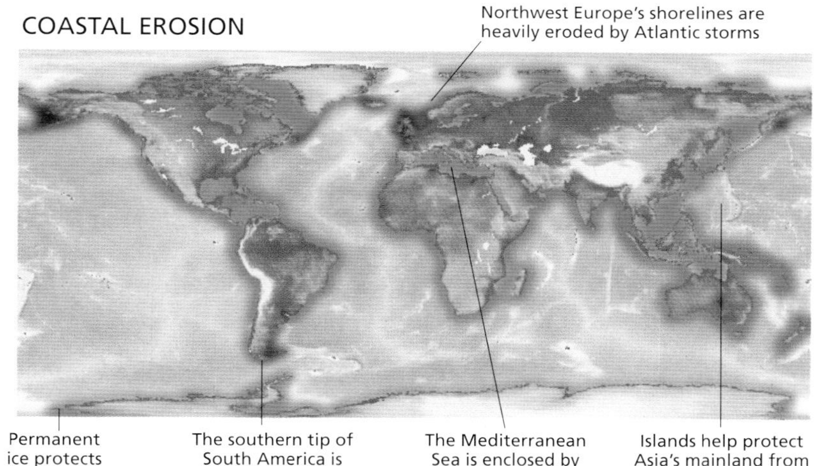
Northwest Europe's shorelines are heavily eroded by Atlantic storms
Permanent ice protects Antarctica's shores
The southern tip of South America is notorious for its devastating storms
The Mediterranean Sea is enclosed by land, so there is little coastal erosion
Islands help protect Asia's mainland from advancing waves

WAVE POWER

The powerful action of waves on an exposed coast can erode a coastline by several metres (feet) a year.

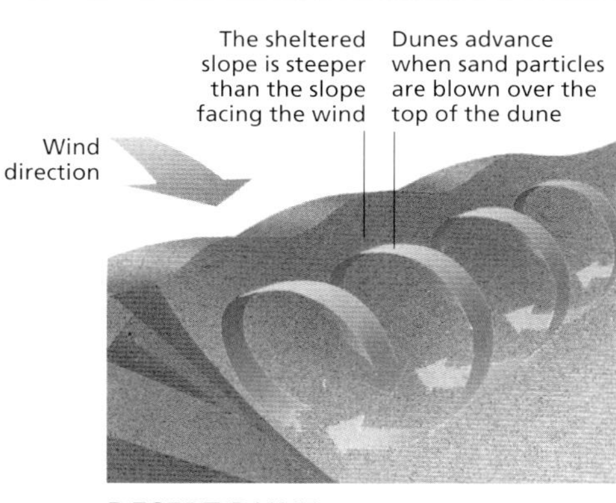
Wind direction
The sheltered slope is steeper than the slope facing the wind
Dunes advance when sand particles are blown over the top of the dune

DESERT DUNE

Dunes are slow-moving mounds or ridges of sand found in deserts and along some coastlines. They only form when the wind's direction and speed is fairly constant.

THE GREAT DESERTS

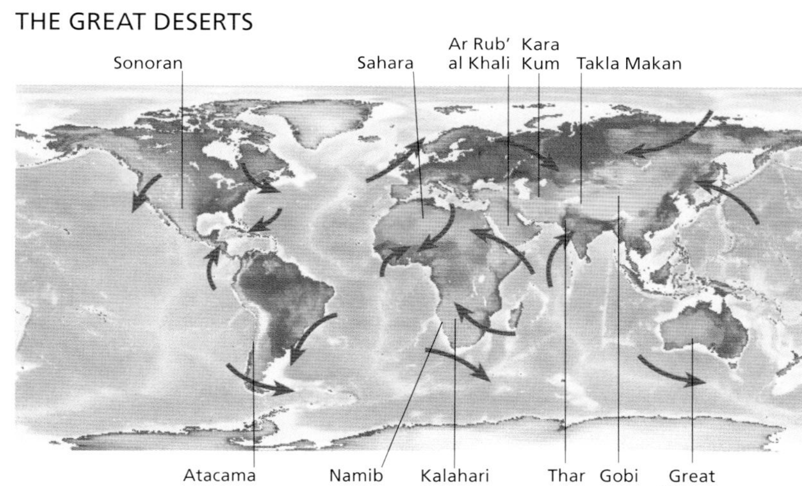
Sonoran
Sahara
Ar Rub' al Khali
Kara Kum
Takla Makan
Atacama
Namib
Kalahari
Thar
Gobi
Great Victoria

NAMIB DESERT, SOUTHERN AFRICA

The sand dunes seen in the centre of the picture are about 50 m (160 ft) high. Winds are driving them slowly but relentlessly towards the right. Not all deserts are sandy. Wind may blow away all the loose sand and gravel, leaving bare rock.

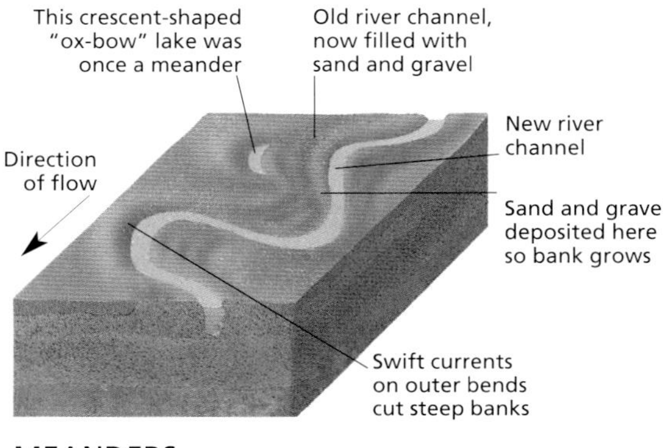
This crescent-shaped "ox-bow" lake was once a meander
Old river channel, now filled with sand and gravel
New river channel
Direction of flow
Sand and gravel deposited here so bank grows
Swift currents on outer bends cut steep banks

MEANDERS

River banks are worn away most on the outside of bends, where water flows fastest. Eroded sand and gravel are built up into banks on the inside of bends in slower-moving water.

THE GREAT RIVER BASINS

Mackenzie
Mississippi
Ob'
Yenisey
Lena
Amur
Amazon
Paraná
Niger
Congo
Nile
Ganges
Yangtze

WINDING RIVER, ALASKA

The more a river meanders across a plain, the longer it becomes and the more slowly it flows.

Climate and Vegetation

The Earth is the only planet in our solar system which supports life. Most of our planet has a breathable atmosphere, and sufficient light, heat and water to support a wide range of plants and animals. The main influences on an area's climate are the amount of sunshine it receives (which varies with latitude and season), how close it is to the influence of ocean currents, and its height above sea level. Since there is more sunlight at the Equator than elsewhere, and rainfall is highest here too, this is where we find the habitats which have more species of plants and animals than anywhere else: rainforests, coral reefs and mangrove swamps. Where rainfall is very low, and where it is either too hot, such as in deserts, or too cold, few plants and animals can survive. Only the icy North and South Poles, and the frozen tops of high mountains, are practically without life of any sort.

WEATHER EXTREMES

Weather is a powerful influence on how we feel, the clothes we wear, the buildings we live in, the colour of our skin, the plants that grow around us, and what we eat and drink. Extreme weather events such as heatwaves, hurricanes, blizzards, tornadoes, sandstorms, droughts and floods, can be terrifyingly destructive.

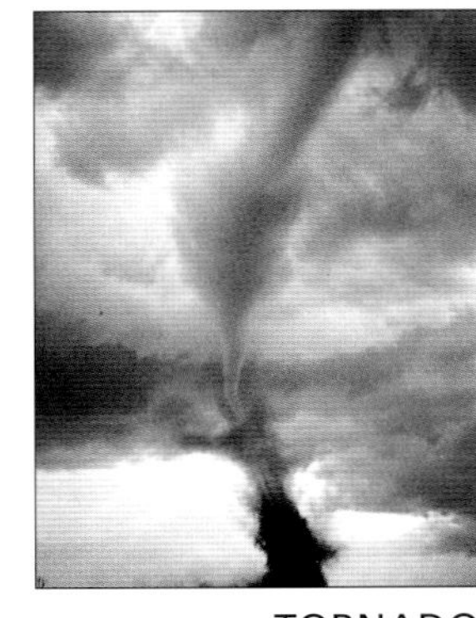

TORNADO

Tornadoes are whirlwinds of cold air that develop when thunderclouds cross warm land. They are extremely violent and unpredictable. Windspeeds often exceed 300 km (180 miles) per hour.

TROPICAL STORMS

These devastating winds develop when air spirals upwards above warm seas. More air is sucked in and the storm begins to move. They bring torrential rain, thunder, lightning and destruction.

DROUGHT

Long periods without water kill plants. Stripped of its protective covering of vegetation, the soil is easily blown away.

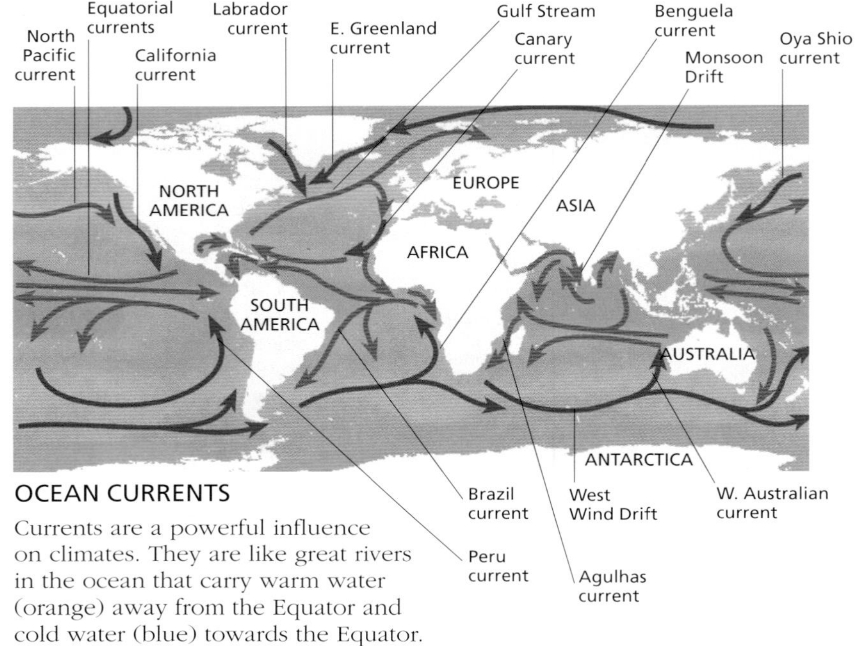
North Pacific current
Equatorial currents
California current
Labrador current
E. Greenland current
Gulf Stream
Canary current
Benguela current
Monsoon Drift
Oya Shio current
NORTH AMERICA
EUROPE
ASIA
AFRICA
SOUTH AMERICA
AUSTRALIA
ANTARCTICA
Brazil current
West Wind Drift
W. Australian current
Peru current
Agulhas current

OCEAN CURRENTS

Currents are a powerful influence on climates. They are like great rivers in the ocean that carry warm water (orange) away from the Equator and cold water (blue) towards the Equator.

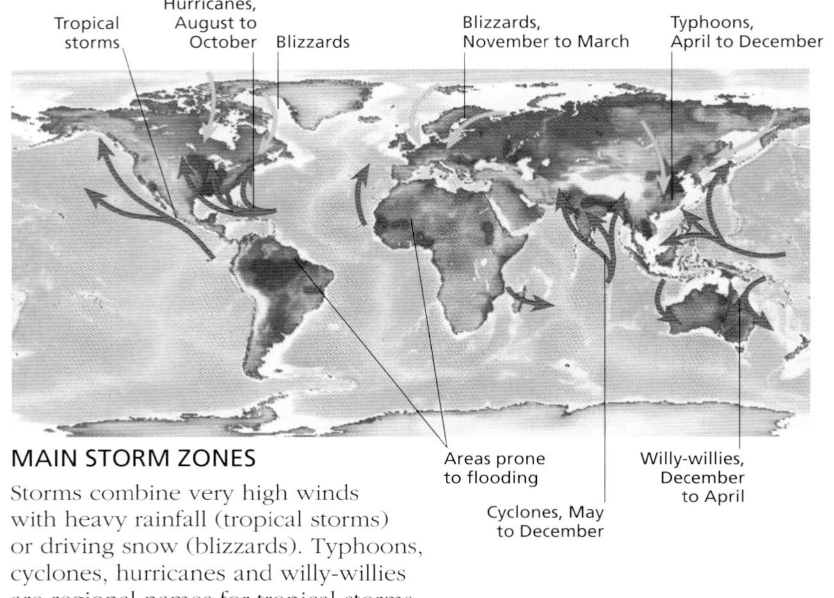
Tropical storms
Hurricanes, August to October
Blizzards
Blizzards, November to March
Typhoons, April to December
Areas prone to flooding
Cyclones, May to December
Willy-willies, December to April

MAIN STORM ZONES

Storms combine very high winds with heavy rainfall (tropical storms) or driving snow (blizzards). Typhoons, cyclones, hurricanes and willy-willies are regional names for tropical storms.

TEMPERATURE

Average temperatures are very different around the world. Areas close to the Equator are usually hot (orange on the map); those close to the Poles usually cold (deep blue). The hottest areas move during the year from the southern to the northern hemispheres.

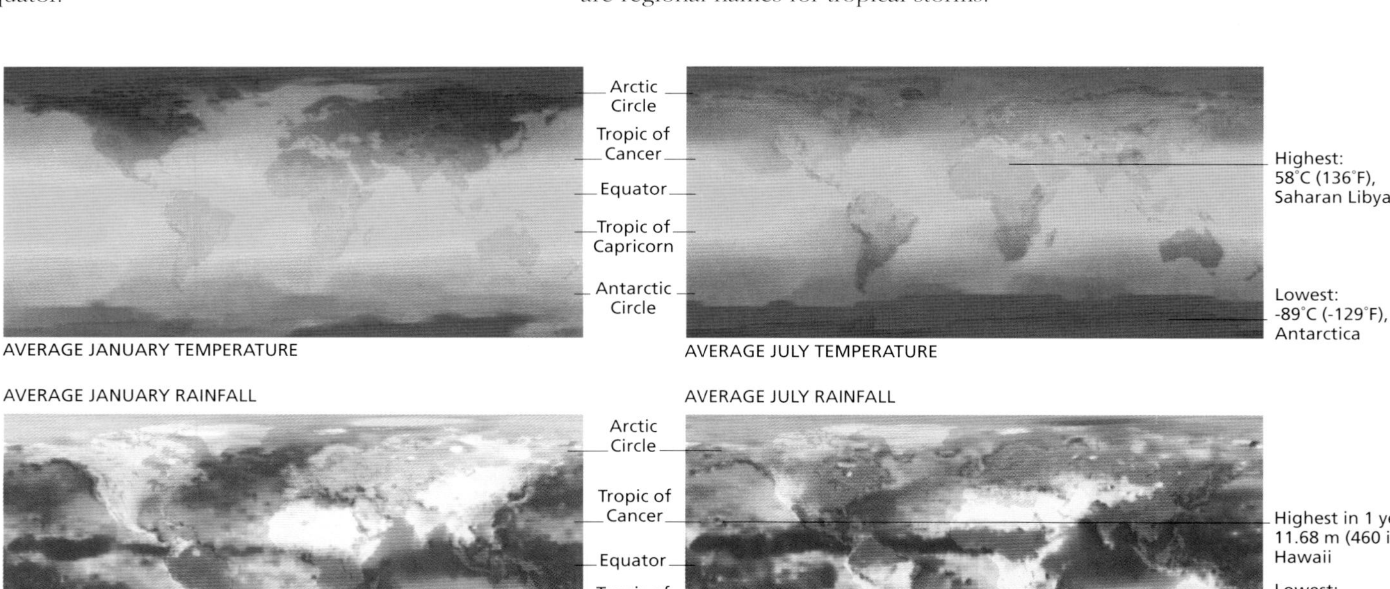
Arctic Circle
Tropic of Cancer
Equator
Tropic of Capricorn
Antarctic Circle
Highest: 58°C (136°F), Saharan Libya
Lowest: -89°C (-129°F), Antarctica
AVERAGE JANUARY TEMPERATURE
AVERAGE JULY TEMPERATURE
AVERAGE JANUARY RAINFALL
AVERAGE JULY RAINFALL
Arctic Circle
Tropic of Cancer
Equator
Tropic of Capricorn
Antarctic Circle
Highest in 1 year: 11.68 m (460 in), Hawaii
Lowest: No rain in more than 14 years, Atacama

RAINFALL

The wettest areas (grey) lie near the Equator. The driest are found close to the tropics, in the centre of continents, or at the poles. Elsewhere, rainfall varies with the season, but it is usually highest in summer. Asia's wet season is known as the monsoon.

BROADLEAF FOREST

Temperate climates have no great extremes of temperature, and drought is unusual. Forests usually contain broad-leaved trees, such as beech or oak, that shed their leaves in autumn.

TUNDRA

As long as frozen soil melts for at least two months of the year, some mosses, lichens and ground-hugging shrubs can survive. They are found around the Arctic Circle and on mountains.

NEEDLELEAF FOREST

Forests of cone-bearing, needleleaf trees such as pine and fir cover much of northern North America, Europe and Asia. They are evergreen and can survive long frozen winters. Most have tall, straight trunks and down-pointing branches. This reduces the amount of snow that can settle on them. The forest floor is dark because leaves absorb most of the incoming sunlight.

Travelling southward from the North Pole, a number of distinct life zones or "biomes" can be seen. Plant and animal life is closely adapted to local climate.

MEDITERRANEAN

The hot dry summers and warm wet winters typical of the Mediterranean region are also found in small areas of southern Africa, the Americas and Australia. Mediterranean-type vegetation can vary from dense forest to thinly spread evergreen shrubs, like these.

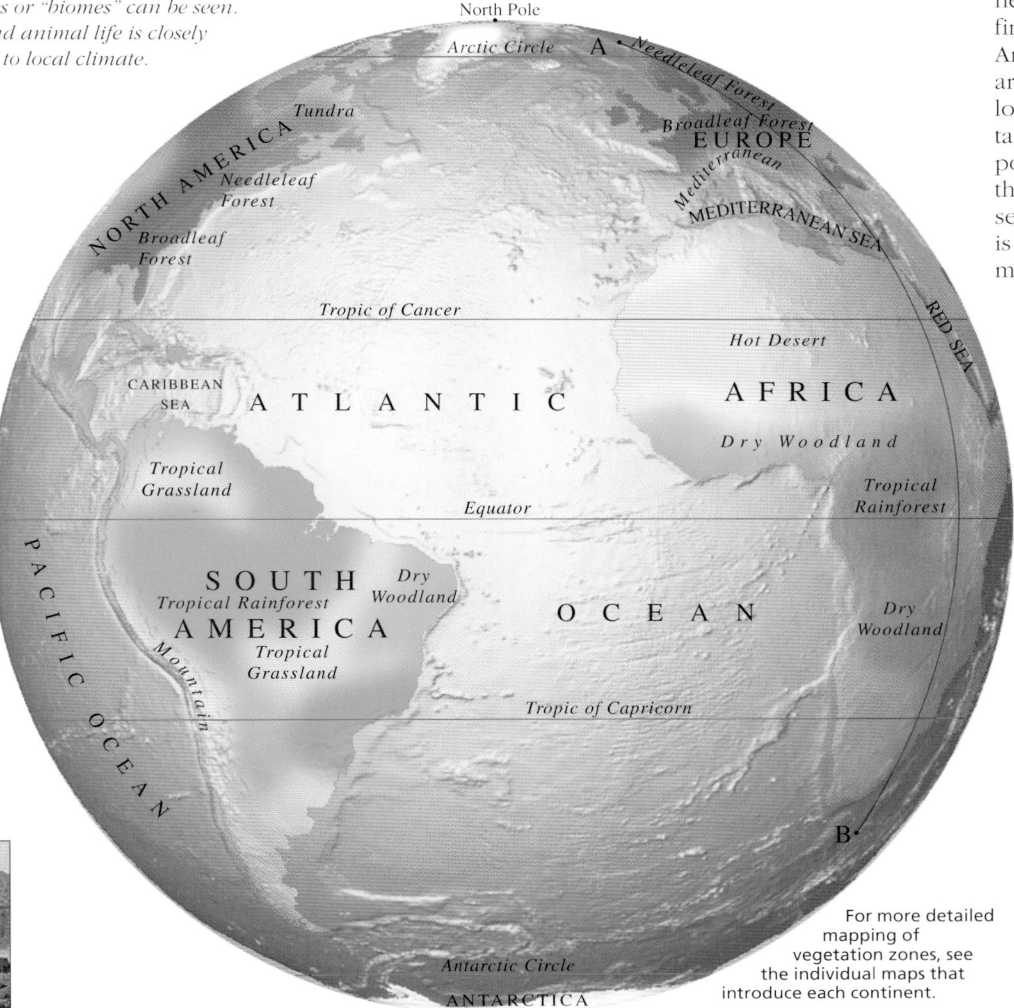
North Pole
Arctic Circle
A
Needleleaf Forest
Broadleaf Forest
EUROPE
Mediterranean
MEDITERRANEAN SEA
Tundra
NORTH AMERICA
Needleleaf Forest
Broadleaf Forest
Tropic of Cancer
RED SEA
Hot Desert
AFRICA
CARIBBEAN SEA
ATLANTIC
Dry Woodland
Tropical Grassland
Tropical Rainforest
Equator
SOUTH AMERICA
Tropical Rainforest
Dry Woodland
OCEAN
Dry Woodland
Mountain
Tropical Grassland
PACIFIC OCEAN
Tropic of Capricorn
B
Antarctic Circle
ANTARCTICA
South Pole

For more detailed mapping of vegetation zones, see the individual maps that introduce each continent.

MOUNTAIN

Vegetation changes with height because the temperature drops and wind increases. Even on the Equator, mountain peaks can be covered in snow. Although trees may cloak the lower slopes, at higher altitudes they give way to sparser vegetation. Near the top, only tundra-type plants can survive.

TROPICAL RAINFOREST

The lush forests found near the Equator depend on year-round high temperatures and heavy rainfall. Worldwide, they may contain 50,000 different kinds of trees and support several million other plant and animal species. Trees are often festooned with climbing plants, or covered with ferns and orchids that have rooted in pockets of water and soil on trunks and branches.

DRY WOODLAND

Plants in many parts of the tropics have to cope with high temperatures and long periods without rain. Some store water in enlarged stems or trunks, or limit water losses by having small, spiny leaves. In dry (but not desert) conditions, trees are widely spaced, with expanses of grassland between, called savannah.

HOT DESERT

Very few plants and animals can survive in hot deserts. Rainfall is low – under 10 cm (4 in) a year. Temperatures often rise above 40°C (104°F) during the day, but drop to freezing point at night. High winds and shifting sands can be a further hazard to life. Only specially adapted plants, such as cacti, can survive.

NORTH-SOUTH CROSS-SECTION THROUGH EUROPE AND AFRICA

The line running between points 'A' and 'B' on the map is the line of the cross-section

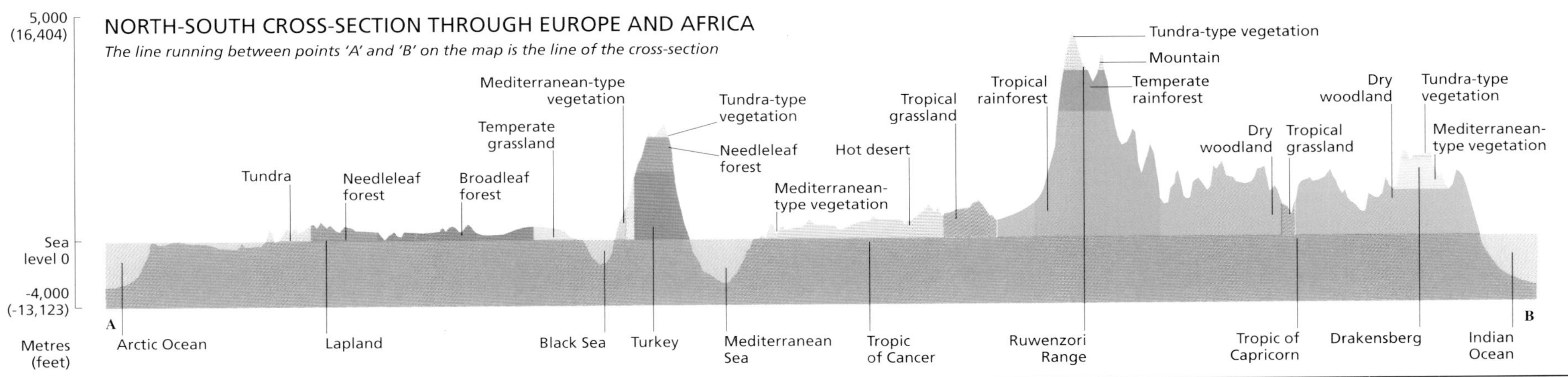
5,000 (16,404)
Sea level 0
-4,000 (-13,123)
Metres (feet)
Tundra
Needleleaf forest
Broadleaf forest
Temperate grassland
Mediterranean-type vegetation
Tundra-type vegetation
Needleleaf forest
Mediterranean-type vegetation
Hot desert
Tropical grassland
Tropical rainforest
Tundra-type vegetation
Mountain
Temperate rainforest
Dry woodland
Tropical grassland
Dry woodland
Tundra-type vegetation
Mediterranean-type vegetation
A
Arctic Ocean
Lapland
Black Sea
Turkey
Mediterranean Sea
Tropic of Cancer
Ruwenzori Range
Tropic of Capricorn
Drakensberg
Indian Ocean
B

PEOPLE AND PLANET

THE EARTH'S POPULATION IS OVER 6,000 million and numbers are rising at the rate of about one million every week. People are not distributed evenly. Some areas, such as parts of Europe, India and China, are very densely populated. Other areas – particularly deserts, polar regions and mountains – can support very few people. Over half of the world's population now lives in towns or cities. This is quite a recent development. Until 1800, most people lived in small villages in the countryside, and worked on the land. But since then more and more people have lived and worked in much larger settlements. A century ago, most of the world's largest cities were in Europe and North America, where new industries and businesses were flourishing. Today, the most rapidly-growing cities are in Asia, South America and Africa. People who move to these cities are usually young adults, so the birth rate amongst these new populations is very high.

A CROWDED PLANET?

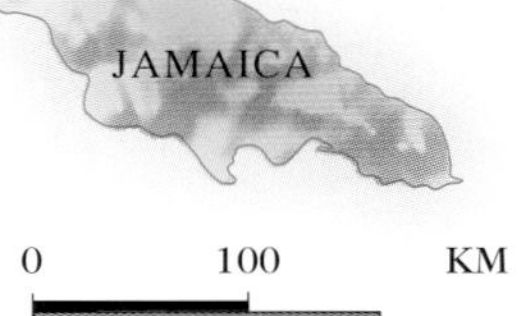
JAMAICA
0
100
KM
0
100
MILES

If the 6 billion people alive today stood close together, they could all fit into an area no larger than the small Caribbean island of Jamaica. Of course, so many people could not live in such a small place. Areas with few people are usually very cold, such as land near the poles and in mountains, or very dry, such as deserts. Areas with large populations often have fertile land and a good climate for crops. Cities support huge populations because they are wealthy enough to buy in everything they need.

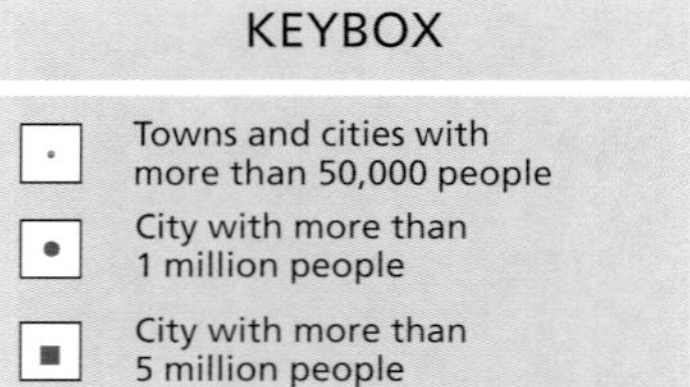
KEYBOX
Towns and cities with more than 50,000 people
City with more than 1 million people
City with more than 5 million people

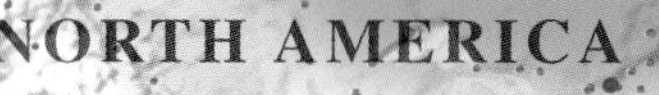
NORTH AMERICA
New York
7.4 million
Mexico City
16.7 million
Jamaica
Bogotá
6 million
SOUTH AMERICA
Lima
6.5 million
Santiago
5.1 million
Rio de Janeiro
10.2 million
Sao Paulo
16.6 million
Buenos Aires
11.7 million

*There are just over 560 million people in **North America**. About 7 in 10 live in a city.*

*There are about 330 million people in **South America**. More than 7 in 10 live in a city.*

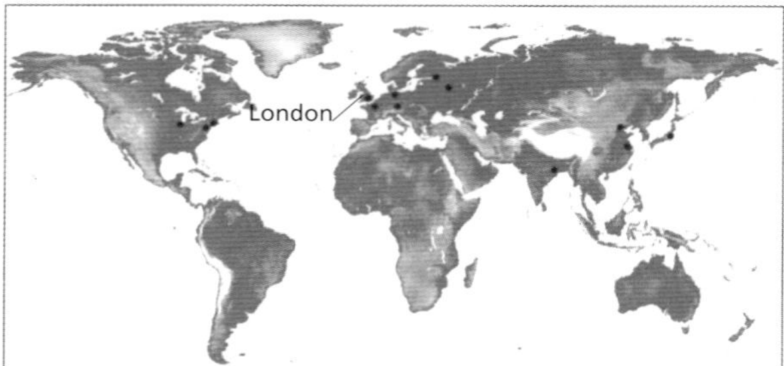
London

MILLIONAIRE CITIES 1900

Less than a century ago there were only 13 cities with more than one million people living in them. All the cities were in the northern hemisphere. The largest was **London**, with seven million people.

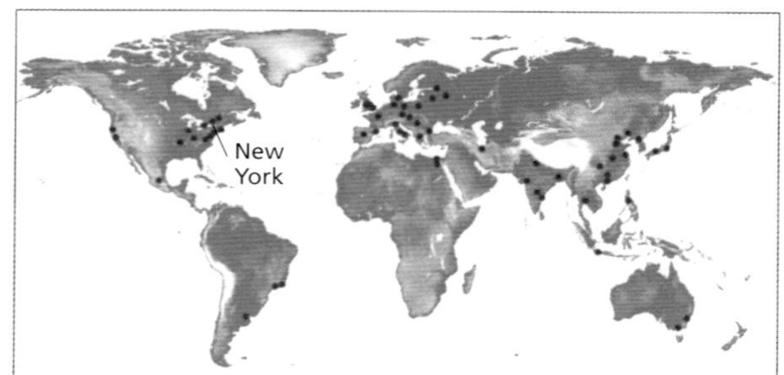
New York

MILLIONAIRE CITIES 1950

By 1950, there were nearly 70 cities with more than one million inhabitants. The largest was **New York**.

SAHARA, AFRICA

The Sahara, like all deserts, is thinly populated. The Tuareg of the northern Sahara are nomads. They travel in small groups because food sources are scarce. Their homes have to be portable.

MONGOLIA, ASIA

Traditionally, Mongolia's nomadic people lived by herding their animals across the steppe. Today, their felt tents, or *gers*, are often set up next to more permanent houses.

AMAZONIA, SOUTH AMERICA

The Yanomami people gather plants in the rainforest and hunt game, but they also grow crops in small forest gardens. Several families live together in a "village" under one huge roof.

MALI, AFRICA

The Dogon people of Mali use mud to construct their elaborate villages. Every family has its own huts and walled areas in which their animals are penned for the night.

WORLD POPULATION GROWTH 1500–2020

Each figure on the graph represents 500 million people.
Note: One billion is 1,000 million.

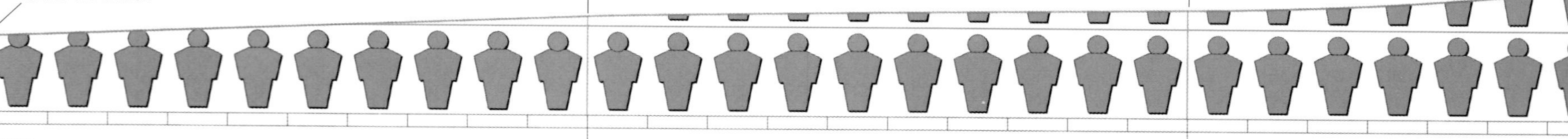
The world's population in 1500 was about 425 million
The world's population in 1600 was about 545 million
The world's population in 1700 was about 610 million.
1500
1600
1700

POOR SUBURB

Densely-populated "shanty towns" have grown on the fringes of many cities in the developing world. Houses are usually built from discarded materials.

RICH SUBURB

Cities are often surrounded by areas where the richest people live. Population densities are low, and the houses may be luxurious, with large gardens or swimming pools. People in these suburbs rely on their cars for transport. This allows them to live a great distance from places of work and leisure in the city centre.

CULTIVATION

Only a small proportion of the Earth's surface can grow crops. It may be possible to bring more land – such as deserts – into production, but yields may be low and costly.

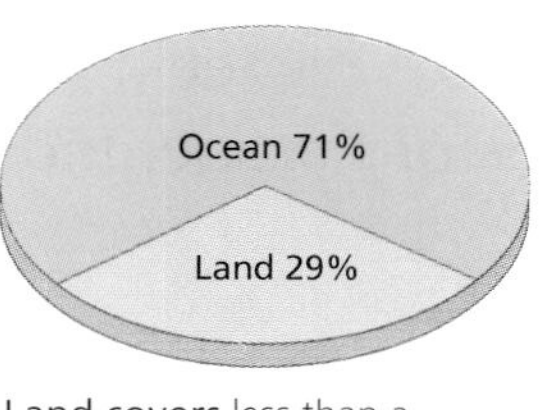
Ocean 71%
Land 29%

Land covers less than a third of the Earth's surface.

Too cold 17%
Too dry 24%
Poor soils 49%
Suitable for crops 10%

Only one-tenth of the total land area can grow crops.

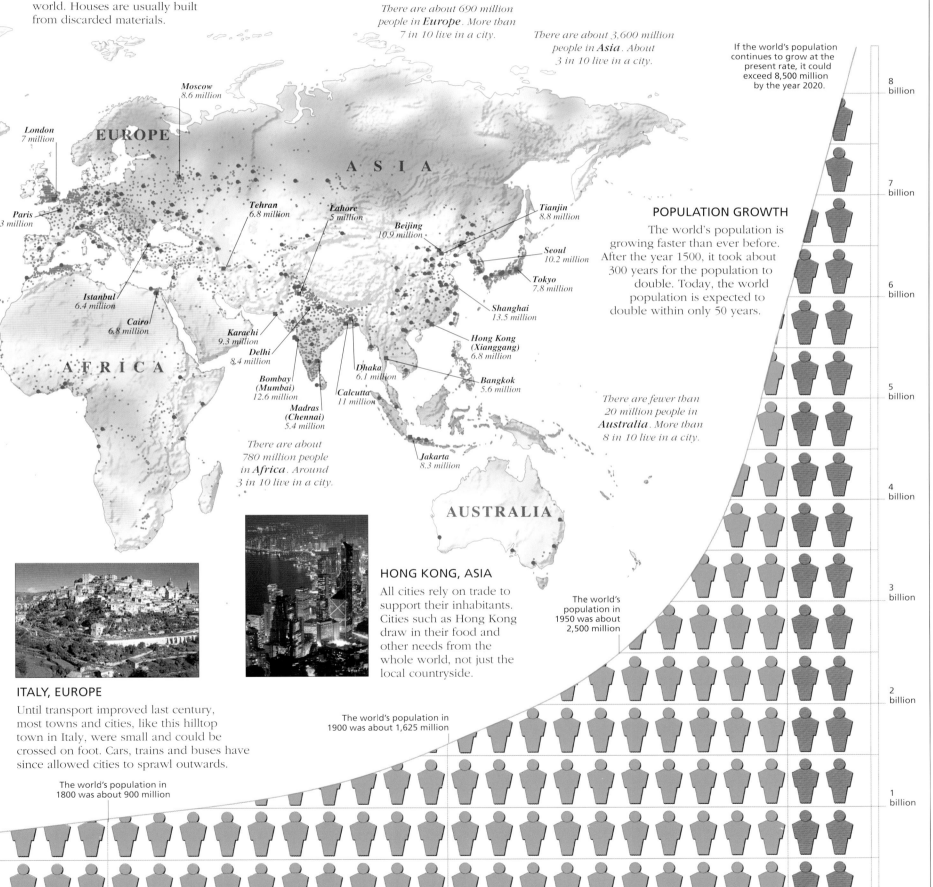

*There are about 690 million people in **Europe**. More than 7 in 10 live in a city.*

*There are about 3,600 million people in **Asia**. About 3 in 10 live in a city.*

EUROPE
ASIA
AFRICA
AUSTRALIA

Moscow 8.6 million
London 7 million
Paris .3 million
Tehran 6.8 million
Lahore 5 million
Beijing 10.9 million
Tianjin 8.8 million
Seoul 10.2 million
Tokyo 7.8 million
Shanghai 13.5 million
Istanbul 6.4 million
Cairo 6.8 million
Karachi 9.3 million
Delhi 8.4 million
Hong Kong (Xianggang) 6.8 million
Dhaka 6.1 million
Bangkok 5.6 million
Bombay (Mumbai) 12.6 million
Calcutta 11 million
Madras (Chennai) 5.4 million
Jakarta 8.3 million

*There are about 780 million people in **Africa**. Around 3 in 10 live in a city.*

*There are fewer than 20 million people in **Australia**. More than 8 in 10 live in a city.*

POPULATION GROWTH

The world's population is growing faster than ever before. After the year 1500, it took about 300 years for the population to double. Today, the world population is expected to double within only 50 years.

If the world's population continues to grow at the present rate, it could exceed 8,500 million by the year 2020.

The world's population in 1950 was about 2,500 million

The world's population in 1900 was about 1,625 million

The world's population in 1800 was about 900 million

8 billion
7 billion
6 billion
5 billion
4 billion
3 billion
2 billion
1 billion

1800
1900
2000

HONG KONG, ASIA

All cities rely on trade to support their inhabitants. Cities such as Hong Kong draw in their food and other needs from the whole world, not just the local countryside.

ITALY, EUROPE

Until transport improved last century, most towns and cities, like this hilltop town in Italy, were small and could be crossed on foot. Cars, trains and buses have since allowed cities to sprawl outwards.

The World Today

There are 192 independent countries in the world today. With the exception of Antarctica every land area of the Earth's surface belongs to, or is claimed by, one country or another. In 1950, there were only 82 countries; but since then many former colonies of the European countries have gained independence. The final stage in this process was the break-up of the Soviet Union after 1990. The world's nations vary enormously in size and shape. The largest country in the world is the Russian Federation; the smallest is the Vatican City.

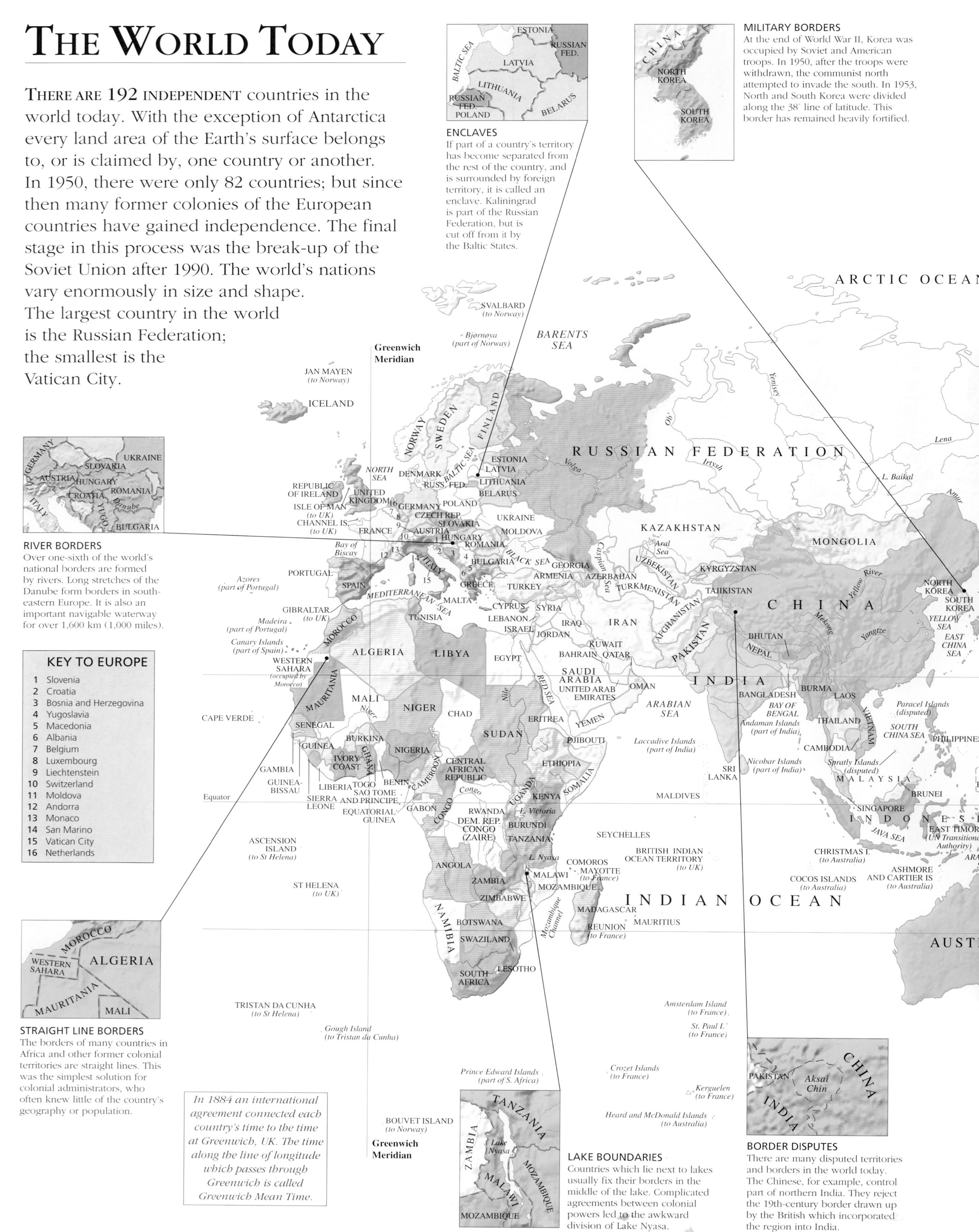

ESTONIA
RUSSIAN FED.
LATVIA
BALTIC SEA
LITHUANIA
RUSSIAN FED.
POLAND
BELARUS
CHINA
NORTH KOREA
SOUTH KOREA
ARCTIC OCEAN
SVALBARD (to Norway)
Bjørnøya (part of Norway)
BARENTS SEA
Greenwich Meridian
JAN MAYEN (to Norway)
ICELAND
NORWAY
SWEDEN
FINLAND
RUSSIAN FEDERATION
Yenisey
Ob'
Lena
Irtysh
Volga
L. Baikal
Amur
GERMANY
UKRAINE
SLOVAKIA
AUSTRIA
HUNGARY
ROMANIA
CROATIA
ITALY
YUGO.
Danube
BULGARIA
NORTH SEA
DENMARK
BALTIC SEA
ESTONIA
LATVIA
LITHUANIA
RUSS. FED.
BELARUS
REPUBLIC OF IRELAND
UNITED KINGDOM
ISLE OF MAN (to UK)
CHANNEL IS. (to UK)
GERMANY
POLAND
CZECH REP.
SLOVAKIA
UKRAINE
MOLDOVA
FRANCE
AUSTRIA
HUNGARY
ROMANIA
KAZAKHSTAN
MONGOLIA
Bay of Biscay
BULGARIA
BLACK SEA
GEORGIA
Caspian Sea
Aral Sea
UZBEKISTAN
KYRGYZSTAN
PORTUGAL
SPAIN
ITALY
GREECE
ARMENIA
AZERBAIJAN
TURKMENISTAN
TAJIKISTAN
Azores (part of Portugal)
MEDITERRANEAN SEA
MALTA
TURKEY
CYPRUS
SYRIA
LEBANON
ISRAEL
JORDAN
IRAQ
IRAN
AFGHANISTAN
PAKISTAN
CHINA
NORTH KOREA
SOUTH KOREA
YELLOW SEA
EAST CHINA SEA
Yellow River
Yangtze
Mekong
GIBRALTAR (to UK)
Madeira (part of Portugal)
TUNISIA
Canary Islands (part of Spain)
MOROCCO
ALGERIA
LIBYA
EGYPT
KUWAIT
BAHRAIN
QATAR
BHUTAN
NEPAL
WESTERN SAHARA (occupied by Morocco)
SAUDI ARABIA
UNITED ARAB EMIRATES
OMAN
INDIA
BANGLADESH
BURMA
LAOS
MAURITANIA
MALI
NIGER
CHAD
Nile
RED SEA
ARABIAN SEA
BAY OF BENGAL
Paracel Islands (disputed)
CAPE VERDE
SENEGAL
ERITREA
YEMEN
Andaman Islands (part of India)
THAILAND
VIETNAM
SOUTH CHINA SEA
PHILIPPINES
SUDAN
BURKINA
DJIBOUTI
Laccadive Islands (part of India)
CAMBODIA
GUINEA
IVORY COAST
GHANA
NIGERIA
CENTRAL AFRICAN REPUBLIC
ETHIOPIA
Nicobar Islands (part of India)
Spratly Islands (disputed)
GAMBIA
GUINEA-BISSAU
SIERRA LEONE
LIBERIA
TOGO
BENIN
CAMEROON
SRI LANKA
MALAYSIA
SAO TOME AND PRINCIPE
Congo
SOMALIA
UGANDA
KENYA
MALDIVES
BRUNEI
Equator
EQUATORIAL GUINEA
GABON
CONGO
RWANDA
L. Victoria
SINGAPORE
INDONESIA
DEM. REP. CONGO (ZAIRE)
BURUNDI
SEYCHELLES
EAST TIMOR (UN Transitional Authority)
ASCENSION ISLAND (to St Helena)
TANZANIA
BRITISH INDIAN OCEAN TERRITORY (to UK)
JAVA SEA
L. Nyasa
COMOROS
MAYOTTE (to France)
CHRISTMAS I. (to Australia)
ANGOLA
MALAWI
ASHMORE AND CARTIER IS (to Australia)
ST HELENA (to UK)
ZAMBIA
MOZAMBIQUE
COCOS ISLANDS (to Australia)
ZIMBABWE
INDIAN OCEAN
NAMIBIA
Mozambique Channel
MADAGASCAR
BOTSWANA
MAURITIUS
REUNION (to France)
SWAZILAND
SOUTH AFRICA
LESOTHO
AUSTR
MOROCCO
WESTERN SAHARA
ALGERIA
MAURITANIA
MALI
TRISTAN DA CUNHA (to St Helena)
Amsterdam Island (to France)
St. Paul I. (to France)
Gough Island (to Tristan da Cunha)
Prince Edward Islands (part of S. Africa)
Crozet Islands (to France)
Kerguelen (to France)
PAKISTAN
Aksai Chin
CHINA
INDIA
Heard and McDonald Islands (to Australia)
BOUVET ISLAND (to Norway)
Greenwich Meridian
TANZANIA
ZAMBIA
Lake Nyasa
MALAWI
MOZAMBIQUE
MOZAMBIQUE

Enclaves

If part of a country's territory has become separated from the rest of the country, and is surrounded by foreign territory, it is called an enclave. Kaliningrad is part of the Russian Federation, but is cut off from it by the Baltic States.

Military Borders

At the end of World War II, Korea was occupied by Soviet and American troops. In 1950, after the troops were withdrawn, the communist north attempted to invade the south. In 1953, North and South Korea were divided along the 38° line of latitude. This border has remained heavily fortified.

River Borders

Over one-sixth of the world's national borders are formed by rivers. Long stretches of the Danube form borders in south-eastern Europe. It is also an important navigable waterway for over 1,600 km (1,000 miles).

Key to Europe

1. Slovenia
2. Croatia
3. Bosnia and Herzegovina
4. Yugoslavia
5. Macedonia
6. Albania
7. Belgium
8. Luxembourg
9. Liechtenstein
10. Switzerland
11. Moldova
12. Andorra
13. Monaco
14. San Marino
15. Vatican City
16. Netherlands

Straight Line Borders

The borders of many countries in Africa and other former colonial territories are straight lines. This was the simplest solution for colonial administrators, who often knew little of the country's geography or population.

In 1884 an international agreement connected each country's time to the time at Greenwich, UK. The time along the line of longitude which passes through Greenwich is called Greenwich Mean Time.

Lake Boundaries

Countries which lie next to lakes usually fix their borders in the middle of the lake. Complicated agreements between colonial powers led to the awkward division of Lake Nyasa.

Border Disputes

There are many disputed territories and borders in the world today. The Chinese, for example, control part of northern India. They reject the 19th-century border drawn up by the British which incorporated the region into India.

THE CHANGING MAP

Borders between nations can change dramatically during their history. In 1634, Poland was Europe's largest nation; between 1772 and 1795 it was absorbed into Prussia, Russia and Austria. After World War I it became an independent country, but its borders changed again in 1945 following German and Russian invasions.

1. 1634
Moscow
POLAND
Warsaw
Kiev

In 1634, Poland was Europe's biggest nation.

2. 1772
Moscow
PRUSSIA
RUSSIA
Warsaw
Kiev
AUSTRIA

From 1772, Poland was part of Austria, Russia and Prussia.

3. 1918
Moscow
POLAND
Warsaw
Kiev

After World War I, Poland became a nation again.

4. 1945
Moscow
POLAND
Warsaw
Kiev

After World War II, the Polish borders were again redrawn.

The world is divided into 24 time zones. The 180° line of longitude is called the International Date Line. Places just west of this line are 24 hours ahead of places to the east. So, by travelling east across the Date Line you can go back a whole day.

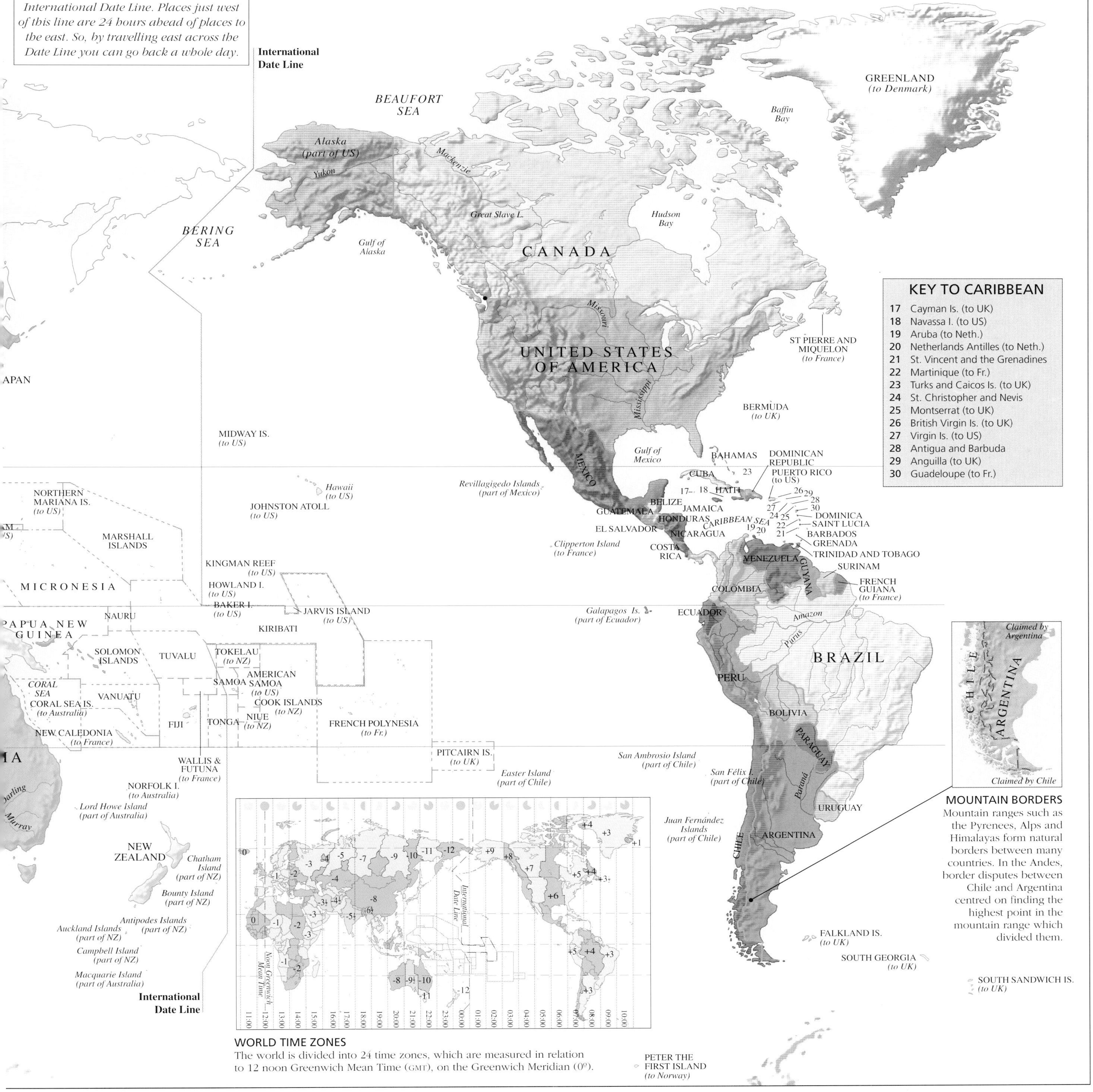

KEY TO CARIBBEAN

17 Cayman Is. (to UK)
18 Navassa I. (to US)
19 Aruba (to Neth.)
20 Netherlands Antilles (to Neth.)
21 St. Vincent and the Grenadines
22 Martinique (to Fr.)
23 Turks and Caicos Is. (to UK)
24 St. Christopher and Nevis
25 Montserrat (to UK)
26 British Virgin Is. (to UK)
27 Virgin Is. (to US)
28 Antigua and Barbuda
29 Anguilla (to UK)
30 Guadeloupe (to Fr.)

MOUNTAIN BORDERS

Mountain ranges such as the Pyrenees, Alps and Himalayas form natural borders between many countries. In the Andes, border disputes between Chile and Argentina centred on finding the highest point in the mountain range which divided them.

WORLD TIME ZONES

The world is divided into 24 time zones, which are measured in relation to 12 noon Greenwich Mean Time (GMT), on the Greenwich Meridian (0°).

KEY TO MAPS

Certain symbols will appear on every spread, and are listed below. These symbols represent physical features, or the country's infrastructure: borders, transport, settlement.

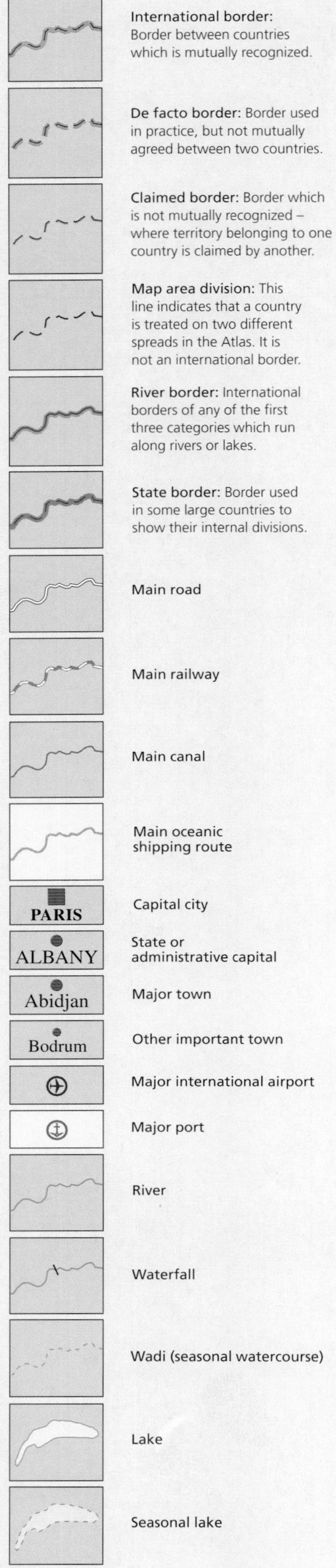

International border: Border between countries which is mutually recognized.
De facto border: Border used in practice, but not mutually agreed between two countries.
Claimed border: Border which is not mutually recognized – where territory belonging to one country is claimed by another.
Map area division: This line indicates that a country is treated on two different spreads in the Atlas. It is not an international border.
River border: International borders of any of the first three categories which run along rivers or lakes.
State border: Border used in some large countries to show their internal divisions.
Main road
Main railway
Main canal
Main oceanic shipping route
PARIS
Capital city
ALBANY
State or administrative capital
Abidjan
Major town
Bodrum
Other important town
Major international airport
Major port
River
Waterfall
Wadi (seasonal watercourse)
Lake
Seasonal lake
▲800m
Spot height of mountains
▼-800m
Spot depth of oceans

ABBREVIATIONS

The following abbreviations are used on maps:

Arch. = Archipelago
C. = Cape
Fr. = France
L. = Lake
I. = Island
Is. = Islands
Mts. = Mountains
Neth. = Netherlands
NZ = New Zealand
Pen. = Peninsula
R. = River
Res. = Reservoir
Fed. = Federation
W. = Wadi
UK = United Kingdom
US = United States of America

HOW TO USE THIS ATLAS

THE MAPS IN THIS ATLAS are organized by continent: North America; Central and South America; Europe; Africa; North and West Asia; South and East Asia; Australasia and Oceania. Each section of the book opens with a large double page spread introducing you to the physical geography – landscapes, climate, animals and vegetation – of the continent. On the following pages, the continent is divided by country, or group of countries. These pages deal with the human geography; each detailed map is supplemented by photographs, illustrations and landscape models. Finally, a glossary defines unfamiliar terms used in the text, and the index provides a list of all place names in the Atlas and facts about each country.

CONTINENT SPREAD

Key to symbols: This keybox lists major physical features which appear on the continental maps

Natural vegetation zones: The world is broken up into areas which are defined by the plants and animals which live there

Locator map: This world map shows where the continent is located

Image key: This natural vegetation colour and symbol box locates the type of landscape to which the photograph refers

! Threatened species: This symbol indicates that the future of certain plants and animals is uncertain

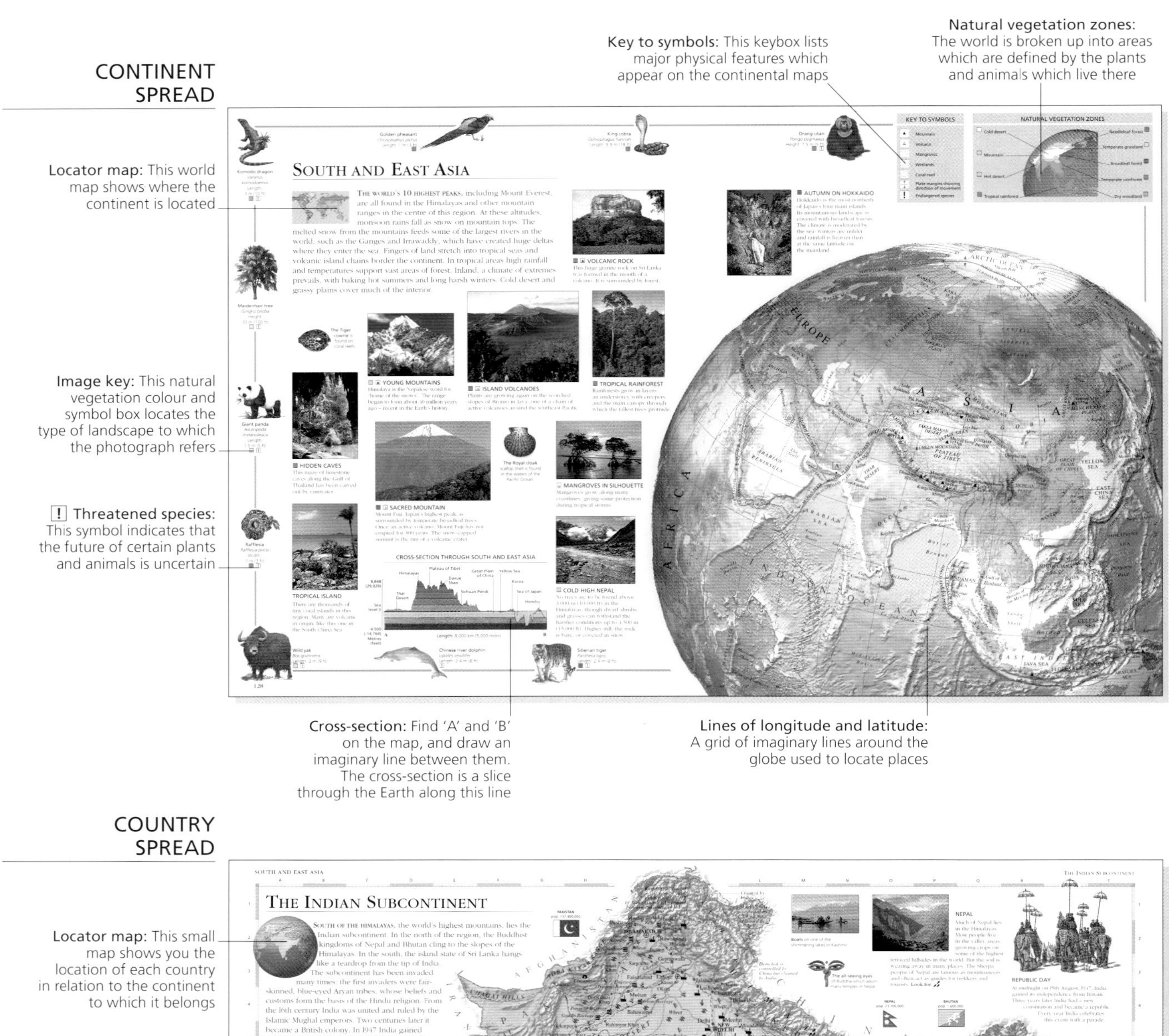

SOUTH AND EAST ASIA

Cross-section: Find 'A' and 'B' on the map, and draw an imaginary line between them. The cross-section is a slice through the Earth along this line

Lines of longitude and latitude: A grid of imaginary lines around the globe used to locate places

COUNTRY SPREAD

Locator map: This small map shows you the location of each country in relation to the continent to which it belongs

Reference grid: The letters and numbers around this grid help you to locate places listed in the index. For an explanation on how to use the grid, see the opening page of the Index

Keybox: A keybox on each spread lists the symbols which appear on the map. These symbols have been chosen to illustrate particularly important or interesting aspects of the country

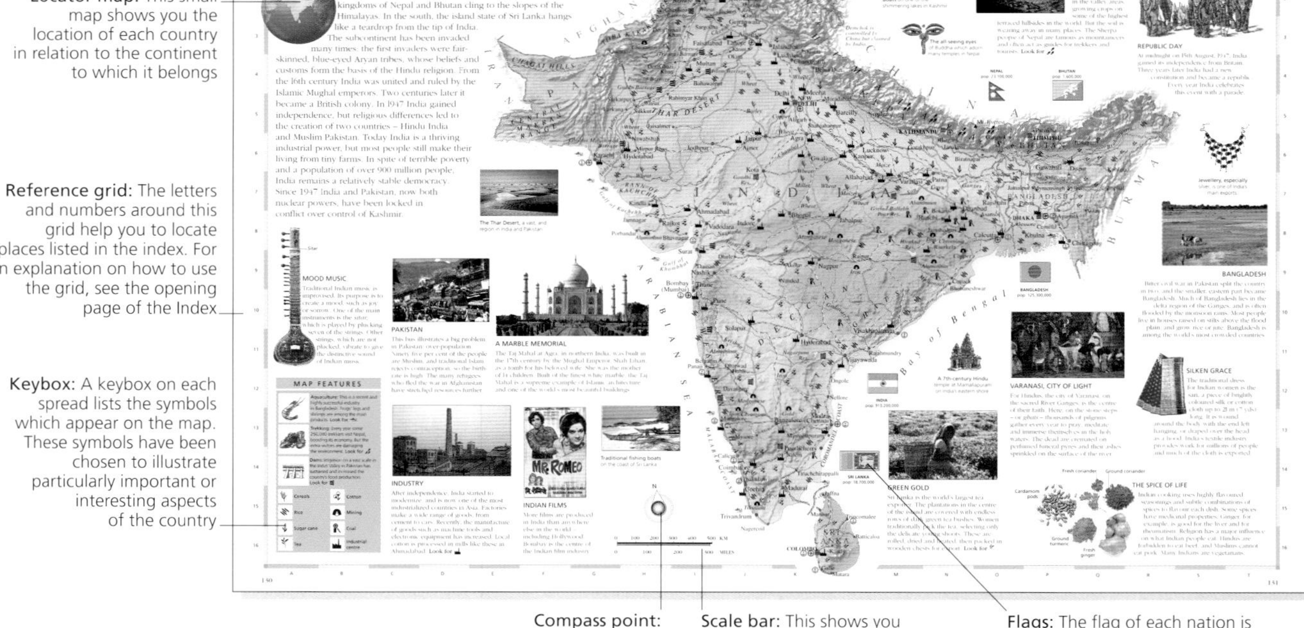

THE INDIAN SUBCONTINENT

Compass point: This will show you the direction of North

Scale bar: This shows you how distance on the map relates to kilometres and miles

Flags: The flag of each nation is positioned next to the country. Population figures are also given

THE BRITISH ISLES

PHYSICAL GEOGRAPHY

The British Isles lie to the northwest of mainland Europe, and were once joined to the continent. Rugged mountains in the north and west are the continuation of a Scandinavian mountain chain. Some 80 million years ago, shallow seas flooded much of southern England, which was blanketed by a thick layer of chalk. Familiar chalk landscapes, such as the South Downs, are a legacy of this period. Much of the British Isles bears the imprint of the last Ice Age, which ended about 10,000 years ago. Ice sheets eroded highlands, carved deep valleys, and indented the Scottish coastline. The Fens of East Anglia are the flattest part of the British Isles. Some land lies below sea level, and is at risk from flooding.

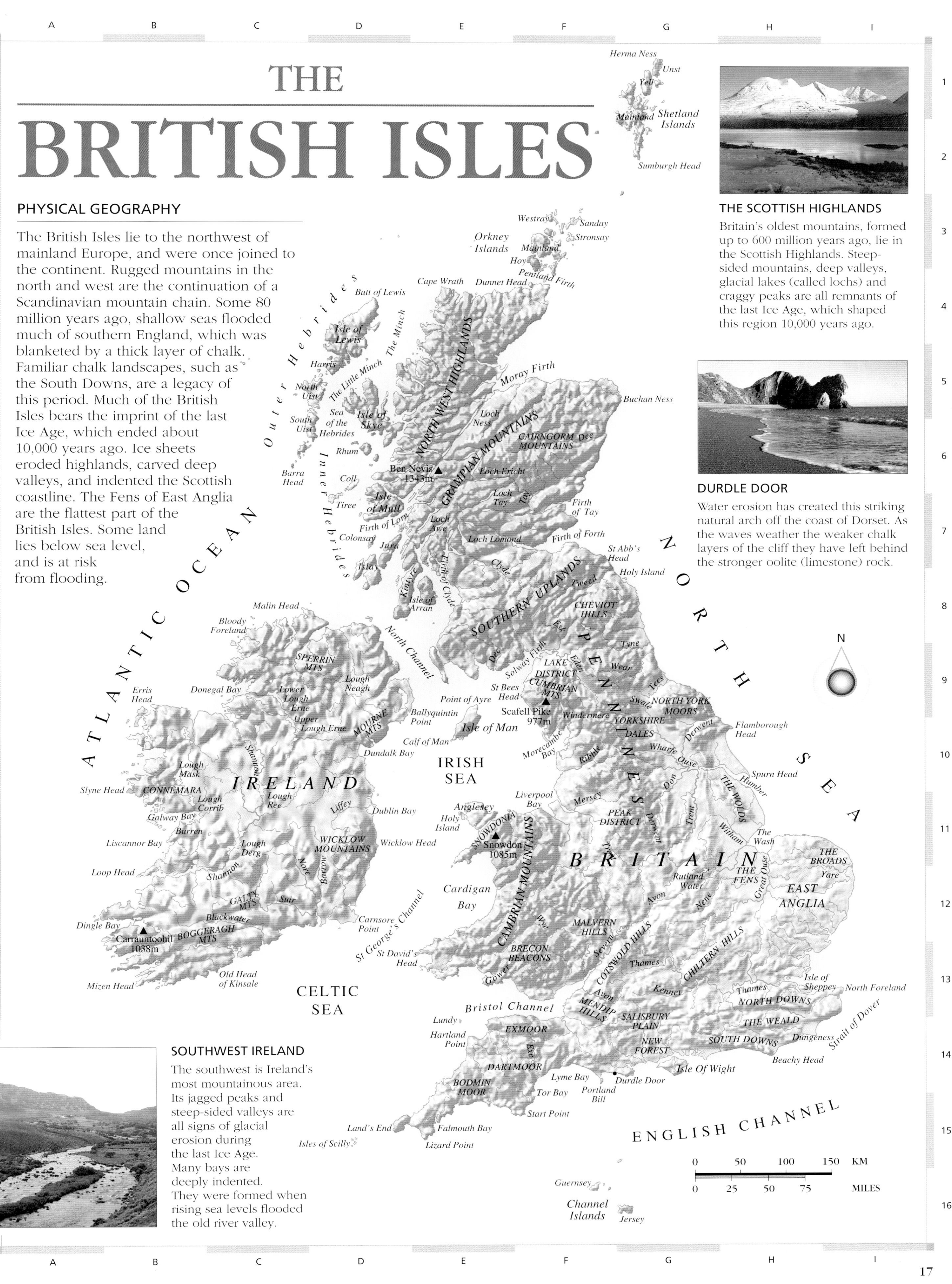

Herma Ness
Unst
Yell
Mainland
Shetland Islands
Sumburgh Head
Westray
Sanday
Stronsay
Orkney Islands
Mainland
Hoy
Pentland Firth
Dunnet Head
Cape Wrath
Butt of Lewis
Outer Hebrides
Isle of Lewis
The Minch
Harris
The Little Minch
North Uist
South Uist
Sea of the Hebrides
Isle of Skye
NORTH WEST HIGHLANDS
Moray Firth
Buchan Ness
Loch Ness
GRAMPIAN MOUNTAINS
CAIRNGORM MOUNTAINS
Dee
Rhum
Barra Head
Inner Hebrides
Ben Nevis 1343m
Coll
Loch Ericht
Loch Tay
Tay
Tiree
Isle of Mull
Firth of Tay
Firth of Lorn
Loch Awe
Colonsay
Jura
Loch Lomond
Firth of Forth
Islay
Kintyre
Firth of Clyde
Clyde
Isle of Arran
St Abb's Head
Holy Island
SOUTHERN UPLANDS
Tweed
CHEVIOT HILLS
ATLANTIC OCEAN
NORTH SEA
Malin Head
Bloody Foreland
North Channel
SPERRIN MTS
Lough Neagh
Donegal Bay
Lower Lough Erne
Upper Lough Erne
MOURNE MTS
Erris Head
Ballyquintin Point
Point of Ayre
Isle of Man
Calf of Man
Dundalk Bay
Esk
Dee
Solway Firth
Eden
LAKE DISTRICT
CUMBRIAN MTS
St Bees Head
Scafell Pike 977m
Windermere
PENNINES
Tyne
Wear
Tees
Swale
NORTH YORK MOORS
YORKSHIRE DALES
Derwent
Flamborough Head
Morecambe Bay
Ribble
Wharfe
Ouse
Lough Mask
Shannon
IRELAND
CONNEMARA
Slyne Head
Lough Corrib
Galway Bay
Lough Ree
Liffey
Dublin Bay
IRISH SEA
Burren
Liscannor Bay
Lough Derg
WICKLOW MOUNTAINS
Wicklow Head
Nore
Barrow
Loop Head
Shannon
GALTY MTS
Suir
Blackwater
Dingle Bay
Carrauntoohil 1038m
BOGGERAGH MTS
Mizen Head
Old Head of Kinsale
Carnsore Point
St George's Channel
CELTIC SEA
Liverpool Bay
Mersey
Anglesey
Holy Island
SNOWDONIA
Snowdon 1085m
CAMBRIAN MOUNTAINS
Cardigan Bay
PEAK DISTRICT
Derwent
Trent
Don
Humber
Spurn Head
THE WOLDS
Witham
The Wash
BRITAIN
Rutland Water
THE FENS
Great Ouse
THE BROADS
Yare
EAST ANGLIA
Nene
Avon
Wye
MALVERN HILLS
Severn
COTSWOLD HILLS
CHILTERN HILLS
Thames
BRECON BEACONS
St David's Head
Gower
Kennet
Isle of Sheppey
North Foreland
Avon
MENDIP HILLS
SALISBURY PLAIN
NORTH DOWNS
THE WEALD
Bristol Channel
Lundy
Hartland Point
EXMOOR
Exe
NEW FOREST
SOUTH DOWNS
Dungeness
Strait of Dover
Beachy Head
DARTMOOR
Isle Of Wight
Lyme Bay
Durdle Door
BODMIN MOOR
Tor Bay
Portland Bill
Start Point
Land's End
Falmouth Bay
Lizard Point
Isles of Scilly
ENGLISH CHANNEL
Guernsey
Channel Islands
Jersey
N
0 50 100 150 KM
0 25 50 75 MILES

THE SCOTTISH HIGHLANDS

Britain's oldest mountains, formed up to 600 million years ago, lie in the Scottish Highlands. Steep-sided mountains, deep valleys, glacial lakes (called lochs) and craggy peaks are all remnants of the last Ice Age, which shaped this region 10,000 years ago.

DURDLE DOOR

Water erosion has created this striking natural arch off the coast of Dorset. As the waves weather the weaker chalk layers of the cliff they have left behind the stronger oolite (limestone) rock.

SOUTHWEST IRELAND

The southwest is Ireland's most mountainous area. Its jagged peaks and steep-sided valleys are all signs of glacial erosion during the last Ice Age. Many bays are deeply indented. They were formed when rising sea levels flooded the old river valley.

Political British Isles

The British Isles contain two separate countries, the United Kingdom and the Republic of Ireland. The UK, one of the longest-lasting parliamentary democracies in the world, includes the nations of England, Scotland and Wales and the province of Northern Ireland. The Queen is the head of state, and the country is governed by the elected House of Commons, based at Westminster in London. Elected local governments administer all local services, from health and education to street-cleaning and refuse-collection and are funded by the central government and by local taxes. Ireland was part of the UK from 1800 to 1921. It is a parliamentary democracy with an elected president as its head of state. The elected house of representatives, headed by the prime minister *(taoiseach)*, is called the Dáil.

THE SCOTTISH PARLIAMENT

In 1999 regional assemblies opened in both Edinburgh and Cardiff, giving both Scotland and Wales the right to govern their own domestic affairs. The UK government in London continues to look after national interests. Other areas, such as Cornwall, are campaigning for more regional independence.

THE CIVIL WAR

King Charles I ruled as an absolute monarch, believing that he was not answerable to parliament or the people. His actions led to his defeat in the English Civil War (1642–45), and his subsequent execution (1649). Civil war battles are still re-enacted today.

LOCAL GOVERNMENT

Elected local authorities have extensive powers in the UK. In rural areas, counties administer services such as health and education, while town councils run services such as refuse collection. In large urban areas, such as Manchester, all aspects of government are run by single authorities.

1: CENTRAL SCOTLAND

CLACKMANNAN
WEST DUNBARTONSHIRE
EAST DUNBARTONSHIRE
NORTH LANARKSHIRE
FALKIRK
WEST LOTHIAN
EDINBURGH
MIDLOTHIAN
INVERCLYDE
GLASGOW
RENFREWSHIRE
EAST RENFREWSHIRE

2: NORTHEAST ENGLAND

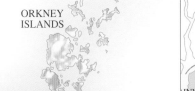

NEWCASTLE UPON TYNE
NORTH TYNESIDE
SOUTH TYNESIDE
GATESHEAD
SUNDERLAND

3: TEESSIDE

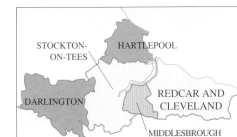

STOCKTON-ON-TEES
HARTLEPOOL
DARLINGTON
REDCAR AND CLEVELAND
MIDDLESBROUGH

7: NORTHWEST ENGLAND

ROCHDALE
BOLTON
BURY
OLDHAM
WIGAN
SALFORD
SEFTON
KNOWSLEY
ST HELENS
TAMESIDE
LIVERPOOL
TRAFFORD
MANCHESTER
STOCKPORT
WIRRAL

SHETLAND ISLANDS
ORKNEY ISLANDS
WESTERN ISLES
OCEAN
NORTH
HIGHLAND
SCOTLAND
MORAY
ABERDEENSHIRE
ABERDEEN
ANGUS
PERTH AND KINROSS
DUNDEE
FIFE
STIRLING
ARGYLL AND BUTE
EAST LOTHIAN
NORTH AYRSHIRE
SOUTH LANARKSHIRE
THE BORDERS
EAST AYRSHIRE
SOUTH

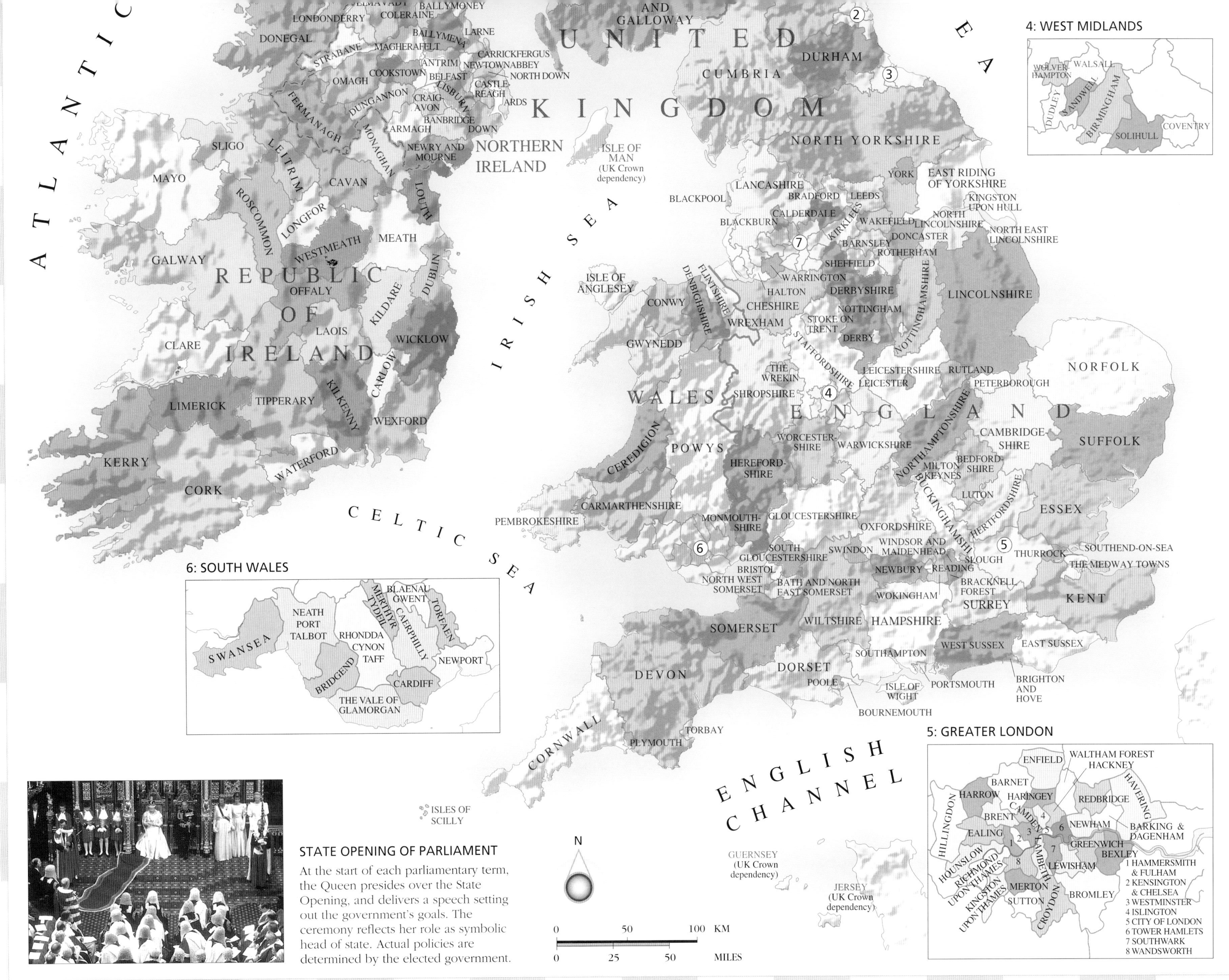

4: WEST MIDLANDS

6: SOUTH WALES

5: GREATER LONDON

1 HAMMERSMITH & FULHAM
2 KENSINGTON & CHELSEA
3 WESTMINSTER
4 ISLINGTON
5 CITY OF LONDON
6 TOWER HAMLETS
7 SOUTHWARK
8 WANDSWORTH

0 50 100 KM

0 25 50 MILES

STATE OPENING OF PARLIAMENT

At the start of each parliamentary term, the Queen presides over the State Opening, and delivers a speech setting out the government's goals. The ceremony reflects her role as symbolic head of state. Actual policies are determined by the elected government.

SOUTHERN ENGLAND

SOUTHERN ENGLAND is dominated by the city of London, the largest in Europe, founded by the Romans in c.AD 50. The city is the historic heart of England, home of the royal court, and its commercial hub. In the 19th century, the port of London was the busiest in the world, the nerve centre of Britain's large overseas empire. Today, London is a major financial, media and cultural centre, with a population of over 7 million. The southeast, England's most prosperous and populous region, is London's "commuter belt". The Thames valley region is the centre of England's computer and electronics industry. Its main town, Oxford, was England's first university, founded in 1167. Further west, wooded river valleys alternate with bare, windswept downland, and dairy and sheep-farms flourish. Cornwall, once an outpost of Celtic culture and early Christianity, is a picturesque region of coastal coves, sheer cliffs, and fishing villages – a magnet for tourists.

COTSWOLD RETREATS

The population of the picturesque villages of southern England is changing. Many Londoners buy weekend and holiday cottages in Cotswold villages. The demand for rural homes pushes up house prices, forcing local people to find work and homes in towns and cities.

NEW TOWNS

In the 20th century, overcrowded, poor-quality housing in London forced the government to establish a number of purpose-built new towns, which could absorb overspill population. Milton Keynes new town was established in 1967.

BATH

The hot springs of Bath were discovered by the Romans, who built a spa complex there. In the 18th century, it once again became fashionable to "take the waters" at Bath. The city's fine architecture reflects its Georgian heyday.

The BAT and BALL

Bars, or public houses, are signalled by vivid signs.

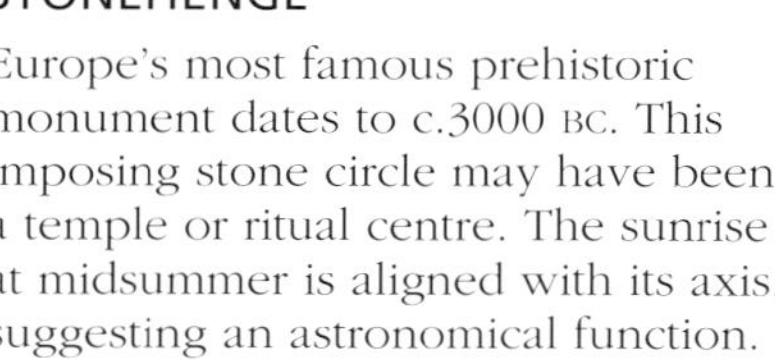

STONEHENGE

Europe's most famous prehistoric monument dates to c.3000 BC. This imposing stone circle may have been a temple or ritual centre. The sunrise at midsummer is aligned with its axis, suggesting an astronomical function.

CRICKET

Although the origins of cricket date back to medieval times, the first recorded match was in 1700. Today, both county cricket matches and international contests are regular events. Local teams, playing on village grounds, are a familiar sight in summer.

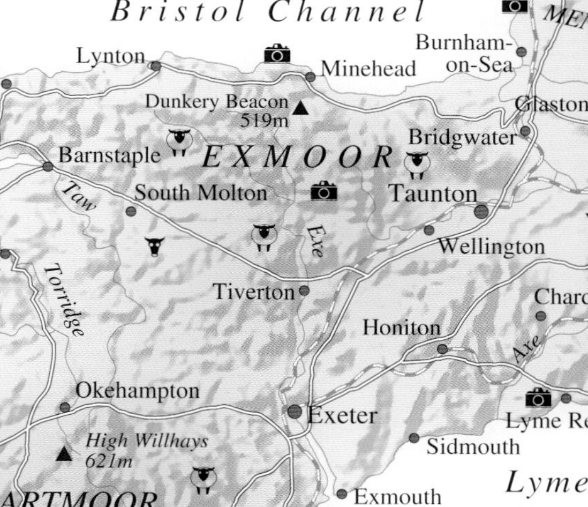
WALES
Avonmouth
Portishead
Clevedon
Weston-super-Mare
Bristol Channel
Burnham-on-Sea
Glastonbury
Lynton
Minehead
Ilfracombe
Lundy
Dunkery Beacon 519m
Barnstaple Bay
Barnstaple
EXMOOR
Bridgwater
Hartland Point
Bideford
Clovelly
South Molton
Taunton
Taw
Wellington
Great Torrington
Torridge
Exe
Tiverton
Chard
Bude
Bude Bay
Honiton
Axe
Tamar
Okehampton
Exeter
Lyme Regis
Port Isaac Bay
Launceston
High Willhays 621m
Sidmouth
BODMIN MOOR
DARTMOOR
Exmouth
Lyme Bay
Wadebridge
Teignmouth
Newton Abbot
ATLANTIC OCEAN
Bodmin
Fowey
Torquay
Newquay
Tor Bay
Paignton
Ligger Bay
St Austell
Saltash
Plymouth
Dart
Dartmouth
St Austell Bay
St Ives
Truro
Bigbury Bay
Start Bay
Redruth
Salcombe
Start Point
Penzance
Falmouth
Land's End
Helston
Mount's Bay
Lizard Point
Isles of Scilly
Hugh Town

MAP FEATURES

Financial centre: The City of London is the headquarters of many corporations and banks, and has an international stock exchange. **Look for**

Tourism: Visitors from all over the world are attracted by the South's cities, churches, countryside and coastline. **Look for**

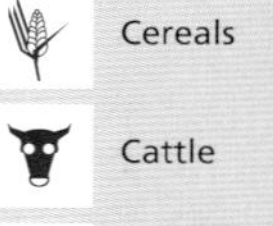

	Cereals		Industrial centre
	Cattle		Hi-tech industry
	Market gardening		Car manufacture
	Sheep		Aerospace
	Food processing		Printing and publishing

The fortress on the island of St Michael's Mount in Cornwall.

CATHEDRAL CITY

Salisbury Cathedral was mainly built between 1220 and 1258. This fine example of Gothic architecture was topped by the tallest spire in England in 1280–1310. The cathedral is surrounded by ancient schools, hospitals and clergy houses. Salisbury, like many of England's cathedral cities, is a major tourist centre.

BRIGHTON

Sea-bathing became popular in the mid-18th century and Brighton was England's first seaside resort. The oriental-style Royal Pavilion, built by the Prince of Wales in 1822, became a landmark. The town is a popular weekend resort for Londoners. **Look for**

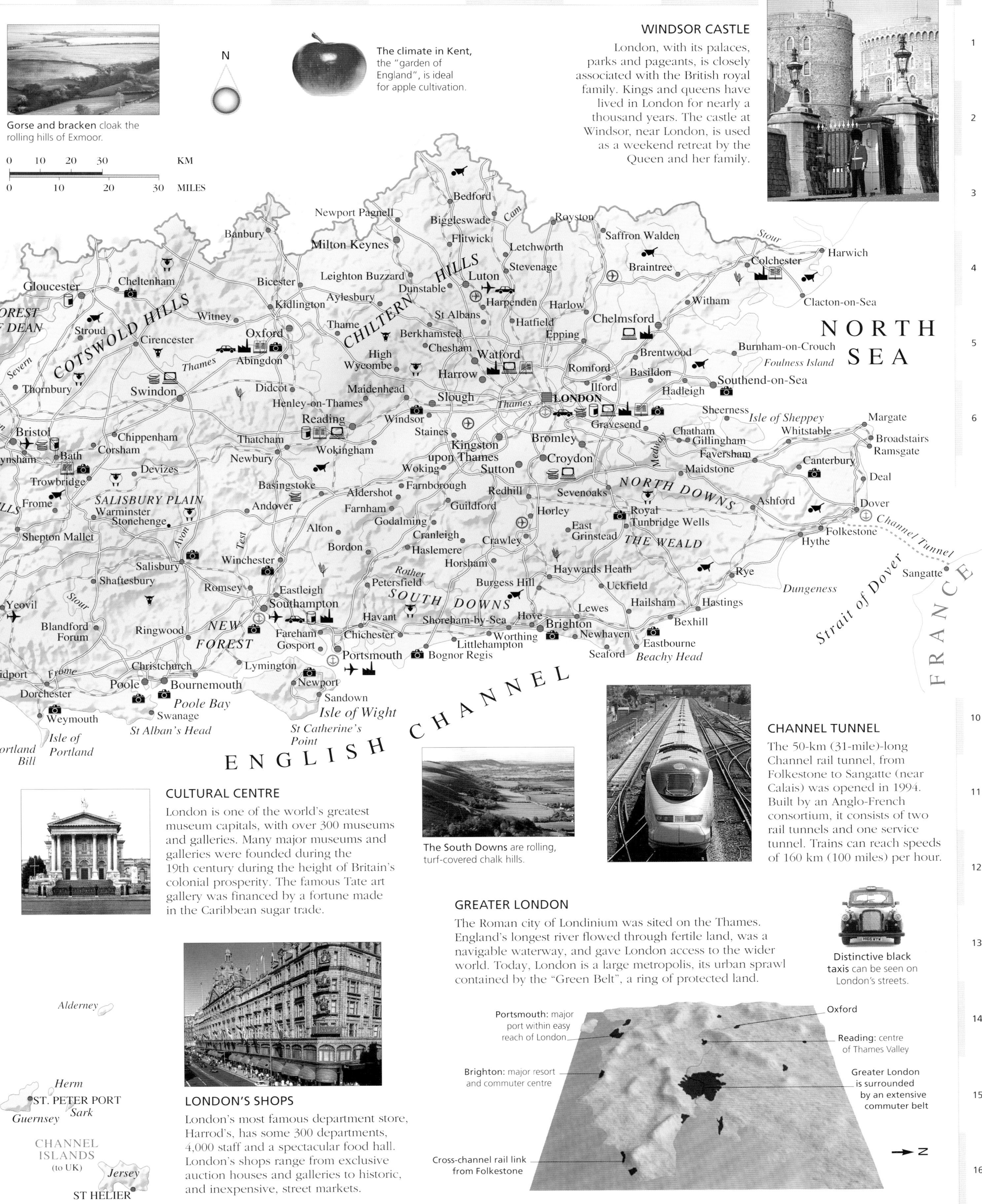

K L M N O P Q R S T
1 2 3 4 5 6 10 11 12 13 14 15 16
N
0 10 20 30 KM
0 10 20 30 MILES
NORTH SEA
ENGLISH CHANNEL
FRANCE
Strait of Dover
Channel Tunnel
COTSWOLD HILLS
CHILTERN HILLS
SALISBURY PLAIN
NORTH DOWNS
SOUTH DOWNS
THE WEALD
NEW FOREST
FOREST OF DEAN
LONDON
Gloucester
Cheltenham
Stroud
Cirencester
Witney
Oxford
Abingdon
Banbury
Bicester
Kidlington
Milton Keynes
Newport Pagnell
Bedford
Biggleswade
Flitwick
Leighton Buzzard
Dunstable
Aylesbury
Thame
Luton
Harpenden
St Albans
Hatfield
Stevenage
Letchworth
Royston
Saffron Walden
Braintree
Colchester
Harwich
Clacton-on-Sea
Witham
Harlow
Chelmsford
Epping
Berkhamsted
Chesham
High Wycombe
Watford
Harrow
Romford
Brentwood
Basildon
Ilford
Hadleigh
Southend-on-Sea
Burnham-on-Crouch
Foulness Island
Sheerness
Isle of Sheppey
Margate
Broadstairs
Ramsgate
Whitstable
Chatham
Gillingham
Faversham
Canterbury
Deal
Dover
Folkestone
Hythe
Ashford
Maidstone
Gravesend
Bromley
Croydon
Sutton
Kingston upon Thames
Woking
Slough
Windsor
Staines
Maidenhead
Henley-on-Thames
Reading
Wokingham
Thatcham
Newbury
Didcot
Swindon
Thornbury
Bristol
Bath
Chippenham
Corsham
Devizes
Trowbridge
Frome
Warminster
Stonehenge
Shepton Mallet
Basingstoke
Andover
Aldershot
Farnborough
Farnham
Guildford
Redhill
Sevenoaks
Royal Tunbridge Wells
East Grinstead
Horley
Crawley
Godalming
Cranleigh
Haslemere
Horsham
Alton
Bordon
Winchester
Salisbury
Shaftesbury
Romsey
Eastleigh
Southampton
Petersfield
Burgess Hill
Haywards Heath
Uckfield
Rye
Dungeness
Sangatte
Hastings
Hailsham
Bexhill
Lewes
Eastbourne
Beachy Head
Seaford
Newhaven
Brighton
Hove
Shoreham-by-Sea
Worthing
Littlehampton
Bognor Regis
Chichester
Havant
Portsmouth
Fareham
Gosport
Lymington
Newport
Sandown
Isle of Wight
St Catherine's Point
Christchurch
Bournemouth
Poole
Poole Bay
Swanage
St Alban's Head
Ringwood
Blandford Forum
Yeovil
Dorchester
Weymouth
Isle of Portland
Portland Bill
Bridport
Thames
Severn
Avon
Test
Stour
Rother
Medway
Cam
Frome
Alderney
Herm
ST. PETER PORT
Guernsey
Sark
CHANNEL ISLANDS (to UK)
Jersey
ST HELIER
Portsmouth: major port within easy reach of London
Brighton: major resort and commuter centre
Cross-channel rail link from Folkestone
Oxford
Reading: centre of Thames Valley
Greater London is surrounded by an extensive commuter belt
N

Gorse and bracken cloak the rolling hills of Exmoor.

The climate in Kent, the "garden of England", is ideal for apple cultivation.

WINDSOR CASTLE

London, with its palaces, parks and pageants, is closely associated with the British royal family. Kings and queens have lived in London for nearly a thousand years. The castle at Windsor, near London, is used as a weekend retreat by the Queen and her family.

CHANNEL TUNNEL

The 50-km (31-mile)-long Channel rail tunnel, from Folkestone to Sangatte (near Calais) was opened in 1994. Built by an Anglo-French consortium, it consists of two rail tunnels and one service tunnel. Trains can reach speeds of 160 km (100 miles) per hour.

CULTURAL CENTRE

London is one of the world's greatest museum capitals, with over 300 museums and galleries. Many major museums and galleries were founded during the 19th century during the height of Britain's colonial prosperity. The famous Tate art gallery was financed by a fortune made in the Caribbean sugar trade.

The South Downs are rolling, turf-covered chalk hills.

GREATER LONDON

The Roman city of Londinium was sited on the Thames. England's longest river flowed through fertile land, was a navigable waterway, and gave London access to the wider world. Today, London is a large metropolis, its urban sprawl contained by the "Green Belt", a ring of protected land.

Distinctive black taxis can be seen on London's streets.

LONDON'S SHOPS

London's most famous department store, Harrod's, has some 300 departments, 4,000 staff and a spectacular food hall. London's shops range from exclusive auction houses and galleries to historic, and inexpensive, street markets.

Central England

From the fertile fens of East Anglia to the industrial cities of the Midlands, Central England is an area of contrasts. The flat marshlands of East Anglia were drained in the 18th century, and the region became Britain's arable heartland. At the same time, the Midlands, with their extensive coalfields and navigable waterways, were at the forefront of the Industrial Revolution. They became major centres of manufacturing, specializing in textiles, ceramics and machinery. Much of Britain's traditional heavy industry is now in decline but its industrial heritage has become a major tourist attraction. Centres such as Nottingham and Derby now specialize in textiles, electronics, aircraft and car manufacture and chemicals. To the north, the bleak industrial landscape gives way to the rolling moors and dales of the Peak District, Britain's first national park.

THE POTTERIES

The Trent valley, with its plentiful supplies of clay and coal (used for firing kilns), became England's main ceramics centre in the 18th century. Josiah Wedgewood founded his pottery works there in 1769. Fine Wedgewood ceramics are still very popular today. Look for [ceramics symbol]

STATELY HOMES

Magnificent country homes reflect the wealth and rank of the English aristocracy. From the 18th century, aristocrats and rich businessmen alike built fine stately homes in large parks, maintained by hundreds of servants and gardeners. Chatsworth, near Bakewell, was completed in 1707.

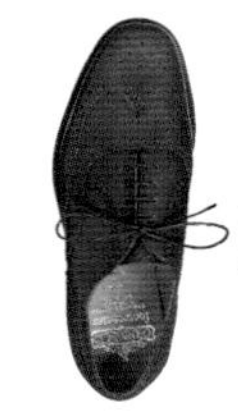

Northampton is a centre of English shoe-making.

The granite rocks and glorious scenery of the Malvern Hills.

Wallasey
Birkenhead
Mersey
Widnes
Warrington
Runcorn
Wilmslow
Glossop
Kinder Scout 636m
Buxton
Ellesmere Port
Northwich
Macclesfield
Chester
Middlewich
Congleton
Sandbach
Crewe
Alsager
Leek
Nantwich
Hanley
Stoke-on-Trent
Newcastle-under-Lyme
Whitchurch
Stone
Uttoxeter
WALES
Oswestry
Stafford
Rugeley
Shrewsbury
Telford
Cannock
Ironbridge
Church Stretton
Wolverhampton
Walsa
West Bromwich
Dudley
Severn
Birminghar
Craven Arms
Ludlow
Kidderminster
Bromsgrove
Stourport-on-Severn
Redditch
Droitwich
Leominster
Worcester
MALVERN HILLS
Great Malvern
Evesham
Wye
Hereford
Ross-on-Wye
N

0 10 20 30 KM
0 10 20 30 MILES

BIRMINGHAM BLIGHT

In the 19th century, Birmingham was a major manufacturing centre, blighted by smoke-belching factories and cramped housing. In the 1960s, much of its centre was cleared and redeveloped; today its 19th-century civic buildings are being restored.

IRONBRIDGE

In the 18th century, Ironbridge Gorge was at the heart of the developing Industrial Revolution. When, in 1709, Abraham Darby pioneered the use of inexpensive coke to smelt iron ore, Ironbridge was transformed into one of the world's great iron-making centres.

Cadbury's chocolates are made at Bourneville, outside Birmingham.

MAP FEATURES

Textiles: The east Midlands, in particular Nottingham and Leicester, are major weaving, clothes-manufacturing and lace-making centres. Look for [textiles symbol]

Pollution: Coal-fired power plants generate much of England's energy, but are a major cause of pollution. Look for [pollution symbol]

Cereals	Chemicals
Root crops	Hi-tech
Cattle	Aerospace
Food processing	Car manufacture
Brewing	Ceramics
Industrial centre	Pharmaceuticals

SHAKESPEARE SHRINE

William Shakespeare, England's most famous writer, was born in Stratford-upon-Avon in 1564. The town is now home to the renowned Royal Shakespeare Company. The cottage that belonged to his wife, Anne Hathaway, is a popular tourist attraction.

SPAGHETTI JUNCTION

Britain's system of motorways dates to the 1960s. Since then, most freight traffic has switched from rail to road, and there is pressure to build more motorways. Spaghetti Junction, on the M6 just north of Birmingham, is Britain's most complex road interchange.

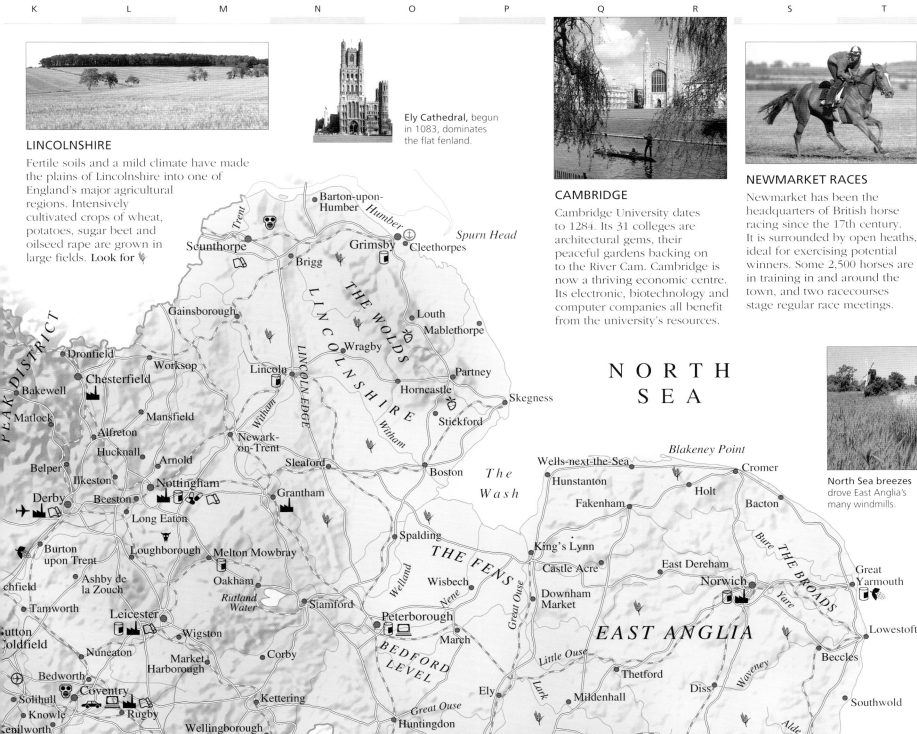

LINCOLNSHIRE

Fertile soils and a mild climate have made the plains of Lincolnshire into one of England's major agricultural regions. Intensively cultivated crops of wheat, potatoes, sugar beet and oilseed rape are grown in large fields. Look for

Ely Cathedral, begun in 1083, dominates the flat fenland.

CAMBRIDGE

Cambridge University dates to 1284. Its 31 colleges are architectural gems, their peaceful gardens backing on to the River Cam. Cambridge is now a thriving economic centre. Its electronic, biotechnology and computer companies all benefit from the university's resources.

NEWMARKET RACES

Newmarket has been the headquarters of British horse racing since the 17th century. It is surrounded by open heaths, ideal for exercising potential winners. Some 2,500 horses are in training in and around the town, and two racecourses stage regular race meetings.

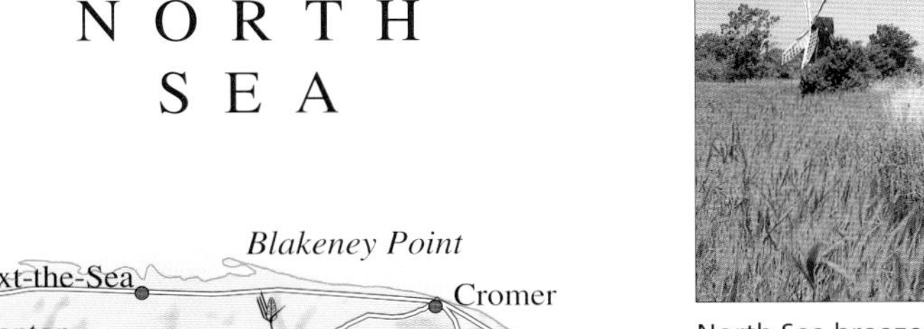

North Sea breezes drove East Anglia's many windmills.

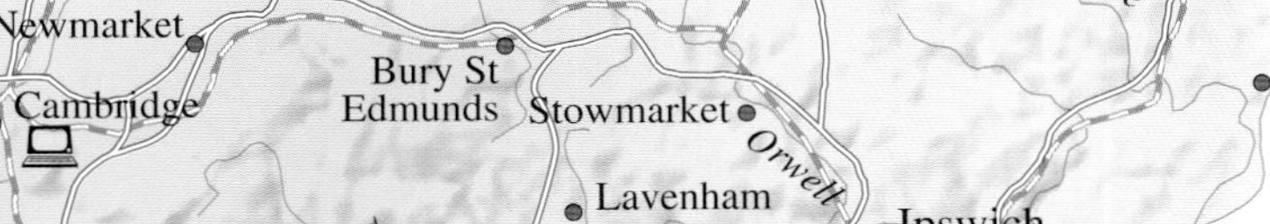

Broad fields of oilseed rape dominate the East Anglian landscape in the spring.

East Anglia's coasts and estuaries are ideal for yachting.

NARROW BOAT

England's canal network dates to the 18th century, when waterways were used to transport goods in bulk between industrial centres. The birthplace of the English canal system, the Midlands still has the biggest concentration of navigable waterways.

LAVENHAM

The flourishing English wool trade was based in East Anglia between the 14th and 16th centuries. The wool trade brought a new prosperity to the region, reflected in its fine churches and houses. Lavenham is a perfectly preserved Tudor wool town.

CONTAINER PORT

Felixstowe, on the Orwell estuary, has been a container port since 1953. One of the largest ports in Britain, it is also the most accessible to Europoort in the Netherlands. Increased trade with Europe in the 1980s has made Felixstowe one of Britain's busiest ports.

NORTHERN ENGLAND

THE WILD AND RUGGED country of northern England is imprinted with an eventful past, ranging from Roman invasions, Celtic Christianity and Viking raids, to skirmishes with Scottish clans. But it is the Industrial Revolution which has left the most vivid legacy. From the mill towns of Lancashire to the shipbuilding ports of the Tyne, Wear and Tees estuaries, the landscape bears the scars of industrialization. In the 19th century, Liverpool and Manchester were England's two largest cities after London. Coal mines, textile mills and dockyards all attracted migrants from the country to the cities, where they lived in cramped and squalid housing. Some industrialists were benefactors to the region, leaving a legacy of fine buildings, art galleries and museums. Today, heavy industry is in decline, the economy of the North is depressed, and unemployment is high. Yet many regions have become shrines to their industrial past, and inner cities are being revitalized and redeveloped.

HADRIAN'S WALL

The Romans began building this 117-km (73-mile) wall across northern England in AD 120. It marked the northwestern boundary of the Roman empire. Troops were stationed all along the wall, and forts were built at 8-km (5-mile) intervals.

A door-knocker from Durham's 900-year-old cathedral.

The rugged peaks and tranquil waters of the Lake District.

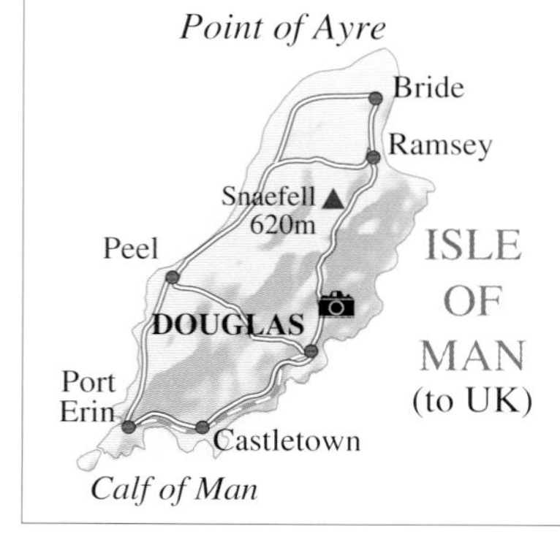

Point of Ayre
Bride
Ramsey
Snaefell 620m
Peel
DOUGLAS
ISLE OF MAN (to UK)
Port Erin
Castletown
Calf of Man

SELLAFIELD

Situated on the wild and windswept Cumbrian coast, Sellafield is a plant which reprocesses spent nuclear reactor fuel. Its construction was very widely opposed because of fears of radioactive discharges into the Irish Sea. Disturbingly high levels of diseases such as childhood leukaemia have further reinforced local opposition to the plant.

THE LAKE DISTRICT

The Lake District contains some of England's most magnificent scenery, and is a magnet for tourists and hikers. During the last Ice Age, 10,000 years ago, glaciers scoured deep basins out of the mountainsides, which filled with water to form lakes when the glaciers melted. Look for 📷

Traditional roast beef is served with Yorkshire pudding, a savoury batter.

BLACKPOOL

Thousands of factory workers from Lancashire once flocked to Blackpool for their holidays. It is still a major resort, offering piers, bingo halls and amusement arcades. The 158-m (418-ft) Tower, illuminated with coloured lights, is a famous landmark.

FUNLAND
FUN

MAP FEATURES

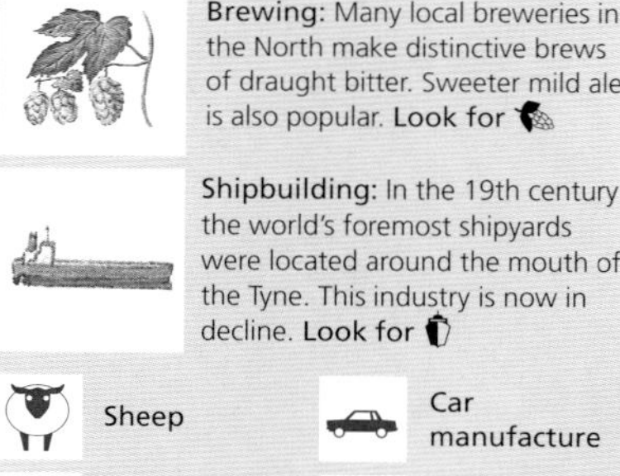

Brewing: Many local breweries in the North make distinctive brews of draught bitter. Sweeter mild ale is also popular. Look for

Shipbuilding: In the 19th century the world's foremost shipyards were located around the mouth of the Tyne. This industry is now in decline. Look for

Sheep	Car manufacture
Cattle	Chemicals
Fishing	Hi-tech
Food processing	Textiles
Industrial centre	Tourism

LIVERPOOL DOCKS

In the 19th century, Liverpool was the main departure point for the Americas, and many would-be emigrants settled there. The container port, based in Bootle, still flourishes and the 19th-century dock area has been transformed into shops, museums and galleries.

Manchester United is a world-famous football team.

SCOTLAND
CHEVIOT
North Tyne
Kielder Water
Hadrian's Wall
Brampton
Haltwhistle
Solway Firth
Carlisle
South Tyne
Wigton
Eden
Cross Fell 893m
Cockermouth
Bassenthwaite Lake
Penrith
Workington
Skiddaw 931m
Whitehaven
Keswick
Ullswater
St Bees Head
Cumbrian Mountains
Helvellyn 949m
Scafell Pike 978m
LAKE DISTRICT
Sellafield
Seascale
Windermere
Kendal
Ravenglass
Whernside 737m
Ulverston
Ingleborough 723m
Barrow-in-Furness
IRISH SEA
Isle of Walney
Morecambe
Lancaster
Morecambe Bay
FOREST OF BOWLAND
Fleetwood
Wyre
Clitheroe
Poulton-le-Fylde
Blackpool
Ribble
Preston
Accrington
Lytham St Anne's
Leyland
Blackburn
Southport
Chorley
Bolton
Ormskirk
Formby
Wigan
Kirkby
Crosby
St Helens
Bootle
Liverpool
Mersey

Berwick-upon-Tweed
Tweedmouth
Holy Island
Lindisfarne
Farne Islands
Bamburgh
Wooler
The Cheviot 816m
Alnwick
Amble
Druridge Bay
Otterburn
Ashington
Morpeth
Ridsdale
Blyth
Whitley Bay
Tynemouth
South Shields
Newcastle upon Tyne
Gateshead
Washington
Sunderland
Stanley
Consett
Chester-le-Street
Durham
Peterlee
Stanhope
Wear
Bishop Auckland
Spennymoor
Hartlepool
Tees
Shildon
Billingham
Redcar
Barnard Castle
Stockton-on-Tees
Middlesbrough
Staithes
Whitby
Darlington
Robin Hood's Bay
Esk
Richmond
Scotch Corner
Catterick
Swale
NORTH YORK MOORS
Northallerton
YORKSHIRE DALES
Hawes
Ure
Scarborough
Thirsk
Helmsley
Pickering
Filey
Rye
Derwent
Filey Bay
Wharfe
Malton
Flamborough Head
Ripon
Bridlington
THE WOLDS
Knaresborough
Driffield
Bridlington Bay
Harrogate
York
Skipton
Ilkley
Wetherby
Hull
Hornsea
Otley
Beverley
Colne
Leeds
Nelson
Burnley
Haworth
Bradford
Selby
Kingston upon Hull
Garforth
Hessle
Withernsea
Halifax
Aire
Ouse
Castleford
Dewsbury
Wakefield
Goole
Huddersfield
Humber
Spurn Head
Barnsley
Don
Oldham
Doncaster
Manchester
Mexborough
Rotherham
Stockport
Sheffield
NORTH SEA
KM 0 15 30
MILES 0 15 30
N

Lindisfarne, a focus of Celtic Christianity.

NEWCASTLE

Once the site of a Roman fort, and for many centuries the base for English campaigns against the Scots, Newcastle flourished as a coal-mining centre, famous for its engineering and steel production. The imposing Tyne Bridge reflects its past prosperity; its derelict quayside buildings are now being restored.

CAR MANUFACTURING

Tyneside was once a major shipbuilding centre. Today, foreign competition has undermined traditional shipbuilding and abandoned docks have been turned into business parks. Foreign investors, including the Japanese car manufacturers Nissan, have started to move in and revitalize the region. Look for 🚗

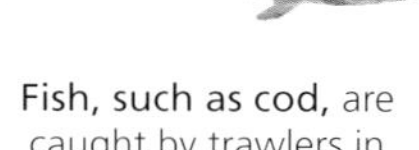

Fish, such as cod, are caught by trawlers in the North Sea.

HAWORTH

Haworth Parsonage, high on the Pennine moorland, was the home from 1820–61 of the novelists Charlotte, Emily and Anne Brontë. Visitors from all over the world come to absorb the bleak landscape which is vividly described in their novels.

WIND POWER

Wind turbines high on the North York Moors are used to generate electricity – wind power now accounts for 10 % of England's electricity. Although turbines are a clean energy source, they are often sited in isolated beauty spots, and are seen as blots on the landscape.

Asian restaurants, serving spicy curries, are very popular.

ETHNIC MINORITIES

Britain's ethnic minorities account for less than 5 per cent of the total population, but they tend to be concentrated in cities, such as Bradford and Sheffield, where there are more economic opportunities. Most immigrants are from former colonies of the British Empire.

Many coal-mining towns boast traditional brass bands.

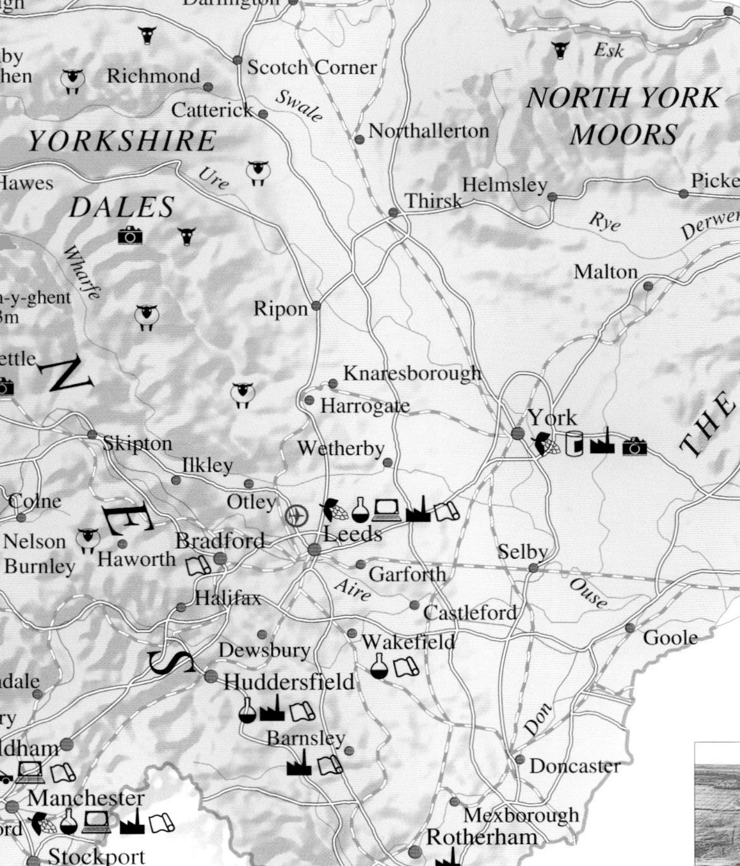

The Pennine uplands form the backbone of northern England.

POWER STATIONS

The coal-fired power stations of northern England, with their distinctive cooling towers, traditionally generated four-fifths of England's electricity. Recently, there has been a change to gas-fired power stations, resulting in coal pit closures.

WALES

THE CAMBRIAN MOUNTAINS form the backbone of the Welsh landmass. Wales was not united with England until 1535 and both Welsh culture and language, rooted in a 3,000 year-old Celtic history, remains very strong. In the 19th century rich reserves of iron and coal were discovered in Glamorgan. Wales became the world's leading coal exporter, and the valleys of the south became major centres of industry and population. Today, these traditional industries have all but disappeared. Working coal mines are living museums, and the Welsh economy is now dominated by electronics, hi-tech industries and oil- and petroleum-refining. The mountainous landscape of Wales and its spectacular coastline have long attracted visitors, and tourism is increasingly important. In 1999, the opening of a Welsh assembly in Cardiff restored a measure of regional self-government to the Welsh people.

RUGBY

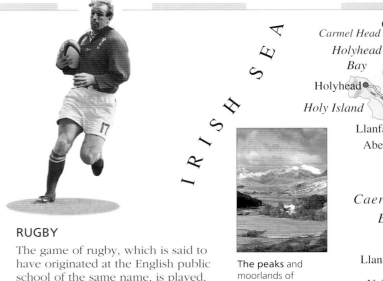

The game of rugby, which is said to have originated at the English public school of the same name, is played, and followed, with great enthusiasm by the Welsh. The new Millennium Stadium in Cardiff was the focus of the 1999 Rugby World Cup.

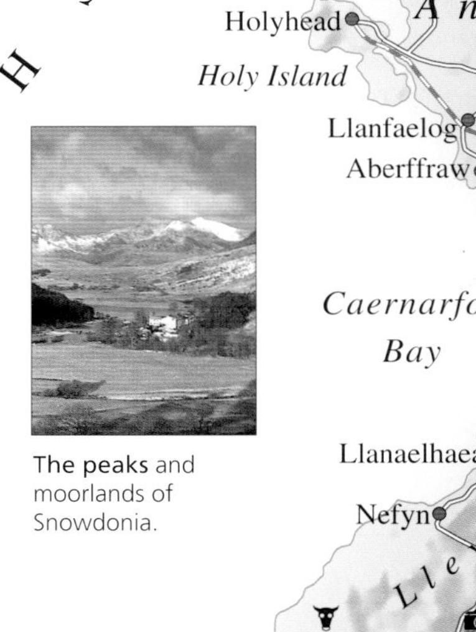
IRISH SEA
Cemae
Carmel Head
Holyhead Bay
Holyhead
An
Holy Island
Llanfaelog
Aberffraw
Caernarfo
Bay
Llanaelhaea
Nefyn
Lle
Aberdaron
Braich y Pwll
Abersoch
Bardsey Island
Trwyn Cilan

The peaks and moorlands of Snowdonia.

SHEEP

Sheep are ideally suited to the rugged Welsh landscape. The native mountain breed thrives in very bleak conditions. But Welsh sheep-farmers have become increasingly angry with EU agricultural policy, and a sharp fall in the price of lamb is putting many out of business. Look for

CHEPSTOW CASTLE

The town of Chepstow, situated on the River Wye, is in a strategic position, guarding the route into south Wales. It was the site of British, Roman and Norman fortifications. Many castles were founded between the 11th and 13th centuries, when Norman barons controlled the borderlands.

The rugged cliffs and rocky bays of the West Wales coast.

MALE-VOICE CHOIR

Much of the Welsh cultural heritage is steeped in legend, poetry and music. Today, male-voice choirs are found in many towns, villages and factories. Choirs compete in *eisteddfods* – festivals celebrating Welsh culture.

TENBY

The magnificent coastal scenery of southwest Wales has long attracted visitors to the region. The fishing port of Tenby, with its medieval centre and fine Georgian houses, is one of the most picturesque coastal towns, a tourist centre for visitors from England since the 19th century. Look for

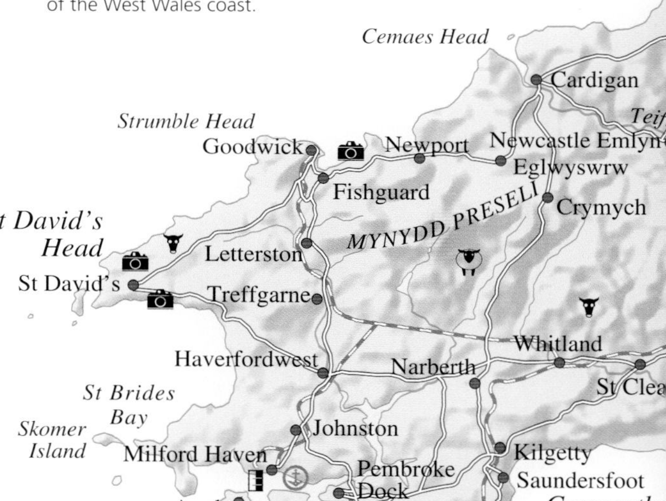
Cemaes Head
Cardigan
Tei
Strumble Head
Goodwick
Newport
Newcastle Emlyn
Eglwyswrw
Fishguard
Crymych
MYNYDD PRESELI
St David's Head
Letterston
St David's
Treffgarne
Whitland
Haverfordwest
Narberth
St Clea
St Brides Bay
Skomer Island
Johnston
Milford Haven
Kilgetty
Pembroke Dock
Saundersfoot
Angle
Pembroke
Carmarthe
Tenby
Bay
Caldey Island
St Govan's Head
CELTIC SEA

Sheepdogs are invaluable helpers on remote hill farms.

MAP FEATURES

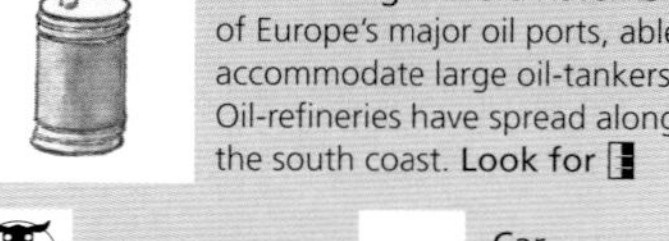

Hydro-electricity: Many valleys have been dammed to create reservoirs which supply water to English cities. Hydro-electricity is a by-product. Look for

Oil refining: Milford Haven is one of Europe's major oil ports, able to accommodate large oil-tankers. Oil-refineries have spread along the south coast. Look for

Sheep

Car manufacture

Cattle

Hi tech industry

Industrial centre

Tourism

URBAN SPRAWL

By the mid-19th century, a great exodus of people from the country to the iron and coal-producing valleys of the southeast was taking place. Rows of terraced houses, with distinctive roofs of Welsh slate, crept across the hills, obliterating the rural landscape.

INDUSTRIAL HEARTLAND

The south coast of Wales has large harbours at Milford Haven and Port Talbot, and west Glamorgan is a petrochemical and oil-refining centre. Energy-producing gas and electricity industries now dominate the economy, but oil spills and pollution are a major problem.

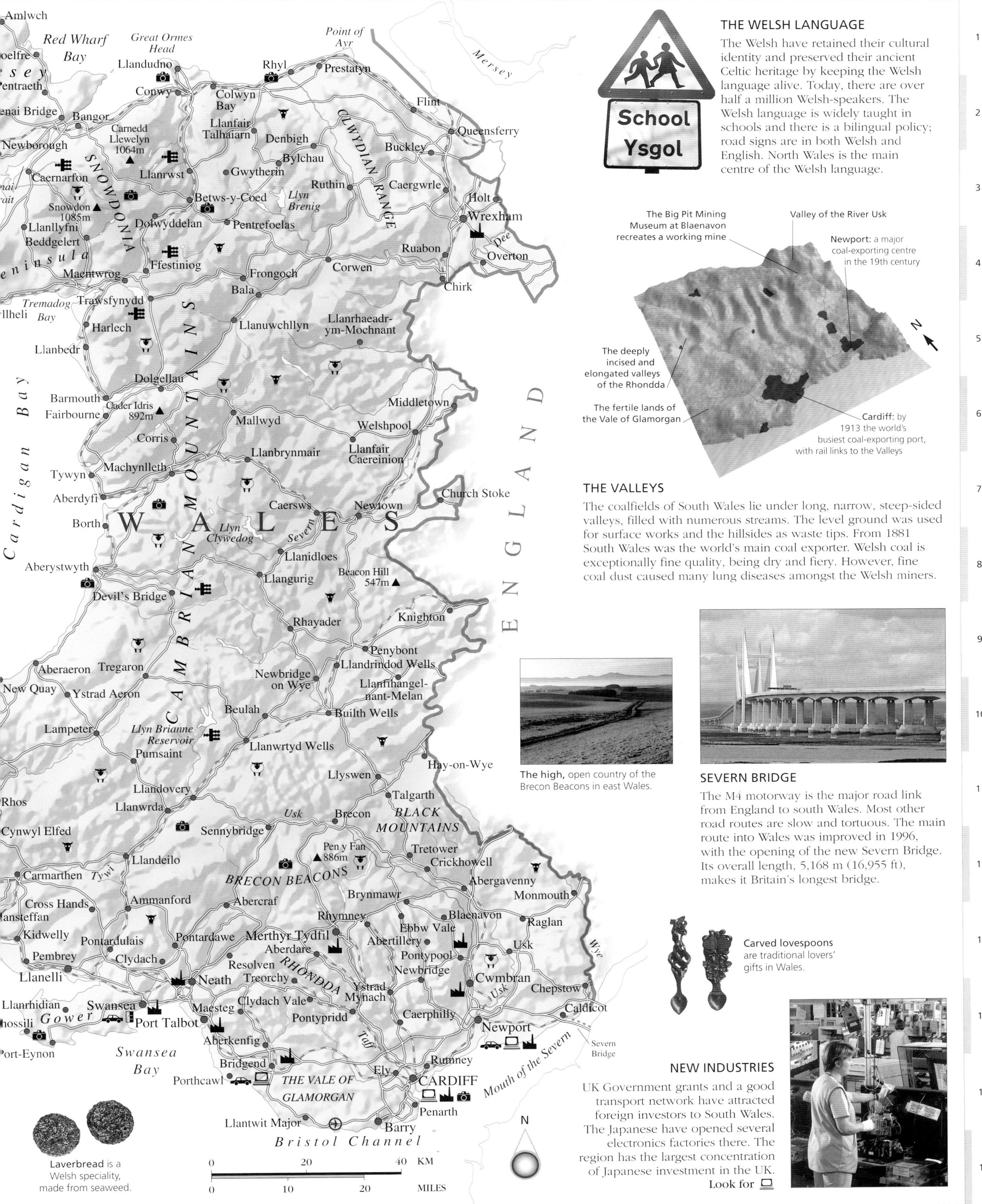
THE WELSH LANGUAGE
The Welsh have retained their cultural identity and preserved their ancient Celtic heritage by keeping the Welsh language alive. Today, there are over half a million Welsh-speakers. The Welsh language is widely taught in schools and there is a bilingual policy; road signs are in both Welsh and English. North Wales is the main centre of the Welsh language.
School
Ysgol
The Big Pit Mining Museum at Blaenavon recreates a working mine
Valley of the River Usk
Newport: a major coal-exporting centre in the 19th century
The deeply incised and elongated valleys of the Rhondda
The fertile lands of the Vale of Glamorgan
Cardiff: by 1913 the world's busiest coal-exporting port, with rail links to the Valleys
THE VALLEYS
The coalfields of South Wales lie under long, narrow, steep-sided valleys, filled with numerous streams. The level ground was used for surface works and the hillsides as waste tips. From 1881 South Wales was the world's main coal exporter. Welsh coal is exceptionally fine quality, being dry and fiery. However, fine coal dust caused many lung diseases amongst the Welsh miners.
The high, open country of the Brecon Beacons in east Wales.
SEVERN BRIDGE
The M4 motorway is the major road link from England to south Wales. Most other road routes are slow and tortuous. The main route into Wales was improved in 1996, with the opening of the new Severn Bridge. Its overall length, 5,168 m (16,955 ft), makes it Britain's longest bridge.
Carved lovespoons are traditional lovers' gifts in Wales.
NEW INDUSTRIES
UK Government grants and a good transport network have attracted foreign investors to South Wales. The Japanese have opened several electronics factories there. The region has the largest concentration of Japanese investment in the UK.
Look for
Laverbread is a Welsh speciality, made from seaweed.
WALES
ENGLAND
CAMBRIAN MOUNTAINS
SNOWDONIA
CLWYDIAN RANGE
BRECON BEACONS
BLACK MOUNTAINS
THE VALE OF GLAMORGAN
Cardigan Bay
Bristol Channel
Swansea Bay
Mouth of the Severn
Snowdon 1085m
Carnedd Llewelyn 1064m
Cader Idris 892m
Pen y Fan 886m
Beacon Hill 547m
Cardiff
Newport
Swansea
Wrexham
Aberystwyth
0 20 40 KM
0 10 20 MILES

SCOTLAND

MUCH OF SCOTLAND is rugged and mountainous and most of the population is concentrated in the Central Lowlands. People from the Highlands are Gaelic-speakers and many Scottish traditions, such as the clans (a tribal system), tartan, bagpipes and Highland Games originate here. The Shetland islanders have a Scandinavian heritage. In the 19th century, the area around the Clyde was one of the world's great industrial regions. Although these industries have declined, the discovery of North Sea oil in the 1970s boosted the Scottish economy. Scotland was united with England in 1707 after centuries of conflict. It retained its own educational and legal system and had its own Protestant church, the Presbyterian Church of Scotland, founded in 1689. In 1999, a separate Scottish assembly opened in Edinburgh, restoring a measure of self-government to the region.

CROFTING

In the remote Highlands, islands and Shetlands a way of life persists that is centuries old. Farmers live in small isolated cottages, or crofts, growing oats, potatoes and root vegetables and raising sheep. Their meagre living is sometimes supplemented by weaving.

HIGHLAND GAMES

Originally contests held at large clan gatherings, the Games were revived in the 1830s and over 40 major meetings are now held annually. Events include shot-putting and tossing the caber, a 5-m (17-ft) long fir pole. There is also bagpipe music and highland dancing.

Scotch whisky is exported all over the world.

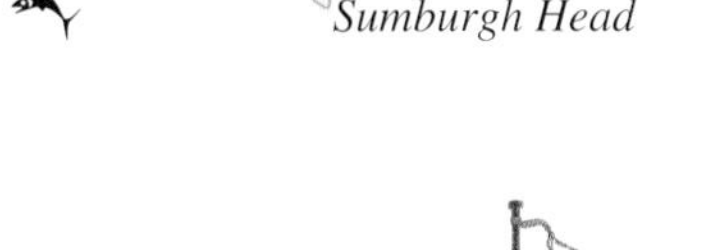

Mournful bagpipes serenaded the Scots into battle.

HIGHLAND CATTLE

Bred in the uplands of the west, highland cattle are sturdy animals with shaggy coats and wide spreading horns. They are hardy, and can thrive on very scant pastureland. Highland beef is of an unsurpassed flavour, and is much sought after. Look for

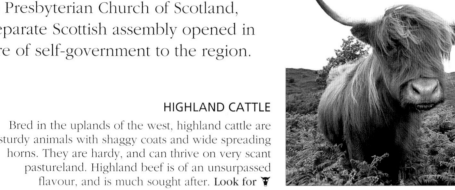

IONA

When the Irish monk and priest, St Columba, travelled to Scotland in 563, he made the island of Iona a centre of Christian learning. The abbey at Iona was the base from which Scottish missionaries rebuilt the shattered fabric of Christianity in northern England.

Red deer are confined to the Scottish Highlands.

The craggy peaks and steep cliffs of Glen Coe in the Highlands.

PETERHEAD

Peterhead is the EU's top whitefish landing port. It is also one of Britain's major fish processing centres. Scotland as a whole accounts for more than 60 per cent of the UK's total fishing catch. Scotland's largest fish market is based at Aberdeen.

N

0 10 20 30 KM

0 10 20 30 MILES

Shetland Islands
Herma Ness
Unst
Fetlar
Yell
Isbister
Yell Sound
St Magnus Bay
Brae
Whalsay
Mainland
Garth
Lerwick
Foula
Scousburgh
Sumburgh Head
Fair Isle
Orkney Islands
The North Sound
Westray
Sanday
Rousay
Eday
Stronsay
Mainland
Shapinsay
Kirkwall
Stromness
Scapa Flow
Hoy
St Margaret's Hope
South Ronaldsay
Pentland Firth
John o'Groats
Duncansby Head
Thurso
Wick
Cape Wrath
Durness
Portskerra
Tongue
Halladale
Halkirk
Kinbrace
Brora
Helmsdale
NORTH SEA
Lochinver
Loch Shin
Oykel
Lairg
Ullapool
Brora
Dornoch
Tarbat Ness
Tain
Invergordon
Cromarty
Moray Firth
Dingwall
Lossiemouth
Elgin
Buckie
Banff
Macduff
Fraserburgh
Forres
Nairn
Keith
Deveron
Turriff
Peterhead
Inverness
Findhorn
Spey
Huntly
Ythan
Buchan Ness
Beauly
Grantown-on-Spey
Ellon
Loch Ness
Tomintoul
Inverurie
Don
Aviemore
CAIRNGORM
GLEN MOR
NORTH WEST HIGHLANDS
Loch Maree
Loch Torridon
Kyle of Lochalsh
Stromeferry
Raasay
Portree
Isle of Skye
Uig
Broadford
Butt of Lewis
Port of Ness
Carloway
Stornoway
Eye Peninsula
Isle of Lewis
The Minch
Tarbert
Harris
Sound of Harris
The Little Minch
North Uist
Lochmaddy
Benbecula
South Uist
Lochboisdale
Outer Hebrides
SEA OF THE HEBRIDES

GLAMIS

From Roman times, the lowlands were engulfed by conflict with their English neighbours. This violent history is reflected in the region's many turretted castles, such as the imposing medieval tower-house of Glamis Castle.

NEW INDUSTRIES

Grangemouth's petrochemical works are an example of the modernization of Scottish industry. The manufacturing of electronics, computers, electrical goods and textiles is replacing Scotland's traditional heavy industry. **Look for**

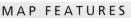

MAP FEATURES

Fishing: Scottish fisheries specialize in both whitefish and herrings, which are smoked to make kippers. **Look for**

Skiing: The Cairngorms, are the site of one of Britain's first ski centres. **Look for**

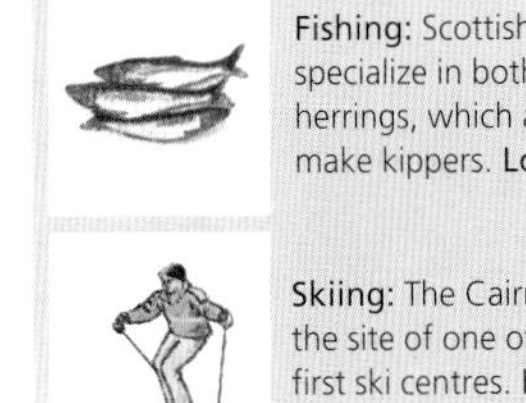
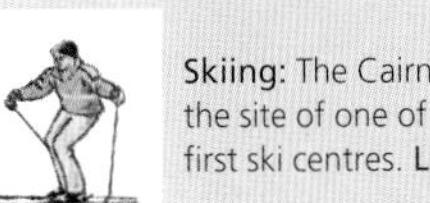
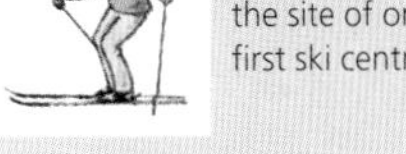
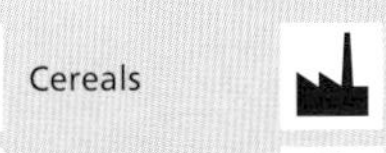
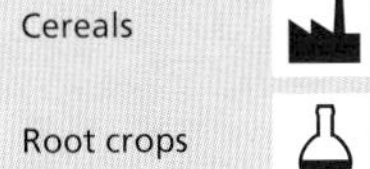
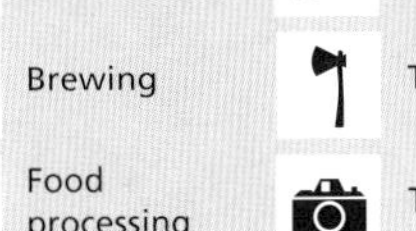

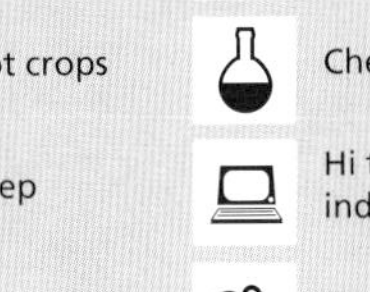

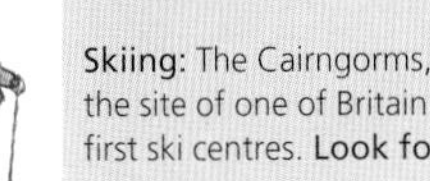

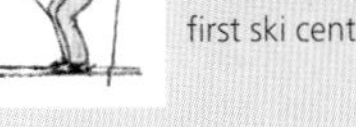

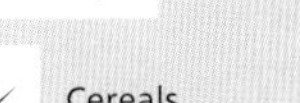
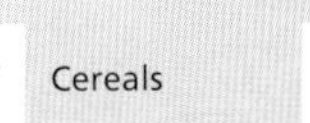
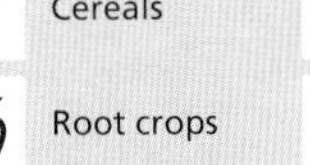

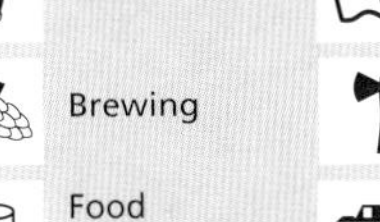
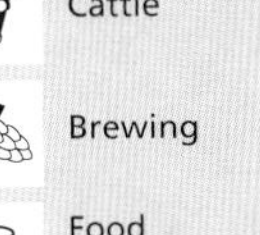

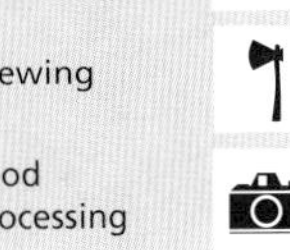

Cereals	Industrial centre
Root crops	Chemicals
Sheep	Hi tech industry
Cattle	Textiles
Brewing	Timber
Food processing	Tourism

ATLANTIC OCEAN

NORTH SEA

SCOTLAND

ENGLAND

Inner Hebrides

North Channel

GRAMPIAN MOUNTAINS

SIDLAW HILLS

PENTLAND HILLS

SOUTHERN UPLANDS

CHEVIOT HILLS

Castlebay, Rhum, Eigg, Muck, Point of Ardnamurchan, Coll, Tobermory, Tiree, Iona, Isle of Mull, Lochdon, Oban, Firth of Lorn, Colonsay, Loch Morar, Loch Linnhe, Fort William, Ben Nevis 1343m, Glen Coe, Lochy, Inveraray, Loch Fyne, Lochgilphead, Helensburgh, Greenock, Jura, Sound of Jura, Port Askaig, Islay, Port Ellen, Mull of Oa, Tarbert, Rothesay, Island of Bute, Firth of Clyde, Kintyre, Brodick, Isle of Arran, Campbeltown, Mull of Kintyre, Largs, Irvine, Troon, Prestwick, Ayr, Maybole, Girvan, Ballantrae, Stranraer, Glenluce, Luce Bay, Mull of Galloway, Wigtown, Whithorn, Wigtown Bay, Newton Stewart, Kirkcudbright, Castle Douglas, Dee, Solway Firth, Dumfries, Thornhill, Nith, Annan, Gretna, Lockerbie, Langholm, Esk, Moffat, Teviot, Hawick, Jedburgh, Selkirk, Tweed, Galashiels, Newtown St Boswells, Kelso, Coldstream, Duns, Eyemouth, Peebles, Lanark, New Lanark, Clyde, Cumnock, Kilmarnock, East Kilbride, Hamilton, Motherwell, Coatbridge, Airdrie, Cumbernauld, Giffnock, Paisley, Clydebank, Glasgow, Dumbarton, Loch Lomond, Stirling, Grangemouth, Falkirk, Alloa, Kinross, Dunfermline, Livingston, Forth, EDINBURGH, Dalkeith, Haddington, North Berwick, Firth of Forth, Kirkcaldy, Glenrothes, St Andrews, Callander, Crieff, Earn, Perth, Ben Lawers 1214m, Aberfeldy, Tummel, Tay, Pitlochry, Blairgowrie, Kirriemuir, Dundee, Carnoustie, Arbroath, Forfar, South Esk, Brechin, Montrose, North Esk, Inverbervie, Stonehaven

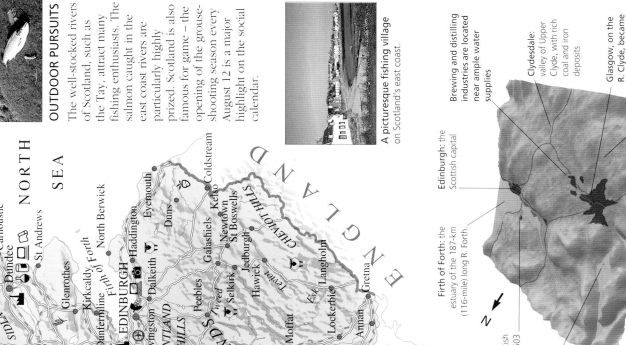

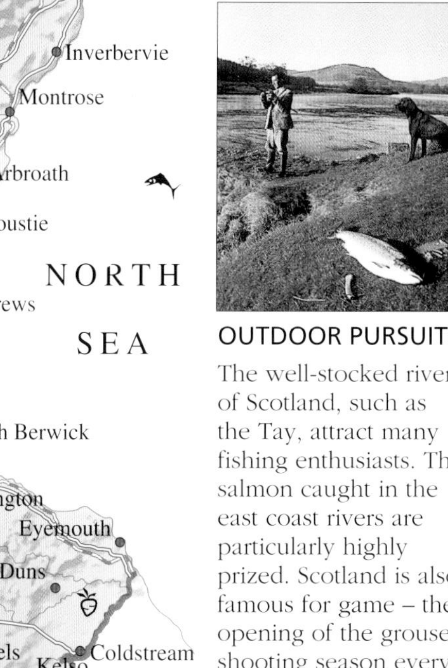

OUTDOOR PURSUITS

The well-stocked rivers of Scotland, such as the Tay, attract many fishing enthusiasts. The salmon caught in the east coast rivers are particularly highly prized. Scotland is also famous for game – the opening of the grouse-shooting season every August 12 is a major highlight on the social calendar.

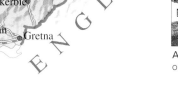

The remote and sandy shores of the Outer Hebrides.

NEW LANARK

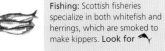

New Lanark was founded in 1785. Its water-powered mills were driven by the River Clyde. By 1800 it had become Britain's largest cotton producer. The village was unusually well laid-out – its commercial success was reflected in the well-being of the workforce.

A picturesque fishing village on Scotland's east coast.

GLASGOW

Glasgow's industrial past, when its cotton mills, shipbuilding and ironworks flourished, is reflected in its fine Victorian architecture. Today, many of its Victorian tenements (slums) have been cleared, and it has become an international cultural centre.

EDINBURGH

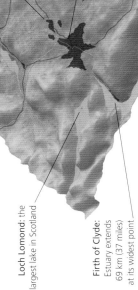

The handsome Scottish capital is bisected by Princes Street, its commercial centre. Its medieval heart is dominated by the promontory of the Castle. To the north, the Georgian New Town was built by affluent merchants. Edinburgh is a major centre of the arts.

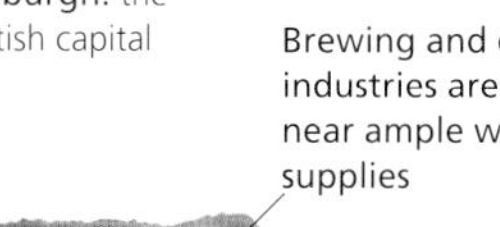
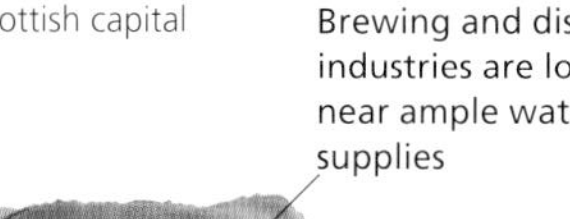
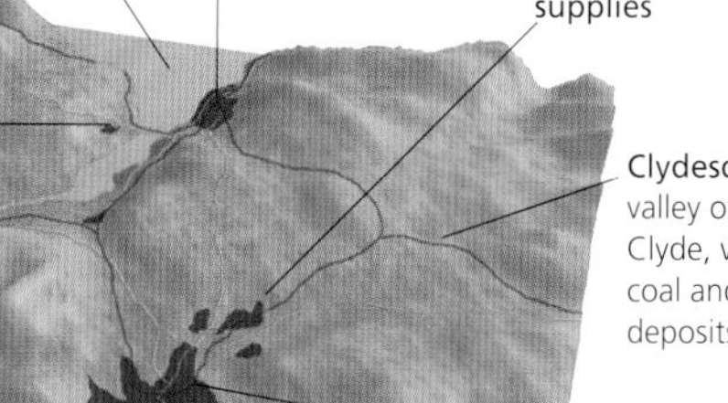

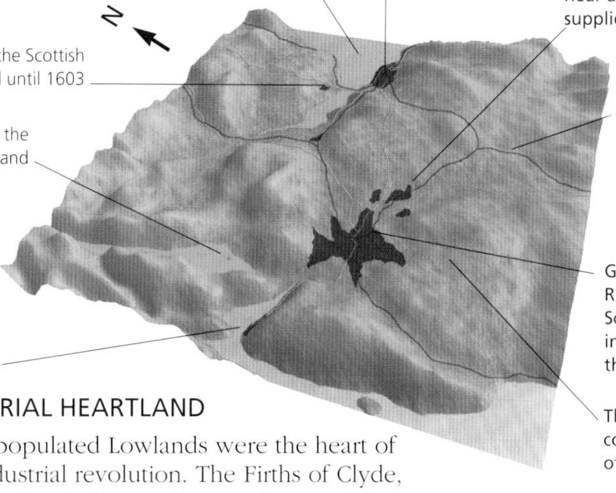

N
Firth of Forth: the estuary of the 187-km (116-mile) long R. Forth.
Edinburgh: the Scottish capital
Brewing and distilling industries are located near ample water supplies
Dunfermline: the Scottish capital until 1603
Loch Lomond: the largest lake in Scotland
Clydesdale: valley of Upper Clyde, with rich coal and iron deposits
Firth of Clyde: Estuary extends 69 km (37 miles) at its widest point
Glasgow, on the R. Clyde, became Scotland's leading industrial city in the 19th century.
The extensive coal deposits of Lanarkshire

THE INDUSTRIAL HEARTLAND

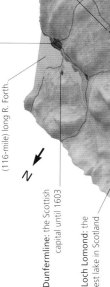

The densely populated Lowlands were the heart of Scotland's industrial revolution. The Firths of Clyde, Tay and Forth deeply indent the coastline, enabling large ships to reach industrial centres. Rich seams of coal in Lanarkshire fuelled industry. The Forth Bridge, opened in 1890, was one of the great engineering achievements of the Victorian era. **Look for**

IRELAND

A REMOTE OUTPOST on Europe's western fringe, Ireland has preserved its rich cultural heritage and language. It was part of the United Kingdom from 1800 to 1921 when a rising against English rule led to the formation of the Republic of Ireland, with its capital in Dublin. The Northern Ireland, with a Protestant majority, remained part of the UK, later to be devastated by conflict between Catholics and Protestants. With the exception of the Northern Irish capital, Belfast, which once had extensive shipbuilding, engineering and textile industries, Ireland did not experience an Industrial Revolution. Entry into the EU in 1973 transformed Ireland's rural economy. The Republic is now dominated by electronic, computer and service industries, such as finance and tourism. Its population is 95 per cent Catholic, and is now three-fifths urban. In 1999, peace agreements in Northern Ireland began to draw Catholic and Protestants together.

FISHING IN DONEGAL

The indented bays of Ireland's west coast provide a base for many small fishing fleets. The most extensive fishing grounds in the EU lie off Ireland's coast, and competition from other nations is fierce. The main Irish catch consists of haddock, plaice, cod and whiting.

Guinness stout is brewed in Dublin and exported to 120 countries worldwide.

The city of Galway on the River Corrib.

KNOCK

In 1879, two local women claimed they had seen an apparition of the Virgin, St Joseph and St John in the small Mayo town of Knock. With the approval of the Catholic church, Knock became a major shrine, and attracts over 1.5 million pilgrims a year.

Cheese, traditionally made in farmhouses and monasteries.

DUNGUAIRE CASTLE

Ireland's history of invasion is reflected in its architecture. Conflict between Irish chieftains and Anglo-Norman barons led to the construction of defensive, walled tower houses between the 15th and 17th centuries. Dunguaire Castle is a typical example, bult in the 16th century.

hurley

GAELIC GAMES

The Irish have worked hard to promote their own native sports of Gaelic football and hurling (a type of hockey), and to resist the influence of English sports. Today, despite the influence of soccer and rugby, Gaelic football is the most popular sport in Ireland, drawing large and passionate crowds.

The lakes, rivers and dramatic mountain scenery of Killarney.

AN COIREÁN
WATERVILLE 21
CATHAIR SAIDHBHIN
CAHERCIVEEN 30½
NEIDÍN
KENMARE 17½
PÁIRC NA SAILEACH
PARKNASILLA 2
KENMARE BAY HOTEL 16
T66

BILINGUAL SIGNS

Ireland was a Gaelic-speaking nation until the 16th century. Although only 11 per cent of the population now speak Gaelic fluently, the Republic is officially bilingual. Knowledge of Gaelic is a requirement of university entrance and a career in the civil service.

MAP FEATURES

Peat: Peat bog covers about 15% of the Irish landscape. Use of peat for fuel and fertilizers has reduced the extent of the peatlands. Look for

Potatoes: Ireland's over-reliance on easily grown potatoes led to a disastrous famine, when potato blight struck in 1848. Potatoes are still a staple crop. Look for

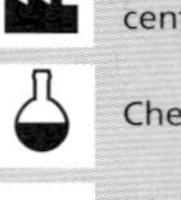

Cereals	Industrial centre
Sheep	Chemicals
Cattle	Hi tech industry
Brewing	Textiles
Food processing	Tourism

CATTLE FARMING

Ireland's fertile grasslands flourish in the wet, mild climate. They provide ample pastureland for beef and dairy cattle, Ireland's main agricultural export. The EU has provided a large market for Irish produce, enabling Ireland's small family farms to survive. Look for

Erris Head
Belmullet
Ballina
Lough Conn
Blacksod Bay
Ballycroy
Nephin 806m
Foxford
Achill Head
Achill Sound
Mullaranny
Bellavary
Clare Island
Clew Bay
Castlebar
Westport
Inishturk
Inishbofin
Mweelrea 817m
Claremorr
PARTRY MOUNTAINS
Lough Mask
Kilmaine
Clifden
CONNEMARA
Slyne Head
Oughtera
Galway
Galway Bay
Inishmore
Aran Islands
Hag's Head
Ennistim
ATLANTIC OCEAN
Ennis
Clarecastle
Kilkee
Kilrush
Shann
Killimer
Shannon
Mouth of the Shannon
Listowel
Rathkeal
Kerry Head
Tralee Bay
Brandon Mountain 953m
Tralee
SLIEVE MISH MOUNTAINS
Castleisland
Dingle
Farranfore
Dingle Bay
Caherciveen
Carrauntoohil 1038m
Killarney
Valencia Island
BOGGERAG MOUNTAIN
Waterville
Kenmare
Macroom
Bolus Head
Ballinskelligs Bay
Glengarriff
Bantry
Dursey Head
Bantry Bay
Ross Carbe
Mizen Head
Clear Island

Volcanic activity formed the approximately 37,000 basalt columns of Giant's Causeway.

STORMONT

The Protestants of Northern Ireland oppose any moves to unite the UK province with the Catholic south. Peace talks in 1999 led to the reopening of the Northern Irish assembly, attended by both Catholics and Protestants, at Stormont, just outside their capital, Belfast.

OSSIAN'S GRAVE

The north was the first part of Ireland to be settled, when hunter-gatherers crossed a land bridge from Scotland, some 9,500 years ago. The first farmers arrived in northern Ireland 4,500 years ago. Traces of their stone field walls and tombs, such as Ossian's Grave in County Antrim, can still be seen.

CELTIC CROSS

Ireland converted to Christianity in the 5th century. A golden age of scholarship centred on newly founded monasteries. Medieval monasteries built distinctive high crosses. Their carved designs, depicting Bible scenes, may have been used to educate the people.

IRISH MUSIC

Traditional Irish music is played in many of Ireland's bars, or pubs. The roots of many Irish ballads can be traced back to medieval times, or to the popular folk songs of the 18th century. The most commonly used instruments are the violin, flute, harp and the uillean pipes (similar to bagpipes).

Hand-blown and hand-cut crystal is made in Waterford.

CUSTOMS HOUSE, DUBLIN

Dublin originated as a Viking trading post, founded on the banks of the River Liffey in the 9th century. Dublin Castle dominates the city's medieval centre. Fine 18th century buildings, such as the Customs House, came to symbolize English oppression, and many were destroyed in the 1916 Easter Rising.

ANGLO-IRISH MANSIONS

The southeast was controlled in the Middle Ages by Anglo-Norman barons. From the 18th century, wealthy Anglo-Irish families were drawn to this stable region, and left a legacy of fine houses. Castletown House was built in 1722–32 for the Speaker of the Irish parliament.

Dublin Bay oysters are a famous delicacy.

THE ENVIRONMENT

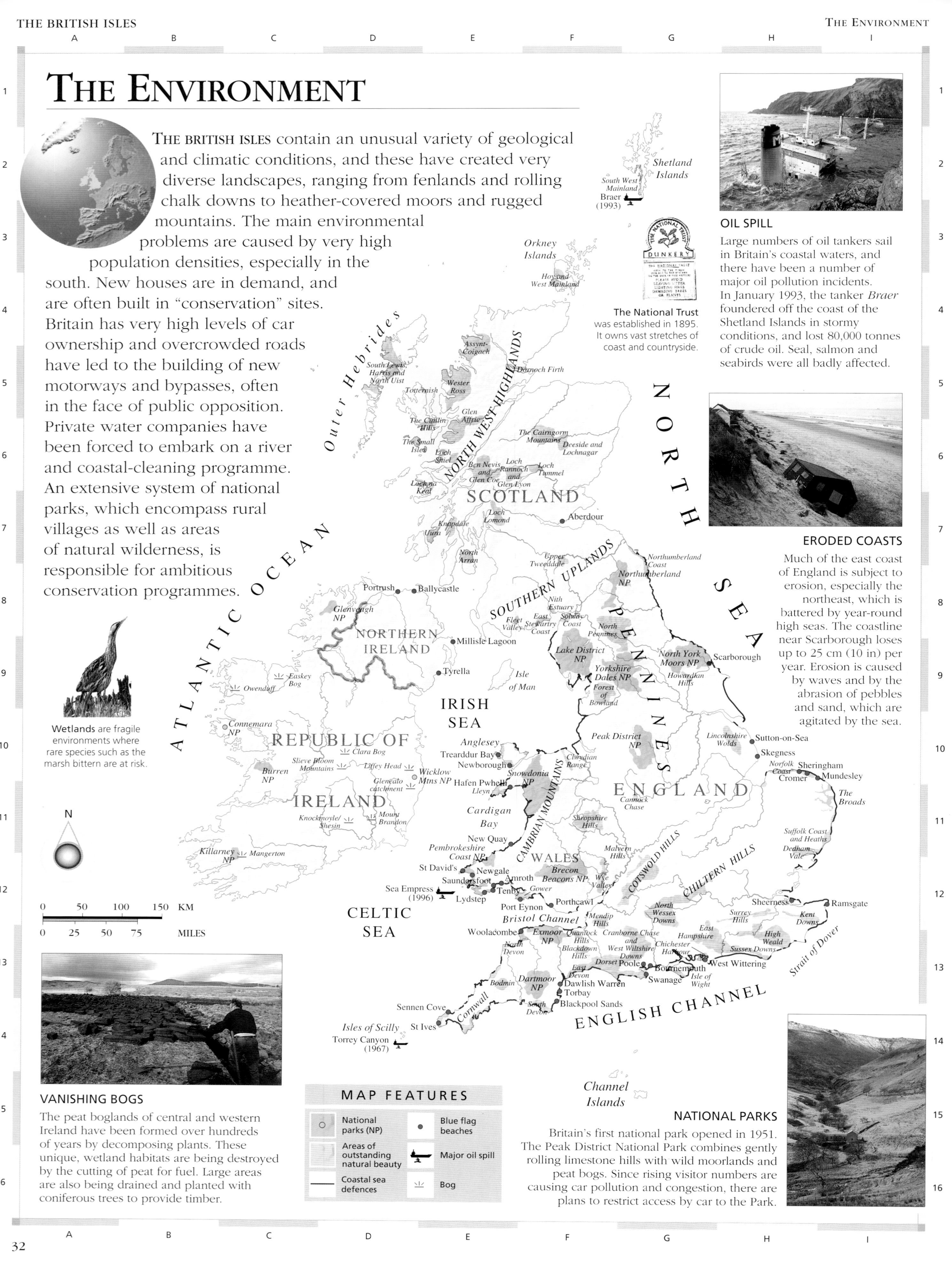
Shetland Islands
South West Mainland
Braer (1993)
Orkney Islands
Hoy and West Mainland
Outer Hebrides
South Lewis, Harris and North Uist
Assynt-Coigach
Wester Ross
Trotternish
Dornoch Firth
NORTH WEST HIGHLANDS
The Cuillin Hills
Glen Affric
The Small Isles
Loch Shiel
The Cairngorm Mountains
Deeside and Lochnagar
Ben Nevis and Glen Coe
Loch Rannoch and Glen Lyon
Loch Tummel
Loch na Keal
SCOTLAND
Loch Lomond
Aberdour
Knapdale
Jura
North Arran
NORTH SEA
ATLANTIC OCEAN
Upper Tweeddale
SOUTHERN UPLANDS
Northumberland Coast
Northumberland NP
Portrush
Ballycastle
Glenveagh NP
Nith Estuary
East Stewartry Coast
Fleet Valley
Solway Coast
North Pennines
PENNINES
NORTHERN IRELAND
Millisle Lagoon
Lake District NP
North York Moors NP
Scarborough
Easkey Bog
Owenduff
Tyrella
Isle of Man
Yorkshire Dales NP
Howardian Hills
Forest of Bowland
IRISH SEA
Connemara NP
REPUBLIC OF IRELAND
Clara Bog
Peak District NP
Lincolnshire Wolds
Sutton-on-Sea
Skegness
Anglesey
Treardduur Bay
Newborough
Clwydian Range
Slieve Bloom Mountains
Liffey Head
Wicklow Mtns NP
Burren NP
Glencalo catchment
Snowdonia NP
Hafen Pwhelli
Lleyn
Norfolk Coast
Sheringham
Cromer
Mundesley
The Broads
ENGLAND
Cannock Chase
Knockmoyle/Shesin
Mount Brandon
Cardigan Bay
CAMBRIAN MOUNTAINS
Shropshire Hills
Suffolk Coast and Heaths
Dedham Vale
Killarney NP
Mangerton
New Quay
Pembrokeshire Coast NP
WALES
Malvern Hills
COTSWOLD HILLS
CHILTERN HILLS
St David's
Newgale
Saundersfoot
Amroth
Brecon Beacons NP
Wye Valley
Sea Empress (1996)
Lydstep
Tenby
Gower
Porthcawl
Port Eynon
Sheerness
Ramsgate
CELTIC SEA
Bristol Channel
Mendip Hills
North Wessex Downs
Surrey Hills
Kent Downs
Woolacombe
Exmoor NP
Quantock Hills
Cranborne Chase and West Wiltshire Downs
East Hampshire
High Weald
North Devon
Blackdown Hills
Chichester Harbour
Sussex Downs
Strait of Dover
Dorset
Poole
Bournemouth
West Wittering
East Devon
Swanage
Isle of Wight
Bodmin
Dartmoor NP
Dawlish Warren
Torbay
Sennen Cove
Cornwall
South Devon
Blackpool Sands
ENGLISH CHANNEL
Isles of Scilly
St Ives
Torrey Canyon (1967)
Channel Islands
N
0 50 100 150 KM
0 25 50 75 MILES
DUNKERY
THE NATIONAL TRUST

THE BRITISH ISLES contain an unusual variety of geological and climatic conditions, and these have created very diverse landscapes, ranging from fenlands and rolling chalk downs to heather-covered moors and rugged mountains. The main environmental problems are caused by very high population densities, especially in the south. New houses are in demand, and are often built in "conservation" sites. Britain has very high levels of car ownership and overcrowded roads have led to the building of new motorways and bypasses, often in the face of public opposition. Private water companies have been forced to embark on a river and coastal-cleaning programme. An extensive system of national parks, which encompass rural villages as well as areas of natural wilderness, is responsible for ambitious conservation programmes.

Wetlands are fragile environments where rare species such as the marsh bittern are at risk.

The National Trust was established in 1895. It owns vast stretches of coast and countryside.

OIL SPILL

Large numbers of oil tankers sail in Britain's coastal waters, and there have been a number of major oil pollution incidents. In January 1993, the tanker *Braer* foundered off the coast of the Shetland Islands in stormy conditions, and lost 80,000 tonnes of crude oil. Seal, salmon and seabirds were all badly affected.

ERODED COASTS

Much of the east coast of England is subject to erosion, especially the northeast, which is battered by year-round high seas. The coastline near Scarborough loses up to 25 cm (10 in) per year. Erosion is caused by waves and by the abrasion of pebbles and sand, which are agitated by the sea.

VANISHING BOGS

The peat boglands of central and western Ireland have been formed over hundreds of years by decomposing plants. These unique, wetland habitats are being destroyed by the cutting of peat for fuel. Large areas are also being drained and planted with coniferous trees to provide timber.

MAP FEATURES

National parks (NP)
Areas of outstanding natural beauty
Coastal sea defences
Blue flag beaches
Major oil spill
Bog

NATIONAL PARKS

Britain's first national park opened in 1951. The Peak District National Park combines gently rolling limestone hills with wild moorlands and peat bogs. Since rising visitor numbers are causing car pollution and congestion, there are plans to restrict access by car to the Park.

ATLAS OF THE WORLD

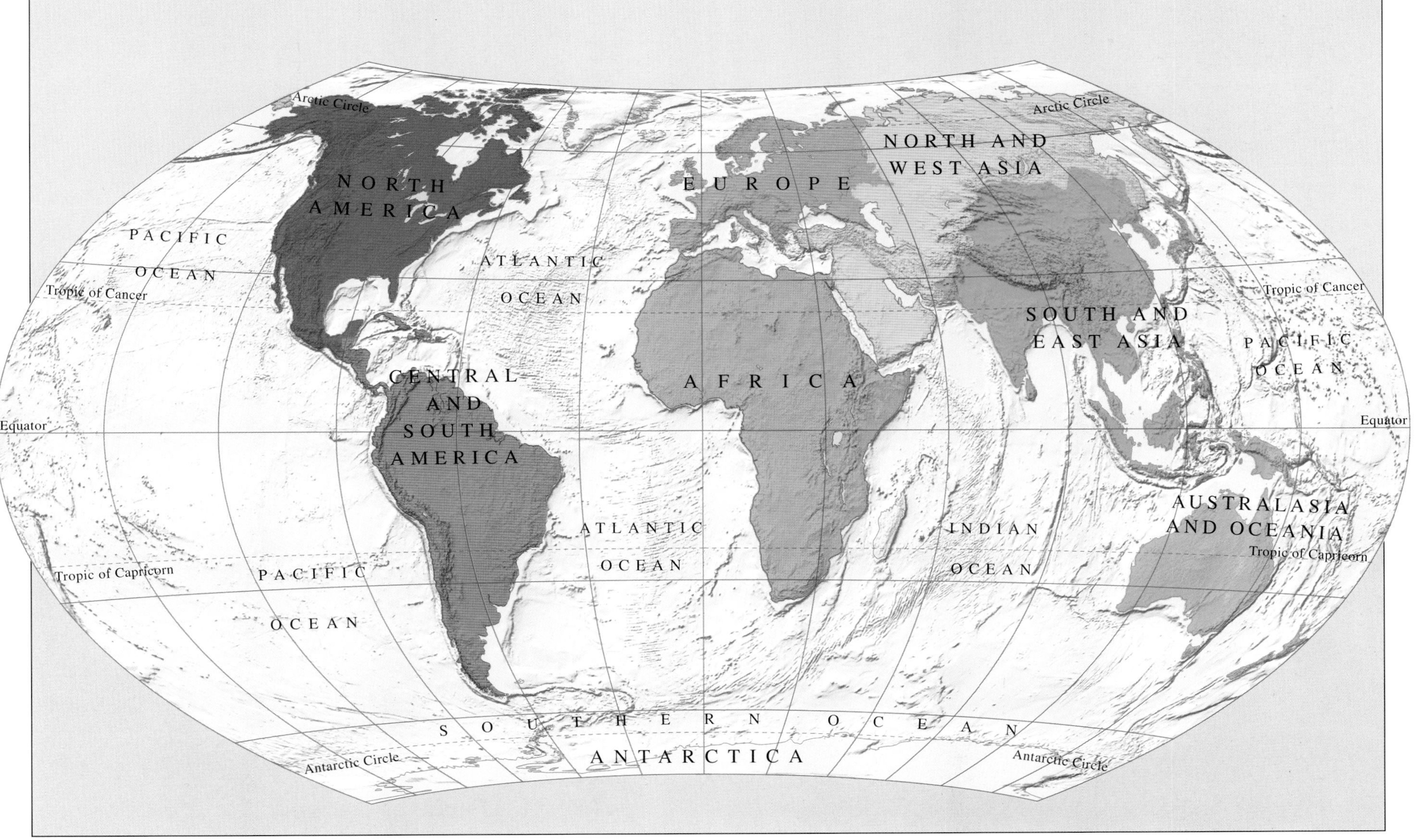
Arctic Circle
Arctic Circle
NORTH AMERICA
EUROPE
NORTH AND WEST ASIA
PACIFIC OCEAN
ATLANTIC OCEAN
Tropic of Cancer
Tropic of Cancer
SOUTH AND EAST ASIA
PACIFIC OCEAN
CENTRAL AND SOUTH AMERICA
AFRICA
Equator
Equator
AUSTRALASIA AND OCEANIA
ATLANTIC OCEAN
INDIAN OCEAN
Tropic of Capricorn
Tropic of Capricorn
PACIFIC OCEAN
SOUTHERN OCEAN
ANTARCTICA
Antarctic Circle
Antarctic Circle

Raccoon
Procyon lotor
Length: 66 cm (26 in)

Desert swallowtail
Papilio coloro
Wingspan: 7 cm (3 in)

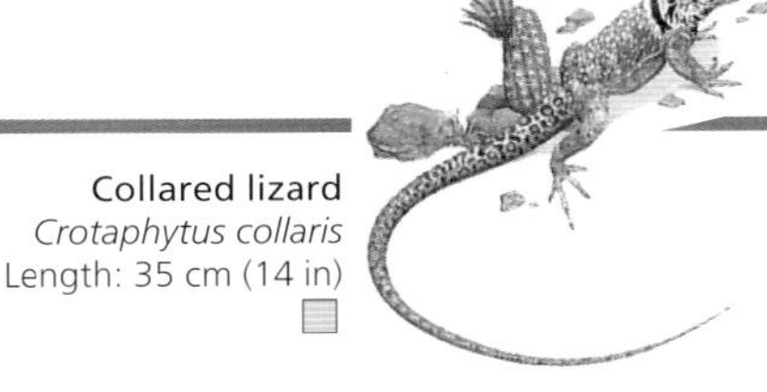

Collared lizard
Crotaphytus collaris
Length: 35 cm (14 in)

North America

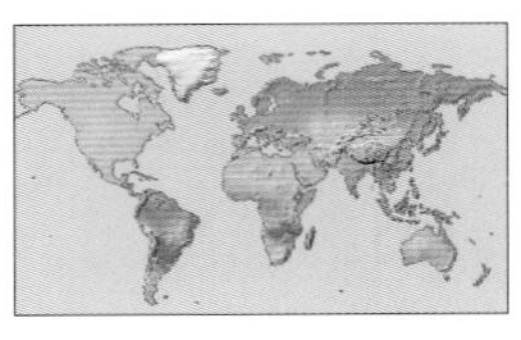

North America forms a gigantic downward-pointing triangle, out of which two great bites have been taken – Hudson Bay and the Gulf of Mexico. Huge parallel mountain chains run down the eastern and western sides. The oldest are the Appalachians to the east, which have been worn away by wind and rain for so long that they are now considerably lower than the younger Rockies to the west. The vast landscape between the mountain chains is very flat. There are large forests in the north, while the central Great Plains are covered by grasslands on which huge herds of bison once roamed. North America is a continent of climatic extremes. In the farthest north, temperatures drop to a freezing -66°C (-87°F), and a dome of ice up to 3 km (2 miles) thick covers Greenland. In the hot deserts of the south-west, temperatures can soar to 57°C (134°F).

Triceratops, a vegetarian dinosaur that lived in western North America 70 million years ago.

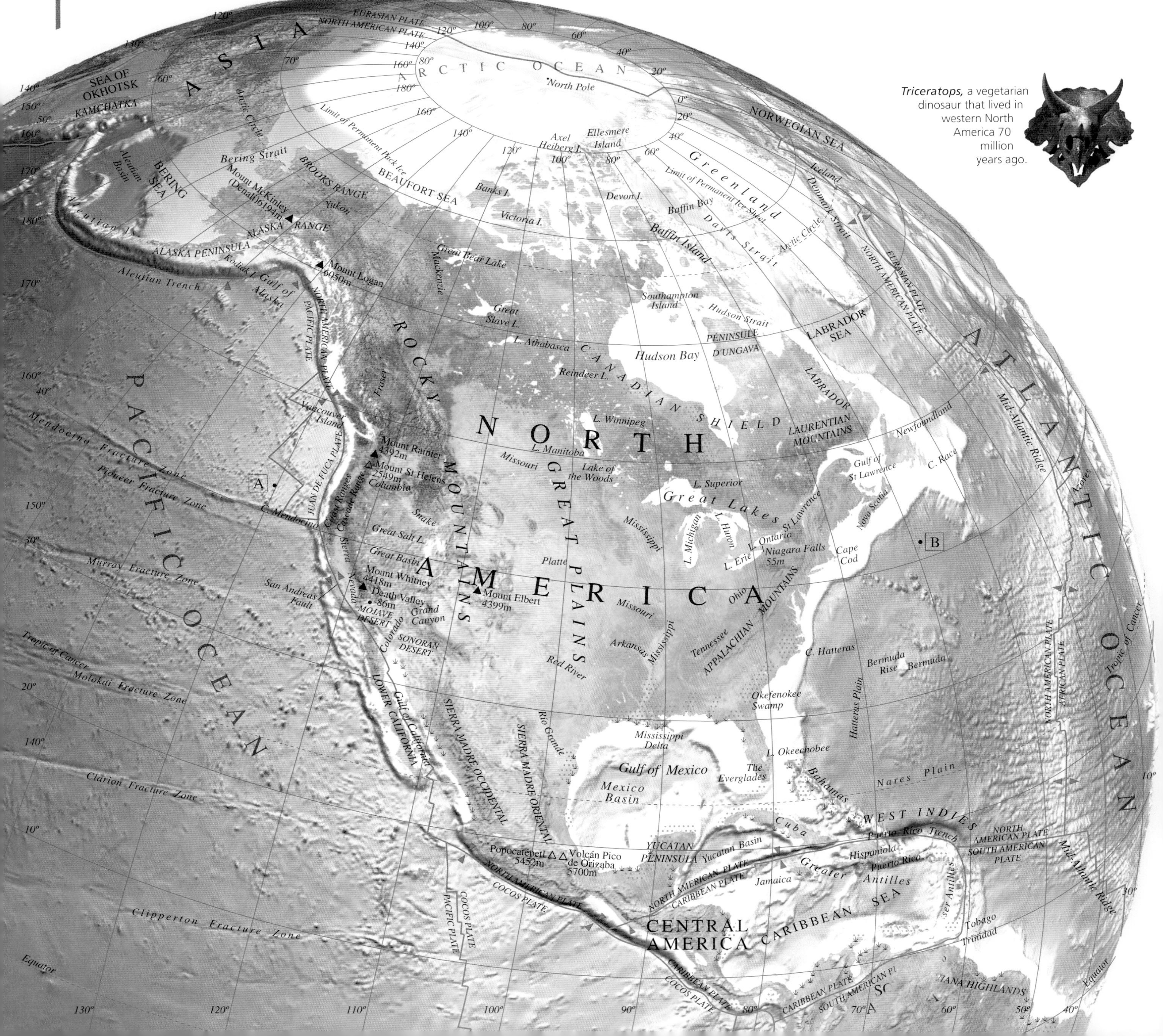

Douglas fir cone
Pseudotsuga menziesii
Length: 8 cm (3 in)

Road runner
Geococcyx californianus
Length: 60 cm (2 ft)

Loggerhead turtle
Caretta caretta
Length: 1.2 m (4 ft)

AUTUMN IN ALASKA

Only tundra – short grasses, low shrubs and small trees – can survive the northern climate. In the brief Alaskan summer plants burst into bloom, changing colour in the autumn.

THE ROOF OF AMERICA

When water-laden ocean air rises over the Alaska Range, moisture freezes and falls as snow. It is so cold that mountain slopes as low as 900 m (3,000 ft) are always snow-covered.

Eutrephoceras, which lived in North America 100 million years ago. It swam by squirting water out of its body cavity.

VOLCANIC ACTIVITY

The volcanic island of Iceland is part of the Mid-Atlantic Ridge. Intense heat generated deep underground creates bubbling hot mud pools and hot springs.

Coast redwood
Sequoia sempervirens
Height: 100 m (330 ft)

Priscacara, a perch that swam in North America's lakes and rivers 50 million years ago.

RIVERS, TREES AND GRASSLAND

For millions of years rivers flowing east from the Rockies have deposited silt on the Great Plains. This has helped to create a deep and very fertile soil which supports huge areas of grassland.

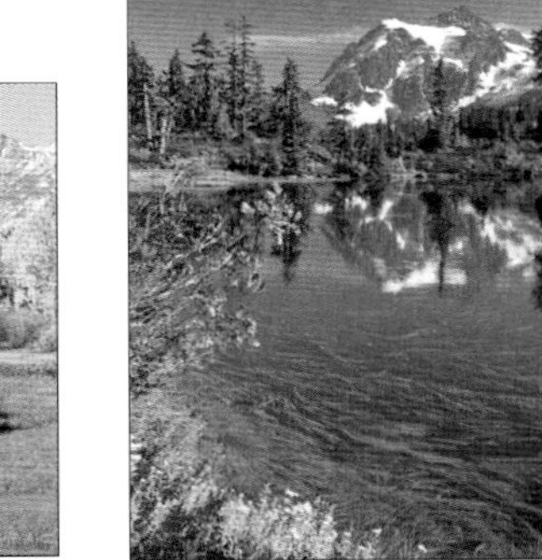

NORTHERN FORESTS

Forests grow across most of the northern region and on cold mountain slopes. These contain mostly needleleaf trees which are well suited to growing in cold conditions.

Bald eagle
Haliaeetus leucocephalus
Wingspan: 2.2 m (7 ft)

RAINFORESTS

Temperate rainforests thrive between the Pacific and the Coast Ranges. Their lush growth is made possible by heavy rainfall carried inland by moist ocean winds.

DRY WINDS AND SAND DUNES

Dry winds blowing from the centre of the continent, combined with the lack of rain, are responsible for the extensive deserts in the south-west. Because the climate is so dry, vegetation is sparse.

DESERT TREES

With searing temperatures and low rainfall, deserts are home to plants which are adapted to conserve water, like cacti and the Joshua Trees shown here.

DESERT RIVER

The brown silt-laden waters of the Colorado River have cut a spectacular gorge through solid rock – the Grand Canyon. It is nearly 2,000 m (6,135 ft) deep.

OKEFENOKEE SWAMP

Okefenokee Swamp is part of the complex river system of the south-east. This large wetland area has a warm climate, providing a haven for reptiles such as alligators and snakes. It is also an important resting place for many migratory birds.

American beaver
Castor canadensis
Length: 1.6 m (5 ft)

KEY TO SYMBOLS

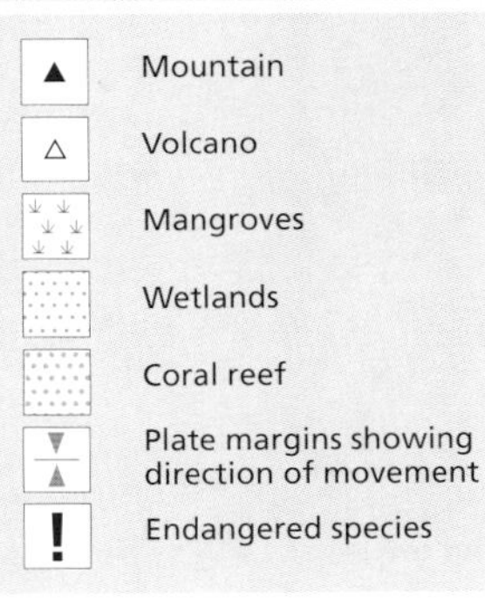

- ▲ Mountain
- △ Volcano
- Mangroves
- Wetlands
- Coral reef
- Plate margins showing direction of movement
- ! Endangered species

NATURAL VEGETATION ZONES

Mountain
Temperate rainforest
Cold desert
Mediterranean-type
Hot desert
Dry woodland
Tundra
Needleleaf forest
Temperate grassland
Broadleaf forest
Tropical rainforest

CROSS-SECTION THROUGH NORTH AMERICA

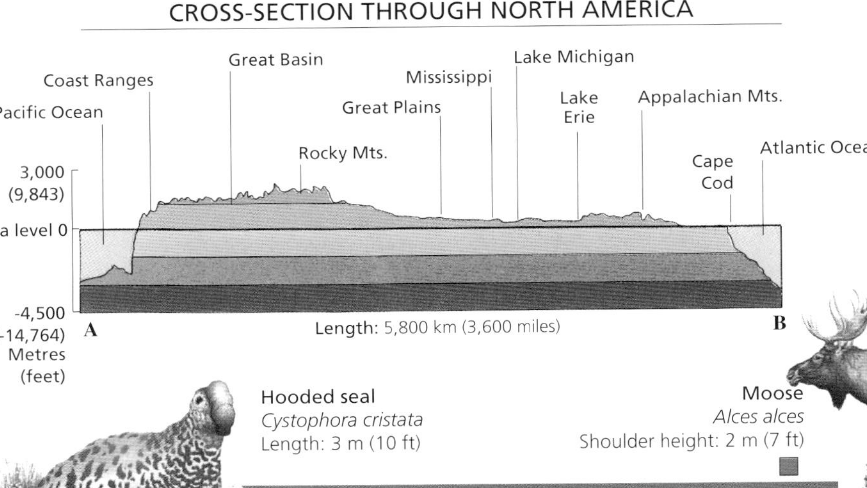
Coast Ranges
Great Basin
Mississippi
Lake Michigan
Pacific Ocean
Great Plains
Lake Erie
Appalachian Mts.
Rocky Mts.
Cape Cod
Atlantic Ocean
3,000 (9,843)
Sea level 0
-4,500 (-14,764)
Metres (feet)
A
B
Length: 5,800 km (3,600 miles)

Hooded seal
Cystophora cristata
Length: 3 m (10 ft)

Moose
Alces alces
Shoulder height: 2 m (7 ft)

WESTERN CANADA AND ALASKA

THOUSANDS OF YEARS AGO the first people to settle in North America crossed the Bering Strait and arrived in present-day Alaska. Their descendants – peoples such as the Inuit (Eskimos) – still inhabit this region. European emigrants began to arrive in large numbers in the 19th century. Alaska was bought by the USA from Russia for $7.2 million in 1867. Many Americans thought this was a waste of money until gold was discovered there in 1896 and then oil in 1968. Canada is a huge country with a small population, most of whom live in cities within about 160 km (100 miles) of the Canada-US border. The fertile plains and dense forest in the south give way to tundra and icefields further north.

ALASKAN OIL

The USA's largest oilfield is at Prudhoe Bay in Alaska. But drilling is made difficult by temperatures as low as -79° C (-110° F), ground that is frozen for most of the year, and long periods of darkness in winter. Look for

UNITED STATES
pop: 268,739,000
(ALASKA)
pop: 609,000

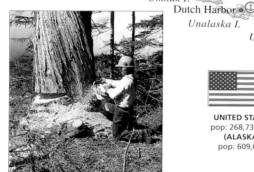

LOGGING

About 40 per cent of Canada is covered in forest. Until recently, there were no controls on logging, and huge areas of forest were cut down. Trees like this one are used to make lumber or plywood. Look for

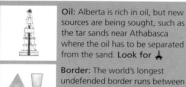

PIPELINE

When the 1,270 km (795 miles) long Trans-Alaskan pipeline from Prudhoe Bay to the ice-free port of Valdez was constructed, it was feared it would harm the environment and wildlife of this remote and beautiful region. To prevent disruption to the moose and caribou migration routes, and to stop the pipeline from freezing, it was raised on stilts above ground. The pipeline crosses plains, mountain ranges and several rivers on its southerly journey.

MAP FEATURES

Oil: Alberta is rich in oil, but new sources are being sought, such as the tar sands near Athabasca where the oil has to be separated from the sand. Look for

Border: The world's longest undefended border runs between Canada and the USA. People and goods can cross it with few restrictions. Look for

Radar: The joint Canada-US Distant Early Warning system has been a key component in the defence of the North American continent since 1957. Look for

Cattle
Mining
Cereals
Coal
Timber
Gas
Fishing
Industrial centre

CALGARY STAMPEDE

The city of Calgary in Alberta started life as a centre of the cattle trade. Although today it is an oil centre, its cowboy traditions are continued in the Stampede, a huge rodeo held every July. For ten days spectators watch displays that include bronco-busting, bull-riding and chuck-wagon racing.

VANCOUVER

This city began as a small settlement for loggers and is now a major port. Grain from Canada's prairies and timber from its forests are shipped from Vancouver's ice-free harbour to countries across the Pacific. The city has attracted many immigrants; at first from Europe, then more recently from Asia.

Brilliant autumn colours in British Columbia.

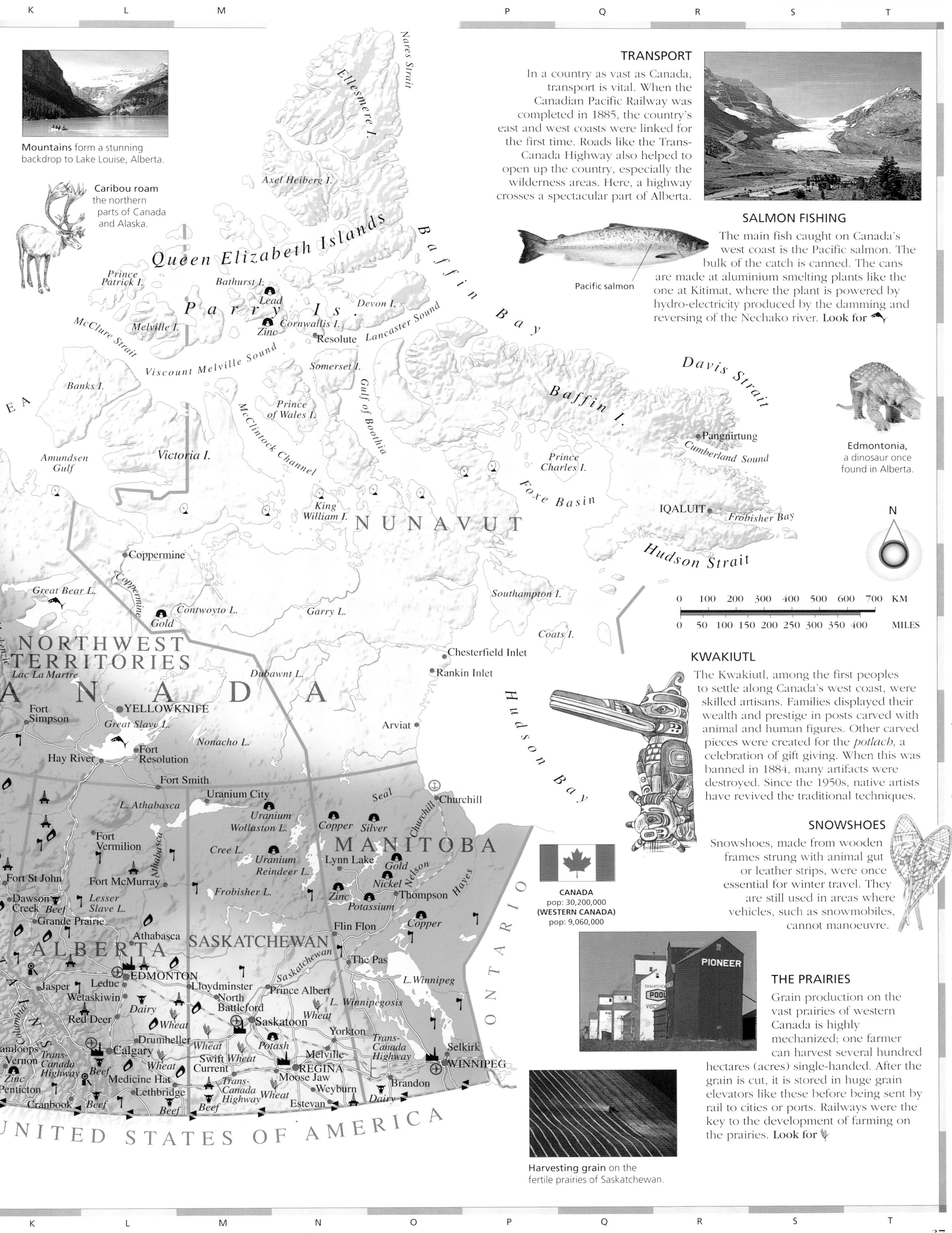
K L M N O P Q R S T
1 2 3 4 5 6 7 8 9 10 11 12 13 14 15 16
Nares Strait
Ellesmere I.
Axel Heiberg I.
Queen Elizabeth Islands
Prince Patrick I.
Bathurst I.
Lead
Parry Is.
Devon I.
Zinc
Cornwallis I.
Resolute
Lancaster Sound
Melville I.
McClure Strait
Viscount Melville Sound
Baffin Bay
Somerset I.
Banks I.
Prince of Wales I.
Gulf of Boothia
McClintock Channel
Davis Strait
Baffin I.
Pangnirtung
Cumberland Sound
Prince Charles I.
Amundsen Gulf
Victoria I.
Foxe Basin
King William I.
NUNAVUT
IQALUIT
Frobisher Bay
Hudson Strait
Coppermine
Great Bear L.
Contwoyto L.
Gold
Garry L.
Southampton I.
Coats I.
0 100 200 300 400 500 600 700 KM
0 50 100 150 200 250 300 350 400 MILES
N
NORTHWEST TERRITORIES
Lac La Martre
Chesterfield Inlet
Rankin Inlet
Dubawnt L.
CANADA
Fort Simpson
YELLOWKNIFE
Great Slave L.
Arviat
Hudson Bay
Nonacho L.
Hay River
Fort Resolution
Fort Smith
Uranium City
L. Athabasca
Uranium
Wollaston L.
Seal
Churchill
Copper
Silver
MANITOBA
Fort Vermilion
Cree L.
Uranium
Reindeer L.
Lynn Lake
Gold
Nickel
Nelson
Fort St John
Fort McMurray
Athabasca
Frobisher L.
Zinc
Potassium
Thompson
Hayes
Dawson Creek
Beef
Lesser Slave L.
Grande Prairie
Flin Flon
Copper
ONTARIO
Athabasca
ALBERTA
SASKATCHEWAN
Saskatchewan
The Pas
EDMONTON
Jasper
Leduc
Wetaskiwin
Lloydminster
North Battleford
Prince Albert
L. Winnipeg
Dairy
L. Winnipegosis
Red Deer
Wheat
Saskatoon
Wheat
Yorkton
Drumheller
Wheat
Potash
Trans-Canada Highway
Kamloops
Vernon
Calgary
Swift Current
Wheat
Melville
Selkirk
Trans-Canada Highway
Zinc
Beef
Wheat
REGINA
WINNIPEG
Medicine Hat
Moose Jaw
Penticton
Lethbridge
Trans-Canada Highway
Weyburn
Brandon
Cranbrook
Beef
Beef
Beef
Wheat
Estevan
Dairy
UNITED STATES OF AMERICA

Mountains form a stunning backdrop to Lake Louise, Alberta.

Caribou roam the northern parts of Canada and Alaska.

TRANSPORT

In a country as vast as Canada, transport is vital. When the Canadian Pacific Railway was completed in 1885, the country's east and west coasts were linked for the first time. Roads like the Trans-Canada Highway also helped to open up the country, especially the wilderness areas. Here, a highway crosses a spectacular part of Alberta.

SALMON FISHING

Pacific salmon

The main fish caught on Canada's west coast is the Pacific salmon. The bulk of the catch is canned. The cans are made at aluminium smelting plants like the one at Kitimat, where the plant is powered by hydro-electricity produced by the damming and reversing of the Nechako river. Look for

Edmontonia, a dinosaur once found in Alberta.

KWAKIUTL

The Kwakiutl, among the first peoples to settle along Canada's west coast, were skilled artisans. Families displayed their wealth and prestige in posts carved with animal and human figures. Other carved pieces were created for the *potlach*, a celebration of gift giving. When this was banned in 1884, many artifacts were destroyed. Since the 1950s, native artists have revived the traditional techniques.

SNOWSHOES

Snowshoes, made from wooden frames strung with animal gut or leather strips, were once essential for winter travel. They are still used in areas where vehicles, such as snowmobiles, cannot manoeuvre.

CANADA
pop: 30,200,000
(WESTERN CANADA)
pop: 9,060,000

THE PRAIRIES

Grain production on the vast prairies of western Canada is highly mechanized; one farmer can harvest several hundred hectares (acres) single-handed. After the grain is cut, it is stored in huge grain elevators like these before being sent by rail to cities or ports. Railways were the key to the development of farming on the prairies. Look for

Harvesting grain on the fertile prairies of Saskatchewan.

EASTERN CANADA

THE VIKINGS WERE THE FIRST Europeans to visit eastern Canada in about AD 986. Then, in the 15th and 16th centuries two expeditions, one from England and one from France, reached Canada and each claimed it. Traders and fur trappers from the two countries followed, setting up rival trading posts and settlements. The struggle for territory led to war between Britain and France. The French were forced to give up their Canadian territories to Britain in 1763, but the French language is still spoken in the province of Quebec today. Canada eventually achieved effective independence from Britain in 1867. Today, southern Quebec and Ontario form eastern Canada's main industrial region, containing most of its population and two of its largest cities – Montréal and Toronto. The Hudson Bay area, while rich in minerals, is a wilderness of forests, rivers and lakes. Snowbound for much of the year, it is sparsely inhabited except by Inuit in the far north.

The Toronto Sky Dome, a huge stadium which seats 50,000.

FRENCH / ENGLISH

Most Canadians speak English, but the country is officially bilingual – as can be seen from the use of both French and English on this stamp which commemorates the province of New Brunswick.

New Brunswick 1784-1984 Nouveau-Brunswick

The sap of the sugar maple tree is made into syrup and sugar. The maple leaf is Canada's national symbol.

A polar bear mother and cubs on the ice in Hudson Bay.

Evergreen and silver birch forests in southern Quebec.

INDUSTRY

Ontario is Canada's most important industrial province, and produces about 55 per cent of the country's manufactured goods. Electronics, steel and food processing are among the major industries, but cars are Ontario's main manufacturing industry and largest export. Many of the factories are owned by US multi-national companies.
Look for [industrial centre symbol]

TORONTO

The CN tower – the world's tallest free-standing structure – dominates the skyline of Toronto, seen here across the waters of Lake Ontario. Toronto is Canada's biggest city, the main commercial and industrial centre, and an important port. Toronto and its surrounding area produce over half Canada's manufactured goods. Its wealthy, multi-cultural population includes Italians, Chinese, Greeks and Poles.

Thousand Island salad dressing

Salad dressing, named after the islands in the St. Lawrence river.

ICE HOCKEY

In winter, Canadians play or watch their favourite sport: ice hockey. The country produces some of the best players in the world.

The Canadian or Horseshoe Falls at Niagara.

MAP FEATURES

Potatoes: The Atlantic provinces, especially Prince Edward Island, grow some of North America's finest potatoes – seed-potatoes in particular. **Look for** [potato symbol]

Mining: Canada is rich in iron ore, nickel, gold, silver and other minerals and is a major uranium exporter – mainly from Ontario. **Look for** [mining symbol]

High-tech industry: Ottawa has most of the electronics and computer companies in Canada, centred on an area known as Silicon Valley North. **Look for** [computer symbol]

- Mixed fruit
- Shellfishing
- Timber
- Hydro-electricity
- Fishing
- Industrial centre

THE MOUNTIES

The Royal Canadian Mounted Police – the Mounties – were established in 1873 during the opening up of the vast areas in the west to trade and industry. Today, they are one of the most efficient and sophisticated police forces, with their headquarters in Ottawa.

OTTAWA

These Parliament Buildings in Ottawa, Canada's capital city, were inspired by the British Houses of Parliament. Many older buildings reflect the city's British origins. Others, such as the National Gallery, are thoroughly modern.

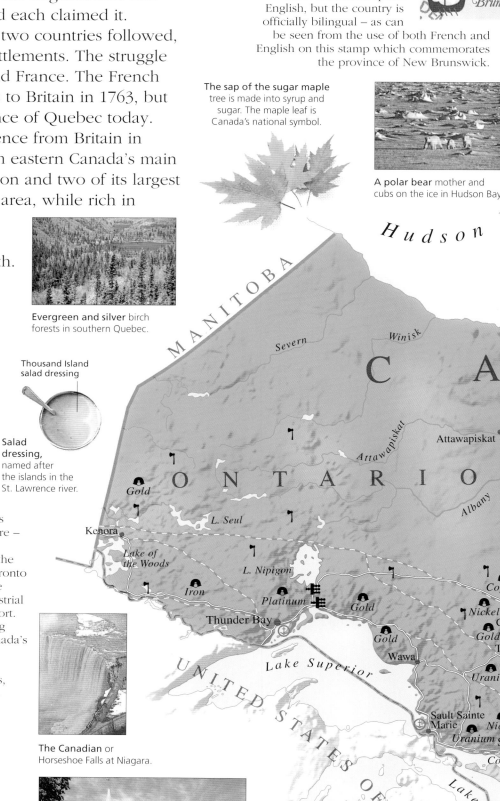

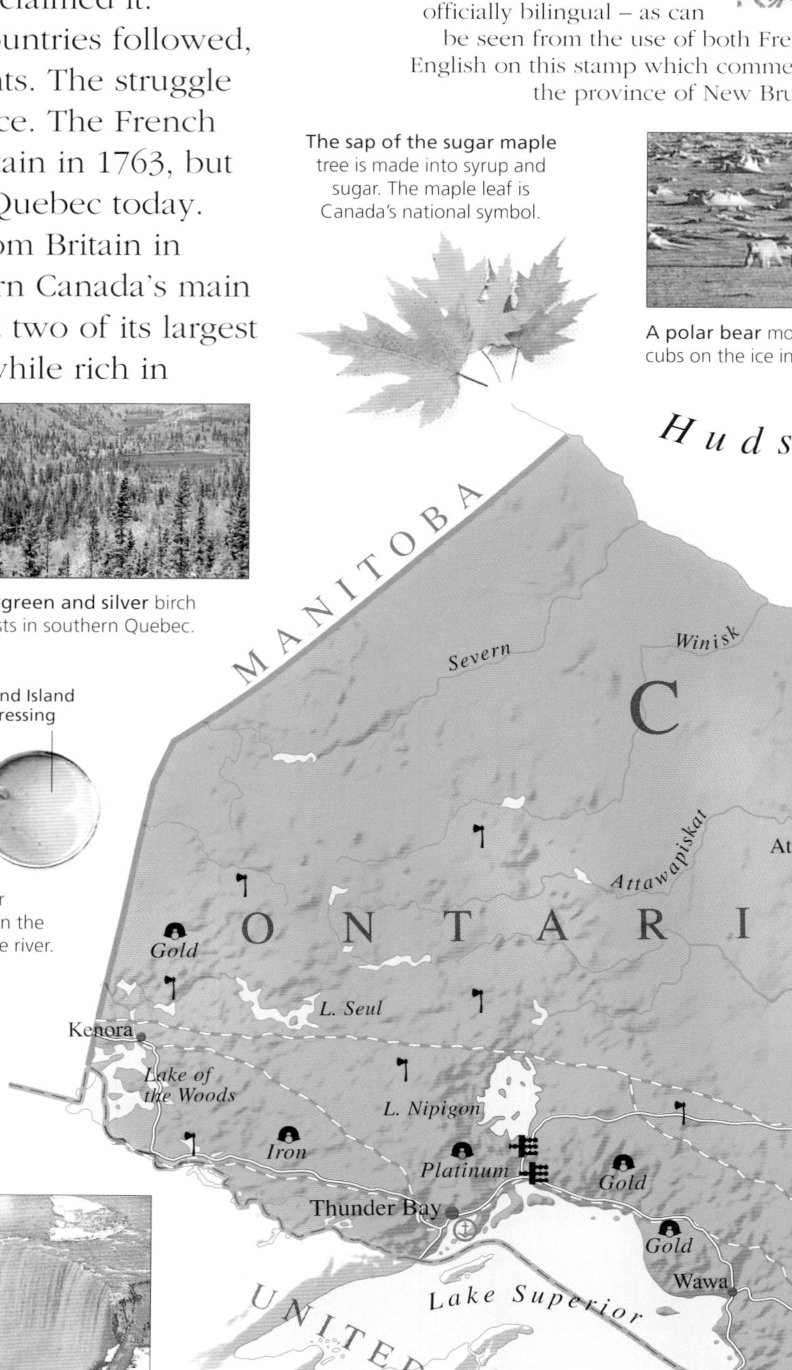
Hudson Bay
MANITOBA
James Bay
C A
ONTARIO
Severn
Winisk
Attawapiskat
Attawapiskat
Albany
Moosone
Gold
Kenora
L. Seul
Lake of the Woods
L. Nipigon
Iron
Platinum
Gold
Thunder Bay
Gold
Wawa
Lake Superior
Copper
Zinc
Nickel
Cochrane
Gold
Timmins
Uranium
Sault Sainte Marie
Nickel
Uranium
Sudbury
Cobal
Copper
Platinu
UNITED STATES OF AMERICA
Lake Huron
Lake Michigan
Owen Sound
Kitchener
Sarnia
London
Windsor
L. Erie

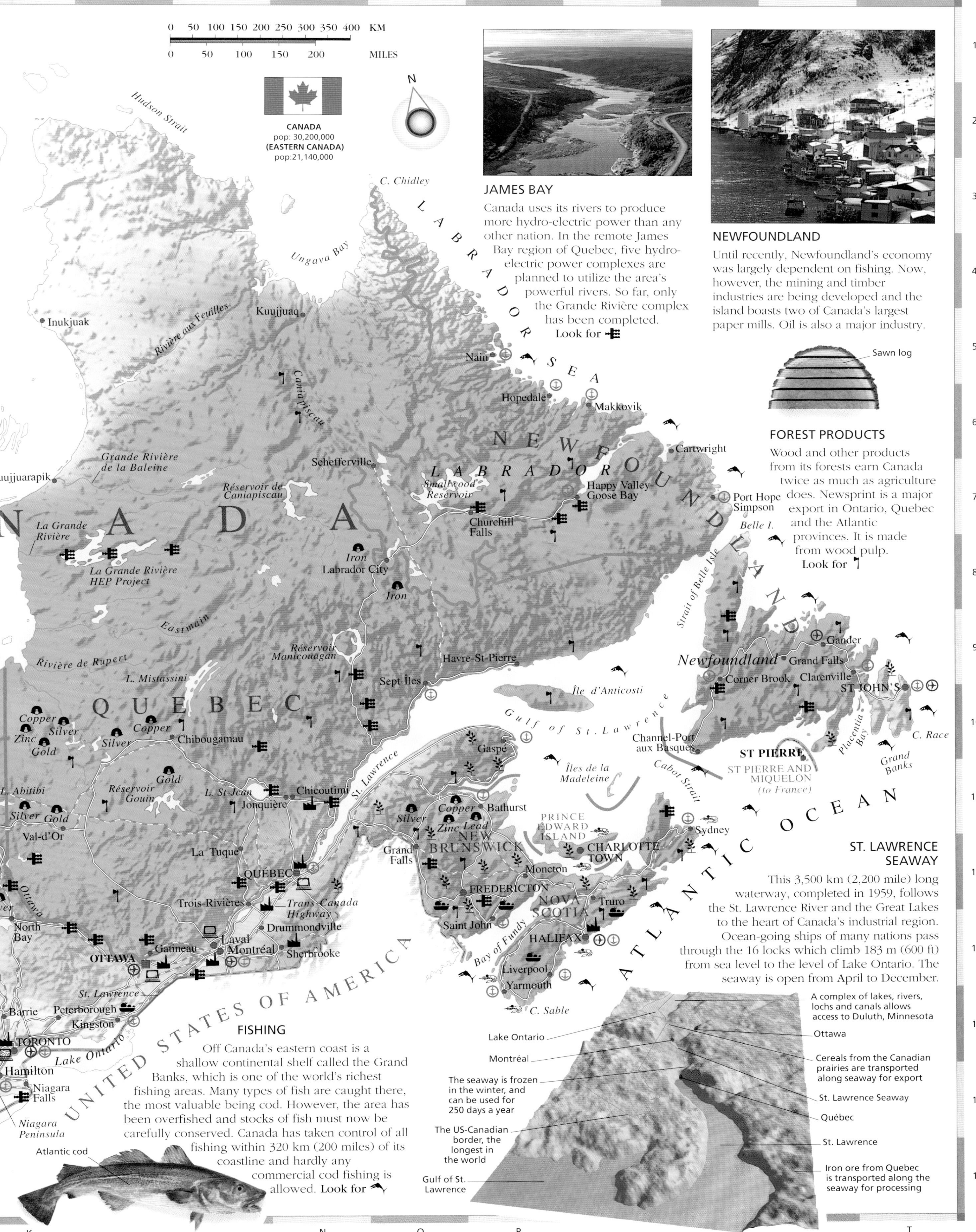

K L M N O P Q R S T
1 2 3 4 5 6 7 8 9 10 11 12 13 14 15 16
0 50 100 150 200 250 300 350 400 KM
0 50 100 150 200 MILES
CANADA
pop: 30,200,000
(EASTERN CANADA)
pop:21,140,000
N
JAMES BAY
Canada uses its rivers to produce more hydro-electric power than any other nation. In the remote James Bay region of Quebec, five hydro-electric power complexes are planned to utilize the area's powerful rivers. So far, only the Grande Rivière complex has been completed.
Look for
NEWFOUNDLAND
Until recently, Newfoundland's economy was largely dependent on fishing. Now, however, the mining and timber industries are being developed and the island boasts two of Canada's largest paper mills. Oil is also a major industry.
Sawn log
FOREST PRODUCTS
Wood and other products from its forests earn Canada twice as much as agriculture does. Newsprint is a major export in Ontario, Quebec and the Atlantic provinces. It is made from wood pulp.
Look for
ST. LAWRENCE SEAWAY
This 3,500 km (2,200 mile) long waterway, completed in 1959, follows the St. Lawrence River and the Great Lakes to the heart of Canada's industrial region. Ocean-going ships of many nations pass through the 16 locks which climb 183 m (600 ft) from sea level to the level of Lake Ontario. The seaway is open from April to December.
FISHING
Off Canada's eastern coast is a shallow continental shelf called the Grand Banks, which is one of the world's richest fishing areas. Many types of fish are caught there, the most valuable being cod. However, the area has been overfished and stocks of fish must now be carefully conserved. Canada has taken control of all fishing within 320 km (200 miles) of its coastline and hardly any commercial cod fishing is allowed. Look for
Atlantic cod
Lake Ontario
Montréal
The seaway is frozen in the winter, and can be used for 250 days a year
The US-Canadian border, the longest in the world
Gulf of St. Lawrence
A complex of lakes, rivers, lochs and canals allows access to Duluth, Minnesota
Ottawa
Cereals from the Canadian prairies are transported along seaway for export
St. Lawrence Seaway
Québec
St. Lawrence
Iron ore from Quebec is transported along the seaway for processing
Hudson Strait
C. Chidley
LABRADOR SEA
Ungava Bay
Inukjuak
Kuujjuaq
Rivière aux Feuilles
Caniapiscau
Nain
Hopedale
Makkovik
NEWFOUNDLAND
LABRADOR
Cartwright
Grande Rivière de la Baleine
Kuujjuarapik
Schefferville
Réservoir de Caniapiscau
Smallwood Reservoir
Happy Valley-Goose Bay
Churchill Falls
Port Hope Simpson
Belle I.
CANADA
La Grande Rivière
La Grande Rivière HEP Project
Iron
Labrador City
Strait of Belle Isle
Eastmain
Réservoir Manicouagan
Havre-St-Pierre
Gander
Newfoundland
Grand Falls
Corner Brook
Clarenville
ST JOHN'S
Rivière de Rupert
L. Mistassini
Sept-Îles
Île d'Anticosti
QUEBEC
Copper
Silver
Zinc
Gold
Chibougamau
Gulf of St. Lawrence
Channel-Port aux Basques
C. Race
Gaspé
ST PIERRE
ST PIERRE AND MIQUELON (to France)
Placentia Bay
Grand Banks
Îles de la Madeleine
Cabot Strait
L. Abitibi
Réservoir Gouin
L. St-Jean
Chicoutimi
Jonquière
St. Lawrence
Bathurst
Lead
PRINCE EDWARD ISLAND
Sydney
ATLANTIC OCEAN
Val-d'Or
La Tuque
Grand Falls
NEW BRUNSWICK
CHARLOTTETOWN
Moncton
QUÉBEC
FREDERICTON
Ottawa
Trois-Rivières
Trans-Canada Highway
NOVA SCOTIA
Truro
North Bay
Drummondville
Saint John
Bay of Fundy
HALIFAX
Gatineau
Laval
OTTAWA
Montréal
Sherbrooke
Liverpool
Yarmouth
C. Sable
UNITED STATES OF AMERICA
Barrie
Peterborough
Kingston
TORONTO
Lake Ontario
Hamilton
Niagara Falls
Niagara Peninsula

NORTHEASTERN UNITED STATES

THE FIRST INHABITANTS of Northeast America were the Native peoples, who made their living for thousands of years from fishing and farming. These peoples were among the first to encounter settlers from Europe in the 16th century, and their numbers were drastically reduced by warfare and contact with European diseases. Many of the first settlers, such as the Puritan pilgrims who sailed to Cape Cod on board the *Mayflower*, were victims of religious persecution, determined to found a brave new world in America. Most settlers were English, and they called the newly-discovered territory New England. They cleared land for farming, founded universities, built churches and established cities. Thanksgiving, celebrated throughout America, commemorates the end of the *Mayflower* pilgrims' first year and their successful harvest. Northeast America, with its rich mineral resources, good harbours and fast-flowing rivers, was the first area on the continent to become industrialized and urbanized. By the mid-19th century, immigrants from Europe were flocking to the USA, many of them settling in New York, or in other East Coast cities. Today, this region is the most densely populated and heavily industrialized area of the United States.

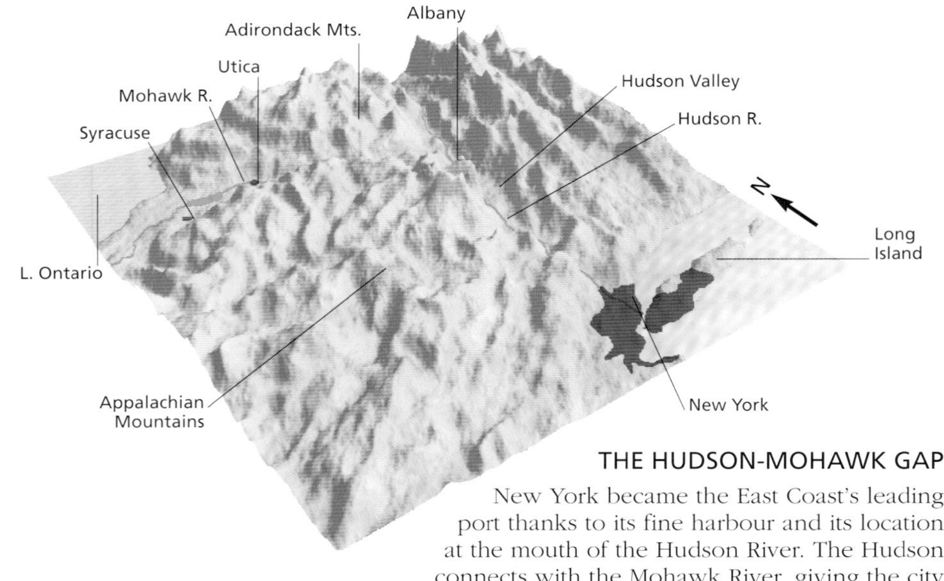
Albany
Adirondack Mts.
Utica
Mohawk R.
Syracuse
Hudson Valley
Hudson R.
N
Long Island
L. Ontario
Appalachian Mountains
New York

THE HUDSON-MOHAWK GAP

New York became the East Coast's leading port thanks to its fine harbour and its location at the mouth of the Hudson River. The Hudson connects with the Mohawk River, giving the city access to the continent's interior; mineral resources and industrial produce were transported along this route.

THE AMISH

This isolated Amish farmstead near Lancaster, Pennsylvania, is run without any modern technology. The Amish are a Protestant sect who came to America from Switzerland in the 18th century. They live by farming, weave all their own clothes and use horses for transport.

The spectacular Niagara Falls near Buffalo, New York State.

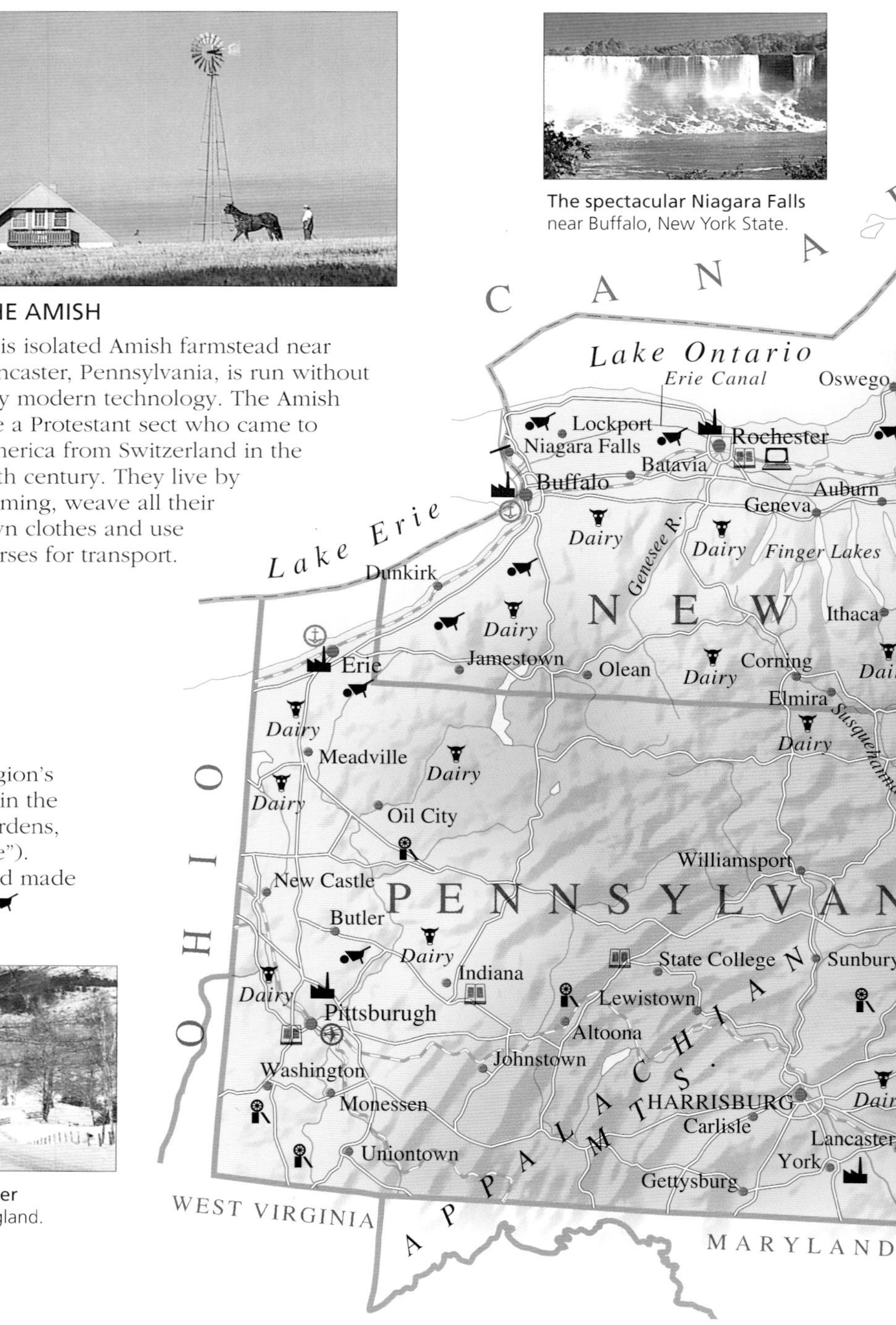
CANADA
Lake Ontario
Erie Canal
Oswego
Lockport
Niagara Falls
Rochester
Batavia
Buffalo
Auburn
Geneva
Dairy
Genesee R.
Finger Lakes
Lake Erie
Dunkirk
NEW
Ithaca
Jamestown
Olean
Corning
Erie
Elmira
Susquehanna
Meadville
OHIO
Oil City
Williamsport
New Castle
PENNSYLVAN
Butler
Indiana
State College
Sunbury
Pittsburgh
Lewistown
Altoona
Johnstown
Washington
APPALACHIAN MTS.
Monessen
HARRISBURG
Carlisle
Lancaster
York
Uniontown
Gettysburg
WEST VIRGINIA
MARYLAND

PUMPKINS

Pumpkins are grown all over New England, and pumpkin pie is a favourite American dish. Pumpkins are also hollowed out to make Jack O'Lanterns for the Hallowe'en festival.

TOMATO SOUP

Many of the fruit and vegetables for the region's big cities, especially New York, are grown in the fruit and vegetable farms, called market gardens, of New Jersey (known as "the Garden State"). Tomatoes are grown in huge quantities, and made locally into tinned tomato soup. Look for

MAP FEATURES
Sailing: Yachting is a popular pastime on New England's Atlantic coast. The Bermuda Race starts from Rhode Island. Look for
Universities: There are more centres of further education and research and development in New England than in any other part of the USA. Look for
Maple syrup: Both sugar and syrup are obtained from the sap of maple trees. Vermont is the USA's main producer. Look for
Cattle
Fishing port
Poultry
Coal
Market gardening
Industrial centre
Fishing
High tech industry

Severe winter weather is common in New England.

Blueberries

Cranberries

NEW ENGLAND BERRIES

Cranberries and blueberries both come from New England and large quantities are grown there. Cranberries are used in sauces, especially to go with roast turkey at Thanksgiving. Blueberries are sweeter, and are often used in pies.

N

0 25 50 75 100 125 150 175 KM

0 25 50 75 100 MILES

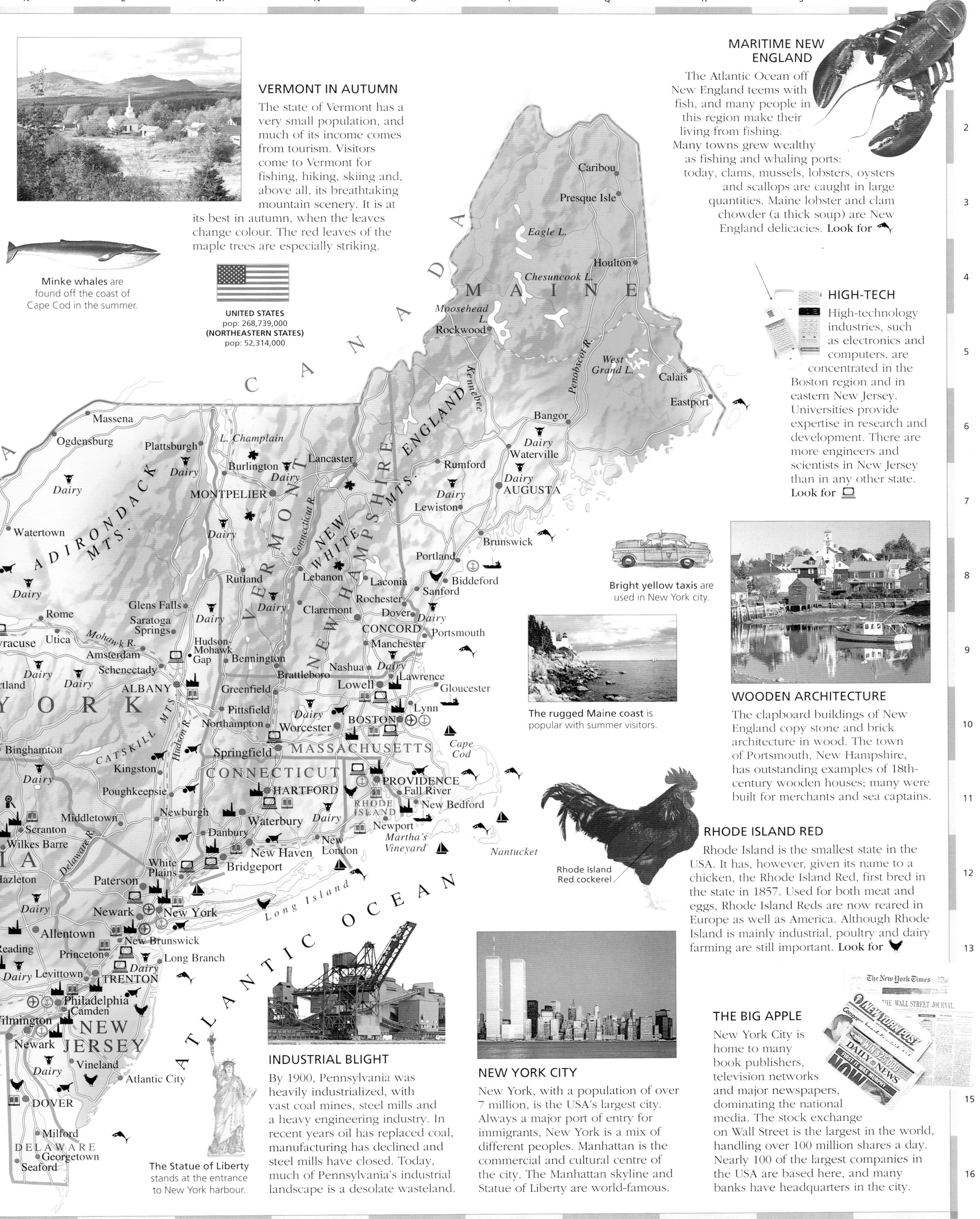
CANADA
MAINE
VERMONT
NEW HAMPSHIRE
NEW ENGLAND
NEW YORK
MASSACHUSETTS
CONNECTICUT
RHODE ISLAND
NEW JERSEY
DELAWARE
ATLANTIC OCEAN
ADIRONDACK MTS.
CATSKILL MTS.
WHITE MTS.
Caribou
Presque Isle
Eagle L.
Houlton
Chesuncook L.
Moosehead L.
Rockwood
West Grand L.
Calais
Eastport
Penobscot R.
Kennebec
Bangor
Waterville
AUGUSTA
Rumford
Lewiston
Brunswick
Portland
Biddeford
Sanford
Dover
Portsmouth
CONCORD
Manchester
Laconia
Rochester
Lebanon
Claremont
Lancaster
Connecticut R.
Nashua
Lawrence
Gloucester
Lowell
Lynn
BOSTON
Cape Cod
Nantucket
Martha's Vineyard
PROVIDENCE
Fall River
New Bedford
Newport
Worcester
Springfield
HARTFORD
Waterbury
New Haven
New London
Bridgeport
Danbury
Long Island
Greenfield
Pittsfield
Northampton
Brattleboro
Bennington
Rutland
MONTPELIER
Burlington
L. Champlain
Plattsburgh
Massena
Ogdensburg
Watertown
Rome
Utica
Syracuse
Mohawk R.
Amsterdam
Schenectady
ALBANY
Glens Falls
Saratoga Springs
Hudson-Mohawk Gap
Hudson R.
Binghamton
Kingston
Poughkeepsie
Newburgh
Middletown
Scranton
Wilkes Barre
Delaware R.
Hazleton
White Plains
Paterson
Newark
New York
Allentown
New Brunswick
Reading
Princeton
Long Branch
Levittown
TRENTON
Philadelphia
Camden
Wilmington
Vineland
Atlantic City
DOVER
Milford
Georgetown
Seaford
Dairy

VERMONT IN AUTUMN

The state of Vermont has a very small population, and much of its income comes from tourism. Visitors come to Vermont for fishing, hiking, skiing and, above all, its breathtaking mountain scenery. It is at its best in autumn, when the leaves change colour. The red leaves of the maple trees are especially striking.

Minke whales are found off the coast of Cape Cod in the summer.

UNITED STATES
pop: 268,739,000
(NORTHEASTERN STATES)
pop: 52,314,000

MARITIME NEW ENGLAND

The Atlantic Ocean off New England teems with fish, and many people in this region make their living from fishing. Many towns grew wealthy as fishing and whaling ports: today, clams, mussels, lobsters, oysters and scallops are caught in large quantities. Maine lobster and clam chowder (a thick soup) are New England delicacies. **Look for**

HIGH-TECH

High-technology industries, such as electronics and computers, are concentrated in the Boston region and in eastern New Jersey. Universities provide expertise in research and development. There are more engineers and scientists in New Jersey than in any other state. **Look for**

Bright yellow taxis are used in New York city.

The rugged Maine coast is popular with summer visitors.

WOODEN ARCHITECTURE

The clapboard buildings of New England copy stone and brick architecture in wood. The town of Portsmouth, New Hampshire, has outstanding examples of 18th-century wooden houses; many were built for merchants and sea captains.

Rhode Island Red cockerel

RHODE ISLAND RED

Rhode Island is the smallest state in the USA. It has, however, given its name to a chicken, the Rhode Island Red, first bred in the state in 1857. Used for both meat and eggs, Rhode Island Reds are now reared in Europe as well as America. Although Rhode Island is mainly industrial, poultry and dairy farming are still important. **Look for**

The Statue of Liberty stands at the entrance to New York harbour.

INDUSTRIAL BLIGHT

By 1900, Pennsylvania was heavily industrialized, with vast coal mines, steel mills and a heavy engineering industry. In recent years oil has replaced coal, manufacturing has declined and steel mills have closed. Today, much of Pennsylvania's industrial landscape is a desolate wasteland.

NEW YORK CITY

New York, with a population of over 7 million, is the USA's largest city. Always a major port of entry for immigrants, New York is a mix of different peoples. Manhattan is the commercial and cultural centre of the city. The Manhattan skyline and Statue of Liberty are world-famous.

THE BIG APPLE

New York City is home to many book publishers, television networks and major newspapers, dominating the national media. The stock exchange on Wall Street is the largest in the world, handling over 100 million shares a day. Nearly 100 of the largest companies in the USA are based here, and many banks have headquarters in the city.

THE SOUTHERN STATES

THIS PART OF THE USA can be divided into three broad regions. To the north, the ridges and valleys of the Appalachian Mountains form a hilly landscape, rich in coal deposits. Immediately to the south and west, the cotton-belt states, with fertile land and a warm, moist climate, are ideal for agriculture. The tropical, humid Gulf region has rich fishing resources; large cargo ports and oil terminals also line the coast. By the 19th century the South had developed an agricultural economy, based on tobacco, rice, indigo and especially cotton, cultivated by African slaves. The northern states believed that slavery in the southern states was wrong, and should be abolished. The South's defeat in the Civil War that followed devastated the region. Today, the South's economy is more varied, thanks to the discovery of oil reserves in the Gulf region and the development of industry. Florida has experienced great population growth in recent years, becoming the fourth-largest state in the 1980s. Its population includes retired people from other states and refugees from Cuba, the Caribbean and Latin America.

Horses graze on a Kentucky farm, in the Bluegrass country.

ATLANTA

The commercial centre of the region is Atlanta, which is the hub of the South's transport network, and has one of the world's busiest airports. Raw materials flood into Atlanta and manufactured goods pour out: clothes, books, iron and steel products and Coca Cola are all made here.

DERBY DAY

Kentucky is called the "Bluegrass State" after the grasslands around the city of Lexington, which provide superb grazing for livestock. This area has the world's greatest concentration of stud farms for breeding thoroughbred horses. The Kentucky Derby, held at Louisville, is one of the world's most famous horse races.

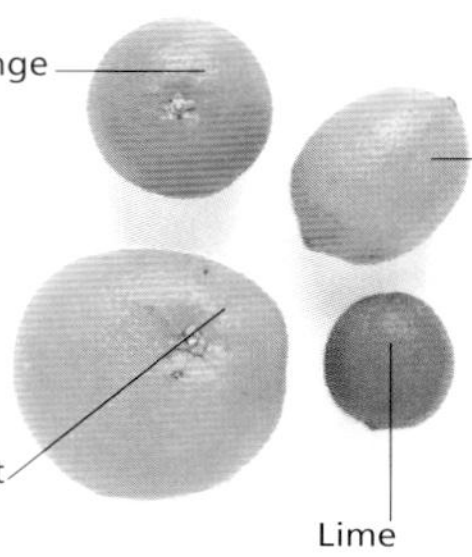

Orange

Lemon

Grapefruit

Lime

Florida produces three-quarters of the USA's oranges and grapefruits.

Jazz saxophone

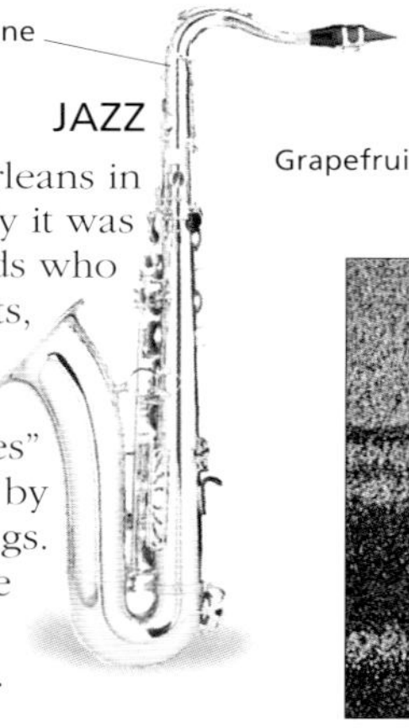

JAZZ

Jazz developed in New Orleans in the early 1900s. Originally it was the music of the bands who marched through the streets, playing at funerals and weddings. Jazz combined many influences – "blues" and spirituals (sung by slaves) and popular songs. Wind instruments are accompanied by drums, piano and double bass.

MAP FEATURES

Soya beans: The main crop in the South is the soya bean. Used for oil, margarine and livestock feed, it has found both domestic and export markets. **Look for**

Coal: Coal, mined from the rich reserves of the Appalachian Mountains, is being overtaken by oil and gas. **Look for**

High-tech industry: The South, with its skilled labour force and good communications, is attracting many high-tech industries. **Look for**

Space centre: The Space Shuttle is launched from the Kennedy Space Center, the launch site of the US Space programme. **Look for**

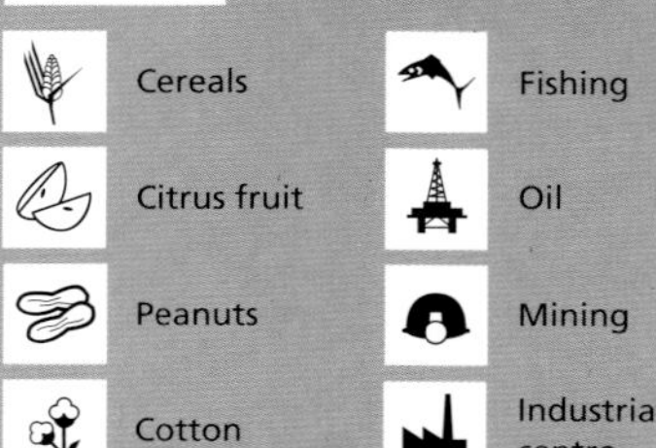

Cereals	Fishing
Citrus fruit	Oil
Peanuts	Mining
Cotton	Industrial centre
Tobacco	Tourism

KING COTTON

Cotton, grown on large plantations using slave labour, was once the basis of the southern economy. Today, it is still grown on farms in some parts of the South. **Look for**

BOURBON

Maize is one of Kentucky's major crops. It is used for making Bourbon whisky, which is a worldwide export.

MISSISSIPPI

Steamboats carry tourists on scenic trips along the Mississippi, one of the world's busiest waterways. Barges transport heavy cargoes from the industrial and agricultural regions near the Great Lakes to the Gulf coast.

Okra

Prawn

Gumbo is a spicy seafood and vegetable stew from Louisiana.

RETIREMENT STATE

Nearly 30 per cent of Florida's inhabitants are over 55 years old. Large numbers of people retire to Florida, lured by its climate and sports facilities. Many settle in retirement developments or in the coastal cities.

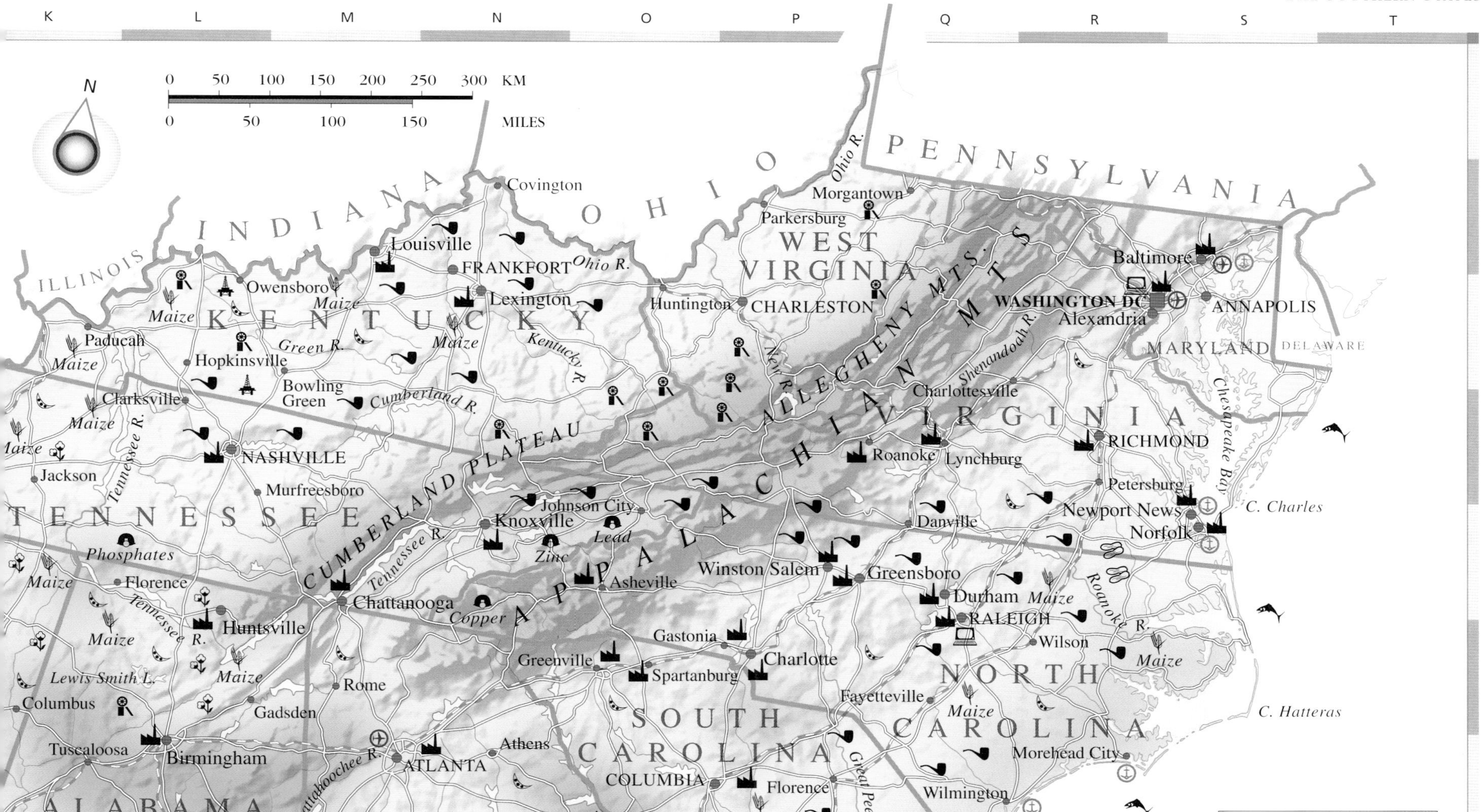

Fields of ripening tobacco in North Carolina.

UNITED STATES
pop: 268,739,000
(SOUTHERN STATES)
pop: 70,532,000

The Everglades – a vast tropical marsh in southern Florida.

AMERICAN CAPITAL

The city of Washington, also known as the District of Columbia, became the USA's capital and seat of the federal government in 1800. This picture shows the lighted dome of the Capitol Building.

The elegant mansions of cotton plantation-owners can still be seen in the South.

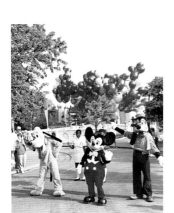

DISNEY WORLD

In 1971, Disney World was opened near Orlando, Florida. Millions of visitors come each year to this vast fantasy land. It occupies a huge area of reclaimed swamp, lake and forest. Tourists also come to Florida to visit the Epcot Center – a trip through a vision of the future – and the Kennedy Space Center.

TOBACCO

The southern states grow high-quality Virginia tobacco. The leaves are cured for 4-6 days in controlled temperatures before being moistened and sorted. Tobacco factories can produce up to 450 million cigarettes a day. Look for

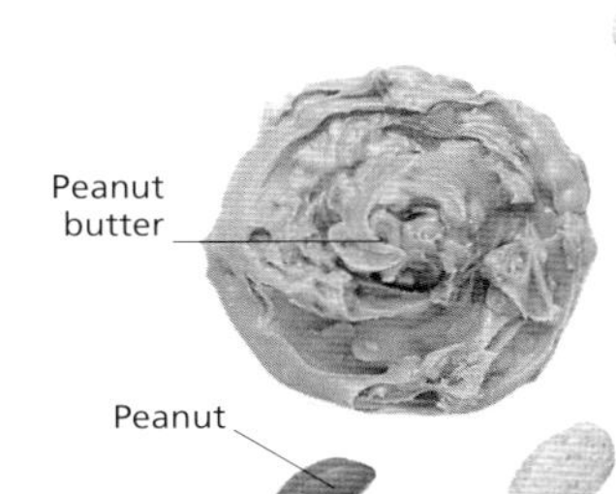
Peanut butter
Peanut

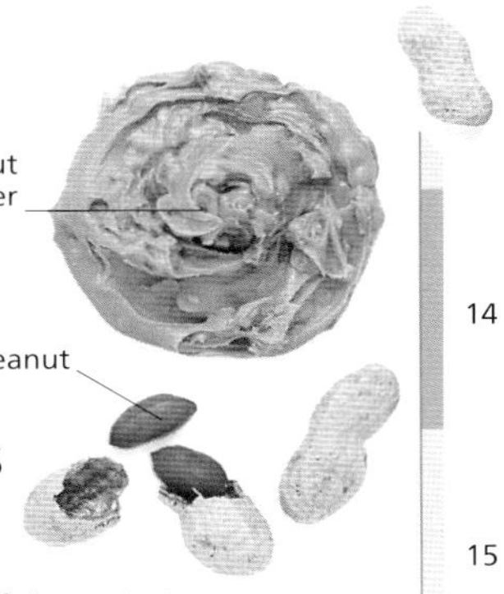

PEANUTS

Georgia grows nearly half the USA's total crop of peanuts. Half of the crop is used for making peanut butter, the rest for edible oil and animal feed. Look for

THE GREAT LAKES

THE FIVE GREAT LAKES of North America – Erie, Ontario, Huron, Michigan and Superior – together form the largest area of fresh water in the world. The states of Indiana, Illinois, Michigan, Ohio, Wisconsin and Minnesota, all of which border on one or more of the lakes, are often called the industrial and agricultural heartland of the United States. This region is rich in natural resources, including coal, iron, copper and timber, and there are large areas of fertile farmland on the flat plains of the prairies. First explored by French traders, fur trappers and missionaries in the 17th century, the region began to attract large numbers of settlers in the early 1800s. Trading links were improved by the opening of the Erie Canal in 1825, which connected the region to the Atlantic coast, while the Mississippi and other rivers gave access to the Gulf of Mexico and the rest of the continent. When railways reached the region in the 1840s, cities such as Chicago grew and prospered as freight-handling centres. Steel production and the car industry later became the main industries in the region. In recent years, a decline in these traditional industries has led to high unemployment in some areas.

Wall-eyes live in the Great Lakes, but their numbers are falling due to pollution.

HOGS

In the 19th century, huge numbers of animals from all over this region were sent to the stock-yards in Chicago for slaughter and processing. Rearing livestock is still important in Illinois. Maize and soya beans, both grown locally, are used as animal feed. **Look for**

HAMBURGERS

Hamburgers are America's own fast food, first produced on a massive scale in Illinois in the 1950s. It has been calculated that in every second of the day, 200 Americans are eating a hamburger. American-style hamburger take-aways can now be found all over the world.

THE WINDY CITY

Chicago is situated at the southern tip of Lake Michigan. It gets its nickname – the Windy City – from the weather conditions in this area. Chicago was ideally positioned for trading with the Midwest region, and quickly became a wealthy modern city. By 1900 it had vast complexes of lumber mills, meat processing factories, railway yards and steel mills.

COLD WINTERS

The Great Lakes region has severe winters, and Minnesota, in particular, suffers from heavy snow-storms. Parts of the Great Lakes themselves can freeze over in winter, and lakeside harbours can be frozen from December to early April.

MAP FEATURES

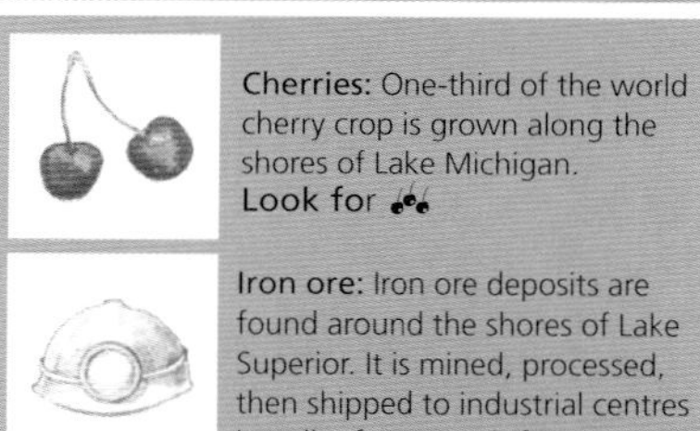

Cherries: One-third of the world cherry crop is grown along the shores of Lake Michigan. **Look for**

Iron ore: Iron ore deposits are found around the shores of Lake Superior. It is mined, processed, then shipped to industrial centres in pellet form. **Look for**

Cattle	Soya beans
Hogs	Coal
Cereals	Oil
Sugar beet	Industrial centre
Market gardening	Vehicle manufacture

An isolated farm on the open prairies of Illinois.

Baseball and fielder's glove. Baseball is the USA's national game.

MILWAUKEE BEER

The Great Lakes region has attracted many immigrants, especially from Germany, the Netherlands and the Scandinavian countries. Milwaukee, where many Germans settled, is home to several of the USA's largest breweries.

PRAIRIE LANDS

The fertile soil and hot, humid summers make the flat expanses of the Midwestern prairies ideal for farming. Nearly half of the world's maize crop is grown on the huge farms in this region.

CORNFLAKES

Food processing is a major industry throughout this agricultural region. Wisconsin, for example, is the major producer of canned peas and sweet corn in the USA. Corn and wheat-based breakfast cereals are exported all over the world from Battle Creek, Michigan. **Look for**

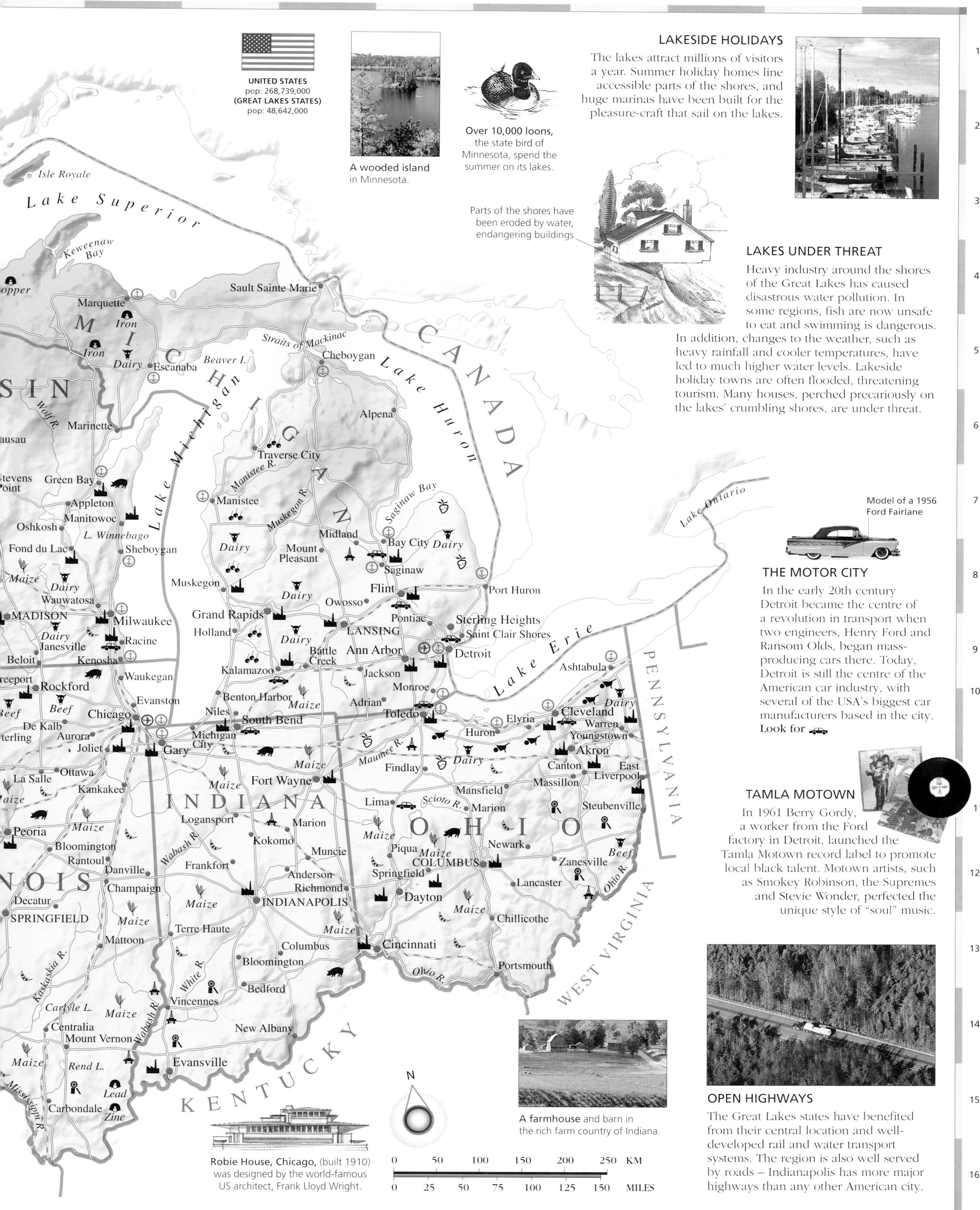

K L M N O P Q R S T
1 2 3 4 5 6 7 8 9 10 11 12 13 14 15 16
UNITED STATES
pop: 268,739,000
(GREAT LAKES STATES)
pop: 48,642,000
Isle Royale
Lake Superior
Keweenaw Bay
Sault Sainte Marie
Marquette
Iron
Dairy
Escanaba
Beaver I.
Straits of Mackinac
Cheboygan
Lake Huron
CANADA
MICHIGAN
Alpena
Marinette
Wolf R.
Lake Michigan
Traverse City
Manistee R.
Manistee
Muskegon R.
Saginaw Bay
Green Bay
Appleton
Manitowoc
Oshkosh
L. Winnebago
Fond du Lac
Sheboygan
Midland
Bay City
Mount Pleasant
Saginaw
Muskegon
Flint
Port Huron
Owosso
Grand Rapids
Holland
Pontiac
Sterling Heights
Saint Clair Shores
LANSING
Ann Arbor
Detroit
Battle Creek
Kalamazoo
Jackson
Monroe
Lake Erie
Ashtabula
Lake Ontario
MADISON
Wauwatosa
Milwaukee
Racine
Janesville
Kenosha
Beloit
Waukegan
Rockford
Evanston
Chicago
Benton Harbor
Niles
South Bend
Adrian
Toledo
Elyria
Cleveland
Warren
Youngstown
Akron
De Kalb
Aurora
Joliet
Gary
Michigan City
Huron
Canton
East Liverpool
Massillon
Ottawa
La Salle
Kankakee
Fort Wayne
Findlay
Maumee R.
Mansfield
INDIANA
Lima
Scioto R.
Marion
Steubenville
OHIO
Logansport
Peoria
Bloomington
Rantoul
Kokomo
Muncie
Newark
Piqua
COLUMBUS
Zanesville
Danville
Champaign
Frankfort
Anderson
Richmond
Springfield
Dayton
Lancaster
Ohio R.
Wabash R.
Decatur
SPRINGFIELD
INDIANAPOLIS
Chillicothe
Terre Haute
Mattoon
Columbus
Cincinnati
Bloomington
Portsmouth
Kaskaskia R.
White R.
Bedford
Vincennes
WEST VIRGINIA
PENNSYLVANIA
Carlyle L.
Centralia
Mount Vernon
New Albany
KENTUCKY
Rend L.
Evansville
Lead
Carbondale
Zinc
Mississippi R.
N
0 50 100 150 200 250 KM
0 25 50 75 100 125 150 MILES

A wooded island in Minnesota.

Over 10,000 loons, the state bird of Minnesota, spend the summer on its lakes.

LAKESIDE HOLIDAYS

The lakes attract millions of visitors a year. Summer holiday homes line accessible parts of the shores, and huge marinas have been built for the pleasure-craft that sail on the lakes.

Parts of the shores have been eroded by water, endangering buildings

LAKES UNDER THREAT

Heavy industry around the shores of the Great Lakes has caused disastrous water pollution. In some regions, fish are now unsafe to eat and swimming is dangerous. In addition, changes to the weather, such as heavy rainfall and cooler temperatures, have led to much higher water levels. Lakeside holiday towns are often flooded, threatening tourism. Many houses, perched precariously on the lakes' crumbling shores, are under threat.

Model of a 1956 Ford Fairlane

THE MOTOR CITY

In the early 20th century Detroit became the centre of a revolution in transport when two engineers, Henry Ford and Ransom Olds, began mass-producing cars there. Today, Detroit is still the centre of the American car industry, with several of the USA's biggest car manufacturers based in the city. **Look for**

TAMLA MOTOWN

In 1961 Berry Gordy, a worker from the Ford factory in Detroit, launched the Tamla Motown record label to promote local black talent. Motown artists, such as Smokey Robinson, the Supremes and Stevie Wonder, perfected the unique style of "soul" music.

A farmhouse and barn in the rich farm country of Indiana.

Robie House, Chicago, (built 1910) was designed by the world-famous US architect, Frank Lloyd Wright.

OPEN HIGHWAYS

The Great Lakes states have benefited from their central location and well-developed rail and water transport systems. The region is also well served by roads – Indianapolis has more major highways than any other American city.

Central and Mountain States

This region includes the lowlands on the west bank of the Mississippi River, the vast expanses of the Great Plains, and the majestic Rocky Mountains. In climate, it is a region of extremes: hot summers alternate with cold winters, and hailstorms, blizzards and tornadoes are frequent events. Once home to large numbers of Native Americans and great herds of buffalo, the plains were settled in the 19th century; the Native Americans were pushed on to reservations and the buffalo slaughtered. Originally dismissed as a desert because of low rainfall and lack of trees, the Great Plains proved to be one of the world's great agricultural regions; today, vast amounts of cereals are grown on mechanized farms, and cattle are grazed on huge ranches. The Rockies are rich in minerals, and reserves of coal, oil and natural gas are being exploited.

The foothills of the snow-covered Rockies in Montana.

CANADA
WASHINGTON
OREGON
NEVADA
UTAH
IDAHO
MONTANA
WYOMING
ROCKY MOUNTAINS
BITTERROOT RANGE
WIND RIVER RANGE
BIGHORN MTS.
Zinc
Lead
Coeur d'Alene
Silver
Kalispell
Flathead L.
Wheat
Beef
Barley
Shelby
L. Elwell
Havre
Missouri R.
Fort Peck
Great Falls
Missoula
Lewiston
HELENA
Canyon Ferry L.
Anaconda
Copper
Butte
Salmon R.
Bozeman
Yellowstone R.
Billings
Bighorn R.
Dillon
Sheridan
Cody
Yellowstone L.
Jackson L.
Grand Teton Mts.
Worland
Uranium
Wind R.
Iron
Nampa
BOISE
Snake R.
Idaho Falls
Phosphate
Pocatello
Twin Falls
Pathfinder Res.
Green R.
Rock Springs
Rawlins
Flaming Gorge Res.

Shredded wheat

AGRICULTURAL INDUSTRIES

A great range of cereals are grown in the Midwest and transported to local cities for processing. Iowa has the largest cereal processing factory in the world, and it is in the cities of this region that many cereals are prepared for the world's breakfast tables. Cities also provide storage facilities for grain and cereals, as well as markets for grain, livestock and farm machinery.

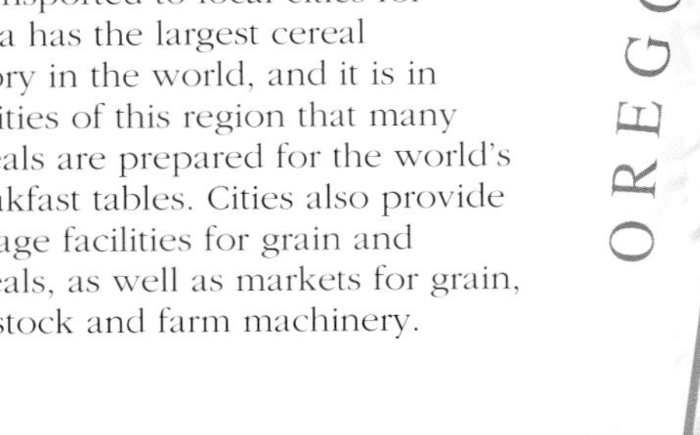

Corn flakes Oats Toasted rice

COWBOYS

Cattle are raised on the Great Plains and foothills of the Rocky Mountains. Ranches often have thousands of cattle. In summer, mounted cowboys herd cattle to upland pastures and drive them back to the ranch for the winter. Cattle are then taken to markets in nearby towns for cattle auctions. **Look for** (cattle symbol)

WYOMING COAL

Wyoming now leads the USA in coal production. Coal from the West is in demand because it has a lower sulphur content than coal mined in the East, and causes less pollution when burnt. Shallow coal reserves are extracted from open-cast mines, like this one, which spoil the landscape. **Look for** (coal symbol)

Fossils of dinosaurs, such as *Tyrannosaurus*, have been found in the foothills of the Rockies.

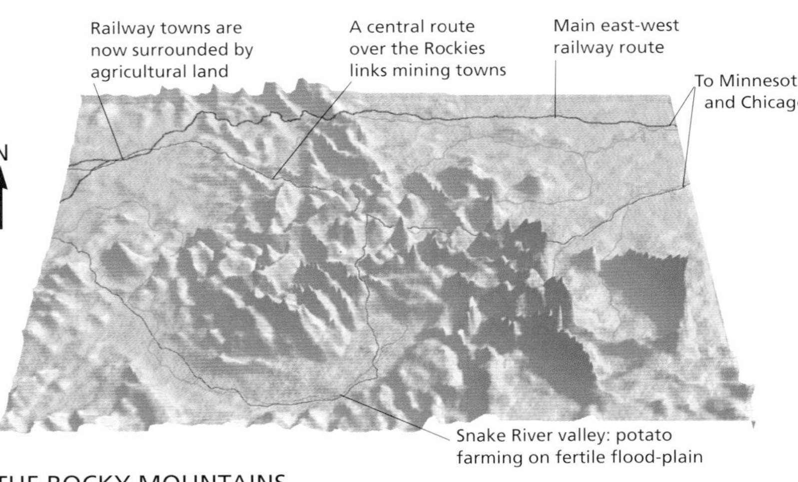

Railway towns are now surrounded by agricultural land
A central route over the Rockies links mining towns
Main east-west railway route
To Minnesota and Chicago
N
Snake River valley: potato farming on fertile flood-plain

THE ROCKY MOUNTAINS

The Rocky Mountains divide the North American continent in two; rivers to the west of the range flow towards the Pacific, while those to the east drain into the Arctic and Atlantic oceans and the Gulf of Mexico. First explored by fur trappers and traders in the 19th century, the mountain passes were used by settlers on their way west. Miners followed the settlers, and the mining towns of Montana were established. By 1869, the Transcontinental railroad had crossed the Rockies, linking the Pacific coast with the rest of the country.

FARMING

Maize is the main crop in Iowa, while wheat is more important in the centre of this region. Nearer the Rockies, the rainfall decreases and wheat farming gives way to cattle ranching. Farming in the Midwest is large-scale and mechanized. These vast wheatfields in Nebraska stretch to the far horizon. Farmers often produce more than they can sell. **Look for** (cereals symbol)

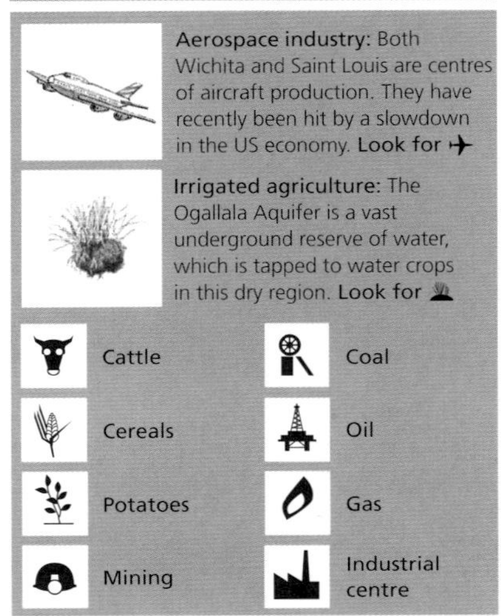

MAP FEATURES

Aerospace industry: Both Wichita and Saint Louis are centres of aircraft production. They have recently been hit by a slowdown in the US economy. **Look for** (aircraft symbol)

Irrigated agriculture: The Ogallala Aquifer is a vast underground reserve of water, which is tapped to water crops in this dry region. **Look for** (irrigation symbol)

Cattle	Coal
Cereals	Oil
Potatoes	Gas
Mining	Industrial centre

TOURISM

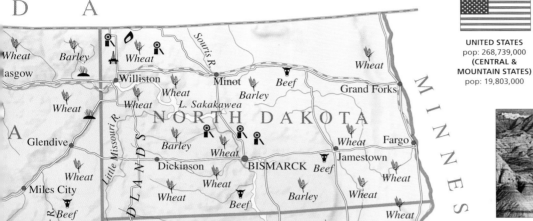

Huge carvings of the heads of four great American presidents – Washington, Lincoln, Jefferson and Theodore Roosevelt – can be seen at Mount Rushmore in South Dakota. Millions of people have visited the monument since its completion in 1927. The mountainous scenery and wildlife of this region attract tourists from all over the world.

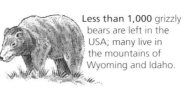

Less than 1,000 grizzly bears are left in the USA; many live in the mountains of Wyoming and Idaho.

BISON

Millions of bison (American buffalo) used to roam the Great Plains. Native Americans hunted them for food and used their hides to make clothing and shelters. Settlers and railway workers virtually wiped out the bison herds in the late 19th century, killing them for food and profit. Today, the bison population is protected and there are now about 50,000 bison living on reserves.

UNITED STATES
pop: 268,739,000
(CENTRAL & MOUNTAIN STATES)
pop: 19,803,000

The Badlands of North and South Dakota have been eroded into hills and gullies.

ON THE ROAD

An extensive road network holds this vast, sparsely-inhabited region together. Highways often run through long stretches of nearly empty land, fringed by gas stations, motels and roadside restaurants. Cars are a necessity in much of the West; in Wyoming, children of 14 can drive to school.

Popcorn, roasted and puffed-up maize, is a Midwestern export.

The Grand Teton Mountains, northern Wyoming.

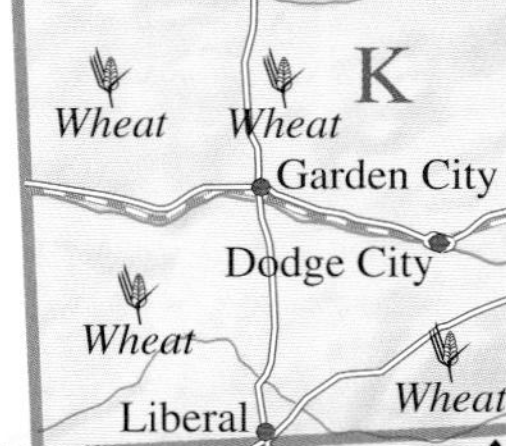
NORTH DAKOTA
SOUTH DAKOTA
NEBRASKA
KANSAS
OKLAHOMA
IOWA
MISSOURI
MINNESOTA
WISCONSIN
ILLINOIS
KENTUCKY
TENNESSEE
ARKANSAS
TEXAS
NEW MEXICO
COLORADO
BISMARCK
PIERRE
LINCOLN
DES MOINES
TOPEKA
JEFFERSON CITY
OKLAHOMA CITY
CHEYENNE

GOLD RUSH

In 1874, gold was found in the Black Hills of South Dakota, a region sacred to the Sioux people. The discovery sparked a major gold rush; towns sprang up overnight, fortunes were won and lost, gambling and crime flourished. The area is still rich in minerals – South Dakota's Homestake gold mine is the biggest in the country. Look for

Broad-brimmed hats are still an essential part of the cowboy's wardrobe.

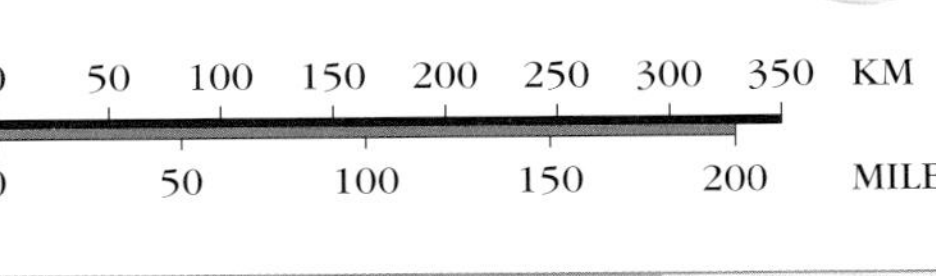
0 50 100 150 200 250 300 350 KM
0 50 100 150 200 MILES

THE SOUTHWESTERN STATES

THE SOUTHWESTERN USA is a region of deserts and high plateaux, broken by the ridges of the southern Rocky Mountains. Many different Native American peoples lived in the Southwest. The region still has the country's largest concentration of Native Americans. The first Europeans to settle in this region were Spaniards who came north from Mexico. This mixed Spanish and Native American heritage is reflected in the region's folk art, architecture and foods. American settlers in Texas rebelled against Mexican rule in 1836, and Texas was annexed to the USA a decade later. The rest of the region became part of the USA after the Mexican War of 1846-48. Gold and silver mining and cattle-ranching attracted settlers to the region in the late 19th century, and oil became a major part of Texas's economy in the 20th century. The region's natural beauty draws tourists from all over the world.

The Saguaro cactus thrives in the deserts of Arizona.

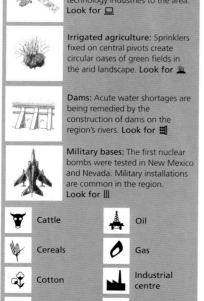

Jordan Mormon Temple, Utah

MORMON CITY

Salt Lake City in Utah is the headquarters of the Latter-day Saints, or Mormons. They settled in Utah in the 1840s, after fleeing from the eastern states, where they had been persecuted for their beliefs. There are now more than six million Mormons worldwide.

NAVAJO RUGS

Many Navajo people live on a vast reservation in Arizona and New Mexico. They still practise weaving, pottery, silver-working and other traditional crafts. Navajo rugs are woven into geometric patterns, and coloured with natural dyes, such as juniper and blackberry.

An 11th-century pottery bowl, made by the Mogollon people.

THE GREAT OUTDOORS

Riding, trekking, canoeing, skiing and fishing are just some of the outdoor activities which draw tourists to the Southwest. But the region's main attraction is the Grand Canyon. About 10,000 visitors each year navigate the Canyon's dangerous waters on rubber rafts, and many others explore it on foot or by donkey.

These strangely shaped rocks in Monument Valley, Arizona, have been carved by the wind.

UNITED STATES
pop: 268,739,000
(SOUTHWESTERN STATES)
pop: 35,552,000

MAP FEATURES

High-tech industry: The space programme has attracted high technology industries to the area. Look for

Irrigated agriculture: Sprinklers fixed on central pivots create circular oases of green fields in the arid landscape. Look for

Dams: Acute water shortages are being remedied by the construction of dams on the region's rivers. Look for

Military bases: The first nuclear bombs were tested in New Mexico and Nevada. Military installations are common in the region. Look for

Cattle | Oil | Cereals | Gas | Cotton | Industrial centre | Mining | Skiing

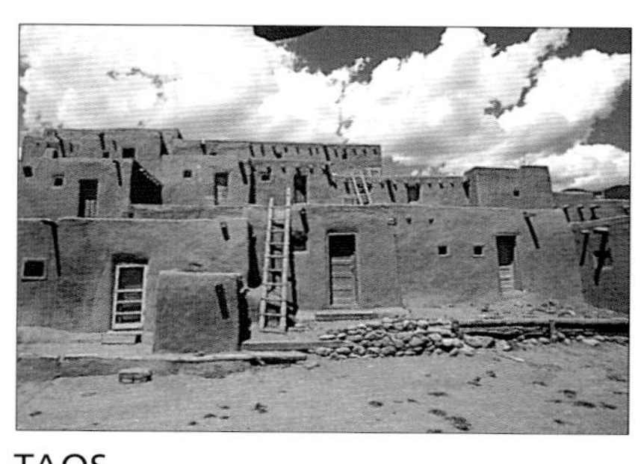

TAOS

The pueblo, or village, of Taos in New Mexico is built of unbaked clay brick, called adobe. This style of building dates back to the Pueblo people, who lived in the region a thousand years ago, farming maize, cotton, beans and squash.

THE GRAND CANYON

Over the last million years, the Colorado River has cut its way through the rocky plateaux of northern Arizona. At the same time, the plateaux have risen. This combined action has formed the largest land gorge in the world – the Grand Canyon. It is more than 1.6 km (1 mile) deep, and 350 km (220 miles) long. Some of the oldest rocks in North America have been found atthe base of the canyon.

Grand Canyon
Bright Angel Point
Colorado River
from Lake Powell
N
Eroded sediment carried down rivers creates fertile plains
to Lake Mead

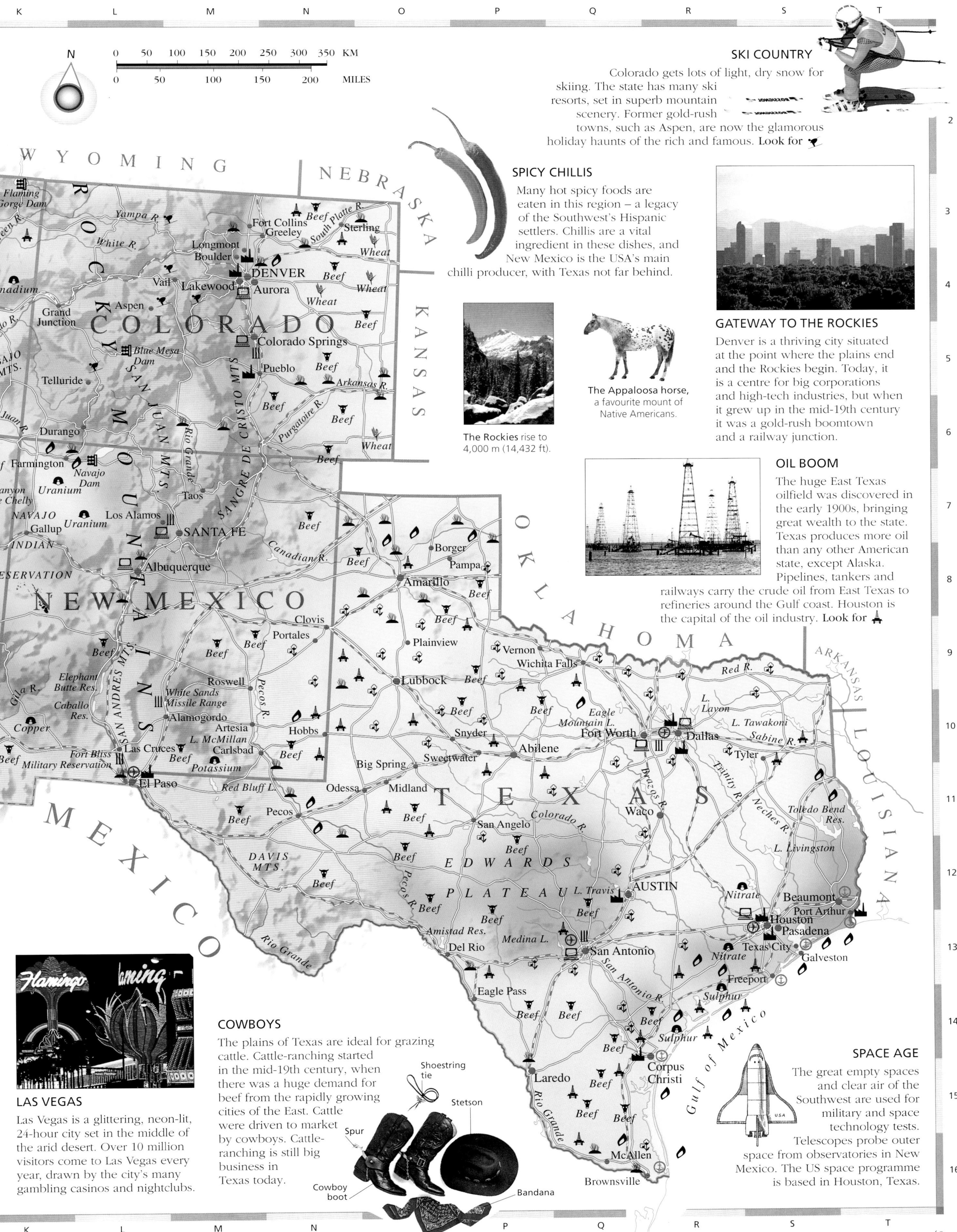
K L M N O P Q R S T
N
0 50 100 150 200 250 300 350 KM
0 50 100 150 200 MILES
WYOMING
NEBRASKA
KANSAS
OKLAHOMA
ARKANSAS
LOUISIANA
MEXICO
COLORADO
NEW MEXICO
TEXAS
ROCKY MOUNTAINS
SAN JUAN MTS.
SANGRE DE CRISTO MTS
SAN ANDRES MTS.
DAVIS MTS.
EDWARDS PLATEAU
NAVAJO INDIAN RESERVATION
Flaming Gorge Dam
Fort Collins
Greeley
Sterling
Longmont
Boulder
DENVER
Lakewood
Aurora
Vail
Aspen
Grand Junction
Colorado Springs
Pueblo
Telluride
Durango
Blue Mesa Dam
Farmington
Navajo Dam
Canyon de Chelly
Gallup
Los Alamos
SANTA FE
Taos
Albuquerque
Clovis
Portales
Roswell
White Sands Missile Range
Alamogordo
Artesia
Carlsbad
L. McMillan
Las Cruces
Fort Bliss Military Reservation
El Paso
Elephant Butte Res.
Caballo Res.
Borger
Pampa
Amarillo
Plainview
Vernon
Wichita Falls
Lubbock
Snyder
Abilene
Fort Worth
Dallas
Tyler
Hobbs
Big Spring
Sweetwater
Odessa
Midland
Pecos
Waco
San Angelo
AUSTIN
Beaumont
Port Arthur
Houston
Pasadena
Texas City
Galveston
San Antonio
Del Rio
Eagle Pass
Freeport
Laredo
Corpus Christi
McAllen
Brownsville
Gulf of Mexico
Yampa R.
White R.
Green R.
South Platte R.
Arkansas R.
Purgatoire R.
Rio Grande
San Juan R.
Canadian R.
Pecos R.
Gila R.
Red R.
Red Bluff L.
Colorado R.
Brazos R.
Trinity R.
Neches R.
Sabine R.
L. Lavon
L. Tawakoni
Eagle Mountain L.
Toledo Bend Res.
L. Livingston
L. Travis
Amistad Res.
Medina L.
San Antonio R.
Beef
Wheat
Uranium
Vanadium
Copper
Potassium
Nitrate
Sulphur
2 3 4 5 6 7 8 9 10 11 12 13 14 15 16

SKI COUNTRY

Colorado gets lots of light, dry snow for skiing. The state has many ski resorts, set in superb mountain scenery. Former gold-rush towns, such as Aspen, are now the glamorous holiday haunts of the rich and famous. **Look for**

SPICY CHILLIS

Many hot spicy foods are eaten in this region – a legacy of the Southwest's Hispanic settlers. Chillis are a vital ingredient in these dishes, and New Mexico is the USA's main chilli producer, with Texas not far behind.

The Rockies rise to 4,000 m (14,432 ft).

The Appaloosa horse, a favourite mount of Native Americans.

GATEWAY TO THE ROCKIES

Denver is a thriving city situated at the point where the plains end and the Rockies begin. Today, it is a centre for big corporations and high-tech industries, but when it grew up in the mid-19th century it was a gold-rush boomtown and a railway junction.

OIL BOOM

The huge East Texas oilfield was discovered in the early 1900s, bringing great wealth to the state. Texas produces more oil than any other American state, except Alaska. Pipelines, tankers and railways carry the crude oil from East Texas to refineries around the Gulf coast. Houston is the capital of the oil industry. **Look for**

LAS VEGAS

Las Vegas is a glittering, neon-lit, 24-hour city set in the middle of the arid desert. Over 10 million visitors come to Las Vegas every year, drawn by the city's many gambling casinos and nightclubs.

COWBOYS

The plains of Texas are ideal for grazing cattle. Cattle-ranching started in the mid-19th century, when there was a huge demand for beef from the rapidly growing cities of the East. Cattle were driven to market by cowboys. Cattle-ranching is still big business in Texas today.

Shoestring tie
Stetson
Spur
Cowboy boot
Bandana

SPACE AGE

The great empty spaces and clear air of the Southwest are used for military and space technology tests. Telescopes probe outer space from observatories in New Mexico. The US space programme is based in Houston, Texas.

THE PACIFIC STATES

THE PACIFIC COAST STATES boast some of the most varied scenery in the USA. California, for example, contains the snow-capped peaks of the Sierra Nevada mountains and the lowest point in North America – Death Valley. Much of California is arid, with farming dependent on irrigation, while vast forests and well-watered fertile valleys are characteristic of Washington and Oregon. American settlers began to cross the Rockies to the Pacific coast in the 1840s. California became part of the USA as a result of the Mexican-American War (1846-48), and the discovery of gold in 1848 led to its rapid settlement. All three states are now major agricultural producers and centres of high-technology industry. In the early 1960s, California became the USA's most highly-populated state. Despite recent problems, the state's economy rivals those of many wealthy nations.

TIMBER

Oregon and Washington are the USA's major timber producers. The region's cedar and fir forests supply one-third of the country's softwood timber. The trees are cut into logs at one of the thousands of sawmills in the forests and then floated down rivers on rafts to the large coastal cities. Some of the wood is made into paper at pulp-mills like the one pictured here. Much of the region's timber is exported to Japan. Tree-felling has reduced the region's stocks of mature trees; efforts are now being made to plant more trees. **Look for**

Almond

Avocado pear

AGRICULTURE

California alone produces half of the USA's fruit and vegetables. Fertile soils and a warm climate have contributed to the state's success, but dry conditions mean that much of the state's farmland has to be irrigated. California's main crops are cotton and grapes. **Look for**

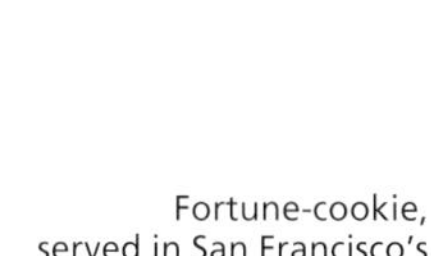

Boeing 767 aircraft

AEROSPACE

The Boeing Corporation, the world's largest aircraft manufacturer, is based in Seattle. Boeing is the city's main employer, and any decline in orders can result in unemployment. California is a major producer of military aeroplanes; cuts in US defence spending have badly affected this region. **Look for**

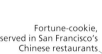

Computer discs capable of storing vast amounts of information

SILICON VALLEY

Santa Clara Valley, south of San Francisco, has one of the largest concentrations of high-technology industry in the world. Over 3,000 firms there specialize in micro-electronics and computer hardware and software. US manufacturers face increasing competition from the Far East. **Look for**

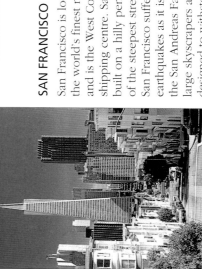

Waves batter the rugged Pacific coast of Oregon.

SAN FRANCISCO

San Francisco is located on one of the world's finest natural harbours, and is the West Coast's trade and shipping centre. San Francisco is built on a hilly peninsula, with some of the steepest streets in the world. San Francisco suffers from frequent earthquakes as it is situated right on the San Andreas Fault. The city's large skyscrapers are specially designed to withstand earthquakes.

Washington's Mount Rainier is permanently snow-covered.

California redwoods are evergreen trees, which can reach 100 m (330 ft).

Fortune-cookie, served in San Francisco's Chinese restaurants

IMMIGRATION

California attracts many immigrants from Asia and South America.

Many Chinese immigrants have settled in San Francisco's Chinatown. This area of the city is a magnet for the Chinese community, and is famous for its exotic shops and restaurants. Immigrants from Latin America, especially Mexico, make up a growing part of the state's population.

HOLLYWOOD

DREAM CITY

Hollywood in Los Angeles is the capital of the world's film and television industry. Although many major studios are no longer based here, the glamour of Hollywood's heyday – from 1915-1950 – lingers on. Many film stars still live here.

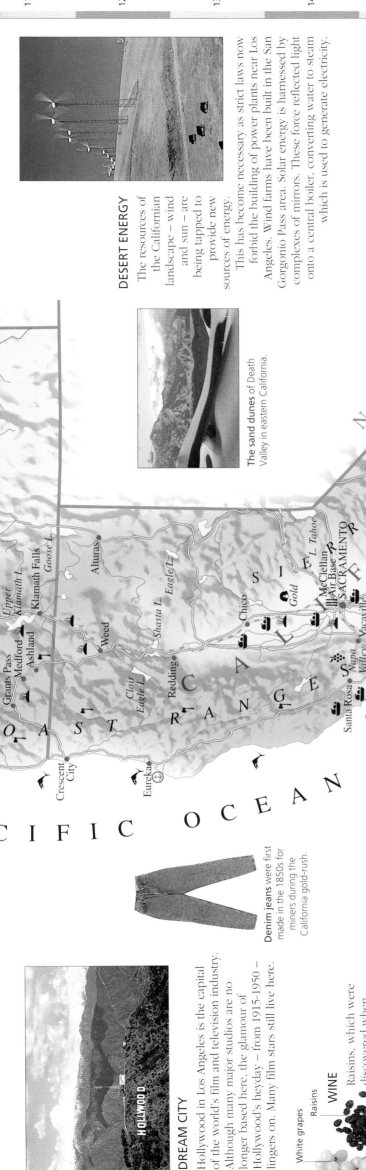

Denim jeans were first made in the 1850s for miners during the California gold-rush.

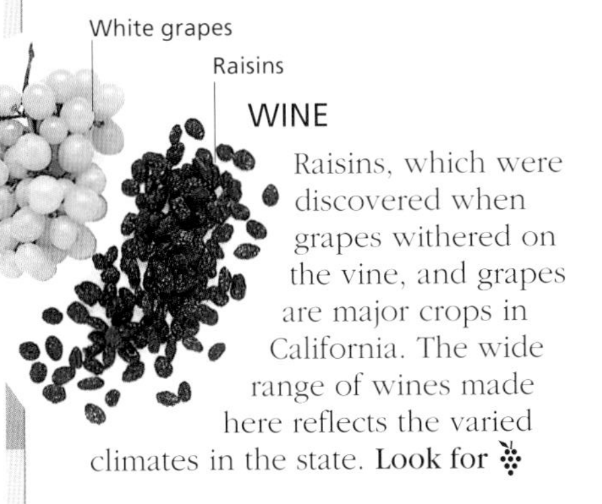
White grapes
Raisins

WINE

Raisins, which were discovered when grapes withered on the vine, and grapes are major crops in California. The wide range of wines made here reflects the varied climates in the state. **Look for** (wine symbol)

MAP FEATURES

Mixed fruit: Washington produces one-third of the USA's apple crop, grown in irrigated valleys east of the Cascade Range. **Look for** (mixed fruit symbol)

Irrigated agriculture: Fertile but dry land in central California is irrigated, via canals and dams, by water from the mountains to the west. **Look for** (irrigated agriculture symbol)

Borders: Millions of Mexicans cross the border into California, many illegally. The border is patrolled by mounted guards and helicopters. **Look for** (border symbol)

Military bases: San Diego has the largest concentration of naval bases in the USA. Deserts in California are also used for weapons testing. **Look for** (military base symbol)

Wine	Oil
Cotton	Industrial centre
Timber	Aerospace industry
Fishing	High-tech industry
Mining	Tourism

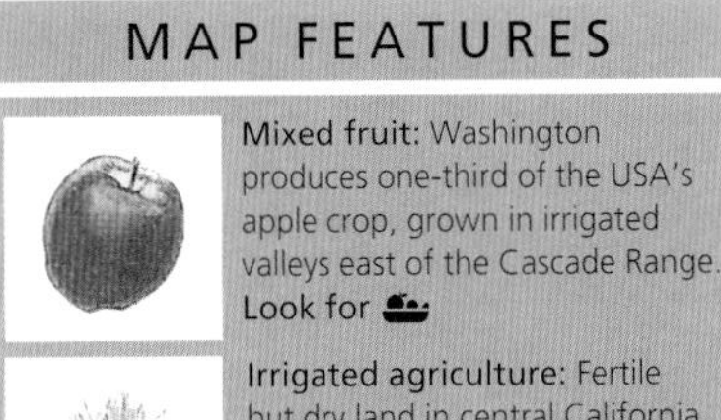

TOURISM

Over 100 million visitors a year come to California. The state offers a wide range of activities: spectacular national parks; attractions such as Disneyland and Hollywood; and the superb Pacific coastline. Venice Beach in Los Angeles is a magnet for visitors. Jugglers, mime artists, folk-singers and body builders throng the sea-front. Fads such as roller-skating and skate-boarding have spread from Venice Beach across the country. **Look for** (tourism symbol)

Green abalone shells found off the Californian coasts are used to make jewellery.

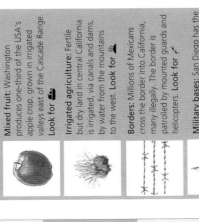

LOS ANGELES

Los Angeles is a vast, sprawling city, stretching for 100 km (60 miles) along the Pacific coast. The city has grown rapidly over the last 100 years, and is a focus for migrants from the rest of the USA. Today, it consists of many separate residential centres, which are linked by an extensive road system, built in the 1930s. Most residents are dependent on cars for transport. The city suffers from pollution because it is surrounded by mountains which stop car fumes escaping.

The sand dunes of Death Valley in eastern California.

DESERT ENERGY

The resources of the Californian landscape – wind and sun – are being tapped to provide new sources of energy.

This has become necessary as strict laws now forbid the building of power plants near Los Angeles. Wind farms have been built in the San Gorgonio Pass area. Solar energy is harnessed by complexes of mirrors. These force reflected light onto a central boiler, converting water to steam which is used to generate electricity.

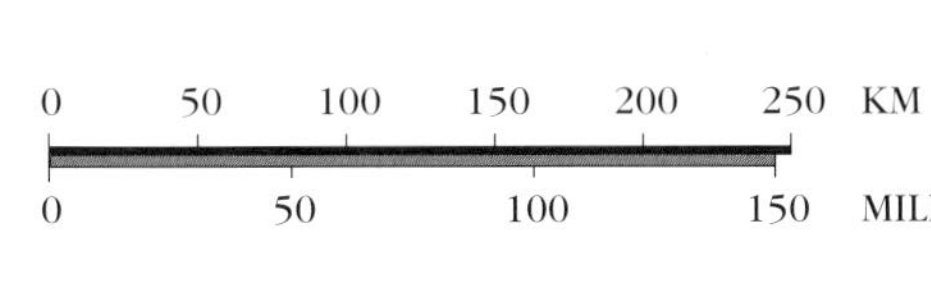
0 50 100 150 200 250 KM
0 50 100 150 MILES

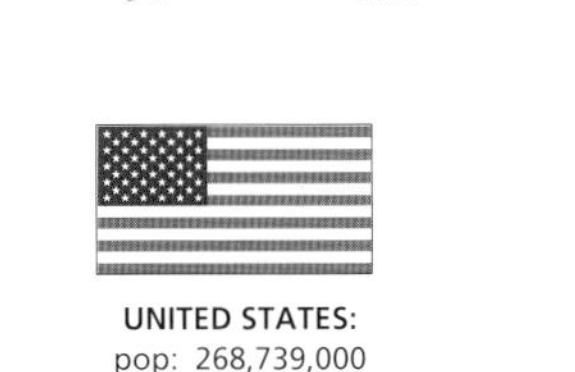
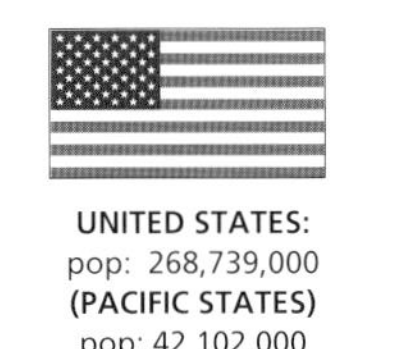
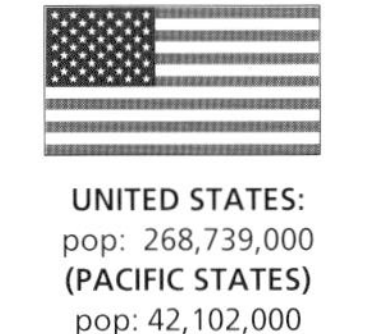
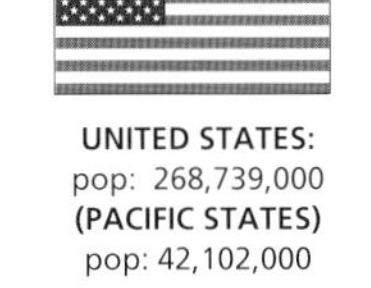
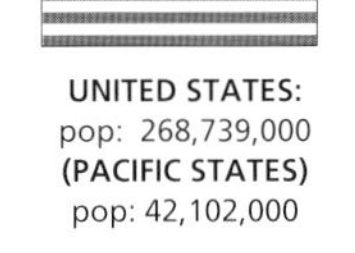

UNITED STATES:
pop: 268,739,000
(PACIFIC STATES)
pop: 42,102,000

N

PACIFIC OCEAN · CALIFORNIA · NEVADA · ARIZONA · MEXICO · COAST RANGES · SIERRA NEVADA · MOJAVE DESERT · SONORAN DESERT

Grants Pass · Medford · Ashland · Upper Klamath L. · Klamath Falls · Goose L. · Crescent City · Weed · Alturas · Eureka · Clair Eagle L. · Shasta L. · Eagle L. · Redding · Chico · Gold · L. Tahoe · McClellan Air Base · SACRAMENTO · Santa Rosa · Napa Valley · Vacaville · Petaluma · Novato · Concord · Stockton · Yosemite National Park · San Francisco · Oakland · Modesto · Mono L. · Santa Clara Valley · San Jose · San Joaquin R. · Merced · Bishop · Santa Cruz · Salinas · Tungsten · Fresno · Monterey · Death Valley · Potassium · China Lake Naval Weapons Center · Bakersfield · San Luis Obispo · Mojave · Barstow · Santa Maria · Vandenburg Air Force Base · Edwards Air Base · Santa Barbara · Ventura · Oxnard · Hollywood · Pasadena · Glendale · San Bernardino · San Gorgonio Pass · Los Angeles · Riverside · Long Beach · Santa Ana · Huntington Beach · Palm Springs · San Clemente · Colorado R. · Salton Sea · Oceanside · Mirimar Naval Air Station · Brawley · San Diego

MEXICO

THE LAND OF MEXICO consists of a dry plateau crossed by broad valleys and enclosed to the west and east by mountains, some of which are volcanic. Lower California, the Yucatan Peninsula and along the country's coasts are the main low-lying areas. Mexico was first occupied by civilizations such as the Maya and Aztec, who built magnificent cities containing plazas, palaces and pyramids. Lured by legends of fabulous hoards of gold and silver, Spanish *conquistadores* invaded Mexico in 1519 and destroyed the existing civilizations. For 300 years the Spanish ruled the country, unifying it with their language and the Roman Catholic religion. Mexico succeeded in winning its independence from Spain by 1821. Today, most Mexicans are *mestizo* – which means they are descendants of the native peoples and the Spanish settlers. Although half the population lives in towns, many people still inhabit areas only accessible on horseback, but rail and air transport are improving. So much of the country is mountainous or dry that only 12 per cent of the land can be used for farming. Mexico has vast oil reserves and mineral riches, but suffers from over-population and huge foreign debts. However, closer links with the USA are strengthening Mexico's economy.

MEXICO
pop: 95,800,000

Tijuana, Mexicali, Ensenada, Colorado, UNITED STATES, LOWER CALIFORNIA, Isla Ángel de la Guarda, Isla Tiburón, Isla Cedros, Nogales, Millet, Copper, Hermosillo, Guaymas, Gulf of California, Santa Rosalia, Manganese, SIERRA DE LA GIGANTA, Ciudad Obregón, SIERRA MADRE, Isla Carmen, Los Mochis, Isla Santa Catalina, Isla San José, Isla del Espíritu Santo, Isla Cerralvo, La Paz, Culiacán, Mazatlán, Lead, Zinc, Conchos, Silver, Maize, Islas Tres Marías

Isla Cedros, off the north-west coast of Mexico.

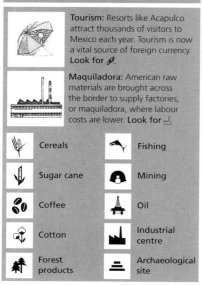

Skeleton made of papier mâché

THE DAY OF THE DEAD

Mexicans believe that life is like a flower; it slowly opens and then closes again. During the annual festival of the Day of the Dead, the streets are decorated with flowers, and ghoulish skeletons are everywhere.

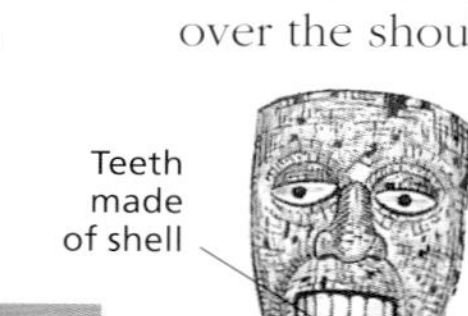

TEXTILES

Although today many fabrics are machine-made, some Mexicans still practise their traditional art of hand-weaving colourful textiles. This *sarape*, part of the traditional Mexican dress for men, is worn over the shoulder.

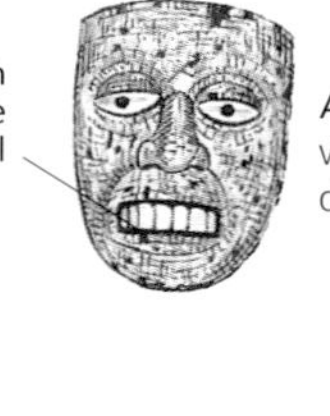
Teeth made of shell

Aztec mask, inlaid with turquoise, depicting a god.

AGRICULTURE

Although Mexico is rapidly industrializing, over half the working population still makes its living from farming. They grow crops like maize, beans and vegetables, and raise cattle, sheep, pigs and chickens.

Cacti growing on Mexico's dry central plateau.

TEHUANA
Sauza
TEQUILA

SPIKED DRINKS

The desert and dry regions of Mexico are home to many varieties of the spiny-leaved *agave* plant. Juice from two varieties is used to make the alcoholic drinks, *tequila* and *mezcal*. The *agave* plant is grown on plantations, then cooked, crushed and fermented. The drink is exported worldwide.

MAP FEATURES

Tourism: Resorts like Acapulco attract thousands of visitors to Mexico each year. Tourism is now a vital source of foreign currency. Look for

Maquiladora: American raw materials are brought across the border to supply factories, or maquiladora, where labour costs are lower. Look for

- Cereals
- Fishing
- Sugar cane
- Mining
- Coffee
- Oil
- Cotton
- Industrial centre
- Forest products
- Archaeological site

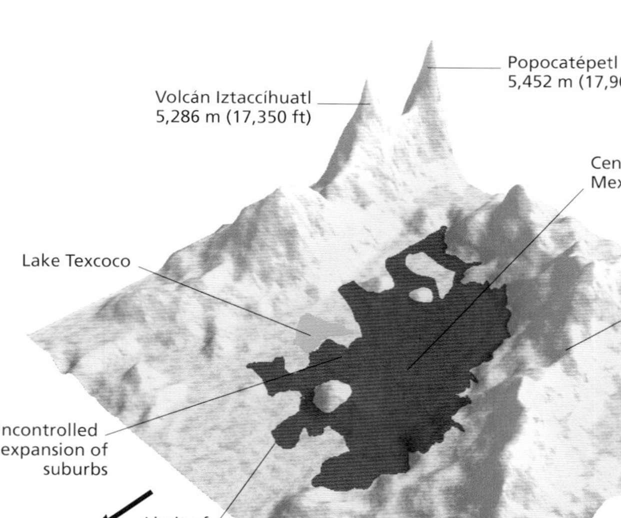
Popocatépetl
5,452 m (17,900 ft)
Volcán Iztaccíhuatl
5,286 m (17,350 ft)
Centre of Mexico City
Mountains prevent pollution escaping
Lake Texcoco
Uncontrolled expansion of suburbs
Limit of urban area
N

MEXICO CITY

The Aztec capital, Tenochtitlán, was built on islands in Lake Texcoco. The city was destroyed by the Spanish, but modern-day Mexico City is built on the ruins. With a population of over 16 million, it is the world's largest city. Mexico City is very polluted because it is surrounded by a ring of mountains which stop polluted air from cars and factories escaping.

K M N O P Q R S T
1 2 3 4 5 6 7 8 9 13 14 15 16
Green pepper
Maize
Avocado
Chilli
Silver brooch
Straps for saddle packs
Saddle horn
Leather stirrup
Pyramid steps
Temple platform
ES OF AMERICA
MEXICO
Río Bravo del Norte
Silver
Chihuahua
Delicias
Lead
Iron
Hidalgo del Parral
Gold
Millet
Manganese
Piedras Negras
Nuevo Laredo
Monclova
Río Grande
Reynosa
Matamoros
Gómez Palacio
Torreón
Monterrey
Saltillo
Mercury
Durango
Maize
SIERRA MADRE ORIENTAL
Ciudad Victoria
Zinc
Zacatecas
Guadalupe
Tabasco
San Luis Potosí
Ciudad Madero
Tampico
Aguascalientes
Río Pánuco
Lagos de Moreno
León
Tequila
Guadalajara
Puerto Vallarta
L. de Chapala
Ocotlán
Irapuato
Querétaro
Celaya
Tuxpan
Poza Rica
Pachuca
Teotihuacán
Zamora de Hidalgo
L. de Cuitzeo
Uruapan
Morelia
Colima
Manzanillo
L. de Pátzcuaro
MEXICO CITY
Volcán Iztaccíhuatl
Tlaxcala
Cholula
Puebla
Popocatépetl
Atlixco
Cuernavaca
Taxco
Río Balsas
Jalapa
Veracruz
Salinas
Orizaba
Gulf of Mexico
Bay of Campeche
Lázaro Cárdenas
SIERRA MADRE DEL SUR
Chilpancingo
Acapulco
Monte Albán
Oaxaca
Coatzacoalcos
Minatitlán
Villahermosa
Frontera
Palenque
Tuxtla
Tehuantepec
Gulf of Tehuantepec
Tapachula
PACIFIC OCEAN
Progreso
Mérida
Sisal
Cancún
Chichén-Itzá
Isla Cozumel
Uxmal
Chicle
Campeche
YUCATAN PENINSULA
Chetumal
BELIZE
GUATEMALA
N
0 50 100 150 200 250 300 350 400 KM
0 50 100 150 200 MILES

HOT DISHES

Mexicans eat a wide variety of foods. Chilli is an important ingredient which is used to add spice and fire to many dishes. Pancakes, or *tortillas*, form the basis of most meals. They are made from maize flour, and can be filled with a mixture of meat, vegetables and cheese.

Red snapper is a favourite dish, fried or grilled.

SILVER

Mexico is rich in minerals. Spanish settlers discovered silver in the mountains of the Sierra Madre in the 16th century. Today, Mexico supplies one-fifth of the world's silver, some of which is made into fine jewellery. **Look for**

SOUVENIR SELLERS

In the crowded streets of Mexico City thousands of people find ways of making a living. Vendors sell food, clothes and lottery tickets; small boys earn a few *pesos* as fire-eaters while others sell souvenirs to tourists.

SUPER SADDLERY

Many horses are bred on the northern grasslands. Horses were brought to Mexico by the Spanish in the 16th century. The Mexicans are expert riders. They use leather saddles, made by local craftsmen.

BLACK GOLD

Mexico's rich reserves of oil and natural gas are vital to its economy. Oil is found mainly along the Bay of Campeche, and is sent to refineries like this one. **Look for**

MUSIC

Traditional folk music is very popular in Mexico. *Mariachi* bands like these wear national costume and play and sing in cafes and plazas all over the country.

THE CHEW IN GUM

In the forests of Mexico grows the wild *sapodilla* tree from which a milky white sap, called *chicle*, is extracted. When processed, the sap becomes a gum, the vital ingredient which makes chewing gum chewy.

LURE OF THE PAST

This 12th-century Maya pyramid in the city of Chichén-Itzá is one of the many buildings left by the ancient civilizations who once inhabited Mexico. Four stairways lead up to a beautifully carved temple. **Look for**

Popocatépetl is a dormant snow-covered volcano.

Isla Cozumel, off the coast of the Yucatan Peninsula.

Colossal stone head made by the Olmec people, the first Central American civilization.

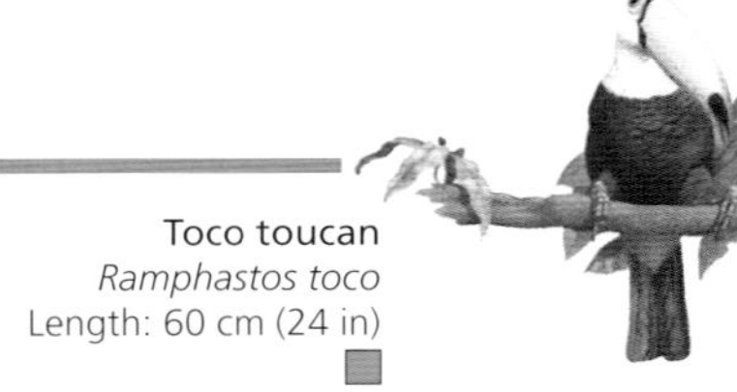

Toco toucan
Ramphastos toco
Length: 60 cm (24 in)

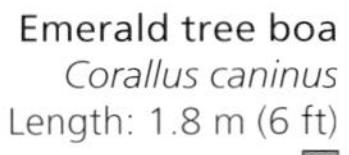

Emerald tree boa
Corallus caninus
Length: 1.8 m (6 ft)

CENTRAL AND SOUTH AMERICA

Geoffroy's spider monkey
Ateles geoffroyi
Length: 1.5 m (5 ft)

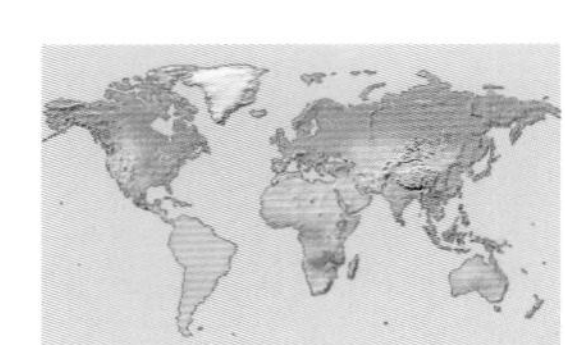

SOUTH AMERICA is shaped like a giant triangle that tapers southward from the Equator to Cape Horn. A huge wall of mountains, the Andes, stretches for 7,250 km (4,500 miles) along the entire Pacific coast. Until three million years ago South America was not connected to North America, so life there evolved in isolation. Several extraordinary animal groups developed, including sloths and anteaters. Many unique plant species originated here too, such as the potato and tomato. South America has the world's largest area of tropical rainforest, through which the River Amazon and its many tributaries run. Central America is mountainous and forested.

TROPICAL TOBAGO

Coconut palms grow along the shores of many Caribbean islands. Palms have flexible trunks that enable them to withstand tropical storms.

Mahogany
Swietenia macrophylla
Height: 25 m (82 ft)

VOLCANIC ISLANDS

One of the extinct volcanic craters of the Galapagos Island group breaks the surface of the Pacific Ocean. Like other isolated regions of the world, many unique species have evolved here, such as the giant tortoise 1.2 m (4 ft) long.

SEA-DWELLING TREES

Mangroves grow along tropical coastlines. The tangled roots of Pinuelo mangroves create ideal homes for tiny aquatic species.

PAMPAS

Giant grasses up to 3 m (10 ft) high grow on Argentina's dry southern Pampas. Here, further north, more plentiful rainfall supports a few scattered trees.

Alpaca
Lama pacos
Height: 1.5 m (5 ft)

Archaeogeryon, a crab that lived in this region 20 million years ago.

VOLCANIC ANDES

Steam and smoke rises from Villarrica, an active volcano. Many peaks in the Andes are active or former volcanoes. Despite the intense heat within these lava-filled mountains, the highest are permanently covered in snow – even those on the Equator.

THE FOREST FLOOR

Tropical rainforest trees form such a dense canopy that little sunlight or rain can reach the ground 70 m (200 ft) below. Rainforest soils are easily washed away when the trees and plants are removed.

THE BLEAK SOUTH

Patagonia's cold desert environment contrasts starkly with the lush hot forests of the Amazon Basin. Plants take root in the cracks of bare rock, and grow close to the ground to survive icy winds.

BIRTH OF A RIVER

The snow-capped peaks of the Andes are the source of the Amazon, the world's second longest river. It is 6,570 km (4,080 miles) long.

Passion flower
Passiflora caerulea
Across flower: 15 cm (6 in)

CROSS-SECTION THROUGH SOUTH AMERICA

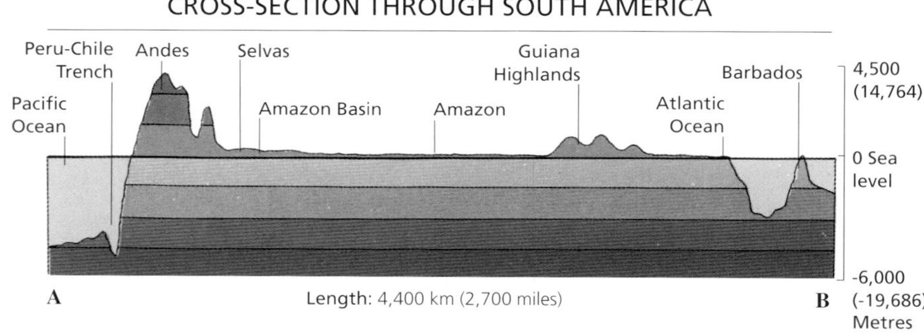

Peru-Chile Trench
Pacific Ocean
Andes
Selvas
Amazon Basin
Amazon
Guiana Highlands
Atlantic Ocean
Barbados
4,500 (14,764)
0 Sea level
-6,000 (-19,686)
Metres (feet)
A
B
Length: 4,400 km (2,700 miles)

DRY ATACAMA DESERT

The Atacama Desert is the world's driest place outside Antarctica. Rain has not fallen in some areas for hundreds of years. Winds that pass over cold coastline currents absorb no moisture.

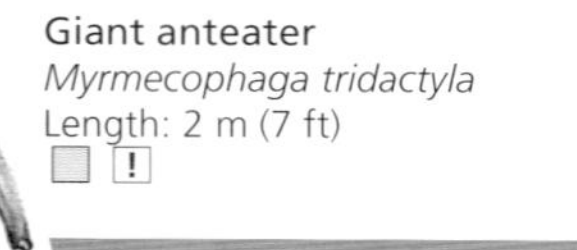

Giant anteater
Myrmecophaga tridactyla
Length: 2 m (7 ft)

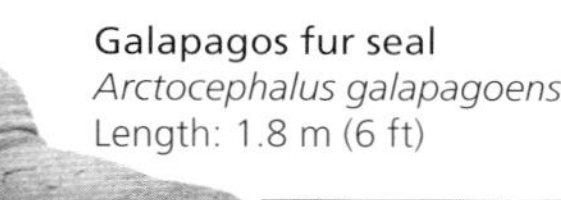

Galapagos fur seal
Arctocephalus galapagoensis
Length: 1.8 m (6 ft)

Ocelot
Felis pardalis
Length: 1.7 m (6 ft)

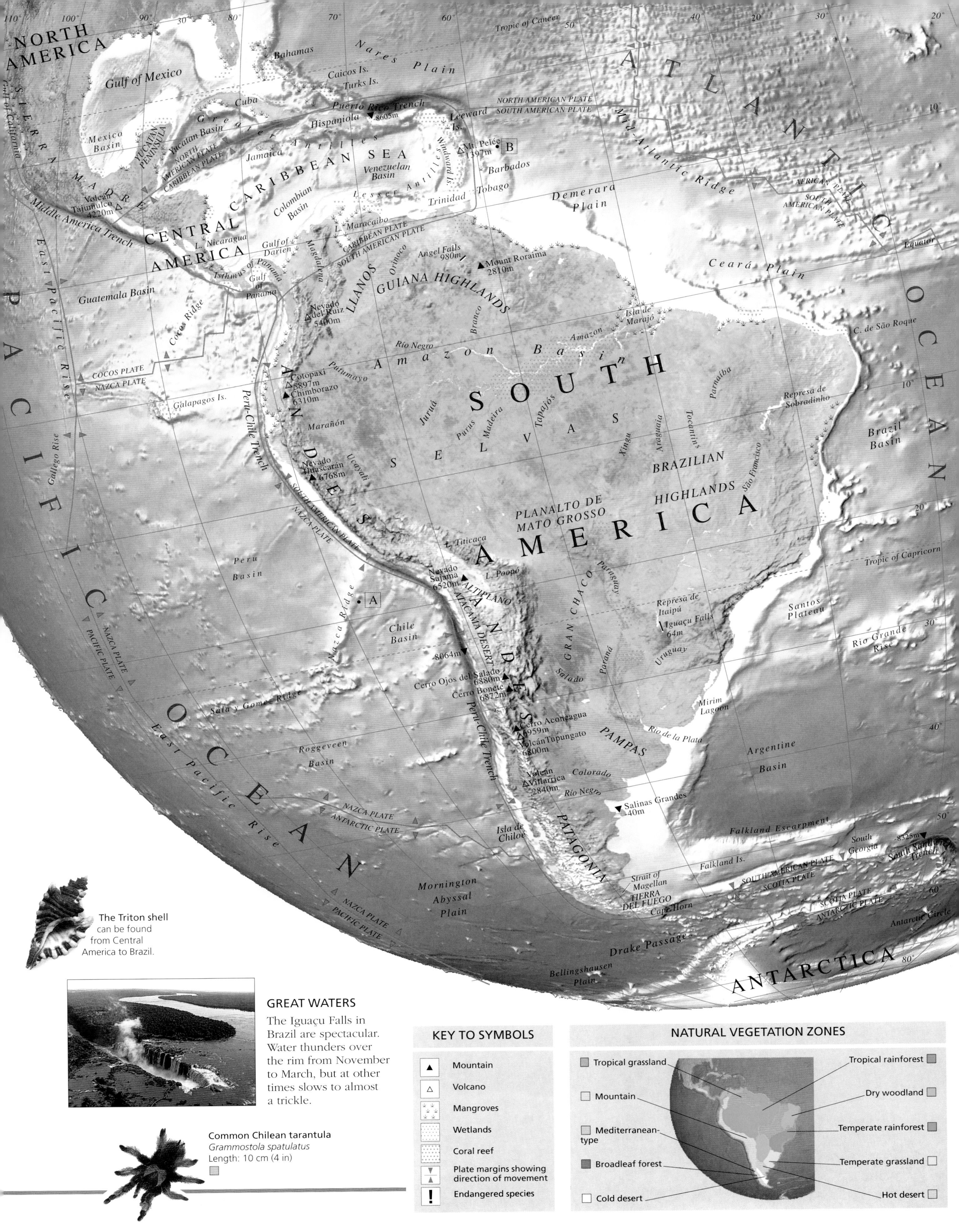
NORTH AMERICA
Gulf of Mexico
Gulf of California
SIERRA MADRE
Bahamas
Nares Plain
Caicos Is.
Turks Is.
Cuba
Puerto Rico Trench
8605m
Hispaniola
NORTH AMERICAN PLATE
SOUTH AMERICAN PLATE
Greater Antilles
Leeward Is.
Mexico Basin
YUCATAN PENINSULA
Yucatan Basin
NORTH AMERICAN PLATE
CARIBBEAN PLATE
Jamaica
CARIBBEAN SEA
Venezuelan Basin
Windward Is.
Mt. Pelée 1397m
B
Barbados
Tobago
Trinidad
Lesser Antilles
Colombian Basin
Volcán Tajumulco 4220m
Middle America Trench
CENTRAL AMERICA
L. Nicaragua
Gulf of Darien
L. Maracaibo
CARIBBEAN PLATE
SOUTH AMERICAN PLATE
Isthmus of Panama
Gulf of Panama
Magdalena
Orinoco
Angel Falls 980m
Mount Roraima 2810m
Demerara Plain
Mid-Atlantic Ridge
ATLANTIC OCEAN
AFRICAN PLATE
SOUTH AMERICAN PLATE
Equator
Ceará Plain
East Pacific Rise
Guatemala Basin
LLANOS
GUIANA HIGHLANDS
Nevado del Ruiz 5400m
Branco
Isla de Marajó
Amazon
C. de São Roque
Cocos Ridge
Río Negro
Amazon Basin
COCOS PLATE
NAZCA PLATE
Cotopaxi 5897m
Chimborazo 6310m
Putumayo
SOUTH
Parnaíba
Represa de Sobradinho
Galapagos Is.
Peru-Chile Trench
Marañón
Juruá
Purus
Madeira
Tapajós
SELVAS
Xingu
Araguaia
Tocantins
Brazil Basin
Gallego Rise
Nevado Huascarán 6768m
Ucayali
ANDES
BRAZILIAN HIGHLANDS
São Francisco
PACIFIC OCEAN
SOUTH AMERICAN PLATE
NAZCA PLATE
PLANALTO DE MATO GROSSO
AMERICA
L. Titicaca
Tropic of Capricorn
Peru Basin
Nevado Sajama 6520m
L. Poopó
ALTIPLANO
A
Paraguay
Represa de Itaipú
Iguaçu Falls 64m
Santos Plateau
GRAN CHACO
Nazca Ridge
Chile Basin
ATACAMA DESERT
NAZCA PLATE
PACIFIC PLATE
8064m
Uruguay
Rio Grande Rise
Paraná
Salado
Cerro Ojos del Salado 6880m
Cerro Bonete 6872m
Sala y Gomez Ridge
Mirim Lagoon
Cerro Aconcagua 6959m
Volcán Tupungato 6800m
PAMPAS
Río de la Plata
Argentine Basin
Roggeveen Basin
Peru-Chile Trench
Colorado
Volcán Villarrica 2840m
Río Negro
Salinas Grandes -40m
NAZCA PLATE
ANTARCTIC PLATE
Isla de Chiloé
PATAGONIA
Falkland Escarpment
South Georgia
8325m
South Sandwich Trench
Falkland Is.
Strait of Magellan
TIERRA DEL FUEGO
SOUTH AMERICAN PLATE
SCOTIA PLATE
SCOTIA PLATE
ANTARCTIC PLATE
Mornington Abyssal Plain
Cape Horn
NAZCA PLATE
PACIFIC PLATE
Antarctic Circle
Drake Passage
Bellingshausen Plain
ANTARCTICA
KEY TO SYMBOLS
Mountain
Volcano
Mangroves
Wetlands
Coral reef
Plate margins showing direction of movement
Endangered species
NATURAL VEGETATION ZONES
Tropical grassland
Mountain
Mediterranean-type
Broadleaf forest
Cold desert
Tropical rainforest
Dry woodland
Temperate rainforest
Temperate grassland
Hot desert

The Triton shell can be found from Central America to Brazil.

GREAT WATERS

The Iguaçu Falls in Brazil are spectacular. Water thunders over the rim from November to March, but at other times slows to almost a trickle.

Common Chilean tarantula
Grammostola spatulatus
Length: 10 cm (4 in)

Central America and the Caribbean

The tropical region of Central America and the Caribbean was settled by hunters and farmers many thousands of years ago. By 300 BC the Maya had established a sophisticated civilization on the mainland – ruins of their pyramids and temples can still be seen deep in the forests of Guatemala. The Maya, as well as the native peoples who lived on the Caribbean islands, were almost wiped out by European explorers who arrived in the 15th century. From this time, European nations, in particular the British, French, Spanish and Dutch, competed for control of the region and some countries did not gain independence until recently. Europeans brought slaves from Africa to work on vast sugar plantations. In the last few decades, tourism has enriched the Caribbean, but in Central America, poverty is still a major problem.

MEXICO
BELIZE
GUATEMALA
HONDURAS
EL SALVADOR
NICARAGUA
COSTA RICA
PANAMA
COLOMBIA
CUBA
JAMAICA
CAYMAN ISLANDS
(to UK)
GREATER
CARIBBEAN
PACIFIC OCEAN
HAVANA (LA HABANA)
Pinar del Río
Copper
Matanzas
I. de la Juventud
Cienfuegos
Santa Clara
Camagüey
Archipiélago de los Jardines de la Reina
Golfo de Guacanayabo
GEORGE TOWN
Grand Cayman
Little Cayman
Cayman Brac
Savanna-La-Mar
Montego Bay
Spanish Town
Tikal
Flores
Altun Ha
Belize City
Belize
BELMOPAN
San Ignacio
Nickel
Huehuetenango
Cobán
Quezaltenango
L. de Izabal
Sololá
Zacapa
Mazatenango
GUATEMALA CITY
Escuintla
Gulf of Honduras
Puerto Barrios
Puerto Cortés
San Pedro Sula
La Ceiba
Trujillo
Copán
Santa Rosa de Copán
Santa Ana
La Esperanza
Comayagua
Juticalpa
Río Patuca
Laguna de Caratasca
SAN SALVADOR
TEGUCIGALPA
La Libertad
San Miguel
Coco
San Lorenzo
Choluteca
Somoto
Gold
Copper
Puerto Cabezas
Estelí
Jinotega
Chinandega
Corinto
León
Matagalpa
Río Grande de Matagalpa
L. Managua
Boaco
MANAGUA
Juigalpa
Granada
Rivas
L. Nicaragua
Bluefields
San Carlos
Río San Juan
Liberia
Puntarenas
Alajuela
SAN JOSÉ
Cartago
Golfo de Nicoya
Limón
Bocas del Toro
Mosquito Gulf
Colón
Panama Canal
David
PANAMA CITY
Penonomé
Chiriquí Gulf
Copper
Santiago
Gulf of Panama
Isla de Coiba
Chitré
Las Tablas
Isla San José
Isla del Rey
La Palma
Gulf of Darien
N
0 50 100 150 200 250 300 350 400 KM
0 50 100 150 200 MILES

GUATEMALA
pop: 11,600,000

CUBA
pop: 11,100,000

BELIZE
pop: 200,000

HONDURAS
pop: 6,100,000

JAMAICA
pop: 2,500,000

EL SALVADOR
pop: 6,100,000

NICARAGUA
pop: 4,500,000

COSTA RICA
pop: 3,700,000

PANAMA
pop: 2,800,000

A Jamaican beach, devastated by a hurricane.

Conches from the shallow waters of the Caribbean are edible.

Jamaican Blue Mountain coffee is prized by experts.

The ancient Maya temple of Altun Ha is hidden deep in the rainforest of Belize.

Swamps near the Honduran coast.

Hot pepper sauce, made with spicy chillis, is used all over the region.

NICARAGUA

Since Nicaragua became independent in 1838 it has been devastated by civil war and foreign interference. During the 1980s, a desperate conflict took place between the socialist government and the right-wing *Contras*, supported by the USA. Although democracy has now been restored, little progress has been made in fighting the huge problems of poverty, ill-health and homelessness.

RURAL MARKETS

Many Guatemalans live in small villages, growing maize and beans and making brightly-coloured cloth, baskets, pottery and wood carvings. These goods, as well as fruit and tobacco, are sold at local markets.

MAP FEATURES

Archaeological sites: Great civilizations, such as the Maya, flourished in Central America from 300 BC. They built temples, palaces and cities. Look for

Shellfishing: Shrimps and lobsters thrive in the mangrove swamps on the coasts of Central America, which provide rich feeding grounds. Look for

Shipping registry: Ships from all over the world fly Panama's flag. They register there because of low fees and limited controls on the labour force. Look for

Sugar cane	Tobacco
Bananas	Timber
Coffee	Mining
Cocoa	Industrial centre
Cotton	Tourism

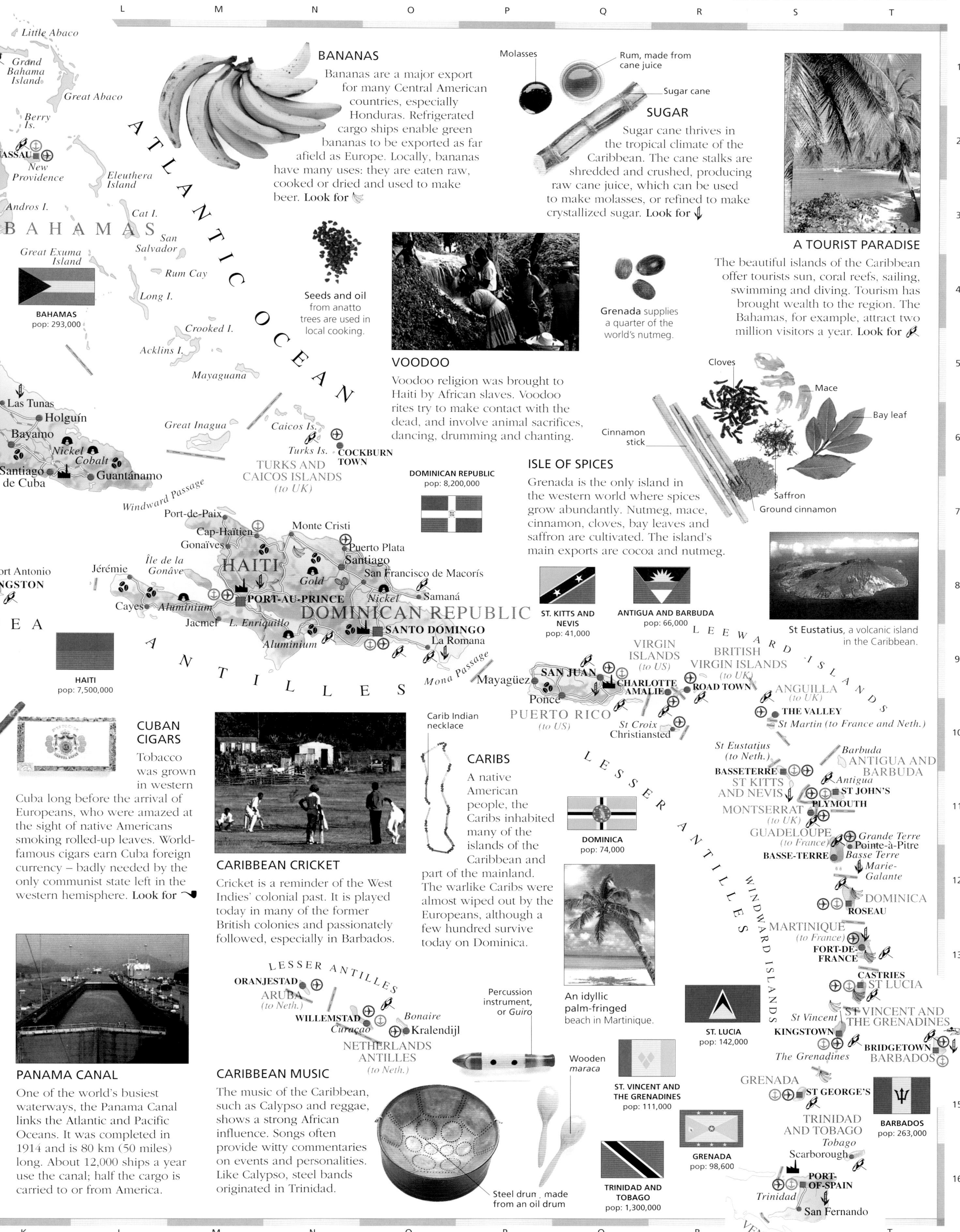
L M N O P Q R S T
1 2 3 4 5 6 7 8 9 10 11 12 13 14 15 16
K L M N O P Q R T
ATLANTIC OCEAN
Little Abaco
Grand Bahama Island
Great Abaco
Berry Is.
NASSAU
New Providence
Eleuthera Island
Andros I.
Cat I.
BAHAMAS
San Salvador
Great Exuma Island
Rum Cay
Long I.
Crooked I.
Acklins I.
Mayaguana
Great Inagua
Caicos Is.
Turks Is.
COCKBURN TOWN
TURKS AND CAICOS ISLANDS (to UK)
Las Tunas
Holguín
Bayamo
Nickel
Cobalt
Santiago de Cuba
Guantánamo
Windward Passage
Port-de-Paix
Cap-Haïtien
Gonaïves
Monte Cristi
Puerto Plata
Santiago
HAITI
Île de la Gonâve
Jérémie
Gold
San Francisco de Macorís
Port Antonio
KINGSTON
PORT-AU-PRINCE
Nickel
Samaná
Cayes
Aluminium
DOMINICAN REPUBLIC
SEA
Jacmel
L. Enriquillo
SANTO DOMINGO
Aluminium
La Romana
ANTILLES
Mona Passage
Mayagüez
SAN JUAN
CHARLOTTE AMALIE
ROAD TOWN
Ponce
PUERTO RICO (to US)
VIRGIN ISLANDS (to US)
BRITISH VIRGIN ISLANDS (to UK)
LEEWARD ISLANDS
ANGUILLA (to UK)
THE VALLEY
St Martin (to France and Neth.)
St Croix
Christiansted
LESSER ANTILLES
St Eustatius (to Neth.)
Barbuda
BASSETERRE
ANTIGUA AND BARBUDA
ST KITTS AND NEVIS
Antigua
ST JOHN'S
MONTSERRAT (to UK)
PLYMOUTH
GUADELOUPE (to France)
Grande Terre
Pointe-à-Pitre
BASSE-TERRE
Basse Terre
Marie-Galante
DOMINICA
ROSEAU
WINDWARD ISLANDS
MARTINIQUE (to France)
FORT-DE-FRANCE
CASTRIES
ST LUCIA
St Vincent
ST VINCENT AND THE GRENADINES
KINGSTOWN
BRIDGETOWN
BARBADOS
The Grenadines
GRENADA
ST GEORGE'S
TRINIDAD AND TOBAGO
Tobago
Scarborough
PORT-OF-SPAIN
Trinidad
San Fernando
VENEZUELA
LESSER ANTILLES
ORANJESTAD
ARUBA (to Neth.)
WILLEMSTAD
Curaçao
Bonaire
Kralendijl
NETHERLANDS ANTILLES (to Neth.)
BAHAMAS pop: 293,000
DOMINICAN REPUBLIC pop: 8,200,000
HAITI pop: 7,500,000
ST. KITTS AND NEVIS pop: 41,000
ANTIGUA AND BARBUDA pop: 66,000
DOMINICA pop: 74,000
ST. LUCIA pop: 142,000
ST. VINCENT AND THE GRENADINES pop: 111,000
GRENADA pop: 98,600
TRINIDAD AND TOBAGO pop: 1,300,000
BARBADOS pop: 263,000
Molasses
Rum, made from cane juice
Sugar cane
Cloves
Mace
Bay leaf
Cinnamon stick
Saffron
Ground cinnamon
Carib Indian necklace
Percussion instrument, or *Guiro*
Wooden *maraca*
Steel drum, made from an oil drum

BANANAS

Bananas are a major export for many Central American countries, especially Honduras. Refrigerated cargo ships enable green bananas to be exported as far afield as Europe. Locally, bananas have many uses: they are eaten raw, cooked or dried and used to make beer. **Look for**

SUGAR

Sugar cane thrives in the tropical climate of the Caribbean. The cane stalks are shredded and crushed, producing raw cane juice, which can be used to make molasses, or refined to make crystallized sugar. **Look for**

A TOURIST PARADISE

The beautiful islands of the Caribbean offer tourists sun, coral reefs, sailing, swimming and diving. Tourism has brought wealth to the region. The Bahamas, for example, attract two million visitors a year. **Look for**

Seeds and oil from anatto trees are used in local cooking.

Grenada supplies a quarter of the world's nutmeg.

VOODOO

Voodoo religion was brought to Haiti by African slaves. Voodoo rites try to make contact with the dead, and involve animal sacrifices, dancing, drumming and chanting.

ISLE OF SPICES

Grenada is the only island in the western world where spices grow abundantly. Nutmeg, mace, cinnamon, cloves, bay leaves and saffron are cultivated. The island's main exports are cocoa and nutmeg.

St Eustatius, a volcanic island in the Caribbean.

CUBAN CIGARS

Tobacco was grown in western Cuba long before the arrival of Europeans, who were amazed at the sight of native Americans smoking rolled-up leaves. World-famous cigars earn Cuba foreign currency – badly needed by the only communist state left in the western hemisphere. **Look for**

CARIBBEAN CRICKET

Cricket is a reminder of the West Indies' colonial past. It is played today in many of the former British colonies and passionately followed, especially in Barbados.

CARIBS

A native American people, the Caribs inhabited many of the islands of the Caribbean and part of the mainland. The warlike Caribs were almost wiped out by the Europeans, although a few hundred survive today on Dominica.

An idyllic palm-fringed beach in Martinique.

PANAMA CANAL

One of the world's busiest waterways, the Panama Canal links the Atlantic and Pacific Oceans. It was completed in 1914 and is 80 km (50 miles) long. About 12,000 ships a year use the canal; half the cargo is carried to or from America.

CARIBBEAN MUSIC

The music of the Caribbean, such as Calypso and reggae, shows a strong African influence. Songs often provide witty commentaries on events and personalities. Like Calypso, steel bands originated in Trinidad.

Northern South America

This region is dominated by the volcanic peaks and mountain ranges of the Andes. The powerful Incas ruled much of this area in the 15th century, and large numbers of their descendants still live in Peru, Bolivia and Ecuador today. In the 16th century, Spanish *conquistadores* reached South America, swept the Incas and other native peoples aside, and colonized the region from Venezuela to Bolivia. Areas to the east were later settled by the French, Dutch and British. Although all the countries except French Guiana are now independent republics, independence has brought many problems, such as military dictatorships, high inflation, organized crime, the illegal drug trade and huge foreign debts. Many of the cities are overcrowded, but large numbers of people still flock there from the countryside, looking for jobs.

CARACAS

The discovery of oil in 1917 made Venezuela the richest country in the region. Its capital, Caracas, was built with oil money. Modern motorways and skyscrapers dominate the city, but many people live in shanty towns on the surrounding hillsides.

MARKET DAY

Brightly dressed in their traditional Andean clothes and hats, local people display their wares in the market of the Peruvian town of Pisac. They sell fruit and vegetables, together with pottery and clothes produced for the tourist trade.

The lush Caribbean coastline of northern Venezuela.

Hammered gold

A figure made by ancient Colombian craftsmen.

GUYANA
pop: 856,000

SURINAM
pop: 442,000

SHRIMPS

Shrimps living in the muddy waters of Ecuador's mangrove swamps have become the country's second most important source of foreign currency, after oil. But, as the industry expands, it is destroying the mangroves – the shrimps' natural habitat. **Look for**

ECUADOR
pop: 12,200,000

COLOMBIA
pop: 37,700,000

VENEZUELA
pop: 23,200,000

The ancient Inca city of Machupicchu in the Peruvian Andes.

Emerald

EMERALDS

Some of the world's finest emeralds are mined near Bogotá, the capital of Colombia. Long before the Spanish invaded the country in search of gold, native peoples mined the emeralds for their gold jewellery and ceremonial objects. **Look for**

N

KM MILES
600
350
500
300
400
250
200
300
150
200
100
100
50
0 0

St Laurent-du-Maroni
Iracoubo
Kourou
CAYENNE
Gold
Albina
Brokopondo
Aluminium
Maroni River
PARAMARIBO
Gold
Aluminium
New Amsterdam
Berbice
Courantyne
(claimed by Surinam)

FRENCH GUIANA (to France)

GEORGETOWN
Bartica
Mazaruni
Gold
Essequibo
Diamonds
Lethem
Beef
(claimed by Venezuela)
Tucupita
Aluminium
Gold
Ciudad Guayana
Ciudad Bolívar
Río Orinoco
Diamonds
Santa Elena de Uairén
Gold
Beef
Cumaná
Barcelona
Maturín
La Asunción
Isla de Margarita
Beef
Beef
La Guaira
Maracay
Valencia
San Juan de los Morros
Beef
San Fernando
Embalse de Guri
Puerto Cabello
Coro
San Felipe
Barquisimeto
Valencia
Beef
Beef
Guanare
Barinas
Trujillo
Mérida
San Cristóbal
Río Apure
Beef
Beef
Beef
Puerto Carreño
Puerto Ayacucho
Puerto Inírida
Beef
Maracaibo
Cabimas
L. Maracaibo
Gulf of Venezuela
Beef

BRAZIL
Santa Marta
Riohacha
Barranquilla
Cartagena
Montería
Sincelejo
Valledupar
San Andrés
Cúcuta
Bucaramanga
Gulf of Darién
Quibdó
Medellín
Bello
Pereira
Manizales
Armenia
Ibagué
BOGOTÁ
Tunja
Yopal
Villavicencio
San José del Guaviare
Buenaventura
Palmira
Cali
Neiva
Río Magdalena
Río Cauca
Beef
Beef
Beef
Beef
Beef
Gold
Río Meta
Río Guaviare
Mitú
Río Caquetá
Leticia
Popayán
Pasto
Mocoa
Florencia
Río Putumayo
Río Caquetá
Río Napo
Río Aguarico
Río Marañón
Amazon
Iquitos
Esmeraldas
Santo Domingo de los Colorados
Manta
Portoviejo
Babahoyo
Milagro
QUITO
Ibarra
Latacunga
Ambato
Riobamba
Guayaquil
Gulf of Guayaquil
Machala
Cuenca
Loja
Sullana

CARIBBEAN SEA

PANAMA

PACIFIC OCEAN

Cinchona leaves

Quinine from the bark of the Peruvian *cinchona* tree is used to treat malaria.

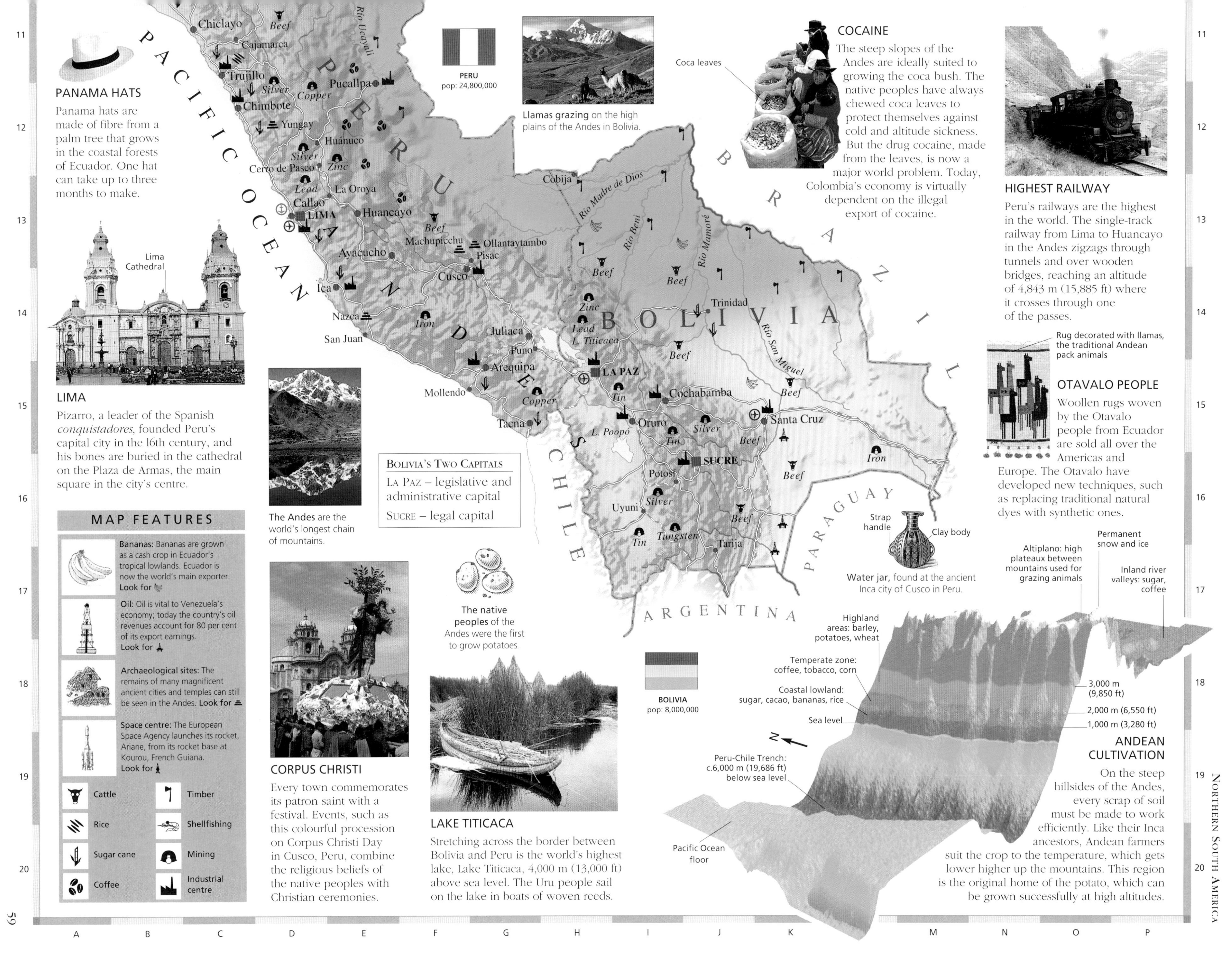
Pacific Ocean
Peru
Bolivia
Brazil
Chile
Argentina
Paraguay
Chiclayo
Cajamarca
Trujillo
Chimbote
Yungay
Huánuco
Cerro de Pasco
La Oroya
Callao
Lima
Huancayo
Ayacucho
Ica
Nazca
San Juan
Pucallpa
Machupicchu
Ollantaytambo
Pisac
Cusco
Juliaca
Puno
Arequipa
Mollendo
Tacna
Cobija
La Paz
L. Titicaca
L. Poopó
Oruro
Cochabamba
Trinidad
Santa Cruz
Sucre
Potosí
Uyuni
Tarija
Río Ucayali
Río Madre de Dios
Río Beni
Río Mamoré
Río San Miguel
Beef
Silver
Copper
Zinc
Lead
Iron
Tin
Tungsten
Coca leaves
Rug decorated with llamas, the traditional Andean pack animals
Strap handle
Clay body
Permanent snow and ice
Altiplano: high plateaux between mountains used for grazing animals
Inland river valleys: sugar, coffee
Highland areas: barley, potatoes, wheat
Temperate zone: coffee, tobacco, corn
Coastal lowland: sugar, cacao, bananas, rice
Sea level
3,000 m (9,850 ft)
2,000 m (6,550 ft)
1,000 m (3,280 ft)
N
Peru-Chile Trench: c.6,000 m (19,686 ft) below sea level
Pacific Ocean floor
Lima Cathedral
PERU pop: 24,800,000
BOLIVIA pop: 8,000,000

PANAMA HATS

Panama hats are made of fibre from a palm tree that grows in the coastal forests of Ecuador. One hat can take up to three months to make.

LIMA

Pizarro, a leader of the Spanish *conquistadores*, founded Peru's capital city in the 16th century, and his bones are buried in the cathedral on the Plaza de Armas, the main square in the city's centre.

MAP FEATURES

Bananas: Bananas are grown as a cash crop in Ecuador's tropical lowlands. Ecuador is now the world's main exporter. **Look for**

Oil: Oil is vital to Venezuela's economy; today the country's oil revenues account for 80 per cent of its export earnings. **Look for**

Archaeological sites: The remains of many magnificent ancient cities and temples can still be seen in the Andes. **Look for**

Space centre: The European Space Agency launches its rocket, Ariane, from its rocket base at Kourou, French Guiana. **Look for**

Cattle · Timber · Rice · Shellfishing · Sugar cane · Mining · Coffee · Industrial centre

Llamas grazing on the high plains of the Andes in Bolivia.

The Andes are the world's longest chain of mountains.

Bolivia's Two Capitals

La Paz – legislative and administrative capital

Sucre – legal capital

The native peoples of the Andes were the first to grow potatoes.

CORPUS CHRISTI

Every town commemorates its patron saint with a festival. Events, such as this colourful procession on Corpus Christi Day in Cusco, Peru, combine the religious beliefs of the native peoples with Christian ceremonies.

LAKE TITICACA

Stretching across the border between Bolivia and Peru is the world's highest lake, Lake Titicaca, 4,000 m (13,000 ft) above sea level. The Uru people sail on the lake in boats of woven reeds.

COCAINE

The steep slopes of the Andes are ideally suited to growing the coca bush. The native peoples have always chewed coca leaves to protect themselves against cold and altitude sickness. But the drug cocaine, made from the leaves, is now a major world problem. Today, Colombia's economy is virtually dependent on the illegal export of cocaine.

HIGHEST RAILWAY

Peru's railways are the highest in the world. The single-track railway from Lima to Huancayo in the Andes zigzags through tunnels and over wooden bridges, reaching an altitude of 4,843 m (15,885 ft) where it crosses through one of the passes.

OTAVALO PEOPLE

Woollen rugs woven by the Otavalo people from Ecuador are sold all over the Americas and Europe. The Otavalo have developed new techniques, such as replacing traditional natural dyes with synthetic ones.

Water jar, found at the ancient Inca city of Cusco in Peru.

ANDEAN CULTIVATION

On the steep hillsides of the Andes, every scrap of soil must be made to work efficiently. Like their Inca ancestors, Andean farmers suit the crop to the temperature, which gets lower higher up the mountains. This region is the original home of the potato, which can be grown successfully at high altitudes.

BRAZIL

OCCUPYING NEARLY HALF of South America, Brazil possesses the greatest river basin in the world. The Amazonian rainforest, which covers some two-thirds of the country, is a vast storehouse of natural riches, still largely untapped. But land is needed for agriculture, ranching and new roads, and each year vast tracts of forest are cleared. The Portuguese colonized the country in the 16th century, intermarrying with the local population. They planted sugar in the northeast, working the plantations with slaves brought from Africa. With a further influx of Europeans, Brazil is now one of the world's most populous and ethnically diverse democracies. A land of opportunity for some – like those in the industrial region round São Paulo – it is one of poverty and deprivation for many, especially in the northeast. In spite of improved industrial output, Brazil still has high unemployment and huge foreign debts.

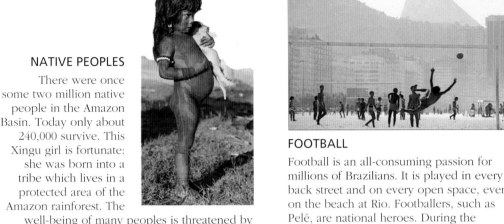

NATIVE PEOPLES

There were once some two million native people in the Amazon Basin. Today only about 240,000 survive. This Xingu girl is fortunate: she was born into a tribe which lives in a protected area of the Amazon rainforest. The well-being of many peoples is threatened by the ever-shrinking rainforest and by disease, logging, farming and gold prospecting.

FOOTBALL

Football is an all-consuming passion for millions of Brazilians. It is played in every back street and on every open space, even on the beach at Rio. Footballers, such as Pelé, are national heroes. During the World Cup, Brazil comes to a standstill.

DANCE MUSIC

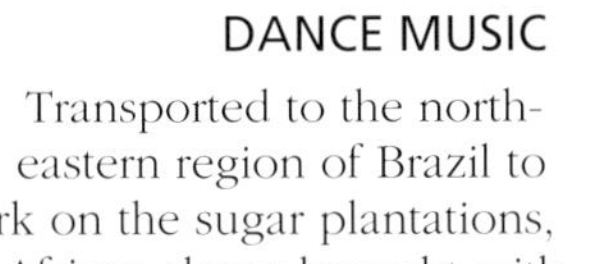

Transported to the north-eastern region of Brazil to work on the sugar plantations, African slaves brought with them the musical rhythms of their homelands. Their music has blended with other musical influences to produce the music for dances, such as the *samba* and the *lambada*. The instruments include this drum, called a *conga*.

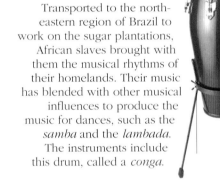

Grandillas, one of the many exotic fruits found in Brazil.

The wings of the *Morpho* butterfly are often used to decorate jewellery.

A huge tree trunk in the depths of the Brazilian rainforest.

BRAZIL
pop: 165,200,000

A stretch of coast near Salvador in the northeast.

0 100 200 300 400 500 600 KM
0 100 200 300 MILES

N

ATLANTIC OCEAN
COLOMBIA VENEZUELA GUYANA SURINAM FRENCH GUIANA (to France) PERU
AMAZON BASIN
BRAZIL
PLANALTO DE MATO GROSSO
Boa Vista, Macapá, Belém, São Luís, Parnaíba, Fortaleza, Manaus, Santarém, Teresina, Mossoró, Natal, João Pessoa, Recife, Maceió, Aracaju, Campina Grande, Picos, Juazeiro, Carolina, Palmas do Tocantins, Serra Pelada, Porto Velho, Cruzeiro do Sul, Rio Branco
C. de São Roque
Rio Negro, Amazon, Rio Madeira, Rio Tapajós, Rio Xingu, Rio Jari, Rio Juruá, Rio Purus, Rio São Manuel, Rio Araguaia, Rio Tocantins, Rio Parnaíba
Represa Balbina, Represa de Tucuruí, Represa de Sobradinho
Gold, Tin, Aluminium, Manganese, Iron, Tungsten, Sisal, Beef, Rubber, Brazil Nuts

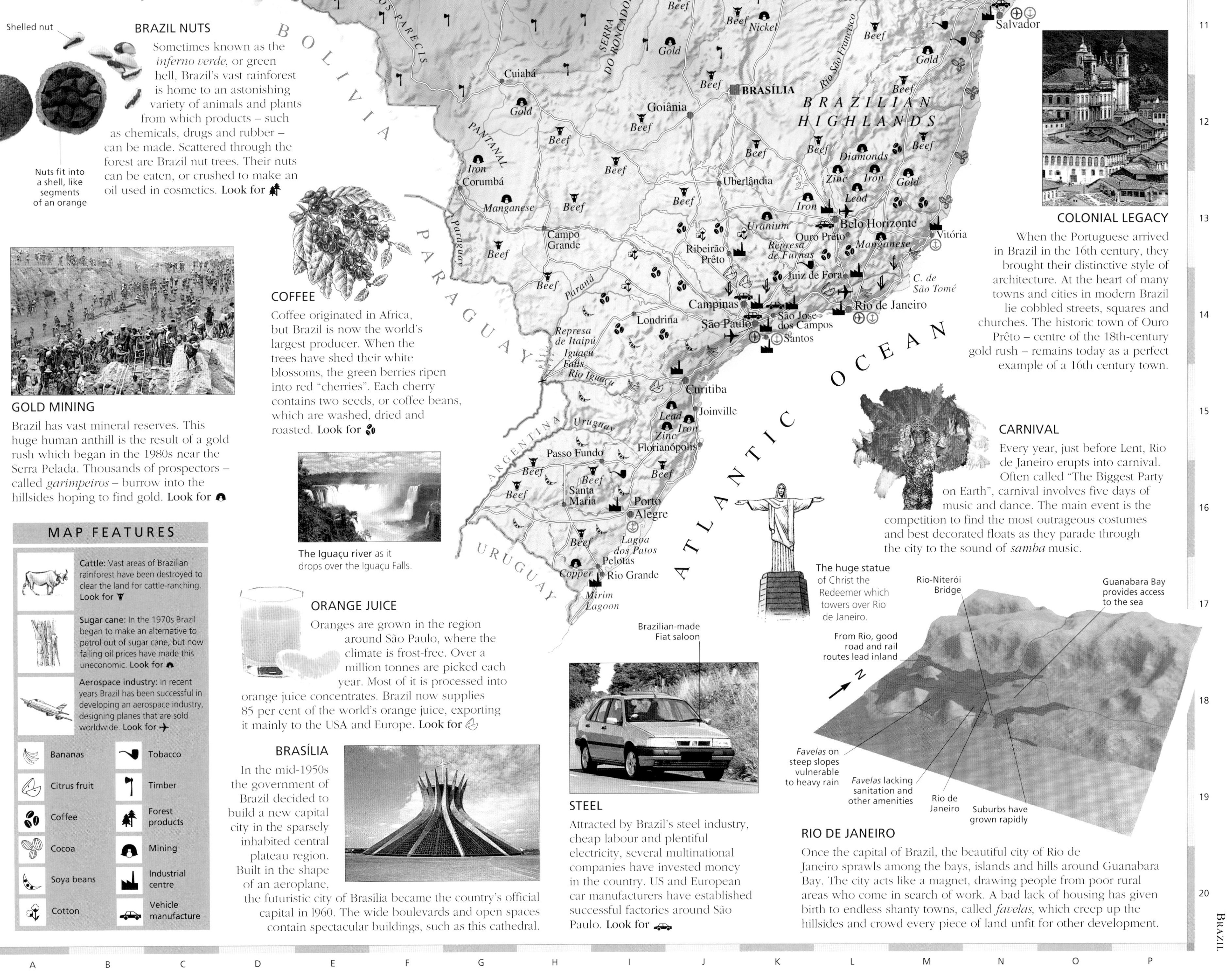
BOLIVIA
PARAGUAY
URUGUAY
ARGENTINA
ATLANTIC OCEAN
BRAZILIAN HIGHLANDS
SERRA DO RONCADOR
PANTANAL
BRASÍLIA
Salvador
Cuiabá
Goiânia
Corumbá
Campo Grande
Uberlândia
Belo Horizonte
Ouro Prêto
Vitória
Ribeirão Prêto
Juiz de Fora
Campinas
São Paulo
São José dos Campos
Santos
Rio de Janeiro
C. de São Tomé
Londrina
Curitiba
Joinville
Florianópolis
Passo Fundo
Santa Maria
Porto Alegre
Lagoa dos Patos
Pelotas
Rio Grande
Mirim Lagoon
Represa de Itaipú
Iguaçu Falls
Rio Iguaçu
Represa de Furnas
Rio São Francisco
Paraná
Paraguay
Uruguay
Shelled nut
Nuts fit into a shell, like segments of an orange
Brazilian-made Fiat saloon
Rio-Niterói Bridge
Guanabara Bay provides access to the sea
From Rio, good road and rail routes lead inland
N
Favelas on steep slopes vulnerable to heavy rain
Favelas lacking sanitation and other amenities
Rio de Janeiro
Suburbs have grown rapidly

BRAZIL NUTS

Sometimes known as the *inferno verde*, or green hell, Brazil's vast rainforest is home to an astonishing variety of animals and plants from which products – such as chemicals, drugs and rubber – can be made. Scattered through the forest are Brazil nut trees. Their nuts can be eaten, or crushed to make an oil used in cosmetics. **Look for**

GOLD MINING

Brazil has vast mineral reserves. This huge human anthill is the result of a gold rush which began in the 1980s near the Serra Pelada. Thousands of prospectors – called *garimpeiros* – burrow into the hillsides hoping to find gold. **Look for**

MAP FEATURES

Cattle: Vast areas of Brazilian rainforest have been destroyed to clear the land for cattle-ranching. **Look for**

Sugar cane: In the 1970s Brazil began to make an alternative to petrol out of sugar cane, but now falling oil prices have made this uneconomic. **Look for**

Aerospace industry: In recent years Brazil has been successful in developing an aerospace industry, designing planes that are sold worldwide. **Look for**

Bananas	Tobacco
Citrus fruit	Timber
Coffee	Forest products
Cocoa	Mining
Soya beans	Industrial centre
Cotton	Vehicle manufacture

COFFEE

Coffee originated in Africa, but Brazil is now the world's largest producer. When the trees have shed their white blossoms, the green berries ripen into red "cherries". Each cherry contains two seeds, or coffee beans, which are washed, dried and roasted. **Look for**

The Iguaçu river as it drops over the Iguaçu Falls.

ORANGE JUICE

Oranges are grown in the region around São Paulo, where the climate is frost-free. Over a million tonnes are picked each year. Most of it is processed into orange juice concentrates. Brazil now supplies 85 per cent of the world's orange juice, exporting it mainly to the USA and Europe. **Look for**

BRASÍLIA

In the mid-1950s the government of Brazil decided to build a new capital city in the sparsely inhabited central plateau region. Built in the shape of an aeroplane, the futuristic city of Brasília became the country's official capital in 1960. The wide boulevards and open spaces contain spectacular buildings, such as this cathedral.

STEEL

Attracted by Brazil's steel industry, cheap labour and plentiful electricity, several multinational companies have invested money in the country. US and European car manufacturers have established successful factories around São Paulo. **Look for**

COLONIAL LEGACY

When the Portuguese arrived in Brazil in the 16th century, they brought their distinctive style of architecture. At the heart of many towns and cities in modern Brazil lie cobbled streets, squares and churches. The historic town of Ouro Prêto – centre of the 18th-century gold rush – remains today as a perfect example of a 16th century town.

CARNIVAL

Every year, just before Lent, Rio de Janeiro erupts into carnival. Often called "The Biggest Party on Earth", carnival involves five days of music and dance. The main event is the competition to find the most outrageous costumes and best decorated floats as they parade through the city to the sound of *samba* music.

The huge statue of Christ the Redeemer which towers over Rio de Janeiro.

RIO DE JANEIRO

Once the capital of Brazil, the beautiful city of Rio de Janeiro sprawls among the bays, islands and hills around Guanabara Bay. The city acts like a magnet, drawing people from poor rural areas who come in search of work. A bad lack of housing has given birth to endless shanty towns, called *favelas*, which creep up the hillsides and crowd every piece of land unfit for other development.

Southern South America

All four countries in this region were colonized in the 16th century by Spain. With the exception of Argentina, their populations are almost entirely *mestizo* – people of mixed Spanish and native descent. In Argentina, 98 per cent of the population is descended from European settlers, as the native peoples were killed or driven out by the immigrants. Argentina falls into three regions: the hot, damp lands of the Gran Chaco in the north, the grasslands of the Pampas in the centre and the barren plateau of Patagonia in the south. Argentina gets its wealth from the rich soil of the Pampas, where cereals are grown and vast herds of sheep and cattle graze. The Pampas spills into neighbouring Uruguay, where sheep provide the country with its main export: wool. Paraguay's economy is mainly dependent on agriculture. Chile is a long, narrow country, stretching along the western side of the Andes, from the mineral-rich Atacama desert to the icy wastes of the south. Both Chile and Argentina, despite a troubled history, are now relatively stable and prosperous.

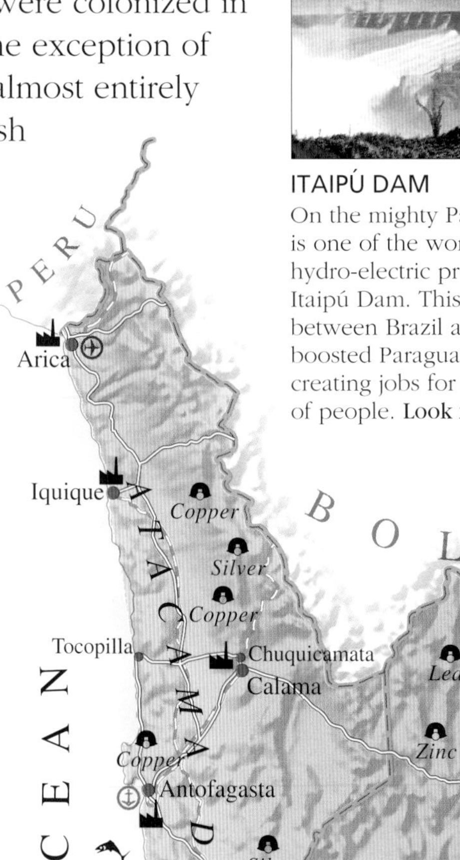
PACIFIC OCEAN
PERU
BOLIVIA
BRAZIL
PARAGUAY
URUGUAY
CHILE
ANDES
ARGENTINA
GRAN CHACO
ATACAMA DESERT
Arica
Iquique
Tocopilla
Chuquicamata
Calama
Antofagasta
Chañaral
Copiapó
Vallenar
La Serena
Coquimbo
Ovalle
Illapel
La Ligua
San Felipe
Quillota
Viña del Mar
Valparaíso
SANTIAGO
San Juan
Mendoza
Godoy Cruz
San Luis
Mercedes
Río Cuarto
Villa María
Córdoba
La Rioja
San Fernando del Valle de Catamarca
Santiago del Estero
San Miguel de Tucumán
Salta
San Salvador de Jujuy
Santa Fe
Paraná
Rosario
San Nicolás de los Arroyos
Junín
BUENOS AIRES
Vera
Resistencia
Corrientes
Formosa
Posadas
Concordia
Gualeguaychú
Colón
Paysandú
Salto
Artigas
Rivera
Tacuarembó
Melo
Treinta y Tres
Fray Bentos
Mercedes
Durazno
Florida
Colonia del Sacramento
Rocha
MONTEVIDEO
ASUNCIÓN
Paraguarí
Villarrica
Caazapá
San Juan Bautista
Encarnación
Pilar
Ciudad del Este
Itaipú Dam
Salto del Guairá
San Pedro
Concepción
Pedro Juan Caballero
Pozo Colorado
Filadelfia
Doctor Pedro P. Peña
General Eugenio A. Garay
Capitán Pablo Lagerenza
Fuerte Olimpo
Mirim Lagoon
Pan-American Highway
Río Bermejo
Pilcomayo
Paraguay
Paraná
Río Salado
Uruguay
Río Negro
Plate
L. Mar Chiquita
Copper
Silver
Lead
Zinc
Iron
Lapis lazuli
Beef
Wheat
Dairy

The Peoples of the Chaco

Only five per cent of Paraguay's population live in the grasslands and swamps of the Gran Chaco. The main people still living there are the Guaranís, the first inhabitants of Paraguay. A smaller group, the Macá, make money by selling colourful hand-woven cloth and goods, like this bag, to tourists.

Itaipú Dam

On the mighty Paraná River is one of the world's largest hydro-electric projects, the Itaipú Dam. This joint venture between Brazil and Paraguay boosted Paraguay's economy, creating jobs for thousands of people. **Look for**

PARAGUAY
pop: 5,200,000

Asunción

Plaza Constitución is just one of many squares whose beautiful Spanish buildings still stand in Asunción, Paraguay's capital and only large city.

Mainly Meat

In the late 19th century, processing and packing meat became an important industry in Uruguay. Today, tinned meats, such as corned beef, are still a major export. Look for

Tomatoes were first grown in South America.

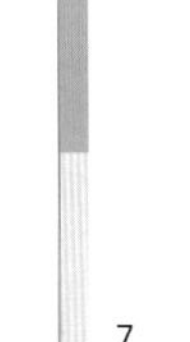

URUGUAY
pop: 3,200,000

Copper

Near Calama, Chile, shining metal is extracted from the largest open-cast copper mine in the world. Giant trucks remove thousands of tonnes (tons) of ore a day. However, the world price of copper is now falling, causing severe economic problems in Chile. **Look for**

CHILE
pop: 13,800,000

The Atacama Desert in Chile is the driest place on Earth.

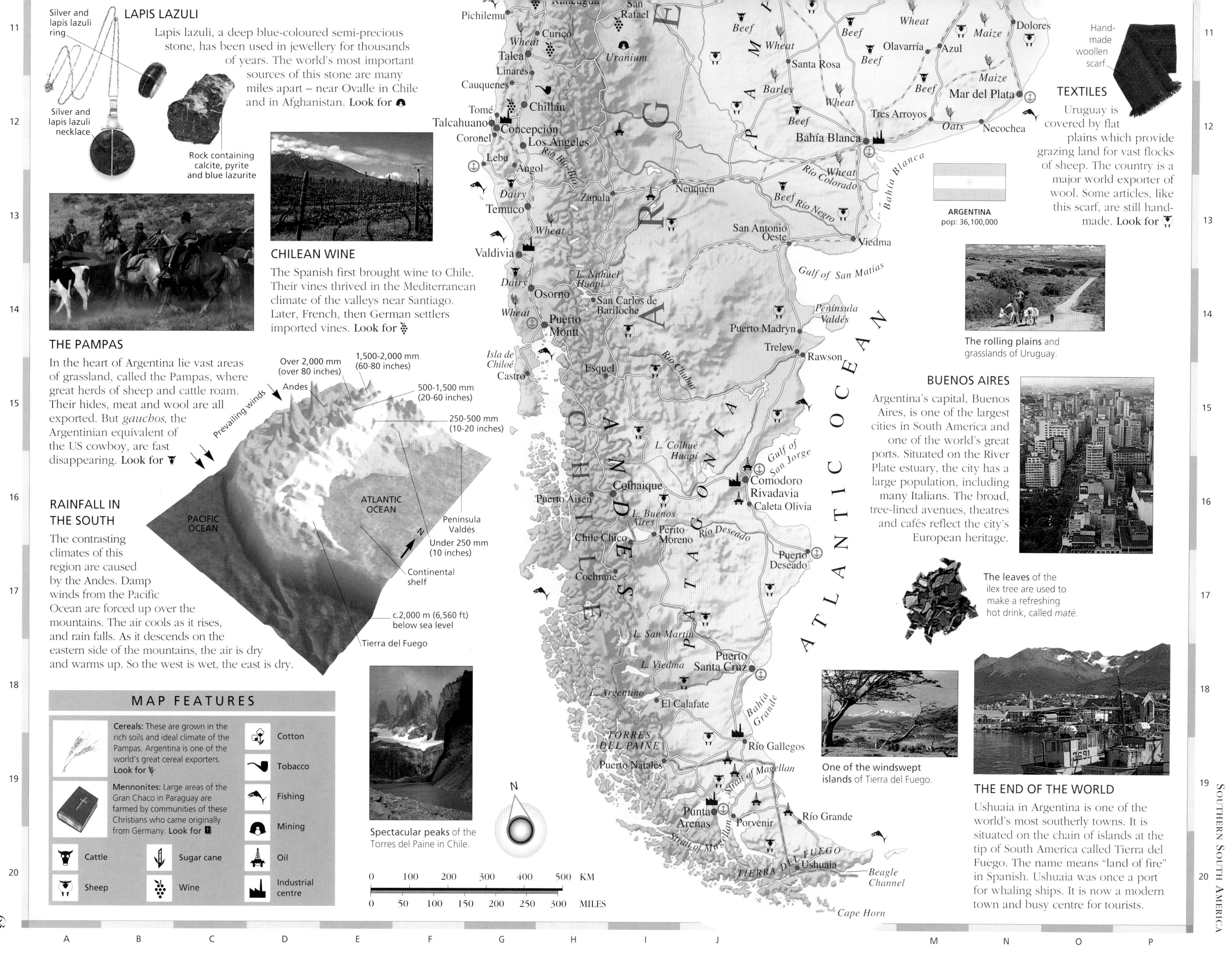

Silver and lapis lazuli ring
Silver and lapis lazuli necklace
Rock containing calcite, pyrite and blue lazurite
Hand-made woollen scarf
ARGENTINA
pop: 36,100,000
Prevailing winds
Andes
Over 2,000 mm (over 80 inches)
1,500-2,000 mm (60-80 inches)
500-1,500 mm (20-60 inches)
250-500 mm (10-20 inches)
PACIFIC OCEAN
ATLANTIC OCEAN
Peninsula Valdés
Under 250 mm (10 inches)
Continental shelf
c.2,000 m (6,560 ft) below sea level
Tierra del Fuego
N
ATLANTIC OCEAN
ARGENTINA
PAMPAS
PATAGONIA
ANDES
CHILE
TIERRA DEL FUEGO
Pichilemu
Curicó
Talca
Linares
Cauquenes
Tomé
Chillán
Talcahuano
Concepción
Coronel
Los Angeles
Lebu
Angol
Río Bío-Bío
Temuco
Valdivia
Osorno
Puerto Montt
Isla de Chiloé
Castro
San Rafael
Uranium
Zapala
Neuquén
L. Nahuel Huapi
San Carlos de Bariloche
Esquel
Río Chubut
L. Colhué Huapí
Coihaique
Puerto Aisén
L. Buenos Aires
Chile Chico
Perito Moreno
Río Deseado
Cochrane
L. San Martín
L. Viedma
L. Argentino
El Calafate
TORRES DEL PAINE
Puerto Natales
Punta Arenas
Strait of Magellan
Porvenir
Río Grande
Ushuaia
Beagle Channel
Cape Horn
Río Gallegos
Bahía Grande
Puerto Santa Cruz
Puerto Deseado
Caleta Olivia
Comodoro Rivadavia
Gulf of San Jorge
Rawson
Trelew
Puerto Madryn
Península Valdés
Gulf of San Matías
San Antonio Oeste
Viedma
Río Negro
Río Colorado
Bahía Blanca
Tres Arroyos
Necochea
Mar del Plata
Olavarría
Azul
Dolores
Santa Rosa
Beef
Wheat
Barley
Maize
Oats
Dairy
0 100 200 300 400 500 KM
0 50 100 150 200 250 300 MILES

LAPIS LAZULI

Lapis lazuli, a deep blue-coloured semi-precious stone, has been used in jewellery for thousands of years. The world's most important sources of this stone are many miles apart – near Ovalle in Chile and in Afghanistan. **Look for**

CHILEAN WINE

The Spanish first brought wine to Chile. Their vines thrived in the Mediterranean climate of the valleys near Santiago. Later, French, then German settlers imported vines. **Look for**

THE PAMPAS

In the heart of Argentina lie vast areas of grassland, called the Pampas, where great herds of sheep and cattle roam. Their hides, meat and wool are all exported. But *gauchos*, the Argentinian equivalent of the US cowboy, are fast disappearing. **Look for**

RAINFALL IN THE SOUTH

The contrasting climates of this region are caused by the Andes. Damp winds from the Pacific Ocean are forced up over the mountains. The air cools as it rises, and rain falls. As it descends on the eastern side of the mountains, the air is dry and warms up. So the west is wet, the east is dry.

MAP FEATURES

Cereals: These are grown in the rich soils and ideal climate of the Pampas. Argentina is one of the world's great cereal exporters. **Look for**

Mennonites: Large areas of the Gran Chaco in Paraguay are farmed by communities of these Christians who came originally from Germany. **Look for**

Cattle
Sheep
Sugar cane
Wine
Cotton
Tobacco
Fishing
Mining
Oil
Industrial centre

Spectacular peaks of the Torres del Paine in Chile.

TEXTILES

Uruguay is covered by flat plains which provide grazing land for vast flocks of sheep. The country is a major world exporter of wool. Some articles, like this scarf, are still hand-made. **Look for**

The rolling plains and grasslands of Uruguay.

BUENOS AIRES

Argentina's capital, Buenos Aires, is one of the largest cities in South America and one of the world's great ports. Situated on the River Plate estuary, the city has a large population, including many Italians. The broad, tree-lined avenues, theatres and cafés reflect the city's European heritage.

The leaves of the ilex tree are used to make a refreshing hot drink, called *maté*.

One of the windswept islands of Tierra del Fuego.

THE END OF THE WORLD

Ushuaia in Argentina is one of the world's most southerly towns. It is situated on the chain of islands at the tip of South America called Tierra del Fuego. The name means "land of fire" in Spanish. Ushuaia was once a port for whaling ships. It is now a modern town and busy centre for tourists.

The Antarctic

The continent of Antarctica has such a cold, harsh climate that no people live there permanently. The land is covered by a huge sheet of ice up to 2 km (1.2 miles) thick, and seas around Antarctica are frozen over. Even during the short summers, the temperature barely climbs above freezing, and the sea-ice only partly melts; in winter, temperatures can plummet to -80° C (-112° F). Few animals and plants can survive on land, but the seas around Antarctica teem with fish and mammals. The only people on the continent are scientists working in the Antarctic research stations and tourists, who come to see the dramatic landscape and the unique creatures that live here. But even these few people have brought waste and pollution to the region.

Icebergs are huge blocks of ice which float in the sea.

KRILL

Krill are the main food of the baleen whale. Japanese and Russian ships catch about 400,000 tonnes (tons) of krill each year, threatening the whales' food supply. Mainly used for animal feed, krill are also considered a delicacy in Japan. Krill gather in such huge numbers that they are visible from aeroplanes or even satellites.

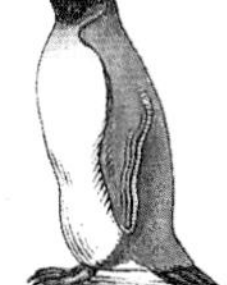

Adélie penguins live in huge colonies on rocks or Antarctic pack ice.

Various nations claimed territory in Antarctica when it was first discovered in the 19th century. These claims have been suspended under the 1959 Antarctic Treaty (signed by 39 nations). Stations can be set up for scientific research, but military bases are forbidden.

ATLANTIC OCEAN
INDIAN OCEAN
PACIFIC OCEAN
SCOTIA SEA
WEDDELL SEA
BELLINGSHAUSEN SEA
AMUNDSEN SEA
ROSS SEA
DAVIS SEA
Drake Passage
South Orkney Is.
Elephant I.
South Shetland Is.
Marambio (to Argentina)
Faraday (to UK)
Larsen Ice Shelf
Adelaide I.
San Martín (to Argentina)
PALMER LAND
Peter I Island (to Norway)
Riiser-Larsen Ice Shelf
Fimbul Ice Shelf
Georg von Neumayer (to Germany)
Novolazarevskaya (to Russian Fed.)
DRONNING MAUD LAND
Lutzow-Holm Bay
Syowa (to Japan)
Molodezhnaya (to Russian Fed.)
ENDERBY LAND
Halley (to UK)
Belgrano II (to Argentina)
Filchner Ice Shelf
Ronne Ice Shelf
Kerguelen (to France)
Crozet Is. (to France)
Heard I. (to Australia)
Mawson (to Australia)
C. Darnley
Mackenzie Bay
Amery Ice Shelf
Lambert Glacier
Prydz Bay
Zhongshan (to China)
West Ice Shelf
GREATER ANTARCTICA
TRANSANTARCTIC MTS.
South Pole
Amundsen-Scott (to US)
ELLSWORTH LAND
LESSER ANTARCTICA
MARIE BYRD LAND
Mirny (to Russian Fed.)
Vostok (to Russian Fed.)
Shackleton Ice Shelf
WILKES LAND
Vincennes Bay
Casey (to Australia)
Cape Poinsett
Getz Ice Shelf
Ross Ice Shelf
Scott Base (to NZ)
VICTORIA LAND
Porpoise Bay
C. Adare
Leningradskaya (to Russian Fed.)
Dumont d'Urville (to France)
Balleny Is.

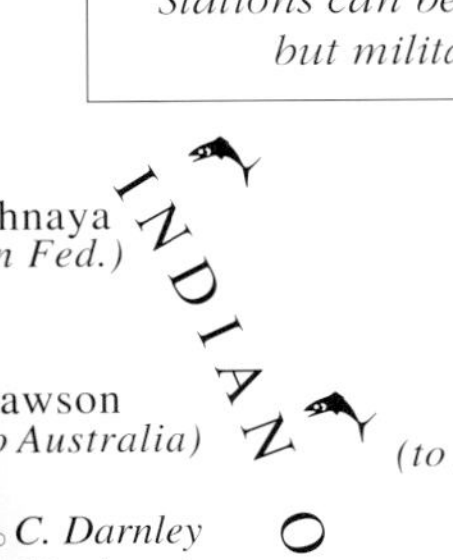

Antarctic fishing fleets are reducing stocks of the cod icefish.

These mountains are on Anvers Island, which lies off the Antarctic Peninsula.

WHALES

Whales thrive in the seas around the Antarctic, which are rich in plankton and krill, their main food sources. Large-scale whale-hunting started in the 20th century, and the numbers of whales soon fell. In 1948 the International Whaling Commission was set up to regulate the numbers and species of whales killed, and to create protected areas. Look for [whale symbol]

Blue whale

ANTARCTIC TOURISM

Cruise liners have been bringing tourists to the Antarctic region since the 1950s. About 2-3,000 visitors a year observe the harsh beauty of the landscape and its extraordinary wildlife from the comfort of cruise ships. Look for [camera symbol]

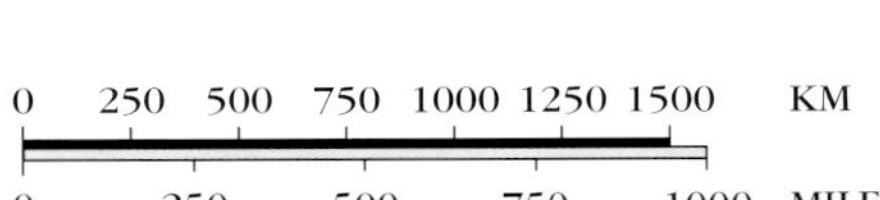

0 250 500 750 1000 1250 1500 KM
0 250 500 750 1000 MILES

POLLUTION

The Antarctic research stations have yet to find effective ways of disposing of their waste. Although some of it is burnt, tins, bottles, machine parts and chemicals are often simply dumped near the bases, spoiling the area's natural beauty. The only solution to the problem is to take the rubbish out of Antarctica. Look for [pollution symbol]

RESEARCH

The scientific base in this picture is the US Amundsen-Scott station, which is built underground at the South Pole. Scientists at the Antarctic research stations are monitoring changes to the weather and environment. Look for [research centre symbol]

MAP FEATURES

Oil: Much of the Arctic region is rich in oil, but the difficulty of drilling and moving oil, as well as environmental concerns, have slowed exploitation. Look for [oil symbol]

Penguin grounds: Penguin breeding grounds are found near Antarctic coasts. Some are being disturbed by tourists, airstrips and construction. Look for [penguin symbol]

Fishing

Polar research centre

Coal

Pollution

Tourism

Whales

THE ARCTIC

THE ARCTIC OCEAN is covered by drifting ice up to 30 metres (98 feet) thick, which partially melts and disperses in the summer. Much of the surrounding land is tundra – plains and moorlands that are carpeted with moss and lichens, but permanently frozen beneath the surface. People have lived around the Arctic for thousands of years, hunting the mammals and fish that live in the ocean. This region has large deposits of oil, but the harsh climate makes it difficult to extract from the ground.

FISHFINGERS

Large numbers of cod, haddock, halibut and other fish live in the Arctic Ocean. Cod and haddock are taken to fish-processing factories in Greenland. Here they are frozen, canned or – in the case of cod – made into fishfingers, and exported to the markets of the USA and Europe. **Look for**

ARCTIC PEOPLES

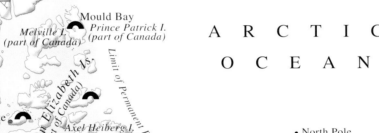

Traditionally, the people of the Arctic survived by hunting animals. They used seal skin for boats and clothing and seal fat (blubber) for fuel. Today, tools, clothes and buildings are made from modern materials. Rifles now replace harpoons and snowmobiles are used for transport.

The northern lights can be seen over the Arctic at night.

ICE-BREAKER

About half the Arctic Ocean is covered with ice in winter, but special ships called ice-breakers can still sail across it. In 1969, a large tanker, the *S.S. Manhattan*, penetrated the pack ice of the Northwest Passage (from eastern Canada to Alaska) for the first time.

Polar bears spend summers on the Arctic ice. They move further south in winter.

GREENLAND

The first Europeans to explore and settle Greenland were Vikings, who arrived in about AD 986. Greenland later came under Danish rule, and is now a self-governing part of Denmark.

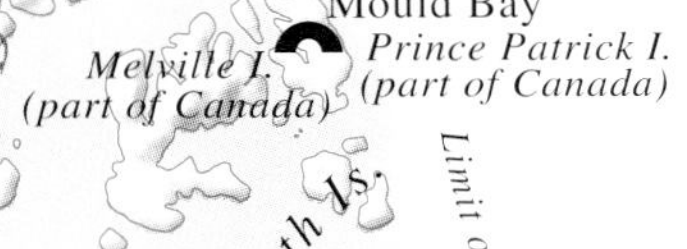

ARCTIC OCEAN
North Pole
CHUKCHI SEA
ALASKA (part of US)
Barrow
Prudhoe Bay
BEAUFORT SEA
Limit of Permanent Pack Ice
Wrangel I. (part of Russian Fed.)
Pevek
Ambarchik
RUSSIAN FEDERATION
EAST SIBERIAN SEA
New Siberian Is. (part of Russian Fed.)
Tiksi
LAPTEV SEA
POLUOSTROV TAYMYR
Severnaya Zemlya (part of Russian Fed.)
Dikson
KARA SEA
Franz Josef Land (part of Russian Fed.)
BARENTS SEA
SVALBARD (to Norway)
LONGYEARBYEN
Spitsbergen
Banks I. (part of Canada)
CANADA
Mould Bay
Prince Patrick I. (part of Canada)
Melville I. (part of Canada)
Queen Elizabeth Is. (part of Canada)
Resolute
Axel Heiberg I. (part of Canada)
Devon I. (part of Canada)
Ellesmere I. (part of Canada)
Alert
Qaanaaq
KNUD RASMUSSEN LAND
Baffin I. (part of Canada)
Baffin Bay
Nord
Upernavik
GREENLAND (to Denmark)
Pangnirtung
Davis Strait
Qeqertarsuaq
Søndre Strømfjord
NUUK
Paamiut
Narsarsuaq
Qaqortoq
Nunap Isua
Danmarkshavn
GREENLAND SEA
Illoqqortoormiut
Tasiilaq
Denmark Strait
JAN MAYEN (to Norway)
ATLANTIC OCEAN
ICELAND
0 250 500 750 1000 KM
0 100 200 300 400 500 MILES

The Arctic tern migrates every year between the Arctic and Antarctica.

Mountains on Svalbard reflected in a melted ice pond.

ARCTIC COAL

The island of Spitsbergen has rich deposits of minerals, especially coal. It is part of Norway, but other countries are allowed to mine there. The Norwegian coal town of Longyearbyen is 1,000 km (620 miles) from the mainland. It can be reached by sea for only eight months a year, making it difficult and expensive to ship coal out. Coal screes and long, severe winters make this a desolate place. **Look for**

The Atlantic Ocean

The world's oceans cover almost three-quarters of the Earth's surface. Beneath the surface of the Atlantic Ocean lie vast, featureless plains and long chains of mountains called ridges. The Mid-Atlantic Ridge is one of the world's longest mountain chains; some of its peaks are so high that they pierce the surface as volcanic islands, such as the Azores. A huge rift valley 24-48 km (15-30 miles) wide runs down the ridge's centre. The deepest part of the Atlantic is 8 km (5 miles) below the surface. On average, the Atlantic has the warmest and saltiest waters of any ocean. Before regular shipping routes were established, the Atlantic isolated America from the prosperous countries of Europe, but today it is crossed by some of the world's most important trade routes. The North Atlantic has always been one of the world's richest fishing grounds, but it has been overfished, and fish stocks are now dangerously low.

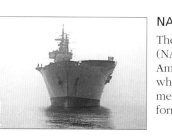

Puffins breed on rocky islands, like the Faeroes.

FISHING

Catches of cod, herring and haddock in the North Atlantic have been severely reduced by over-fishing. Fishing fleets must now travel long distances and remain at sea for months at a time. The fish are processed on the fleet's factory ship to keep them fresh. **Look for**

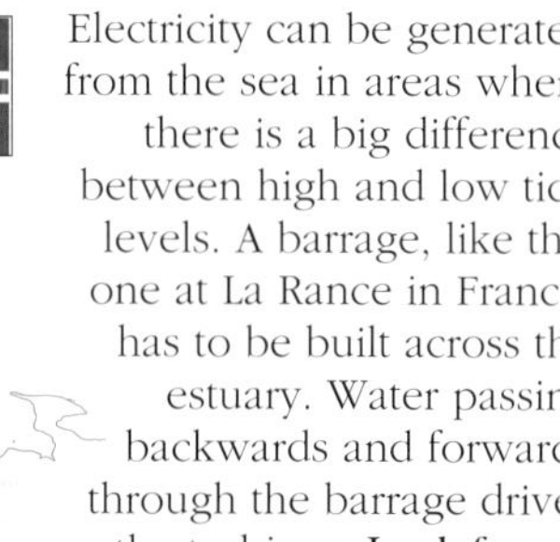

"LAND OF ICE AND FIRE"

There are more than 100 volcanoes on Iceland. Many of them are still active. Beneath the island's harsh, rocky surface lie vast natural heat reserves. This energy is used to provide hot water and central heating for much of the population. Iceland's economy is based on fishing, which accounts for about 70 per cent of its exports.

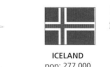

NATO

The North Atlantic Treaty Organization (NATO) is an association of North American and European countries which was established to defend its members – principally against the former Soviet Union. **Look for**

WHALING

Whaling has been going on in the world's oceans for hundreds of years. But with the invention of the explosive harpoon, catches increased rapidly. Today some species of whales are threatened with extinction. Attempts are being made to ban whaling worldwide until numbers recover. **Look for**

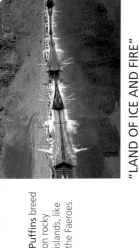

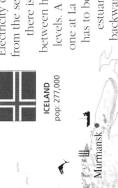

TIDAL ENERGY

Electricity can be generated from the sea in areas where there is a big difference between high and low tide levels. A barrage, like this one at La Rance in France, has to be built across the estuary. Water passing backwards and forwards through the barrage drives the turbines. **Look for**

ICELAND
pop: 277,000

SARGASSO SEA

At the centre of three great North Atlantic currents lies the Sargasso Sea – an area of calm water, covered with sargassum weed. Sailors once believed their ships would be trapped by the weed, and sink.

Fish like these live amongst the sargassum weed

ARCTIC OCEAN
Greenland
Baffin Bay
Davis Strait
Denmark Strait
GREENLAND SEA
ICELAND
REYKJAVIK
FAEROE ISLANDS (to Denmark)
NORTH SEA
Hudson Bay
LABRADOR SEA
NORTH AMERICA
Newfoundland
St. John's
Bay of Fundy
St. Lawrence
Saint John
Halifax
Grand Banks
Newfoundland Basin
Portland
Gloucester
New York
Baltimore
Mississippi
New Orleans
Gulf of Mexico
Bermuda (to UK)
SARGASSO SEA
West Indies
Mid-Atlantic Ridge
Azores (part of Portugal)
Madeira (part of Portugal)
Canary Islands (part of Spain)
Rockall (part of UK)
Murmansk
Kristiansund
Alesund
Bergen
Haugesund
Stavanger
Aberdeen
Skagen
Esbjerg
BALTIC SEA
Tallinn
Liepāja
Grimsby
Bremerhaven
Rotterdam
Boulogne-sur-Mer
La Rance
Lorient
EUROPE
A Coruña
Oporto
Marseille
Livorno
Ancona
Naples
BLACK SEA
MEDITERRANEAN SEA
Gibraltar
Algiers
Sfax
Casablanca
Safi
Port Said
Nile
AFRICA
CAPE VERDE

Tomatoes and other fruit are grown in the warm climate of the Canary Islands.

CAPE VERDE
pop: 417,000

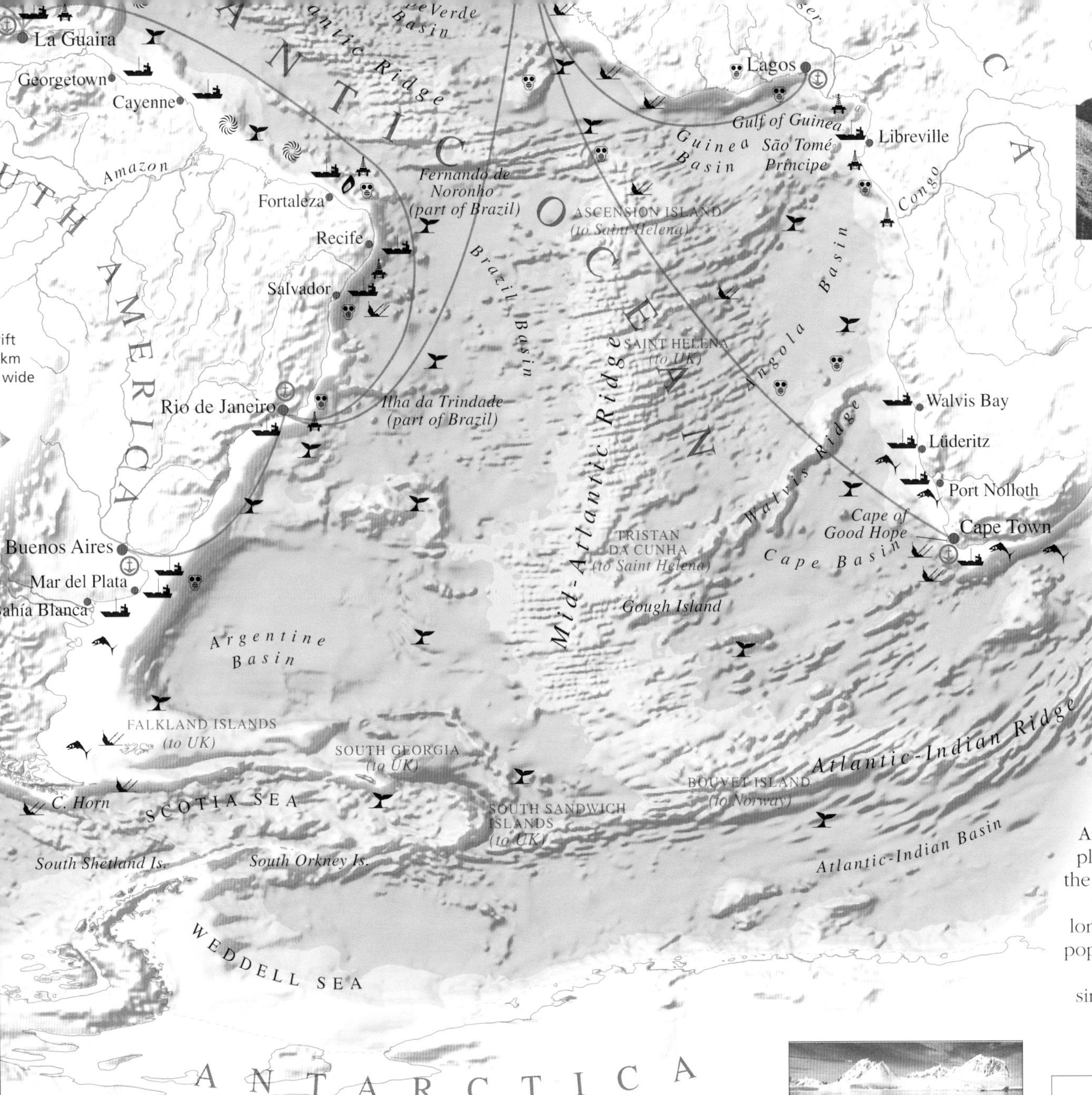

Ocean basins descend to 5,000 m (18,000 ft) below sea level

Brazil Basin

St Helena

Angola Basin

Walvis Ridge

Mid-Atlantic Ridge. At its centre is a rift valley up to 48 km (10 miles) wide

Abyssal plains: The deep ocean bed, occasionally interrupted by volcanic hills and mountains

Tristan da Cuhna

ATLANTIC OCEAN

The Atlantic Ocean floor is spreading at a rate of 2.5 cm (1 in) a year. As the South American and African plates move apart, molten rock spills onto the ocean floor, cools and forms solid rock. This is the Mid-Atlantic ridge, the world's longest mountain range. Although most of the ridge lies beneath the sea, some of its peaks emerge as volcanic islands.

MAP FEATURES

Underwater wrecks: Marine archaeology and location of wrecks was greatly advanced by the development of deep-sea diving equipment. **Look for**

Pollution: Oil rig blow-outs and spills from oil tankers along the coastlines and round the Gulf of Mexico are a major problem in the North Atlantic. **Look for**

Hurricane: The warm Atlantic waters off the north coast of Brazil are the gathering grounds for hurricanes, which then sweep north-westward. **Look for**

Fishing

Fishing ports

Oil

Gas

Alternative power

Tourism

Military bases

Whales

An extinct volcano on an island in the West Indies.

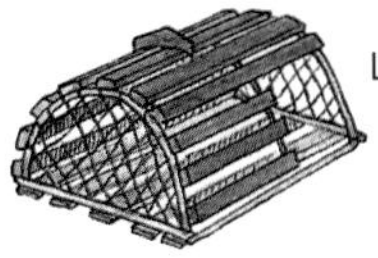

Lobsters are caught in wickerwork lobster pots, baited with dead fish.

SALMON

The early years of an Atlantic salmon are spent in the river where it was born. Then it swims down river to the ocean. In the rich feeding grounds of the North Atlantic it rapidly gains weight. When ready to breed, the salmon's amazing homing device enables it to return to its native river. Here, on their long, hard journey upriver, salmon negotiate a waterfall. Few salmon survive this endurance test to breed a second time.

An isolated settlement on the Falkland Islands in the South Atlantic.

Massive icebergs drift among the pack ice, a threat to shipping in the Atlantic.

TOURISM

A number of islands in the Atlantic, such as the Canaries and Madeira, are great tourist attractions, especially during winter in the Northern hemisphere. The Canaries are a chain of seven mountainous islands; some areas are green and lush, others volcanic. The volcanic lava produces dramatic black landscapes. Look for

SAILING

Areas of the Atlantic have become pleasure grounds. Sailing is one of the main activities, much of it in the warm seas of the Caribbean, but long distance races are increasingly popular, some of them transatlantic. Boats range from yachts sailed single-handed to ships like this tea clipper, sailed by large crews.

CABLES

Snaking across the ocean floor are cables carrying many forms of modern communication, such as telephone calls and fax messages. The first transatlantic cable was laid in 1866. The cables are laid by special ships, like this one in the North Atlantic.

EUROPE

EUROPE, THE SMALLEST CONTINENT after Australia, is less than half the size of North America and a quarter that of Asia. Yet it has a remarkable variety of climates, landforms and types of vegetation. Europe's main mountain ranges, including the Pyrenees and the Alps, roughly divide the continent north and south. They form a barrier that protects the south from the cold winds that blow from the north during winter. As a result, the south is much warmer and drier than the cool, wet, heavily-forested north. Europe has an irregular shape, with many interlocking fingers of land and sea. Because much of the land is close to the sea, coastal areas have fewer temperature extremes. Currents also affect the climate. Thanks to the powerful Gulf Stream, which brings immense amounts of warm water northwards from the Equator, even seas within the Arctic Circle stay ice-free throughout the year.

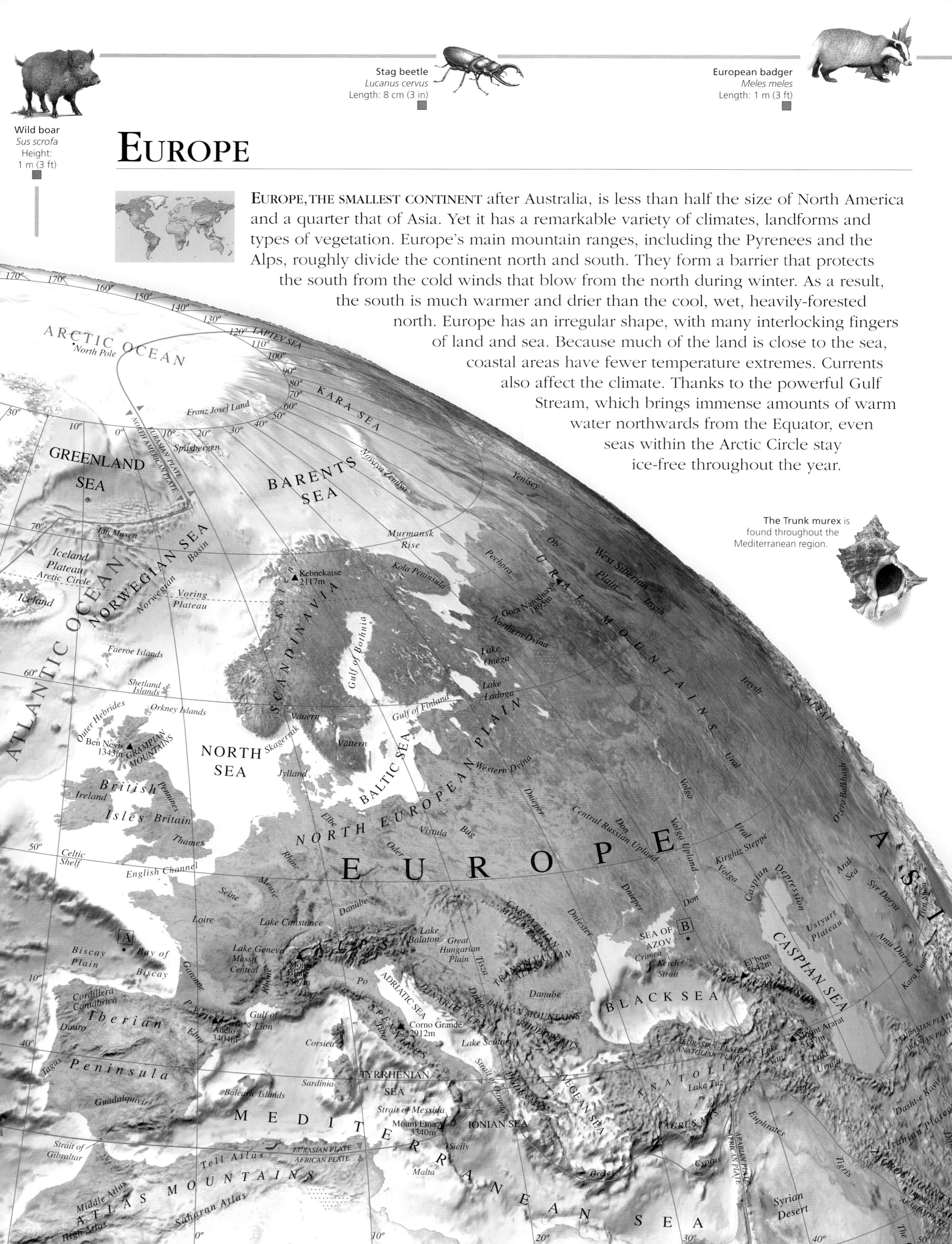

ARCTIC OCEAN
North Pole
LAPTEV SEA
KARA SEA
Franz Josef Land
Spitsbergen
GREENLAND SEA
BARENTS SEA
Novaya Zemlya
Yenisey
Jan Mayen
Iceland Plateau
Arctic Circle
Iceland
NORWEGIAN SEA
Norwegian Basin
Voring Plateau
Murmansk Rise
Kola Peninsula
Pechora
Ob'
West Siberian Plain
Kebnekaise 2117m
Kölen
SCANDINAVIA
Gulf of Bothnia
URAL MOUNTAINS
Gora Narodnaya 1895m
Northern Dvina
Irtysh
ATLANTIC OCEAN
Faeroe Islands
Lake Onega
Lake Ladoga
Gulf of Finland
Shetland Islands
Orkney Islands
Outer Hebrides
Ben Nevis 1343m
GRAMPIAN MOUNTAINS
NORTH SEA
Skagerrak
Vänern
Vättern
Jylland
BALTIC SEA
NORTH EUROPEAN PLAIN
Western Dvina
Ural
Altai
Ozero Balkhash
British Isles
Ireland
Pennines
Britain
Thames
Celtic Shelf
English Channel
Elbe
Vistula
Bug
Oder
Rhine
Dnieper
Don
Central Russian Upland
Volga
Volga Upland
Kirghiz Steppe
EUROPE
ASIA
Caspian Depression
Aral Sea
Syr Darya
Seine
Meuse
Danube
Loire
Lake Constance
Lake Balaton
Great Hungarian Plain
CARPATHIAN MOUNTAINS
Dniester
SEA OF AZOV
Crimea
Kerch Strait
Ustyurt Plateau
Amu Darya
CASPIAN SEA
Biscay Plain
Bay of Biscay
Lake Geneva
Massif Central
Mont Blanc 4807m
ALPS
Tisza
TRANSYLVANIAN ALPS
El'brus 5642m
CAUCASUS
Garonne
Rhône
Po
ADRIATIC SEA
DINARIC ALPS
Drina
BALKAN MOUNTAINS
BLACK SEA
Cordillera Cantabrica
Iberian Peninsula
Douro
PYRENEES
Aneto 3404m
Gulf of Lion
Ebro
APENNINES
Corno Grande 2912m
Tiber
RHODOPE MTS
Lake Scutari
Mount Ararat 5137m
Lake Van
Lake Urmia
EURASIAN PLATE
ANATOLIAN PLATE
Tagus
Corsica
Sardinia
TYRRHENIAN SEA
Strait of Otranto
PINDUS MTS
AEGEAN SEA
ANATOLIA
Lake Tuz
Guadalquivir
Balearic Islands
MEDITERRANEAN SEA
Strait of Messina
Mount Etna 3340m
IONIAN SEA
TAURUS MTS
Euphrates
Dasht-e Kavir
Iranian Plateau
Strait of Gibraltar
EURASIAN PLATE
AFRICAN PLATE
Sicily
Malta
Crete
Cyprus
ARABIAN PLATE
Tigris
ZAGROS MOUNTAINS
Tell Atlas
ATLAS MOUNTAINS
Middle Atlas
High Atlas
Saharan Atlas
Syrian Desert
The Gulf

Wild boar
Sus scrofa
Height: 1 m (3 ft)

Stag beetle
Lucanus cervus
Length: 8 cm (3 in)

European badger
Meles meles
Length: 1 m (3 ft)

The Trunk murex is found throughout the Mediterranean region.

Siberian tit
Parus cinctus
Length: 13 cm (5 in)

Green toad
Bufo viridis
Length: 10 cm (4 in)

BOGLANDS

Bogs cover many of northern Europe's wettest areas. Mosses and reeds are among the few plants that grow in waterlogged soils. Wetlands take thousands of years to develop because plants grow so slowly there.

WAVE POWER

Waves can wear away the shore, creating odd landforms. This seastack off the Orkneys in the British Isles is 135 m (450 ft) high.

Ammonites, fossil relatives of today's octopus, were once found in Europe. They died out 65 million years ago.

PIONEERING BIRCH

Light-loving silver birches are often the first trees to appear on open land. Although quick-growing, they are short-lived. After a few years birches are replaced by trees that can survive shade, such as oaks.

Osprey
Pandion haliaetus
Wingspan: 1.6 m (5 ft)

English oak
Quercus robur
Height: 40 m (130 ft)

BARE MOUNTAIN

Ice, rain, wind and gravity strip steep slopes of all soil. Rocks pile up at the foot of peaks, where plants can take root.

FJORDS

Glaciers have cut hundreds of narrow inlets, or fjords, into Scandinavia's Atlantic coastline. The water in the inlet is calmer than in the open sea.

NEEDLELEAF FOREST

Cone-bearing trees such as pine, larch and fir cover Scandinavia. Most are evergreen: they keep their needle-like leaves even when covered in snow for many months of the year.

TREELESS TUNDRA

Arctic summers are so cool that only the topmost layer of frozen soil thaws. Only shallow-rooted plants can survive in the tundra.

Pine marten
Martes martes
Length: 52 cm (20 in)

ANCIENT WOODLANDS

Relics of Europe's ancient forests, such as these oaks stunted by the rain and wind, are found only in a few valleys in southwest Britain.

This fossil of *Stauranderaster*, a starfish once found in this region, dates from around 70 million years ago.

DRY SOUTH

Crete is a mountainous Mediterranean island with hot dry summers. Many plants survive the summer as underground bulbs, blooming briefly in the wet spring.

YOUNG MOUNTAINS

The Alps are some of western Europe's highest mountains. They are part of an almost continuous belt that stretches from the Pyrenees in the west to the Himalayas in Asia. The Alps are still rising because of plate movements in the Mediterranean region.

CROSS-SECTION THROUGH EUROPE

Atlantic Ocean
Bay of Biscay
Massif Central
Alps
Adriatic Sea
Dinaric Alps
Great Hungarian Plain
Transylvanian Alps
Black Sea
Crimea
Kerch Strait
3,000 (9,843)
0 Sea level
-4,500 (-14,764)
A
Length: 4,500 km (2,800 miles)
B
Metres (feet)

Sweet briar
Rosa rubiginosa
Height: 3 m (10 ft)

KEY TO SYMBOLS

- Mountain
- Volcano
- Wetlands
- Plate margins showing direction of movement
- Endangered species

NATURAL VEGETATION ZONES

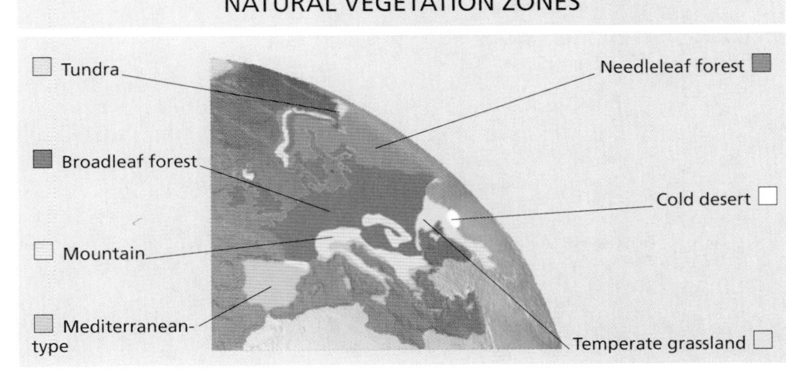
Tundra
Needleleaf forest
Broadleaf forest
Cold desert
Mountain
Mediterranean-type
Temperate grassland

Spanish lynx
Felis lynx
Length: 1.3 m (4 ft)

Scandinavia and Finland

THE SCANDINAVIAN COUNTRIES of Norway, Sweden and Denmark and neighbouring Finland are situated around the Baltic Sea in northern Europe. During past ice ages, glaciers gouged and scoured the land, leaving deep fjords, lakes and valleys in their wake. Much of Norway and Sweden, and nearly two-thirds of Finland, is covered by dense forests of pine, spruce and birch trees. In the far north, winters are long and dark, and snow falls for about eight months of the year. Most Swedish people live in the central lowlands. Norway's economy depends on its shipbuilding, fishing and merchant fleets. Denmark is flat and low-lying, with abundant rainfall and excellent farmland. The Finnish people originally came from the east, via Russia, and consequently differ from the Scandinavians both in language and culture. All four countries have small populations, are highly industrialized and enjoy some of the highest standards of living in the world.

Meadow crops grown for livestock

Cultivation limited to warm, south-facing slopes

Rough upland grazing for sheep and goats

Fish farming of salmon in sheltered waters

Deep water enables ships to reach far inland

Coastal fishing communities are declining

Coastal islands form natural breakwaters

N

A NORWEGIAN FJORD

Norway is so mountainous that only three per cent of the land can be cultivated. Long inlets of sea, called fjords, cut into Norway's west coast. The best farmland is found around the head of the fjords and in the lowland areas around them. Over 70 per cent of Norway's population lives in cities, many of them in towns situated along the sheltered fjords.

The still waters of a Norwegian fjord.

FISHING

As Norway has so little farmland, fishing has always been a vital source of food. Today, about 95 per cent of the total catch is processed, about half of which is made into fishmeal and oil. Fishfarming is on the increase, especially of salmon in the fjords. Look for

Vast shoals of herring gather in the seas around Scandinavia

LAPLAND

Lapland is a land of tundra, forests and lakes. Here the *Samer*, or Lapps, still herd reindeer for their meat and milk. Development in the north now threatens their way of life.

NORWAY
pop: 4,400,000

Fantoft Church, Bergen

STAVE CHURCHES

The wooden stave churches of Norway were built between AD 1000 and 1300. There were once 600 of them, but today only 25 are still standing. A stave church has a stone foundation with a wooden frame on top. The four wooden corner posts are called staves. Further wooden extensions can be added to the basic framework.

Lego building bricks were invented in Denmark.

SKIING

For thousands of years skiing has been the most efficient way of crossing deep snow on foot. This region is often thought to be the original home of skiing – in fact "ski" is the Norwegian word for a strip of wood. Long-distance cross-country skiing, or *langlaufen*, is a popular sport in Norway, Finland and Sweden.

SMÖRGÅSBORD

Smörgåsbord means "sandwich table" in Swedish. Other countries in this region have their own versions, but the idea is the same: a great spread of local delicacies, served cold on bread, which can include ingredients such as reindeer, fish, cheese and salad.

Scrambled egg

Prawn

Caviar

Asparagus

Smoked salmon

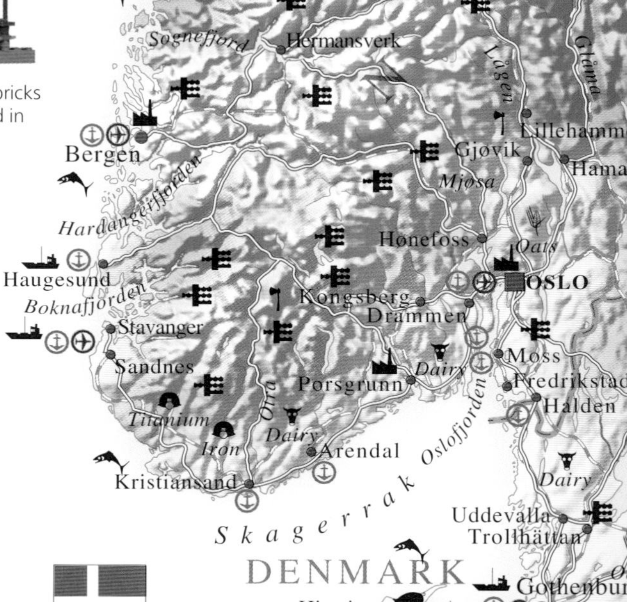
Vikn
Steinkjer
Hitra
Smøla
Vanadium
Trondheim
Molde
Ålesund
Iron
Coppe
Røros
Nordfjord
L. Femunden
Sognefjord
Hermansverk
Lågen
Glåma
Lillehammer
Bergen
Gjøvik
Hamar
Mjøsa
Hardangerfjorden
Hønefoss
Oats
Haugesund
OSLO
Boknafjorden
Kongsberg
Drammen
Stavanger
Moss
Sandnes
Porsgrunn
Dairy
Fredrikstad
Halden
Titanium
Iron
Arendal
Oslofjorden
Kristiansand
Skagerrak

MAP FEATURES

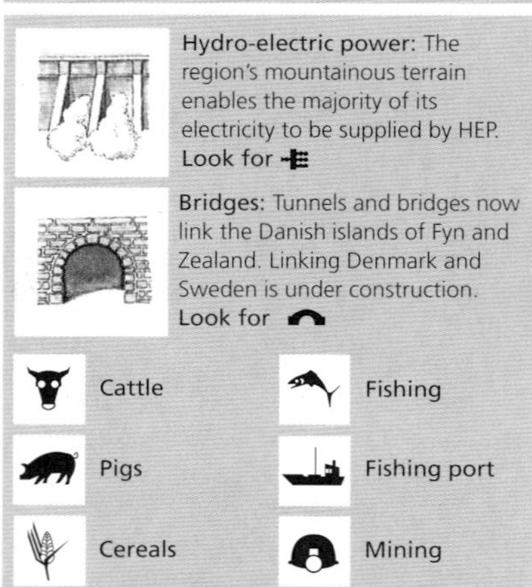

Hydro-electric power: The region's mountainous terrain enables the majority of its electricity to be supplied by HEP. Look for

Bridges: Tunnels and bridges now link the Danish islands of Fyn and Zealand. Linking Denmark and Sweden is under construction. Look for

Cattle
Fishing
Pigs
Fishing port
Cereals
Mining
Timber
Industrial centre

COPENHAGEN

Copenhagen's fine natural harbour and its position at the main entrance to the Baltic Sea, helped it to become a major port and Denmark's capital city. The city's tiny shops, cobbled streets, museums and cafés attract over a million tourists each year.

Danish bacon for export

DENMARK
pop: 5,300,000

DANISH AGRICULTURE

Two-thirds of the total area of Denmark is used for farming. Denmark exports agricultural products all over the world. The main exports are bacon, dairy products, cereals and beef. Cereals are widely grown, but mainly as fodder for pigs. Look for

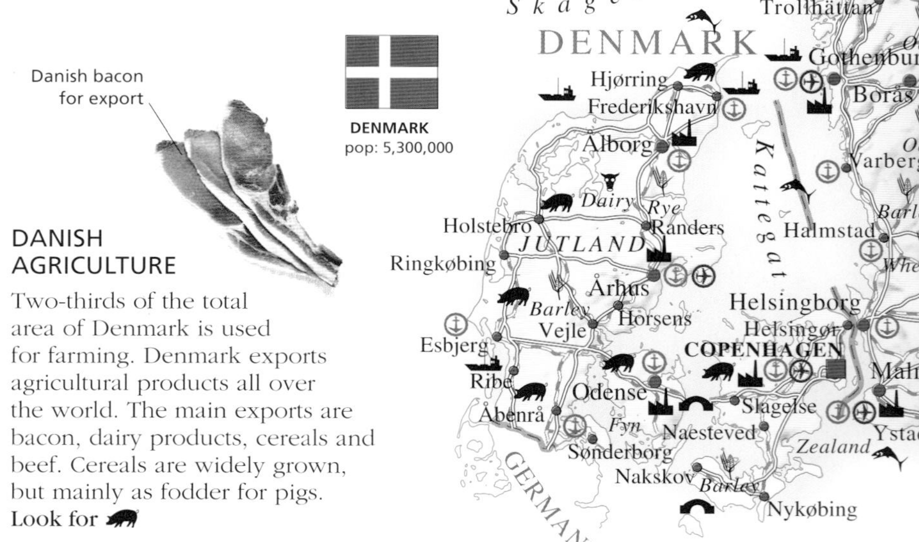
Uddevalla
Trollhättan
DENMARK
Gothenburg
Hjørring
Frederikshavn
Borås
Ålborg
Varberg
Kattegat
Dairy
Rye
Holstebro
Randers
Halmstad
JUTLAND
Ringkøbing
Århus
Barley
Vejle
Horsens
Helsingborg
Helsingør
Esbjerg
COPENHAGEN
Ribe
Odense
Malmö
Åbenrå
Slagelse
Fyn
Naestved
Ystad
Sønderborg
Zealand
Nakskov
Barley
Nykøbing
GERMANY

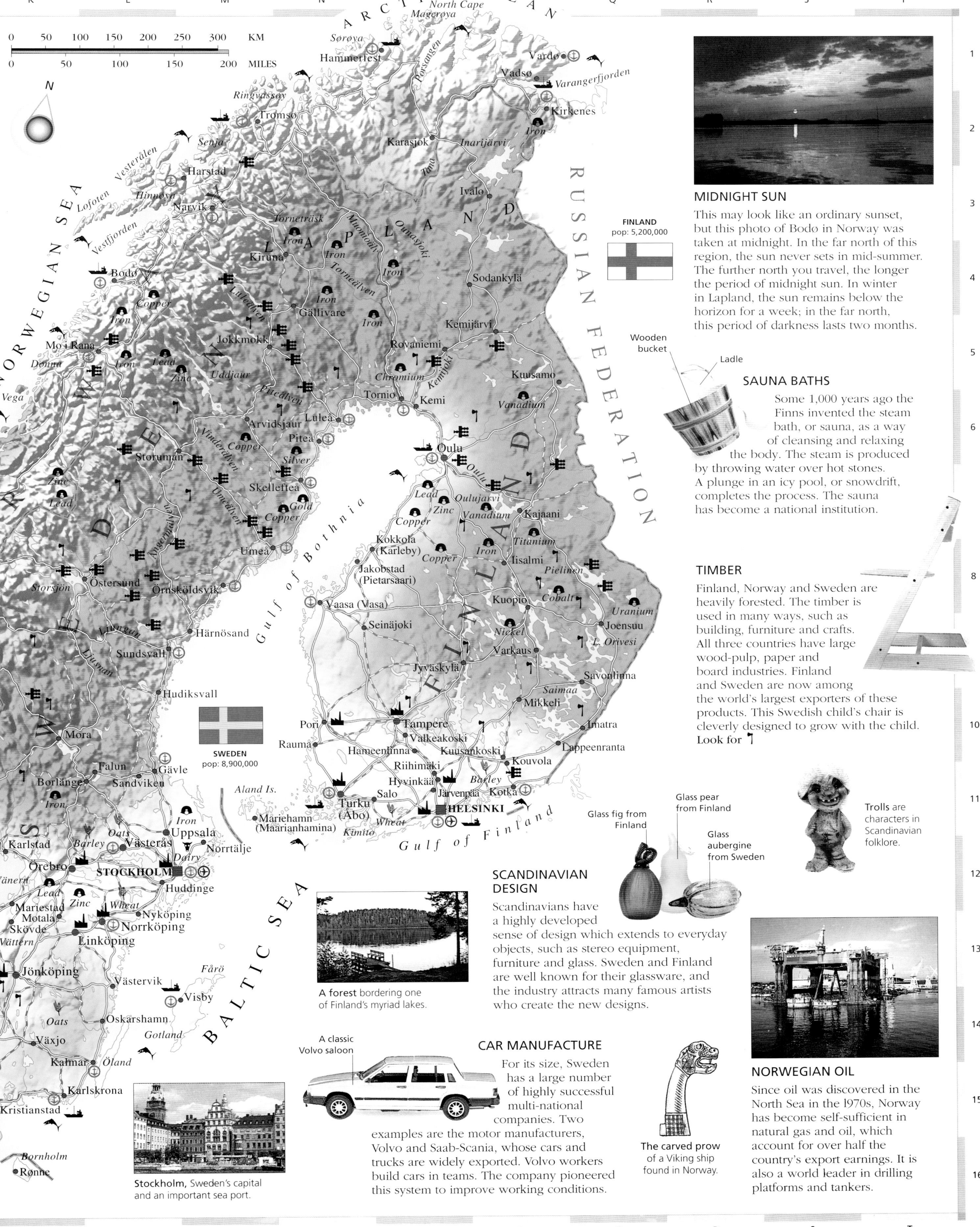
K L M N O P Q R S T
1 2 3 4 5 6 7 8 9 10 11 12 13 14 15 16
0 50 100 150 200 250 300 KM
0 50 100 150 200 MILES
N
ARCTIC OCEAN
North Cape
Magerøya
Sørøya
Hammerfest
Porsangen
Vardø
Vadsø
Varangerfjorden
Kirkenes
Iron
Ringvassøy
Tromsø
Senja
Karasjok
Inarijärvi
Tana
Harstad
Vesterålen
Lofoten
Hinnøya
Narvik
Ivalo
RUSSIAN FEDERATION
NORWEGIAN SEA
Vestfjorden
Torneträsk
Kiruna
LAPLAND
Muonioälv
Ounasjoki
Torneälven
Bodø
Copper
Gällivare
Sodankylä
Luleälven
Jokkmokk
Kemijärvi
Mo i Rana
Dønna
Lead
Zinc
Uddjaur
Rovaniemi
Chromium
Kemijoki
Kuusamo
Vega
Piteälven
Tornio
Kemi
Vanadium
Arvidsjaur
Luleå
Piteå
Silver
Oulu
Storuman
Vindelälven
Skellefteå
Gold
Umeälven
Oulujärvi
Kajaani
Gulf of Bothnia
Ångermanälven
Umeå
Kokkola (Karleby)
Jakobstad (Pietarsaari)
Titanium
Iisalmi
Pielinen
Östersund
Storsjön
Örnsköldsvik
Kuopio
Cobalt
Uranium
Vaasa (Vasa)
Seinäjoki
Nickel
Joensuu
L. Orivesi
Härnösand
Ljungan
Sundsvall
Ljusnan
Varkaus
Jyväskylä
Savonlinna
Saimaa
Mikkeli
FINLAND
Hudiksvall
Pori
Tampere
Imatra
Rauma
Valkeakoski
Hameenlinna
Kuusankoski
Lappeenranta
Riihimäki
Kouvola
Hyvinkää
Barley
Mora
Falun
Gävle
SWEDEN pop: 8,900,000
FINLAND pop: 5,200,000
Borlänge
Sandviken
Aland Is.
Turku (Åbo)
Salo
Järvenpää
Kotka
HELSINKI
Mariehamn (Maarianhamina)
Kimito
Wheat
Gulf of Finland
Oats
Uppsala
Karlstad
Västerås
Norrtälje
Dairy
Örebro
STOCKHOLM
Vänern
Huddinge
Mariestad
Motala
Skövde
Nyköping
Norrköping
Vättern
Linköping
BALTIC SEA
Jönköping
Västervik
Fårö
Visby
Oskarshamn
Gotland
Växjo
Kalmar
Öland
Karlskrona
Kristianstad
Bornholm
Rønne
Wooden bucket
Ladle
Glass fig from Finland
Glass pear from Finland
Glass aubergine from Sweden
A classic Volvo saloon

MIDNIGHT SUN

This may look like an ordinary sunset, but this photo of Bodø in Norway was taken at midnight. In the far north of this region, the sun never sets in mid-summer. The further north you travel, the longer the period of midnight sun. In winter in Lapland, the sun remains below the horizon for a week; in the far north, this period of darkness lasts two months.

SAUNA BATHS

Some 1,000 years ago the Finns invented the steam bath, or sauna, as a way of cleansing and relaxing the body. The steam is produced by throwing water over hot stones. A plunge in an icy pool, or snowdrift, completes the process. The sauna has become a national institution.

TIMBER

Finland, Norway and Sweden are heavily forested. The timber is used in many ways, such as building, furniture and crafts. All three countries have large wood-pulp, paper and board industries. Finland and Sweden are now among the world's largest exporters of these products. This Swedish child's chair is cleverly designed to grow with the child. Look for ⸢

Trolls are characters in Scandinavian folklore.

SCANDINAVIAN DESIGN

Scandinavians have a highly developed sense of design which extends to everyday objects, such as stereo equipment, furniture and glass. Sweden and Finland are well known for their glassware, and the industry attracts many famous artists who create the new designs.

A forest bordering one of Finland's myriad lakes.

CAR MANUFACTURE

For its size, Sweden has a large number of highly successful multi-national companies. Two examples are the motor manufacturers, Volvo and Saab-Scania, whose cars and trucks are widely exported. Volvo workers build cars in teams. The company pioneered this system to improve working conditions.

The carved prow of a Viking ship found in Norway.

NORWEGIAN OIL

Since oil was discovered in the North Sea in the 1970s, Norway has become self-sufficient in natural gas and oil, which account for over half the country's export earnings. It is also a world leader in drilling platforms and tankers.

Stockholm, Sweden's capital and an important sea port.

The British Isles

The British isles consist of two large islands – Britain and Ireland – surrounded by many smaller ones. They are divided into two countries: the United Kingdom (UK), and the Republic of Ireland. At the end of the 18th century, the UK became the first country in the world to undergo an industrial revolution. It became the world's leading manufacturing and trading nation, and built up an empire that covered more than a quarter of the world. The UK's traditional industries, such as coal mining, textiles and car manufacturing, have declined in recent years, but service industries such as banking and insurance have been extremely successful. The Republic of Ireland, which became independent from the UK in 1921, is still a mainly rural country and many Irish people make their living from farming. However, tourism and high-tech industries, such as computers and pharmaceuticals, are increasingly important. The UK and Ireland still have close trading links and many Irish people go to the UK to find work.

A deep inlet of water – or loch – in the north of Scotland.

Tartan scarf

Scottish shortbread

TARTAN TOURISM

Tourism is an important source of income for Scotland. People come to enjoy the beautiful highland scenery, and visit the ancient castles. For centuries, Scotland was dominated by struggles between rival families, known as clans. Today one of the most popular tourist souvenirs is tartan – textiles woven in the colours of the clans.

OIL

Rich reserves of both oil and natural gas were found under the North Sea in the 1960s. By the late 1970s, natural gas was being piped to most homes, factories and businesses in the UK.

Massive oil rigs were moored in the North Sea, and wells were dug by drilling into the ocean bed below the platforms. Oil rigs and onshore refineries brought employment to many areas, especially in eastern Scotland. But oil reserves are being steadily used up, and oil production is now in decline. **Look for**

Bright red letter boxes are a common sight on British streets.

FISHING

The waters of the north-east Atlantic are amongst the world's richest fishing grounds, well-stocked with mackerel, herring, cod, haddock and shellfish. The British Isles has many fishing ports, like this one in the north-east of England. But EU regulations designed to reduce catches and conserve fish stocks, are causing widespread discontent amongst fishermen. **Look for**

"THE TROUBLES"

British Protestants, who settled in Ireland in the 17th century, celebrate their history with parades and marching bands. In 1922, when the Protestants in the north refused to join the newly-independent Catholic south, Catholics were discriminated against and violence erupted. In the 1960s British troops were sent to police the province. The peace process of the 1990s was disrupted by sporadic violence.

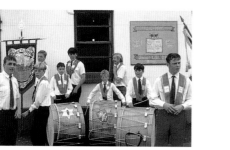

Irish butter

AGRICULTURE AND INDUSTRY

Farming has always been Ireland's principal source of income. Dairy products, beef and potatoes are still important, but recently, the number of high-tech industries has increased.

Outer Hebrides
Shetland Islands
Lerwick
Orkney Islands
Stromness
Kirkwall
C. Wrath
Isle of Lewis
Stornoway
Beef
Thurso
Loch Shin
The Minch
Ullapool
Harris
North Uist
The Little Minch
South Uist
Isle of Skye
Barra
Canna
Rhum
Eigg
Muck
Mallaig
Coll
Tiree
Mull
Fort William
Oats
Inverness
Moray Firth
Elgin
Spey
Loch Ness
Barley
Fraserburgh
Peterhead
Aberdeen
Dee
GRAMPIAN MTS.
SCOTLAND
Oban
Perth
Dundee
Colonsay
Jura
Islay
Loch Lomond
Forth
Stirling
Greenock
Grangemouth
Firth of Forth
Glasgow
Edinburgh
Kintyre
Isle of Arran
Clyde
Dairy
Tweed
Ayr
SOUTHERN UPLANDS
Lough Foyle
ATLANTIC OCEAN
NORTH SEA

Education
The Guardian
THE TIMES
20p
Daily Mirror
£50,000
SCANDAL AT THE COMMONS

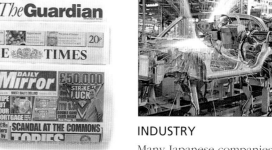

MEDIA CENTRE

The British media is highly influential around the English-speaking world. There are several high-quality national newspapers, including *The Times, The Guardian,* and *The Observer*. The state-owned British Broadcasting Corporation (BBC) has an international reputation, and sells its television programmes all over the world. London is a major centre of publishing, advertising and video production.

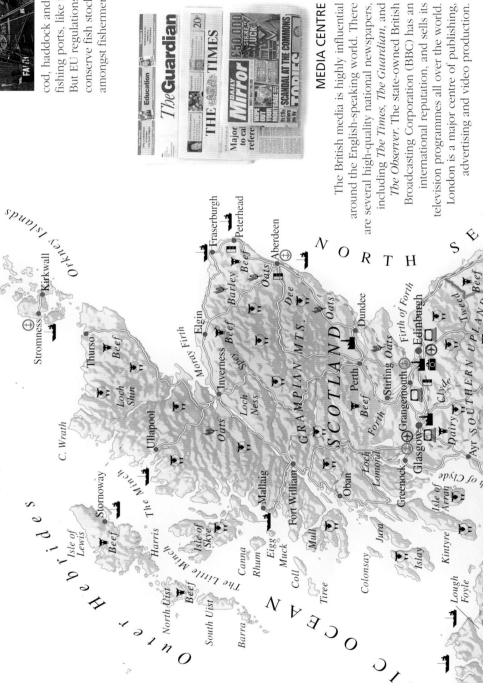

INDUSTRY

Many Japanese companies, car and electronics manufacturers in particular, are now based in the UK, attracted by a skilled labour force and access to European markets. Britain's traditional industries, such as textiles, steel and pottery have been joined by newer, high-tech industries. **Look for**

UNITED KINGDOM
pop: 58,200,000
REPUBLIC OF IRELAND
pop: 3,600,000
REPUBLIC OF IRELAND
IRISH SEA
NORTH SEA
ENGLISH CHANNEL
ENGLAND
WALES
PENNINES
CAMBRIAN MTS.
LAKE DISTRICT
BRECON BEACONS
EXMOOR
DARTMOOR
CORNWALL
EAST ANGLIA
WICKLOW MTS.
ISLE OF MAN (to UK)
DOUGLAS
Donegal Bay
Galway Bay
Dingle Bay
Bantry Bay
St George's Channel
Cardigan Bay
Bristol Channel
Morecambe Bay
Solway Firth
Lyme Bay
Strait of Dover
The Wash
Humber
Lough Neagh
Lower Lough Erne
Lough Corrib
Lough Ree
Lough Derg
Shannon
Liffey
Barrow
Blackwater
Severn
Thames
Ouse
Tees
The Fens
Anglesey
Holy I.
Lundy
Isles of Scilly
Land's End
Isle of Wight
Channel Tunnel
Stranraer
Bangor
Belfast
Newry
Dundalk
Sligo
Galway
Athlone
DUBLIN
Dún Laoghaire
Shannon
Limerick
Tralee
Killarney
Waterford
Wexford
Cork
Dumfries
Carlisle
Whitehaven
Newcastle upon Tyne
Sunderland
Middlesbrough
Lancaster
Blackpool
Preston
Bolton
Liverpool
Birkenhead
Manchester
Bradford
Leeds
Huddersfield
York
Sheffield
Kingston upon Hull
Grimsby
Lincoln
Holyhead
Caernarfon
Chester
Stoke-on-Trent
Derby
Nottingham
Shrewsbury
Aberystwyth
Wolverhampton
Birmingham
Leicester
Coventry
Peterborough
King's Lynn
Norwich
Great Yarmouth
Fishguard
Milford Haven
Swansea
Merthyr Tydfil
Newport
Cardiff
Worcester
Stratford-upon-Avon
Northampton
Cambridge
Ipswich
Felixstowe
Gloucester
Luton
Colchester
Oxford
Swindon
Watford
Bristol
Bath
LONDON
Reading
Heathrow
Southend-on-Sea
Barnstaple
Taunton
Stonehenge
Salisbury
Yeovil
Crawley
Canterbury
Southampton
Dover
Exeter
Bournemouth
Newport
Portsmouth
Brighton
Hastings
Plymouth
Falmouth
Penzance
Beef
Dairy
Oats
Barley
Wheat
Channel Is.
ST. PETER PORT
GUERNSEY (to UK)
JERSEY (to UK)
ST. HELIER
N
0 50 100 150 KM
0 25 50 75 MILES
Big Ben
The Houses of Parliament, London
Cricket ball
Soccer ball
Rugby ball
Mitre

LONDON

The Romans founded the town they called Londinium on the River Thames in AD 43. The UK's capital is now a huge, sprawling city with seven million inhabitants. London is the country's centre of finance, politics, law, and culture, and contains many famous historical buildings, shops, museums and theatres.

MULTICULTURAL BRITAIN

Since the 1960s, the UK has become an increasingly multicultural society. Large numbers of immigrants have come to the UK from former colonies in Africa, the Caribbean and Asia and have greatly enriched British culture with their own traditions.

English beers are made from barley, malt and hops.

Dublin's fine O'Connell bridge over the R. Liffey.

The rocky coast of Cornwall in southwest England.

Tea, served with milk, is Britain's national drink.

MAP FEATURES

High-tech industry: Companies making scientific instruments, electronics and computers are based in southern England, Scotland and Ireland. **Look for**

Tourism: Millions of visitors a year come to the UK to see palaces, castles, ancient monuments, cathedrals and museums. **Look for**

Tunnel: The Channel Tunnel, linking England and France, is 50 km (31 miles) long. Passenger and freight trains use the tunnel. **Look for**

Airport: Heathrow, 20 km (12 miles) from London, is the world's busiest international airport. It handles 60 million passengers a year. **Look for**

Cattle | Coal
Sheep | Industrial centre
Cereals | Oil refining
Market gardening | Aerospace industry
Fishing port | Vehicle manufacturing

SPORT

Many sports which are now played all over the world originated in the UK. Rugby, cricket and golf were all British inventions, while the rules of modern soccer were established on the sports fields of English schools.

FARMING

About three-quarters of the land in the UK is used for farming. The crops vary from region to region and reflect the country's varied climate and soils. Barley, wheat, vegetables and sugar beet are the main crops in the east of the country, while beef and dairy farming is a speciality in the west.

HIGH FINANCE

The skyscrapers and office blocks that surround St. Paul's Cathedral in the City of London are home to one of the world's biggest financial centres. City companies specialize in banking and insurance, and lead the world in foreign currency deals. The City covers only a small area, but every day it is filled with more than half a million office workers.

Spain and Portugal

Spain and Portugal are located on the Iberian Peninsula, which is cut off from the rest of Europe by the Pyrenees. This isolation, combined with the region's closeness to Africa and the Atlantic Ocean, has shaped the history of the two countries. The Moors, an Islamic people from North Africa, occupied the peninsula in the 8th century AD, leaving an Islamic legacy that is still evident today. In 1492 the Moors were finally expelled from Catholic Spain. The oceangoing Spanish and Portuguese took the lead in exploring and colonizing the New World, and both nations acquired substantial overseas empires. During this era, Portugal was ruled by Spain from about 1580 to 1640. Eventually, both nations lost most of their colonies, and their once-great wealth and power declined. Spain was torn apart by a vicious civil war from 1936-39, and right-wing dictators ruled both Spain and Portugal for much of the 20th century. In the 1970s, both countries emerged as modern democracies, and have since experienced rapid economic growth, benefiting from their membership of the European Union. Today, their economies are dominated by tourism and agriculture, although Spanish industry is expanding rapidly.

PORTUGAL
pop: 9,800,000

Portugal exports large numbers of oysters caught in the Atlantic.

The Cordillera Cantábrica in northwestern Spain.

ATLANTIC OCEAN
Ferrol
A Coruña
Eucalyptus
Avilés
Gijón
Oviedo
GALICIA
Lugo
Santiago
Iron
CORDILLERA CANTÁBRICA
Tin
León
Pontevedra
Ourense
Vigo
Tungsten
Minho

ORANGES

Oranges were introduced to Spain by the Moors in about the 9th century AD. They are grown along the Mediterranean coast and are an important export. The best Spanish oranges come from Valencia. Oranges from Seville are used for making fine marmalade. **Look for**

GROWING CORKS

Spain and Portugal produce two-thirds of the world's cork. It is made from the outer bark of these evergreen oak trees. The bark is stripped off, seasoned, flattened, then laid out in sheets.

MAP FEATURES

Forest products: Spain and Portugal are Europe's only source of eucalyptus, which is grown for its gum, resin, oil and wood. **Look for**

Fishing: Spanish fishing fleets are amongst the largest in Europe, concentrated around the northwest Atlantic coast. **Look for**

Vehicle manufacture: Spain ranks sixth in world car exports, specializing in small cars. **Look for**

Sheep
Fishing ports
Citrus fruit
Mining
Wine
Industrial centre
Vegetable oil
Tourism

Sherry
Port

FORTIFIED WINES

This region is famous for its fortified wines. They are made by adding extra alcohol to the wine during the fermentation process. Sherry is named after Jeréz de la Frontera, while port comes from Oporto. **Look for**

LISBON

Portugal's great navigators and explorers set sail from Lisbon, on the mouth of the River Tagus. The city, which grew rich on global trade, was completely rebuilt after an earthquake destroyed two thirds of it in 1755.

A castle is visible on the wooded hills north of Lisbon.

Spain is one of the world's leading olive producers.

FISH DISHES

Paella is a classic Spanish dish from the Valencia region, where rice is grown. It consists of a variety of meat, fish, fresh vegetables and saffron-flavoured rice, simmered in a stock. Spaniards eat a lot of fish, and fish stew is another popular dish. Spain is also famous for its cured meats, especially ham, or *jamón serrano.*

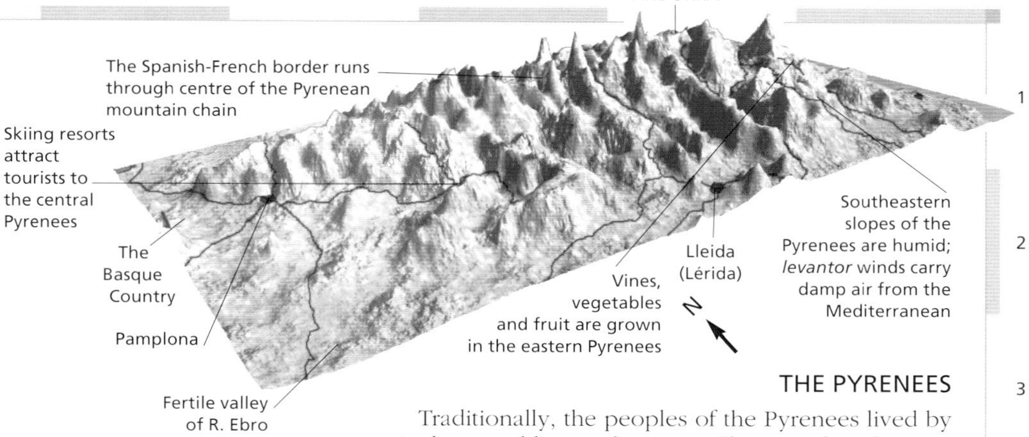

The Spanish-French border runs through centre of the Pyrenean mountain chain

Skiing resorts attract tourists to the central Pyrenees

The Basque Country

Pamplona

Fertile valley of R. Ebro

Vines, vegetables and fruit are grown in the eastern Pyrenees

Lleida (Lérida)

Southeastern slopes of the Pyrenees are humid; *levantor* winds carry damp air from the Mediterranean

THE PYRENEES

Traditionally, the peoples of the Pyrenees lived by agriculture and livestock-raising. Sheep and cattle were moved seasonally up and down the mountains, grazing the high snow-free pastures in summer. Fast-flowing rivers have great potential for hydro-electric power and – in the 19th century – steel and paper mills were built in the Pyrenean foothills. Today, the region is in decline, as young people abandon traditional mountain communities for cities. The area's abundant natural beauty is, however, attracting increasing numbers of tourists.

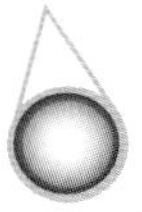

Many tourists visit the beautiful Balearic Islands.

TOURISM

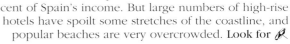

Fifty million visitors a year visit Spain's Mediterranean coast alone, and tourism accounts for 10 per cent of Spain's income. But large numbers of high-rise hotels have spoilt some stretches of the coastline, and popular beaches are very overcrowded. **Look for**

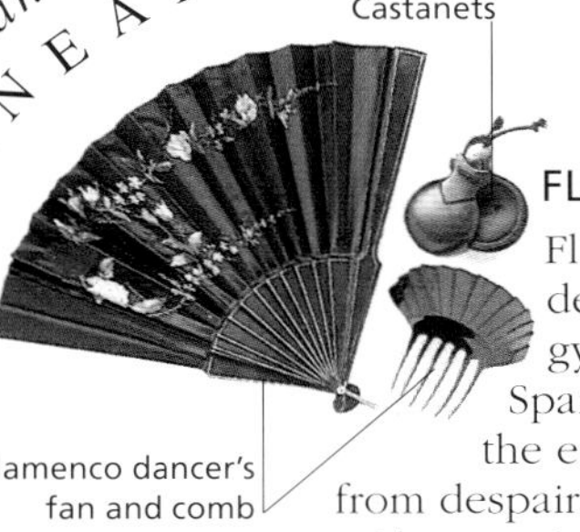

Castanets

FLAMENCO

Flamenco music and dance, developed by the Andalusian gypsies, are the major folk arts of Spain. Flamenco songs deal with the entire range of human emotion, from despair to ecstasy, and are performed with a passionate intensity. Dancers dress in traditional costume and accompany themselves on castanets and guitars.

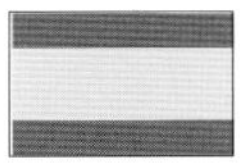

Flamenco dancer's fan and comb

SPAIN
pop: 39,800,000

THE ALHAMBRA

The Alhambra, at Granada in southern Spain, is a Moorish palace and fortress built during the 13th-14th centuries. It was the Moors' last stronghold in Spain. It is a beautiful example of Moorish architecture, famous for its delicately carved stone, brilliantly patterned mosaics and tiles, and alabaster fountains.

Gibraltar has been a British colony since the 18th century.

BULLFIGHTING

In Spain, bullfighting is a national sport. During a bullfight, brightly coloured capes are fluttered to tempt the bull to charge. When it charges, the matador sticks long, pointed barbs into the bull's shoulders. Once it is exhausted, the matador uses his sword to kill the bull, exposing himself to mortal danger.

CATHOLICISM

Like the Portuguese, the Spanish blend Roman Catholicism with customs and superstitions dating back to pre-Christian times. Their *fiestas* combine religious ceremonies with wine and dancing.

A B C D E F G H I J

FRANCE

FOR CENTURIES FRANCE has played a central role in European civilization. Reminders of its long history can be found throughout the land; prehistoric cave-dwellings, Roman amphitheatres, medieval cathedrals, castles, and the 17th- and 18th-century palaces of the powerful French monarchs. The French Revolution of 1789 swept away the monarchy and changed the face of France forever. The country survived the Napoleonic wars and occupation during World Wars I and II, and now has a thriving economy based on farming and industry. It is a land of varied scenery and strong regional traditions, the only country which belongs to both northern and southern Europe. Farming is still important, but many people have moved from the country to the cities. France still administers a number of overseas territories, all that remain of its once widespread empire. Today, France's population includes immigrants from its former colonies, especially Muslims from North Africa. France is one of the most enthusiastic members of the European Union.

PARIS

Paris, the capital of France, is the largest and most important city in the country. It lies on both banks of the River Seine. One of the world's great cities, Paris contains magnificent buildings, art treasures and elegant shops. The wrought-iron Eiffel Tower looms above the city, the symbol of Paris.

A cyclist in the *Tour de France*, the world's most famous cycle race.

FRANCE
pop: 58,700,000

AGRICULTURE

France is a mainly rural country producing a wide range of farm products. Some farms still use traditional methods but modern technology has transformed regions like the Paris Basin, where cereals are grown on a large scale. **Look for**

THE AIRBUS

Developing new aircraft is so costly that sometimes several countries form a company together to share the costs. One example is Airbus Industrie: the main factory is at Toulouse, but costs are shared by France, Germany, the UK and Spain. With successful aircraft already flying, Airbus Industrie is planning a jumbo jet. **Look for**

MAP FEATURES

Market gardening: In the northwest the mild climate and sheltered conditions are ideal for growing early vegetables, called primeurs. **Look for**

Nuclear power: Lacking its own energy sources, France has developed its nuclear power industry. It now produces 70% of its electricity. **Look for**

Tourism: In the underdeveloped Mediterranean region tourism has been encouraged by the construction of attractive holiday resorts. **Look for**

Rail routes: France has Europe's largest rail network. Inter-city trains (TGVs), travel at speeds of up to 300 km (186 miles) per hour. **Look for**

	Cheese		Coal
	Cereals		Industrial centre
	Sugar beet		Aerospace industry
	Wine		Vehicle manufacturing
	Mining		Skiing

CHATEAUS

France has many beautiful historic buildings. Along the banks of the River Loire and its tributaries are royal palaces, or chateaus, built by the royalty of France from the 15th-17th centuries. Chambord, originally a hunting lodge, has 440 rooms and 85 staircases. Fairytale palaces like these attract thousands of visitors each year.

Fields of sunflowers can be seen in many areas of France.

Head of garlic
Snail
Clove of garlic

Snails, served with butter and garlic, are a great French delicacy.

Camembert

LE RUSTIQUE

Brie

CHEESE

France is famous for its cheese. Over 300 different varieties are made. Many, like Camembert, Roquefort and Brie, are world-famous and copied in many other countries. Each region has its traditional way of making and packaging its cheeses. Goat and sheep's milk is used as well as cow's. **Look for**

The principality of Andorra is situated in the Pyrenees.

ANDORRA
pop: 65,000

ENGLISH CHANNEL
Cherbourg
le Havre
Channel Islands (to UK)
Caen
St-Lô
Wheat
NORMANDY (NORMANDIE)
Camembert
Iron
St-Malo
Île d'Ouessant
Brest
St-Brieuc
Wheat
BRITTANY (BRETAGNE)
Barley
Oats
Wheat
Oats
Alençon
Rennes
Quimper
Barley
Laval
le Mans
Lorient
Iron
Vannes
Barley
Angers
Belle Île
St-Nazaire
Nantes
Loire
Tours
FRANCE
Wheat
la Roche-sur-Yon
les Sables-d'Olonne
Wheat
Poitiers
ATLANTIC OCEAN
la Rochelle
Charente
Wheat
Saintes
Angoulême
Barley
Bordeaux
Dordogne
Garonne
Arcachon
TGV
Mont-de-Marsan
Maize
Bayonne
Maize
Pau
Maize
Tarbes
PYRENEES

A B C D E F G H I J

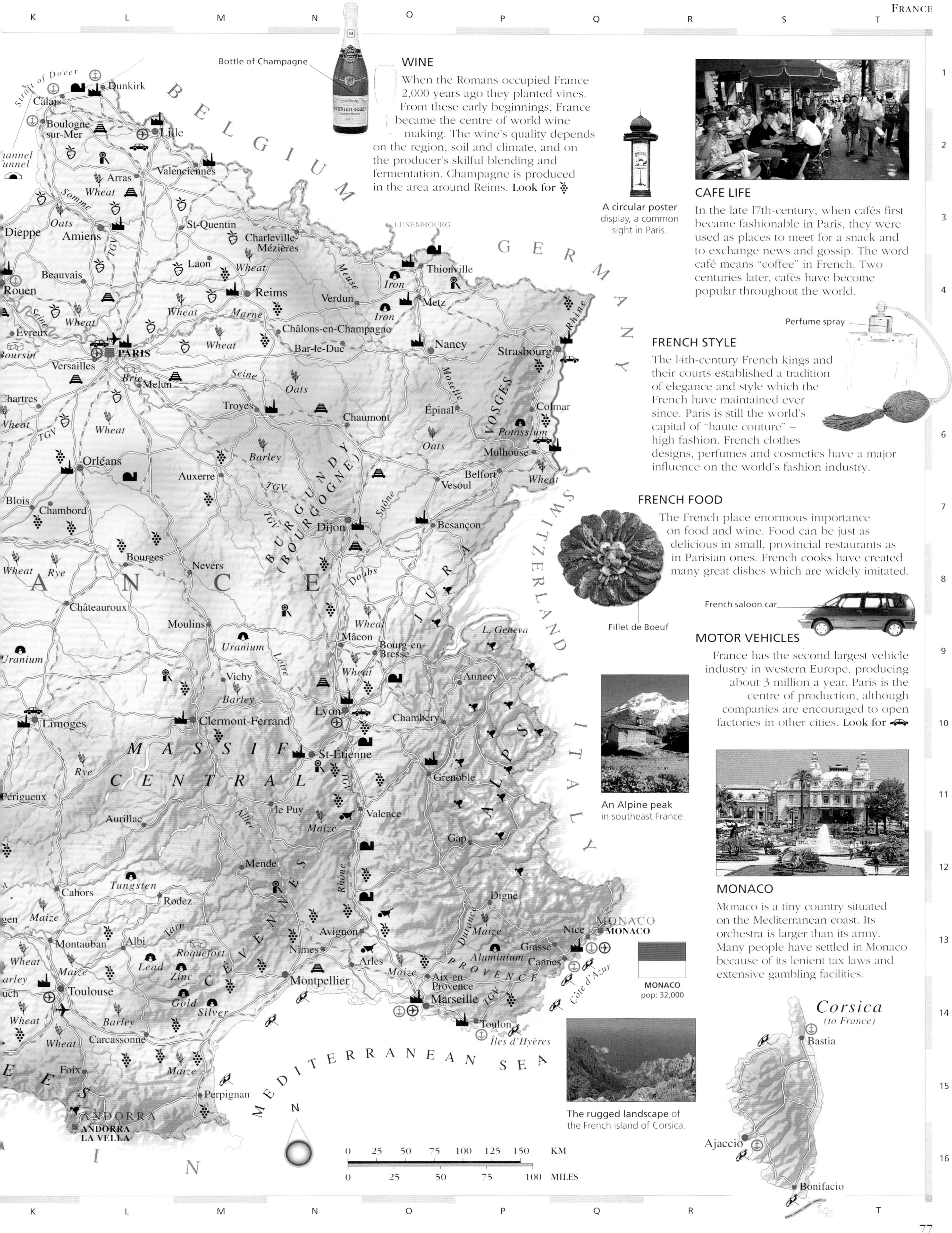
BELGIUM
GERMANY
LUXEMBOURG
SWITZERLAND
ITALY
ANDORRA
ANDORRA LA VELLA
MONACO
FRANCE
SPAIN
MEDITERRANEAN SEA
Strait of Dover
Channel Tunnel
Dunkirk
Calais
Boulogne-sur-Mer
Lille
Valenciennes
Arras
Somme
Dieppe
Amiens
St-Quentin
Charleville-Mézières
Laon
Beauvais
Rouen
Reims
Verdun
Thionville
Metz
Seine
Marne
Évreux
Châlons-en-Champagne
Nancy
Strasbourg
Rhine
Bar-le-Duc
PARIS
Versailles
Melun
Brie
Boursin
Chartres
Troyes
Chaumont
Moselle
Épinal
VOSGES
Colmar
Mulhouse
Belfort
Vesoul
Orléans
Auxerre
BURGUNDY (BOURGOGNE)
Saône
Blois
Chambord
Dijon
Besançon
Bourges
Nevers
Doubs
JURA
Châteauroux
Moulins
Mâcon
Bourg-en-Bresse
L. Geneva
Loire
Vichy
Annecy
Limoges
Clermont-Ferrand
Lyon
Chambéry
MASSIF CENTRAL
St-Étienne
Grenoble
ALPS
Périgueux
le Puy
Valence
Aurillac
Allier
Gap
Mende
Rhône
CÉVENNES
Cahors
Rodez
Digne
Durance
Tarn
Avignon
Nice
Montauban
Albi
Roquefort
Nîmes
Grasse
Cannes
Arles
PROVENCE
Côte d'Azur
Toulouse
Montpellier
Aix-en-Provence
Marseille
Toulon
Îles d'Hyères
Carcassonne
Foix
Perpignan
Corsica (to France)
Bastia
Ajaccio
Bonifacio
0 25 50 75 100 125 150 KM
0 25 50 75 100 MILES

Bottle of Champagne

WINE

When the Romans occupied France 2,000 years ago they planted vines. From these early beginnings, France became the centre of world wine making. The wine's quality depends on the region, soil and climate, and on the producer's skilful blending and fermentation. Champagne is produced in the area around Reims. **Look for**

A circular poster display, a common sight in Paris.

CAFE LIFE

In the late 17th-century, when cafés first became fashionable in Paris, they were used as places to meet for a snack and to exchange news and gossip. The word café means "coffee" in French. Two centuries later, cafés have become popular throughout the world.

Perfume spray

FRENCH STYLE

The 14th-century French kings and their courts established a tradition of elegance and style which the French have maintained ever since. Paris is still the world's capital of "haute couture" – high fashion. French clothes designs, perfumes and cosmetics have a major influence on the world's fashion industry.

FRENCH FOOD

The French place enormous importance on food and wine. Food can be just as delicious in small, provincial restaurants as in Parisian ones. French cooks have created many great dishes which are widely imitated.

Fillet de Boeuf

French saloon car

MOTOR VEHICLES

France has the second largest vehicle industry in western Europe, producing about 3 million a year. Paris is the centre of production, although companies are encouraged to open factories in other cities. **Look for**

An Alpine peak in southeast France.

MONACO

Monaco is a tiny country situated on the Mediterranean coast. Its orchestra is larger than its army. Many people have settled in Monaco because of its lenient tax laws and extensive gambling facilities.

MONACO
pop: 32,000

The rugged landscape of the French island of Corsica.

THE LOW COUNTRIES

BELGIUM, THE NETHERLANDS and Luxembourg are the most densely populated countries in Europe. They are known as the "Low Countries" because much of the land is flat and low-lying. In the Netherlands, much of the land lies below sea level, and has been reclaimed from the sea over the centuries by ingenious technology. The marshy, drained soils are extremely fertile. All three countries enjoy high living standards, with well-developed industries and excellent rail, road and waterway communications with the rest of Europe. During the course of their history, the Low Countries have often been the battleground between warring nations, and both Belgium and Luxembourg only achieved independence in the 19th century. Belgium is still divided by language – Dutch is spoken in the north, while the Walloons in the south speak French. The northern Netherlands are mainly Protestant; the rest of the region is basically Roman Catholic. Today, the Low Countries are unswerving supporters of the European Union. The cities of Brussels, The Hague and Luxembourg are all headquarters of important European institutions.

FLOWERS

Tulip

The Netherlands are Europe's largest producers of flowers, and spectacular fields of spring flowers in full bloom are a major tourist attraction. Cut flowers are flown daily from the Netherlands to cities all over the world. Cultivation of bulbs such as crocuses, hyacinths, daffodils and tulips is a speciality. They have been grown here since about 1600, when they were introduced from Turkey and the Middle East. **Look for**

DELTA PROJECT

Much of the Netherlands lies below sea level, and is at risk from flooding. Over the centuries, barriers, called dykes, have been built to keep the sea out and water has been drained and pumped into canals. The Delta Project, completed in 1986, used dykes to close off the Rhine, Maas and Scheldt estuaries from the North Sea, creating freshwater lakes. The region had long been exposed to the destructive power of the North Sea; in 1953 floods killed 1,835.

Rhine
Rotterdam
Maas
Bergen op Zoom
Freshwater lakes created by dams
Scheldt
NORTH SEA
Total length of dams: 30 km (18.5 miles)
Roads across dykes make isolated areas more accessible
Oosterschelde Dam is 2.8 km (1.75 miles) long. Adjustable gates allow tidal seawater to ebb and flow
Vlissingen
Middelburg

IMMIGRATION

Beef Rendang
Peanuts
Satay (barbecued meat)
Egg-fried rice
Prawns and garlic
Salad in peanut sauce
Pickled vegetables

Immigrants from theNetherlands' former colonies of Surinam, the Antilles and Indonesia have had a strong impact on Dutch life and culture. Indonesian restaurants are a common sight in Dutch cities, and *rijstafel* (rice surrounded by side dishes of egg, vegetables, meat and fish) is now a national dish.

CITY OF CANALS

The Dutch capital, Amsterdam, is a city of islands, built on swampy land. It is criss-crossed by 160 canals. Many of the city's finest gabled houses date from the 16th-18th centuries, when merchants grew rich from trade and exploration. Amsterdam is not only the country's historic centre, it is also its second-largest port.

DELFT TILE

Delft pottery has been made in the Netherlands since the 17th century. The technique of glazing pottery with tin, used in Delft, came to the Netherlands from the Middle East via Spain and Italy. This Delft tile is decorated with a windmill, a familiar sight in the Netherlands. There are about 1,000 windmills still standing today, dating mainly from the 18th and 19th centuries.

ROTTERDAM

Rotterdam is one of the world's largest ports, lying within a massive built-up and industrialized area called Randstad Holland. Rotterdam is situated near the mouth of the Rhine, which is an important trade route. Imported oil is refined locally; the port also handles minerals, grain, timber and coal.

NETHERLANDS
pop: 15,700,000

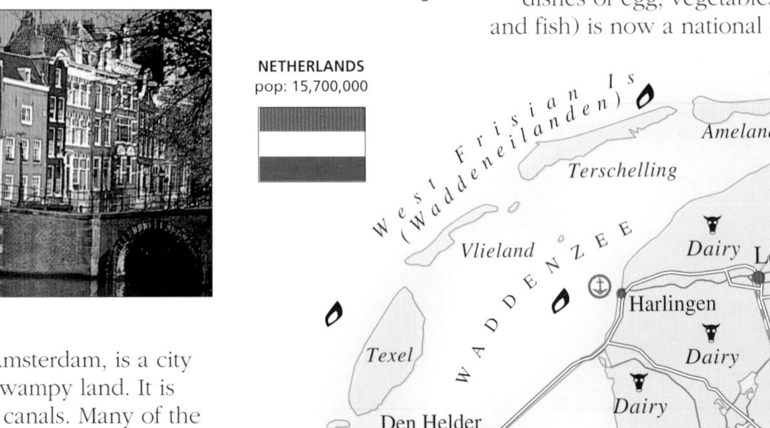
West Frisian Is (Waddeneilanden)
Schiermonnikoog
Ameland
Terschelling
Vlieland
Texel
WADDENZEE
IJSSELMEER
Flevoland
IJssel
NETHERLANDS
GERMANY
SEA
Delfzijl
Groningen
Winschoten
Leeuwarden
Harlingen
Drachten
Heerenveen
Assen
Emmen
Hoogeveen
Meppel
Den Helder
Alkmaar
Hoorn
Purmerend
Lelystad
Zwolle
Velsen-Noord
IJmuiden
Zaanstad
Haarlem
AMSTERDAM
Amstelveen
Harderwijk
Almelo
Hilversum
Apeldoorn
Deventer
Hengelo
Enschede
Leiden
Amersfoort
Zutphen
Wheat
Dairy
Beef

The rind of Dutch Edam cheese is coloured with anatto dye.

Both Belgium and the Netherlands are major beer exporters.

NORTH SEA
NETHERLANDS
BELGIUM
LUXEMBOURG
GERMANY
FRANCE
ARDENNES
Hoek van Holland
Europoort
Rotterdam
Gouda
Dordrecht
Nijmegen
Oss
's-Hertogenbosch
Waalwijk
Breda
Tilburg
Roosendaal
Bergen op Zoom
Middelburg
Vlissingen
Terneuzen
Zeebrugge
Ostend (Oostende)
Bruges (Brugge)
Veurne
Torhout
Roeselare
Ieper
Kortrijk
Mouscron
Ghent (Gent)
Sint-Niklaas
Aalst
Antwerp (Antwerpen)
Mechelen
Turnhout
Baarle-Hertog (part of Belgium)
Eindhoven
Helmond
Weert
Venlo
Roermond
Heerlen
Maastricht
Genk
Hasselt
Leuven
BRUSSELS (BRUSSEL/BRUXELLES)
Tienen
Ronse
Ath
Tournai
Nivelles
Soignies
La Louvière
Mons
Gosselies
Charleroi
Namur
Huy
Seraing
Liège
Herstal
Verviers
Eupen
Malmédy
Sankt-Vith
Dinant
Philippeville
Marche-en-Famenne
Bastogne
Neufchâteau
Arlon
Vianden
Diekirch
LUXEMBOURG
Esch-sur-Alzette
Rhine (Rijn)
Waal
Maas
Lek
Oosterschelde
Westerschelde
Scheldt
Albert Canal
Meuse
Sambre
Ourthe
Lesse
Moselle
IJzer
Overflakkee
Delta Project
Wheat
Barley
Rye
Oats
Dairy
Beef
N
0 25 50 75 KM
0 10 20 30 40 MILES

DIAMONDS

Diamonds from Africa and Australia are cut, polished and sold in the cities of Antwerp and Amsterdam. Most of the diamonds are used in industry for sawing, drilling and grinding.

The medieval city of Bruges is famous for its canals and fine houses.

BELGIUM
pop: 10,200,000

Flax, which is used to make linen, is grown on the flat plains of northern Belgium.

MAP FEATURES

Gas: Offshore reserves in the North Sea are the fifth largest in the world. Gas is the main domestic fuel in the Netherlands. **Look for**

Dams: The Netherlands' Delta Project is the world's largest water control project. Five dams prevent flooding and provide fresh water. **Look for**

Shipping canals: Most of Belgium's main inland industrial centres are linked with the North Sea ports and Antwerp by canals. **Look for**

Cattle — Market gardening — Cereals — Flowers — Sugar beet — Industrial centre

Belgium, especially Brussels, is famous for its rich chocolates.

The EU flag is a symbol of unity in Europe

COMMUNITY CAPITAL

The EU (European Union) was set up in 1957 to encourage free trade between member nations and administer shared economic, social and legal policies. There are 15 member nations. Brussels with Strasbourg, is the headquarters of the European Parliament and Luxembourg is the headquarters of the Court of Justice and Investment Bank.

The medieval town hall at Leuven in Belgium.

DAIRY PRODUCTS

More than one-third of Dutch farmland is used for dairy production. Dutch black and white Friesian cattle, which graze on the low-lying fertile land, are one of the finest dairy breeds in the world. The Netherlands exports more cheese than any other country. Cheese was originally made on a small scale in farmhouses, but today cheese-making is highly mechanized. **Look for**

NETHERLANDS' TWO CAPITALS
AMSTERDAM – capital
THE HAGUE – seat of government

HIGH TECHNOLOGY

All three countries have well-established electronics industries, making everything from razors to X-ray machines. Their position at the heart of Europe, good transport links, easy access to European markets and raw materials, as well as large pools of skilled labour, have all helped to make high technology industry a success.

LUXEMBOURG
pop: 422,000

LUXEMBOURG BANKING

Luxembourg is a centre of international banking and finance. It is the headquarters of the European Investment Bank, and more than 100 major banks are based there. Financial services are fast becoming more important than Luxembourg's traditional steel-manufacturing industries.

The picturesque fortress of Vianden overlooking the River Our in Luxembourg.

GERMANY

SITUATED IN THE CENTRE OF EUROPE, Germany is now the continent's leading economic power. In the past it has been an area of great conflict; it was not until 1871 that a patchwork of independent states, who had fought bitterly for centuries, were united under Prussian leadership to form Germany. Last century Germany was defeated in two world wars. By 1945 the economy was shattered and the country divided between a Soviet-dominated communist East and a democratic West. The post-war years saw an amazing recovery in West Germany's economy. Natural advantages, such as a central position in Europe, large reserves of coal and iron, along with the construction of an efficient transport system and the determination to succeed, have all helped to create a dynamic economy. The East, on the other hand, lagged behind. In 1989, the Soviet Union began to disintegrate, and communism collapsed throughout Eastern Europe. The two halves of Germany were reunified in 1990, but problems soon became apparent. West Germans resented the huge amounts of money invested in the East to bring it up to their standards. East Germans became impatient with the slow pace of change. These resentments have led to violence against refugees, immigrants and "guest-workers", many of whom have lived in Germany for most of their lives.

CARS

Germany is Europe's largest vehicle producer, specializing in high-quality cars. American and Japanese car companies are based here, attracted by the skilled workforce. **Look for**

AGRICULTURE

Germany produces all its own food, and is one of the world's main growers of sugar beet, barley and rye. Oats, rye and barley thrive in the mild, wet north, while wheat is grown in the warmer south. **Look for**

Green pastures and woodland on the flat, Baltic coast.

This decorated mug is called a *stein*, and is used for beer.

Brandenburg Gate

BERLIN

At the end of World War II, Germany's capital city, Berlin, was divided between the four victorious Allies. In 1961 the Berlin Wall was built to separate the Russian sector from the other three. In 1989 the wall came down: thousands of East Germans came through this Gate into the west.

DRESDEN

Once Dresden was a beautiful old city, with many 18th-century buildings. But in World War II it was devastated by bombing. After extensive reconstruction, the city's historic buildings have now been restored to their former state.

Salami

Peppered salami

SAUSAGES

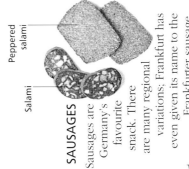

Sausages are Germany's favourite snack. There are many regional variations; Frankfurt has even given its name to the Frankfurter sausage. Germany also has over 200 varieties of bread.

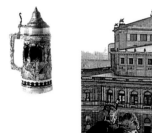

A windmill in the fertile farmland of the northeast.

Many German towns have half-timbered buildings dating back to the Middle Ages.

BELGIUM
LUXEMBOURG
FRANCE
SWITZERLAND
AUSTRIA
CZECH REPUBLIC
THURINGIA
BAVARIA (BAYERN)
Thuringian Forest
ORE MTS. (ERZGEBIRGE)
FRÄNKISCHE ALB
SCHWÄBISCHE ALB
Black Forest (Schwarzwald)
Bohemian Forest
BAVARIAN ALPS
Mönchengladbach
Düsseldorf
Wuppertal
Remscheid
Leverkusen
Bergisch Gladbach
Cologne (Köln)
Aachen
Bonn
Siegen
Giessen
Koblenz
Eltz
Rheinfels
Kaub
Wiesbaden
Mainz
Frankfurt am Main
Offenbach
Darmstadt
Fulda
Trier
Kaiserslautern
Saarbrücken
Mannheim
Heidelberg
Heilbronn
Karlsruhe
Pforzheim
Stuttgart
Tübingen
Ulm
Freiburg im Breisgau
Konstanz
Friedrichshafen
L. Constance
Hohenschwangau
Neuschwanstein
Linderhof
Garmisch-Partenkirchen
Ammersee
Starnberger See
Augsburg
Munich (München)
Herrenchiemsee
Rosenheim
Chiemsee
Ingolstadt
Landshut
Passau
Regensburg
Nuremberg (Nürnberg)
Erlangen
Bamberg
Bayreuth
Würzburg
Schweinfurt
Suhl
Gotha
Erfurt
Wartburg
Mühlhausen
Jena
Gera
Plauen
Hof
Zwickau
Chemnitz
Colditz
Dresden
Rhine (Rhein)
Mosel
Main
Neckar
Danube (Donau)
Inn
Fulda
Eder
Lead
Zinc
Potassium
Copper
Uranium
Iron
Wheat
Barley
Dairy
N
0 25 50 75 100 125 150
0 25 50 75

Beethoven, Germany's most famous composer, wrote many pieces for the piano.

GERMANY
pop: 82,400,000

OPTICAL SKILLS

Germany has a large number of optical instrument manufacturers, who make cameras, microscopes and telescopes. East Germany led the former Soviet bloc in this field. However, since reunification, many of these companies in the East have closed down as they were over-staffed and heavily subsidized, and now cannot compete without government support.

RHINE BARGES

The River Rhine stretches from the North Sea deep into the German industrial heartland. Freight, such as coal, grain and timber, is often carried by barges like these. Many tourists also travel on the southern part of the Rhine to see the beautiful scenery, vineyards and castles on its banks.

BROWN COAL

In eastern Germany, large amounts of lignite (brown coal) are mined from vast open pits. Lignite is used for generating electricity. When burnt, it causes severe pollution. **Look for**

MAP FEATURES

Shipbuilding: Once a major industry in Germany's North Sea ports, shipbuilding is now in decline, and unemployment is growing. **Look for**

Castles: The Rhine trade route was protected by castles. Now they are a popular sight on tourist cruises. **Look for**

Pollution: The Rhine is polluted by industry, especially chemical works. Companies are beginning to find ways of cleaning up plants. **Look for**

Cattle	Mining
Cereals	Coal
Sugar beet	Industrial centre
Wine	Vehicle manufacture
Hops	High-tech industry

BAVARIA

The Bavarian Alps rise behind the Catholic church of St. Koloman, near Hohenschwangau. Bavaria is mainly Catholic, with a strong regional identity. The beautiful scenery and historic towns all make Bavaria a popular tourist destination.

BEER FESTIVALS

Many small Bavarian towns have annual beer festivals. Local people wear traditional costume, and spend several days drinking beer, dancing and singing to the accompaniment of brass bands.

The Bavarian Alps are popular for winter sports.

Flask, used in chemical experiments

CHEMICALS

Over half a million people are employed in Germany's chemical industry. Germany is the leading producer in Europe, and still dominates world markets, despite competition from the Far East. Raw materials for the chemical industry are transported along the River Rhine. Chemicals are widely used in industry to produce paints, detergents, cosmetics and medicines.

PRECISION ENGINEERING

While heavy industry tends to be concentrated in north Germany, the south has become a centre for the manufacture of special steels, cutlery and precision instruments. This region lacks coal, so industry could not develop here until gas was piped in from the Netherlands. **Look for**

THE ALPINE STATES

RUNNING THROUGH the middle of Austria and Switzerland are the Alps, the highest mountains in Europe. Both countries lie on Europe's main north-south trading routes, with access to the heart of Europe via the great Danube and Rhine waterways. Switzerland was formed in the Middle Ages, when a number of Alpine communities united in defensive leagues against their more powerful neighbours. Modern Switzerland is a confederation of 26 separate provinces, called cantons. The country has three main languages – German, French and Italian. In contrast, Austria was once the centre of the mighty Habsburg Empire. When the Empire collapsed in 1918, Austria became an independent country. Both Austria and Slovenia, which became independent from communist Yugoslavia in 1991, have mineral resources and thriving industries. With few natural resources, Switzerland has concentrated instead on skilled, high-technology manufacturing.

20 g.
FINE GOLD
999.9

Gold bar

BANKING

Switzerland is one of the world's main financial centres. People from all over the world put their money into Swiss bank accounts as the country is well-known for its political stability. Liechtenstein is also a major banking centre. Look for

DAIRY FARMING

Swiss dairy cattle spend winter in the Alpine valleys, and in summer are taken up to the Alpine pastures for grazing. The milk is used to make many varieties of cheese, such as Gruyère. Look for

Porcelain teeth

FALSE TEETH

Liechtenstein is the headquarters of world dental manufacture. False teeth, filling materials and plastic for crown and bridge dental work are exported to more than 100 countries.

Mount Eiger can be glimpsed through clouds.

Liechtenstein is famous for its beautiful stamps.

St. Bernard dogs were trained to rescue travellers lost in the Alps.

LIECHTENSTEIN
pop: 31,000

The castle at Vaduz, the capital of Liechtenstein.

The Swiss consume more chocolate than any other nationality in the world.

SWITZERLAND
pop: 7,300,000

GENEVA

Switzerland has not been at war for 150 years and is therefore seen as a neutral meeting place. Many international organizations have their headquarters in the city of Geneva.

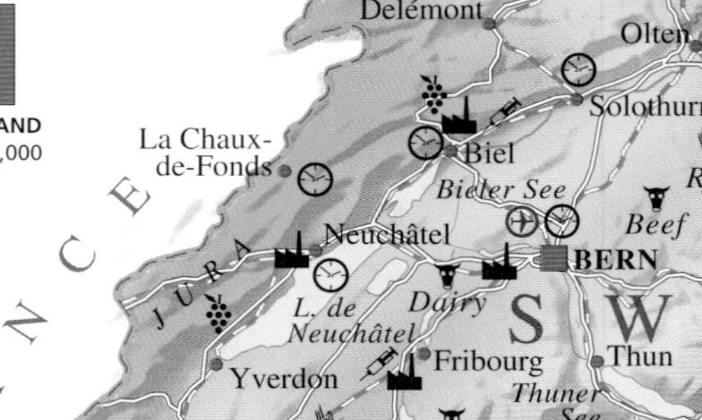

GERMANY
FRANCE
ITALY
SWITZERLAND
LIECHTENSTEIN
Schaffhausen
L. Constance
Basel
Liestal
Rhine (Rhein)
Frauenfeld
Winterthur
Zürich
Herisau
Sankt Gallen
Bregenz
Dornbirn
Delémont
Aarau
Olten
Aare
L. Zurich (Zürichsee)
Appenzell
Feldkirch
Landeck
St. Anton
Arlberg Tunnel
VADUZ
Linth Walensee
Glarus
Solothurn
Biel
Bieler See
La Chaux-de-Fonds
Zug
Luzern
Schwyz
Vierwaldstätter See
Neuchâtel
BERN
Sarnen
Stans
Altdorf
Chur
JURA
L. de Neuchâtel
Fribourg
Thun
Thuner See
Brienzer See
Interlaken
Yverdon
Lötschberg Tunnel
Eiger
Jungfrau
St. Gotthard Tunnel
San Bernardino Tunnel
St. Moritz
RHAETIAN ALPS
LEPONTINE ALPS
BERNER ALPEN
Lausanne
Gstaad
Montreux
L. Geneva
Brig
Simplon Tunnel
Simplon Pass
Sierre
Sion
Rhône
Locarno
Bellinzona
Geneva (Genève)
Martigny
PENNINE ALPS
Matterhorn
L. Maggiore
Lugano
L. di Lugano
Great St. Bernard Tunnel
Dairy
Beef
Rye
Wheat
N
0 25 50 75 100 KM
0 25 50 MILES

MAP FEATURES

Hydro-electric power: The Swiss pioneered hydro-electricity. Today, Austria is an important producer, tapping the potential of the Danube. Look for

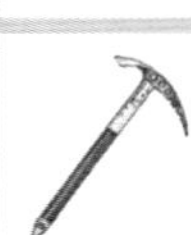
Climbing: Mountaineers first started climbing the Alps in the 19th century. Some of the peaks are stil thought to be the world's toughest climbs. Look for

Tunnels: There are only a few road passes through the Alps, but railway routes through tunnels are helping to ease the traffic. Look for

Pollution: Tourism in the Alps, especially the heavy use of roads, is causing environmental problems. Look for

	Cereals		Watchmaking
	Cattle		Pharmaceuticals
	Wine		Financial centre
	Industrial centre		Skiing

The spectacular scenery of northern Slovenia.

ALPINE PASSES

Although the Alps are a formidable obstacle to communications, mountain passes have been used since prehistoric times. Since the 19th century, major engineering feats have made the Alps more accessible: bridges cross gorges and deep valleys and tunnels pass under the mountains.

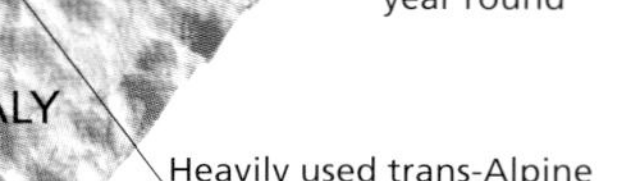

Rhône valley offers route into the heart of the Alps
Simplon rail tunnel, built in 1906
Berner Alpen
Brig
SWITZERLAND
ITALY
Simplon Pass, built 1801-06, open to cars all year round
Heavily used trans-Alpine routes are congested and difficult to cross in winter

VIENNA

For many centuries, Austria was ruled by the Habsburg family. Their empire included Hungary; their capital was Vienna. The city contained many grand buildings and elegant palaces such as this one, the Schönbrunn Palace, which was the Habsburg family's summer residence. The Habsburg empire finally collapsed in 1918.

AUSTRIAN INDUSTRY

Hydro-electric power from the Austrian Alps is a major source of energy for heavy industry. Iron ore deposits around Linz and Donawitz fuel the Austrian steel industry. Some Austrian steel plants have been forced to close by lower world steel prices. **Look for**

Iron ore

PHARMACEUTICALS

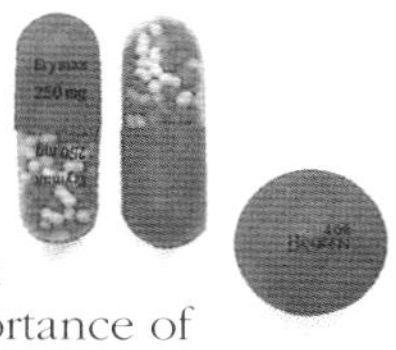

One of Switzerland's main industries is pharmaceuticals (making drugs and medicines). The industry has benefited from the Swiss emphasis on the importance of research and product development, the latest technology and a highly skilled workforce. Perfumes, cosmetics and drugs are all made in the Basel area. **Look for**

Edelweiss is a rare Alpine flower.

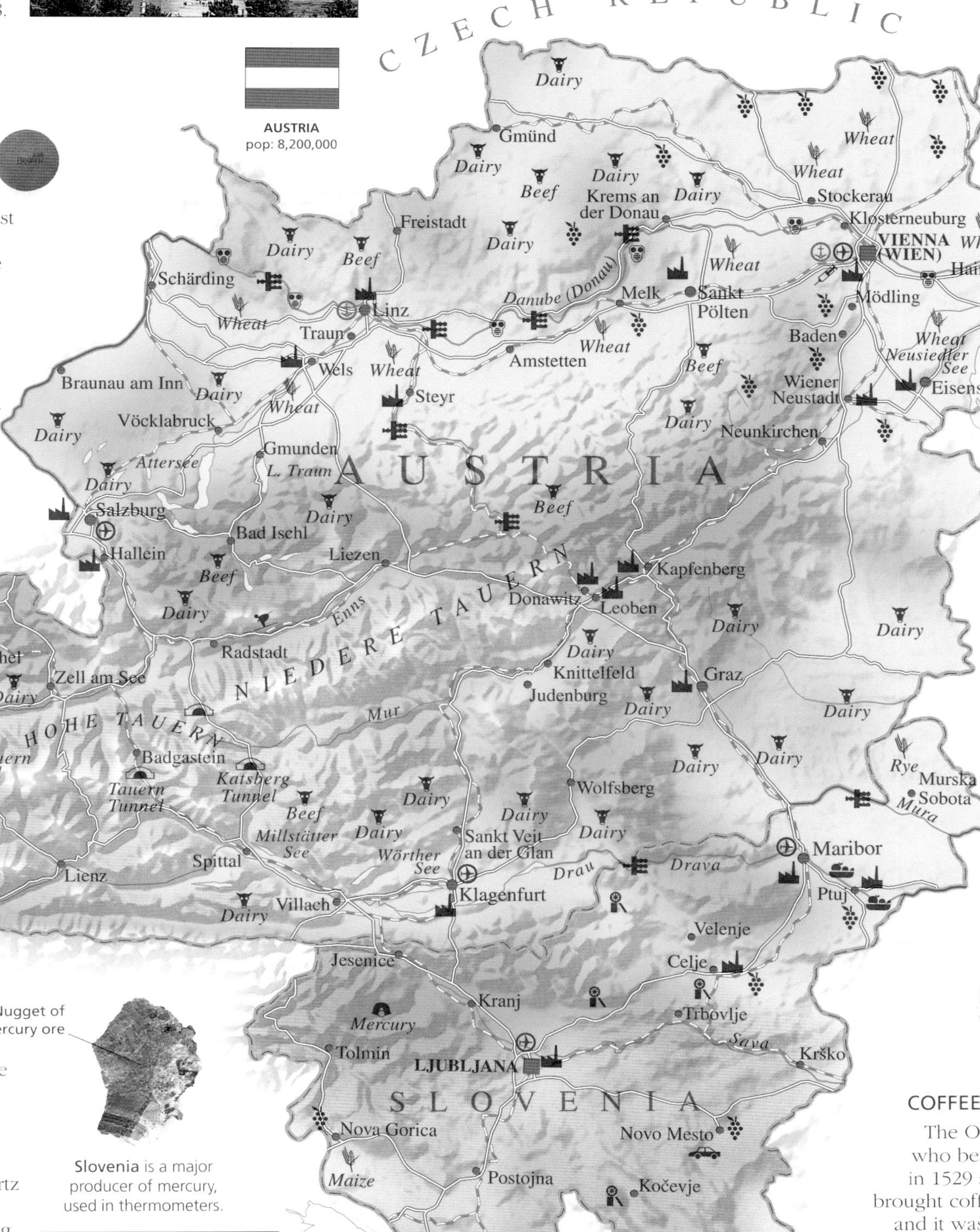

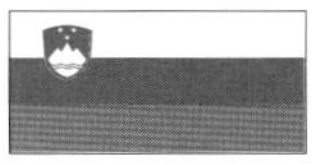

Cow bells help farmers to locate animals in remote Alpine pastures.

WATCHMAKING

Watches and clocks have been made in Switzerland since the 16th century. Recently, however, Swiss companies have been under pressure from the Japanese and Americans who developed quartz technology. The Swiss have saved their industry by making certain of their more famous watches cheaper. **Look for**

Nugget of mercury ore

Slovenia is a major producer of mercury, used in thermometers.

The Abbey at Melk in Austria was built in the 18th century.

COFFEE AND CAKES

The Ottoman Turks, who besieged Vienna in 1529 and 1683, first brought coffee to the city, and it was here that the first coffee-shop in Western Europe was opened. There are still many cafés in Vienna, where people drink coffee and eat Austria's famous chocolate cakes. *Sachertorte* is named after the Viennese pastryshop where it is made.

Sachertorte

SKI CENTRE

The Alps are visited by over 100 million people each year. But ski-runs, improved roads and expanding resorts are all having a harmful effect on the environment. Huge numbers of trees have been cut down to make way for ski-runs, but these can provide routes for avalanches. **Look for**

AUSTRIAN TOURISM

Austria's tourist industry is booming due to the attractions of its beautiful scenery, historical towns, picturesque villages and winter sports facilities. Tourism is now one of Austria's most profitable industries. A quarter of Austria's tourists visit during the winter; many of the visitors come from nearby Germany.

LJUBLJANA

The Slovenian capital, Ljubljana, is a major centre of manufacturing, textiles, electronics and chemical industries. One in seven Slovenes live in the capital. The recent conflict to the south has hit Slovenia's tourist industry, which is now slowly recovering. Visitors are attracted by its historic towns and villages, mountains and beaches.

CENTRAL EUROPE

IN 1989 THE COMMUNIST governments of Central Europe collapsed and the region entered a period of momentous change. All four countries of Central Europe only became independent states early in the last century. After World War II they were incorporated into the Soviet bloc and ruled by communist governments. These states started to industrialize rapidly, but they were heavily dependent on the former Soviet Union for their raw materials and markets. When communism collapsed in 1989, the new, democratically elected governments were faced with many problems: modernizing industry, huge foreign debts, soaring inflation, rising unemployment and terrible pollution. In 1993 the former state of Czechoslovakia was split into two countries, the Czech Republic and Slovakia.

Grudziądz, a medieval Polish town on the River Vistula.

POLAND
pop: 38,700,000

POLLUTION

Central European industry has blighted the forests of the Czech Republic. Acid rain, caused by emission of various pollutants into the air, is killing the forests. Lakes and streams are also becoming acidified, creating impossible living conditions for many organisms. The poisoned and scarred landscape will take decades to recover. Look for

PUPPETS

Puppet shows are popular throughout Central Europe, but the former Czechoslovakia is acknowledged as the original home of European puppetry. Today, over a thousand Czech Republic and Slovak puppet companies perform plays.

Wooden puppet

GLASS

The Czech Republic's glass industry is centuries old. Glassware, such as this decanter and glasses, is often intricate and brightly coloured. The industry uses local supplies of sand to make the glass. Bohemian crystal is manufactured principally in the northwest around Karlovy Vary, and is also popular with the ever-increasing number of tourists.

PRAGUE

The Czech Republic's capital, Prague, has some of the most beautiful and well-preserved architecture in Europe. Since 1989, when the country was opened to tourists, thousands of people have flocked to the city. Look for

CZECH REPUBLIC
pop: 10,200,000

MAP FEATURES

Mining: Poland is one of the world's largest coal producers, but recently the industry has been affected by competition from abroad. Look for

Financial centre: In Hungary, the Budapest stock exchange opened in 1990, and many new banks have now opened in the city. Look for

Dam: The dam built by the Slovaks on the Danube at Gabčíkovo has caused a major dispute between Hungary and Slovakia. Look for

Cereals
Industrial centre
Sugar beet
Shipbuilding
Mixed fruit
Tourism
Timber
Spas
Mining
Pollution

HUNGARIAN INDUSTRY

Since the end of World War II Hungary has industrialized rapidly. It manufactures products such as aluminium, steel, electronic goods and vehicles, especially buses. But when the Soviet Union disintegrated, Hungarian manufacturers lost many of the traditional markets for their products – especially in heavy industry – and now face many problems. Look for

BEER

Some of Europe's finest beers and lagers are brewed in the Czech Republic. Pilsener lager originated in the town of Plzeň; Budweiser beer has been brewed at České Budějovice for over a century. Huge quantities of beer, the Budweiser beer in particular, are exported, principally to European countries such as Germany and the UK.

Beautifully painted eggs are sold in the Czech Republic and Slovakia at Easter.

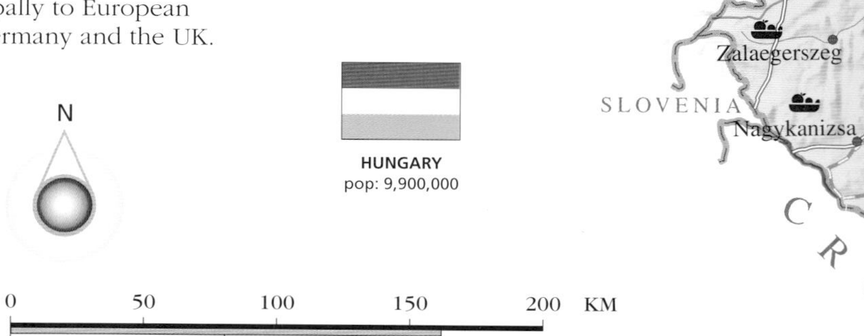

N
0
50
100
150
200
KM
0
50
100
MILES

HUNGARY
pop: 9,900,000

SOLIDARITY

Many Polish people work in heavy industries, such as coal mining and shipbuilding. In 1980 discontent over poor working conditions led to a strike at this shipyard in Gdansk, and to the birth of Solidarity, the Soviet bloc's first independent trade union. Solidarity has significantly influenced Polish politics.

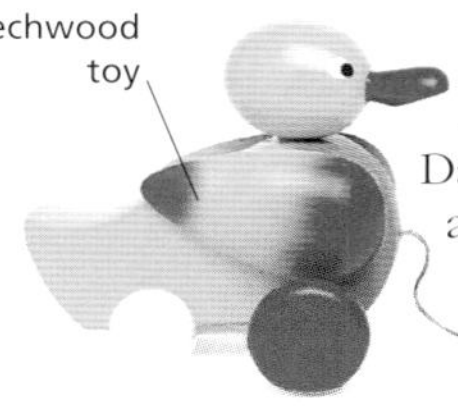

Beechwood toy

TIMBER

Apart from the lowland area around the River Danube, the landscape of the Czech Republic and Slovakia is mountainous. Both countries have relatively small populations and much of the land is still covered with forest. Both countries have large timber industries. Some timber – mainly pine – is used to make furniture. Beech is often used for the manufacture of toys. **Look for**

RELIGION

For a thousand years, through invasions, wars, repression – and times when the country almost ceased to exist – the Polish people have found strength in their religious faith. Even during the last 40 years of communist government – which actively discouraged religion of any kind – 90 per cent of the population remained devout Catholics.

150
POLSKA

Wild boar, shown on this Polish stamp, are still found in the region.

PAPRIKA

The flat plains in Hungary are amongst the most fertile farming areas in Europe. Cereals, sugar beet and fruit are among the main crops. Sweet red peppers – from which paprika is made – are also grown. Paprika is a vital ingredient in many spicy Hungarian dishes.

Morning mist rising over the western Carpathians.

SLOVAKIA
pop: 5,400,000

BUDAPEST

Budapest, the Hungarian capital, was once two towns, Buda on the Danube's right bank, and Pest on the left. The town was very badly damaged during World War II, but many of its historic buildings have since been carefully restored. This vast, domed parliament building in Pest faces across the river to Buda.

Ernö Rubik, a Hungarian, invented this complex puzzle.

SPA BATHS

Hot thermal springs were used for medicinal purposes in ancient Greece and Rome. The Romans were the first to develop baths – like this one in Budapest where bathers enjoy a game of chess. Hungary now has 154 hot-spring baths, which are open to the public. The Czech Republic and Slovakia have 900 mineral springs and 58 health spas, which are reserved for medicinal purposes only. It is hoped that more foreigners will come to the region to use the thermal springs. **Look for**

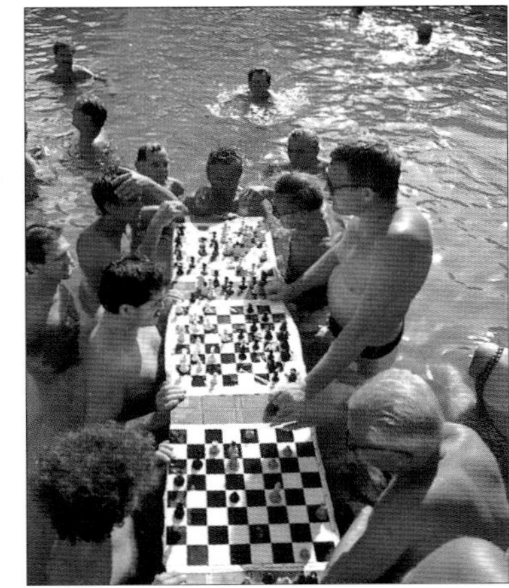

Hungary's famous horses are bred on the Great Hungarian Plain.

Italy and Malta

At various times in the past 2,000 years Italy has influenced the development of European civilization. From this narrow, boot-shaped peninsula the Romans established a vast empire throughout Europe and North Africa; Christianity was first adopted as an official religion by a Roman emperor, and Rome later became the centre of the Catholic Church. In the 14th century, an extraordinary flowering of the arts and sciences, known as the Renaissance, or "rebirth", started in Italy and transformed European thought and culture. Italy at this time was divided into independent city states, and was later ruled by foreign nations, including France and Austria. But in 1870, after centuries of foreign domination, Italy became an independent and unified country. Despite a lack of natural resources, and defeat in World War II, Italy has become a major industrial power. The country has long suffered from corruption and organized crime, but recent changes show promise of more political stability in the future.

PASTA

Orecchioni (large ears)

Cappelletti (little hats)

Round tortellini (small pies)

The Italian explorer, Marco Polo, is said to have brought the recipe for pasta to Italy when he returned from his great journey to China. Pasta is a type of dough made by adding water to wheat flour. It has become one of the world's most popular foods. It can be made into different shapes, and filled with meat or vegetables.

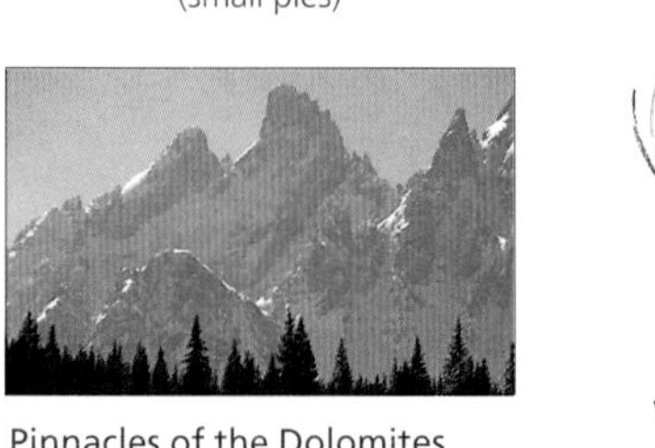
Pinnacles of the Dolomites in northeastern Italy.

Masks like these are worn during the February carnival in Venice, which includes plays, masked balls and fireworks.

VERONA

The ancient Romans were skilful engineers, and many of their remarkable buildings are still standing today. The foundations of much of Italy's road system was also built by the Romans. Verona is based on the Roman grid street plan. The town's ancient amphitheatre seats 22,000, and is still used.

VENICE

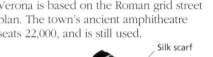

This historic city is built on a number of islands in a shallow lagoon. Many buildings stand on wooden stilts driven into the mud. Venice's future is in the balance, threatened by flooding and pollution.

Silk scarf
Suede shoe

DESIGN

Italians place great emphasis on design and produce beautiful looking products. This flair for design is particularly obvious in their cars and clothes. The fashion houses of Rome, Florence, Milan and Venice rival those of Paris, and Italian shoes and clothes are widely exported.

THE PO VALLEY

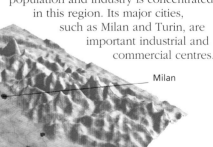

Between the Alps and the Apennines lies a huge triangular plain, drained by Italy's greatest river, the Po. The majority of the country's agriculture, population and industry is concentrated in this region. Its major cities, such as Milan and Turin, are important industrial and commercial centres.

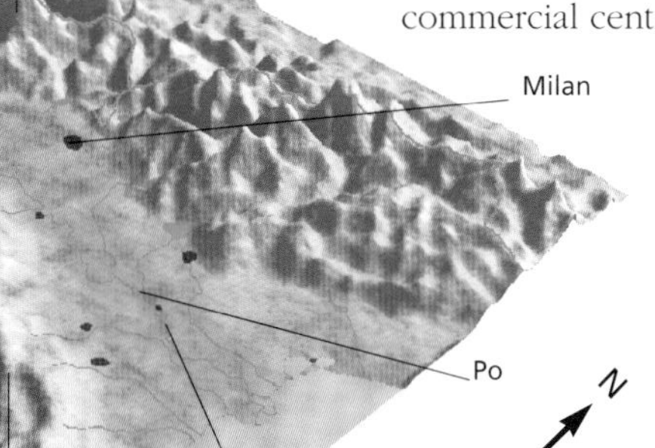
Alps
Turin
Mountain passes link Italy to the rest of Europe
Milan
Alpine rivers supply water for HEP and irrigation
Po
Genoa: major sea port and industrial centre
N
Apennines
Farming of maize, wheat and rice

ITALY
pop: 57,200,000

SAN MARINO
pop: 25,000

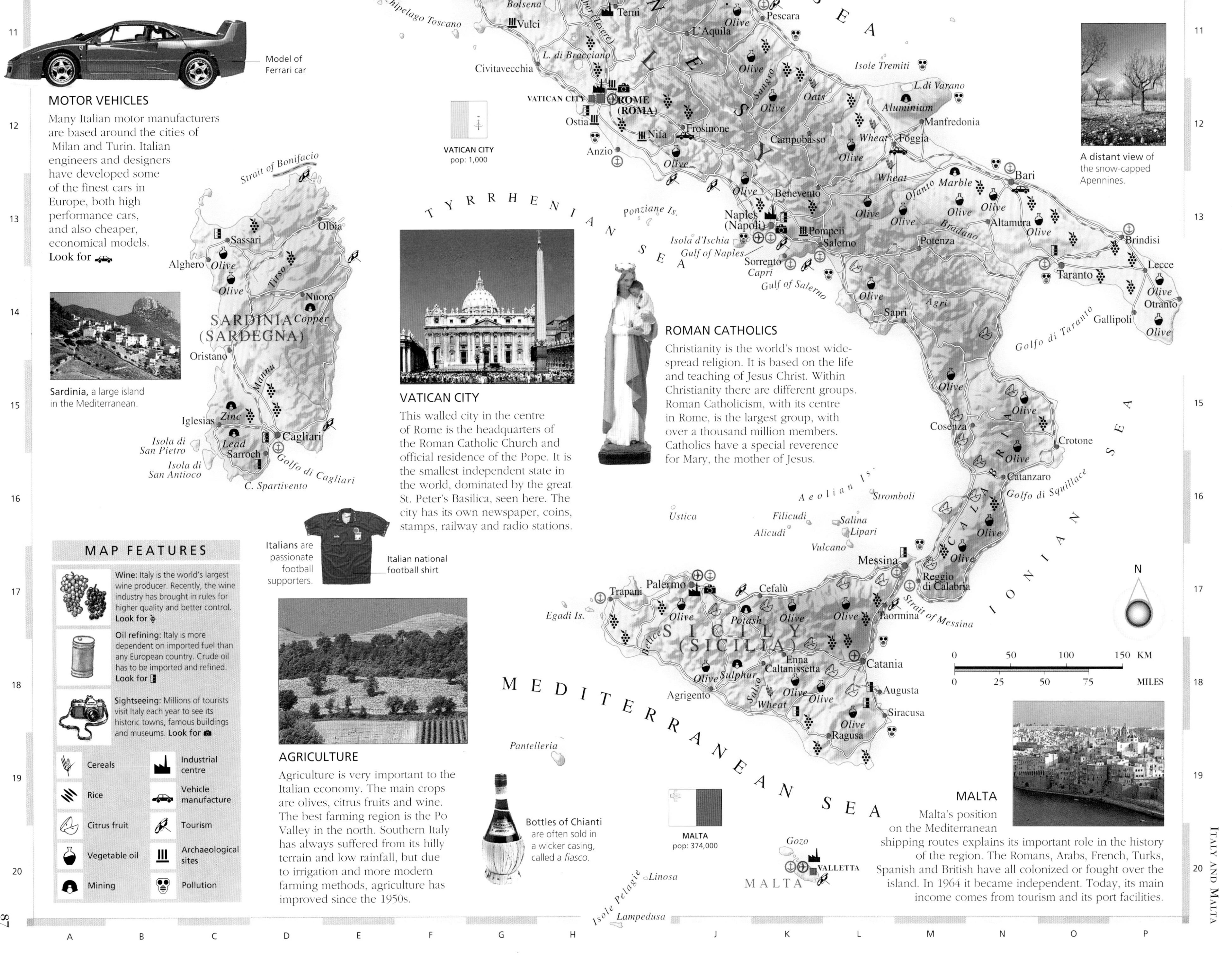
TYRRHENIAN SEA
MEDITERRANEAN SEA
IONIAN SEA
SARDINIA (SARDEGNA)
SICILY (SICILIA)
CALABRIA
MALTA
VATICAN CITY
ROME (ROMA)
Naples (Napoli)
Civitavecchia
Ostia
Anzio
Nila
Frosinone
L'Aquila
Terni
Vulci
Bolsena
L. di Bracciano
Pescara
Campobasso
Benevento
Pompeii
Salerno
Sorrento
Capri
Gulf of Naples
Gulf of Salerno
Isola d'Ischia
Ponziane Is.
Isole Tremiti
L.di Varano
Manfredonia
Foggia
Bari
Altamura
Potenza
Brindisi
Lecce
Otranto
Taranto
Gallipoli
Golfo di Taranto
Sapri
Cosenza
Crotone
Catanzaro
Golfo di Squillace
Reggio di Calabria
Strait of Messina
Messina
Taormina
Catania
Augusta
Siracusa
Ragusa
Enna
Caltanissetta
Agrigento
Cefalù
Palermo
Trapani
Egadi Is.
Ustica
Aeolian Is.
Stromboli
Filicudi
Alicudi
Salina
Lipari
Vulcano
Pantelleria
Isole Pelagie
Linosa
Lampedusa
Gozo
VALLETTA
Strait of Bonifacio
Olbia
Sassari
Alghero
Nuoro
Oristano
Iglesias
Cagliari
Golfo di Cagliari
Sarroch
C. Spartivento
Isola di San Pietro
Isola di San Antioco
Arcipelago Toscano
Tirso
Mannu
Belice
Salso
Sangro
Ofanto
Bradano
Agri
Aluminium
Marble
Copper
Zinc
Lead
Potash
Sulphur
Oats
Wheat
Olive
N
0 50 100 150 KM
0 25 50 75 MILES

Model of Ferrari car

MOTOR VEHICLES

Many Italian motor manufacturers are based around the cities of Milan and Turin. Italian engineers and designers have developed some of the finest cars in Europe, both high performance cars, and also cheaper, economical models. **Look for**

Sardinia, a large island in the Mediterranean.

VATICAN CITY
pop: 1,000

VATICAN CITY

This walled city in the centre of Rome is the headquarters of the Roman Catholic Church and official residence of the Pope. It is the smallest independent state in the world, dominated by the great St. Peter's Basilica, seen here. The city has its own newspaper, coins, stamps, railway and radio stations.

ROMAN CATHOLICS

Christianity is the world's most widespread religion. It is based on the life and teaching of Jesus Christ. Within Christianity there are different groups. Roman Catholicism, with its centre in Rome, is the largest group, with over a thousand million members. Catholics have a special reverence for Mary, the mother of Jesus.

A distant view of the snow-capped Apennines.

Italians are passionate football supporters.

Italian national football shirt

MAP FEATURES

Wine: Italy is the world's largest wine producer. Recently, the wine industry has brought in rules for higher quality and better control. **Look for**

Oil refining: Italy is more dependent on imported fuel than any European country. Crude oil has to be imported and refined. **Look for**

Sightseeing: Millions of tourists visit Italy each year to see its historic towns, famous buildings and museums. **Look for**

Cereals	Industrial centre
Rice	Vehicle manufacture
Citrus fruit	Tourism
Vegetable oil	Archaeological sites
Mining	Pollution

AGRICULTURE

Agriculture is very important to the Italian economy. The main crops are olives, citrus fruits and wine. The best farming region is the Po Valley in the north. Southern Italy has always suffered from its hilly terrain and low rainfall, but due to irrigation and more modern farming methods, agriculture has improved since the 1950s.

Bottles of Chianti are often sold in a wicker casing, called a *fiasco*.

MALTA
pop: 374,000

MALTA

Malta's position on the Mediterranean shipping routes explains its important role in the history of the region. The Romans, Arabs, French, Turks, Spanish and British have all colonized or fought over the island. In 1964 it became independent. Today, its main income comes from tourism and its port facilities.

Southeast Europe

This troubled region of southeastern Europe consists of a wide variety of landscapes, religions, peoples and languages. The region was invaded many times, and from the 14th-19th centuries was occupied by the Turks. After World War II, both Albania and Yugoslavia were ruled by communist governments. When the communist leader, General Tito, died in 1980 the Yugoslav government became less centralized, and former republics now demanded their independence. Serbia, the largest and most powerful republic, resisted the break-up of Yugoslavia. In 1991, a bloody civil war broke out between Serbia and Croatia and, eventually, between Serbs and Muslims in Bosnia. In 1999, when conflict broke out between Serbia and its Albanian minority population in Kosovo, NATO bombing raids destroyed much of the Serbian infrastructure, forcing the Serbs to seek a peace agreement. Albania was isolated by its communist government from the rest of Europe and became economically backward. But the country has now shaken off its communist rulers and held democratic elections.

CROATIA
pop: 4,500,000

SLOVENIA
CROATIA
BOSNIA HERZEGOVINA
ADRIATIC SEA
DINARIC ALPS
DALMATIA
Čakovec
Varaždin
Koprivnica
Rye
Maize
Bjelovar
Virovitica
Česma
Samobor
ZAGREB
Karlovac
Kupa
Sisak
Rijeka
Aluminium
Ogulin
Krk
Kvarner
Nova Gradiška
Sava
Iron
Wheat
Oats
Prijedor
Bosanska Gradiška
Una
Bosanska Krupa
Bihać
Banja Luka
Vrbas
Pula
Rt Kamenjak
Cres
Kvarnerička Vrata
Lošinj
Gospić
Ključ
Jajce
Pag
Zadar
Knin
Peručko Jezero
Livno
Dugi Otok
Kornat
Krka
Šibenik
Žirje
Čiovo
Split
Šolta
Brač
Hvar
Vis
Korčulanski Kanal
Metković
Pelješac
Korčula
Lastovski Kanal
Lastovo
Mljet

Walnuts flourish in the warm summers and well-drained soils of Yugoslavia.

YUGO

This car, the Yugo, is manufactured in the Serbian city of Kragujevac. It was designed for foreign export, but the economic disruption caused by the civil war and the NATO bombing of Serbia in 1999 have dealt a death blow to this industry. International trade sanctions, combined with a lack of foreign investment, have crippled Serbia's manufacturing industry.

BOSNIA AND HERZEGOVINA
pop: 4,000,000

TOURISM

Many tourists are attracted to Croatia's Dalmatian coast, which is famous for its beautiful scenery, warm climate and stunning coastline. The conflict of the early 1990s brought Croatia's tourist industry to a violent halt, but over the last five years visitors have gradually returned, and are helping to revitalize Croatia's economy. Look for [tourism symbol]

UNDER FIRE

The world looked on in horror as Dubrovnik, a beautiful city with an untouched centre dating back 1,000 years, came under Serbian attack in 1991. Sarajevo, the Bosnian capital, was another casualty; many of its historic mosques and churches were hit by shells. Other historic towns in Bosnia and Croatia have also suffered irreparable damage during the war.

Mixed valley farming gives way to barren mountains in central Albania.

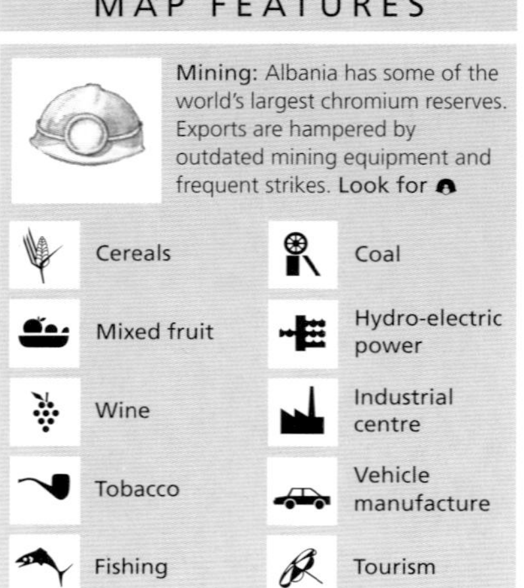
MAP FEATURES
Mining: Albania has some of the world's largest chromium reserves. Exports are hampered by outdated mining equipment and frequent strikes. Look for
Cereals
Coal
Mixed fruit
Hydro-electric power
Wine
Industrial centre
Tobacco
Vehicle manufacture
Fishing
Tourism

MARKETS

In peacetime, local markets in the region are packed with people and well-stocked with a wide range of produce from nearby farms. Large quantities of fruit and vegetables are grown in the mild, warm climate of the Croatian coast and in western Bosnia. Look for [mixed fruit symbol]

FOLKLORE

Variations in national costume reflect the contrasting cultural traditions and the great ethnic variety of the people living in this region. The oriental influence, for example, can be seen clearly in the Turkish-style costumes of the south. The Dubrovnik region is famous for its costume of white dresses, embroidered blouses and waistcoats. Folk-music and dancing take place at religious festivals and on market-days, and are also laid on for tourist groups.

N

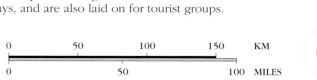

0 50 100 150 KM
0 50 100 MILES

YUGOSLAVIA
pop: 10,400,000

IRON GATES

The Danube, the second-longest river in Europe, passes through Serbia on its journey from Germany to the Black Sea. As the river leaves the broad plains of northern Serbia, it is forced through this narrow gorge, called the Iron Gates. In 1972, Romania and Yugoslavia built a power station here to use the water to make electricity.

Look for

CIVIL WAR

When Yugoslavia broke up into independent countries in 1990, civil war broke out between the Serbs and both Croatia and Bosnia. The Serbs cleared and resettled Bosnian Muslim homes, a policy called "ethnic cleansing". In 1999, conflict erupted again, caused by discrimination against Serbia's Albanian minority, which make up 80% of the population of Kosovo. Many were forced to flee to adjacent countries.

LANGUAGE DIFFERENCES

The main language of the former Yugoslavia is Serbo-Croatian. It can be written in two different ways, reflecting both ethnic origin and religion. The Eastern Orthodox Serbs use Cyrillic, a Slavic alphabet created in the 9th century by two Greek brothers, who were Christian. Croats, on the other hand, use the Roman alphabet.

200
ЈУГОСЛАВИЈА

Postage stamp using Roman alphabet

Postage stamp using Cyrillic alphabet

MACEDONIA
pop: 2,200,000

ALBANIA

There is little traffic in the central square in Albania's capital, Tirana: until recently, private cars were banned. Albania is now emerging from 50 years of isolation. Under communism, free speech and religion were forbidden. Even beards were not allowed. In 1997, the catastrophic failure of private investment schemes left many people penniless and the economy collapsed. Many Albanians fled the country, which was forced to accept international aid. Although a new democratic government has been installed, the impact of these events on the economy is still being felt.

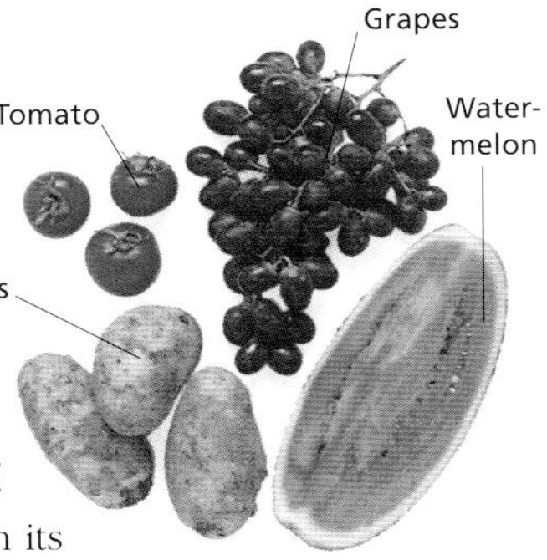

Tomato

Potatoes

Grapes

Water-melon

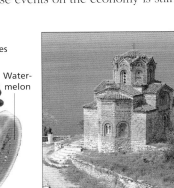

ALBANIAN AGRICULTURE

Although its economy is based on farming, Albania still has difficulties feeding its own population, which is the fastest-growing in Europe. The main crops are potatoes, maize, wheat, sugar beet, fruit and vegetables. Until recently, most of the land was owned and farmed by the state, but today it is farmed by individual families.

There is very little farming in the mountains of Montenegro.

RELIGION

This beautiful church on the shores of Lake Ohrid dates back to the medieval period, when Macedonia followed the Eastern Orthodox church. Later, Bosnia, Montenegro and Serbia were occupied by the Ottoman Turks and became largely Muslim countries.

ALBANIA
pop: 3,400,000

Romania and Bulgaria

Romania and Bulgaria are located in the southeast of Europe, on the shores of the Black Sea. The River Danube forms the border between the two countries, and the most fertile land in the region is found in the river's vast valley and delta. Forests of oak, pine and fir trees grow on the slopes of the Carpathian and Balkan Mountains. Romania and Bulgaria were occupied by Romans, Bulgars, Hungarians and Turkish Ottomans, but this troubled history ended when they became independent countries in the late 19th and early 20th centuries. After two world wars, both countries became part of the Soviet communist bloc. Although they are no longer communist, economic reform has been slow, and unemployment, high prices and food shortages are still constant problems.

THE PRESIDENTIAL PALACE

Under Romania's repressive communist leader, President Ceauşescu, food and energy supplies were rationed. Despite this, the President started a series of expensive building projects, such as this presidential palace in Bucharest. In 1989, the Romanian people rose up against communism, and executed their president.

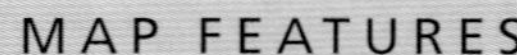

MAP FEATURES

Vehicle manufacture: Romanian factories make copies of French vehicles for export to China, Russia and many Western countries. **Look for**

High-tech industry: Electronics earn Bulgaria foreign currency, although the computer industry is suffering from international competition. **Look for**

Spas: Mineral springs and health treatments are provided by many spa resorts, which are a popular tourist attraction. **Look for**

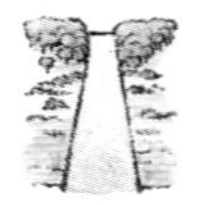

Shipping canal: The Danube-Black Sea Canal enables ships to avoid the slow journey through the Danube Delta. **Look for**

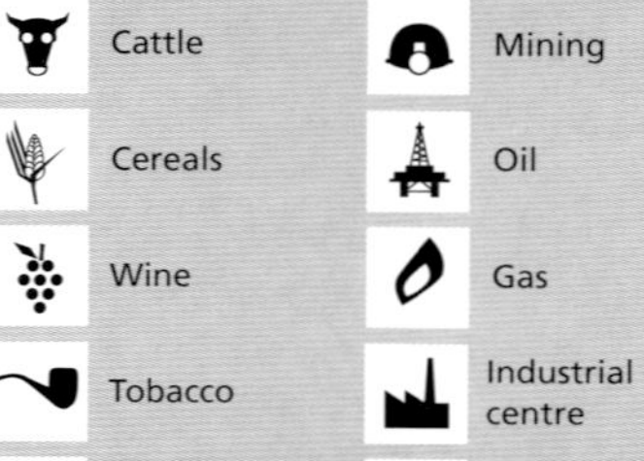

Cattle
Mining
Cereals
Oil
Wine
Gas
Tobacco
Industrial centre
Roses
Tourism

Rose-petal

ROSE-OIL

Used in perfume, rose-oil is literally worth its weight in gold. Central Bulgaria produces most of the world's supply. The world's largest rose gardens are at Kazanlûk. **Look for**

TOBACCO

Bulgaria is the world's second largest exporter of cigarettes. Tobacco is grown in the fertile valleys of the River Maritsa. This woman is sorting tobacco leaves, ready for selling. **Look for**

Small farms in the wooded valleys of central Romania.

YOGHURT

Yoghurt, made from the milk of cows, sheep or goats, is an important part of the Bulgarian diet. Many Bulgarians claim that eating yoghurt helps them live to a ripe old age.

The Alexander Nevsky church in Sofia celebrates liberation from Turkish rule.

Bulgaria is the world's fourth largest wine exporter.

RILA MONASTERY

The walls of Rila monastery are decorated with no less than 1,200 superb wall-paintings. The monastery became a symbol of the Bulgarians' struggle to preserve the Christian faith during centuries of Turkish rule. The monastery was originally founded in 1335, and was rebuilt after it burnt to the ground in the 19th century.

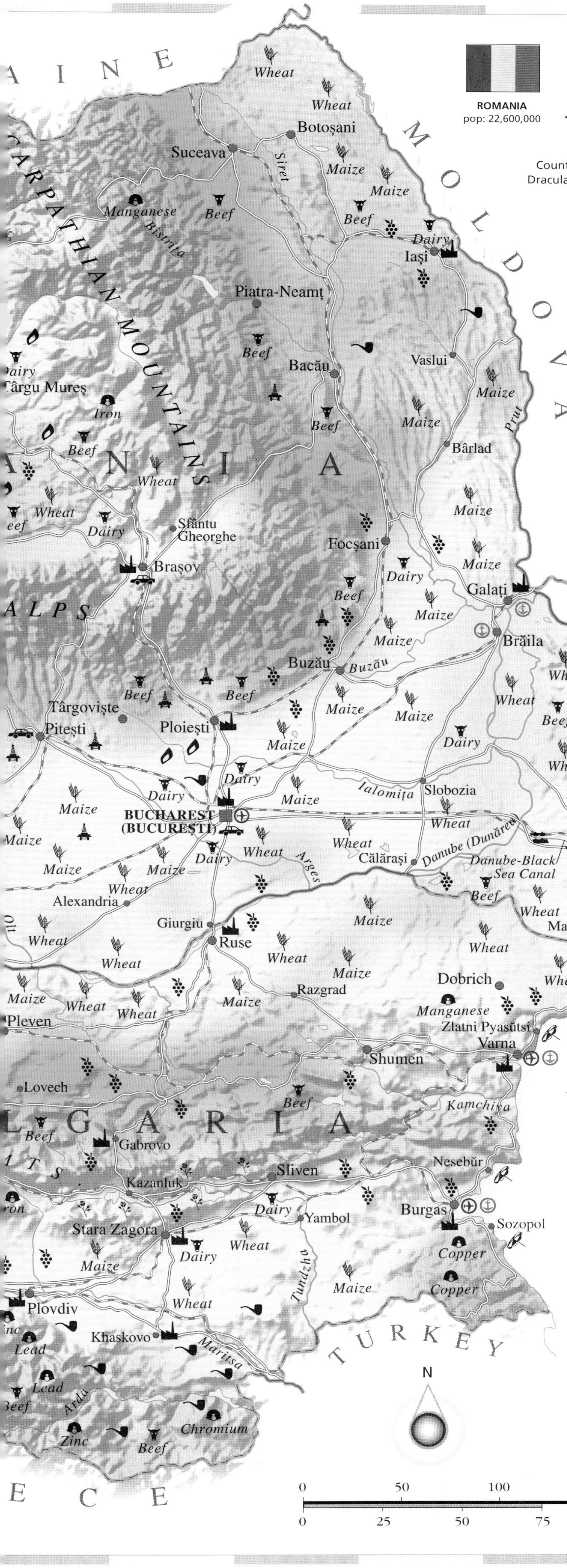

ROMANIA
pop: 22,600,000

Count Dracula

DRACULA

The story of Dracula is linked to Transylvania, and attracts many tourists to the region. Tales of the blood-sucking Count, complete with vampire bats, garlic cloves and wooden stakes, are thought to be based on Vlad the Impaler, a 15th-century prince who resisted Turkish rule. His name is explained by his habit of impaling his enemies on wooden stakes.

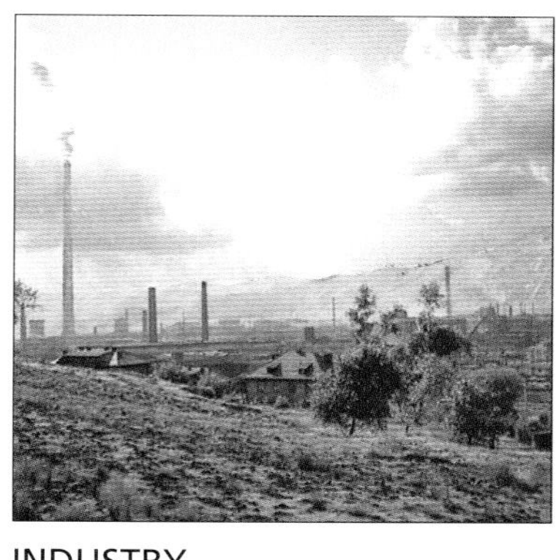

INDUSTRY

These chimneys at Copsa Micâ in Romania are belching out hydro-carbons, which pollute the air, water and soil. Romania's industrialization was not subject to pollution controls.

The heights of the Carpathian Mountains.

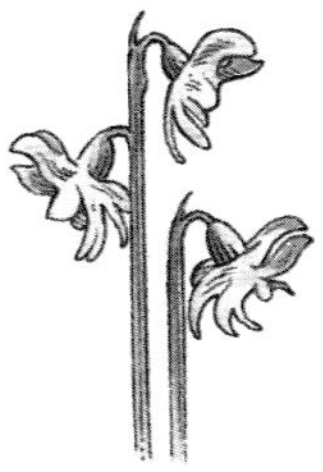

This rare ghost orchid grows in shady parts of Bulgarian forests.

FARMING

The fertile lands of the Danube valley and the Black Sea plains are rich farming country: wheat, maize, potatoes and fruit are the main crops. Country traditions continue, especially in Romania, where many village scenes seem unchanged since medieval times.

POSTAGE STAMPS

The lettering on these Bulgarian postage stamps is in the Cyrillic alphabet. It dates back to the 9th century AD, when Saints Cyril and Methodius devised the alphabet so that they could translate the Bible into Old Bulgarian. The Cyrillic alphabet is also used in the Russian Federation.

Traditional houses are preserved in rural Bulgaria.

GYPSIES

Large numbers of gypsies (or Romanies) live in both Romania and Bulgaria. The gypsies are thought to have arrived from India, via the Middle East, in the 5th century AD. Many gypsies still wander from place to place, trading goods for a living. Gypsies are often persecuted by their host countries, who find it hard to understand their different customs and way of life.

TOURISM

This region has experienced a great surge in package holidays since the 1980s. International airports at Varna and Burgas serve visitors from western Europe, while Russian tourists cross the Black Sea by ferry. Many new resorts have been built, and the natural beauty of the coastline, with its sandy beaches, pine forests and old fishing villages, is often spoiled by ugly, high-rise developments. Look for

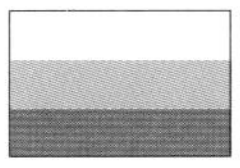

BULGARIA
pop: 8,400,000

0 50 100 150 KM
0 25 50 75 MILES

GREECE

FROM THE EARLIEST TIMES, the life and economy of Greece has been shaped by its geography. It is a country of rugged mountains, isolated valleys, remote peninsulas and more than 1,400 scattered islands. The difficulty of travelling by land has turned Greece into a seafaring nation, which owns the second largest fleet of merchant ships in the world. Ninety per cent of its imports and exports are carried by sea rather than by road. Most people in Greece make their living from farming, but in recent years, tourism has become an important source of income. Tourists visit Greece not only for its warm, Mediterranean climate and beautiful landscape, but also for its ancient ruins. Many of these date from the 5th century BC, when the country was the cultural centre of the western world, the birthplace of democracy, and home of great thinkers such as Socrates, Plato and Aristotle.

Greek Orthodox bishop

THE ORTHODOX CHURCH

Most Greek Christians belong to the Orthodox Church. This was founded in Constantinople (modern Istanbul) in the 4th century AD. The Eastern Orthodox Church established there still flourishes in Greece, Eastern Europe and Russia.

ATHENS

Athens is famous for its Acropolis ("high place"), crowned by the Parthenon temple. Smog all too often obscures the Acropolis, and cars are banned from the city on certain days to reduce pollution.

GREEK SALAD

Parsley
Aubergine
Cucumber
Beef tomato

Many Greek farms are small, growing just enough vegetables and fruit for the farmer's family. Lettuces, cucumbers, tomatoes, olives, herbs and cheese are the most common produce.

MAP FEATURES

Archaeological sites: Remains from ancient Greece are found all over the country, attracting many visitors. **Look for Ⅲ**

Sultanas and currants: Greece is the world's largest exporter of these fruits. Small, black currants are named after the town of Corinth. **Look for** 🍇

The Olympic Games: The event started in Olympia in 776 BC. Sports included running, wrestling, boxing, horse racing, javelin and discus. **Look for** ◯◯◯

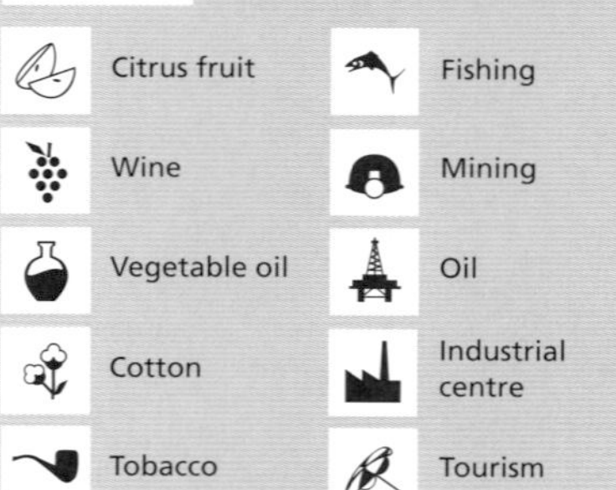

Citrus fruit
Fishing
Wine
Mining
Vegetable oil
Oil
Cotton
Industrial centre
Tobacco
Tourism

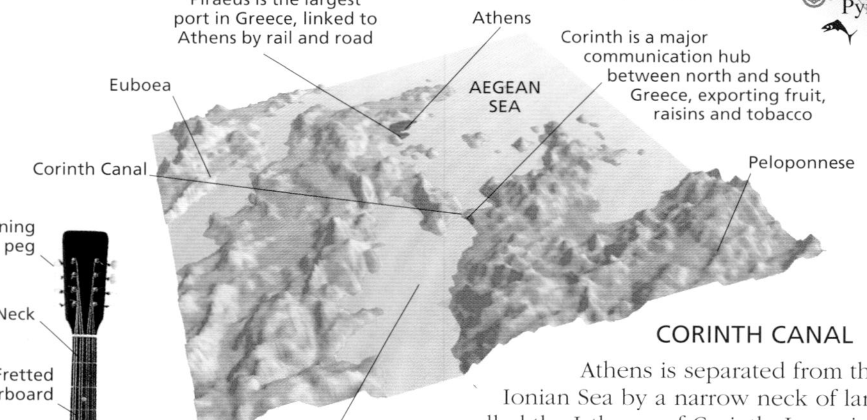

Piraeus is the largest port in Greece, linked to Athens by rail and road
Athens
Corinth is a major communication hub between north and south Greece, exporting fruit, raisins and tobacco
Euboea
AEGEAN SEA
Corinth Canal
Peloponnese
N
Gulf of Corinth

CORINTH CANAL

Athens is separated from the Ionian Sea by a narrow neck of land called the Isthmus of Corinth. In ancient times, ships were dragged across the isthmus. In 1893 the Greeks cut a canal through the isthmus. It is 6.3 km (3.9 miles) long, but only just wide enough for a ship to squeeze between the cliffs on either side. The canal shortened the journey from the Ionian Sea to Athens' main port, Piraeus, by 320 km (200 miles).

Tuning peg
Neck
Fretted fingerboard
String
Pegbox inlaid with mother-of-pearl
Soundhole
Body
Bridge

CLASSICAL MUSIC

The bouzouki is a stringed instrument, similar to a lute or a guitar, which is used in traditional Greek music. Folk dances, national costumes and music are still very popular at religious festivals such as Easter, and on special occasions such as weddings.

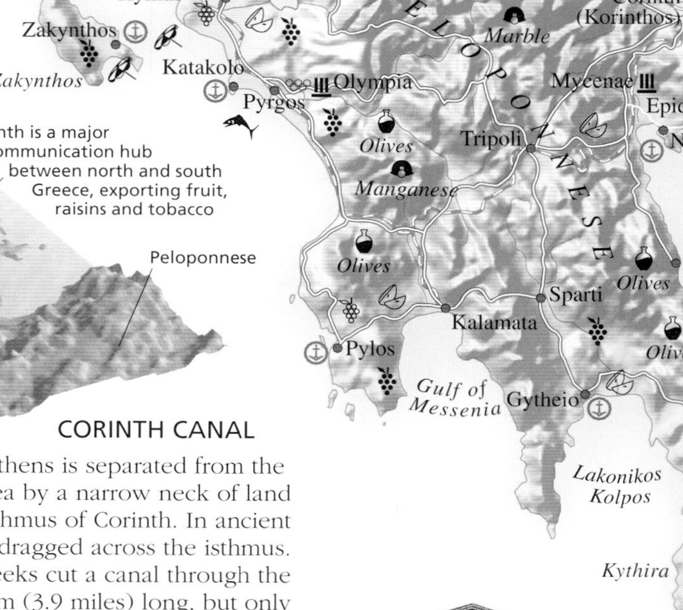

MACEDONIA
ALBANIA
GREECE
PINDUS MOUNTAINS
IONIAN SEA
Ionian Is.
PELOPONNESE
Lake Prespa
Florina
Edessa
L. Vegoritis
Kilkis
Vardar
Salonica (Thessaloniki)
Kastoria
L. Kastoria
Veroia
Chromium
Kozani
Aliakmonas
Katerini
Thermaic Gulf
Grevena
Corfu (Kerkyra)
Corfu (Kerkyra)
Olives
Igoumenitsa
Ioannina
Pineios
Trikala
Larisa
Karditsa
Volos
Arta
Acheloos
Preveza
Lefkada
Lefkada
Stylida
Lamia
Loutra Aidipsou
Nickel
Aluminium
L. Trichonis
Astakos
Amfissa
Itea
Delphi
Mesolongi
Lixouri
Argostoli
Kefalonia
Patra
Gulf of Patra
Gulf of Corinth
Corinth Canal
Kyllini
Andravida
Corinth (Korinthos)
Zakynthos
Zakynthos
Katakolo
Marble
Pyrgos
Olympia
Mycenae
Epidaurus
Nafplio
Tripoli
Manganese
Leonidio
Sparti
Kalamata
Pylos
Gulf of Messenia
Gytheio
Lakonikos Kolpos
Neapoli
Kythira

The Parthenon temple (built 432 BC) was the centre of religious life in Classical Athens.

SACRED OIL

Olives have been grown in Greece for over two thousand years. In ancient times, the olive was sacred to Athena, the goddess of war, and olive wreaths were worn as a symbol of victory. Today, olives and olive oil are major exports. **Look for** 🏺

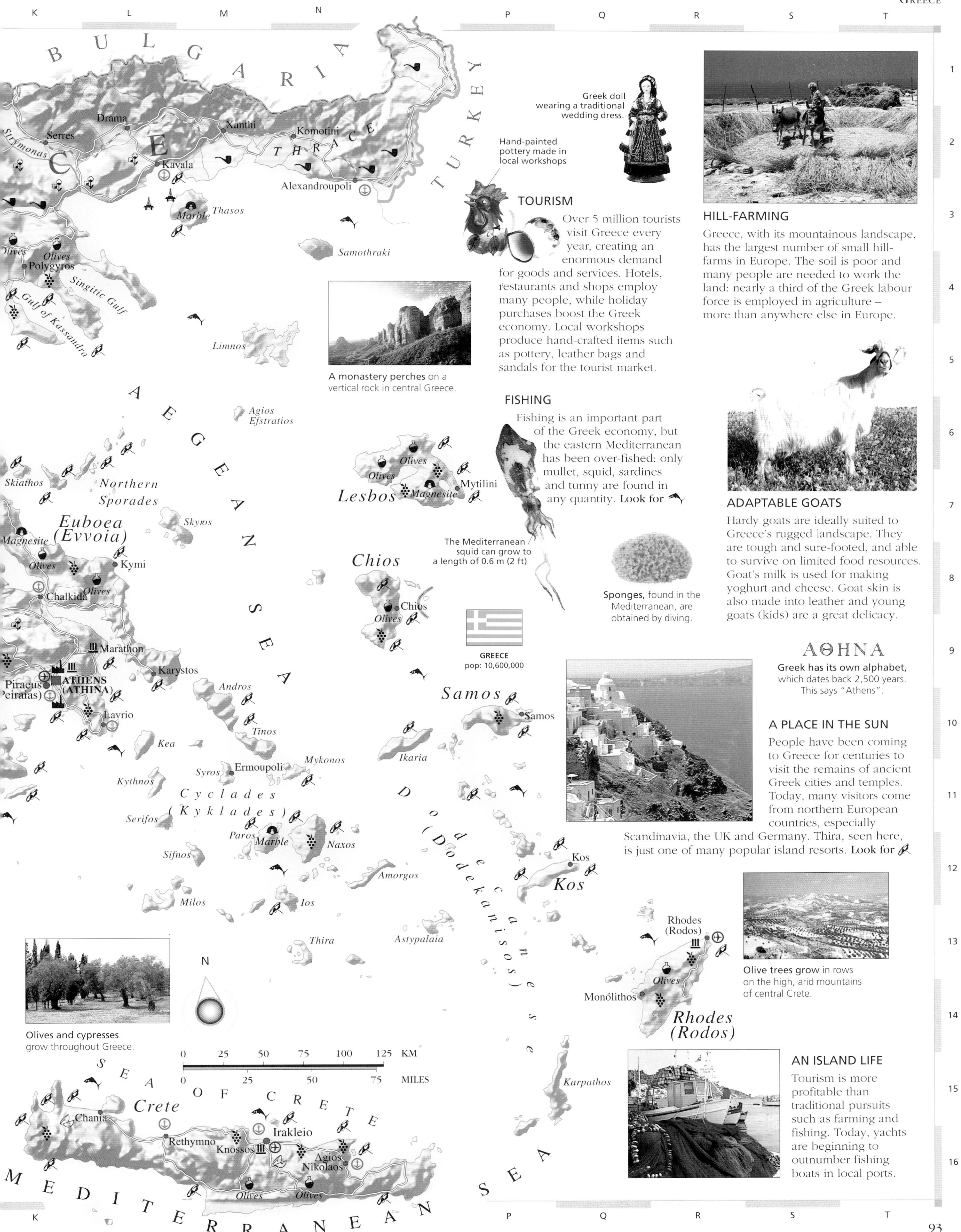
BULGARIA
TURKEY
GREECE
THRACE
Drama
Serres
Strymonas
Xanthi
Komotini
Kavala
Alexandroupoli
Thasos
Marble
Samothraki
Olives
Polygyros
Singitic Gulf
Gulf of Kassandra
Limnos
AEGEAN SEA
Agios Efstratios
Skiathos
Northern Sporades
Skyros
Euboea (Evvoia)
Magnesite
Kymi
Chalkida
Marathon
Karystos
Piraeus (Peiraias)
ATHENS (ATHINA)
Lavrio
Lesbos
Mytilini
Chios
Samos
Ikaria
Andros
Tinos
Kea
Syros
Ermoupoli
Mykonos
Kythnos
Cyclades (Kyklades)
Serifos
Sifnos
Paros
Naxos
Milos
Amorgos
Ios
Thira
Astypalaia
Dodecanese (Dodekanisos)
Kos
Rhodes (Rodos)
Monólithos
Karpathos
N
0 25 50 75 100 125 KM
0 25 50 75 MILES
SEA OF CRETE
Crete
Chania
Rethymno
Knossos
Irakleio
Agios Nikolaos
MEDITERRANEAN SEA
GREECE
pop: 10,600,000
ΑΘΗΝΑ

Greek doll wearing a traditional wedding dress.

Hand-painted pottery made in local workshops

TOURISM

Over 5 million tourists visit Greece every year, creating an enormous demand for goods and services. Hotels, restaurants and shops employ many people, while holiday purchases boost the Greek economy. Local workshops produce hand-crafted items such as pottery, leather bags and sandals for the tourist market.

A monastery perches on a vertical rock in central Greece.

FISHING

Fishing is an important part of the Greek economy, but the eastern Mediterranean has been over-fished: only mullet, squid, sardines and tunny are found in any quantity. Look for

The Mediterranean squid can grow to a length of 0.6 m (2 ft)

Sponges, found in the Mediterranean, are obtained by diving.

HILL-FARMING

Greece, with its mountainous landscape, has the largest number of small hill-farms in Europe. The soil is poor and many people are needed to work the land: nearly a third of the Greek labour force is employed in agriculture – more than anywhere else in Europe.

ADAPTABLE GOATS

Hardy goats are ideally suited to Greece's rugged landscape. They are tough and sure-footed, and able to survive on limited food resources. Goat's milk is used for making yoghurt and cheese. Goat skin is also made into leather and young goats (kids) are a great delicacy.

ΑΘΗΝΑ

Greek has its own alphabet, which dates back 2,500 years. This says "Athens".

A PLACE IN THE SUN

People have been coming to Greece for centuries to visit the remains of ancient Greek cities and temples. Today, many visitors come from northern European countries, especially Scandinavia, the UK and Germany. Thira, seen here, is just one of many popular island resorts. Look for

Olive trees grow in rows on the high, arid mountains of central Crete.

Olives and cypresses grow throughout Greece.

AN ISLAND LIFE

Tourism is more profitable than traditional pursuits such as farming and fishing. Today, yachts are beginning to outnumber fishing boats in local ports.

THE BALTIC STATES AND BELARUS

THE THREE BALTIC STATES – Latvia, Lithuania and Estonia – made history in 1990-91 when they became the first republics to declare their independence from the Soviet Union. This was the end of a long series of invasions and occupations by the Vikings, Germans, Danes, Poles and Russians. A new era had begun, but many of the old problems – food shortages, pollution, weak economies – still remained. The region's flat landscape is well-drained by lakes and rivers and is ideal for farming. The main crops are grains, sugar beet and potatoes. In Belarus heavy industry such as machine-building and metal-working is important, while the Baltic states manufacture electronics and consumer goods. Following independence, many Russians who moved to the Baltic states to work in industry were returned to their homeland. The Baltic Sea, although much of it is frozen in the winter months, gives access to the markets of northern Europe. Industrialization has left a terrible legacy. Summer resorts along the Baltic coast have been closed to visitors because of polluted seawater, and Belarus was badly hit by the nuclear accident at Chornobyl' in the Ukraine in 1986, when 70 per cent of the radioactive fall-out landed on its territory.

ESTONIA
pop: 1,400,000

LITHUANIA
pop: 3,700,000

ПРАВАЯ СТОРОНА

KALININGRAD

A statue of Lenin dominates the centre of Kaliningrad, capital of Russia's Baltic enclave. This historic city dates to the 13th century. It was once a major German Baltic port, but was devastated by Russian forces in 1945. It is now a major industrial and commercial centre.

One of the many lakes of Lithuania.

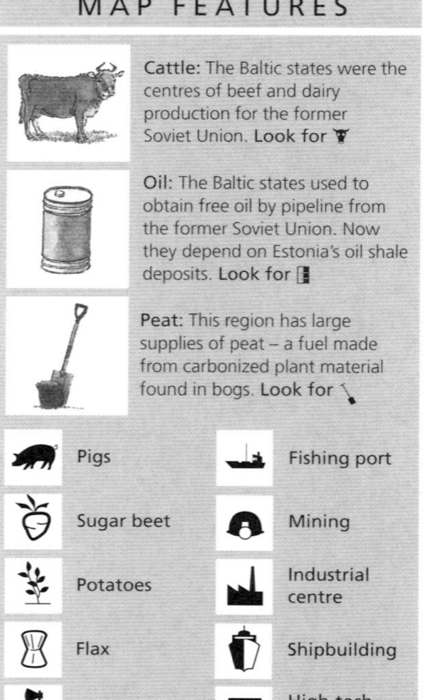
MAP FEATURES
Cattle: The Baltic states were the centres of beef and dairy production for the former Soviet Union. Look for
Oil: The Baltic states used to obtain free oil by pipeline from the former Soviet Union. Now they depend on Estonia's oil shale deposits. Look for
Peat: This region has large supplies of peat – a fuel made from carbonized plant material found in bogs. Look for
Pigs
Fishing port
Sugar beet
Mining
Potatoes
Industrial centre
Flax
Shipbuilding
Timber
High-tech industry

Spider, trapped in amber

BALTIC GOLD

Amber is the fossilized sap of ancient trees. The Baltic states produce two-thirds of the world's amber, most of it found along Lithuania's "amber coast". Amber has been collected and traded since prehistoric times. It is a precious stone, but is also valued for its medical properties. Even today it is used to treat rheumatism. Look for

MINSK

Although Minsk was founded over 900 years ago, it has no historic buildings. The city was virtually destroyed by bombing during World War II, when half of Minsk's population is estimated to have been killed. After the war, the city was rebuilt, and became one of the industrial centres of the former Soviet Union.

Sour cream
Beetroot, mixed with sour cream
Draniki

NATIONAL DISH

Draniki is the national dish of Belarus. It is made of grated potatoes fried in vegetable oil and served with sour cream. Potatoes are grown everywhere, and are one of Belarus's main products. Large numbers of dairy cattle are kept on its extensive pastureland.

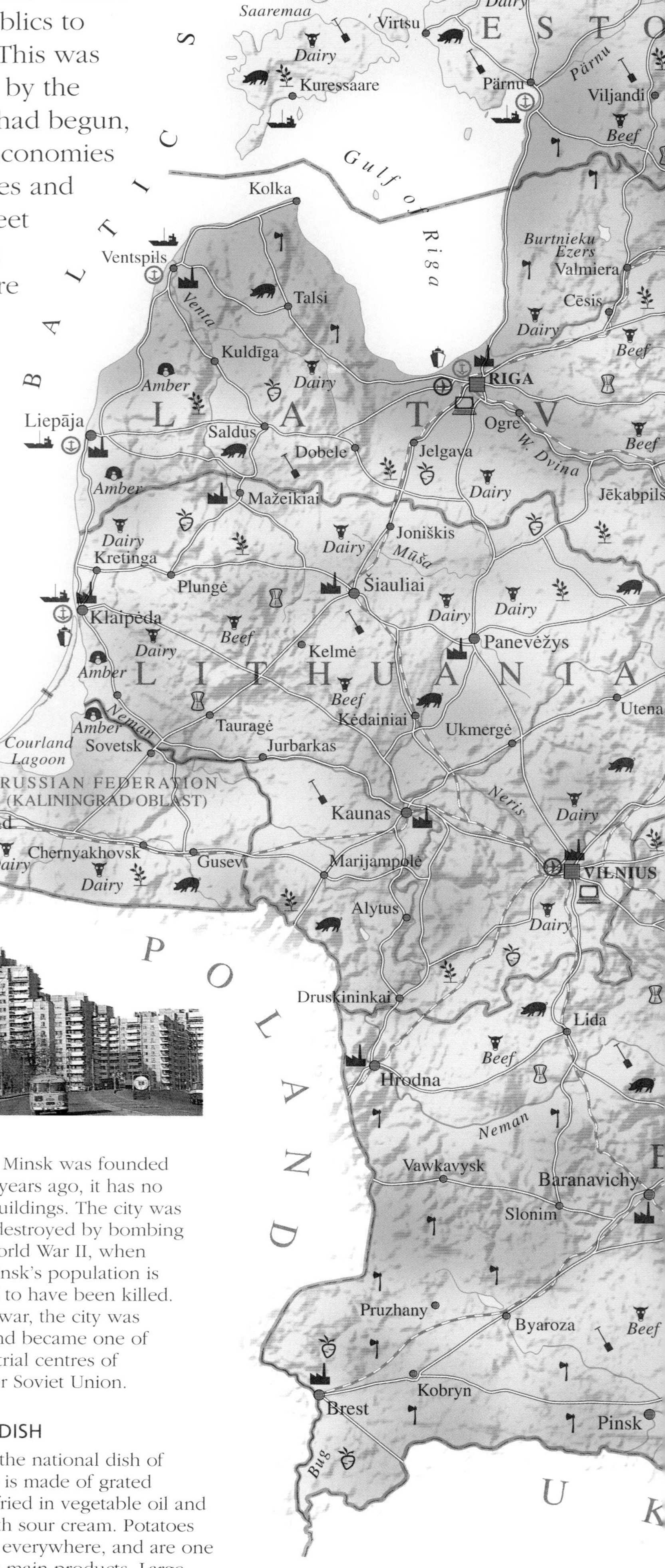
BALTIC SEA
Gulf of Riga
Naissaar
TALLINN
Paldiski
Kärdla
Vormsi
Hiiumaa
Haapsalu
Paide
Saaremaa
Virtsu
ESTONIA
Kuressaare
Pärnu
Viljandi
Kolka
Ventspils
Talsi
Burtnieku Ezers
Valmiera
Cēsis
Kuldīga
RIGA
Liepāja
LATVIA
Saldus
Dobele
Jelgava
Ogre
W. Dvina
Jēkabpils
Mažeikiai
Joniškis
Mūša
Kretinga
Plungė
Šiauliai
Klaipėda
Panevėžys
Kelmė
LITHUANIA
Utena
Kėdainiai
Ukmergė
Tauragė
Jurbarkas
Neman
Sovetsk
Courland Lagoon
RUSSIAN FEDERATION (KALININGRAD OBLAST)
Baltiysk
Kaliningrad
Chernyakhovsk
Gusev
Kaunas
Neris
Marijampolė
VILNIUS
Alytus
POLAND
Druskininkai
Lida
Hrodna
Vawkavysk
Baranavichy
Slonim
Pruzhany
Byaroza
Brest
Kobryn
Pinsk
Bug
Amber
Dairy
Beef

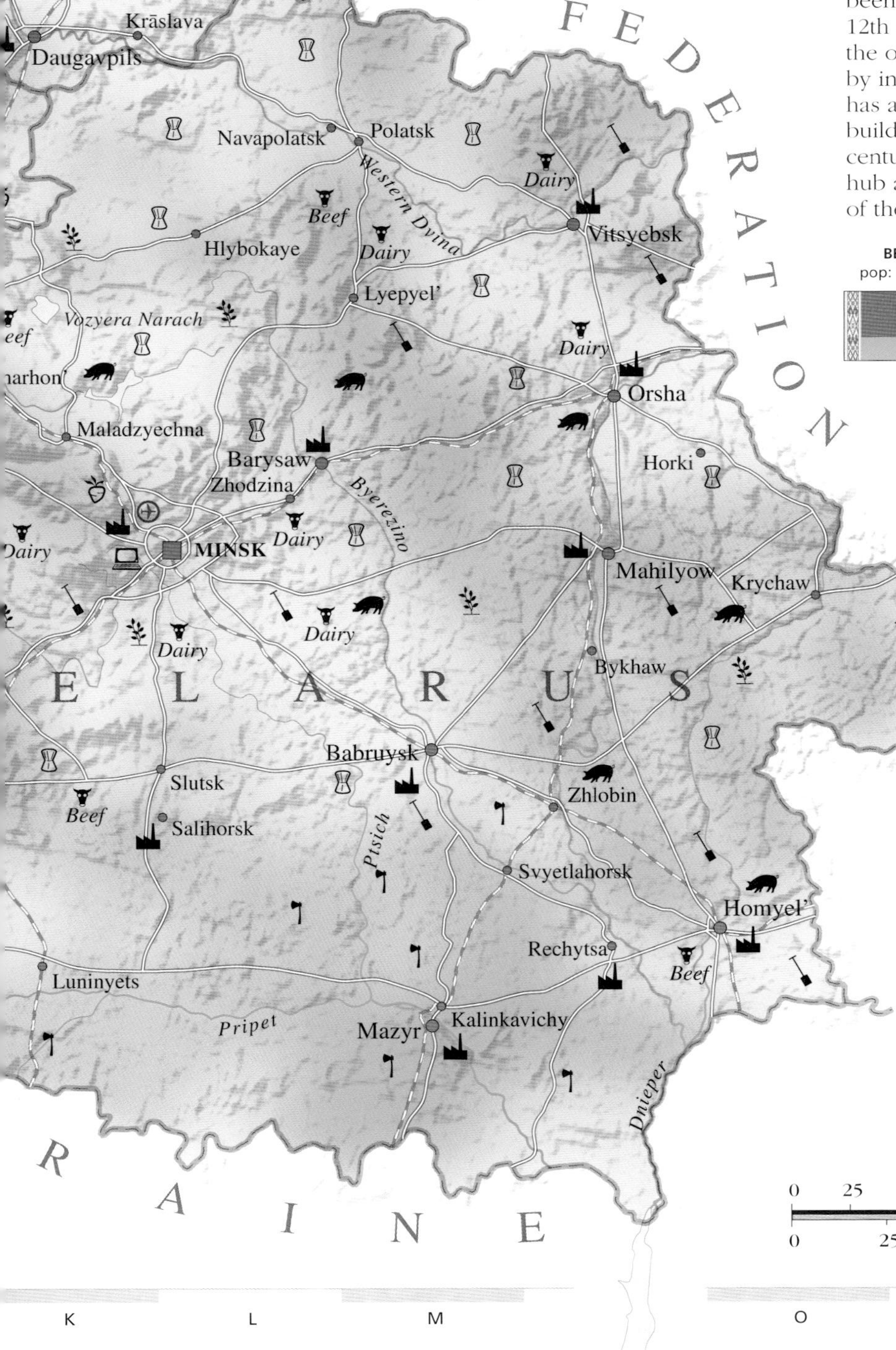

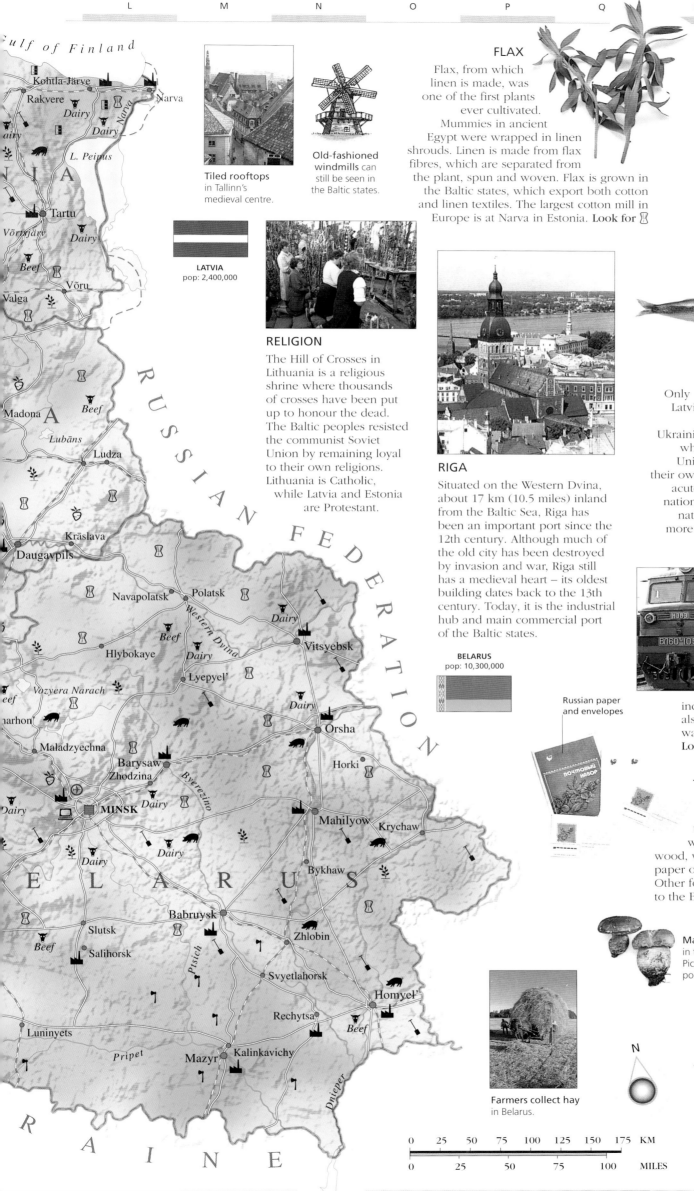

FLAX

Flax, from which linen is made, was one of the first plants ever cultivated. Mummies in ancient Egypt were wrapped in linen shrouds. Linen is made from flax fibres, which are separated from the plant, spun and woven. Flax is grown in the Baltic states, which export both cotton and linen textiles. The largest cotton mill in Europe is at Narva in Estonia. **Look for**

Tiled rooftops in Tallinn's medieval centre.

Old-fashioned windmills can still be seen in the Baltic states.

TALLINN

Tallinn, Estonia's capital, is an important Baltic port, with regular ferries to Finland. In contrast to the modern port, the city centre has changed little since medieval times, with cobbled streets, ancient walls, turrets and gables.

LATVIA
pop: 2,400,000

RELIGION

The Hill of Crosses in Lithuania is a religious shrine where thousands of crosses have been put up to honour the dead. The Baltic peoples resisted the communist Soviet Union by remaining loyal to their own religions. Lithuania is Catholic, while Latvia and Estonia are Protestant.

Sprats are caught in the Baltic Sea, and are served with onions.

A LATVIAN IDENTITY

Only 55 per cent of the people of Latvia were born in the country. Russians, Belarusians and Ukrainians were resettled in Latvia when it was part of the Soviet Union. As a near minority in their own country, Latvians are acutely aware of their own national identity. They promote their language, national dress, dances and music – there are more than a million known Latvian folk songs.

RIGA

Situated on the Western Dvina, about 17 km (10.5 miles) inland from the Baltic Sea, Riga has been an important port since the 12th century. Although much of the old city has been destroyed by invasion and war, Riga still has a medieval heart – its oldest building dates back to the 13th century. Today, it is the industrial hub and main commercial port of the Baltic states.

BELARUS
pop: 10,300,000

HEAVY INDUSTRY

Many of the former Soviet Union's trains and railway carriages were manufactured in Latvia, the most industrialized of the Baltic States. Latvia also produces minibuses, trams, mopeds, washing machines and tape recorders. **Look for**

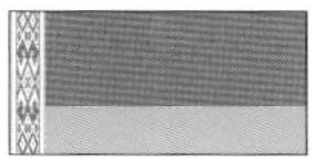

Russian paper and envelopes

TIMBER

About one-third of this region is still covered with fir and pine forest, and timber is an important industry. Inland waterways are used to transport the wood, which is either made into wood-pulp for paper or used to make furniture and matches. Other former Soviet states also send their timber to the Baltic region for processing. **Look for**

Many mushrooms grow in the Belarusian forests. Picking mushrooms is a popular summer outing.

Farmers collect hay in Belarus.

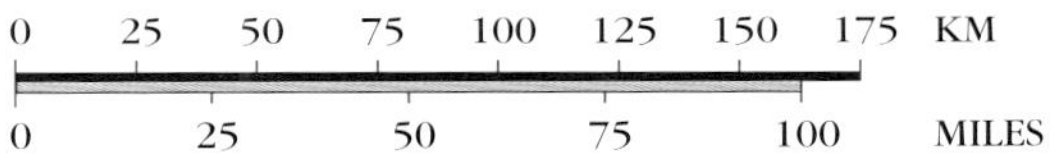

VODKA

Potatoes are one of the most important crops in Belarus. They are exported to the Russian Federation where they are fermented and used to make the national drink, vodka. The name vodka comes from the Russian word *voda* which means "water". Cheap vodka has led to a high rate of alcoholism, which governments have tried to curb by heavily taxing alcohol.

European Russia

THE RUSSIAN FEDERATION is the largest country in the world. Stretching across two continents – Europe in the west and Asia in the east – it is twice the size of the USA. The Ural Mountains form the division between the European and Asian parts of the country. The Russian Federation has fertile farmlands, vast mineral deposits and abundant timber, oil and other natural resources. Despite its size and natural wealth, Russia is currently in a state of political and economic turmoil. After centuries of rule by czars (emperors), the world's first communist government took power in Russia in 1917. The Union of Soviet Socialist Republics (USSR) included many of the territories that were formerly parts of the Russian Empire. During 74 years of communist rule, the Soviet Union became an industrial and military superpower, but at an appalling cost to its people and environment. Economic problems led to liberal reforms beginning in the mid-1980s, and ultimately to the fall of the communist regime in December 1991. By then most of the non-Russian republics had declared independence. The new Russian Federation is now governed by a democratic multi-party system, but the economy is stagnating. Conflict with ethnic and religious enclaves, such as Muslim Chechnya, in the south is an ongoing problem.

SAINT PETERSBURG

Saint Petersburg, the capital of Russia from 1712-1918, was founded by Czar Peter the Great in 1703. It is built on 12 islands, linked by bridges, and has many elegant 18th-century buildings.

RELIGION

Moscow is the spiritual centre of the Russian Orthodox church. For many decades, the Church was persecuted in Russia; today, churches are re-opening, and many Russian people are turning back to religion. Beautiful icons (religious images painted on wood), like this one, adorn the churches and people's homes.

САНКТ-ПЕТЕРБУРГ

The name "Saint Petersburg", written in Russia's Cyrillic alphabet, which was devised by Christian missionaries in the 10th century.

Northern Russia is covered with coniferous forest, called taiga.

NORWAY
FINLAND
ESTONIA
LATVIA
BELARUS
BARENTS SEA
WHITE SEA
KARA SEA (KARSKOYE MORE)
Novaya Zemlya
Kara Strait
Ostrov Vaygach
Ostrov Kolguyev
Cheshskaya Guba
Baydaratskaya Guba
KOLA PENINSULA (KOL'SKIY POLUOSTROV)
Murmansk
Nickel
Copper
Iron
Ozero Imandra
Ozero Umbozero
Ozero Pyaozero
Ozero Topozero
Phosphate
Aluminium
Kem'
Ozero Segozero
L. Ladoga
L. Onega
Onega
Petrozavodsk
Gulf of Finland
Saint Petersburg (Sankt-Peterburg)
Pskov
Novgorod
Archangel (Arkhangel'sk)
Northern Dvina
Mezen'
Pinega
Pechora
Izhma
Uranium
Usa
Vorkuta
RUSSIAN FEDERATION
URAL MOUNTAINS (URAL'SKIYE GORY)
Kotlas
Syktyvkar
Vologda
Cherepovets
Rybinsk Reservoir
Yaroslavl'
Kostroma
Moscow-Volga Canal
Ivanovo
Gzhel'
MOSCOW (MOSKVA)
Tver'
Volga
Smolensk
Dnieper
Nevel'
Vetluga
Kama
Rye
Oats
Barley

RUSSIAN FEDERATION
pop: 147,200,000
(EUROPEAN RUSSIA)
pop: 105,837,000

Many wooden churches built in the 17th century still stand on small islands in Lake Onega.

St. Basil's, Moscow, built in the 16th century

MOSCOW

The city of Moscow was founded in the 12th century. At its centre is a fortified citadel called the Kremlin. Its stone walls enclose the grand palace of the czars, four cathedrals and a church. The Kremlin became – and is now – the country's seat of government.

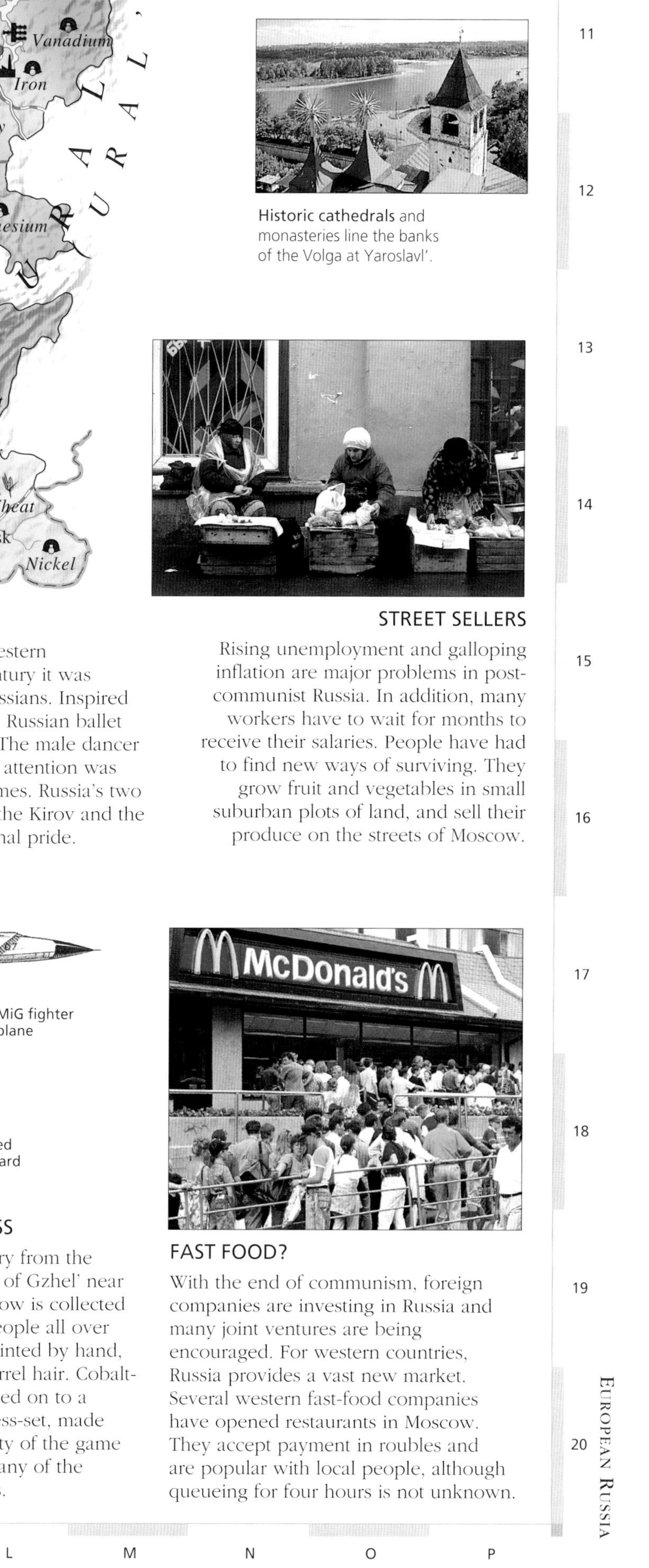
UKRAINE
KAZAKHSTAN
GEORGIA
AZERBAIJAN
CHECHNYA
CAUCASUS
URAL
BLACK SEA
SEA OF AZOV
CASPIAN SEA
Kerch Strait
Tula
Orël
Kursk
Belgorod
Voronezh
Lipetsk
Ryazan'
Tambov
Penza
Saransk
Nizhniy Novgorod
Yoshkar-Ola
Cheboksary
Kazan'
Izhevsk
Perm'
Naberezhnyye Chelny
Ul'yanovsk
Tol'yatti
Samara
Ufa
Saratov
Balakovo
Krasnoarmeysk
Volgograd
Rostov-na-Donu
Krasnodar
Maykop
Sochi
Cherkessk
Stavropol'
Elista
Astrakhan
Nal'chik
Vladikavkaz
Groznyy
Makhachkala
Orenburg
Orsk
Volga
Don
Kuban
Kuma
Vyatka
Severskiy Donets
Tsimlyanskoye Vodokhranilishche
Vodokhranilishche
Wheat
Maize
Barley
Oats
Rye
Iron
Copper
Nickel
Sulphur
Magnesium
Vanadium
Platinum
Lead
Zinc
N
0 100 200 300 400 500 KM
0 50 100 150 200 250 300 MILES

MINERAL WEALTH

Mines are a common sight in Russia. There are large reserves of coal around Moscow. Nickel, copper, phosphates and cobalt are found in the far north. Iron, sulphur, copper, gold and nickel are mined in the south and southwest. **Look for**

Traditional hand-made wooden toy, in the form of a child and dancing bear.

MAP FEATURES

Reindeer: Nomads in the north herd reindeer, which are used to carry loads and for their meat, milk and skins. **Look for**

Hydro-electric power: vast dams on the Dneiper and Volga rivers power electricity generators, which supply large cities and other republics. **Look for**

Vehicle manufacture: Cars are manufactured along the Volga. The truck plant at Naberezhnyye Chelny is the largest in the world. **Look for**

Pollution: Huge numbers of factories, which have grown without environmental controls, are polluting the region's rivers. **Look for**

Cereals	Mining
Sugar beet	Coal
Citrus fruit	Industrial centre
Tobacco	Aerospace industry

Fur hats with ear-flaps are essential in Russia's freezing winters.

A tutu, the costume worn by ballerinas

Ballet shoe

BALLET

Ballet originally developed in western Europe, but in the late 19th century it was completely changed by the Russians. Inspired largely by one man, Diaghilev, Russian ballet became creative and exciting. The male dancer was more important, and more attention was paid to the music and the costumes. Russia's two most famous ballet companies are the Kirov and the Bolshoi. Both are a source of national pride.

MAKING WAVES

The manufacture and sale of weapons, such as this MiG fighter plane, has been badly hit by the end of the Cold War. At Nizhniy Novgorod, where nuclear submarines used to be built, many shipyard workers are now making a semi-automatic washing machine, called the "Wave". Large numbers of unsold machines fill the former shipyard's warehouses. **Look for**

MiG fighter plane

Model of a Lada hatchback

LADA

In 1965, the Russians signed a deal with the Italian car company, Fiat. A factory was built at Tol'yatti and is the largest car plant in the former Soviet Union. Ladas (based on the Fiat) are manufactured here, and some are exported to the West. Few Russians own a car, but the demand for imported western cars is growing. **Look for**

Chess piece

Enamelled chess-board

CHESS

Pottery from the town of Gzhel' near Moscow is collected by people all over the world. The patterns are painted by hand, using brushes made from squirrel hair. Cobalt-blue patterns are then enamelled on to a background of white. This chess-set, made in Gzhel', reflects the popularity of the game here – Russia has produced many of the world's grand masters of chess.

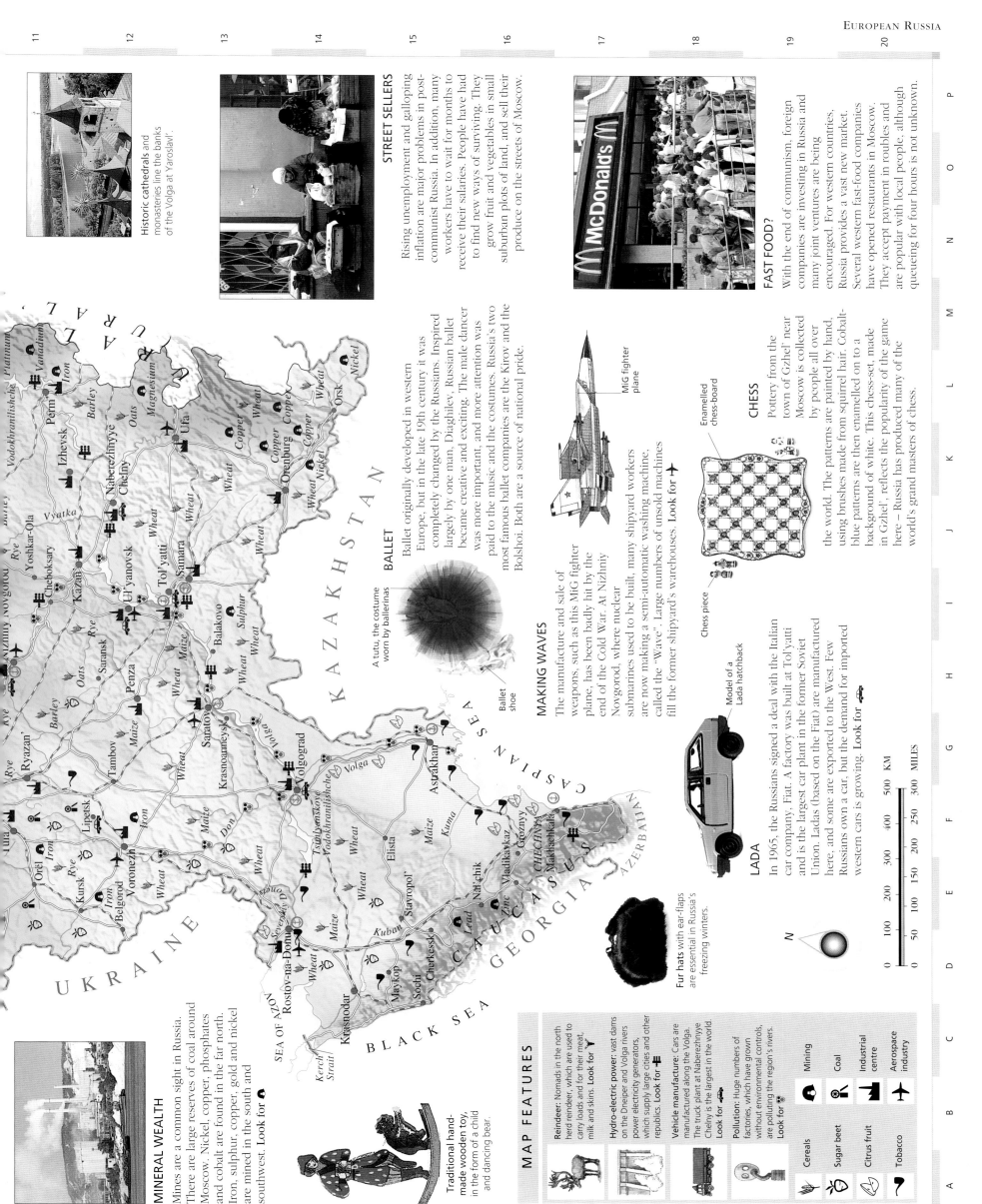

Historic cathedrals and monasteries line the banks of the Volga at Yaroslavl'.

STREET SELLERS

Rising unemployment and galloping inflation are major problems in post-communist Russia. In addition, many workers have to wait for months to receive their salaries. People have had to find new ways of surviving. They grow fruit and vegetables in small suburban plots of land, and sell their produce on the streets of Moscow.

FAST FOOD?

With the end of communism, foreign companies are investing in Russia and many joint ventures are being encouraged. For western countries, Russia provides a vast new market. Several western fast-food companies have opened restaurants in Moscow. They accept payment in roubles and are popular with local people, although queueing for four hours is not unknown.

UKRAINE, MOLDOVA AND THE CAUCASUS REPUBLICS

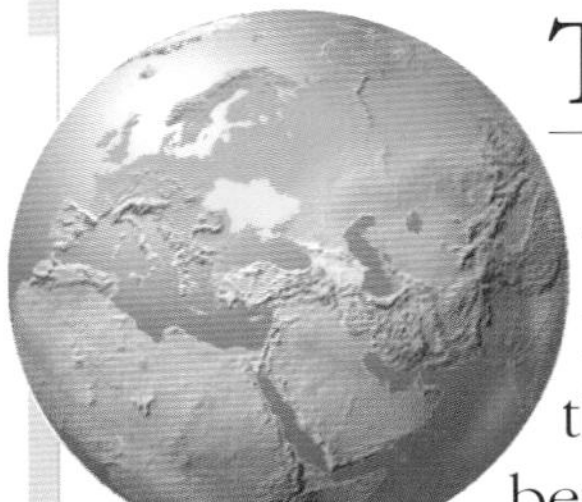

THE CAUCASUS MOUNTAINS run between the Black and Caspian Seas. Higher in places than the Alps, they form a natural barrier between the flat steppes of the Russian Federation to the north and the plateaux of Southwest Asia. The newly independent states which lie to the south of the Russian Federation are rich in a variety of natural resources. Ukraine is dominated by a flat and fertile plain, where huge quantities of cereals are grown on large farms. Ukraine also possesses extensive coal and iron ore deposits and is heavily industrialized. Wine and fruit are produced in Moldova and Georgia, where the climate is mild and the soil fertile. Mountainous Armenia is rich in minerals, while Azerbaijan has plentiful oil.

Cereals being harvested in the fertile fields of Ukraine.

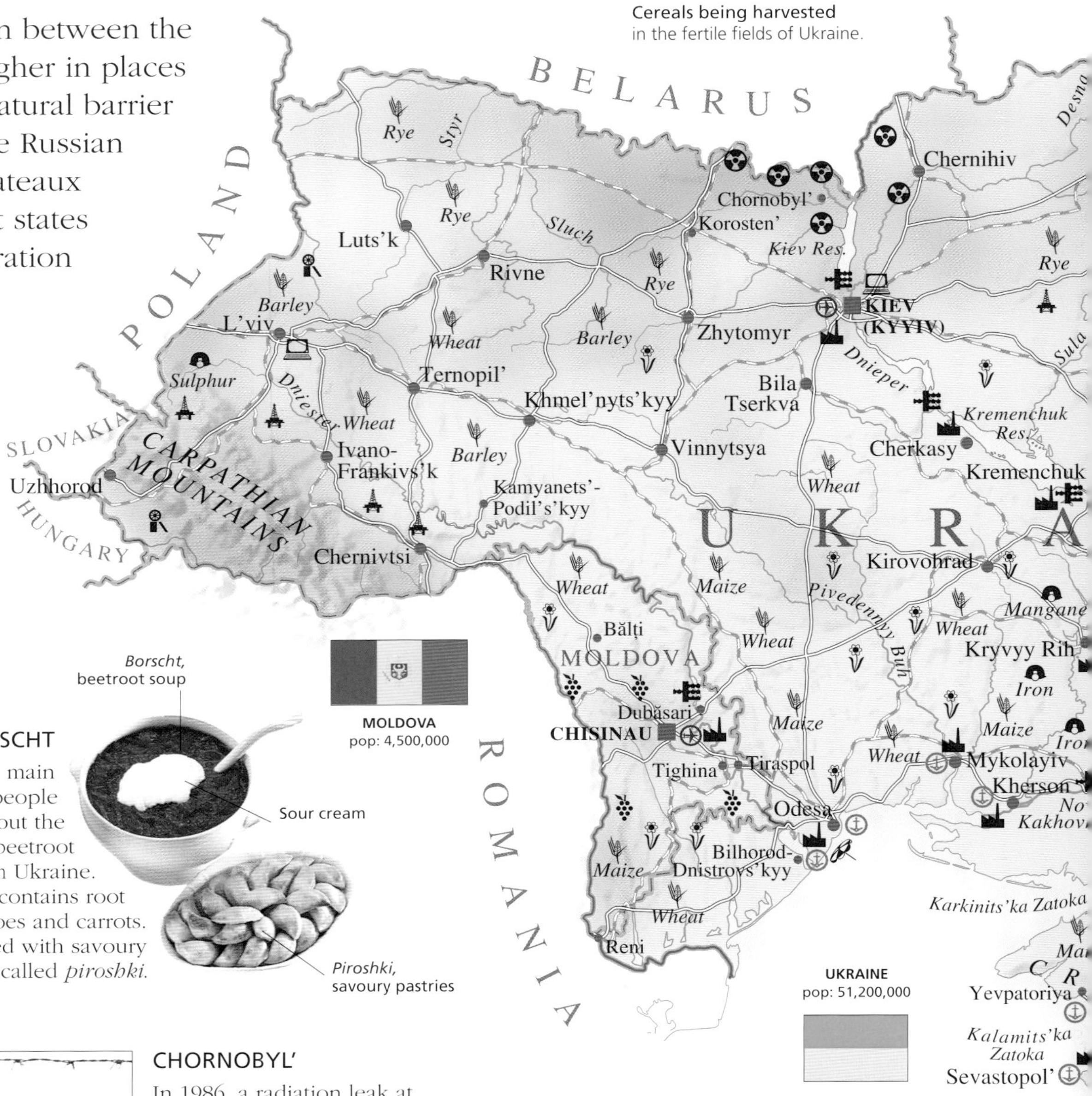

MOLDOVA
pop: 4,500,000

UKRAINE
pop: 51,200,000

BORSCHT

Vegetable soups are the main food for many country people in cold regions throughout the world. Russia's famous beetroot soup, *borscht*, comes from Ukraine. There, the *borscht* also contains root vegetables, such as potatoes and carrots. *Borscht* is often served with savoury turnovers, called *piroshki*.

Borscht, beetroot soup

Sour cream

Piroshki, savoury pastries

WINE

Georgian brandy

Moldovan wine

A quarter of the former Soviet Union's wine was produced in Moldova, which is well known for its champagne. Vines also thrive on the warm, sunny hills of eastern Georgia, where wine and brandy are produced. **Look for** (wine symbol)

CHORNOBYL'

In 1986, a radiation leak at Chornobyl' nuclear power station caused panic all over Europe. More than 100,000 people were evacuated from the area around the plant, where towns now stand desolate and empty. More than two million people still live, in fear and uncertainty, in the contaminated areas. **Look for** (nuclear pollution symbol)

MAP FEATURES

Oil: There is a large oilfield under the delta of the River Kura in Azerbaijan. Offshore wells are also being dug in the Caspian Sea. Look for (oil symbol)

Hydro-electric power: Dams on the River Dnieper supply water for crops and for electricity. The rivers of the Caucasus also provide electricity. Look for (hydro-electric symbol)

High-tech: Electrical and electronic equipment, such as TVs and computers, are made in the Caucasus republics. Look for (high-tech symbol)

Cereals	Mining
Wine	Coal
Tea	Industrial centre
Sunflowers	Tourism
Fishing	Nuclear pollution

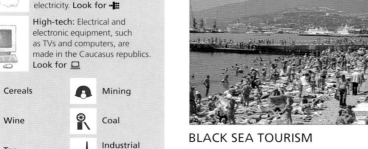

BLACK SEA TOURISM

The Crimea attracts millions of visitors who cram onto the crowded beaches to enjoy the warm sun. Many visitors come for their health, rest and a regime of healthy eating, massage and exercise. **Look for** (tourism symbol)

Hardy crops, such as maize which can withstand frosts, are grown on lowlands

Black Sea

The barrier of the Caucasus mountains blocks cold air from the north

Tbilisi

TURKEY
GEORGIA
ARMENIA
RUSSIAN FEDERATION
AZERBAIJAN
CASPIAN SEA

Mountains force humid air to rise. It falls as rain in Georgia

Grapes and fruits grown in valleys

Baku

Cotton production along lower R. Kura

THE CAUCASUS

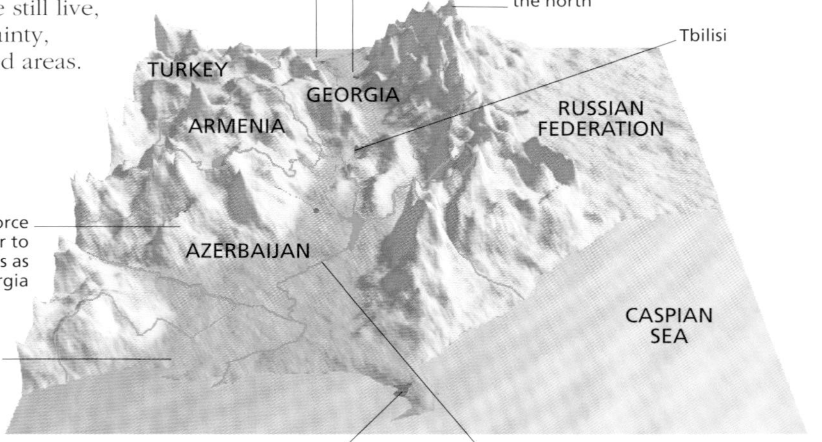

Armenia, Azerbaijan and Georgia – the Caucasus Republics – are isolated from the Russian Federation by the Caucasus mountains. The warm sub-tropical climate of the region allows an exotic range of crops to be grown. Georgia has a humid climate, so tea and citrus fruits are cultivated. In the drier east, the rivers running down from the mountains are used to water the fields.

BLACK BREAD

Ukraine was known as the former Soviet Union's "breadbasket". Its broad flat steppes, with their fertile black earth, are intensively cultivated: wheat, buckwheat, potatoes, rye and flax are grown on vast farms. Much of Ukraine's countryside consists of endless fields of cereals, the view broken only by the occasional haystack.

Matrioshka dolls are hand-painted. Each is made from a single piece of wood.

KIEV

Kiev, founded in the 9th century, is the capital of Ukraine. St. Sophia's Cathedral, with its gilded domes, has been Kiev's most famous landmark since 1037. Kiev is situated on the banks of the River Dnieper, the republic's main waterway. It is within easy reach of the Black Sea ports, as well as being near Ukraine's industrial centre.

The Ukraine is the world's largest producer of buckwheat. Although it is ground up to make flour, buckwheat is not a true cereal.

COAL

About a third of the former Soviet Union's coal came from the area around Donets'k in Ukraine, where there are about 40 deep mines. Miners working here are reasonably well-paid, but gas explosions and the frequent breakdown of equipment put them at risk. Death rates in these mines are 10 times higher than in mines in the USA. Look for

INDUSTRIAL HEARTLAND

Ukraine's Donbass region, with its rich reserves of coal, iron, manganese and other minerals, is a major industrial area. Heavy industry, such as iron and steel works, engineering and chemicals, still dominate the region, but today, cars, aircraft, televisions and computers are also manufactured here. Look for

CAUCASUS CONFLICT

When the Caucasus republics were part of the Soviet Union, many different peoples were forced to live side by side. Since these countries became independent, many pent-up resentments have been unleashed. Within Muslim Azerbaijan, the Christian, mainly Armenian, region of Nagornyy-Karabakh has caused great tension and conflict. A peace agreement has now been negotiated.

TEA

Tea is a popular drink throughout the former Soviet Union, and over 90 per cent of the tea consumed here is grown in Georgia. Both black and green teas are grown on large tea plantations. Tea is served black and strong, with sugar or lemon. Look for

SUNFLOWERS

Sunflowers are an important crop in southern Ukraine. The seeds, which can be eaten, contain oil and protein. Sunflower oil is used for cooking. The seeds are also used in the manufacture of margarine and soap, and are mixed with maize and peas for cattle feed. Look for

Decorated Black Sea fiddle, from Georgia.

The snow-capped peaks of the Caucasus mountains.

AZERBAIJAN
pop: 7,700,000

Caviar, served on toast

CAVIAR

The Russian sturgeon is a large fish, which can grow up to 7 m (23 ft) in length. Its eggs, called caviar, are an expensive delicacy. Sturgeon live in the Black and Caspian Seas and swim up rivers, such as the Dnieper, to breed in fresh water. Hydro-electric dams on these rivers have disrupted the sturgeons' routes, and polluted water is causing concern about falling numbers of fish. Look for

GEORGIA
pop:5,400,000

The Swallow's Nest Castle, high on a rock near Yalta.

TEXTILES

Georgia is famous for its silk and textiles. Brightly coloured and patterned cotton fabrics are woven with gold and silver thread. Worn by women as headscarves, these fabrics are seen throughout the Caucasus.

ARMENIA
pop: 3,600,000

0 50 100 150 200 250 300 KM
0 50 100 150 MILES

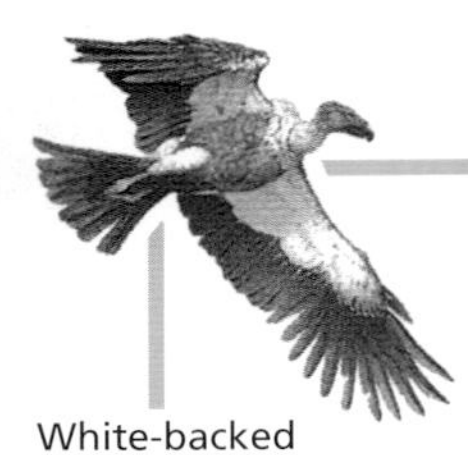

White-backed vulture
Gyps bengalensis
Wingspan: 2.2 m (7 ft)

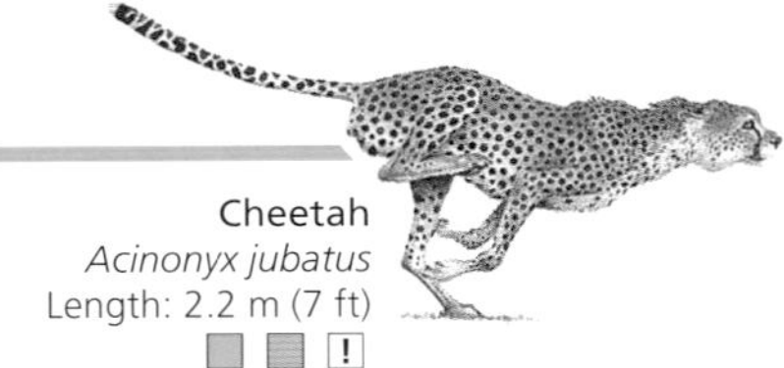

Cheetah
Acinonyx jubatus
Length: 2.2 m (7 ft)

Aye-aye
Daubentonia madagascariensis
Length: 45 cm (18 in)

AFRICA

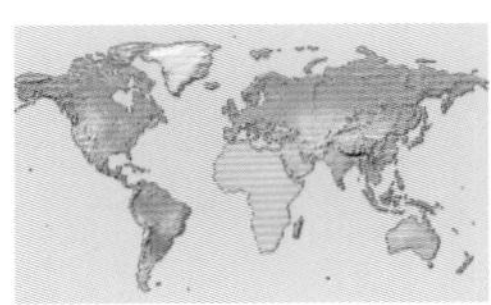

AFRICA IS THE SECOND largest continent after Asia, and the only one through which the Equator and both tropics run. It is also home to the world's longest river, the Nile. The climate and vegetation roughly mirror each other on either side of the Equator. In the extreme south, and along the Mediterranean coast in the north, hot dry summers are followed by mild wet winters. Similarly, the land around each tropic is hot and starved of rain, so great deserts have formed. Africa's immense tropical savannah grasslands are prone to drought, but around the Equator high rainfall has produced lush tropical rainforests. The volcanoes and strangely elongated lakes in the Great Rift Valley are evidence of cracks in the Earth's crust that threaten eventually to split Africa apart.

HOT SAHARA

The inhospitable Sahara desert covers one-third of Africa. Temperatures can exceed 50°C (120°F).

Burchell's zebra
Equus burchelli
Height: 1.2 m (4 ft)

MISTY RAINFOREST

Tropical rainforests only grow where temperatures are always high, and rain is abundant. Here in central Africa, it rains every day – more than 2 m (7 ft) falls each year.

THUNDERING WATERFALL

The Zambezi River winds slowly through dry woodlands before reaching the Victoria Falls. Here it plummets 108 m (354 ft), creating so much noise and spray that local people call it "the smoke that thunders".

Malachite is a copper-rich ore found in many parts of eastern Africa.

GREAT RIFT VALLEY

Cracks in the Earth's crust have made a valley 6,000 km (3,750 miles) long, and up to 90 km (55 miles) wide.

Umbrella thorn acacia
Acacia tortillis
Height: 18 m (60 ft)

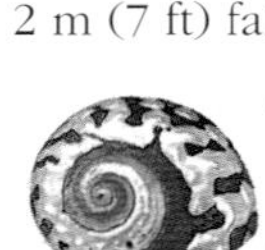

The South African Turban shell looks like a headdress made of coiled cloth.

SAND DUNES IN THE NAMIB

The intensely hot Namib Desert forms a narrow strip down Africa's southwest coast. Rainfall is less than 15 cm (6 in) a year, but sea mists from the cold currents along the coast provide enough moisture for some plants and animals to survive.

SERENGETI PLAIN

Savannah – grassland and open woodland – is home to huge herds of grazing animals, including wildebeest and zebra.

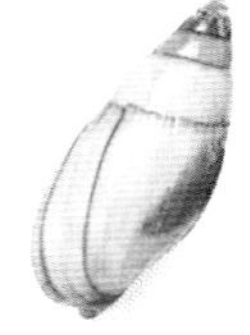

Shells like this Black Mitre can be found in shallow water along the west African coast.

OKAVANGO DELTA

Not all rivers run to the sea. The Okavango River ends in a huge inland swamp that attracts thousands of water-loving animals, such as hippopotamuses.

Gaboon viper
Bitis gabonica
Length: 2 m (7 ft)

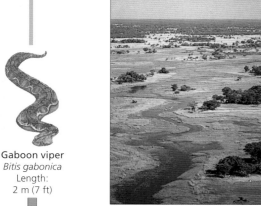

CROSS-SECTION THROUGH AFRICA

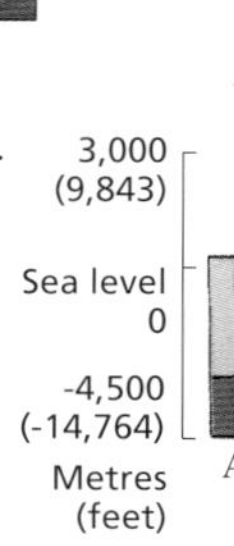

L. Victoria
Serengeti Plain
Great Rift Valley (western)
Ruwenzori Mountains
Great Rift Valley (eastern)
Atlantic Ocean
Congo Basin
Indian Ocean
3,000 (9,843)
Sea level 0
-4,500 (-14,764)
Metres (feet)
A
B
Length: 4,500 km (2,800 miles)

SOUTHERN AFRICA

Rainfall is so low in southern Africa that for most of the year few plants show themselves above ground. But as soon as the rains come, a barren landscape is transformed, covered by a brilliant mass of flowers.

African elephant
Loxodonta africana
Height: 4 m (13 ft)

Desert scorpion
Androctonus australis
Length: 8 cm (3 in)

Mountain gorilla
Gorilla gorilla
Height: 1.8 m (6 ft)

MEDITERRANEAN SEA
ASIA
Strait of Gibraltar
EURASIAN PLATE
AFRICAN PLATE
C. Bon
Madeira Ridge
Madeira
ATLAS MTS.
Chott el Jerid
Gulf of Sirte
Nile Delta
IRANIAN PLATE
ARABIAN PLATE
The Gulf
Tropic of Cancer
Jbel Toubkal 4165m
Canary Is.
Qattara Depression -133m
LIBYAN DESERT
Nile
RED SEA
ARABIAN PENINSULA
TASSILI-N-AJJER
Tahat 2918m
AHAGGAR
L. Nasser
NUBIAN DESERT
SAHARA
TIBESTI
Emi Koussi 3415m
Cape Verde Is.
ARABIAN PLATE
AFRICAN PLATE
Senegal
Niger
Blue Nile
Socotra
Raas Xaafuun
Gulf of Aden
Ras Dashen 4620m
L. Tana
SAHEL
L. Chad
Black Volta
AFRICA
White Nile
ETHIOPIAN HIGHLANDS
Niger
Benue
Sudd
Shebeli
L. Volta
ADAMAWA HIGHLANDS
L. Rudolf
Great Rift Valley
Equator
Niger Delta
Mt. Cameroon 4070m
Ubangi
Somali Basin
Gulf of Guinea
Bioko
Congo Basin
L. Albert
Kirinyaga 5200m
Guinea Basin
Príncipe
São Tomé
L. Victoria
SERENGETI PLAIN
Kilimanjaro 5895m
INDIAN OCEAN
Mid-Atlantic Ridge
Congo
Ngorongoro Crater
Zanzibar
L. Tanganyika
L. Rukwa
Comoro Is.
L. Mweru
L. Nyasa
Angola Basin
SOUTH AMERICAN PLATE
AFRICAN PLATE
Zambezi
Mozambique Channel
Madagascar
L. Kariba
Okavango
Victoria Falls 108m
Tropic of Capricorn
C. Fria
NAMIB DESERT
Okavango Delta
Limpopo
Madagascar Basin
Walvis Ridge
KALAHARI DESERT
Natal Basin
Phofung 3282m
Orange R.
Mid-Atlantic Ridge
DRAKENSBERG
Cape Basin
Cape of Good Hope
C. Agulhas
Southwest Indian Ridge
Agulhas Basin
AFRICAN PLATE
ANTARCTICA PLATE
ATLANTIC OCEAN
A
B
Black rhinoceros
Diceros bicornis
Length: 3.6 m (12 ft)
KEY TO SYMBOLS
Mountain
Volcano
Mangroves
Wetlands
Coral reef
Plate margins showing direction of movement
Endangered species
NATURAL VEGETATION ZONES
Mediterranean-type
Temperate grassland
Hot desert
Mountain
Tropical grassland
Tropical rainforest
Dry woodland

BOTTLE TREES
Plants can resist drought by reducing their leaf-size and enlarging their stems to store water. Here in Madagascar's dry woodlands, huge-trunked baobabs, or "bottle trees", grow alongside spiny Dideria.

Northwest Africa

Over the centuries, Northwest Africa has been invaded by many peoples. The entire north coast from the Red Sea to the Atlantic was once part of the Roman Empire. While subsequent colonization by Italy, Great Britain, Turkey, Spain and France contributed to the culture of the countries, it was the 7th-century Arab conquest which fundamentally changed the region. The conversion of the original peoples – the Berbers – to Islam, and the use of Arabic as a common language, gave these countries a sense of unity which remains today. In fact, the region is sometimes called the Maghreb, which means "west" in Arabic. In the northwest, the Atlas Mountains form a barrier between the wetter, cooler areas along the coast and the arid Sahara. This desert is the biggest on Earth, and is still growing. Water shortages and lack of land for farming are problems throughout the region, especially as the population of the Maghreb is increasing rapidly. In Algeria and Libya, however, the desert has revealed hidden riches – abundant oil and natural gas.

FEZ – AN ISLAMIC CITY

This view of the city of Fez in Morocco shows the flat-roofed houses that are traditional in this region. Seen from the narrow streets, the houses look blank and windowless, but this is because they are designed to face inwards on to central courtyards which are cool and private. Islamic cities may appear to be a chaotic maze of streets, but in fact they are laid out following guidelines set in the holy book of Islam, the *Koran*.

The Moroccans make a refreshing tea from the spearmint plant.

MOROCCO
pop: 28,000,000
Strait of Gibraltar
Tangier
Ceuta (part of Spain)
Tétouan
Al-Hoceima
Melilla (part of Spain)
Kenitra
Tlemcen
RABAT
Oujda
Casablanca
Meknès
Fez
MOROCCO
Safi
Phosphates
Khouribga
Essaouira
Beni Mellal
Er Rachidia
Marrakech
Figuig
Phosphates
Agadir
Boumalne-Dadès
Béchar
ATLAS
Tiznit
Olive
ATLANTIC OCEAN
Tan-Tan
LAAYOUNE
Tindouf
Smara
Phosphates
ALG
Adra
WESTERN SAHARA
MAURITANIA
Ad Dakhla
Morocco occupied the whole of Western Sahara in 1979
Lagouira
WESTERN SAHARA
pop: 230,000
MALI
S

BERBERS

Berbers were the original people of northwest Africa. When the Arabs invaded, they were driven out of the fertile coastal areas. Many Berbers still live in remote villages or towns – such as here at Boumalne-Dadès – high in the Atlas Mountains, where their lifestyle and language have remained unchanged for centuries.

Couscous is the basic ingredient of many North African dishes. It is made of tiny pellets of flour, called semolina.

MAP FEATURES

Mining: Huge quantities of phosphates come from the sands of Western Sahara and Morocco. They are the vital raw material for fertilizers. **Look for**

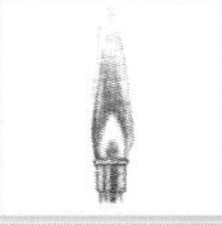

Gas: Algeria has vast reserves of natural gas, much of it exported to Europe – some by pipeline to Italy across the Mediterranean Sea. **Look for**

Archaeological sites: Early civilizations, such as the Romans, built cities in the desert and along the coast of North Africa. **Look for**

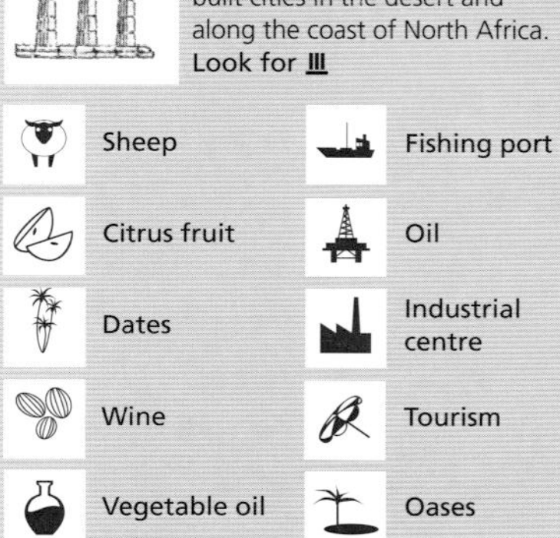
Sheep
Fishing port
Citrus fruit
Oil
Dates
Industrial centre
Wine
Tourism
Vegetable oil
Oases

CARPETS AND RUGS

Hand-knotted carpets and rugs, with their distinctive bold patterns and deep pile, are made throughout the region. In Morocco the most important carpet factories are in Rabat and Fez. Craftworkers often work together in cooperatives to maintain high quality and to control prices.

WESTERN SAHARA

Western Sahara is a sparsely populated desert area lying between Morocco and Mauritania. It was a Spanish colony until 1976, but is now fighting for independence from Morocco which claims the country, and the phosphates found there. This photo shows young members of the liberation movement.

The Ahaggar mountains, Algeria, jut up in the middle of the Sahara.

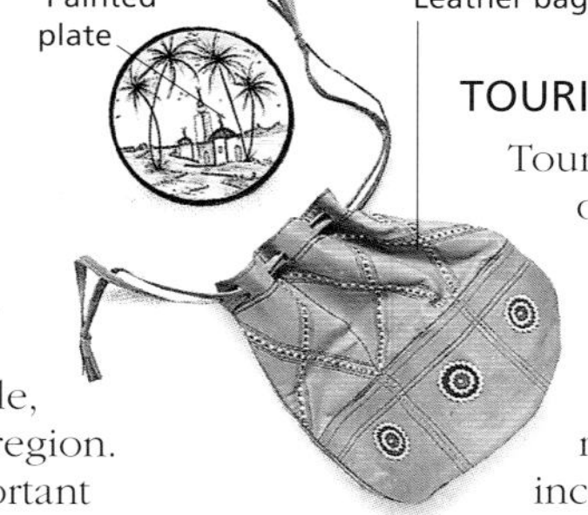

Painted plate

Leather bag

TOURISM

Tourism is a vital source of foreign income for Morocco and Tunisia. When oil prices fell in the 1980s, tourism took the place of oil as the main source of foreign income. Modern hotels, built in traditional styles, have sprung up along the coast. Both countries produce handicrafts for tourists, such as leather and brassware. **Look for**

THE TUAREG

The Tuareg are a nomadic tribe who inhabit a huge area of the Sahara. In the past they controlled the great camel caravans which crossed the desert to the Mediterranean, carrying slaves, ivory, gold and salt. Today, some Tuareg still follow the traditional desert way of life, but many have become settled farmers.

NORTH COAST AGRICULTURE

Along the Mediterranean coast, and in sheltered valleys in the Atlas Mountains, the soil is rich and the climate mild. In these areas, farmers can grow crops such as grapes, olives, cereals and citrus fruit. Sheep, goats and cattle are kept throughout the region, especially in Tunisia.

"BREAD OF THE DESERT"

The fruit of the date palm has been eaten for centuries. Dates are rich in protein and provide food for people and animals. They grow around desert oases, where the climate is hot and dry and there is water in the ground. Every part of a date palm has some use. **Look for**

Ruins of the Roman port of Leptis Magna in Libya.

KAIROUAN

For Muslims, the 9th-century Great Mosque in the desert at Kairouan, Tunisia, is the holiest place in Africa. The enormous courtyard – where the people pray – is paved in marble and surrounded by a forest of columns. The interior is decorated with beautiful glazed tiles.

TUNISIA
POP: 9,500,000

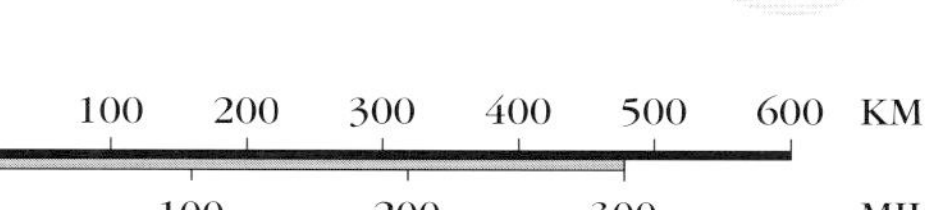

N
0 100 200 300 400 500 600 KM
0 100 200 300 MILES

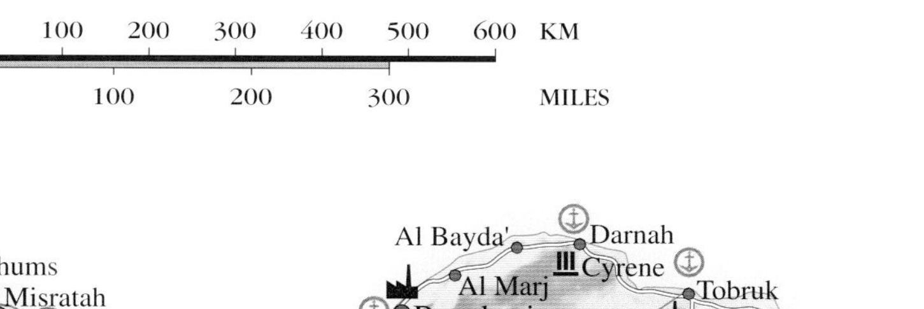

MEDITERRANEAN SEA
ALGIERS
Béjaïa
Skikda
Annaba
Bizerte
TUNIS
Blida
Olive
Mostaganem
Constantine
Jendouba
Sousse
Monastir
Sétif
Tiaret
Batna
Iron
Tébessa
Kairouan
Timgad
Biskra
Phosphates
Sfax
Chott Melghir
Tozeur
Gafsa
Gabès
Djerba
Laghouat
Chott el Jerid
El Oued
Medenine
Touggourt
Ghardaïa
TRIPOLI (TARABULUS)
Al Khums
Misratah
Gharyan
Leptis Magna
Yafran
Ouargla
GRAND ERG OCCIDENTAL
GRAND ERG ORIENTAL
TUNISIA
TRIPOLITANIA
Ghadāmis
Gulf of Sirte
Surt
Al Bayda'
Darnah
Cyrene
Al Marj
Benghazi (Banghazi)
Tobruk
Ajdabiya
Marsa al Burayqah
Great Man-made River Project
Al Jaghbub
CYRENAICA
Hun
LIBYA
ALGERIA
Adiri
Birak
Sabha
Awbari
Illizi
FEZZAN
Murzuq
TASSILI-N-AJJER
Ghat
SAHARA
Al Khufrah
AHAGGAR
Tamanrasset
EGYPT
NIGER
CHAD
SUDAN

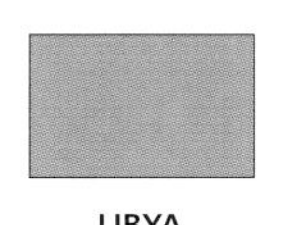

A Saharan oasis – an island of green in a sea of sand.

LIBYA
pop: 6,000,000

OIL IN LIBYA

Until the discovery of oil in 1958, many people in Libya were very poor. The money from oil has enabled Libya to construct roads and railways, improve education and develop industry and agriculture. Libyan oil is in great demand because it has no sulphur in it. This means that when it is burned, it gives out very little pollution. **Look for**

Classical Arab lute from Morocco.

ALGERIA
pop: 30,200,000

WOOD SHORTAGE

The main source of energy for many African people is burning wood. But tree roots help to bind the soil together, and when large numbers of trees are cut down, the soil can be blown or worn away. This allows the desert to spread. People who live in treeless areas spend hours searching for wood to burn, and must then carry it long distances to their villages. Collecting wood is traditionally women's work.

An Algerian stamp showing the traditional dress for men.

WATER PIPELINE

Deep beneath the Sahara are vast underground supplies of water. The Libyans are building a series of huge pipelines like the one shown under construction here, which will carry this water across the desert to the coastal areas. It will be used to water the farmland and increase crop production. This is known as the Great Man-made River project, and two cross-desert pipelines have already been completed.

NORTHEAST AFRICA

WATERED AND FERTILIZED BY THE NILE, the longest river in the world, Egypt is a fertile strip running through the Sahara desert. The first people settled there about 8,000 years ago and, by the time of the pharaohs, Egypt had become one of the world's first great civilizations. Today, Egypt is a relatively stable democracy, with a growing number of industries and control of the Suez Canal, one of the world's most important waterways. To the south are the highlands of Ethiopia and Eritrea. This area is fertile and well-watered in places, but recent droughts have made life precarious for the farmers and nomads who live there. The countries of Somalia, Sudan and Ethiopia have been beset by terrible problems, including drought, famine, religious conflicts and civil war. Thousands of refugees from these areas depend on international aid. In 1993, Eritrea gained independence from Ethiopia, after a civil war which lasted 30 years.

The pyramids at El Giza were built as tombs for the pharaohs.

EGYPT
pop: 65,700,000

THE GIFT OF THE NILE

The River Nile floods in the summer, carrying rich mud from the highlands of Sudan and Ethiopia to the deserts of Egypt. This creates some of the most fertile land in the world. Nearly 99 per cent of the Egyptian population live along the banks of the Nile.

TOURIST SOUVENIRS

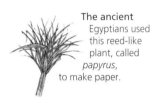

Large numbers of "ancient Egyptian" scarabs (beetles) and other fake antiques are made locally and sold to tourists. City streets are lined with market stalls and the small workshops where these goods are made. Tourism has stimulated this informal economy.

CAIRO AND THE DELTA

Cairo is the largest city in the Islamic world and is also one of the fastest-growing. Its current population is estimated at 13 million. To the north, dams and irrigation canals have disturbed the flow of the River Nile, reducing the amount of sediment it deposits at the Delta. This causes a reduction in cultivable land, forcing more farmers into the cities.

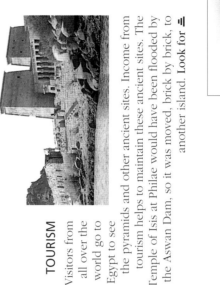

Nile
Gulf of Suez
WESTERN DESERT
El Faiyum oasis is cultivated with vines, olives, wheat and legumes
Cairo, centre of the rail and road network, lies at the foot of the Delta
Suez Canal is 121miles (195km) long, and links the Mediterranean and Red Seas
Site of pyramids at El Giza
DELTA
Alexandria marks the western limit of the Delta.
Port Said marks the eastern limit of the Delta
MEDITERRANEAN SEA
MEDITERRANEAN SEA
The Nile Delta is extensively cultivated, but is gradually shrinking and becoming salinated
N

SUEZ CANAL

Opened in 1869, The Suez Canal is one of the world's largest artificial waterways and a vital source of income for Egypt. It connects the Red Sea with the Mediterranean, offering a short cut from Europe to The Gulf, India and the Far East. On average, 21,250 ships a year use the canal.

The ancient Egyptians used this reed-like plant, called *papyrus*, to make paper.

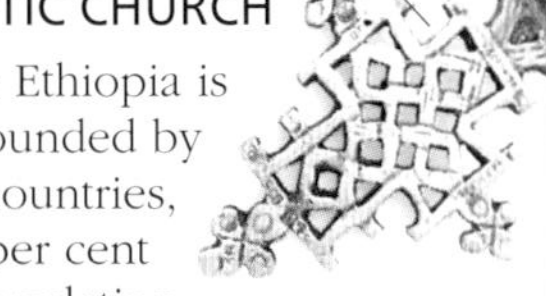
Coptic cross

THE COPTIC CHURCH

Although Ethiopia is surrounded by Islamic countries, about 40 per cent of its population is Christian. The isolated Ethiopian church developed into a unique branch of Christianity, called the Coptic Church.

TOURISM

Visitors from all over the world go to Egypt to see the pyramids and other ancient sites. Income from tourism helps to maintain these ancient sites. The Temple of Isis at Philae would have been flooded by the Aswan Dam, so it was moved, brick by brick, to another island. Look for

The gold death-mask of the Pharaoh Tutankhamun, c. 1352 BC

Cotton *jelaba*

COTTON

Egypt produces about a third of the world's high-quality cotton. Textile industries, such as spinning, weaving and dyeing cotton are also important. Cotton is the coolest fabric to wear during hot summers. Egyptian men often wear a long-sleeved cotton garment, or *jelaba*. Look for

AGRICULTURE

Although there is fertile land in southern Ethiopia, farming methods are inefficient. The scratch plough is widely used, and – as its name implies – is only able to turn over the surface of the soil. After a few years, the goodness in the soil is used up, and crops will no longer grow.

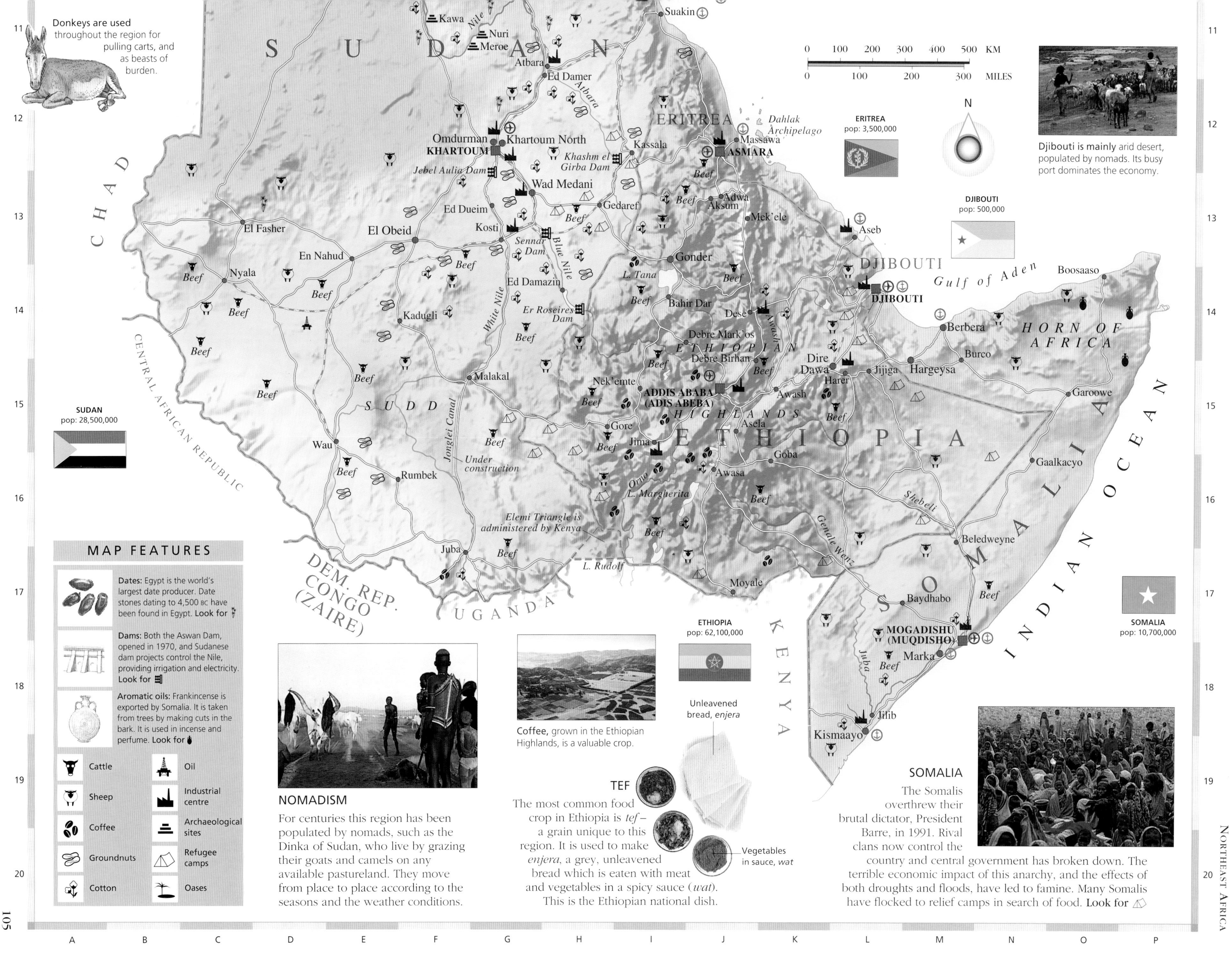
SUDAN
CHAD
CENTRAL AFRICAN REPUBLIC
DEM. REP. CONGO (ZAIRE)
UGANDA
KENYA
ETHIOPIA
ERITREA
DJIBOUTI
SOMALIA
INDIAN OCEAN
Gulf of Aden
HORN OF AFRICA
ETHIOPIAN HIGHLANDS
SUDD
KHARTOUM
Omdurman
Khartoum North
ASMARA
ADDIS ABABA (ADIS ABEBA)
DJIBOUTI
MOGADISHU (MUQDISHO)
Kawa
Nuri
Meroe
Atbara
Ed Damer
Suakin
Kassala
Massawa
Dahlak Archipelago
Khashm el Girba Dam
Jebel Aulia Dam
Wad Medani
Gedaref
Adwa
Aksum
Mek'ele
Aseb
El Fasher
Ed Dueim
El Obeid
Kosti
Sennar Dam
Blue Nile
Gonder
L. Tana
Bahir Dar
En Nahud
Nyala
Ed Damazin
Er Roseires Dam
Kadugli
White Nile
Dese
Awash
Debre Mark'os
Debre Birhan
Dire Dawa
Harer
Jijiga
Hargeyska
Berbera
Burco
Boosaaso
Malakal
Nek'emte
Gore
Jima
Asela
Goba
Awasa
Jonglei Canal
Under construction
Wau
Rumbek
Orno
L. Margherita
Elemi Triangle is administered by Kenya
Juba
L. Rudolf
Moyale
Genale Wenz
Shebeli
Beledweyne
Gaalkacyo
Garoowe
Baydhabo
Marka
Juba
Jilib
Kismaayo
Beef
Nile
Atbara
0 100 200 300 400 500 KM
0 100 200 300 MILES
N
ERITREA
pop: 3,500,000
DJIBOUTI
pop: 500,000
SUDAN
pop: 28,500,000
ETHIOPIA
pop: 62,100,000
SOMALIA
pop: 10,700,000
Unleavened bread, *enjera*
Vegetables in sauce, *wat*

Donkeys are used throughout the region for pulling carts, and as beasts of burden.

Djibouti is mainly arid desert, populated by nomads. Its busy port dominates the economy.

MAP FEATURES

Dates: Egypt is the world's largest date producer. Date stones dating to 4,500 BC have been found in Egypt. **Look for**

Dams: Both the Aswan Dam, opened in 1970, and Sudanese dam projects control the Nile, providing irrigation and electricity. **Look for**

Aromatic oils: Frankincense is exported by Somalia. It is taken from trees by making cuts in the bark. It is used in incense and perfume. **Look for**

Cattle	Oil
Sheep	Industrial centre
Coffee	Archaeological sites
Groundnuts	Refugee camps
Cotton	Oases

NOMADISM

For centuries this region has been populated by nomads, such as the Dinka of Sudan, who live by grazing their goats and camels on any available pastureland. They move from place to place according to the seasons and the weather conditions.

Coffee, grown in the Ethiopian Highlands, is a valuable crop.

TEF

The most common food crop in Ethiopia is *tef* – a grain unique to this region. It is used to make *enjera*, a grey, unleavened bread which is eaten with meat and vegetables in a spicy sauce (*wat*). This is the Ethiopian national dish.

SOMALIA

The Somalis overthrew their brutal dictator, President Barre, in 1991. Rival clans now control the country and central government has broken down. The terrible economic impact of this anarchy, and the effects of both droughts and floods, have led to famine. Many Somalis have flocked to relief camps in search of food. **Look for**

WEST AFRICA

Calabash (bowl) made from a vegetable called a gourd, then decorated.

MAURITANIA
pop: 2,500,000

THE LANDSCAPE OF WEST AFRICA ranges from the sand dunes of the Sahara, through the dry grasslands of the Sahel region, to the tropical rainforests in the south. There is just as much variety in the peoples of the region – more than 250 different tribes live in Nigeria alone. In the north, most people are Muslim, a legacy of the Arab traders who controlled the great caravan routes across the Sahara and brought the religion with them. It was from West Africa, particularly the coastal regions, that hundreds of thousands of Africans were transported to North and South America as slaves. Today many people in West Africa make their living from farming or herding animals. Crops such as coffee and cocoa are grown on large plantations. Like the logging industry, which is also a major source of earnings, these plantations are often owned by foreign multinational companies who take most of the profits out of the region. Recent discoveries of oil and minerals offered the promise of economic prosperity, but this has been prevented by falling world prices, huge foreign debts, corruption and civil wars.

WESTERN SAHARA
MAURITANIA
Zouérat
Fdérik
Iron
Gum arabic
Atar
Nouâdhibou
Râs Nouâdhibou
Râs Timirist
NOUAKCHOTT
Copper
Tidjikja

SENEGAL
pop: 9,000,000

GAMBIA
pop: 1,900,000

Kano mosque, built to serve the largely Islamic population in northern Nigeria.

GUINEA-BISSAU
pop: 1,100,000

DAKAR

Dakar, the capital of Senegal, is one of the main ports in West Africa. It lies on the Atlantic coast and has a fine natural harbour, large modern docks and ship repair facilities. It is the country's main industrial centre.

TOURISM

Tourism in this region has expanded rapidly. In the Gambia, the number of visitors rose from 300 in 1965 to over 100,000 a year in the 1990s. Most tourists stay along the Atlantic coast, but many also go on trips into the bush.

GUINEA
pop: 7,700,000

SIERRA LEONE
pop: 4,600,000

Rosso
Saint Louis
Louga
SENEGAL
Phosphates
Kaédi
Matam
Kiffa
Néma
Nioro
DAKAR
Diourbel
Kaolack
Kayes
BANJUL
GAMBIA
Georgetown
Tambacounda
Kolda
Ziguinchor
Bafatá
BISSAU
GUINEA-BISSAU
Bijagós Archipelago
BAMAKO
Bougouni
Sikasso
Labé
Aluminium
Gold
Kindia
Kankan
CONAKRY
GUINEA
Odienné
Korhogo
SIERRA LEONE
Makeni
FREETOWN
Diamonds
Voinjama
Bo
Kenema
Nzérékoré
Gbanga
Robertsport
MONROVIA
YAMOUSSOUKRO
Buchanan
LIBERIA
Greenville
Harper
Zwedru
Gagnoa
Daloa
ATLANTIC OCEAN

Cocoa pod

Cocoa beans

Pulp

COCOA

The ancient Aztec people of Mexico were the first to make a drink called *chocolatl* from the seeds of the cacao tree – brought to West Africa by European colonizers. The region now produces over half the world's supply of cocoa beans. Look for

LIBERIA
pop: 2,700,000

IVORY COAST
pop: 14,600,000

MAP FEATURES

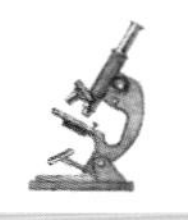

Vegetable oil: The oil palm is widely grown throughout West Africa. Palm oil is used by people in the region and some is exported. **Look for**

Research centre: At a centre in Ibadan, Nigeria, new disease-resistant varieties of maize, cassava, and other crops have been bred. **Look for**

Film industry: Burkina has a large film industry, subsidized by the government, with studios in Ouagadougou and an annual film festival. **Look for**

Shipping registry: Many of the world's shipping countries register their ships in Liberia because of low taxes and lax employment rules. **Look for**

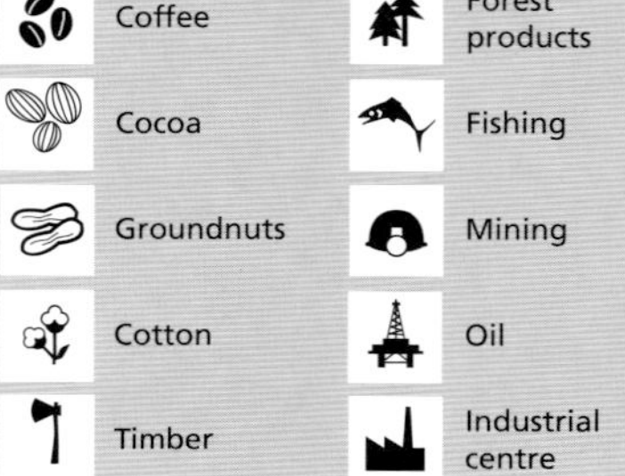

Coffee		Forest products	
Cocoa		Fishing	
Groundnuts		Mining	
Cotton		Oil	
Timber		Industrial centre	

DEFORESTATION

The population of West Africa is growing rapidly. Vast areas of forest have been cut down, either for wood or to clear farmland to feed these extra people. This problem is particularly bad in the Ivory Coast, where little forest is left. **Look for**

AFTER INDEPENDENCE

Since independence, some African countries have been plagued by many problems, such as unstable governments and foreign debts. Ivory Coast, however, is one of West Africa's most prosperous countries. Its last president built this cathedral when he had the capital moved to his family village at Yamoussoukro.

GROUNDNUTS

Groundnuts, or peanuts, grow on low, bushy plants and ripen in the ground – hence their name. They are grown throughout West Africa. Most of the crop is made into groundnut oil, which is used for cooking. Look for

MALI
pop: 11,800,000

A deserted village at the bottom of dramatic rocky outcrops in Mali.

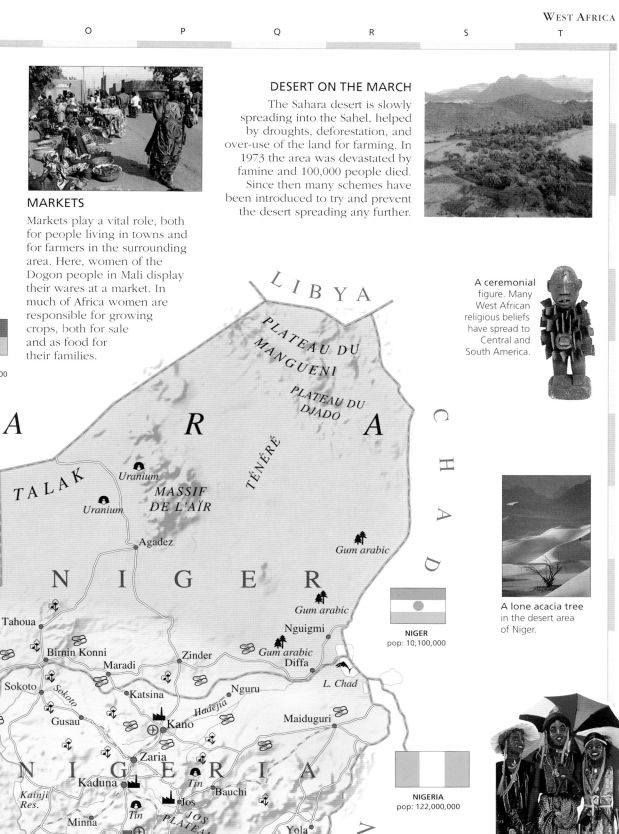

MARKETS

Markets play a vital role, both for people living in towns and for farmers in the surrounding area. Here, women of the Dogon people in Mali display their wares at a market. In much of Africa women are responsible for growing crops, both for sale and as food for their families.

BURKINA
pop: 11,400,000

DESERT ON THE MARCH

The Sahara desert is slowly spreading into the Sahel, helped by droughts, deforestation, and over-use of the land for farming. In 1973 the area was devastated by famine and 100,000 people died. Since then many schemes have been introduced to try and prevent the desert spreading any further.

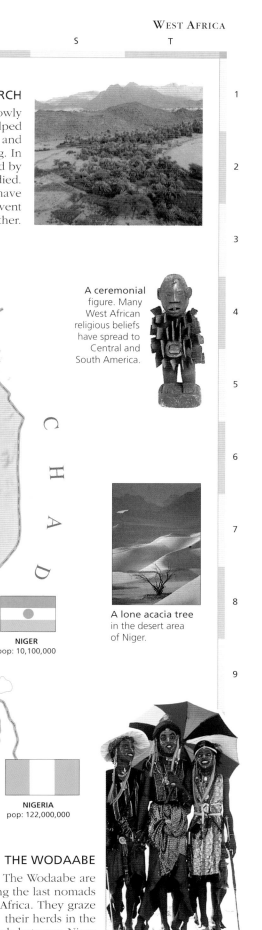

A ceremonial figure. Many West African religious beliefs have spread to Central and South America.

A lone acacia tree in the desert area of Niger.

NIGER
pop: 10,100,000

NIGERIA
pop: 122,000,000

THE WODAABE

The Wodaabe are among the last nomads in Africa. They graze their herds in the borderlands between Niger and Nigeria. Every year they hold a festival at which the men compete for the title of "most beautiful and charming man." The judges are women. The men wear make-up which emphasizes their eyes and teeth.

GHANA
pop: 18,900,000

TOGO
pop: 4,400,000

BENIN
pop: 5,900,000

OIL IN NIGERIA

Nigeria's economy has been transformed by oil. Discovered in the 1950s, oil accounts for about 95 per cent of export earnings, and has paid for the development of new industries. Look for

RIVER NIGER

The Niger flows both north and south during its long journey to the Atlantic. Much of its course passes through the Sahel, where the persistent droughts have reduced water levels. In this region the river often evaporates completely during the dry season. As it reaches the wetter tropics in Nigeria, the amount of water increases, and farmers use large amounts of it for crops and livestock.

N

0 100 200 300 400 500 KM
0 50 100 150 200 250 300 MILES

CENTRAL AFRICA

MUCH OF THIS REGION IS COVERED in dense tropical rainforest, drained by the great Congo (Zaire) River and its tributaries. The climate is hot and humid. All the countries in the area have small populations – although some are increasing rapidly. French is the official language in many of the countries – a legacy from the days when they were French colonies. The third largest country in Africa, Dem. Rep. Congo (Zaire), has rich mineral deposits, but has declined economically since independence. Chad has been torn apart by civil wars, and the Central African Republic has suffered from corrupt governments. Both countries are desperately poor. Equatorial Guinea has suffered so much from bad government that one-third of its population now lives in exile. Abundant minerals and oil have made Gabon the richest country in the region. Oil is also of major importance in the Congo, and both countries have relatively large city populations. Cameroon is home to more than 200 different peoples, and is relatively prosperous.

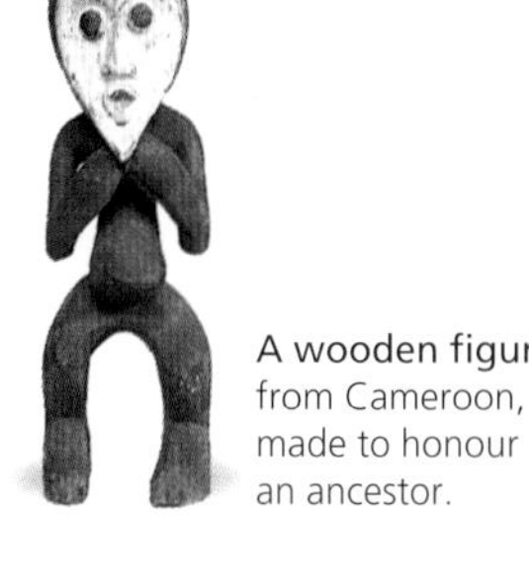

A wooden figure from Cameroon, made to honour an ancestor.

CHILDRENS HOSPITAL
WAD SHERIFAY

HEALTH CLINIC

Traditional African medicine is still widely practised in this region, and western medicine has also been successfully used to cure or control many diseases. Medicines are often dispensed at village clinics like this one. But there are still major problems – many babies do not survive and there is a great shortage of doctors. In Chad, for example, over 30,000 people have to share one doctor.

CHAD
pop: 6,900,000

LAKE CHAD

Lake Chad lies at the point where Chad, Cameroon, Niger and Nigeria meet. Due to a series of droughts, the rivers that feed the lake have shrunk to little more than streams and reduced it to a tenth of its former size. Fish from Lake Chad – such as this *tilapia* – are a major source of food for the people who live in the surrounding areas. But each year the fishermen must haul their boats further to reach the lake's receding water.

PYGMIES

Several groups of pygmies live scattered through the rainforests of Central Africa. They still survive mainly by hunting and gathering, but also trade with their neighbours and have learnt to speak their languages. Pygmies rarely reach a height of more than 125 cms (4 ft). This pygmy hut, made of banana fronds, is in a forest clearing in the Central African Republic.

CENTRAL AFRICAN REPUBLIC
pop: 3,500,000

Forested valleys and hills around Dolisie, Congo.

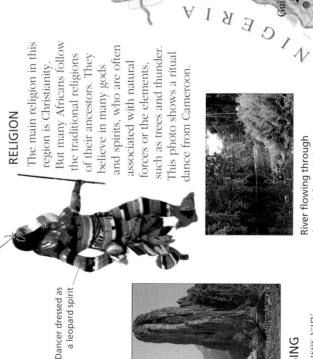

RELIGION

The main religion in this region is Christianity. But many Africans follow the traditional religions of their ancestors. They believe in many gods and spirits, who are often associated with natural forces or the elements, such as trees and thunder. This photo shows a ritual dance from Cameroon.

Dancer dressed as a leopard spirit

TRADITIONAL HOUSING

Traditional African houses vary from area to area, according to the building materials that are available locally. The walls of these houses in Cameroon are made of mud, and the roofs of straw. Building a house is one of the regular family tasks. As the family grows, so new houses are added to the group.

River flowing through dense rainforest in Cameroon.

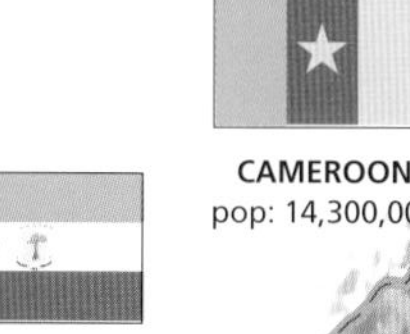

CAMEROON
pop: 14,300,000

EQUATORIAL GUINEA
pop: 430,000

LIBYA
NIGER
NIGERIA
SUDAN
CHAD
CENTRAL AFRICAN REPUBLIC
CAMEROON
TIBESTI
Faya
Biltine
Abéché
Mao
Bol
L. Chad
Ati
NDJAMENA
Kousseri
Mongo
Bahr Erguig
Chari
Bahr Salamat
Am Timan
Maroua
Bongor
Guider
Garoua
Laï
Sarh
Moundou
L. de Lagdo
Goré
Ngaoundéré
Birao
Copper
Ndélé
Chromium
Diamonds
Banyo
Aluminium
Kaga Bandoro
Bria
Kotto
Bamenda
Tin
Bafoussam
Gold
Bouar
Bossangoa
Sibut
Iron
Ubangi
Bambari
Uranium
Obo
Palm
Bangassou

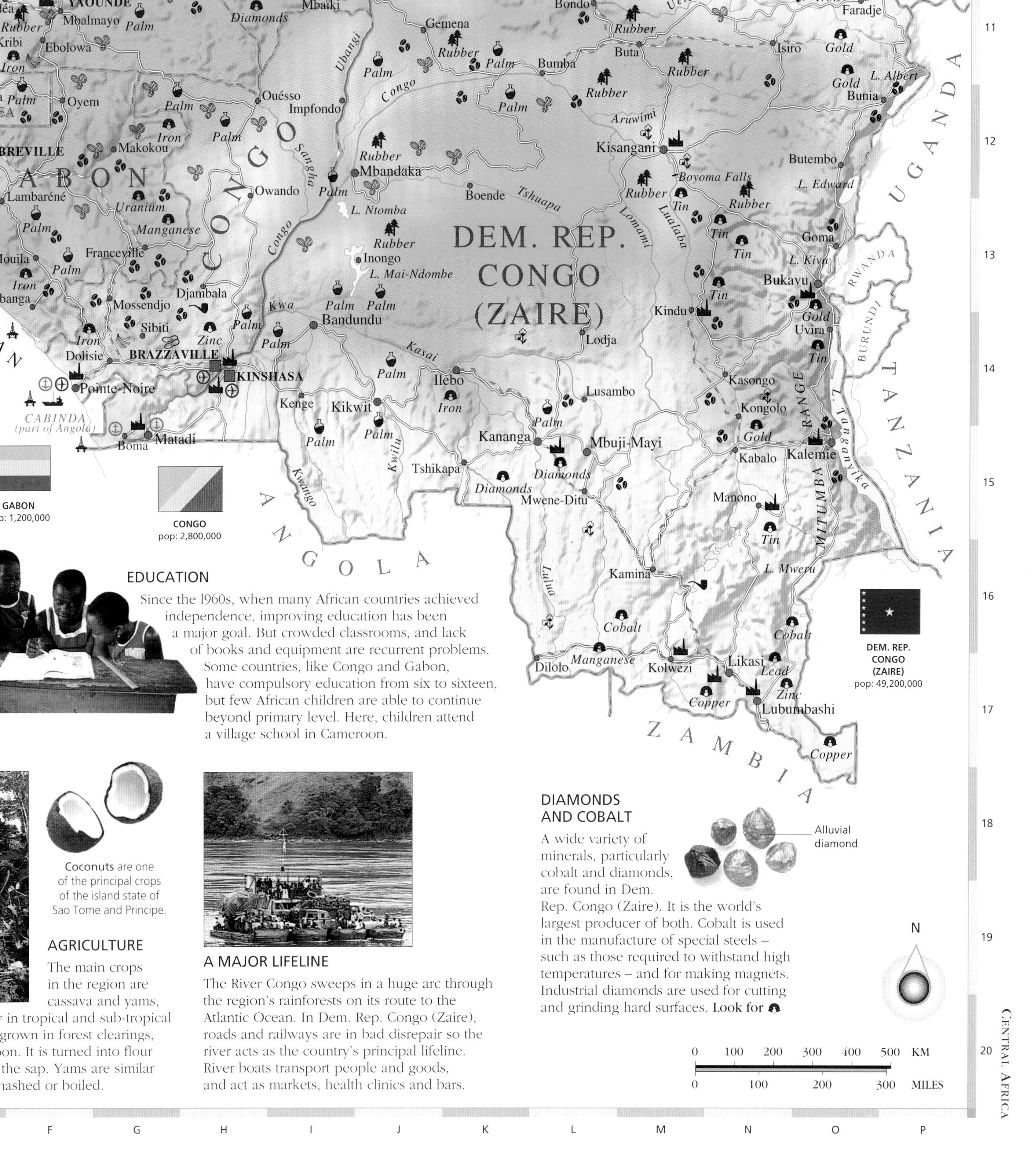

DEM. REP. CONGO (ZAIRE)
CONGO
GABON
EQUATORIAL GUINEA
SAO TOME AND PRINCIPE
ANGOLA
ZAMBIA
TANZANIA
UGANDA
RWANDA
BURUNDI
ATLANTIC OCEAN
Gulf of Guinea
CABINDA (part of Angola)
MALABO
YAOUNDÉ
LIBREVILLE
SÃO TOMÉ
BRAZZAVILLE
KINSHASA
Príncipe
Edéa
Kribi
Mbalmayo
Ebolowa
Bata
Oyem
Makokou
Lambaréné
Port-Gentil
Mouila
Tchibanga
Franceville
Mossendjo
Sibiti
Djambala
Dolisie
Pointe-Noire
Boma
Matadi
Ouésso
Impfondo
Owando
Mbaïki
Gemena
Bumba
Bondo
Buta
Isiro
Faradje
Bunia
Kisangani
Mbandaka
Boende
Inongo
Bandundu
Kenge
Kikwit
Ilebo
Lodja
Lusambo
Tshikapa
Kananga
Mbuji-Mayi
Mwene-Ditu
Kamina
Kindu
Kasongo
Kongolo
Kabalo
Kalemie
Manono
Butembo
Goma
Bukavu
Uvira
Dilolo
Kolwezi
Likasi
Lubumbashi
L. Albert
L. Edward
L. Kivu
L. Tanganyika
L. Mweru
L. Ntomba
L. Mai-Ndombe
Congo
Ubangi
Sangha
Ogooué
Kwa
Kasai
Kwilu
Kwango
Lulua
Tshuapa
Lomami
Lualaba
Aruwimi
Uele
Boyoma Falls
MITUMBA RANGE
N
0 100 200 300 400 500 KM
0 100 200 300 MILES

LIBREVILLE

Libreville, Gabon's capital, was founded in the mid-19th century as a settlement for freed French slaves. In fact, its name means "free town" in French. The city has expanded rapidly since the discovery of oil in the 1970s, and is now a major port.

SAO TOME AND PRINCIPE
pop: 131,000

GABON
pop: 1,200,000

CONGO
pop: 2,800,000

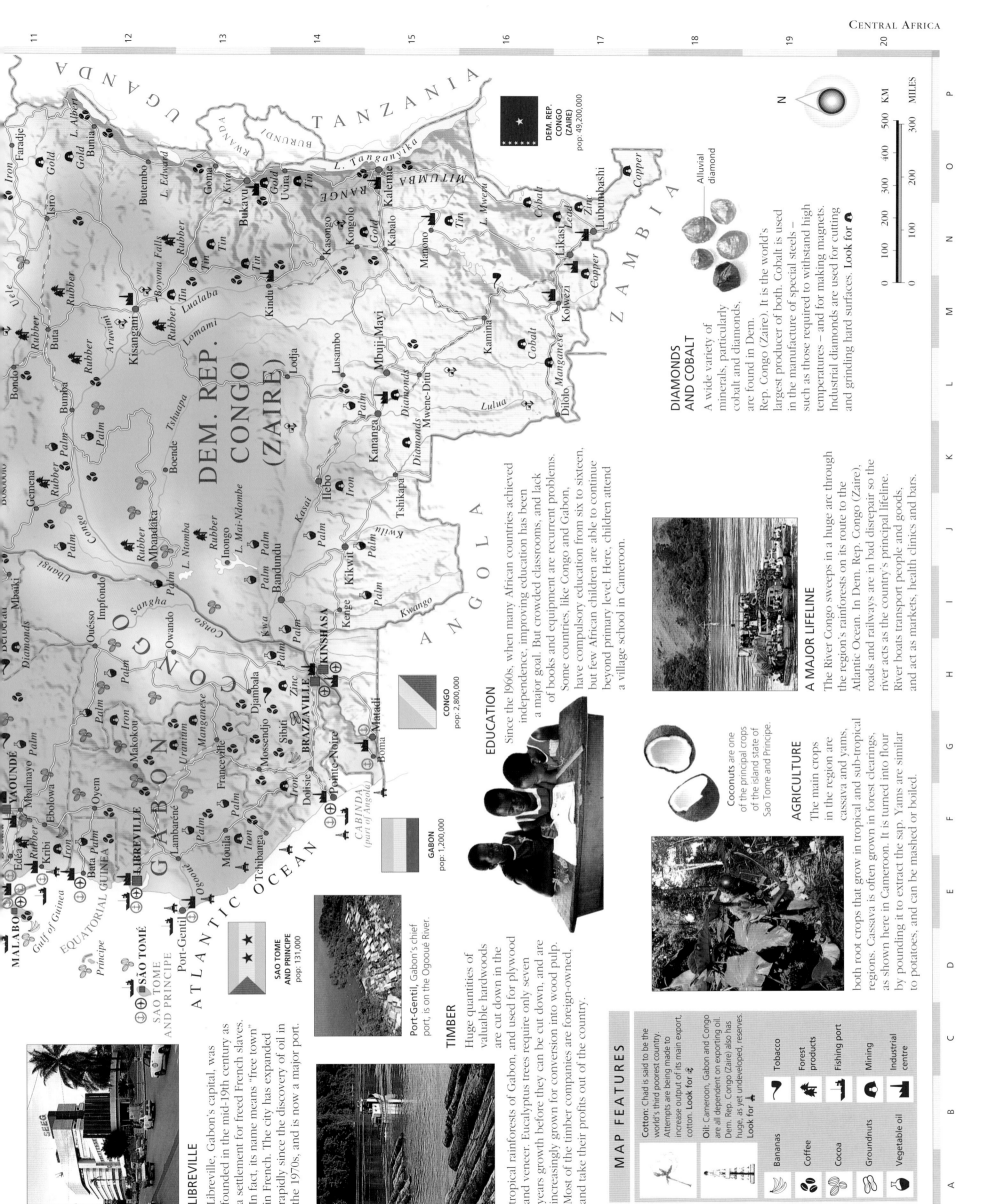

DEM. REP. CONGO (ZAIRE)
pop: 49,200,000

Port-Gentil, Gabon's chief port, is on the Ogooué River.

TIMBER

Huge quantities of valuable hardwoods are cut down in the tropical rainforests of Gabon, and used for plywood and veneer. Eucalyptus trees require only seven years growth before they can be cut down, and are increasingly grown for conversion into wood pulp. Most of the timber companies are foreign-owned, and take their profits out of the country.

EDUCATION

Since the 1960s, when many African countries achieved independence, improving education has been a major goal. But crowded classrooms, and lack of books and equipment are recurrent problems. Some countries, like Congo and Gabon, have compulsory education from six to sixteen, but few African children are able to continue beyond primary level. Here, children attend a village school in Cameroon.

MAP FEATURES

Cotton: Chad is said to be the world's third poorest country. Attempts are being made to increase output of its main export, cotton. **Look for**

Oil: Cameroon, Gabon and Congo are all dependent on exporting oil. Dem. Rep. Congo (Zaire) also has huge, as yet undeveloped, reserves. **Look for**

Bananas	Tobacco
Coffee	Forest products
Cocoa	Fishing port
Groundnuts	Mining
Vegetable oil	Industrial centre

Coconuts are one of the principal crops of the island state of Sao Tome and Principe.

AGRICULTURE

The main crops in the region are cassava and yams, both root crops that grow in tropical and sub-tropical regions. Cassava is often grown in forest clearings, as shown here in Cameroon. It is turned into flour by pounding it to extract the sap. Yams are similar to potatoes, and can be mashed or boiled.

A MAJOR LIFELINE

The River Congo sweeps in a huge arc through the region's rainforests on its route to the Atlantic Ocean. In Dem. Rep. Congo (Zaire), roads and railways are in bad disrepair so the river acts as the country's principal lifeline. River boats transport people and goods, and act as markets, health clinics and bars.

DIAMONDS AND COBALT

Alluvial diamond

A wide variety of minerals, particularly cobalt and diamonds, are found in Dem. Rep. Congo (Zaire). It is the world's largest producer of both. Cobalt is used in the manufacture of special steels – such as those required to withstand high temperatures – and for making magnets. Industrial diamonds are used for cutting and grinding hard surfaces. **Look for**

Central East Africa

East Africa's wealth lies in its land. Most people make their living from farming or cattle herding. Large areas covered with long grass, scrub and scattered trees, called savannah, provide grazing for domestic and wild animals alike. Tea, coffee and tobacco are grown as cash crops throughout the area, especially in Kenya and Malawi. The economy of Uganda, crippled by civil wars over the last 20 years, is being reformed with the help of international aid. However, Uganda's great agricultural potential is still not being exploited. Zambia, Rwanda, Burundi and Uganda all suffer from having no sea ports. Except in Kenya, industry everywhere is poorly developed. Only Zambia is rich in minerals. After economic decline in the 1980s, Tanzania is slowly recovering. In Rwanda, conflict between two ethnic groups, the Hutu and Tutsi, led to the slaughter of up to 500,000 Tutsis in 1994, and a mass exodus of refugees.

THE SAMBURU

In Kenya's northern plateau region, tribes such as the Samburu continue to follow the traditional way of life of their ancestors. They live by grazing their herds of cattle, sheep and goats on the savannah. This *moran*, or warrior, wears numerous strings of beads, distinctive ivory earrings and always carries two spears and a knife.

TRAINS

Countries with no coastline are very dependent on road and rail transport to link them to industrial centres and main ports. Although the African rail network is expanding, tracks are often poorly maintained. Here, people board a train at Kampala in Uganda.

PREDATORY FISH

The Nile perch was introduced into Lake Victoria to increase fish production in the 1960s. Although the lake is vast, this fish now occupies every corner, and is killing off the original fish population. Look for

Tsetse fly carries a disease which can kill cattle and humans.

AIDS

AIDS is a worldwide problem, but it is particularly widespread in Africa. Many people on the continent already suffer from diseases and malnutrition, which makes them more vulnerable to the illnesses associated with AIDS.

WILDLIFE RESERVES

Africa's great plains contain some of the world's most spectacular species of wildlife. All the countries in the region have set aside huge areas as national parks where animals are protected. Wildlife safaris attract thousands of tourists and provide countries with much needed foreign income. Look for

POACHING

Africa's wildlife parks have helped preserve the animals, but poaching remains a major problem. In an attempt to save the elephants, a worldwide ban on the sale of ivory has been imposed. But policing the parks is very costly; poachers are armed and dangerous. Here, in Tanzania, wardens are burning a poacher's hut.

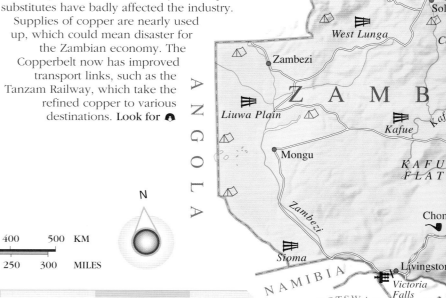

Vultures cluster in a lone tree on the Tanzanian grasslands.

MAP FEATURES

Coffee: A valuable cash crop, coffee is grown in Uganda, Kenya, Tanzania and Rwanda. In recent years, coffee production in Kenya has increased rapidly. **Look for**

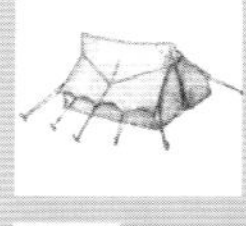

Market gardening: Kenya has ideal conditions for growing vegetables and fruit, which are exported in large quantities, mainly to Europe. **Look for**

Hydro-electric power: The Kariba Dam on the Zambezi River, built by Zambia and Zimbabwe, supplies both nations with electricity. **Look for**

Refugee camps: Warfare in neighbouring countries has caused thousands of refugees to flee to temporary camps in the region. **Look for**

	Sugar cane		Forest products
	Coconuts		Fishing
	Tea		Mining
	Cotton		Industrial centre
	Tobacco		Wildlife reserves

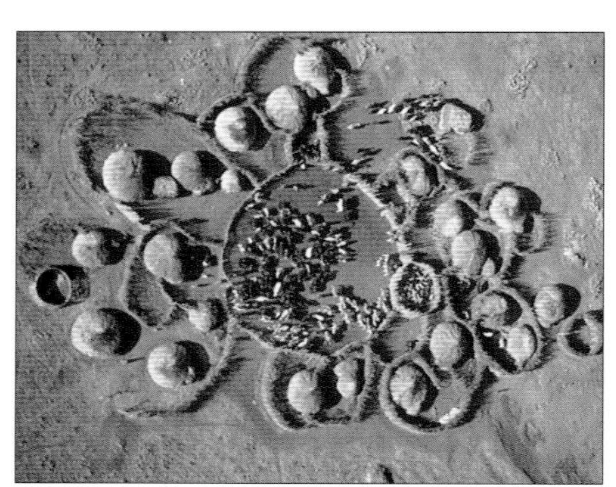

AFRICAN VILLAGE

East African villages usually consist of a series of huts enclosed by thorn fences. This aerial photo shows a village belonging to the Masai tribe. A Masai man may have several wives. Each wife has her own huts, enclosed by a fence. The live-stock is taken out to graze by day, and driven into the fenced enclosure at night.

COPPER

Copper bracelets

There are huge desposits of copper in central Africa, centred around Ndola in Zambia. This region is often called the Copperbelt. Copper accounts for 90 per cent of Zambia's export earnings, but low prices in recent years and the discovery of cheaper substitutes have badly affected the industry. Supplies of copper are nearly used up, which could mean disaster for the Zambian economy. The Copperbelt now has improved transport links, such as the Tanzam Railway, which take the refined copper to various destinations. Look for

0 100 200 300 400 500 KM

0 50 100 150 200 250 300 MILES

ANGOLA
ZAMB
West Lunga
Zambezi
Liuwa Plain
Kafue
Mongu
KAFUE FLATS
Zambezi
Choma
Sioma
Livingstone
Victoria Falls
NAMIBIA
BOTSWANA
ZIM

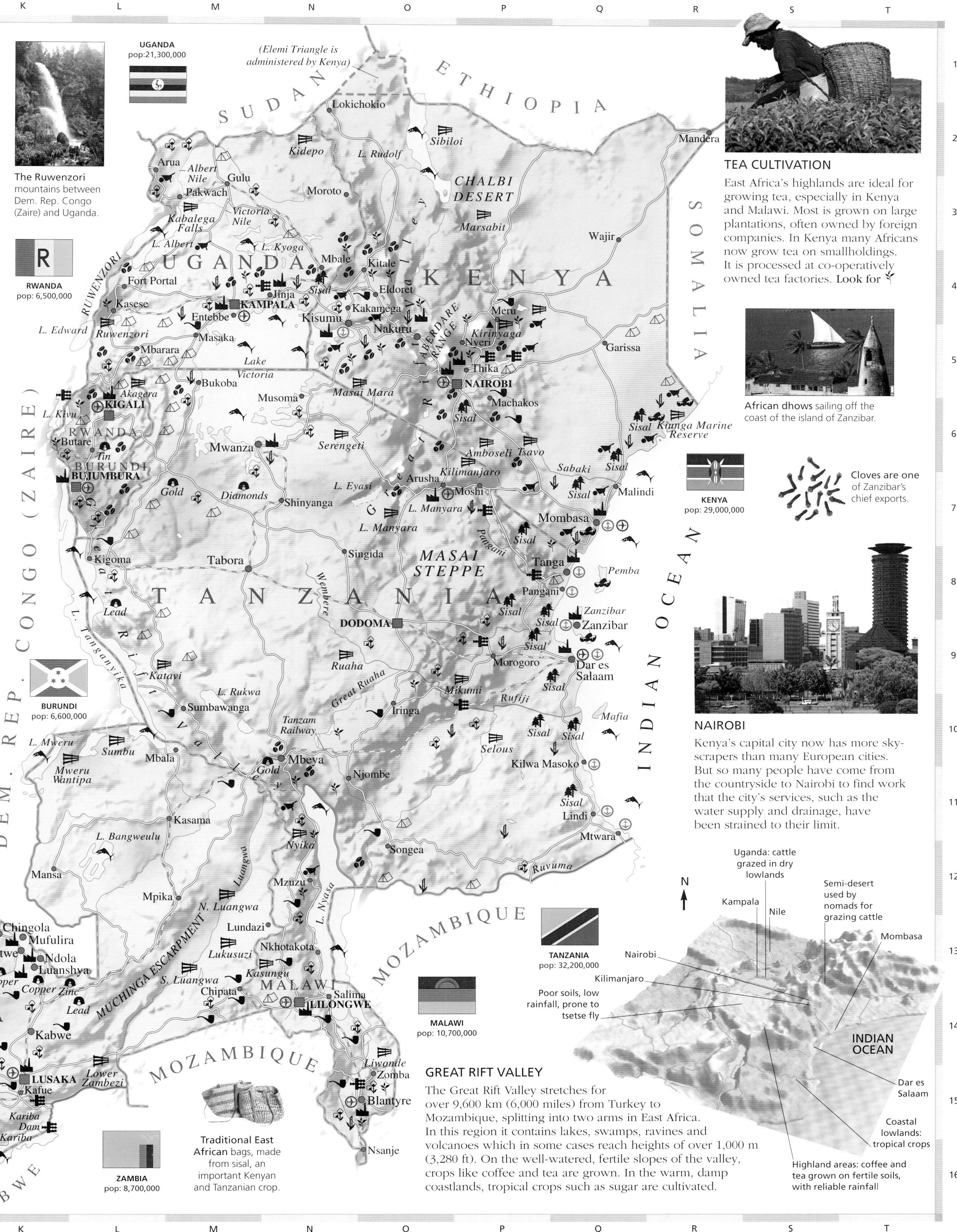
K L M N O P Q R S T
1 2 3 4 5 6 7 8 9 10 11 12 13 14 15 16
UGANDA
pop:21,300,000
RWANDA
pop: 6,500,000
BURUNDI
pop: 6,600,000
KENYA
pop: 29,000,000
TANZANIA
pop: 32,200,000
MALAWI
pop: 10,700,000
ZAMBIA
pop: 8,700,000
(Elemi Triangle is administered by Kenya)
SUDAN
ETHIOPIA
SOMALIA
KENYA
UGANDA
RWANDA
BURUNDI
TANZANIA
MALAWI
MOZAMBIQUE
DEM. REP. CONGO (ZAIRE)
INDIAN OCEAN
CHALBI DESERT
MASAI STEPPE
Great Rift Valley
RUWENZORI
ABERDARE RANGE
MUCHINGA ESCARPMENT
Lokichokio
Sibiloi
Kidepo
L. Rudolf
Mandera
Arua
Albert Nile
Gulu
Pakwach
Moroto
Marsabit
Kabalega Falls
Victoria Nile
L. Albert
L. Kyoga
Wajir
Mbale
Kitale
Fort Portal
Eldoret
Jinja
Sisal
KAMPALA
Kasese
Entebbe
Kisumu
Kakamega
Meru
L. Edward
Ruwenzori
Nakuru
Kirinyaga
Masaka
Nyeri
Garissa
Mbarara
Lake Victoria
Thika
Bukoba
NAIROBI
Akagera
Musoma
Masai Mara
Machakos
L. Kivu
KIGALI
Kiunga Marine Reserve
Butare
Tin
Mwanza
Serengeti
Amboseli
Tsavo
BUJUMBURA
Sabaki
Gold
Diamonds
L. Eyasi
Arusha
Kilimanjaro
Moshi
Malindi
Shinyanga
L. Manyara
Mombasa
Pangani
Kigoma
Singida
Tabora
Tanga
Pemba
Wembere
Lead
L. Tanganyika
DODOMA
Zanzibar
Katavi
Ruaha
Morogoro
Dar es Salaam
L. Rukwa
Great Ruaha
Mikumi
Rufiji
Sumbawanga
Tanzam Railway
Iringa
Mafia
L. Mweru
Sumbu
Mbala
Selous
Mweru Wantipa
Mbeya
Kilwa Masoko
Njombe
Kasama
Lindi
L. Bangweulu
Nyika
Mtwara
Songea
Luangwa
Mansa
Mzuzu
Ruvuma
L. Nyasa
Mpika
N. Luangwa
Chingola
Mufulira
Lundazi
Kitwe
Ndola
Nkhotakota
Luanshya
Lukusuzi
Copper
Zinc
Kasungu
S. Luangwa
Chipata
Salima
LILONGWE
Kabwe
LUSAKA
Lower Zambezi
Kafue
Liwonde
Zomba
Blantyre
Kariba Dam
L. Kariba
Nsanje
N
Uganda: cattle grazed in dry lowlands
Kampala
Nile
Semi-desert used by nomads for grazing cattle
Mombasa
Nairobi
Kilimanjaro
Poor soils, low rainfall, prone to tsetse fly
INDIAN OCEAN
Dar es Salaam
Coastal lowlands: tropical crops
Highland areas: coffee and tea grown on fertile soils, with reliable rainfall

The Ruwenzori mountains between Dem. Rep. Congo (Zaire) and Uganda.

TEA CULTIVATION

East Africa's highlands are ideal for growing tea, especially in Kenya and Malawi. Most is grown on large plantations, often owned by foreign companies. In Kenya many Africans now grow tea on smallholdings. It is processed at co-operatively owned tea factories. **Look for**

African dhows sailing off the coast of the island of Zanzibar.

Cloves are one of Zanzibar's chief exports.

NAIROBI

Kenya's capital city now has more skyscrapers than many European cities. But so many people have come from the countryside to Nairobi to find work that the city's services, such as the water supply and drainage, have been strained to their limit.

GREAT RIFT VALLEY

The Great Rift Valley stretches for over 9,600 km (6,000 miles) from Turkey to Mozambique, splitting into two arms in East Africa. In this region it contains lakes, swamps, ravines and volcanoes which in some cases reach heights of over 1,000 m (3,280 ft). On the well-watered, fertile slopes of the valley, crops like coffee and tea are grown. In the warm, damp coastlands, tropical crops such as sugar are cultivated.

Traditional East African bags, made from sisal, an important Kenyan and Tanzanian crop.

SOUTHERN AFRICA

THE WEALTHIEST and most dominant country in this region is South Africa. Black African lands were gradually settled in the 19th century by Dutch colonists, their descendants – the Afrikaners – and the British. When vast deposits of gold and diamonds were discovered in the late 19th century, the country became rich. In 1948 the government introduced a system of "separate development", called apartheid, which separated people according to their colour, and gave political power to whites only. This policy led to isolation and sanctions from the rest of the world's nations, which only ended after the abolition of apartheid. The first democratic elections were held in 1994. After years of conflict, South Africa has now become a more integrated society. Most of the countries around South Africa rely on its industries for trade and work. After 30 years of unrest, Namibia has now won independence from South Africa. Mozambique and Angola are both struggling for survival after years of civil war. Zimbabwe has a relatively diverse economy, based on agriculture and its rich mineral resources.

SOUTH AFRICA'S THREE CAPITALS
PRETORIA – administrative capital
CAPE TOWN – legislative capital
BLOEMFONTEIN – judicial capital

The Ndebele people of South Africa often paint their houses in bright colours.

ANGOLA
pop: 12,000,000

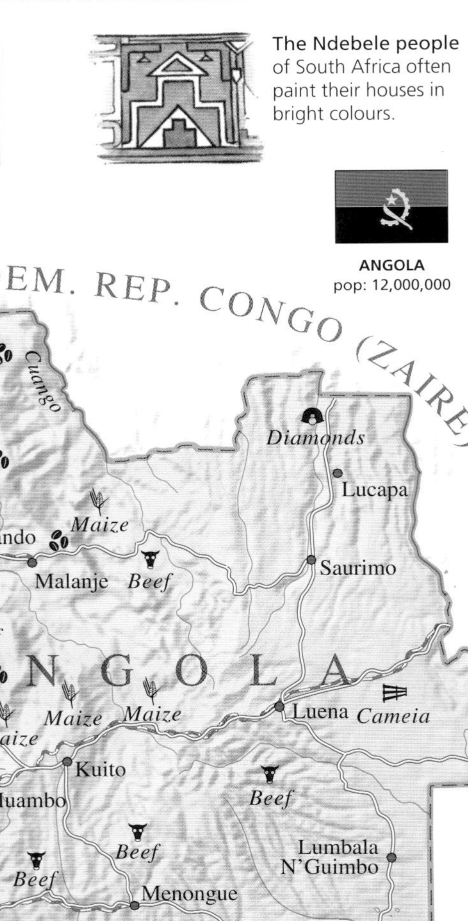

CONGO
DEM. REP. CONGO (ZAIRE)
CABINDA (part of Angola)
Cabinda
Congo
ATLANTIC OCEAN
Ambriz
Uíge
Caxito
LUANDA
N'Dalatando
Malanje
Cuango
Cuanza
Quicama
Maize
Beef
Diamonds
Lucapa
Saurimo
Manganese
Sumbe
ANGOLA
Luena
Cameia
Lobito
Benguela
Kuito
Huambo
Lumbala N'Guimbo
Menongue
Cuito Cuanavale
Lubango
Phosphates
Namibe
Bicuari
Mupa
Cubango
Iona
Cunene
N'Giva
Ondangwa
Rundu
Etosha Pan
Copper
Okavango Delta
C. Fria
Etosha
Tsumeb
Skeleton Coast
Zinc
Grootfontein
Lead
Otjiwarongo
Tin
NAMIBIA
NAMIB DESERT
Ghanzi
Okahandja
Rössing
Swakopmund
Uranium
WINDHOEK
Gobabis
Walvis Bay
Rehoboth
KALAHARI DESERT
BOTSWANA
Dairy
Maltahöhe
Mariental
Gemsbok
Namib Naukluft
Kalahari Gemsbok
Keetmanshoop
Lüderitz
Iron
Diamonds
Karasburg
Orange R.
Upington
Augrabies Falls
Manganese
SOUTH AFRICA
Calvinia
Beaufort West
Cape Columbine
Wheat
Saldanha
Table Bay
Oudtshoorn
CAPE TOWN
Table Mt.
Cape of Good Hope
C. Agulhas

NAMIBIA
pop: 1,700,000

SOUTH AFRICA
pop: 44,300,000

INDUSTRY

South Africa is the region's industrial leader. Johannesburg, the country's largest city, is seen here behind the huge mounds of earth excavated from the gold mines. Look for [industrial centre symbol]

URANIUM

Namibia is rich in copper, diamonds, tin and other minerals. Its mining industry accounts for 90 per cent of its export earnings. At Rössing, in the Namib Desert, uranium is extracted from a huge open-cast mine, and exported abroad. Look for [mining symbol]

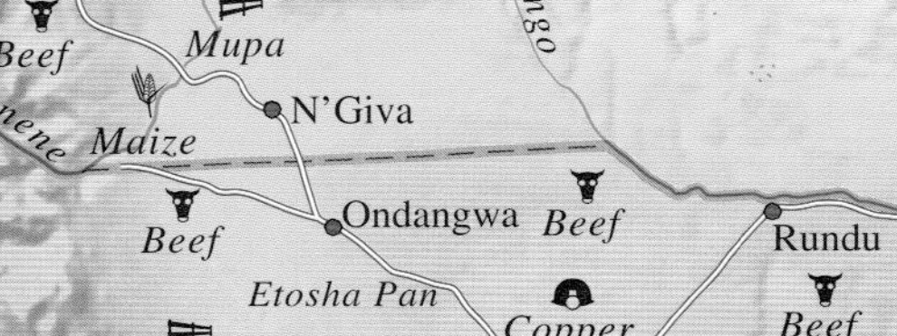

The *ilimba* drum from Zimbabwe is made from the hard shell of a fruit called a gourd.

MAP FEATURES

Fishing: Overfishing, by both foreign and local fleets, is a major threat to Namibia's once rich fishing grounds. Controls are in operation. Look for [fishing symbol]

Oil: Civil war in Angola has disrupted industry, but its oil reserves – the only major ones in the region – so far have been little affected. Look for [oil symbol]

Wildlife reserves: Most of the region's countries have set aside large areas as wildlife parks, which are popular tourist attractions. Look for [wildlife reserve symbol]

Cattle	Tea
Cereals	Tobacco
Citrus fruit	Mining
Wine	Coal
Coffee	Industrial centre

BUSHMEN

Bushmen – or *San* – are one of the few groups of hunter-gatherers left in Africa. These tiny people can be traced far back into African history. Today some 1,000 bushmen still live in the harsh environment of the Kalahari Desert.

A lone thorn tree in the hot, sandy Namib Desert.

CAPE TOWN

Sprawled along the lower slopes of Table Mountain, and overlooking Table Bay, Cape Town has a spectacular setting. It is a busy port and the city where South Africa's parliament meets. Until the Suez Canal was opened, Cape Town lay on the main shipping route between Europe and Asia. Its harbour was often used by ships sheltering from the gales and stormy seas off the Cape of Good Hope.

THE SANGOMA

In most African tribal societies there is a person called a *sangoma* (sometimes known as a "witch doctor"), who heals people, predicts the future and generally looks after the well-being of the people.

Fresh maize

MAIZE

Maize is one of the main crops grown in this region. In the 1980s, the introduction of new kinds of seed and wider use of fertilizer greatly increased the production of maize. As most men work in industry, women cultivate the crops required to feed the family. Look for

DIAMONDS

Botswana was one of the world's poorest nations when it became independent. But since the discovery of diamonds in the Kalahari Desert, its economy has been transformed, and diamonds now make up 80 per cent of its exports. Look for

Acacias are a common sight on the savannah.

SUN CITY

The tourist resort of Sun City lies to the west of Johannesburg. Visitors from the region, and the rest of the world, are drawn to its luxury hotels, casino, game park and other attractions.

CIVIL WARS

Both the former Portuguese colonies of Mozambique and Angola were plunged into civil war following independence in 1975. Today, there is a fragile peace and both countries are beginning to rebuild their shattered economies.

0 100 200 300 400 500 600 KM

0 100 200 300 MILES

N

ZIMBABWE
pop: 11,900,000

BOTSWANA
pop: 1,600,000

MOZAMBIQUE
pop: 18,700,000

Lake Kariba is a huge, artificially constructed lake.

OSTRICH FARMS

Ostrich feathers were once in great demand as fashion accessories. Ostrich farmers grew rich, and were known as Feather Barons. Feathers are no longer fashionable, but ostriches are still farmed for their meat around Oudtshoorn, in South Africa.

"TOWNSHIPS"

The apartheid system meant that many black people were forced to live in "townships", often some distance from their work. The largest and best known is Soweto. People from Soweto – which means "South-Western Townships" – travel daily to work in Johannesburg.

Platinum is mined in northwestern South Africa

Platinum crystal

SWAZILAND
pop: 931,000

GOLD

Southern Africa has the richest deposits of valuable minerals in Africa. These miners are drilling for gold near Johannesburg, the area where gold was first discovered in 1886. This work is usually done by black Africans, but a mixed labour force will be more common in future. Gold from South Africa is often sold abroad in the form of coins called *Krugerrands*. Look for

LESOTHO
pop: 2,200,000

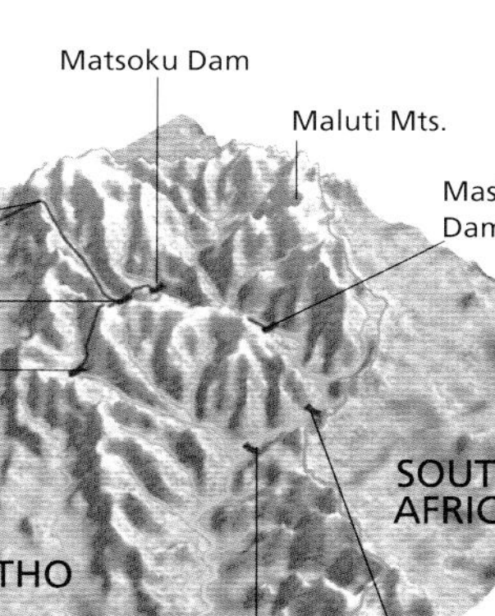
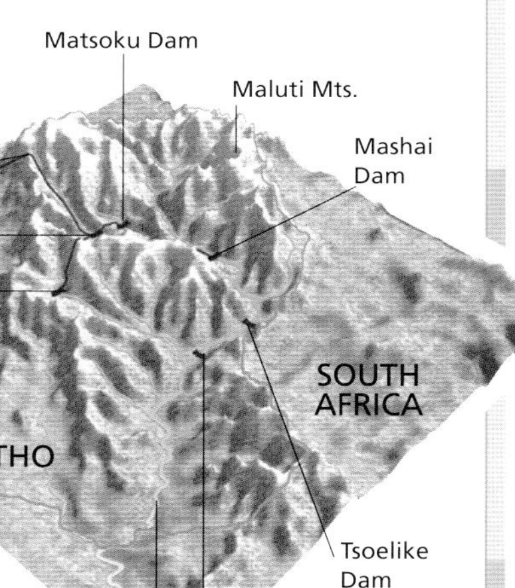
Matsoku Dam
Maluti Mts.
Lengthy tunnels transfer water between dams
Mashai Dam
Katse Dam
Mohale Dam
SOUTH AFRICA
LESOTHO
Tsoelike Dam
Ntoahae Dam
Orange R.
N

LESOTHO'S WATER PROJECT

In contrast with surrounding areas, Lesotho's Maluti Mountains have plenty of water. A huge project is underway building dams and tunnels to transfer water and electricity to neighbouring South Africa.

The Indian Ocean

Some 5,000 islands – many of them surrounded by coral reefs – are scattered across the Indian Ocean. Beneath its surface three great mountain ranges converge towards the ocean's centre – an area of strong seismic and volcanic activity. The ocean reaches its greatest depth – 7,440 m (24,400 ft) – in the Java Trench. Over 1,000 million people – about a fifth of the world's population – live in the countries that surround the Indian Ocean, representing an immense range of cultures and religions. Heavy monsoon rain and tropical storms cause flooding along the ocean's northern coasts. The world's largest oil-fields are located around The Gulf.

KARACHI

In the mid-19th century a railway line was built along the Indus valley to Karachi, and it developed into a large port and industrial city. When Pakistan was created an independent nation in 1947, Karachi became the country's capital. It has now been replaced by the new city of Islamabad in the north.

FISHING

Large-scale fishing is far less developed in the Indian Ocean than in either the Atlantic or Pacific. Fishing is difficult because there are relatively few areas of shallow sea. Small-scale fishing, however, provides a valuable source of food. Many fishermen, like these Sri Lankans, use basic, often inefficient methods. Tuna is the most important catch in the area. Look for

ISLANDS

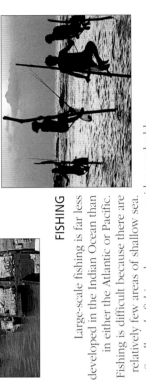

The islands of the Indian Ocean include enormous ones like Madagascar, coral atolls like the Maldives, and volcanic islands like Réunion. All are threatened by rising sea levels which reduce the area of land available. Coral reefs are being eroded, leaving islands increasingly exposed to ocean tides and flooding.

The loggerhead turtle is one of the Indian Ocean's many endangered species.

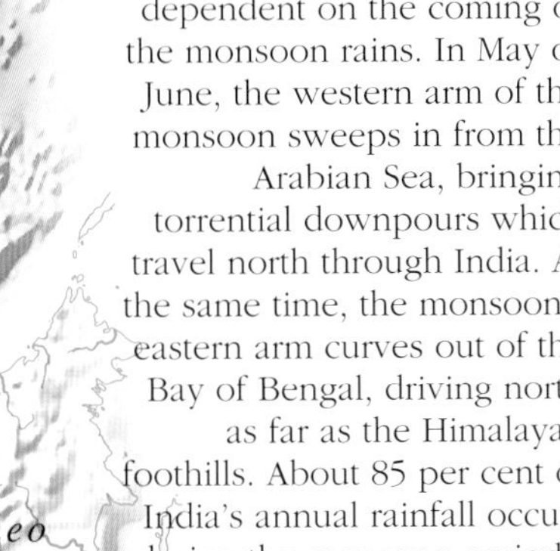

MONSOON

Farmers in the lands around the Indian Ocean are wholly dependent on the coming of the monsoon rains. In May or June, the western arm of the monsoon sweeps in from the Arabian Sea, bringing torrential downpours which travel north through India. At the same time, the monsoon's eastern arm curves out of the Bay of Bengal, driving north as far as the Himalayan foothills. About 85 per cent of India's annual rainfall occurs during the monsoon periods.

Sugar cane

SUGAR

Sugar was first brought to Mauritius by the Dutch in the 1600s. Ninety per cent of the island's arable farm-land is covered by sugar plantations. But today sugar has been replaced in importance by textiles, which now account for nearly half the island's exports. **Look for**

Hotel complex on an island in Mauritius

TOURISM

The Indian Ocean islands are great tourist attractions. They welcome the money this brings, but the sheer number of visitors threatens to destroy the islands' environment. **Look for**

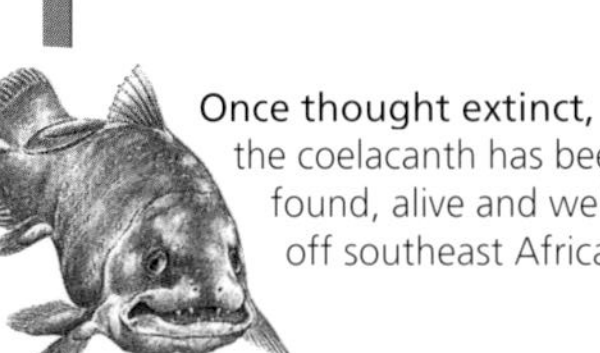

Once thought extinct, the coelacanth has been found, alive and well, off southeast Africa.

MALDIVES
pop: 282,000

COMOROS
pop: 672,000

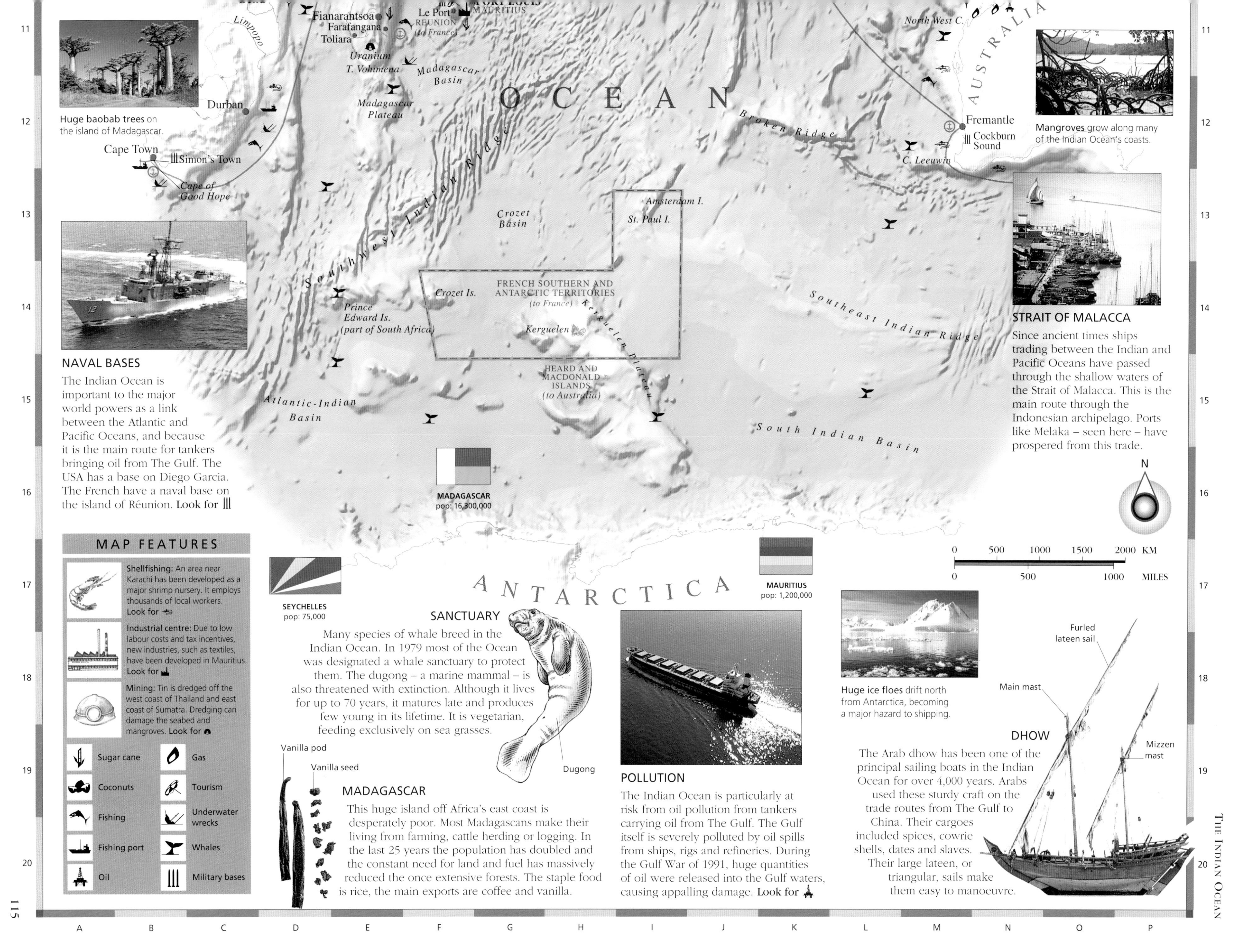
OCEAN
ANTARCTICA
AUSTRALIA
Limpopo
Durban
Cape Town
Simon's Town
Cape of Good Hope
Fianarantsoa
Farafangana
Toliara
Uranium
T. Vohimena
Le Port
RÉUNION (to France)
MAURITIUS
Madagascar Basin
Madagascar Plateau
Southwest Indian Ridge
Prince Edward Is. (part of South Africa)
Atlantic-Indian Basin
Crozet Basin
Crozet Is.
FRENCH SOUTHERN AND ANTARCTIC TERRITORIES (to France)
Kerguelen
Kerguelen Plateau
HEARD AND MACDONALD ISLANDS (to Australia)
Amsterdam I.
St. Paul I.
Broken Ridge
Southeast Indian Ridge
South Indian Basin
North West C.
Fremantle
Cockburn Sound
C. Leeuwin
N
0 500 1000 1500 2000 KM
0 500 1000 MILES
MADAGASCAR
pop: 16,300,000
SEYCHELLES
pop: 75,000
MAURITIUS
pop: 1,200,000
Dugong
Vanilla pod
Vanilla seed
Furled lateen sail
Main mast
Mizzen mast

Huge baobab trees on the island of Madagascar.

NAVAL BASES

The Indian Ocean is important to the major world powers as a link between the Atlantic and Pacific Oceans, and because it is the main route for tankers bringing oil from The Gulf. The USA has a base on Diego Garcia. The French have a naval base on the island of Réunion. **Look for** |||

MAP FEATURES

Shellfishing: An area near Karachi has been developed as a major shrimp nursery. It employs thousands of local workers. **Look for**

Industrial centre: Due to low labour costs and tax incentives, new industries, such as textiles, have been developed in Mauritius. **Look for**

Mining: Tin is dredged off the west coast of Thailand and east coast of Sumatra. Dredging can damage the seabed and mangroves. **Look for**

Sugar cane
Coconuts
Fishing
Fishing port
Oil
Gas
Tourism
Underwater wrecks
Whales
Military bases

SANCTUARY

Many species of whale breed in the Indian Ocean. In 1979 most of the Ocean was designated a whale sanctuary to protect them. The dugong – a marine mammal – is also threatened with extinction. Although it lives for up to 70 years, it matures late and produces few young in its lifetime. It is vegetarian, feeding exclusively on sea grasses.

MADAGASCAR

This huge island off Africa's east coast is desperately poor. Most Madagascans make their living from farming, cattle herding or logging. In the last 25 years the population has doubled and the constant need for land and fuel has massively reduced the once extensive forests. The staple food is rice, the main exports are coffee and vanilla.

POLLUTION

The Indian Ocean is particularly at risk from oil pollution from tankers carrying oil from The Gulf. The Gulf itself is severely polluted by oil spills from ships, rigs and refineries. During the Gulf War of 1991, huge quantities of oil were released into the Gulf waters, causing appalling damage. **Look for**

Huge ice floes drift north from Antarctica, becoming a major hazard to shipping.

Mangroves grow along many of the Indian Ocean's coasts.

STRAIT OF MALACCA

Since ancient times ships trading between the Indian and Pacific Oceans have passed through the shallow waters of the Strait of Malacca. This is the main route through the Indonesian archipelago. Ports like Melaka – seen here – have prospered from this trade.

DHOW

The Arab dhow has been one of the principal sailing boats in the Indian Ocean for over 4,000 years. Arabs used these sturdy craft on the trade routes from The Gulf to China. Their cargoes included spices, cowrie shells, dates and slaves. Their large lateen, or triangular, sails make them easy to manoeuvre.

Cedar of Lebanon
Cedrus libani
Height: 40 m (130 ft)

Common hamster
Cricetus cricetus
Length: 30 cm (12 in)

Waxwing
Bombycilla garrulus
Length: 18 cm (8 in)

NORTH AND WEST ASIA

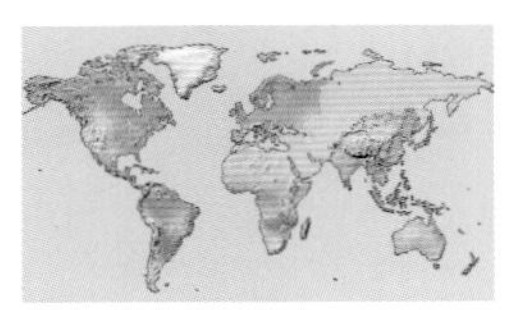

NORTH AND WEST ASIA contains some of the world's most inhospitable environments. In the south, the Arabian Peninsula is almost entirely a baking hot desert, where no plants can grow. To the north, a belt of rugged, snow-capped mountains and high plateaux cross the continent. The climate becomes drier and more extreme towards the centre of the continent. Dry hot summers contrast with bitterly cold winters. Cold deserts give way to treeless plains known as steppe, then to huge marshes, and to the world's largest needleleaf forest. In the extreme north, both land and sea are frozen for most of the year. Only in summer do the top layers of soil thaw briefly allowing plants of the tundra, such as moss and lichen, to cover the land.

COLD FOREST
Strong but flexible trunks and a tent-like shape help needleleaf trees to withstand the great weight of snow that covers them throughout the long winter.

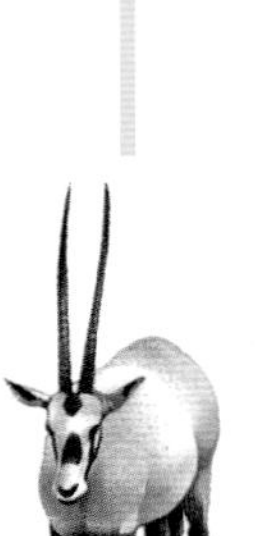

Arabian oryx
Oryx leucoryx
Height: 1.2 m (4 ft)

HOT BATHS
These strange white terraces formed in the south-west of Asia in much the same way that a kettle "furs". Underground water heated by volcanic activity dissolves minerals in rocks. These are deposited when the water reaches the surface and cools.

DROUGHT-TOLERANT TREES
Plants growing near the Black Sea minimize water-loss during the long hot summers. Most have wax-covered leaves through which little water can escape.

Blue turquoise, a semi-precious stone mainly found in cold areas of north Asia.

REGENERATING FOREST
Juniper trees, unlike many plants, are able to withstand the acid soils of needleleaf forests. Here junipers cover the floor of a dense pine forest.

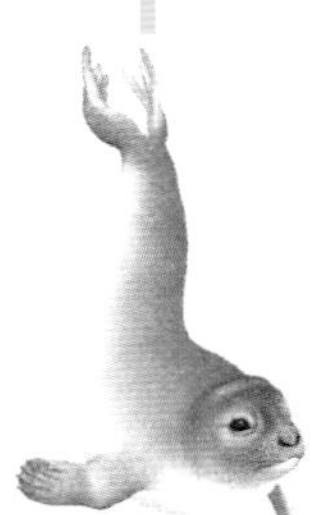

Baikal seal
Phoca sibirica
Length: 1.5 m (5 ft)
Only found in Lake Baikal

The fossilized head of Gallimimus, an ostrich-like dinosaur that once lived in Asia.

SINAI'S ROCK "MUSHROOMS"
In deserts, sand particles whipped along by high-speed winds create natural sculptures. Rock at the base of the "mushroom" has been more heavily eroded than rock above, leading to these unusual landforms.

VOLCANO
There are more than 30 active volcanoes on the Kamchatka peninsula, on the Pacific Ocean's "Ring of Fire". Volcanic activity is due to the deep underground movements of the Eurasian plate.

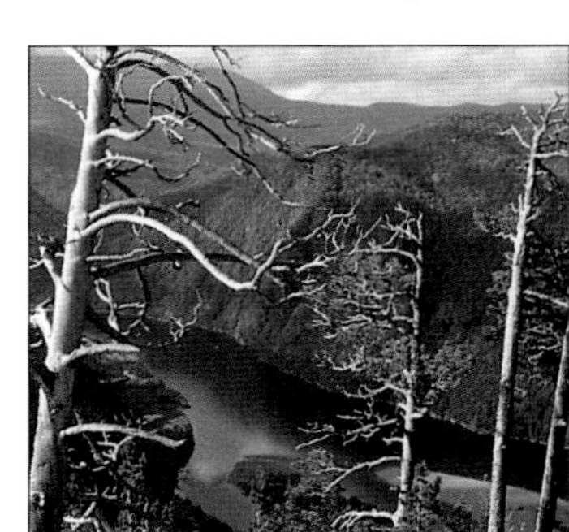

FROZEN RIVER
The River Lena rises near Lake Baikal, the world's deepest and oldest freshwater lake. Like other Siberian rivers, it flows into the Arctic Ocean and is frozen over for eight or nine months of the year.

Darkling beetle
Sternodes species
Length: 2 cm (1 in)

HOT DESERTS
The Arabian desert is one of the hottest and driest places in the world. Temperatures frequently reach 45°C (120°F), and very little rain falls.

CROSS-SECTION THROUGH NORTH AND WEST ASIA

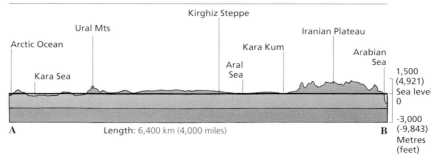

Arctic Ocean
Kara Sea
Ural Mts
Kirghiz Steppe
Aral Sea
Kara Kum
Iranian Plateau
Arabian Sea
1,500 (4,921)
Sea level 0
-3,000 (-9,843)
Metres (feet)
A
Length: 6,400 km (4,000 miles)
B

COLD WINTER DESERT
Large parts of Central Asia are covered in deserts that are hot in summer, but very cold in winter. A river has been naturally dammed to form this lake, which is unusual in this dry region.

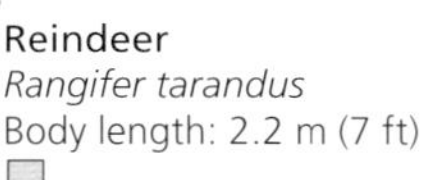

Reindeer
Rangifer tarandus
Body length: 2.2 m (7 ft)

Pallas's cat
Felis manul
Length: 65 cm (26 in)

Grey wolf
Canis lupus
Length: 1.4 m (5 ft)

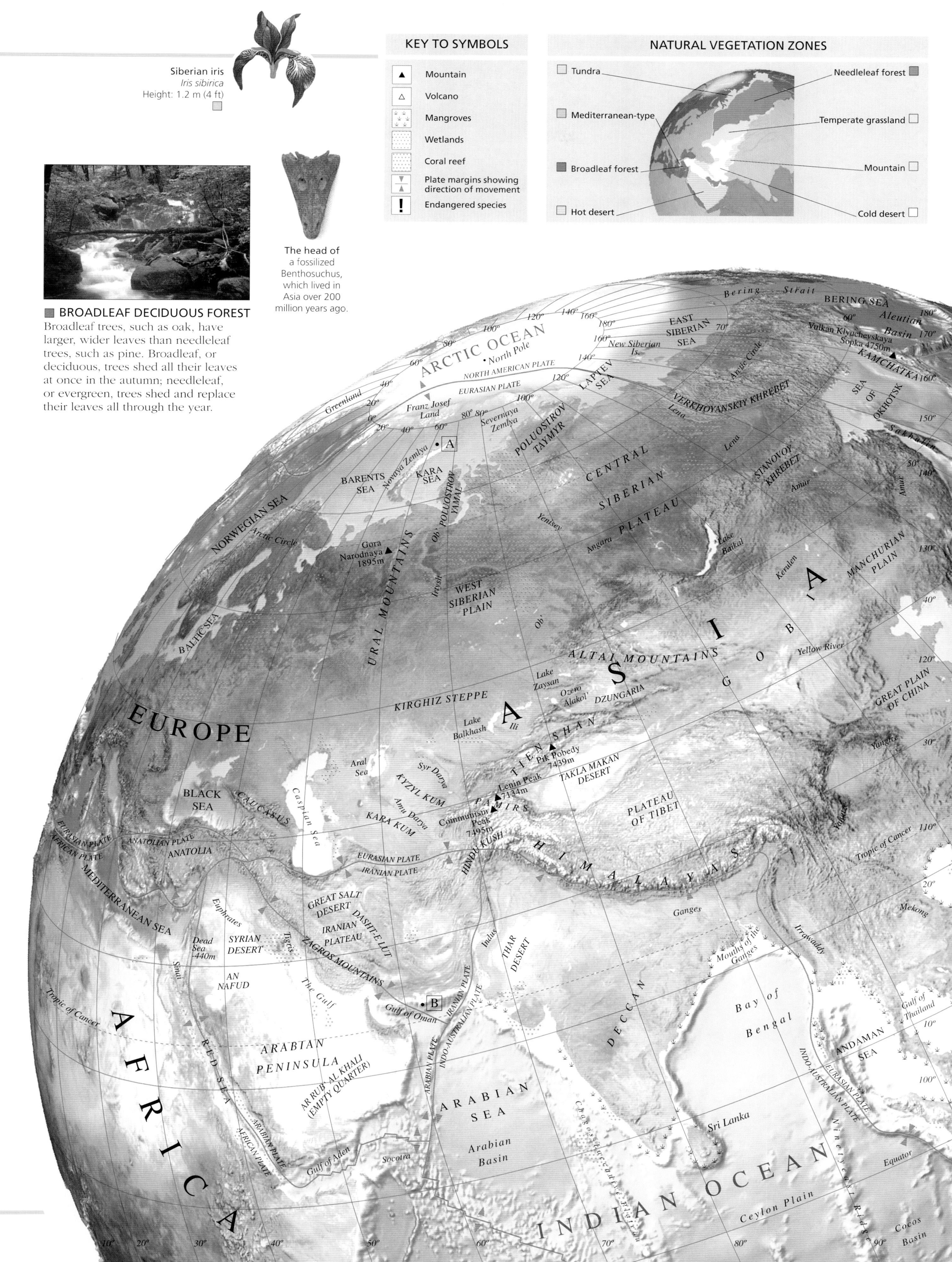
KEY TO SYMBOLS
Mountain
Volcano
Mangroves
Wetlands
Coral reef
Plate margins showing direction of movement
Endangered species
NATURAL VEGETATION ZONES
Tundra
Needleleaf forest
Mediterranean-type
Temperate grassland
Broadleaf forest
Mountain
Hot desert
Cold desert
ARCTIC OCEAN
North Pole
NORTH AMERICAN PLATE
EURASIAN PLATE
Greenland
Franz Josef Land
Severnaya Zemlya
LAPTEV SEA
EAST SIBERIAN SEA
New Siberian Is.
Bering Strait
BERING SEA
Aleutian Basin
Vulkan Klyuchevskaya Sopka 4750m
KAMCHATKA
SEA OF OKHOTSK
Sakhalin
VERKHOYANSKIY KHREBET
Lena
Arctic Circle
POLUOSTROV TAYMYR
A
BARENTS SEA
Novaya Zemlya
KARA SEA
POLUOSTROV YAMAL
CENTRAL SIBERIAN PLATEAU
STANOVOY KHREBET
Amur
NORWEGIAN SEA
Gora Narodnaya 1895m
URAL MOUNTAINS
Ob'
Yenisey
Angara
Lake Baikal
Kerulen
MANCHURIAN PLAIN
Irtysh
WEST SIBERIAN PLAIN
BALTIC SEA
ASIA
GOBI
Yellow River
ALTAI MOUNTAINS
Lake Zaysan
Ozero Alakol'
DZUNGARIA
GREAT PLAIN OF CHINA
KIRGHIZ STEPPE
EUROPE
Lake Balkhash
Ili
TIEN SHAN
Pik Pobedy 7439m
TAKLA MAKAN DESERT
Yangtze
Aral Sea
Syr Darya
KYZYL KUM
Lenin Peak 7134m
PAMIRS
Communism Peak 7495m
PLATEAU OF TIBET
BLACK SEA
CAUCASUS
Caspian Sea
Amu Darya
KARA KUM
HINDU KUSH
HIMALAYAS
EURASIAN PLATE
AFRICAN PLATE
ANATOLIAN PLATE
ANATOLIA
IRANIAN PLATE
Tropic of Cancer
MEDITERRANEAN SEA
Euphrates
GREAT SALT DESERT
DASHT-E LUT
IRANIAN PLATEAU
Ganges
Mekong
Dead Sea -440m
SYRIAN DESERT
Tigris
ZAGROS MOUNTAINS
Indus
THAR DESERT
Mouths of the Ganges
Irrawaddy
Sinai
AN NAFUD
The Gulf
B
Gulf of Oman
IRANIAN PLATE
INDO-AUSTRALIAN PLATE
DECCAN
Bay of Bengal
Gulf of Thailand
AFRICA
RED SEA
ARABIAN PENINSULA
AR RUB' AL KHALI (EMPTY QUARTER)
ARABIAN PLATE
ANDAMAN SEA
ARABIAN SEA
Chagos-Laccadive Plateau
Sri Lanka
Ninetyeast Ridge
Arabian Basin
Gulf of Aden
Socotra
INDIAN OCEAN
Ceylon Plain
Equator
Cocos Basin

Siberian iris
Iris sibirica
Height: 1.2 m (4 ft)

The head of a fossilized Benthosuchus, which lived in Asia over 200 million years ago.

BROADLEAF DECIDUOUS FOREST
Broadleaf trees, such as oak, have larger, wider leaves than needleleaf trees, such as pine. Broadleaf, or deciduous, trees shed all their leaves at once in the autumn; needleleaf, or evergreen, trees shed and replace their leaves all through the year.

TURKEY AND CYPRUS

SITUATED PARTLY IN EUROPE and partly in Asia, Turkey is also balanced between modern Europe and its Islamic past. For 600 years, the Ottoman Turks ruled over a great empire covering a quarter of Europe, but by the early 20th century their empire had disappeared. In the 1920s, Mustapha Kemal (Atatürk) forcibly modernized Turkish society. Today, Turkey is becoming increasingly industrialized; textile and food-processing industries dominate the economy. In the central plateau, however, farmers and herders live as they have done for centuries, adapting their lives to the harsh environment. To the north, the Black Sea is rich in fish, and the fertile areas around its shores are well-suited to farming. The beautiful western and southern coasts are strewn with the remains of ancient Greek sites, and attract 1.5 million tourists to Turkey every year.

The harbour and castle of St. Peter at Bodrum.

ISTANBUL

Istanbul is divided in two by a strait of water called the Bosporus. One part of the city is in Europe, the other in Asia. Its buildings are also a mix of East and West: grand mosques, graceful minarets and exotic bazaars rub shoulders with modern shops, offices and restaurants.

TURKEY
pop: 63,800,000

BULGARIA
GREECE
Edirne
Kırklareli
Wheat
Tekirdağ
Sariyer
Bosporus
İstanbul
Beykoz
İzmit
Adapazarı
Sea of Marmara
Gallipoli
Dardanelles
Bandırma
Gemlik
İznik
Bilecik
Çanakkale
Bursa
Sakarya
Troy
Olives
Balikesir
Eskişehir
Ayvalık
Kütahya
Pergamon
Akhisar
Demirköprü Baraji
Manisa
İzmir
Uşak
Afyon
Bolvadin
Ephesus
Kuşadası
Aydın
Nazilli
Priene
Aphrodisias
Pamukkale
Denizli
Eğirdir Gölü
Miletus
Didyma
Milas
Isparta
Burdur
Halicarnassus
Muğla
Bodrum
Marmaris
Dalaman
Fethiye
Ölüdeniz
Perge
Antalya
Side
AEGEAN SEA
MEDITERRANEAN

STREET TRADERS

Large numbers of people from the countryside go to Turkey's cities to try to make a living. Many of them sell goods, food or drink on the streets or from makeshift market stalls. Others work as shoe-shiners, carrying their equipment in highly decorated brass cases.

A CLASSICAL LEGACY

The temple of Athena in Priene is one of Turkey's many ancient treasures. The Aegean coast was colonized by the ancient Greeks as early as 700 BC. Many people go to Turkey to visit the dramatic remains of Greek cities and temples. Look for Ⅲ

Blue Mosque, Istanbul

MOSQUE

Modern Turkey does not have a state religion. It was once an Islamic country, but in the 20th century reforms limited the powers of the clerics and introduced civil law. Recently, however, there has been an Islamic revival and modern Turks are going back to many customs from their rich Islamic past.

MAP FEATURES

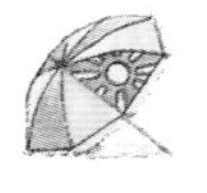

Tobacco: Turkey is a major producer. Dark, Turkish tobacco is grown around the Black Sea and Aegean coasts. **Look for**

Tourism: Coastal resorts are developing rapidly. Airports cater for growing numbers of visitors from northern Europe. **Look for**

Dams: Ambitious dam-building programmes, especially in the south-east, are being used for hydro-electric power and for watering farmland. **Look for**

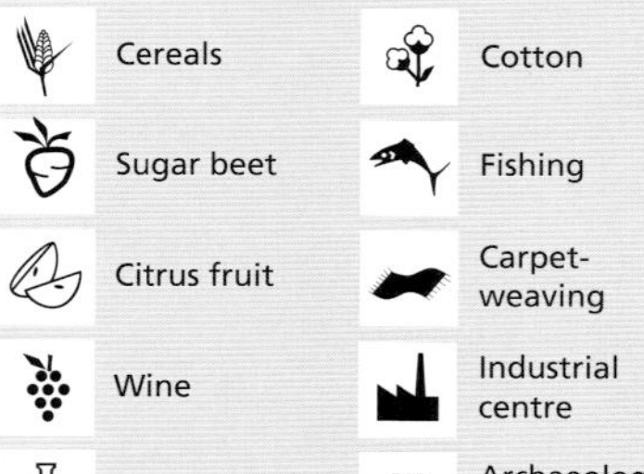

	Cereals		Cotton
	Sugar beet		Fishing
	Citrus fruit		Carpet-weaving
	Wine		Industrial centre
	Vegetable oil	Ⅲ	Archaeological site

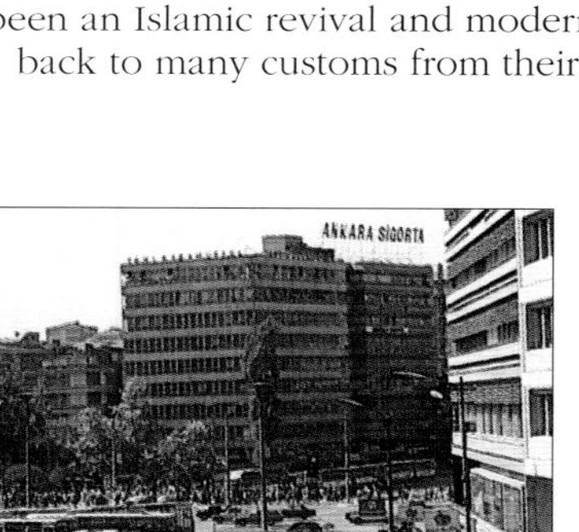

ANKARA

Ankara has been the capital of Turkey since 1923. It is a planned, modern city with boulevards, parks and many high-rise flats. Until recently, the city suffered from terrible pollution, caused by people burning brown coal, or lignite, for heating. Now, clean natural gas is piped into the city from the Russian Federation.

Dried apricot

Almond

Hazelnut

Peach

Fig

This strange landscape is in Cappadocia, central Turkey.

AGRICULTURE

Turkey has a varied landscape and climate. This means that many different types of crop can be grown there and the Turks are able to produce all their own food. Cereals, sugar beet, grapes, nuts, cotton and tobacco are all major exports. Hazelnuts are grown along the shores of the Black Sea. Figs, peaches, olives and grapes are grown along the Mediterranean coast and in the coastal lowlands. Cereals are cultivated on the central plateau. Farms are still relatively small and only gradually being modernized, but despite this productivity is high.

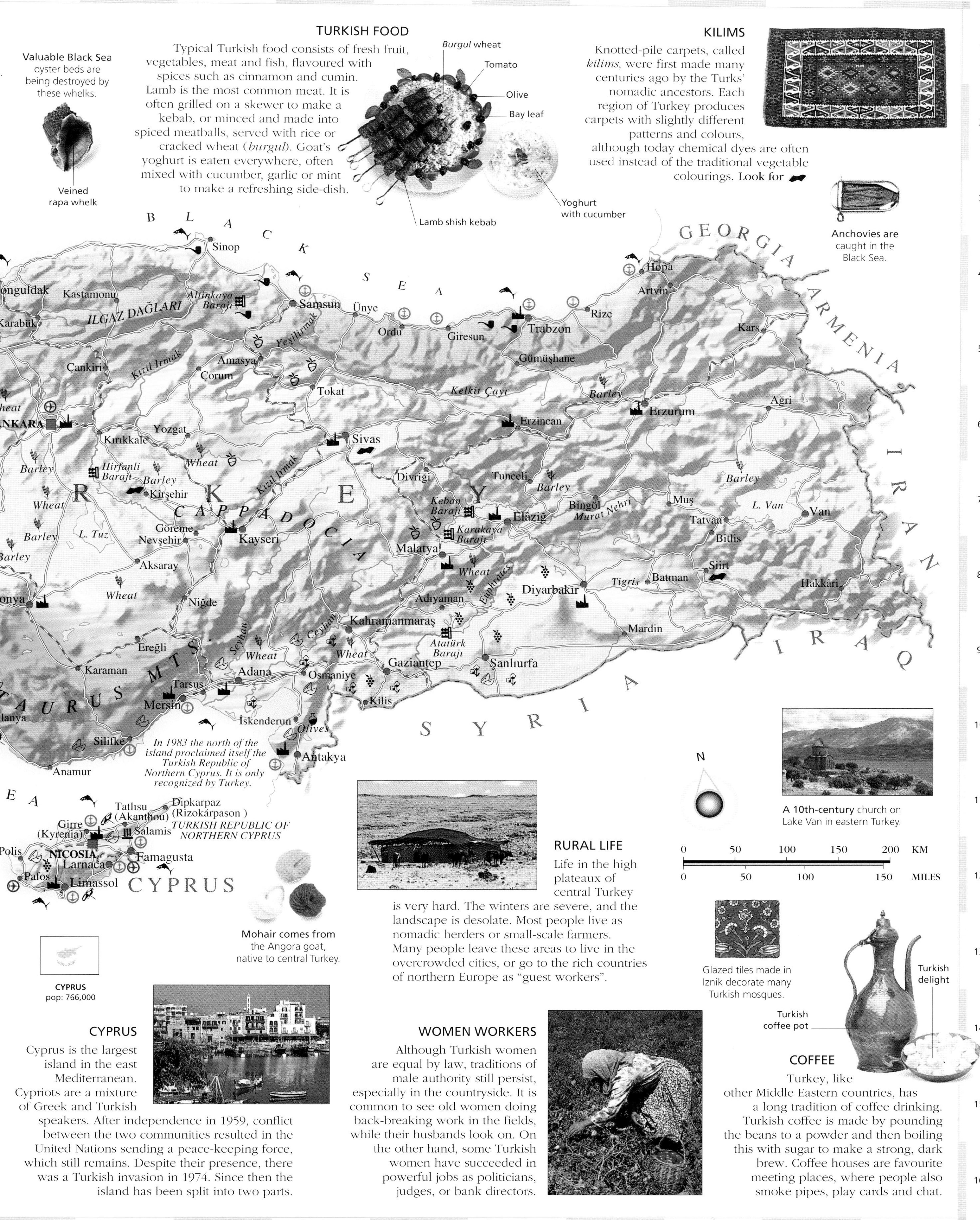
K L M N O P Q R S T
1 2 3 4 5 6 7 8 9 10 11 12 13 14 15 16
Burgul wheat
Tomato
Olive
Bay leaf
Lamb shish kebab
Yoghurt with cucumber
BLACK SEA
GEORGIA
ARMENIA
IRAN
IRAQ
SYRIA
Sinop
Zonguldak
Kastamonu
Karabük
ILGAZ DAĞLARI
Altinkaya Barajı
Samsun
Ünye
Ordu
Giresun
Trabzon
Rize
Hopa
Artvin
Kars
Gümüşhane
Yeşilırmak
Kızıl Irmak
Amasya
Çorum
Çankiri
Tokat
Kelkit Çayı
Barley
Erzurum
Ağri
Wheat
ANKARA
Erzincan
Yozgat
Kırıkkale
Sivas
Hirfanli Barajı
Kırşehir
CAPPADOCIA
Divriği
Tunceli
TURKEY
Keban Barajı
Elâzığ
Bingöl
Murat Nehri
Muş
L. Van
Van
Tatvan
Bitlis
Göreme
Nevşehir
Kayseri
L. Tuz
Karakaya Barajı
Malatya
Siirt
Aksaray
Euphrates
Diyarbakir
Tigris
Batman
Hakkâri
Konya
Niğde
Adıyaman
Kahramanmaraş
Mardin
Seyhan
Ceyhan
Ereğli
Atatürk Barajı
Gaziantep
Şanlıurfa
Karaman
Adana
Osmaniye
TAURUS MTS
Tarsus
Mersin
Kilis
Alanya
İskenderun
Olives
Silifke
Antakya
Anamur
In 1983 the north of the island proclaimed itself the Turkish Republic of Northern Cyprus. It is only recognized by Turkey.
N
Dipkarpaz (Rizokárpason)
Tatlısu (Akanthou)
Girne (Kyrenia)
Salamis
TURKISH REPUBLIC OF NORTHERN CYPRUS
Polis
NICOSIA
Larnaca
Famagusta
Pafos
Limassol
CYPRUS
0 50 100 150 200 KM
0 50 100 150 MILES
Turkish delight
Turkish coffee pot

TURKISH FOOD

Typical Turkish food consists of fresh fruit, vegetables, meat and fish, flavoured with spices such as cinnamon and cumin. Lamb is the most common meat. It is often grilled on a skewer to make a kebab, or minced and made into spiced meatballs, served with rice or cracked wheat (*burgul*). Goat's yoghurt is eaten everywhere, often mixed with cucumber, garlic or mint to make a refreshing side-dish.

Valuable Black Sea oyster beds are being destroyed by these whelks.

Veined rapa whelk

KILIMS

Knotted-pile carpets, called *kilims*, were first made many centuries ago by the Turks' nomadic ancestors. Each region of Turkey produces carpets with slightly different patterns and colours, although today chemical dyes are often used instead of the traditional vegetable colourings. Look for

Anchovies are caught in the Black Sea.

A 10th-century church on Lake Van in eastern Turkey.

RURAL LIFE

Life in the high plateaux of central Turkey is very hard. The winters are severe, and the landscape is desolate. Most people live as nomadic herders or small-scale farmers. Many people leave these areas to live in the overcrowded cities, or go to the rich countries of northern Europe as "guest workers".

Mohair comes from the Angora goat, native to central Turkey.

Glazed tiles made in Iznik decorate many Turkish mosques.

CYPRUS
pop: 766,000

CYPRUS

Cyprus is the largest island in the east Mediterranean. Cypriots are a mixture of Greek and Turkish speakers. After independence in 1959, conflict between the two communities resulted in the United Nations sending a peace-keeping force, which still remains. Despite their presence, there was a Turkish invasion in 1974. Since then the island has been split into two parts.

WOMEN WORKERS

Although Turkish women are equal by law, traditions of male authority still persist, especially in the countryside. It is common to see old women doing back-breaking work in the fields, while their husbands look on. On the other hand, some Turkish women have succeeded in powerful jobs as politicians, judges, or bank directors.

COFFEE

Turkey, like other Middle Eastern countries, has a long tradition of coffee drinking. Turkish coffee is made by pounding the beans to a powder and then boiling this with sugar to make a strong, dark brew. Coffee houses are favourite meeting places, where people also smoke pipes, play cards and chat.

THE NEAR EAST

CAUGHT BETWEEN the two worlds of Europe and Asia, the Near East is bordered on the west by the fertile coasts of the Mediterranean Sea, and on the east by the arid deserts of Arabia. Some of the world's earliest civilizations were born here, while the history of all three of the world's great religions – Judaism, Christianity and Islam – is closely bound up with the region. Imperial conquerors and Christian and Muslim crusaders battled fiercely over this territory, and by the 17th century much of the region was part of the Turkish Ottoman empire. In 1918, the Near East came under the control of Britain and France; a dangerous mixture of religions and passionate nationalism plunged the area into conflict. Today, Lebanon is emerging from a fierce civil war between Christians and Muslims. Israel, which became a Jewish state in 1948, has been involved in numerous wars with its neighbours and there is considerable unrest among its minority Palestinian population. Many Palestinian refugees, who have left Israel, are living in camps in Jordan and Lebanon. Despite these problems, the Near East continues to survive economically. Israel is highly industrialized and a world leader in advanced farming techniques. Syria has its own reserves of oil, and is gradually becoming more industrialized.

Carnation

Rose

Grapefruit

Lemon

Orange

Lime

FARMING

Although about half of Israel is desert, it is self-sufficient in most food, and actually exports agricultural produce, especially citrus fruits and flowers. Israeli farming uses advanced irrigation techniques and is highly mechanized. Many farms are run as *kibbutzim;* the land is owned by members, who share work and profits. Look for

JERUSALEM THE GOLDEN

The historic city of Jerusalem is held sacred by three major religions: Judaism, Christianity and Islam. Throughout its history, it has been the object of pilgrimage and religious crusades. For Jews, the Wailing Wall, seen here, is the most sacred site, while the Dome of the Rock is sacred to Muslims, reflecting divisions within Israel.

UZI GUNS

Israel is a major arms producer, developing weapons for her own army, such as this Uzi gun, as well as medium-range missiles to deter Arab enemies. Military service in the Israel Defence Force (IDF) is compulsory for all Israeli citizens. Men must serve three years, unmarried women two years.

Lake Tiberias, known in the Bible as the Sea of Galilee.

Skull-cap, yarmulke

JUDAISM

Judaism is one of the oldest religions in the world. Jews believe in one God, and the most devout (Orthodox) follow codes of behaviour based on laws contained in their holy book, the *Torah*. This is the first part of Old Testament and is written in Hebrew. Modern Hebrew is the language of Israel.

The *Torah*

Prayer shawl

WATER WARS

Throughout this region, water is in very short supply. Where water resources are shared (for example, Israel and Jordan share the Jordan River), disputes can occur. Israel leads the way in irrigation techniques. Fields are watered by drip irrigation – holes in pipes dispense exactly the right amount of water required, avoiding wastage.

DEAD SEA MUD

The Dead Sea, 400 m (1,300 ft) below sea level, is an enclosed salt lake. Salt levels are six times higher than in other seas, so no fish live in these waters. The Dead Sea is rich in minerals, some of which have medical properties.

Dead Sea mud is used as a skin conditioner, and cure for arthritis

Soap made from Dead Sea mud

MAP FEATURES

Cotton: Syria's most profitable cash crop is cotton. The area of land devoted to cotton has been expanded in recent years. Look for

Tourism: People come to this region from all over the world to visit archaeological sites, ancient cities, and holy places. Look for

Refugee camps: Palestinian refugees have fled from Israel to Jordan and Lebanon. Many fled to Jordan from Kuwait after the 1991 Gulf War. Look for

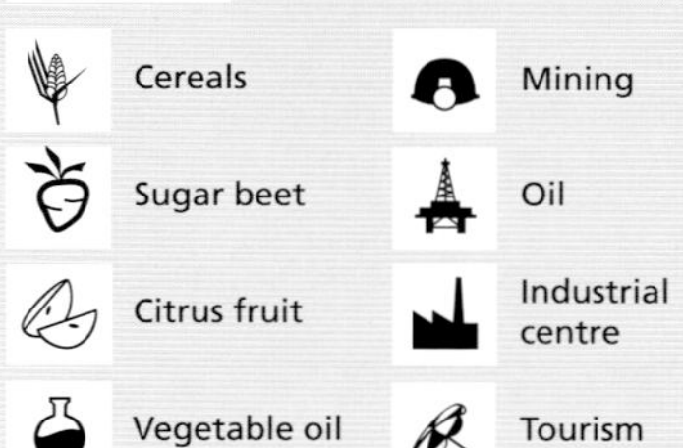

	Cereals		Mining
	Sugar beet		Oil
	Citrus fruit		Industrial centre
	Vegetable oil		Tourism
	Tobacco		Irrigated agriculture

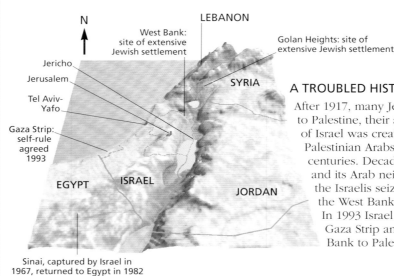

N

LEBANON

West Bank: site of extensive Jewish settlement

Golan Heights: site of extensive Jewish settlement

Jericho

Jerusalem

Tel Aviv-Yafo

SYRIA

Gaza Strip: self-rule agreed 1993

EGYPT

ISRAEL

JORDAN

Sinai, captured by Israel in 1967, returned to Egypt in 1982

A TROUBLED HISTORY

After 1917, many Jews emigrated from Europe to Palestine, their ancient homeland. The State of Israel was created in 1948, driving out the Palestinian Arabs who had also lived there for centuries. Decades of conflict between Israel and its Arab neighbours followed. In 1967 the Israelis seized Sinai, the Gaza Strip, the West Bank and the Golan Heights. In 1993 Israel agreed to restore the Gaza Strip and parts of the West Bank to Palestinian home rule.

N

0 50 100 150 KM

0 25 50 75 100 MILES

SIN

Gulf of Suez

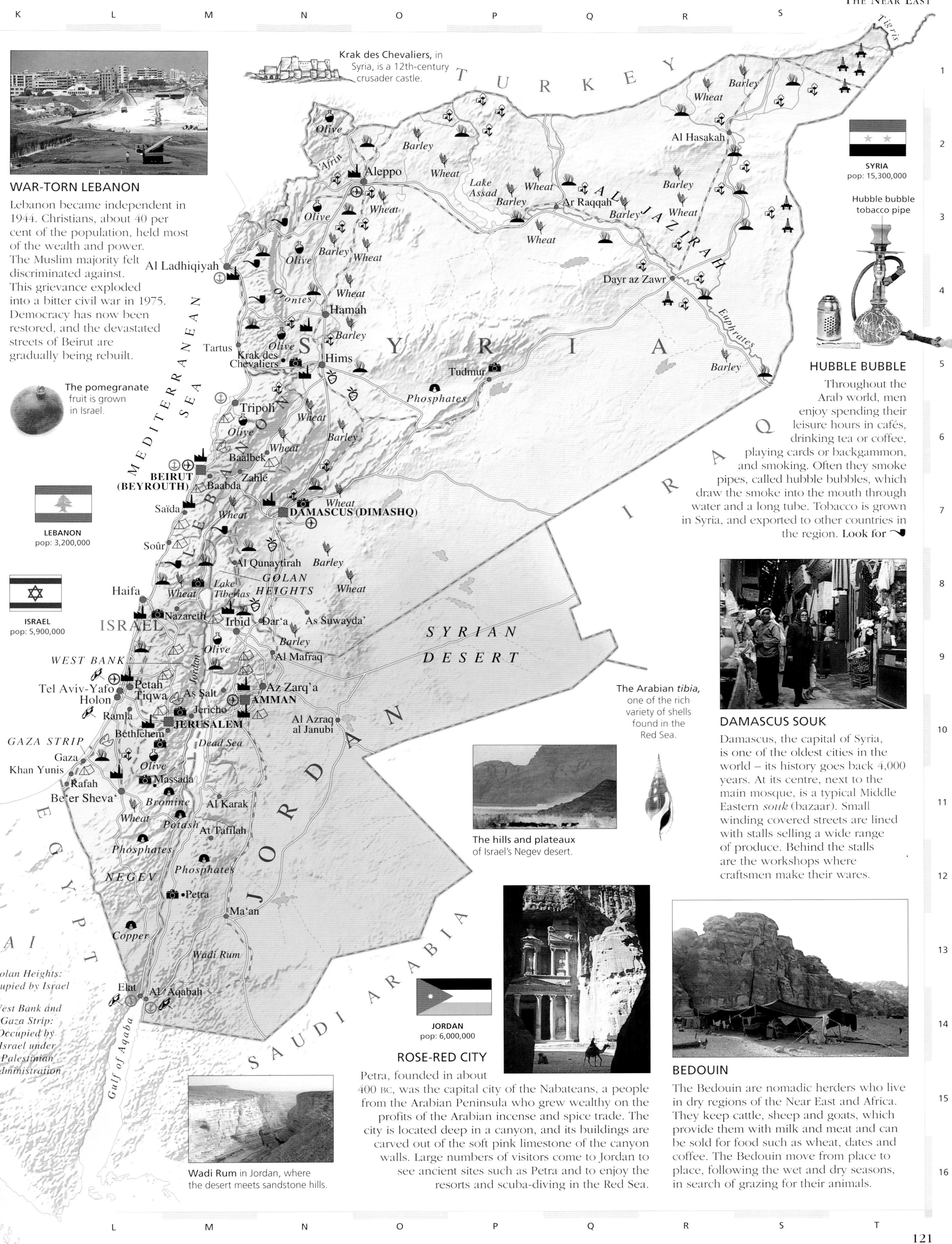

K L M N O P Q R S
T U R K E Y
S Y R I A
I R A Q
J O R D A N
S A U D I   A R A B I A
E G Y P T
M E D I T E R R A N E A N   S E A
L E B A N O N
ISRAEL
SYRIAN DESERT
AL JAZIRAH
GOLAN HEIGHTS
WEST BANK
GAZA STRIP
NEGEV
Aleppo
Al Hasakah
Ar Raqqah
Lake Assad
Dayr az Zawr
Al Ladhiqiyah
Hamah
Tartus
Krak des Chevaliers
Hims
Tudmur
Tripoli
Baalbek
Zahlé
BEIRUT (BEYROUTH)
Baabda
Saïda
DAMASCUS (DIMASHQ)
Soûr
Al Qunaytirah
Haifa
Lake Tiberias
Nazareth
Irbid
Dar'a
As Suwayda'
Al Mafraq
Tel Aviv-Yafo
Holon
Petah Tiqwa
As Salt
Az Zarq'a
AMMAN
Ramla
Jericho
JERUSALEM
Bethlehem
Dead Sea
Al Azraq al Janubi
Gaza
Khan Yunis
Rafah
Massada
Be'er Sheva'
Al Karak
At Tafilah
Petra
Ma'an
Wadi Rum
Elat
Al Aqabah
Gulf of Aqaba
Tigris
Euphrates
Orontes
'Afrin
Jordan
Wheat
Barley
Olive
Phosphates
Bromine
Potash
Copper
Golan Heights: occupied by Israel
West Bank and Gaza Strip: Occupied by Israel under Palestinian administration
1 2 3 4 5 6 7 8 9 10 11 12 13 14 15 16
L M N O P Q R S T

Krak des Chevaliers, in Syria, is a 12th-century crusader castle.

WAR-TORN LEBANON

Lebanon became independent in 1944. Christians, about 40 per cent of the population, held most of the wealth and power. The Muslim majority felt discriminated against. This grievance exploded into a bitter civil war in 1975. Democracy has now been restored, and the devastated streets of Beirut are gradually being rebuilt.

The pomegranate fruit is grown in Israel.

LEBANON
pop: 3,200,000

ISRAEL
pop: 5,900,000

SYRIA
pop: 15,300,000

Hubble bubble tobacco pipe

HUBBLE BUBBLE

Throughout the Arab world, men enjoy spending their leisure hours in cafés, drinking tea or coffee, playing cards or backgammon, and smoking. Often they smoke pipes, called hubble bubbles, which draw the smoke into the mouth through water and a long tube. Tobacco is grown in Syria, and exported to other countries in the region. **Look for**

DAMASCUS SOUK

Damascus, the capital of Syria, is one of the oldest cities in the world – its history goes back 4,000 years. At its centre, next to the main mosque, is a typical Middle Eastern *souk* (bazaar). Small winding covered streets are lined with stalls selling a wide range of produce. Behind the stalls are the workshops where craftsmen make their wares.

The Arabian *tibia*, one of the rich variety of shells found in the Red Sea.

The hills and plateaux of Israel's Negev desert.

JORDAN
pop: 6,000,000

ROSE-RED CITY

Petra, founded in about 400 BC, was the capital city of the Nabateans, a people from the Arabian Peninsula who grew wealthy on the profits of the Arabian incense and spice trade. The city is located deep in a canyon, and its buildings are carved out of the soft pink limestone of the canyon walls. Large numbers of visitors come to Jordan to see ancient sites such as Petra and to enjoy the resorts and scuba-diving in the Red Sea.

Wadi Rum in Jordan, where the desert meets sandstone hills.

BEDOUIN

The Bedouin are nomadic herders who live in dry regions of the Near East and Africa. They keep cattle, sheep and goats, which provide them with milk and meat and can be sold for food such as wheat, dates and coffee. The Bedouin move from place to place, following the wet and dry seasons, in search of grazing for their animals.

The Middle East

THE WORLD'S FIRST CITIES grew up about 5,500 years ago in the area between the Tigris and Euphrates rivers. The land in this region is dry, but these early people created ingenious irrigation techniques to direct the river water on to their fields of crops. In AD 570, the Prophet Mohammed, founder of the Islamic religion, was born in Mecca, in modern-day Saudi Arabia. Islam soon spread throughout the Middle East, where it is now the dominant religion, and into Africa. In recent years, the discovery of oil has brought great wealth to the countries around The Gulf, and with it, rapid industrial and social change. Both Iran and Iraq earn huge revenues from oil, but they have been troubled by dictatorship and political unrest, as well as by a ten-year war. In 1991, the region was devastated by the Gulf War, which brought UN troops to the Middle East to fight against Iraq.

MIDDLE EASTERN FOOD

Farming in the Arabian Peninsula has been transformed by new irrigation methods. Saudi Arabia now exports wheat; the United Arab Emirates vegetables. Pulses such as lentils and chickpeas are the main food crops elsewhere.

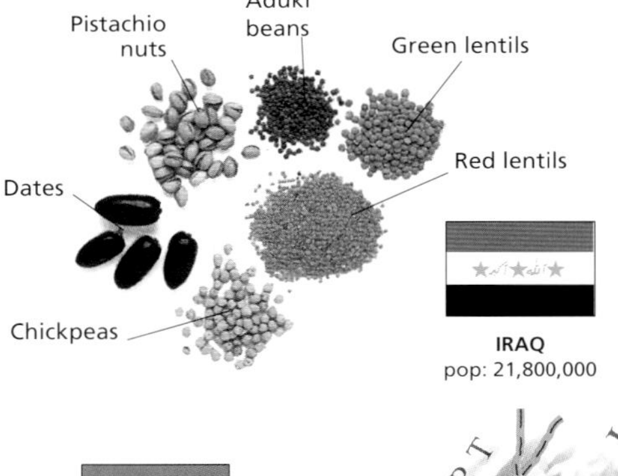
Pistachio nuts
Aduki beans
Green lentils
Red lentils
Dates
Chickpeas

BAGHDAD

Baghdad, Iraq's capital since 1918, has grown dramatically over the last 20 years, but was badly damaged during the Gulf War. The city has been rebuilt. Massive monuments to President Hussein once again adorn its streets.

KUWAIT
pop: 1,800,000

IRAQ
pop: 21,800,000

SAUDI ARABIA
pop: 20,200,000

For centuries Marsh Arabs have lived in the swampy delta of the Tigris and Euphrates.

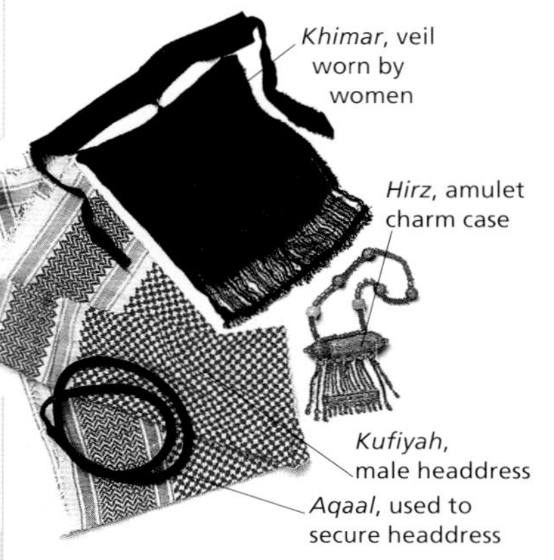
Khimar, veil worn by women
Hirz, amulet charm case
Kufiyah, male headdress
Aqaal, used to secure headdress

ARAB DRESS

In summer, when temperatures in the Gulf reach 50° C (122° F), layers of loose robes and a headdress are worn to make the heat bearable.

ISLAM

Mecca is Islam's holiest place and a centre of pilgrimage. Muslims believe in one God, *Allah*. They worship in mosques, and should pray five times a day, give alms, and fast for the month-long period of *Ramadan*.

Camels, known as "ships of the desert", can go for days without water, and are used to carry loads.

MAKING THE DESERT BLOOM

Water is scarce all over this region, and is carefully managed. More than 60 per cent of the world's desalination plants are in the Arabian Peninsula. They are used to extract the salt from sea water to make it drinkable. **Look for** 💧

MAP FEATURES

Archaeological sites: The ancient cities of the Middle East, such as Ur, date back to 3,500 BC. They are the oldest cities in the world. **Look for**

Dams: A series of dams and barrages have been built along the Tigris and Euphrates to provide water for the dry plains of southern Iraq. **Look for**

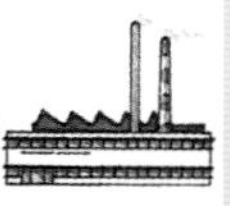

Industrial centre: Saudi Arabia's economy has been dominated by oil. It is seeking to widen its range of industries. **Look for**

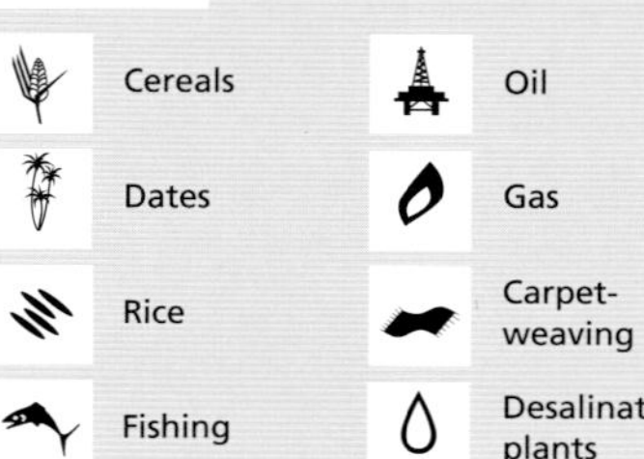
Cereals
Oil
Dates
Gas
Rice
Carpet-weaving
Fishing
Desalination plants

YEMEN

Unlike the rest of the Arabian Peninsula, Yemen has enough rainfall to water its crops. Most crops are grown on mountain terraces in the highlands. The country is self-sufficient in barley, lentils, sorghum, maize and coffee. **Look for**

The minaret of the Great Mosque at Samarra, Iraq.

Yemen's capital, Sana, dates back to the 7th century.

YEMEN
pop: 16,900,000

SYRIA
JORDAN
EGYPT
Gulf of Aqaba
SYRIAN DESERT
Wadi Hawran
Wadi al Ghadaf
An Nabk
'Ar'ar
Al Jawf
Sakakah
Tabuk
AN NAFUD
Wheat
HEJAZ
Ha'il
Buraydah
NEJD
Yanbu al Bahr
Medina
RED SEA
Jedda
Mecca
Ta'if
SAUDI ARABIA
Al Bahah
ASIR
Barley
Abha
Khamis Mushayt
AR RUB
Najran
Jizan
Sa'dah
RAMLAT
Kamaran
Hajjah
Hodeida
SANA
Mar'ib
YEMEN
Millet
Dhamar
Ibb
Ta'izz
Al Bayda
Al Mukha
Lahij
Aden
Zinjibar
Bab el Mandeb

K M N O P Q R S T
1 2 3 4 5 6 7 8 9 10 11 12 13 14 15 16
TURKEY
ARMENIA
AZERBAIJAN
CASPIAN SEA
TURKMENISTAN
AFGHANISTAN
PAKISTAN
KUWAIT
BAHRAIN
QATAR
UNITED ARAB EMIRATES
OMAN
ELBURZ MTS
ZAGROS MTS
DASHT-E KAVIR
DASHT-E LUT
The Gulf
Gulf of Oman
Strait of Hormuz
Gulf of Masira
ARABIAN SEA
AD DAHNA
AD DAFRAH
AL KHALI (EMPTY QUARTER)
L. Urmia
Tabriz
Orumiyeh
Ardabil
Rasht
Zanjan
Qazvin
Amol
Sari
Gorgan
Karaj
TEHRAN
Hamadan
Sanandaj
Bakhtaran
Qom
Semnan
Sabzevar
Neyshabur
Mashhad
Kashan
Arak
Borujerd
Ilam
Dezful
Isfahan
Shahr-e Kord
Ahvaz
Khorramshahr
Abadan
Yazd
Yasuj
Pasargadae
Persepolis
Shiraz
Bushire
Kerman
Zahedan
Bandar-e 'Abbas
Qeshm I.
Hamun-e Jaz Murian
Jask
Chabahar
Dahuk
Nineveh
Mosul
Arbil
As Sulaymaniyah
Kirkuk
Tikrit
Samarra'
Khanaqin
Ramadi
BAGHDAD
Karbala
Al Hillah
Najaf
Al Kut
Ad Diwaniyah
Al 'Amarah
An Nasiriyah
Al Qurnah
Ur
Hawr al Hammar
Basra
Az Zubayr
Tigris
Euphrates
Jazirat Bubiyan
KUWAIT
Ash Shu'aybah
Al Jubayl
Ad Damman
Dhahran
MANAMA
Al Hufuf
Dukhan
DOHA
RIYADH (AR RIYAD)
Harad
Ras al Khaimah
Sharjah
Khasab (part of Oman)
Dubai
Fujairah
ABU DHABI
Al Buraymi
Suhar
Al Khaburah
Ibri
Ar Rustaq
MUSCAT (MASQAT)
Nizwa
Sama'il
Sur
Jasirat Masirah
Kuria Muria Is.
Salalah
Raysut
Al Ghaydah
Al Mukalla
Wheat
Barley
Millet
N
0 100 200 300 400 500 KM
0 50 100 150 200 250 300 MILES

KURDS

There are 25 million Kurds. They are one of the largest groups of stateless people in the world. Their homeland, Kurdistan, straddles three countries: Turkey, Iraq and Iran. Many Kurds were forced into refugee camps by the Gulf War. Kurdish separatists are in open conflict with the Turkish government.

Shahyad Monument

TEHRAN

The last Shah (king) of Iran used his great wealth to modernize the country by building dams, power stations, factories and roads. He ruled as a dictator, and the cities of Iran were filled with monuments in his name. Islamic fundamentalists overthrew the Shah in 1979.

IRAN
pop: 73,100,000

TEXTILES

Iran is famous for its superb, hand-made carpets. They are produced by a combination of weaving and knotting the wool, often using patterns which are several hundred years old. They are coloured with vegetable dyes. **Look for**

Finely embroidered textiles, such as this saddlebag, are typically Kurdish.

BAHRAIN
pop: 594,000

UNITED ARAB EMIRATES
pop: 2,400,000

OMAN
pop: 2,500,000

The Zagros Mountains lie in the southwest of Iran.

QATAR
pop: 579,000

An oil pipeline snakes across the Arabian desert.

OIL

The discovery of oil in the Gulf region has brought enormous wealth to the Middle East. The region now supplies 30 per cent of the world's oil and Saudi Arabia alone produces a tenth of the world's total. Pipelines cross the desert and huge tankers pick up oil from the coastal terminals, making the Gulf one of the world's busiest seaways. **Look for**

CENTRAL ASIA

THE CENTRAL ASIAN REPUBLICS lie on the ancient Silk Road between Asia and Europe, and their historic cities grew up along this route. Afghanistan controlled the route south into Pakistan and India, through the Khyber Pass in the Hindu Kush mountains. The hot, dry deserts of Central Asia and high, rugged mountain ranges of the Pamirs and Tien Shan were not suited to agriculture. For centuries people lived as nomads, herding sheep across the empty plains, or settled as merchants and traders in the Silk Road cities. When Central Asia became part of the communist Soviet Union, everything changed: local languages and the Islamic religion (which had come to the region from the Middle East in the 8th century) were restricted; irrigation schemes made farming the arid land possible; oil, gas and other minerals were exploited; industry was developed. Today, these newly-independent republics are returning to the languages, religion and traditions of their past. Afghanistan, independent since 1750, has recently suffered terrible conflict and economic collapse.

Akhal-Teke racehorse

HORSEMEN OF THE STEPPES

The nomadic peoples of the steppes travel great distances on horseback, and horse fairs and races are important events in their calendar. Ashgabat in Turkmenistan is the main breeding centre for the Akhal-Teke, a much prized racehorse, able to maintain its speed in desert conditions.

UZBEKISTAN
pop: 24,100,000

TURKMENISTAN
pop: 4,300,000

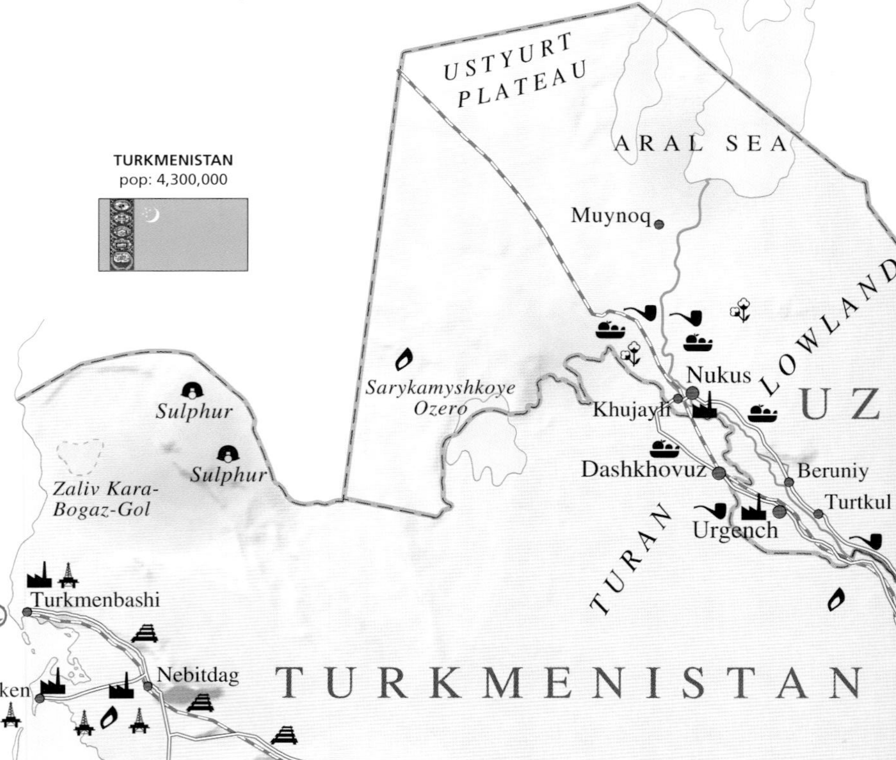

USTYURT PLATEAU
ARAL SEA
Muynoq
LOWLAND
Nukus
UZ
Khujayli
Sarykamyshkoye Ozero
Sulphur
Sulphur
Zaliv Kara-Bogaz-Gol
Dashkhovuz
Beruniy
Turtkul
Urgench
TURAN
CASPIAN SEA
Turkmenbashi
Cheleken
Nebitdag
TURKMENISTAN
Gyzylarbat
Kizyl-Atrek
Byuzmeyin
ASHGABAT
IRAN
Bayramaly
Mary
Tedzhen
Tedzhen
Gushgy
Herat
Namakzar
AFG
Hamun-e-Saberi
Dasht-e Gowd-e-Zereh

AGRICULTURE

Farming in this dry region depends on irrigation. The Kara Kum Canal is 1,100 km (683 miles) long – the longest canal in the world. It carries water from the Amu Darya towards the Caspian Sea, and waters vast areas of land. Draining the river, however, has also created desert landscapes.

Opium poppies are grown all over the region. They provide illegal money for many farmers, who supply the international drug trade.

SULPHUR

Turkmenistan's sulphur deposits are amongst the largest in the world. Sulphur is used in the manufacture of gunpowder, as well as in medicine, ointment and drugs. Turkmenistan also has large reserves of oil and gas, but has been slow to make money from its resources.

MARKETS

Towns such as Samarqand have changed little since the days of the Silk Road, and are still full of merchants and traders. Bazaars and street-side stalls sell local fruit and vegetables, herbs, spices, silk and cotton.

MAP FEATURES

Alternative energy: Sunlight is used to generate power in Central Asia, providing a clean alternative to nuclear power. Look for ⚡

Rail route: The planned Trans-Asian Railway will connect Beijing and Istanbul, via Central Asia and the Caspian Sea. Look for [rail symbol]

Cattle	Mining
Sheep	Oil
Mixed fruit	Gas
Tobacco	Carpet weaving
Cotton	Industrial centre

Carrots were first grown for food in Afghanistan.

CARPETS

Carpets from Uzbekistan, Turkmenistan, northern Afghanistan and other parts of this region are world-famous. They are made by hand-knotting, and are woven from fine Karakul wool. They follow distinctive geometric patterns in a range of red, brown and maroon colours. Carpets are used as saddle-cloths, tent hangings and prayer mats. Look for [carpet weaving symbol]

KARAKUL SHEEP

Karakul sheep are bred for their distinctive curly fleece. They are especially important in Afghanistan. Nomadic people have herded sheep in this region for many centuries. Each summer they take their flocks up to the lush mountain pastures, and in winter they are herded down onto the plains. Look for [sheep symbol]

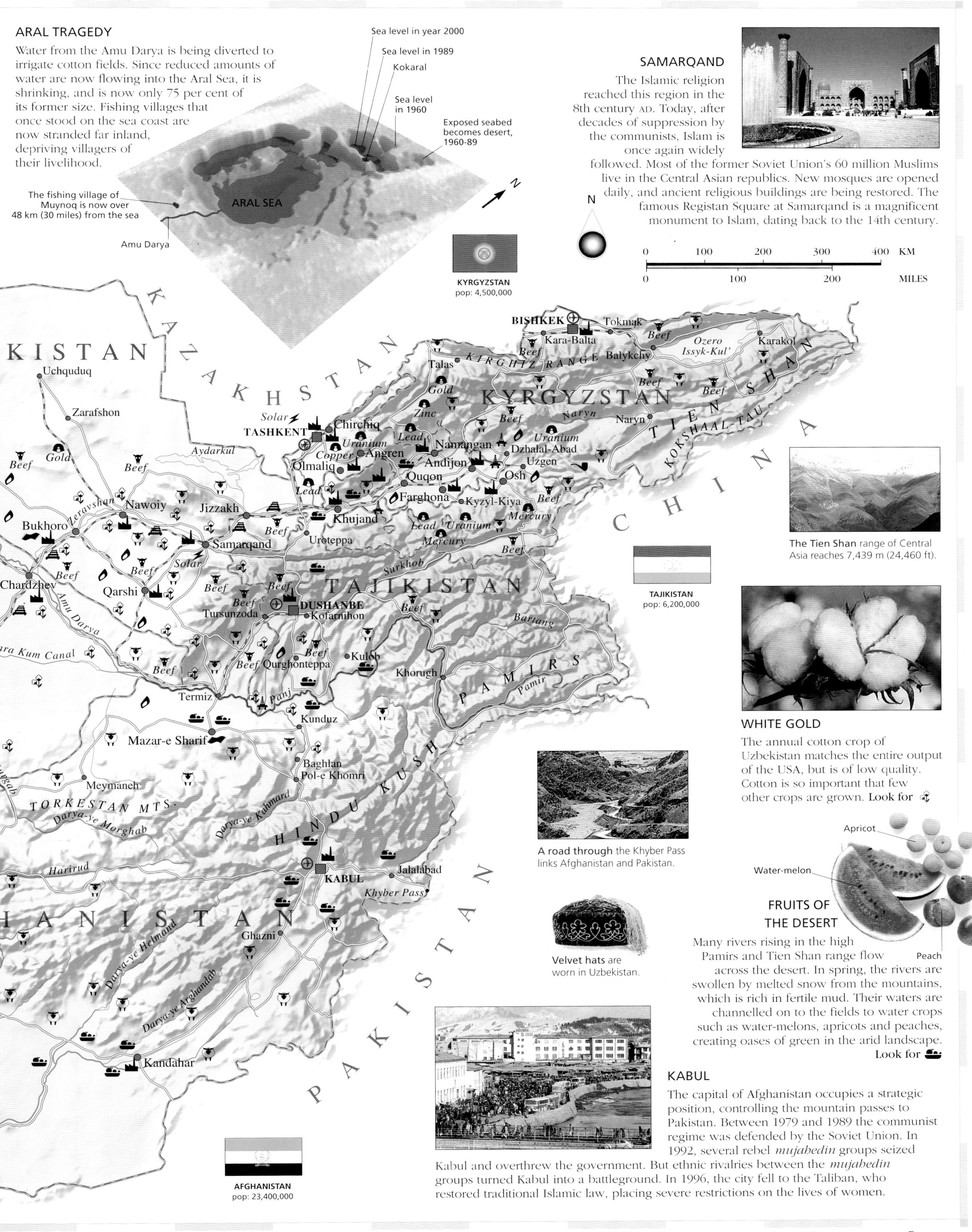
Sea level in year 2000
Sea level in 1989
Kokaral
Sea level in 1960
Exposed seabed becomes desert, 1960-89
The fishing village of Muynoq is now over 48 km (30 miles) from the sea
ARAL SEA
Amu Darya
N
KYRGYZSTAN
pop: 4,500,000
0 100 200 300 400 KM
0 100 200 MILES
KAZAKHSTAN
KYRGYZSTAN
TAJIKISTAN
CHINA
PAKISTAN
BISHKEK
Tokmak
Kara-Balta
Balykchy
Ozero Issyk-Kul'
Karakol
KIRGHIZ RANGE
TIEN SHAN
KOKSHAAL-TAU
Talas
Naryn
Uchquduq
Zarafshon
Aydarkul
TASHKENT
Chirchiq
Olmaliq
Angren
Namangan
Andijon
Dzhalal-Abad
Uzgen
Osh
Quqon
Farghona
Kyzyl-Kiya
Khujand
Uroteppa
Jizzakh
Nawoiy
Bukhoro
Zeravshan
Samarqand
Qarshi
Chardzhev
Amu Darya
Kara Kum Canal
Tursunzoda
DUSHANBE
Kofarnihon
Surkhob
Bartang
Kulob
Qurghonteppa
Khorugh
PAMIRS
Pamir
Panj
Termiz
Kunduz
Mazar-e Sharif
Baghlan
Pol-e Khomri
Meymaneh
Murghab
TORKESTAN MTS.
Darya-ye Morghab
Darya-ye Kahmard
HINDU KUSH
Harirud
KABUL
Jalalabad
Khyber Pass
Ghazni
Darya-ye Helmand
Darya-ye Arghandab
Kandahar
Gold
Zinc
Lead
Uranium
Copper
Mercury
Solar
Beef
TAJIKISTAN
pop: 6,200,000
AFGHANISTAN
pop: 23,400,000
Apricot
Water-melon
Peach

ARAL TRAGEDY

Water from the Amu Darya is being diverted to irrigate cotton fields. Since reduced amounts of water are now flowing into the Aral Sea, it is shrinking, and is now only 75 per cent of its former size. Fishing villages that once stood on the sea coast are now stranded far inland, depriving villagers of their livelihood.

SAMARQAND

The Islamic religion reached this region in the 8th century AD. Today, after decades of suppression by the communists, Islam is once again widely followed. Most of the former Soviet Union's 60 million Muslims live in the Central Asian republics. New mosques are opened daily, and ancient religious buildings are being restored. The famous Registan Square at Samarqand is a magnificent monument to Islam, dating back to the 14th century.

The Tien Shan range of Central Asia reaches 7,439 m (24,460 ft).

WHITE GOLD

The annual cotton crop of Uzbekistan matches the entire output of the USA, but is of low quality. Cotton is so important that few other crops are grown. Look for

A road through the Khyber Pass links Afghanistan and Pakistan.

Velvet hats are worn in Uzbekistan.

FRUITS OF THE DESERT

Many rivers rising in the high Pamirs and Tien Shan range flow across the desert. In spring, the rivers are swollen by melted snow from the mountains, which is rich in fertile mud. Their waters are channelled on to the fields to water crops such as water-melons, apricots and peaches, creating oases of green in the arid landscape. Look for

KABUL

The capital of Afghanistan occupies a strategic position, controlling the mountain passes to Pakistan. Between 1979 and 1989 the communist regime was defended by the Soviet Union. In 1992, several rebel *mujahedin* groups seized Kabul and overthrew the government. But ethnic rivalries between the *mujahedin* groups turned Kabul into a battleground. In 1996, the city fell to the Taliban, who restored traditional Islamic law, placing severe restrictions on the lives of women.

Russia and Kazakhstan

The Ural Mountains form a natural barrier between the European and the Asian parts of Russia. Although over 77 per cent of the country lies in Asia, only 27 per cent of the population live here. Siberia dominates Russia east of the Urals, stretching to the Pacific Ocean and northwards into the Arctic. The climate is severe, parts of Siberia are colder in winter than the North Pole. Siberia has huge deposits of gold, coal, diamonds, gas and oil, but workers had to be offered high wages and housing to work there. Today, both Russia and Kazakhstan have great economic potential, but are still coping with a legacy of severe industrial pollution.

HYDRO-ELECTRIC POWER

Siberia's rivers provide 80 per cent of Russia's hydro-electric power, fuelling industry throughout eastern Russia. Massive dams, such as this one on the River Angara, provide the power for the aluminium industry.
Look for

Ear of wheat

VIRGIN LANDS

In the 1950s, the Soviet Union tried to increase grain production. The empty steppes of Kazakhstan, known as the "Virgin Lands", were ploughed up to grow crops. Today, much of this farmland is reverting to steppe.
Look for

MAP FEATURES

Industrial centre: This region produces one-third of the former USSR's iron and steel. Timber processing is also very important. Look for

Pollution: Nearly 500 Soviet nuclear devices were detonated in Kazakhstan from 1949-1989. Many children in this area are malformed at birth. Look for

Military bases: Russia's far east is a highly militarized area. The Russian Pacific fleet is based at Vladivostok. Look for

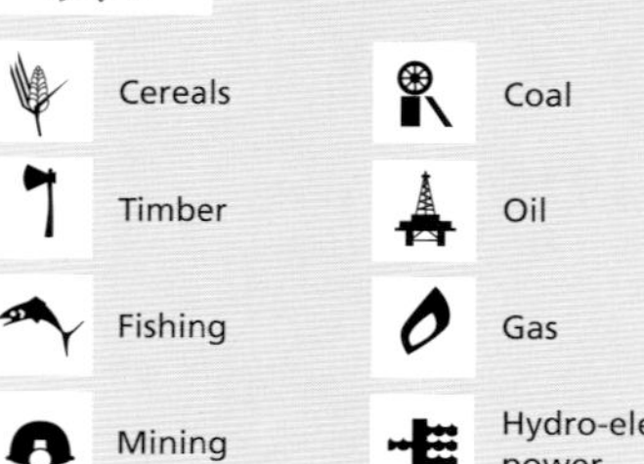
Cereals
Coal
Timber
Oil
Fishing
Gas
Mining
Hydro-electric power

A child's toy wooden sledge from Siberia.

KAZAKH HORSEMEN

The first inhabitants of the steppe were a nomadic people who travelled on horseback, herding their sheep with them. They slept in felt tents like these, called *yurts*. Their descendants, the Kazakhs, still place great value on horses and riding skills, and horse-racing is a popular sport. The Kazakh national drink is *kumiss* – fermented mare's milk. The traditional nomadic lifestyle of the steppe has gradually been replaced by large-scale agriculture and industry.

KAZAKHSTAN
pop: 16,900,000

SPACE CENTRE

The Russian space programme is based at Baykonur in Kazakhstan, where this Buran unmanned shuttle was launched in 1988. Russia's achievements in space technology started with the launch of the Sputnik satellite in 1957. Since then, Russia has been responsible for the first man in space, the first woman cosmonaut, and the first space walk. The Mir orbital station, in space since 1986, was manned by cosmonauts until 1999.

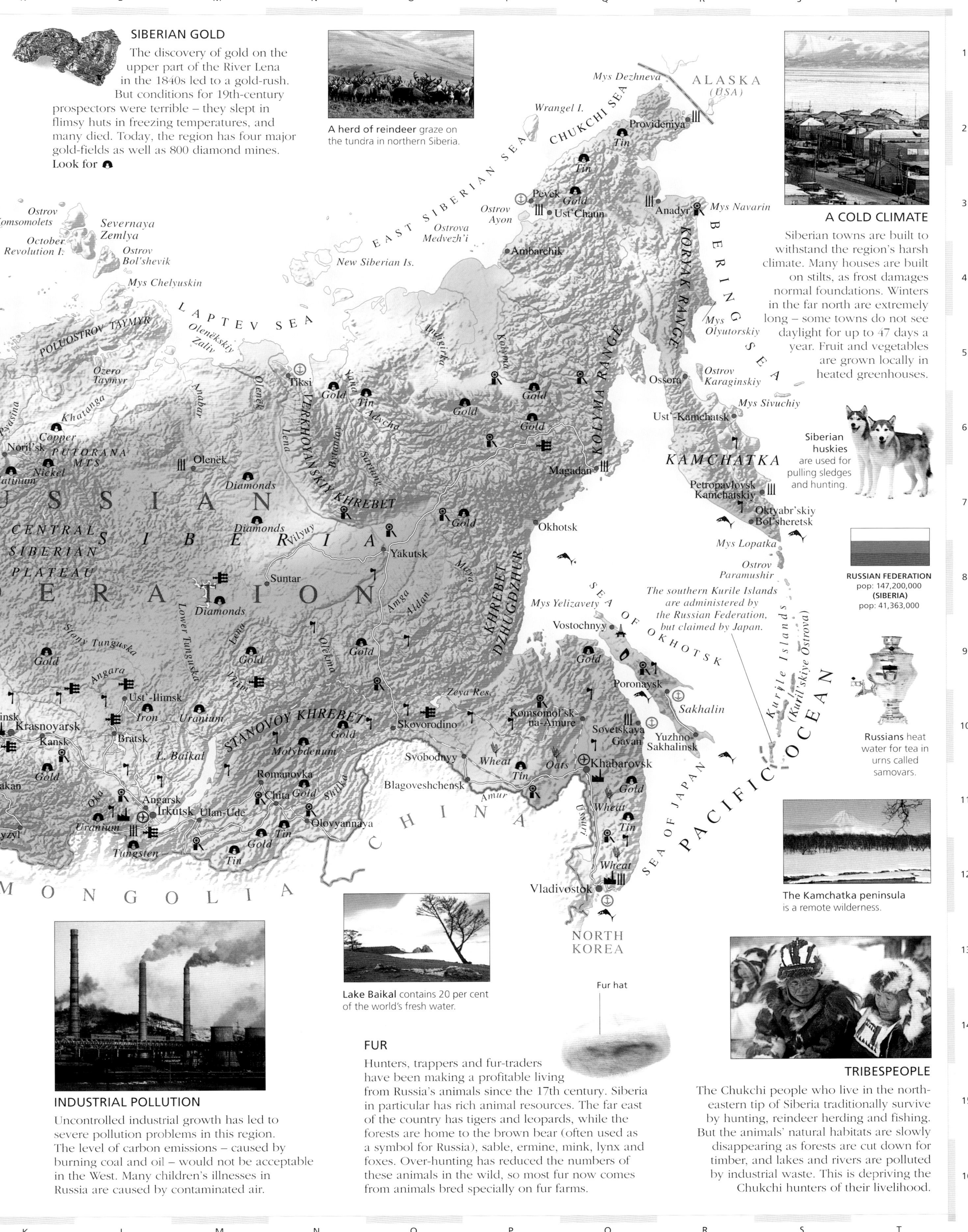
ALASKA (USA)
Mys Dezhneva
Wrangel I.
CHUKCHI SEA
Provideniya
EAST SIBERIAN SEA
Ostrov Ayon
Ostrova Medvezh'i
New Siberian Is.
Pevek
Ust'Chaun
Ambarchik
Anadyr'
Mys Navarin
KORYAK RANGE
BERING SEA
Mys Olyutorskiy
Ostrov Karaginskiy
Ossora
Mys Sivuchiy
Ust'-Kamchatsk
KAMCHATKA
Petropavlovsk Kamchatskiy
Oktyabr'skiy
Bol'sheretsk
Mys Lopatka
Ostrov Paramushir
The southern Kurile Islands are administered by the Russian Federation, but claimed by Japan.
Kurile Islands (Kuril'skiye Ostrova)
PACIFIC OCEAN
SEA OF OKHOTSK
Mys Yelizaveta
Vostochnyy
Poronaysk
Sakhalin
Yuzhno-Sakhalinsk
Sovetskaya Gavan'
Komsomol'sk-na-Amure
Khabarovsk
SEA OF JAPAN
Vladivostok
NORTH KOREA
Okhotsk
Magadan
KOLYMA RANGE
KHREBET DZHUGDZHUR
Yakutsk
VERKHOYANSKIY KHREBET
Tiksi
LAPTEV SEA
Olenëkskiy Zaliv
Mys Chelyuskin
Ostrov Komsomolets
Severnaya Zemlya
October Revolution I.
Ostrov Bol'shevik
POLUOSTROV TAYMYR
Ozero Taymyr
Noril'sk
PUTORANA MTS.
Olenëk
RUSSIAN FEDERATION
SIBERIA
CENTRAL SIBERIAN PLATEAU
Suntar
Ust'-Ilimsk
Krasnoyarsk
Kansk
Bratsk
L. Baikal
Angarsk
Irkutsk
Ulan-Ude
Chita
Romanovka
Olovyannaya
STANOVOY KHREBET
Skovorodino
Zeya Res.
Svobodnyy
Blagoveshchensk
Amur
CHINA
MONGOLIA
Kyzyl
Gold
Tin
Diamonds
Copper
Nickel
Iron
Uranium
Molybdenum
Tungsten
Wheat
Oats
Lena
Yana
Indigirka
Kolyma
Vilyuy
Aldan
Amga
Olëkma
Vitim
Angara
Lower Tunguska
Stony Tunguska
Shilka
Ussuri
Khatanga
Anabar
Pyasina
Adycha
Bytantay
Sartang
Maya
Oka

SIBERIAN GOLD

The discovery of gold on the upper part of the River Lena in the 1840s led to a gold-rush. But conditions for 19th-century prospectors were terrible – they slept in flimsy huts in freezing temperatures, and many died. Today, the region has four major gold-fields as well as 800 diamond mines. Look for

A herd of reindeer graze on the tundra in northern Siberia.

A COLD CLIMATE

Siberian towns are built to withstand the region's harsh climate. Many houses are built on stilts, as frost damages normal foundations. Winters in the far north are extremely long – some towns do not see daylight for up to 47 days a year. Fruit and vegetables are grown locally in heated greenhouses.

Siberian huskies are used for pulling sledges and hunting.

RUSSIAN FEDERATION
pop: 147,200,000
(SIBERIA)
pop: 41,363,000

Russians heat water for tea in urns called samovars.

The Kamchatka peninsula is a remote wilderness.

Lake Baikal contains 20 per cent of the world's fresh water.

Fur hat

INDUSTRIAL POLLUTION

Uncontrolled industrial growth has led to severe pollution problems in this region. The level of carbon emissions – caused by burning coal and oil – would not be acceptable in the West. Many children's illnesses in Russia are caused by contaminated air.

FUR

Hunters, trappers and fur-traders have been making a profitable living from Russia's animals since the 17th century. Siberia in particular has rich animal resources. The far east of the country has tigers and leopards, while the forests are home to the brown bear (often used as a symbol for Russia), sable, ermine, mink, lynx and foxes. Over-hunting has reduced the numbers of these animals in the wild, so most fur now comes from animals bred specially on fur farms.

TRIBESPEOPLE

The Chukchi people who live in the north-eastern tip of Siberia traditionally survive by hunting, reindeer herding and fishing. But the animals' natural habitats are slowly disappearing as forests are cut down for timber, and lakes and rivers are polluted by industrial waste. This is depriving the Chukchi hunters of their livelihood.

Golden pheasant
Chrysolophus pictus
Length: 1 m (3 ft)

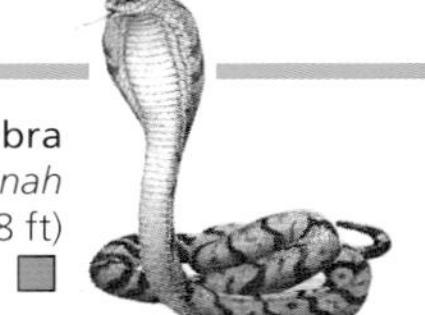

King cobra
Ophiophagus hannah
Length: 5.5 m (18 ft)

Komodo dragon
Varanus komodoensis
Length: 3 m (10 ft)

SOUTH AND EAST ASIA

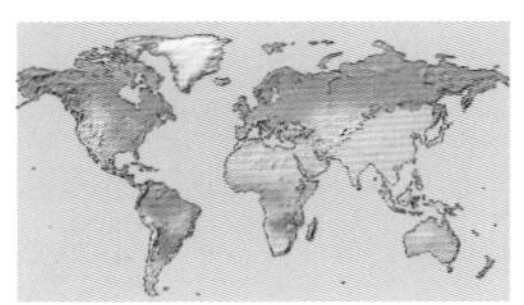

THE WORLD'S 10 HIGHEST PEAKS, including Mount Everest, are all found in the Himalayas and other mountain ranges in the centre of this region. At these altitudes, monsoon rains fall as snow on mountain tops. The melted snow from the mountains feeds some of the largest rivers in the world, such as the Ganges and Irrawaddy, which have created huge deltas where they enter the sea. Fingers of land stretch into tropical seas and volcanic island chains border the continent. In tropical areas high rainfall and temperatures support vast areas of forest. Inland, a climate of extremes prevails, with baking hot summers and long harsh winters. Cold desert and grassy plains cover much of the interior.

VOLCANIC ROCK
This huge granite rock on Sri Lanka was formed in the mouth of a volcano. It is surrounded by forest.

Maidenhair tree
Gingko biloba
Height: 30 m (100 ft)

The Tiger cowrie is found on coral reefs.

YOUNG MOUNTAINS
Himalaya is the Nepalese word for "home of the snows". The range began to form about 40 million years ago – recent in the Earth's history.

ISLAND VOLCANOES
Plants are growing again on the scorched slopes of Bromo in Java, one of a chain of active volcanoes around the southeast Pacific.

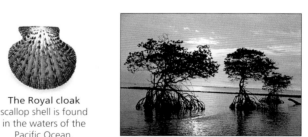

TROPICAL RAINFOREST
Rainforests grow in layers: an understorey with creepers, and the main canopy through which the tallest trees protrude.

Giant panda
Ailuropoda melanoleuca
Length: 1.5 m (5 ft)

HIDDEN CAVES
This maze of limestone caves along the Gulf of Thailand has been carved out by rainwater.

SACRED MOUNTAIN
Mount Fuji, Japan's highest peak, is surrounded by temperate broadleaf trees. Once an active volcano, Mount Fuji has not erupted for 300 years. The snow-capped summit is the rim of a volcanic crater.

The Royal cloak scallop shell is found in the waters of the Pacific Ocean.

MANGROVES IN SILHOUETTE
Mangroves grow along many coastlines, giving some protection during tropical storms.

Rafflesia
Rafflesia pricei
Width: 1 m (3 ft)

TROPICAL ISLAND
There are thousands of tiny coral islands in this region. Many are volcanic in origin, like this one in the South China Sea.

CROSS-SECTION THROUGH SOUTH AND EAST ASIA

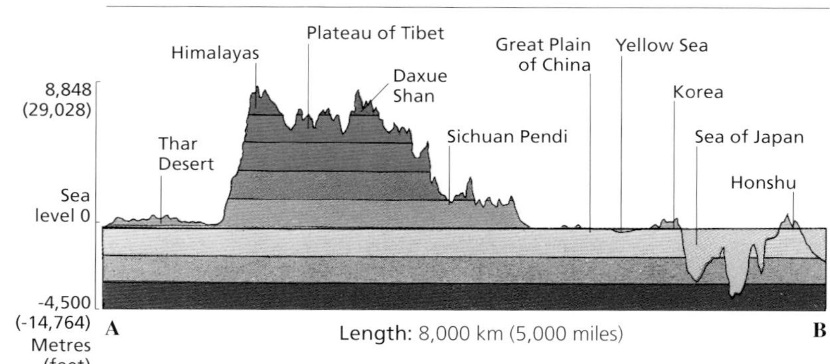

Himalayas
Plateau of Tibet
Daxue Shan
Great Plain of China
Yellow Sea
Korea
Sichuan Pendi
Sea of Japan
Honshu
Thar Desert
8,848 (29,028)
Sea level 0
-4,500 (-14,764)
Metres (feet)
A
B
Length: 8,000 km (5,000 miles)

COLD HIGH NEPAL
No trees are to be found above 3,000 m (10,000 ft) in the Himalayas, though dwarf shrubs and grasses can withstand the harsher conditions up to 4,500 m (15,000 ft). Higher still, the rock is bare, or covered in snow.

Wild yak
Bos grunniens
Length: 3 m (9 ft)

Chinese river dolphin
Lipotes vexillifer
Length: 2.4 m (8 ft)

Siberian tiger
Panthera tigris
Length: 2.4 m (8 ft)

AFRICA

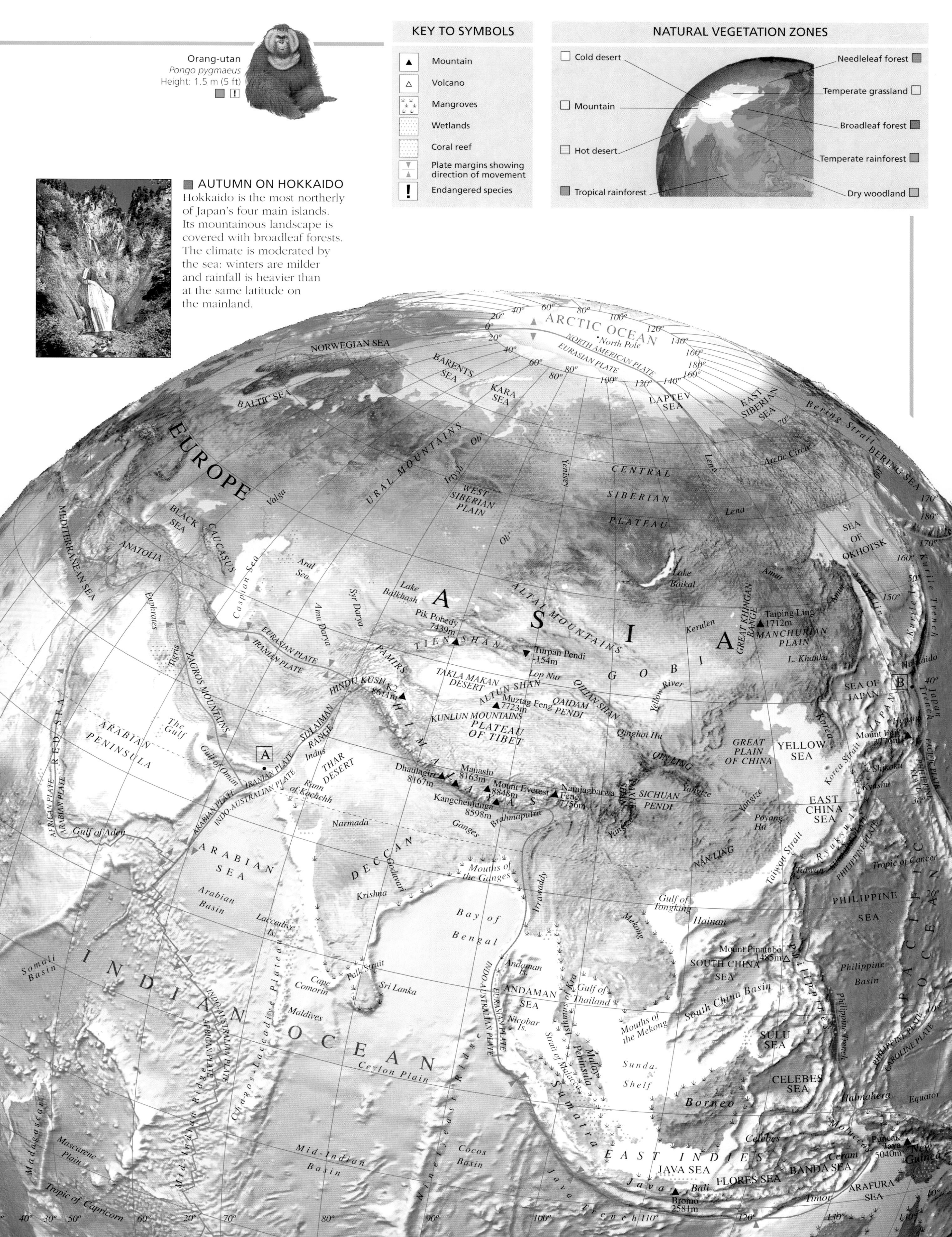
Orang-utan
Pongo pygmaeus
Height: 1.5 m (5 ft)
KEY TO SYMBOLS
Mountain
Volcano
Mangroves
Wetlands
Coral reef
Plate margins showing direction of movement
Endangered species
NATURAL VEGETATION ZONES
Cold desert
Mountain
Hot desert
Tropical rainforest
Needleleaf forest
Temperate grassland
Broadleaf forest
Temperate rainforest
Dry woodland
AUTUMN ON HOKKAIDO
Hokkaido is the most northerly of Japan's four main islands. Its mountainous landscape is covered with broadleaf forests. The climate is moderated by the sea: winters are milder and rainfall is heavier than at the same latitude on the mainland.
ARCTIC OCEAN
North Pole
NORTH AMERICAN PLATE
EURASIAN PLATE
NORWEGIAN SEA
BARENTS SEA
KARA SEA
LAPTEV SEA
EAST SIBERIAN SEA
BALTIC SEA
Bering Strait
BERING SEA
Arctic Circle
EUROPE
URAL MOUNTAINS
Ob'
Irtysh
WEST SIBERIAN PLAIN
Yenisey
Lena
CENTRAL SIBERIAN PLATEAU
Volga
BLACK SEA
CAUCASUS
MEDITERRANEAN SEA
ANATOLIA
Caspian Sea
Aral Sea
SEA OF OKHOTSK
Kurile Trench
Amur
Lake Baikal
Lake Balkhash
ASIA
ALTAI MOUNTAINS
Pik Pobedy 7439m
TIEN SHAN
Turpan Pendi -154m
Euphrates
Tigris
Amu Darya
Syr Darya
EURASIAN PLATE
IRANIAN PLATE
ZAGROS MOUNTAINS
PAMIRS
HINDU KUSH
K2 8611m
TAKLA MAKAN DESERT
Lop Nur
GOBI
ALTUN SHAN
QILIAN SHAN
QAIDAM PENDI
Muztag Feng 7723m
KUNLUN MOUNTAINS
PLATEAU OF TIBET
Kerulen
GREAT KHINGAN RANGE
Taiping Ling 1712m
MANCHURIAN PLAIN
L. Khanka
Hokkaido
SEA OF JAPAN
Japan Trench
Yellow River
Qinghai Hu
QIN LING
GREAT PLAIN OF CHINA
YELLOW SEA
Korea
Korea Strait
JAPAN
Honshu
Mount Fuji 3776m
Shikoku
Kyushu
PACIFIC PLATE
PHILIPPINE PLATE
ARABIAN PENINSULA
The Gulf
Gulf of Oman
SULAIMAN RANGE
Indus
THAR DESERT
HIMALAYAS
Dhaulagiri 8167m
Manaslu 8163m
Mount Everest 8848m
Kangchenjunga 8598m
Namjagbarwa Feng 7756m
DAXUE SHAN
SICHUAN PENDI
Yangtze
Poyang Hu
EAST CHINA SEA
RED SEA
AFRICAN PLATE
ARABIAN PLATE
IRANIAN PLATE
INDO-AUSTRALIAN PLATE
Rann of Kachchh
Narmada
Ganges
Brahmaputra
Gulf of Aden
ARABIAN SEA
DECCAN
Godavari
Krishna
Mouths of the Ganges
Irrawaddy
NAN LING
Taiwan Strait
Taiwan
Ryukyu Is.
Tropic of Cancer
PHILIPPINE SEA
Arabian Basin
Laccadive Is.
Bay of Bengal
Gulf of Tongking
Hainan
Mekong
Mount Pinatubo 1485m
SOUTH CHINA SEA
Philippines
Philippine Basin
Somali Basin
INDIAN OCEAN
Palk Strait
Cape Comorin
Sri Lanka
Andaman Is.
ANDAMAN SEA
Kra Isthmus
Gulf of Thailand
South China Basin
Maldives
Nicobar Is.
Malay Peninsula
Strait of Malacca
Mouths of the Mekong
SULU SEA
Philippine Trench
PACIFIC OCEAN
Ceylon Plain
Sunda Shelf
CELEBES SEA
CAROLINE PLATE
Chagos-Laccadive Plateau
Ninetyeast Ridge
Mid-Indian Ridge
Sumatra
Borneo
Halmahera
Equator
Madagascar
Mascarene Plain
Mid-Indian Basin
Cocos Basin
Celebes
Moluccas
Puncak Jaya 5040m
New Guinea
EAST INDIES
JAVA SEA
Ceram
BANDA SEA
Java
Bali
FLORES SEA
Bromo 2581m
Timor
ARAFURA SEA
Java Trench
Tropic of Capricorn

THE INDIAN SUBCONTINENT

SOUTH OF THE HIMALAYAS, the world's highest mountains, lies the Indian subcontinent. In the north of the region, the Buddhist kingdoms of Nepal and Bhutan cling to the slopes of the Himalayas. In the south, the island state of Sri Lanka hangs like a teardrop from the tip of India.

The subcontinent has been invaded many times: the first invaders were fair-skinned, blue-eyed Aryan tribes, whose beliefs and customs form the basis of the Hindu religion. From the 16th century India was united and ruled by the Islamic Mughal emperors. Two centuries later it became a British colony. In 1947 India gained independence, but religious differences led to the creation of two countries – Hindu India and Muslim Pakistan. Today India is a thriving industrial power, but most people still make their living from tiny farms. In spite of terrible poverty and a population of over 900 million people, India remains a relatively stable democracy. Since 1947 India and Pakistan, now both nuclear powers, have been locked in conflict over control of Kashmir.

PAKISTAN
pop: 137,400,000

Kashmir: a "line of control" was established in 1972 by Simla (shimla) Agreement between Pakistan and India

AFGHANISTAN · IRAN · PAKISTAN · INDIA · ARABIAN SEA · CHAGAI HILLS · CENTRAL MAKRAN RANGE · TOBA KAKAR RANGE · THAR DESERT · RANN OF KACHCHH · *Gulf of Kachchh* · *Gulf of Khambhat* · WESTERN GHATS · MALABAR COAST

Peshawar · ISLAMABAD · Rawalpindi · Srinagar · Mardan · Jhelum · Gujrat · Gujranwala · Sargodha · Amritsar · Faisalabad · Lahore · Kasur · Okara · Dera Ismail Khan · Quetta · Dera Ghazi Khan · Multan · Bahawalpur · Rahimyar Khan · Shikarpur · Larkana · Sukkur · Jaisalmer · Nawabshah · Mirpur Khas · Karachi · Hyderabad · Jodhpur · Jaipur · Ajmer · Kota · Kandla · Ahmadabad · Jamnagar · Rajkot · Vadodara · Indore · Porbandar · Bhavnagar · Surat · Dhule · Daman · Nashik · Bombay (Mumbai) · Thane · Pune · Solapur · Belgaum · Panaji · Dharwad · Hubli · Davangere · Mangalore · Mysore · Calicut · Coimbatore · Ernakulam · Cochin · Trivandrum · Nagercoil

Tarbela Dam · *Tarbela Res.* · *Mangla Res.* · *Jinnah Barrage* · *Chashma Barrage* · *Chromium* · *Emerson (Trimmu) Barrage* · *Islam Barrage* · *Panjnad Barrage* · *Guddu Barrage* · *Ghulam Muhammad Barrage* · *Gandhi Res.* · *Aluminium* · *Iron* · *Chromium* · *Manganese* · *Wheat* · *Barley* · *Indus* · *Chenab* · *Narmada* · *Tapti* · *Krishna*

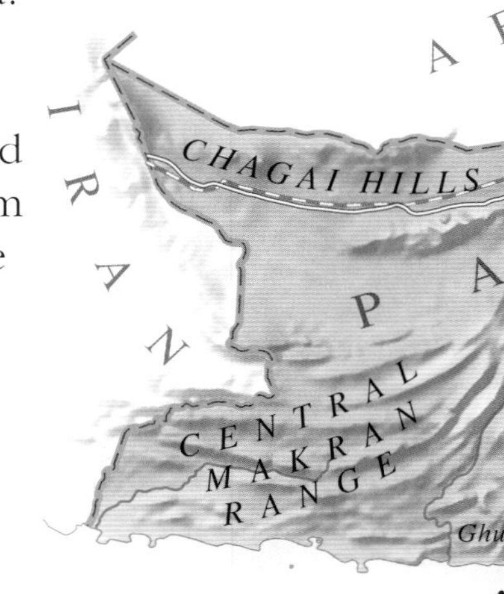

The Thar Desert, a vast, arid region in India and Pakistan.

Sitar

MOOD MUSIC

Traditional Indian music is improvised. Its purpose is to create a mood, such as joy or sorrow. One of the main instruments is the *sitar*, which is played by plucking seven of the strings. Other strings, which are not plucked, vibrate to give the distinctive sound of Indian music.

PAKISTAN

This bus illustrates a big problem in Pakistan: over-population. Ninety-five per cent of the people are Muslim, and traditional Islam rejects contraception, so the birth-rate is high. The many refugees who fled the war in Afghanistan have stretched resources further.

A MARBLE MEMORIAL

The Taj Mahal at Agra, in northern India, was built in the 17th century by the Mughal Emperor, Shah Jahan, as a tomb for his beloved wife. She was the mother of 14 children. Built of the finest white marble, the Taj Mahal is a supreme example of Islamic architecture and one of the world's most beautiful buildings.

MAP FEATURES

Aquaculture: This is a recent and highly successful industry in Bangladesh. Frogs' legs and shrimps are among the main products. **Look for**

Trekking: Every year some 250,000 trekkers visit Nepal, boosting its economy. But the extra visitors are damaging the environment. **Look for**

Dams: Irrigation on a vast scale in the Indus Valley in Pakistan has sustained and increased the country's food production. **Look for**

Cereals	Cotton
Rice	Mining
Sugar cane	Coal
Tea	Industrial centre

INDUSTRY

After independence, India started to modernize, and is now one of the most industrialized countries in Asia. Factories make a wide range of goods, from cement to cars. Recently, the manufacture of goods such as machine tools and electronic equipment has increased. Local cotton is processed in mills like these in Ahmadabad. **Look for**

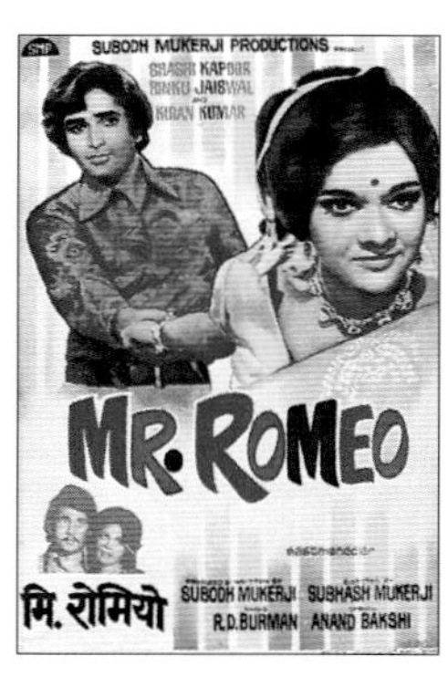
MR. ROMEO
मि. रोमियो

INDIAN FILMS

More films are produced in India than anywhere else in the world – including Hollywood. Bombay is the centre of the Indian film industry.

Traditional fishing boats on the coast of Sri Lanka.

N

0 100 200 300 400 500 KM

0 100 200 300 MILES

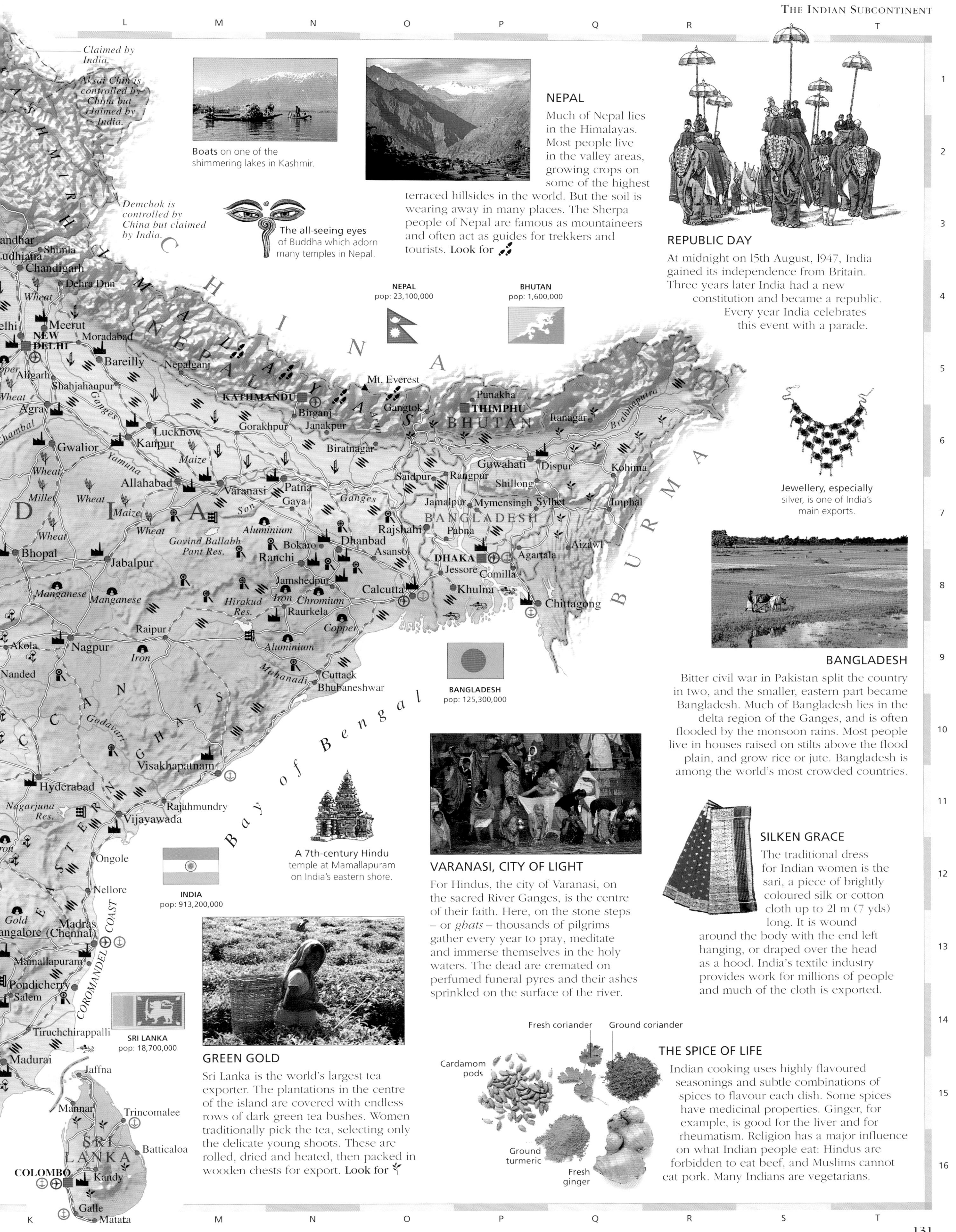
Claimed by India.
Aksai Chin is controlled by China but claimed by India.
Demchok is controlled by China but claimed by India.
KASHMIR
HIMALAYAS
CHINA
NEPAL
BHUTAN
BANGLADESH
BURMA
INDIA
DECCAN
EASTERN GHATS
COROMANDEL COAST
SRI LANKA
Bay of Bengal
Shimla
Chandigarh
Dehra Dun
Meerut
NEW DELHI
Moradabad
Bareilly
Nepalganj
Aligarh
Shahjahanpur
Agra
Gwalior
Lucknow
Kanpur
Allahabad
Varanasi
Patna
Gaya
Gorakhpur
KATHMANDU
Birganj
Janakpur
Biratnagar
Mt. Everest
Gangtok
Punakha
THIMPHU
Itanagar
Guwahati
Dispur
Shillong
Kohima
Imphal
Saidpur
Rangpur
Jamalpur
Mymensingh
Sylhet
Rajshahi
Pabna
Dhanbad
Asansol
Bokaro
Ranchi
Jamshedpur
Calcutta
DHAKA
Jessore
Comilla
Agartala
Aizawl
Khulna
Chittagong
Bhopal
Jabalpur
Raipur
Nagpur
Akola
Nanded
Raurkela
Cuttack
Bhubaneshwar
Visakhapatnam
Hyderabad
Rajahmundry
Vijayawada
Ongole
Nellore
Madras (Chennai)
Mamallapuram
Pondicherry
Salem
Tiruchchirappalli
Madurai
Jaffna
Mannar
Trincomalee
Batticaloa
COLOMBO
Kandy
Galle
Matara
Ganges
Yamuna
Son
Chambal
Mahanadi
Godavari
Brahmaputra
Govind Ballabh Pant Res.
Hirakud Res.
Nagarjuna Res.
Wheat
Maize
Millet
Manganese
Aluminium
Iron
Chromium
Copper
Gold

Boats on one of the shimmering lakes in Kashmir.

The all-seeing eyes of Buddha which adorn many temples in Nepal.

NEPAL

Much of Nepal lies in the Himalayas. Most people live in the valley areas, growing crops on some of the highest terraced hillsides in the world. But the soil is wearing away in many places. The Sherpa people of Nepal are famous as mountaineers and often act as guides for trekkers and tourists. Look for

NEPAL
pop: 23,100,000

BHUTAN
pop: 1,600,000

REPUBLIC DAY

At midnight on 15th August, 1947, India gained its independence from Britain. Three years later India had a new constitution and became a republic. Every year India celebrates this event with a parade.

Jewellery, especially silver, is one of India's main exports.

BANGLADESH

Bitter civil war in Pakistan split the country in two, and the smaller, eastern part became Bangladesh. Much of Bangladesh lies in the delta region of the Ganges, and is often flooded by the monsoon rains. Most people live in houses raised on stilts above the flood plain, and grow rice or jute. Bangladesh is among the world's most crowded countries.

BANGLADESH
pop: 125,300,000

A 7th-century Hindu temple at Mamallapuram on India's eastern shore.

INDIA
pop: 913,200,000

VARANASI, CITY OF LIGHT

For Hindus, the city of Varanasi, on the sacred River Ganges, is the centre of their faith. Here, on the stone steps – or *ghats* – thousands of pilgrims gather every year to pray, meditate and immerse themselves in the holy waters. The dead are cremated on perfumed funeral pyres and their ashes sprinkled on the surface of the river.

SILKEN GRACE

The traditional dress for Indian women is the sari, a piece of brightly coloured silk or cotton cloth up to 21 m (7 yds) long. It is wound around the body with the end left hanging, or draped over the head as a hood. India's textile industry provides work for millions of people and much of the cloth is exported.

SRI LANKA
pop: 18,700,000

GREEN GOLD

Sri Lanka is the world's largest tea exporter. The plantations in the centre of the island are covered with endless rows of dark green tea bushes. Women traditionally pick the tea, selecting only the delicate young shoots. These are rolled, dried and heated, then packed in wooden chests for export. Look for

Fresh coriander

Ground coriander

Cardamom pods

Ground turmeric

Fresh ginger

THE SPICE OF LIFE

Indian cooking uses highly flavoured seasonings and subtle combinations of spices to flavour each dish. Some spices have medicinal properties. Ginger, for example, is good for the liver and for rheumatism. Religion has a major influence on what Indian people eat: Hindus are forbidden to eat beef, and Muslims cannot eat pork. Many Indians are vegetarians.

China and Mongolia

The remote mountains, deserts and steppes of Mongolia and the northwestern part of China are harsh landscapes; temperatures are extreme, the terrain is rugged and distances between places are vast. Three large Autonomous Regions of China lie here – Inner Mongolia, Xinjiang Uygur and Tibet.

Remote Tibet, situated on a high plateau and ringed by mountains, was invaded by China in 1950. The Chinese have systematically destroyed Tibet's traditional agricultural society and Buddhist monasteries. Most of China's ethnic minorities and Muslims (a legacy of Silk Road trade with the Middle East) are located in Inner Mongolia and Xinjiang. Roads and railways are being built to make these isolated areas accessible, and rich resources of coal are being exploited. Mongolia is a vast, isolated country. It became a communist republic in 1924, but has now re-established democracy. Most people still live by herding animals, although new industries have begun to develop.

The Tien Shan range in central Xinjiang Uygur.

MONGOLIAN STEPPES

About half the Mongolian population still live in the countryside, many as nomadic herders. Nomads live in *gers* – circular tents made of felt and canvas stretched over a wooden frame. They herd yak, sheep, goats, cattle and camels, and travel great distances on horseback.

Cylinder containing written prayer

In Tibet, written prayers are placed in prayer wheels. These small cylinders are rotated by hand.

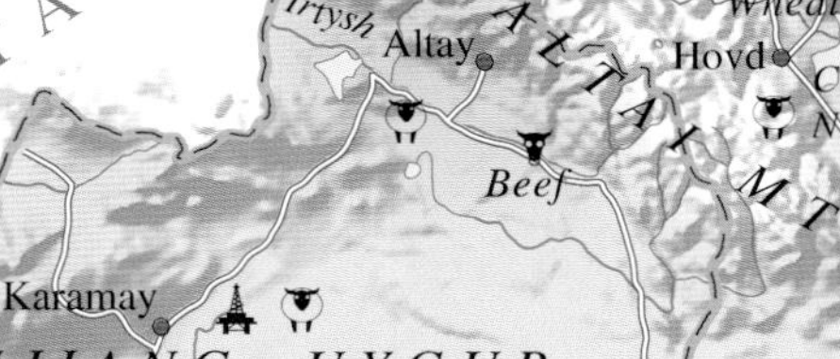
KAZAKHSTAN
Irtysh
Altay
ALTAI MTS.
Uvs Nuur
Ulaangom
Hyargas Nuur
Olgiy
Hovd
Char Nuur
Karamay
XINJIANG UYGUR AUTONOMOUS REGION
Yining
Kuytun
Shihezi
Urumqi
Hami
Turpan
TIEN SHAN
Aksu
Korla
Bosten Hu
Tarim He
KYRGYZSTAN
Kashi
Tarim Basin
TAJIKISTAN
Shache
AFGHANISTAN
PAKISTAN
KARAKORAM RANGE
TAKLA MAKAN DESERT
Hotan
Lop Nur
CHINA
Lenghu
Da Qaidam
ALTUN SHAN
KUNLUN MTS.
Golmud
Aksai Chin is controlled by China, but claimed by India
INDIA

Tongtian He
TANGGULA SHAN

Demchok is controlled by China, but claimed by India
Gar
GANGDISE SHAN
Tangra Yumco
TIBET
Siling Co
Nam Co
Salween
Nagqu
Brahmaputra
Lhasa
Nyingchi
Xigazê
Yamzho Yumco
Gyangzê
Mt. Everest
Nyalam
HIMALAYAS
NEPAL
BHUTAN
INDIA

KASHI MARKET

The city of Kashi is located in the far west of China. With its Muslim mosques, minarets and lively bazaar it is more like a city in the Middle East than China. Its Sunday market, the biggest in Asia, attracts up to 60,000 visitors. A vast array of goods are sold there: horses, camels, livestock, grains, spices and cloth.

ADAPTABLE YAKS

Herders in Mongolia and Tibet keep yaks. They thrive at high altitudes, surviving extreme cold and even burrowing under snow for grass. Yaks provide milk, butter, meat, wool and leather. In Tibet, yak's butter is served with tea. **Look for**

MAP FEATURES

Timber: Forests in eastern Tibet have been cut down by the Chinese. Bare hillsides encourage soil erosion, flooding and landslides. **Look for**

Coal: Mongolia is a major exporter of coal to the Russian Federation. There are also open-cast mines in Xinjiang Uygur and Inner Mongolia. **Look for**

Pollution: Nuclear tests in Xinjiang Uygur have caused radiation fallout, pollution and many birth defects. **Look for**

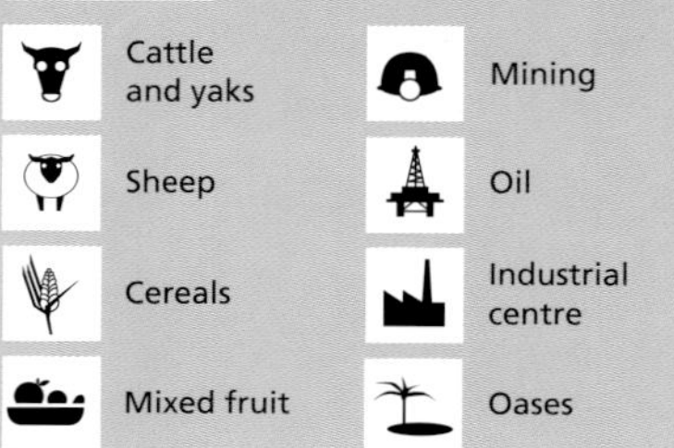
Cattle and yaks
Mining
Sheep
Oil
Cereals
Industrial centre
Mixed fruit
Oases

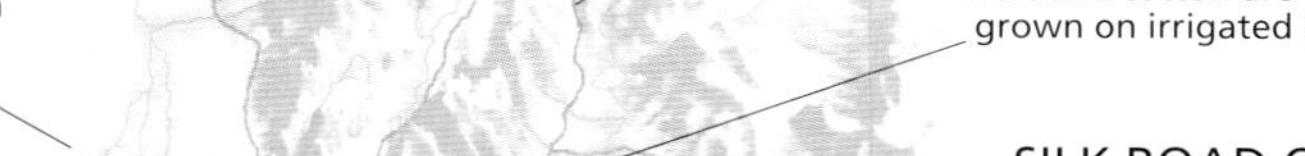
Oases: winter and spring wheat, corn, rice and cotton are grown
N
Passes through Tien Shan range
Takla Makan Desert
Tarim He
Lop Nur: saline lake
Boston Hu: fruit and cotton are grown on irrigated land

SILK ROAD OASES

The oases of Xinjiang Uygur lie on the edge of the Takla Makan Desert, in the foothills of the Tien Shan range. They are watered by melted snow from the mountains, and sheltered by warm winds coming down the mountain slopes. Towns grew up next to the oases, which lie along the ancient Silk Road.

The high plateau of Tibet, known as "the roof of the world".

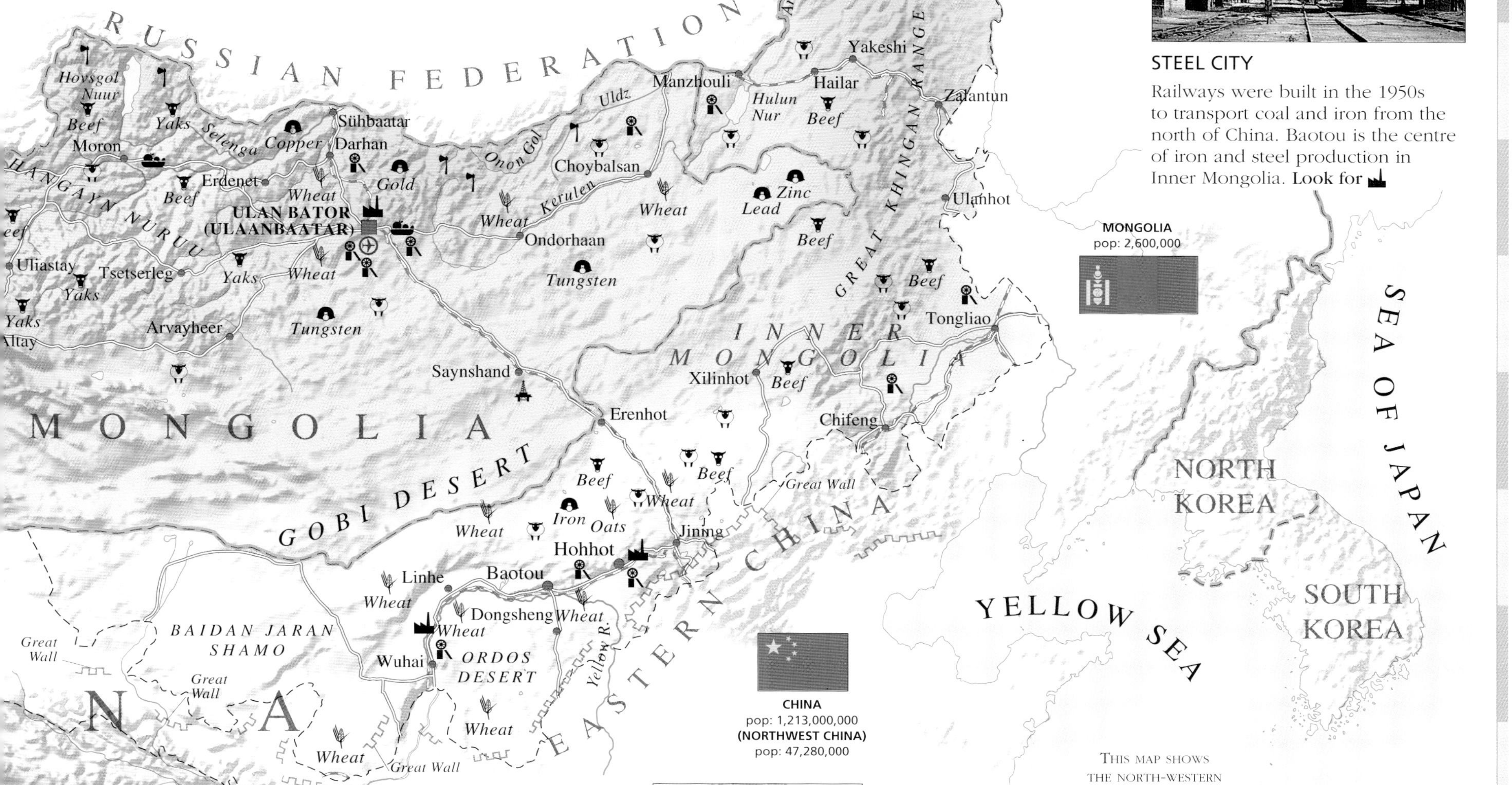

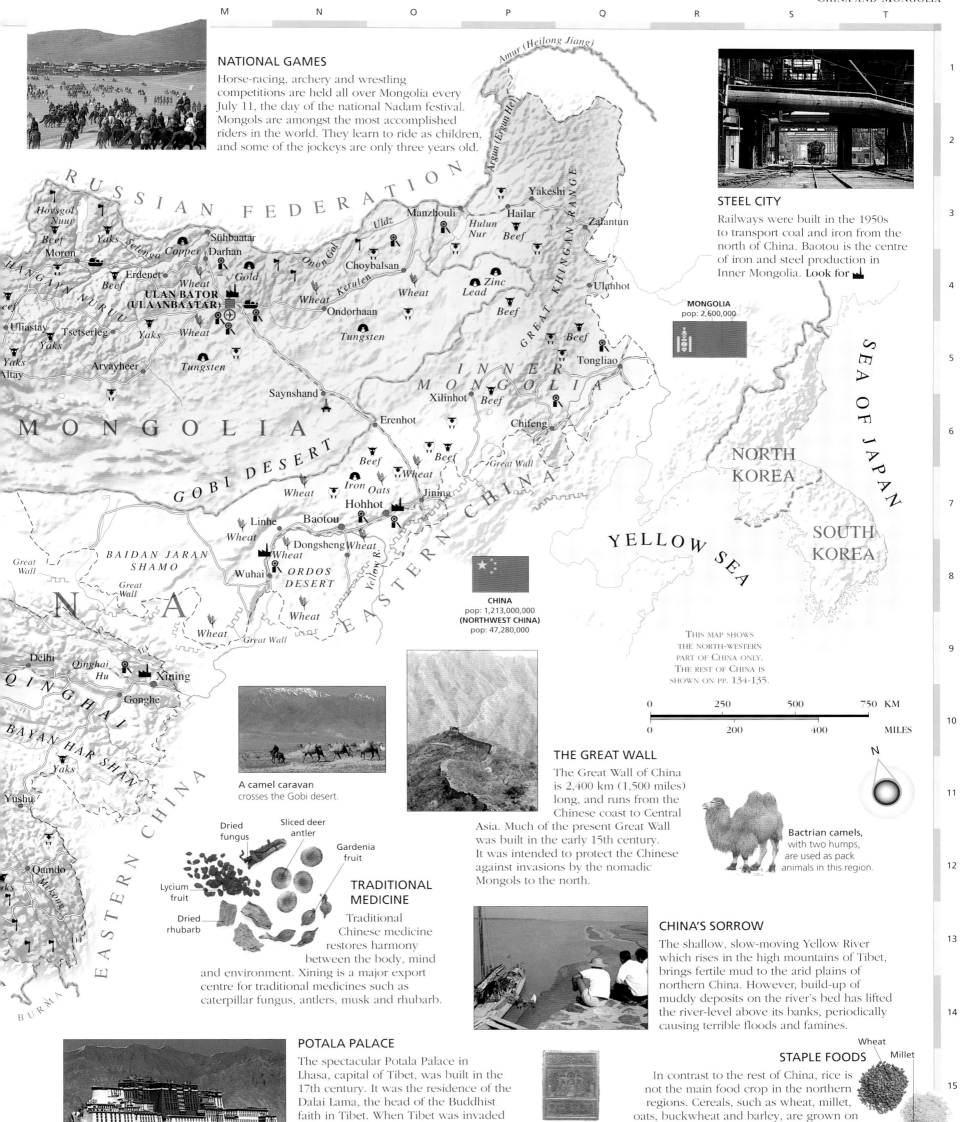

NATIONAL GAMES

Horse-racing, archery and wrestling competitions are held all over Mongolia every July 11, the day of the national Nadam festival. Mongols are amongst the most accomplished riders in the world. They learn to ride as children, and some of the jockeys are only three years old.

STEEL CITY

Railways were built in the 1950s to transport coal and iron from the north of China. Baotou is the centre of iron and steel production in Inner Mongolia. **Look for**

MONGOLIA
pop: 2,600,000

CHINA
pop: 1,213,000,000
(NORTHWEST CHINA)
pop: 47,280,000

This map shows the north-western part of China only. The rest of China is shown on pp. 134-135.

0 250 500 750 KM
0 200 400 MILES

A camel caravan crosses the Gobi desert.

THE GREAT WALL

The Great Wall of China is 2,400 km (1,500 miles) long, and runs from the Chinese coast to Central Asia. Much of the present Great Wall was built in the early 15th century. It was intended to protect the Chinese against invasions by the nomadic Mongols to the north.

Bactrian camels, with two humps, are used as pack animals in this region.

Dried fungus
Sliced deer antler
Gardenia fruit
Lycium fruit
Dried rhubarb

TRADITIONAL MEDICINE

Traditional Chinese medicine restores harmony between the body, mind and environment. Xining is a major export centre for traditional medicines such as caterpillar fungus, antlers, musk and rhubarb.

CHINA'S SORROW

The shallow, slow-moving Yellow River which rises in the high mountains of Tibet, brings fertile mud to the arid plains of northern China. However, build-up of muddy deposits on the river's bed has lifted the river-level above its banks, periodically causing terrible floods and famines.

POTALA PALACE

The spectacular Potala Palace in Lhasa, capital of Tibet, was built in the 17th century. It was the residence of the Dalai Lama, the head of the Buddhist faith in Tibet. When Tibet was invaded by China in 1950, Buddhism was brutally repressed by the Chinese. In 1959 there were over 6,000 monasteries in Tibet – by 1979 only five remained.

Loose tea leaves are compressed into hard blocks, easily carried by Tibetan nomads.

STAPLE FOODS

In contrast to the rest of China, rice is not the main food crop in the northern regions. Cereals, such as wheat, millet, oats, buckwheat and barley, are grown on irrigated land or oases. Noodles and steamed buns (*mantou*) are the main bulk food of the north, served with spicy, barbecued meat. **Look for**

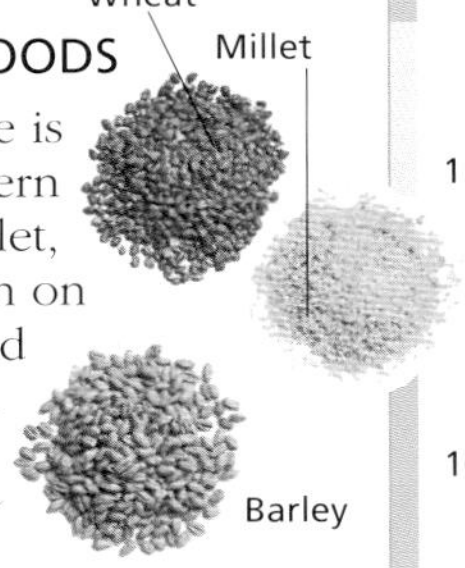

Wheat
Millet
Barley

CHINA AND KOREA

THE LANDSCAPE OF SOUTHEASTERN CHINA ranges from mountains and plateaux to wide river valleys and plains. One- fifth of all the people on Earth live in China – most of them in the eastern part of the country. For centuries, China was isolated from the rest of the world, ruled by powerful emperors and known to only a handful of traders. In the 19th century the European powers forced China to open its borders to trade, starting a period of rapid change. In 1949, after a long struggle between nationalists and communists, the People's Republic of China was established as a communist state. Taiwan became a separate country. The communist government has encouraged foreign investment, technological innovation and private enterprise, although calls for democracy have been suppressed. Korea has been dominated by its powerful Chinese and Japanese neighbours for many years. After World War II, Korea was divided in two. North Korea became one of the most isolated and repressive communist regimes in the world. South Korea transformed itself into a highly industrial economy.

BEIJING OPERA

Traditional Chinese opera dates back 2,000 years and combines many different elements – songs, dance, mime and acrobatics. The stories are based on folktales. Make-up shows the characters' personalities – kind, loyal or wicked, for example.

INDUSTRY

Although China has extensive reserves of coal, iron ore and oil, its heavy industry is state-run, old-fashioned and inefficient. Seventy per cent of China's energy is provided by coal. About half China's coal comes from large, well-equipped mines; the rest is extracted from small local pits. These mines are notorious for their high accident rates. Look for ⛏

Sesame oil

Dried mushroom

FOOD

Chinese food varies widely from region to region. Its most famous cuisine comes from the area around Guangzhou, and uses a huge range of ingredients – it is said that the people from this region will "eat everything with wings except aeroplanes and everything with legs except the table". Chinese food has become popular all over the world, transported to many countries by Chinese migrants.

Soy sauce

Dried prawn

MONGOLIA
INNER
Yumen
Great Wall
QINGHAI
Yinchuan
Wuwei
NINGXIA AUTONOMOUS REGION
Lanzhou
Wheat
Wheat
Wheat
CH
Yalong Jiang
Dadu He
Mianyang
Chengdu
Maize
Litang
Chongqing
Leshan
Zigong
Jinsha Jiang
Xichang
Zunyi
Aluminium
Panzhihua
Copper
Guiyang
Dongchuan
BURMA
Salween
Dali
Kunming
Hongshui He
Maize
Maize
Gejiu
Tin
Maize
Mekong
VIETNAM
Pingxiang
LAOS

THIS MAP SHOWS THE SOUTH-EASTERN PART OF CHINA ONLY. THE REST OF CHINA IS SHOWN ON PP. 132-133.

PLAN YOUR FAMILY FOR A BETTER FUTURE

BABY BOOM

China's population is now over a billion, stretching resources such as land, food and education to the limit. Couples with only one child receive various benefits. If a second child is born, these benefits are withdrawn.

The Great Wild Goose pagoda at Xi'an was built in the 7th century AD. It formed part of a Buddhist monastery.

Tea, China's national drink, is grown on terraced hillsides in the south of the country.

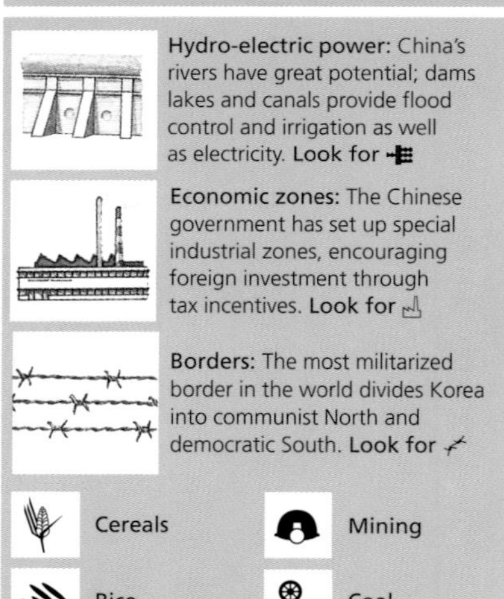
MAP FEATURES
Hydro-electric power: China's rivers have great potential; dams lakes and canals provide flood control and irrigation as well as electricity. Look for
Economic zones: The Chinese government has set up special industrial zones, encouraging foreign investment through tax incentives. Look for
Borders: The most militarized border in the world divides Korea into communist North and democratic South. Look for
Cereals
Mining
Rice
Coal
Tea
Oil
Timber
Industrial centre
Fishing
Shipbuilding

AGRICULTURE

China feeds its vast population from only seven per cent of the world's farm-land. In the fertile southern part of the country, the fields can yield three harvests every year – two crops of rice and a third crop of vegetables or cereals. Look for

RACIAL MINORITIES

This woman comes from the Hani people, one of the many different ethnic minorities who live in southwest China. Most minority groups live in remote, sparsely-inhabited regions. Many still follow traditional lifestyles based on herding, hunting, or growing food for their families.

N

0 100 200 300 400 500 600 KM
0 100 200 300 MILES

THE DRAGON THRONE

The Hall of Supreme Harmony houses the Dragon Throne, seat of the former emperors of China. It is the largest building in Beijing's Forbidden City, and dates back to the 15th century. Ordinary citizens were banned from this area, which was reserved for the Emperor and his courtiers. Today, the Forbidden City has been restored and opened to the public: it attracts millions of tourists every year.

北京

The word "Beijing", written in Chinese. Each symbol stands for a word or an idea.

A jade vase. Jade is China's most precious stone.

COMMUNISM

In the 1960s, China suffered a campaign of terror against artists, politicians and intellectuals. Although the regime is now more liberal, political messages displayed on walls are often the only way of challenging the government.

NORTH KOREA
pop: 23,200,000

GINSENG

Korea exports this precious root, which is widely used in traditional Asian medicine. It is also popular in the West where it is thought to improve health and promote long life and vigour.

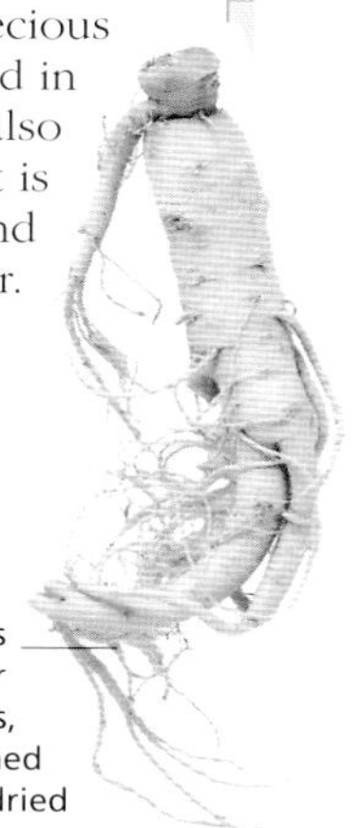

Ginseng roots are grown for 4-6 years, then steamed and dried

Rice fields in South Korea. Rice thrives in the mild south.

SOUTH KOREA
pop: 46,100,000

CHINA
pop: 1,213,000,000
(SOUTHEAST CHINA)
pop: 1,165,670,000

LAND OF MIRACLES

The Korean economy was devastated by World War II, but during the last 40 years South Korea has undergone an economic miracle. Today, it has a major shipbuilding industry and modern steelworks; textiles, cars, computers, and televisions pour off production lines. A quarter of all South Koreans live in the capital, Seoul, which has become one of the world's largest cities.

Playing table tennis is a national passion in China.

Carp-fishing with cormorants, nets and bamboo rafts in Guangxi Zhuangzu Autonomous Region.

SHANGHAI

The port of Shanghai is the largest city in China. In the 19th century foreign countries, who were involved in trade with China, claimed sections of the city, establishing commercial buildings and warehouses, and giving central Shanghai the appearance of a European city. Today, Shanghai has become important as a centre of heavy industry.

TAIWAN
pop: 21,500,000

HONG KONG

The rocky island of Hong Kong became a British Crown Colony in the 19th century. In 1997 it was returned to China, and became a "special administrative region". Hong Kong has the busiest container port in the world, and is a centre of trade, finance, manufacturing and tourism.

THE LITTLE DRAGON

Taiwan is one of Asia's wealthiest economies. The country produces about 10 per cent of the world's computers, and also specializes in textiles and shoe-manufacturing. The Taiwanese refer to their country as the Republic of China, but China does not recognize the country under this name.

JAPAN

THE LAND OF THE RISING SUN, as Japan is sometimes called, was ruled for centuries by powerful warlords called *shoguns,* who discouraged any contact with the outside world. When traders from America and Europe arrived, Japan's isolation suddenly ended, the *shogun* was overthrown and an emperor ruled the country. Over the next century, Japan transformed itself into one of the world's richest nations, a change in fortune all the more remarkable considering the country's geography. Japan consists of four main islands and 4,000 smaller islands. The majority of its 126 million people live closely packed together around the coast, since two-thirds of the land is mountainous and thickly forested. Japan has few natural resources and has to import most of its fuel and raw materials. The Japanese have concentrated on improving and adapting technology imported from abroad. Today, Japanese companies are world leaders in many areas of research and development, a success partly due to their management techniques which ensure a well paid and loyal workforce.

RICE CULTIVATION

Rice is Japan's main food. Although only about 11 per cent of the land is suitable for farming, Japan produces enough rice for its own needs. The crop is intensively cultivated on small plots of land using fertilizers and sophisticated machinery, like this rice planter. The warm, wet summers in southern Japan are ideal for growing rice. **Look for**

FISHING

Fish is a very popular food in Japan. Huge quantities are caught each year by the country's fishing fleet – the world's largest. One million tonnes of fish and shellfish are also bred every year in fish farms. These tuna are on sale in Tokyo's fish market. **Look for**

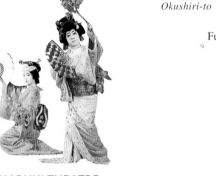

KABUKI THEATRE

There are two forms of traditional Japanese theatre: Noh and Kabuki. Noh is very old: the plays are based on myths of the gods and contain music and symbolic dancing. Kabuki theatres have plays based on stories of great heroes of the past. This photo shows a scene from a Kabuki play.

Silk *kimono*

TRADITIONAL DRESS

Until the 19th century Japanese traditional dress varied greatly between the social classes. In the royal courts long-sleeved robes called *kimonos* were worn. Made of silk, these were wound round the body and tied with a sash. *Kimonos* are still worn on special occasions.

A miniature television, produced in Japan.

The Japanese are skilled at *bonsai* – the art of producing miniature trees and shrubs.

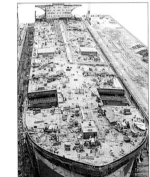

The southern Kurile Islands are administered by the Russian Federation but claimed by Japan.

The Hidaka-sanmyaku mountains on the large island of Hokkaido.

FOOD

Rice

Seaweed

Marinated raw fish

Lacquer dish

The Japanese eat a lot of fish because there is not enough farmland to keep cattle for meat or dairy produce.

JAPAN
pop: 125,900,000

SHIPBUILDING

A large number of the ships sailing the world today were made in Japan. Countries such as South Korea can now build ships more cheaply, however, and Japan's industry is declining. To remain competitive, Japanese shipbuilders are building specialized ships – such as cruise liners, and developing new products like oil-drilling platforms. **Look for**

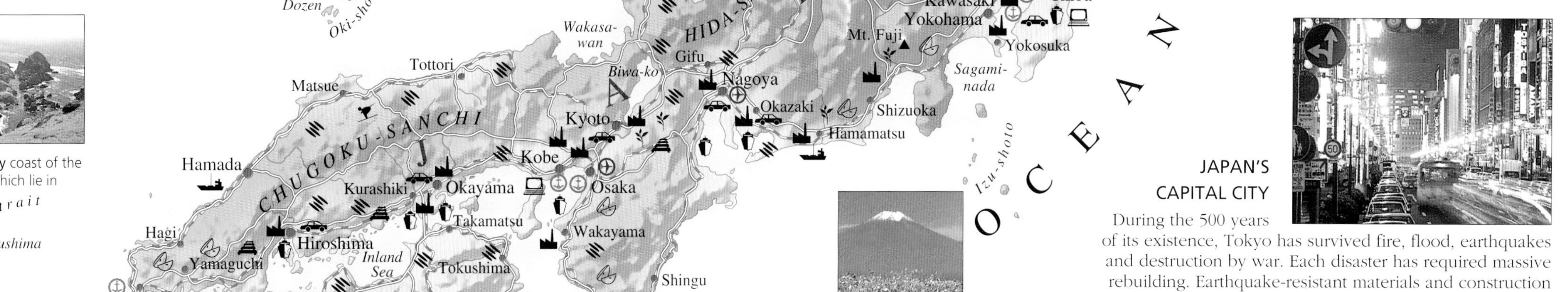

PACIFIC OCEAN
EAST CHINA SEA
Ryukyu Is.
Kyushu
Shikoku
CHUGOKU-SANCHI
HIDA-SAN
Kitakyushu
Fukuoka
Saga
Sasebo
Nagasaki
Kumamoto
Beppu
Oita
Nobeoka
Miyazaki
Kagoshima
Hiroshima
Yamaguchi
Shimonoseki
Matsuyama
Uwajima
Nakamura
Kōchi
Tokushima
Takamatsu
Okayama
Kurashiki
Hamada
Matsue
Tottori
Kobe
Osaka
Kyoto
Wakayama
Shingu
Nagoya
Gifu
Okazaki
Hamamatsu
Shizuoka
Mt. Fuji
Yokohama
Kawasaki
Chiba
Yokosuka
Sagami-nada
Izu-shoto
Biwa-ko
Wakasa-wan
Dozen
Oki-shoto
Hagi
Inland Sea
Iki
Tsushima
Korea Strait
Goto-retto
Shimo-jima
AMAKUSA-NADA
Osumi-kaikyo
Osumi-shoto
Tanega-shima
Yaku-shima
Tokara-retto
Amami-gunto
Amami o-shima
Tokuno-shima
Okinoerabu-jima
Okinawa
Okinawa-shoto
Naha
N
0 50 100 150 200 250 KM
0 50 100 150 MILES

The beautiful rocky coast of the Oki-shoto islands, which lie in the Sea of Japan.

Mount Fuji, Japan's sacred mountain, is crowned with snow.

JAPAN'S CAPITAL CITY

During the 500 years of its existence, Tokyo has survived fire, flood, earthquakes and destruction by war. Each disaster has required massive rebuilding. Earthquake-resistant materials and construction techniques, which enable a building to sway rather than fall, have allowed new skyscrapers to replace older buildings. But the danger of earthquakes remains, and there are plans to move the capital to a safer site further north.

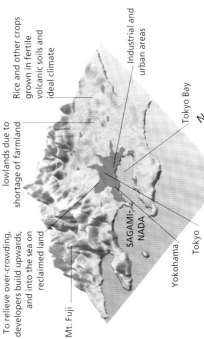

Japanese motorbike

VEHICLE INDUSTRY

Japanese vehicle manufacturers became world leaders in the 1980s thanks to their stylish designs, new technology and efficient production methods. Today, motor vehicles are the country's biggest export. Japanese vehicle manufacturers have also opened a number of factories overseas – in Europe, the USA and elsewhere. Countries in areas like eastern Europe can supply cheaper labour than in Japan. **Look for**

RELIGION

There are two main religions in Japan – Buddhism and Shinto. People often follow both: it is common to be married with Shinto rituals, but buried with Buddhist. There are numerous Buddhist and Shinto shrines and temples in Japan. They were usually built of wood – and therefore vulnerable to fire – and temples like Ginkakuji in Kyoto have been rebuilt several times.

COMMUTING

Most Japanese people live in the cities, but few people can afford to live in the city centres, so most people have to commute to work. Trains are fast and efficient, but so overcrowded that special guards are employed to push commuters into the carriages.

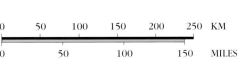

A bottle of rice wine, or *sake*, Japan's national drink.

COMPUTERS

The Japanese excel at producing miniature electronic goods, such as computers and televisions. They have set such high standards that few countries can match them. A silicon "chip" able to hold 1,000 pages of newsprint in its memory is being developed.

To relieve over-crowding, developers build upwards, and into the sea on reclaimed land
Intensively cultivated lowlands due to shortage of farmland
Rice and other crops grown in fertile volcanic soils and ideal climate
Mt. Fuji
SAGAMI-NADA
Industrial and urban areas
Yokohama
Tokyo
Tokyo Bay
N

SITE OF TOKYO

Built around Tokyo Bay, and hemmed in by mountains, Tokyo is unable to spread further inland or along the coast. The sprawling built-up region around Tokyo and Yokohama is the world's largest urban area, and is sometimes called a megalopolis. It has a population of over 27 million people, and accounts for 25 per cent of Japan's industrial production.

MAP FEATURES

Financial centre: Japan is a leading member of the world financial community. Its stock exchange ranks second in the world. **Look for**

Skiing: The Hida-sanmyaku mountains in Honshu are excellent for skiing. In 1998, the Winter Olympics were held in Nagano. **Look for**

Rail routes: The Shinkansen, or bullet train, runs from Tokyo to Fukuoka at an average speed of 195 km (122 miles) per hour. **Look for**

- Rice
- Mixed fruit
- Citrus fruit
- Tea
- Tobacco
- Fishing ports
- Industrial centre
- Vehicle manufacture
- Shipbuilding
- High-tech industry

Mainland Southeast Asia

Much of this region is mountainous and covered with forest. Most of the people live in the great river valleys, plateaux or fertile plains. Farming is the main occupation, with rice the principal crop. Of the seven countries, only Thailand was not a British or French colony. Thais are deeply devoted to their royal family and Buddhist faith. The Federation of Malaysia includes 11 states on the mainland, joined in 1963 by Sabah and Sarawak in Borneo. This union of east and west has produced one of the world's most successful developing countries. Singapore, at first part of Malaysia, became a republic in 1965. The island controls the busy shipping routes between the Indian and Pacific Oceans. Cambodia, Laos and Vietnam have all suffered from many years of warfare. Cambodia's future is still uncertain, but the other two countries show signs of economic recovery. Burma has become increasingly isolated from the world by its repressive government.

Ruby

Calcite

RUBIES

Several types of precious stone are mined in the northeast of Burma. The glowing red rubies from this region are considered the finest in the world. Many people in the East believe that wearing a ruby protects you from harm. Today Burma has a virtual monopoly over the ruby trade. Look for

BURMA (MYANMAR)
pop: 47,600,000

FISHING

Fish is one of the main foods in this area. Thailand has a thriving fish canning industry. Fish farming in the inland lake of Tonle Sap, Cambodia, is also successful. Here, in Burma, fish are caught from small huts built over the water. Look for

TIMBER

Thailand was once a major producer of teak, but so much of the country's forests have been cut down that commercial logging was banned in 1989 – until forests recover. Burma is now the world's principal teak exporter. Here, huge logs float down the Irrawaddy river. Look for

Boats on the Irrawaddy, the great river of Burma.

Lacquer tray

Making lacquer ware is a traditional craft in Thailand.

BUDDHISM

Except for Malaysia, the main religion in this region is Buddhism. In Thailand and Burma, where almost all the people are Buddhists, every young man puts on the saffron robe, shaves his head and enters a monastery for several months.

OPIUM

Poppy seeds

Dried opium poppy

For the poor hill tribes of the "Golden Triangle" – the remote area where Burma, Laos and Thailand meet – growing opium poppies is one of the few sources of income. Useful painkillers can be made from the poppies, but so too are dangerous drugs, such as heroin and opium. The government is encouraging people in this area to grow other crops, such as flowers and tobacco.

LAOS
pop: 5,400,000

VIETNAM

Rice is the principal crop in this country. As Vietnam is so mountainous, most people live in the two main river deltas. Two-thirds of the farmed land is devoted to growing rice. The wet-field, or *paddy*, is planted by women. Look for

VIETNAM
pop: 77,900,000

Durian fruit is grown throughout the region.

Fruit of the oil palm

PALM OIL

The oil palm comes from West Africa, but has been successfully introduced into Malaysia and Indonesia. Palm oil and palm kernel oil, which are used in soap and as edible oils, are made from the fruit. Malaysia started production to lessen its dependence on the rubber crop – increasingly replaced by synthetic alternatives. **Look for** (vegetable oil symbol)

ELEPHANTS

Compared to a tractor, a working elephant needs little fuel, does not rust and needs no spare parts. A tractor lasts for about six years, an elephant for 30, and it is less harmful to the environment. Elephants are used to move timber and to take tourists for rides in the forest.

Pineapple fruit

Pineapple ring

PINEAPPLES

Thailand has become the world's biggest exporter of canned pineapple, 50 per cent of the product going to the USA. The pineapples are processed in factories where the skin is removed, the stem cut out and the fruit sliced into rings or chunks. Some of the largest factories in Thailand are owned by Japanese companies.

Siamese cats originally came from Thailand – once called Siam.

MAP FEATURES

Mining: Malaysia is the world's biggest producer of tin, but its resources are becoming depleted. **Look for** (mining symbol)

Dam: A series of dams is planned on the Mekong to provide HEP and irrigation. All six countries involved must first reach agreement. **Look for** (dam symbol)

Tourism: Over 3 million tourists visit Thailand each year, and tourism has become a major source of foreign currency. **Look for** (tourism symbol)

Rice · Fishing · Coconuts · Coal · Vegetable oil · Gas · Timber · Industrial centre · Forest products · Archaeological site

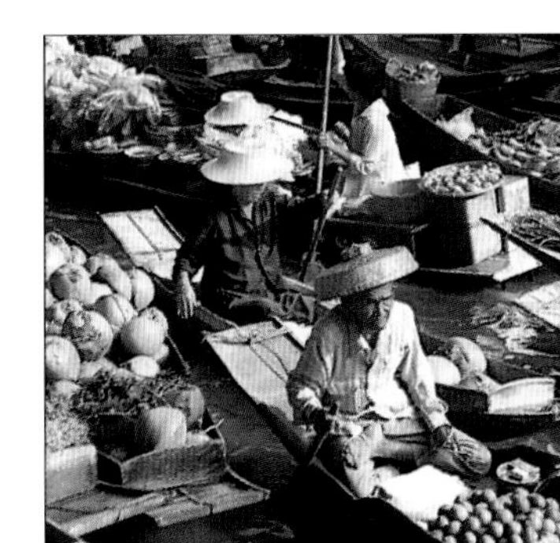

FLOATING MARKET

Bangkok, Thailand's capital, is a noisy, hectic city, full of Buddhist temples – *wats* – and congested with traffic. The city was built on an island in the river, and the canals – or *klongs* – were once the city's streets. The few canals that remain are still used by flat boats – called *sampans* – to transport fresh fruit and vegetables from the countryside to the floating markets where the *sampans* act as shops.

The Cameron High-lands, Malaysia.

ELECTRONICS

Thailand and Malaysia are both industrializing rapidly. They have many factories where electronic products, like this pocket calculator, are assembled. Both countries now export a large number of manufactured goods. Malaysia makes its own car, the Proton; Thailand is a leading manufacturer of integrated circuits.

THAILAND pop: 59,600,000

CAMBODIA pop: 10,800,000

WEST MALAYSIA pop: 16,952,000

Orchids are grown in northern Thailand as an alternative to opium, and are widely exported.

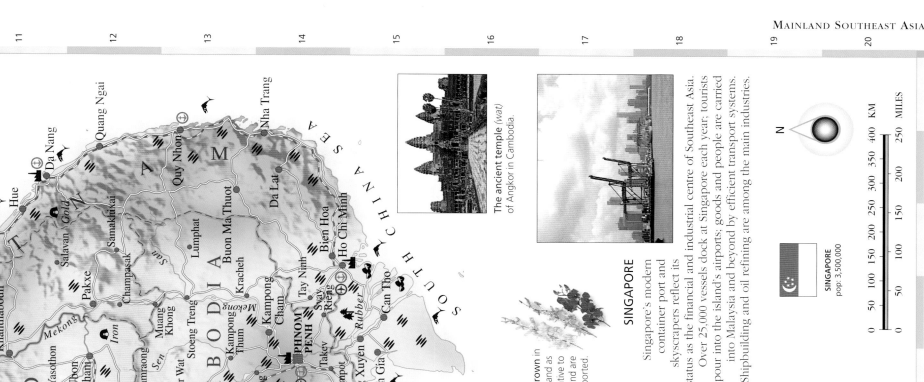

The ancient temple *(wat)* of Angkor in Cambodia.

SINGAPORE

Singapore's modern container port and skyscrapers reflect its status as the financial and industrial centre of Southeast Asia. Over 25,000 vessels dock at Singapore each year; tourists pour into the island's airports; goods and people are carried into Malaysia and beyond by efficient transport systems. Shipbuilding and oil refining are among the main industries.

SINGAPORE pop: 3,500,000

0 50 100 150 200 250 300 350 400 KM
0 50 100 150 200 250 MILES

THAILAND · CAMBODIA · VIETNAM · MALAYSIA · ANDAMAN SEA · Gulf of Thailand · SOUTH CHINA SEA · Gulf of Martaban · Strait of Malacca · Singapore Strait · BANGKOK · PHNOM PENH · KUALA LUMPUR · SINGAPORE · Moulmein · Pyapon · Kyaikkami · Ye · Tavoy · Mergui · Phitsanulok · Phetchabun · Khon Kaen · Khanthabouli · Hue · Da Nang · Quang Ngai · Nakhon Sawan · Nakhon Ratchasima · Yasothon · Ubon Ratchathani · Pakxe · Salavan · Samakhixai · Champasak · Sara Buri · Ayutthaya · Prachin Buri · Kanchanaburi · Ratchaburi · Phetchaburi · Chon Buri · Pattaya · Rayong · Chanthaburi · Phumi Samraong · Angkor Wat · Batdambang · Muang Khong · Stoeng Treng · Lumphat · Quy Nhon · Pouthisat · Kampong Thum · Kracheh · Buon Ma Thuot · Kampong Chhnang · Kampong Cham · Krong Kaoh Kong · Kampong Saom · Takev · Svay Rieng · Tay Ninh · Bien Hoa · Ho Chi Minh · Da Lat · Nha Trang · Kampot · Long Xuyen · Rach Gia · Can Tho · Prachuap Khiri Khan · Chumphon · Ko Phangan · Ko Samui · Surat Thani · Nakhon Si Thammarat · Phuket · Ko Phuket · Trang · Thale Luang · Songkhla · Hat Yai · Pattani · Yala · Narathiwat · Kota Bharu · Pulau Langkawi · Alor Setar · George Town · Butterworth · Taiping · Ipoh · Kuala Terengganu · Dungun · Teluk Intan · Kuantan · Klang · Seremban · Port Dickson · Melaka · Johor Bahru · C. Negrais · Isthmus of Kra · Mergui Archipelago · Cameron Highlands · Srinagarind Res. · Mekong · Mae Nam Mun · Nam Ping · Tonle Sap · Sen · San · Sungai Pahang

Maritime Southeast Asia

Scattered between the Indian and Pacific Oceans lies a huge crescent of mountainous tropical islands – the East Indies. The largest country in this region is Indonesia, which was ruled by the Dutch for nearly 350 years. Over half its 13,677 islands are still uninhabited. The island of Borneo is shared between Indonesia, the Malaysian states of Sabah and Sarawak, and the Sultanate of Brunei. Indonesia's national motto, "Unity in diversity", ideally suits a country made up of 362 different peoples speaking over 250 dialects and languages. Indonesia seized East Timor in 1975. In 1999, an overwhelming vote for independence led to violent clashes, and a UN peacekeeping force was sent to the island. The Philippines, ruled for three centuries by Spain, then for 50 years by the USA, consists of over 7,000 islands. It is the only mainly Christian country in Asia. Much of the region is covered by forests, which contain some of the finest timber in the world.

COCONUTS

Kernel

Indonesia and the Philippines are the world's major coconut growers. Every part of the tree has its uses, even the leaves. The kernel is dried to make copra from which a valuable oil is obtained. Look for [coconuts symbol]

STILT VILLAGES

Many of the villages in this region are built over water. The houses are made of local materials, like wood and bamboo, and built on stilts to protect them from vermin and flooding. For houses built on land, raised floors also provide shelter for the owner's animals which live underneath.

BRUNEI

The Sultanate of Brunei became rich when oil was discovered in 1929. This golden-domed mosque, built with the country's new-found wealth, towers above the capital, Bandar Seri Begawan. The small, predominantly Muslim, population pays no taxes, and enjoys free education and health care.

Helicopter

AIRCRAFT INDUSTRY

Indonesia has developed a thriving aircraft industry. About 12,000 workers assemble helicopters and aircraft at Bandung in Java. The factories are jointly owned by five international aircraft manufacturers. The first solely Indonesian-designed aircraft will soon be completed.

RELIGION

Although about 90 per cent of Indonesians are Muslim, many of their religious ceremonies contain elements of other religions – like Hinduism and Buddhism – which blend with local traditions and beliefs. Recently, Islam has become more dominant. More girls now wear the Islamic headdress, like these pupils at a school in Sumatra.

MALAYSIA
pop: 21,500,000
(EAST MALAYSIA: SABAH AND SARAWAK)
pop: 4,548,000

BRUNEI
pop: 313,000

Dense rainforest on Sumatra is home to elephants and tigers.

Borobudur, the great 8th-century Buddhist temple on Java.

SOUTH CHINA SEA
Kota Kinabalu
BANDAR SERI BEGAWAN
Kuala Belait
Miri
BRUNEI
MALAYSIA (EAST)
Bandaaceh
Rubber
Belawan
Medan
Pematangsiantar
Pulau Simeulue
Danau Toba
Palm
Sibolga
Pulau Natuna Besar
Kepulauan Natuna
Kepulauan Anambas
Sibu
Sarikei
Batang Rajang
SARAWAK
Kuching
Singapore Strait
Pulau Bintan
Pulau Nias
Sumatra
Tanjungpinang
Pekanbaru
Borneo
Sungai Kapuas
PEGUNUNGAN MULLER
Pontianak
Kepulauan Batu
Pulau Pini
Pulau Lingga
Pulau Singkep
PEGUNUNGAN SCHWANER
Padang
Batang Hari
Jambi
Kepulauan Karimata
Pulau Siberut
PEGUNUNGAN BARISAN
Pulau Bangka
Tin
Pangkalpinang
Pulau Sipura
Pulau Pagai Utara
Pulau Pagai Selatan
Palembang
Pulau Belitung
Kualakapuas
Banjarmasin
Bengkulu
JAVA SEA
Pulau Enggano
Bandarlampung
JAKARTA
Bogor
Sukabumi
Bandung
Cirebon
Semarang
Surabaya
Pulau Bawean
Pulau Madura
Borobudur
Yogyakarta
Kediri
Malang
Jember
Banyuwangi
Java
Denpasar
Bali
INDIAN OCEAN

JAKARTA

Situated on the island of Java, Indonesia's capital Jakarta has the largest population of any city in Southeast Asia – and is still growing rapidly. It was once the centre of the region's Dutch trading empire and many typical Dutch buildings still stand in the old part of the city. At night, skyscrapers glitter above the city's modern centre.

MAP FEATURES

Vegetable oil: Indonesia is now one of the world's major producers of palm oil. It has many uses, from hydraulic brake fluids to cooking oil. Look for [palm oil symbol]

Research centre: Near Manila in the Philippines the Rice Research Institute has developed many of the world's modern high-yield types of rice. Look for [research symbol]

Pirates: Pirate attacks on vessels in the area are increasing, especially at night and in the busy shipping lanes of the Singapore Strait. Look for [pirate symbol]

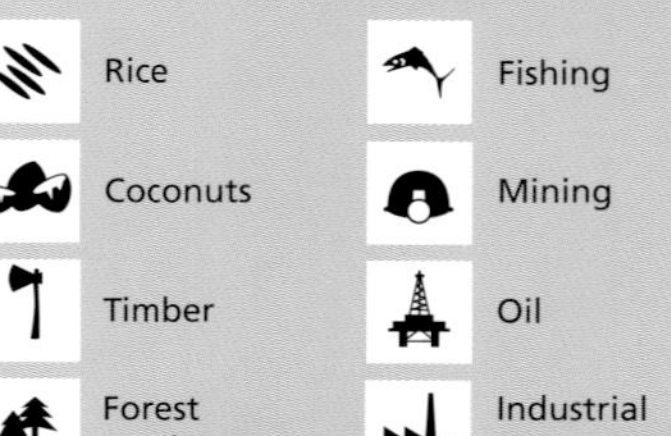

Rice
Fishing
Coconuts
Mining
Timber
Oil
Forest products
Industrial centre

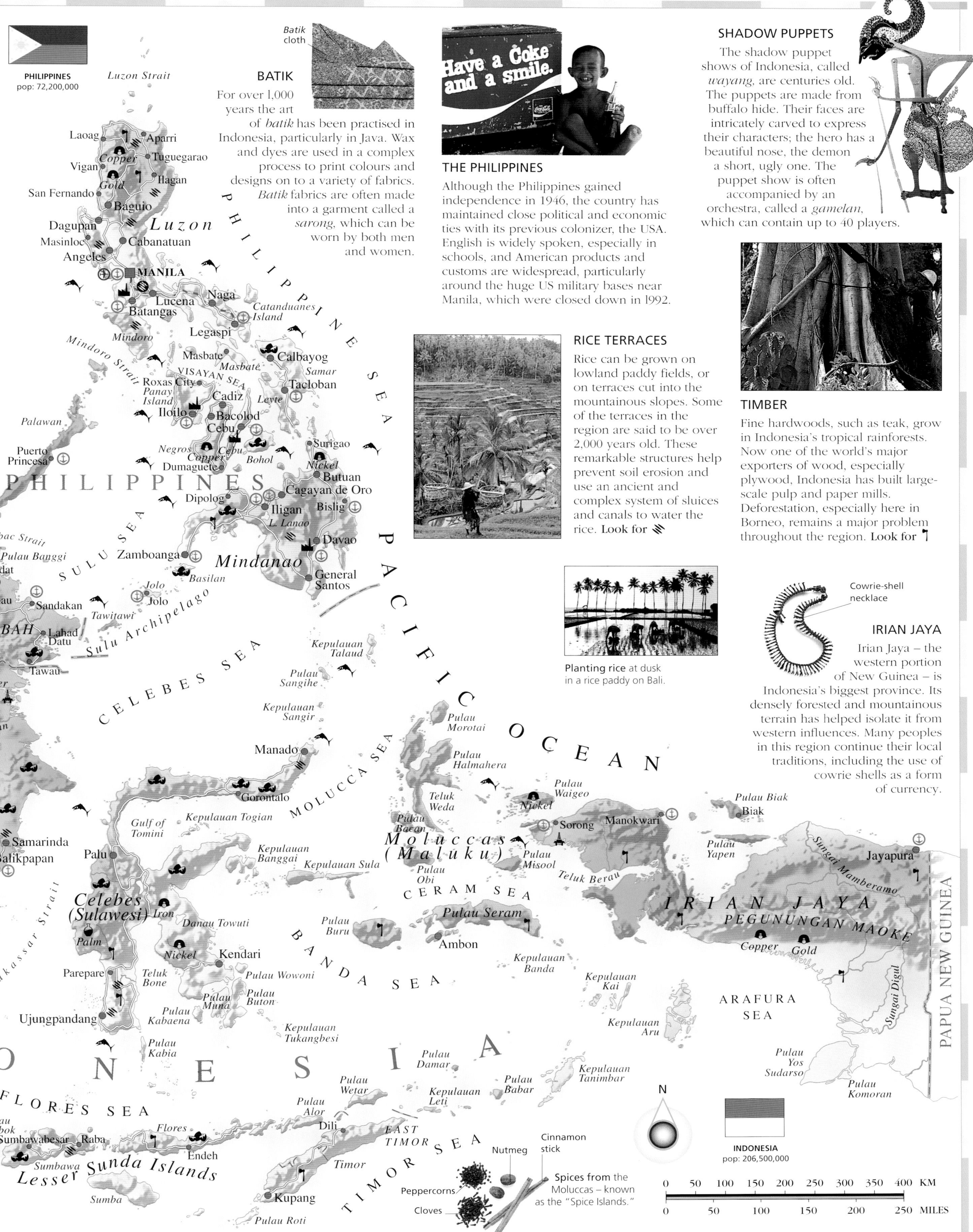

PHILIPPINES
pop: 72,200,000
Luzon Strait
Laoag
Aparri
Vigan
Tuguegarao
Copper
Gold
Ilagan
San Fernando
Baguio
Dagupan
Luzon
Masinloc
Cabanatuan
Angeles
MANILA
Lucena
Naga
Batangas
Catanduanes Island
Mindoro
Legaspi
Mindoro Strait
Masbate
Calbayog
Samar
VISAYAN SEA
Roxas City
Panay Island
Cadiz
Tacloban
Leyte
Iloilo
Bacolod
Palawan
Cebu
Puerto Princesa
Negros
Copper
Surigao
Bohol
Nickel
Dumaguete
Butuan
PHILIPPINES
Dipolog
Cagayan de Oro
Iligan
Bislig
L. Lanao
Davao
Zamboanga
Mindanao
General Santos
Basilan
Jolo
SULU SEA
PHILIPPINE SEA
Pulau Banggi
Kudat
Sandakan
Tawitawi
Sulu Archipelago
SABAH
Lahad Datu
Tawau
CELEBES SEA
PACIFIC OCEAN
Kepulauan Talaud
Pulau Sangihe
Kepulauan Sangir
Pulau Morotai
Pulau Halmahera
Manado
MOLUCCA SEA
Gorontalo
Teluk Weda
Pulau Waigeo
Nickel
Sorong
Manokwari
Pulau Biak
Biak
Gulf of Tomini
Kepulauan Togian
Pulau Bacan
Moluccas (Maluku)
Pulau Misool
Pulau Yapen
Jayapura
Samarinda
Balikpapan
Palu
Kepulauan Banggai
Kepulauan Sula
Pulau Obi
Teluk Berau
Sungai Mamberamo
CERAM SEA
Celebes (Sulawesi)
Iron
Makassar Strait
Danau Towuti
Pulau Buru
Pulau Seram
IRIAN JAYA
PEGUNUNGAN MAOKE
Palm
BANDA SEA
Ambon
Copper
Gold
Nickel
Kendari
Kepulauan Banda
Parepare
Teluk Bone
Pulau Wowoni
Kepulauan Kai
Pulau Muna
Pulau Buton
ARAFURA SEA
Sungai Digul
PAPUA NEW GUINEA
Pulau Kabaena
Kepulauan Aru
Ujungpandang
Kepulauan Tukangbesi
Pulau Kabia
INDONESIA
Pulau Damar
Kepulauan Tanimbar
Pulau Yos Sudarso
Pulau Wetar
Pulau Babar
Pulau Komoran
FLORES SEA
Pulau Alor
Kepulauan Leti
Pulau Lombok
Sumbawabesar
Raba
Flores
Dili
EAST TIMOR
Endeh
TIMOR SEA
Sumbawa
Lesser Sunda Islands
Timor
Sumba
Kupang
Pulau Roti
INDONESIA
pop: 206,500,000
N
0 50 100 150 200 250 300 350 400 KM
0 50 100 150 200 250 MILES
Batik cloth
Have a Coke and a smile.
Cowrie-shell necklace
Nutmeg
Cinnamon stick
Peppercorns
Cloves

BATIK

For over 1,000 years the art of *batik* has been practised in Indonesia, particularly in Java. Wax and dyes are used in a complex process to print colours and designs on to a variety of fabrics. *Batik* fabrics are often made into a garment called a *sarong*, which can be worn by both men and women.

THE PHILIPPINES

Although the Philippines gained independence in 1946, the country has maintained close political and economic ties with its previous colonizer, the USA. English is widely spoken, especially in schools, and American products and customs are widespread, particularly around the huge US military bases near Manila, which were closed down in 1992.

SHADOW PUPPETS

The shadow puppet shows of Indonesia, called *wayang*, are centuries old. The puppets are made from buffalo hide. Their faces are intricately carved to express their characters; the hero has a beautiful nose, the demon a short, ugly one. The puppet show is often accompanied by an orchestra, called a *gamelan*, which can contain up to 40 players.

RICE TERRACES

Rice can be grown on lowland paddy fields, or on terraces cut into the mountainous slopes. Some of the terraces in the region are said to be over 2,000 years old. These remarkable structures help prevent soil erosion and use an ancient and complex system of sluices and canals to water the rice. **Look for**

TIMBER

Fine hardwoods, such as teak, grow in Indonesia's tropical rainforests. Now one of the world's major exporters of wood, especially plywood, Indonesia has built large-scale pulp and paper mills. Deforestation, especially here in Borneo, remains a major problem throughout the region. **Look for**

Planting rice at dusk in a rice paddy on Bali.

IRIAN JAYA

Irian Jaya – the western portion of New Guinea – is Indonesia's biggest province. Its densely forested and mountainous terrain has helped isolate it from western influences. Many peoples in this region continue their local traditions, including the use of cowrie shells as a form of currency.

Spices from the Moluccas – known as the "Spice Islands."

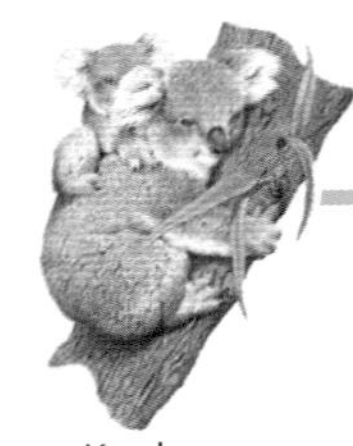

Koala
Phascolarctos cinereus
Length: 80 cm (31 in)

Funnel-web spider
Atrax robustus
Length: 3 cm (1 in)

Raggiana's bird of paradise
Paradisaea raggiana
Length: 1.4 m (4 ft)

AUSTRALASIA AND OCEANIA

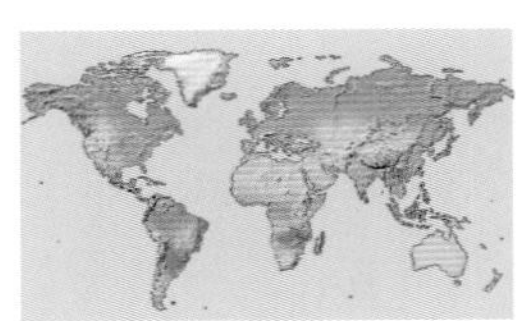

AUSTRALASIA AND OCEANIA includes Australia, New Zealand and numerous island groups in the Pacific. Australia – the smallest, flattest and driest continent – has been worn down by 3,000 million years of exposure to wind and rain. Away from Australia, along the edges of the continental plates, volcanic activity is common because the plates are still moving. These plate movements greatly affect New Guinea, many Pacific islands and New Zealand. Elsewhere in the Pacific Ocean, thousands of tiny coral islands have grown on the tops of undersea volcanic mountains. Climates vary greatly across the region, from the wet tropical climates of the islands in the outer Pacific, to the hot, dry deserts of central Australia. Tropical rainforest can be found in northeastern Australia and much of New Guinea.

Cider gum tree
Eucalyptus gunnii
Height: 25 m (76 ft)

SURF AND SAND
Powerful waves from the Tasman Sea wash the southeast coast of Australia, creating long, sandy beaches.

AUSTRALIA'S RAINFOREST
Over 600 different types of trees grow in the tropical rainforest on the Cape York Peninsula. Mists often hang over the forest.

DESERT MOUNTAINS
For millions of years, erosion has scoured the centre of Australia. Rocky outcrops like Kata Tjuta have been reduced to sandstone domes.

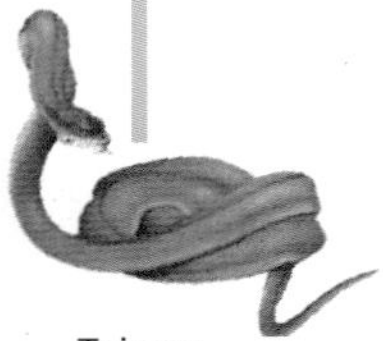

Taipan
Oxyuranuus scutellatus
Length: 3.6 m (12 ft)

TROPICAL GRASSLAND
Deserts with arid shrubs and tussock grasses dominate the central third of Australia. Across northern Australia, is a tropical grassland with scattered trees.

DRY WOODLAND
Eucalyptus – otherwise known as gum trees – abound in Australia. Most species are adapted to dry conditions, their tough, leathery leaves resisting the drying effect of the sun.

TEMPERATE RAINFOREST
Far from other land and surrounded by ocean, much of New Zealand has high rainfall and is mild all year round. These conditions encourage the unique plants of the temperate rainforest.

HOT NEW ZEALAND
Steam rises from pools of sulphurous boiling water and mud, signs of volcanic activity along the plate margins. The heat comes from deep within the Earth.

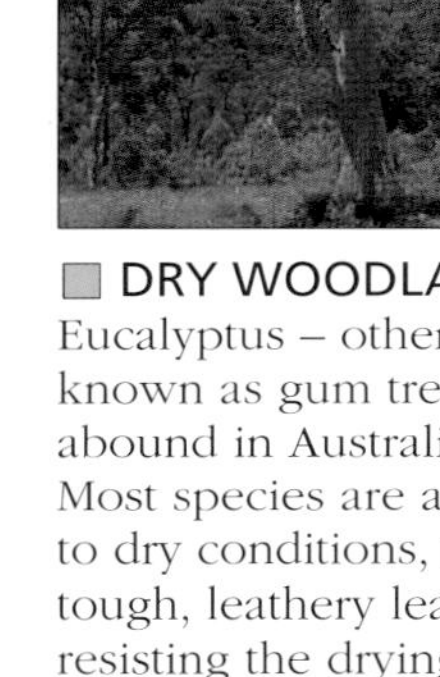

Black opal, a precious stone found in Australia.

Giant white buttercup
Ranunculus lyalii
Size: 1 m (3 ft)

THE PINNACLES
Western Australia's weird limestone pinnacles stand out in the sandy desert. Rain and plant roots have shaped the pillars over the last 25,000 years.

CROSS-SECTION THROUGH AUSTRALASIA AND OCEANIA

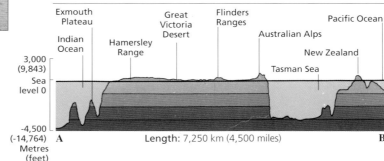

Exmouth Plateau
Indian Ocean
Hamersley Range
Great Victoria Desert
Flinders Ranges
Australian Alps
Tasman Sea
New Zealand
Pacific Ocean
3,000 (9,843)
Sea level 0
-4,500 (-14,764)
Metres (feet)
A
Length: 7,250 km (4,500 miles)
B

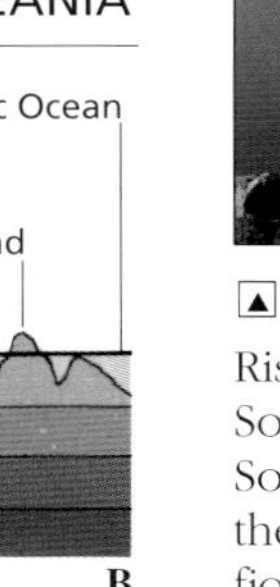

NEW ZEALAND'S ALPS
Rising steeply from the west coast, the Southern Alps cover 80 per cent of South Island. Glaciers moving down the mountains carved deep inlets – fjords – along the southwest coast.

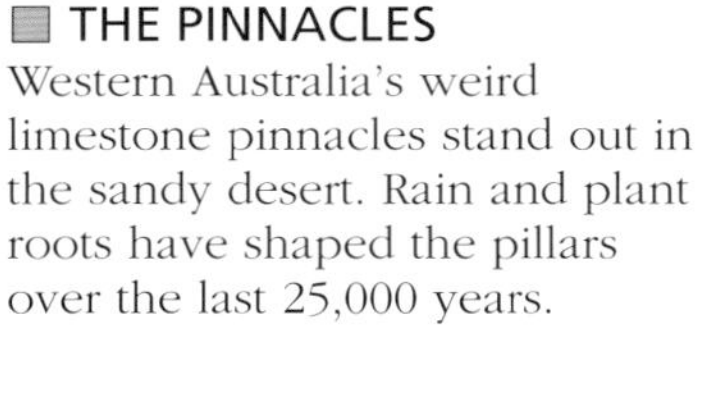

Red kangaroo
Macropus rufus
Height: 2 m (6 ft)

Brown kiwi
Apteryx australis
Height: 35 cm (14 in)

Giant clam
Tridacna gigas
Shell: 1.5 m (5 ft)

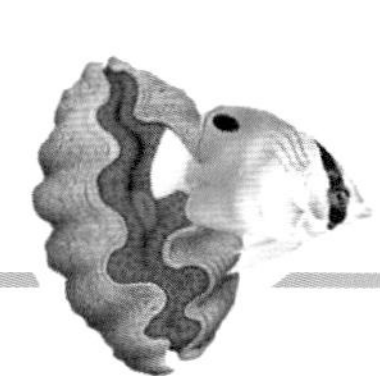

Butterfly fish
Chaetodon auriga
Length: 20 cm (8 in)

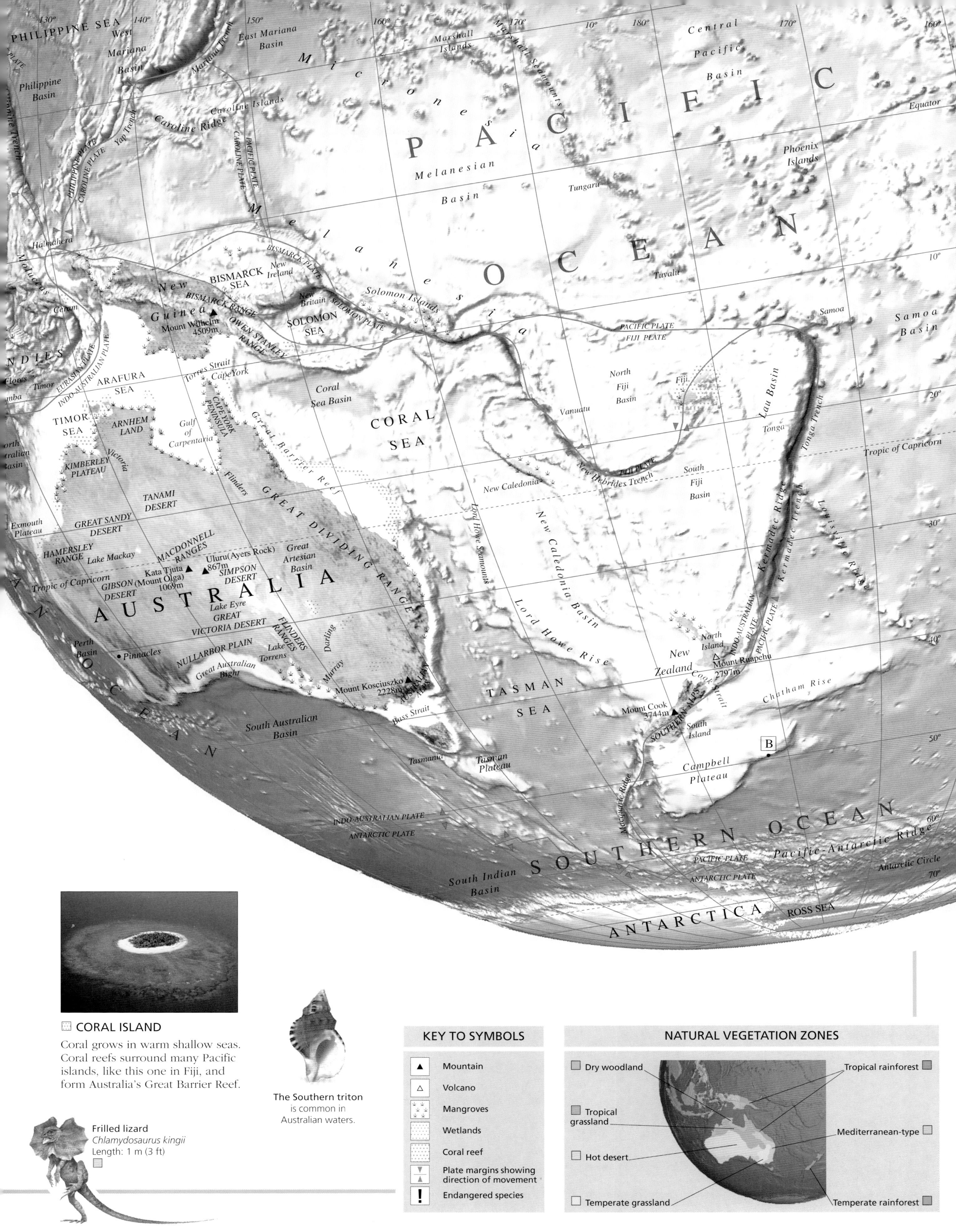

PHILIPPINE SEA
West Mariana Basin
Philippine Basin
East Mariana Basin
Mariana Trench
Marshall Islands
Marshall Seamounts
Central Pacific Basin
Micronesia
Caroline Islands
Caroline Ridge
Yap Trench
PHILIPPINE PLATE
CAROLINE PLATE
PACIFIC PLATE
PACIFIC OCEAN
Equator
Melanesian Basin
Tungaru
Phoenix Islands
Melanesia
Halmahera
Moluccas
BISMARCK PLATE
BISMARCK SEA
New Ireland
New Guinea
BISMARCK RANGE
OWEN STANLEY RANGE
Mount Wilhelm 4509m
Tuvalu
New Britain
SOLOMON PLATE
Solomon Islands
SOLOMON SEA
Ceram
Samoa
Samoa Basin
PACIFIC PLATE
FIJI PLATE
EURASIAN PLATE
INDO-AUSTRALIAN PLATE
Torres Strait
Cape York
ARAFURA SEA
Flores
Timor
North Fiji Basin
Fiji
Lau Basin
Coral Sea Basin
CORAL SEA
Vanuatu
Tonga
Tonga Trench
TIMOR SEA
ARNHEM LAND
Gulf of Carpentaria
CAPE YORK PENINSULA
Great Barrier Reef
Tropic of Capricorn
KIMBERLEY PLATEAU
Victoria
Flinders
New Caledonia
New Hebrides Trench
South Fiji Basin
TANAMI DESERT
GREAT DIVIDING RANGE
Exmouth Plateau
GREAT SANDY DESERT
Lord Howe Seamounts
New Caledonia Basin
Kermadec Ridge
Kermadec Trench
Louisville Ridge
HAMERSLEY RANGE
Lake Mackay
MACDONNELL RANGES
Uluru (Ayers Rock) 867m
Great Artesian Basin
Kata Tjuta (Mount Olga) 1069m
SIMPSON DESERT
Tropic of Capricorn
GIBSON DESERT
AUSTRALIA
Lake Eyre
GREAT VICTORIA DESERT
FLINDERS RANGES
Darling
Lord Howe Rise
North Island
INDO-AUSTRALIAN PLATE
PACIFIC PLATE
Perth Basin
Pinnacles
NULLARBOR PLAIN
Lake Torrens
New Zealand
Mount Ruapehu 2797m
Great Australian Bight
Murray
Mount Kosciuszko 2228m
AUSTRALIAN ALPS
Cook Strait
Chatham Rise
INDIAN OCEAN
TASMAN SEA
Mount Cook 3744m
SOUTHERN ALPS
South Island
Bass Strait
South Australian Basin
B
Tasmania
Tasman Plateau
Campbell Plateau
Macquarie Ridge
INDO-AUSTRALIAN PLATE
ANTARCTIC PLATE
SOUTHERN OCEAN
Pacific-Antarctic Ridge
PACIFIC PLATE
ANTARCTIC PLATE
South Indian Basin
Antarctic Circle
ANTARCTICA
ROSS SEA
130° 140° 150° 160° 170° 180° 170° 160°
10° 20° 30° 40° 50° 60° 70°
KEY TO SYMBOLS
Mountain
Volcano
Mangroves
Wetlands
Coral reef
Plate margins showing direction of movement
Endangered species
NATURAL VEGETATION ZONES
Dry woodland
Tropical rainforest
Tropical grassland
Mediterranean-type
Hot desert
Temperate grassland
Temperate rainforest

CORAL ISLAND

Coral grows in warm shallow seas. Coral reefs surround many Pacific islands, like this one in Fiji, and form Australia's Great Barrier Reef.

The Southern triton is common in Australian waters.

Frilled lizard
Chlamydosaurus kingii
Length: 1 m (3 ft)

THE PACIFIC OCEAN

THE PACIFIC IS THE LARGEST and deepest of the world's oceans. It covers a greater area of the Earth's surface than all the land areas combined. At its deepest point – 11,033 m (36,197 ft) down in the Mariana Trench – it is deep enough to cover Mount Everest. More than half the world's population lives around the shores of the Pacific. The ocean's northern and western edges, known as the outer Pacific, are fringed with chains of islands, such as the Aleutians. The inner Pacific islands fall into three main groups: Melanesia, Micronesia and Polynesia. With the development of modern communications, trade and co-operation between countries surrounding the ocean – sometimes referred to as the "Pacific Rim" – is increasing. Countries such as Japan, Australia and New Zealand want the south Pacific made into a Nuclear-Free Zone, which would prevent all testing of nuclear weapons.

The Aleutians, a chain of volcanic islands in the Pacific.

MICRONESIA
pop: 109,000

NAURU
pop: 11,000

PALAU
pop: 17,700

A coral atoll in French Polynesia.

CONTAINER PORTS

Today, fruit, meat and many other goods are moved round the world in huge metal containers. Here, a ship waits to be loaded at Kobe, one of Japan's main container ports.

FISHING

Pacific islanders fish mainly for food, although any surplus catch may be sold. Many fish are caught in the north Pacific by commercial shipping fleets operating far from their home bases. The biggest catches are made by Japan, South Korea, Taiwan and the USA. The main fish caught is tuna. **Look for**

Skipjack tuna

COCONUTS

The coconut palm is called "tree of life" by Pacific islanders because it provides so many of their daily needs, such as food and building materials. Here the white "meat" of the coconut is dried to make copra, which is exported. **Look for**

SOLOMON ISLANDS
pop: 417,000

MAP FEATURES

Fishing: Since the first salmon farms were set up in 1982 around Chiloé island, Chile, salmon farming became a major industry. **Look for**

Mining: The Pacific island of Nauru became prosperous through the export of phosphates, used to make fertilizers. **Look for**

Pollution: Nuclear testing carried out by the USA and France has polluted certain islands in the Pacific. **Look for**

Sugar cane
Coconuts
Timber
Shellfishing
Fishing ports
Tourism
Whales
Military bases

FIJI

Fiji is a group of volcanic islands surrounded by coral reefs. Although one of the few south Pacific islands to develop tourism, Fiji's economy is still dominated by the sugar cane crop – shown here being harvested. A number of tax-free factories have been set up which export a variety of products overseas; clothing, in particular, has proved very successful. **Look for**

Tropical growth on an island in the Tonga group.

ISLANDS

The Pacific islands are scattered over a huge area, far from any industrial centre and from each other. Some of the islands are high and volcanic, others low coral atolls. They are home to over five million people whose one great shared resource is the sea. A huge variety of fish and shellfish are caught from small boats and by diving. In general, the soil of the islands is poor.

VANUATU
pop: 200,000

FIJI
pop: 822,000

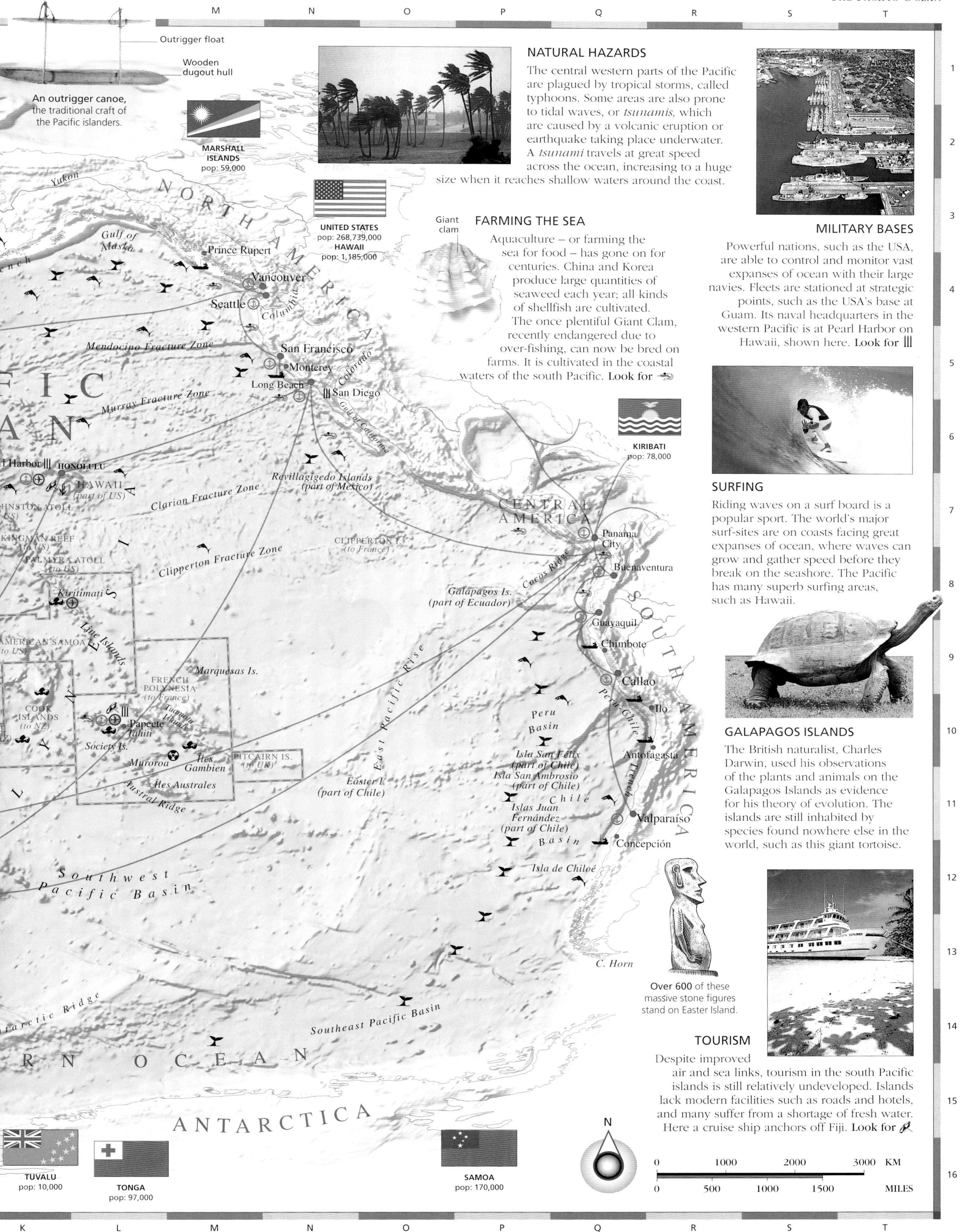

Outrigger float
Wooden dugout hull
MARSHALL ISLANDS pop: 59,000
UNITED STATES pop: 268,739,000
HAWAII pop: 1,185,000
Giant clam
KIRIBATI pop: 78,000
TUVALU pop: 10,000
TONGA pop: 97,000
SAMOA pop: 170,000
NORTH AMERICA
CENTRAL AMERICA
SOUTH AMERICA
ANTARCTICA
Yukon
Gulf of Alaska
Prince Rupert
Vancouver
Seattle
Columbia
Mendocino Fracture Zone
San Francisco
Monterey
Colorado
Long Beach
San Diego
Murray Fracture Zone
Gulf of California
Pearl Harbor
HONOLULU
HAWAII (part of US)
Revillagigedo Islands (part of Mexico)
Clarion Fracture Zone
KINGMAN REEF
PALMYRA ATOLL (to US)
Clipperton Fracture Zone
CLIPPERTON I. (to France)
Panama City
Buenaventura
Cocos Ridge
Galápagos Is. (part of Ecuador)
Kiritimati
Line Islands
AMERICAN SAMOA (to US)
Guayaquil
Chimbote
Marquesas Is.
FRENCH POLYNESIA (to France)
COOK ISLANDS (to NZ)
Papeete
Tahiti
Society Is.
Tuamotu Islands
Mururoa
Îles Gambier
PITCAIRN IS. (to UK)
Îles Australes
Austral Ridge
East Pacific Rise
Easter I. (part of Chile)
Callao
Peru Basin
Ilo
Peru-Chile Trench
Antofagasta
Isla San Félix (part of Chile)
Isla San Ambrosio (part of Chile)
Chile Basin
Islas Juan Fernández (part of Chile)
Valparaíso
Concepción
Isla de Chiloé
C. Horn
Southwest Pacific Basin
Southeast Pacific Basin
N
0 1000 2000 3000 KM
0 500 1000 1500 MILES

An outrigger canoe, the traditional craft of the Pacific islanders.

NATURAL HAZARDS

The central western parts of the Pacific are plagued by tropical storms, called typhoons. Some areas are also prone to tidal waves, or *tsunamis*, which are caused by a volcanic eruption or earthquake taking place underwater. A *tsunami* travels at great speed across the ocean, increasing to a huge size when it reaches shallow waters around the coast.

FARMING THE SEA

Aquaculture – or farming the sea for food – has gone on for centuries. China and Korea produce large quantities of seaweed each year; all kinds of shellfish are cultivated. The once plentiful Giant Clam, recently endangered due to over-fishing, can now be bred on farms. It is cultivated in the coastal waters of the south Pacific. **Look for**

MILITARY BASES

Powerful nations, such as the USA, are able to control and monitor vast expanses of ocean with their large navies. Fleets are stationed at strategic points, such as the USA's base at Guam. Its naval headquarters in the western Pacific is at Pearl Harbor on Hawaii, shown here. **Look for** |||

SURFING

Riding waves on a surf board is a popular sport. The world's major surf-sites are on coasts facing great expanses of ocean, where waves can grow and gather speed before they break on the seashore. The Pacific has many superb surfing areas, such as Hawaii.

GALAPAGOS ISLANDS

The British naturalist, Charles Darwin, used his observations of the plants and animals on the Galapagos Islands as evidence for his theory of evolution. The islands are still inhabited by species found nowhere else in the world, such as this giant tortoise.

Over 600 of these massive stone figures stand on Easter Island.

TOURISM

Despite improved air and sea links, tourism in the south Pacific islands is still relatively undeveloped. Islands lack modern facilities such as roads and hotels, and many suffer from a shortage of fresh water. Here a cruise ship anchors off Fiji. **Look for**

Australia and Papua New Guinea

Australia is a land of extremes. It is the world's smallest, flattest continent, with the lowest rainfall. The landscape ranges from scattered areas of rainforest along the northeast coast to arid desert – called the Outback – in the centre, to snowfields in the southeast. It is also one of the most urbanized countries; 70 per cent of the population live in towns and cities in the coastal regions, while much of the interior remains sparsely inhabited. Until two centuries ago this vast land was solely occupied by Aboriginal peoples, but in 1788 settlers from Britain established a colony on the southeast coast. Since then immigration, originally from Europe but now from Asia, has played a vital part in Australia's development. Australia is a wealthy and politically stable country with rich natural resources, steady population growth and increasingly strong trade links in the Pacific area, especially with Japan and the USA. Papua New Guinea, the eastern half of the mountainous island of New Guinea, was once an Australian colony, but became independent in 1975.

AUSTRALIA
pop: 18,966,800

Flying Doctors

In the Australian Outback, the nearest neighbour can live vast distances away. For a doctor to cover such huge areas by road would be impossible. About 60 years ago the Royal Flying Doctor Service was established. In an emergency a caller can contact the service by radio, 24 hours a day, and receive medical treatment within hours.

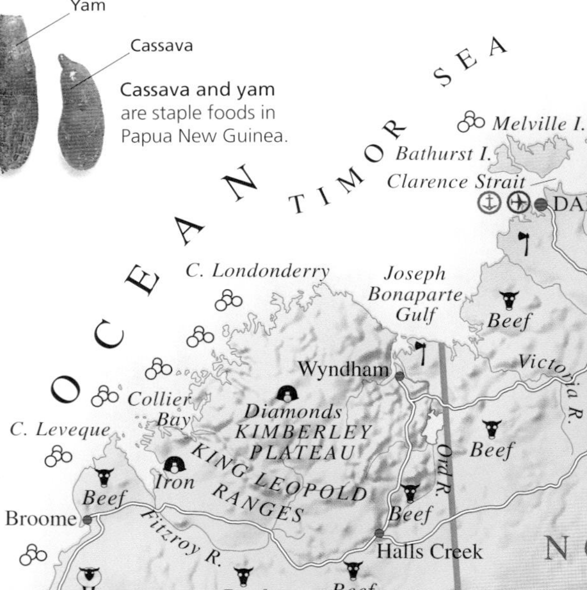

Yam

Cassava

Cassava and yam are staple foods in Papua New Guinea.

Gold

Quartz

Mining

Australia has large deposits of minerals such as gold, uranium, coal, iron ore, aluminium and diamonds. The mining of these minerals played an important part in the early development of the continent. Improved mining techniques have led to a resurgence in gold mining in Western Australia. Look for ⛑

The Great Outdoors

Australia's climate is ideal for watersports and other outdoor activities. But Australians are increasingly aware of the danger of skin cancer from the country's intense sunshine, and are learning to take precautions when in the sun.

WHAT'S THERE TO CELEBRATE
TO CELEBRATE
200 YEARS OF WHITE

First Inhabitants

Aboriginal peoples believe they have occupied Australia since "before time began". Early Aboriginal societies survived by hunting and gathering. They had their own traditions of story telling, distinctive ceremonies and art styles. Today, 66 per cent of Aboriginal peoples live in towns. Here, 200 years after the first European settlement, activists march through Sydney demanding land rights. The government has introduced programmes to improve Aboriginal standards of living, education and employment.

Map Features

Cattle: Australia has about 24 million cattle and exports beef and veal to over 100 countries, especially Japan and the USA. Look for 🐂

Mining: Papua New Guinea has recently become a major producer of gold, which is mined on the mainland and on one of the outlying islands. Look for ⛑

Pearls: Large South Sea pearls are cultivated in oysters in the waters along Australia's north-west coast. These are called "cultured" pearls. Look for ∞

Sheep	Fishing ports
Cereals	Coal
Sugar cane	Industrial centre
Timber	Major airstrips
Wine	Tourism

INDIAN OCEAN
TIMOR SEA
Melville I. · Bathurst I. · Clarence Strait · DARWIN · Croker
C. Londonderry · Joseph Bonaparte Gulf · Wyndham · Beef · Victoria R.
C. Leveque · Collier Bay · Diamonds · KIMBERLEY PLATEAU · KING LEOPOLD RANGES · Iron · Ord R. · Beef
Broome · Fitzroy R. · Halls Creek · NORTHERN TERRITORY · Copper
Monte Bello Is. · Barrow I. · Port Hedland · GREAT SANDY DESERT · Iron
Dampier · North West C. · Manganese · HAMERSLEY RANGE · Ashburton R. · Iron · L. Disappointment · L. Mackay · MACDONNELL
WESTERN AUSTRALIA · Gold · GIBSON DESERT
L. Macleod · Carnarvon · Shark Bay · Dirk Hartog I. · Murchison R. · Gold · Uluru (Ayers Rock)
Meekatharra · L. Carnegie · Gold · L. Wells
Mount Magnet · Gold · Nickel · GREAT VICTORIA DESERT
Geraldton · Oats · Gold · Zinc · Nickel · L. Barlee · Gold · Nickel
Dairy · L. Moore · Kalgoorlie · NULLARBOR PLAIN
Wheat · PERTH · Fremantle · Dairy · Gold · Gold · Nickel · Rockingham · Gold
C. Naturaliste · Bunbury · Barley · Esperance · C. Pasley · Great Australian Bight
Augusta · C. Leeuwin · Albany

Australia's Watershed

The Great Dividing Range is a series of rugged hill-lands and plateaux extending along Australia's east coast from the Cape York Peninsula to Tasmania. When Europeans first crossed the barrier in 1813, they opened up the Outback to immigration and settlement. Today, the highlands include many major tourist centres, but farming, timber and mining are also important.

Australian Alps: an important tourist and skiing centre

Gentle western slopes, drained by Murray, Lachlan, Murrumbidgee and Goulburn rivers

Grazing and fruit and vegetable farming on the well-watered eastern areas

Sydney

PACIFIC OCEAN

N

Coastal plain is the most densely populated region of Australia

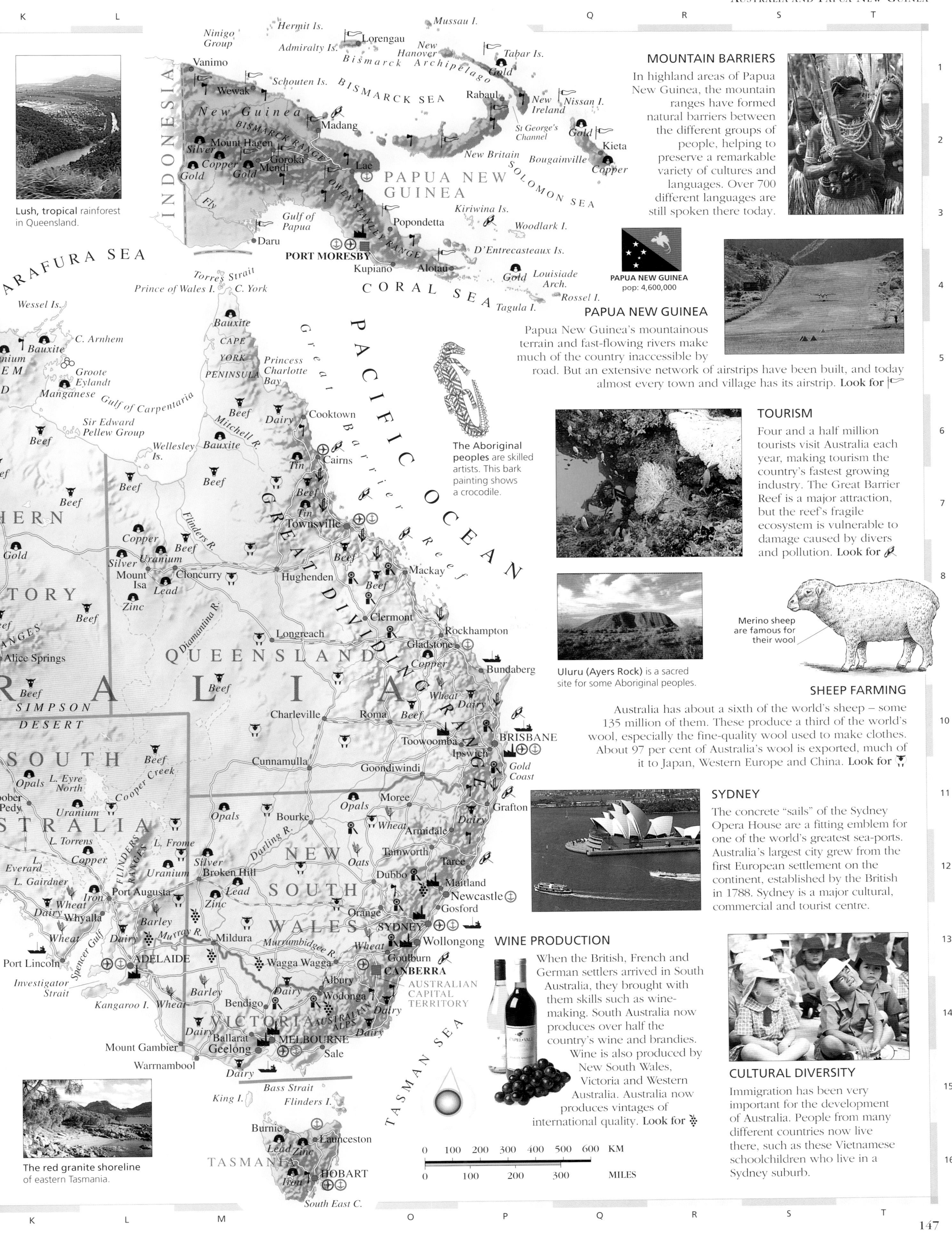
ARAFURA SEA
INDONESIA
PAPUA NEW GUINEA
New Guinea
BISMARCK SEA
Bismarck Archipelago
SOLOMON SEA
CORAL SEA
PACIFIC OCEAN
Great Barrier Reef
GREAT DIVIDING RANGE
QUEENSLAND
NEW SOUTH WALES
VICTORIA
TASMANIA
TASMAN SEA
AUSTRALIAN CAPITAL TERRITORY
PORT MORESBY
BRISBANE
SYDNEY
CANBERRA
MELBOURNE
ADELAIDE
HOBART
Gulf of Carpentaria
CAPE YORK PENINSULA
Torres Strait
Bass Strait
SIMPSON DESERT
0 100 200 300 400 500 600 KM
0 100 200 300 MILES
PAPUA NEW GUINEA
pop: 4,600,000

Lush, tropical rainforest in Queensland.

MOUNTAIN BARRIERS

In highland areas of Papua New Guinea, the mountain ranges have formed natural barriers between the different groups of people, helping to preserve a remarkable variety of cultures and languages. Over 700 different languages are still spoken there today.

PAPUA NEW GUINEA

Papua New Guinea's mountainous terrain and fast-flowing rivers make much of the country inaccessible by road. But an extensive network of airstrips have been built, and today almost every town and village has its airstrip. Look for

The Aboriginal peoples are skilled artists. This bark painting shows a crocodile.

TOURISM

Four and a half million tourists visit Australia each year, making tourism the country's fastest growing industry. The Great Barrier Reef is a major attraction, but the reef's fragile ecosystem is vulnerable to damage caused by divers and pollution. Look for

Uluru (Ayers Rock) is a sacred site for some Aboriginal peoples.

Merino sheep are famous for their wool

SHEEP FARMING

Australia has about a sixth of the world's sheep – some 135 million of them. These produce a third of the world's wool, especially the fine-quality wool used to make clothes. About 97 per cent of Australia's wool is exported, much of it to Japan, Western Europe and China. Look for

SYDNEY

The concrete "sails" of the Sydney Opera House are a fitting emblem for one of the world's greatest sea-ports. Australia's largest city grew from the first European settlement on the continent, established by the British in 1788. Sydney is a major cultural, commercial and tourist centre.

WINE PRODUCTION

When the British, French and German settlers arrived in South Australia, they brought with them skills such as wine-making. South Australia now produces over half the country's wine and brandies. Wine is also produced by New South Wales, Victoria and Western Australia. Australia now produces vintages of international quality. Look for

CULTURAL DIVERSITY

Immigration has been very important for the development of Australia. People from many different countries now live there, such as these Vietnamese schoolchildren who live in a Sydney suburb.

The red granite shoreline of eastern Tasmania.

NEW ZEALAND

NEW ZEALAND LIES deep in the southern Pacific, about halfway between the Equator and the South Pole, 1,500 km (932 miles) from Australia, its nearest large neighbour. New Zealand was one of the last places on Earth to be inhabited by people. The first settlers were Maoris from the Polynesian islands in the Pacific. They were followed by Europeans, who now make up about 86 per cent of the population. From 1840 to 1907 New Zealand was a British colony. Sheep farming was the main source of wealth. But since the 1970s – when Britain joined the EU and cut its imports from New Zealand dramatically – new markets have had to be found in Southeast Asia.

RUGBY

Rugby was first played in New Zealand in 1870. Since then it has become the country's favourite sport. The national team, the "All Blacks", are world famous. They are named after their black shirts and shorts.

The volcanic peak of Mount Ngauruhoe in North Island.

AUCKLAND

Most New Zealanders live in towns. About one-third of the population lives in the city of Auckland. It is the country's main port and industrial centre, and has the world's largest Polynesian population.

GEOTHERMAL POWER

In the volcanic region of North Island, geothermal power stations like this one tap the vast underground supplies of hot water to generate electricity. Look for ⚡

NEW ZEALAND
pop: 3,700,000

Cheddar cheese

Butter

DAIRY PRODUCTS

Huge herds of dairy cattle are kept in New Zealand, mainly on North Island. Dairy produce is an important export. Large quantities of butter and cheese are sent overseas in chilled container ships. Look for [sheep/cattle symbol]

Queen scallop

Oysters and queen scallops are bred on fish farms.

The Southern Alps in South Island.

TOURISM

Tourism is now New Zealand's largest source of foreign currency. The mild climate and spectacular scenery are ideal for trekking and the varied coastline is a sailor's paradise. National parks occupy 13 per cent of the land area. Look for [trekking symbol]

Great Exhibition Bay · Waipapakauri · Dairy · Beef · Whangarei · Great Barrier I. · Kaipara Harbour · Coromandel · Auckland · Thames · North Island · Bay of Plenty · Dairy · Tauranga · Hamilton · Beef · Rotorua · Dairy · Beef · Beef · L. Taupo · Taupo · Gisborne · New Plymouth · Mt. Ngauruhoe 2291m · Hawke Bay · Dairy · Napier · Beef · Hastings · Wanganui · Dairy · Palmerston North · Levin · Cook Strait · Dairy · Beef · Masterton · WELLINGTON · Dairy · TASMAN SEA · NEW ZEALAND · PACIFIC OCEAN · Beef · Tasman Bay · Nelson · Picton · Beef · Blenheim · Dairy · Wairau · Westport · Kaikoura · Greymouth · Hurunui · Dairy · Pegasus Bay · Beef · Christchurch · Rakaia · Beef · SOUTHERN ALPS · Beef · Canterbury Bight · Timaru · Waitaki · Milford Sound · Queenstown · L. Te Anau · L. Wakatipu · Taieri · Dairy · Beef · Dunedin · Dairy · Invercargill · Foveaux Strait · Stewart I. · South Island · N

0 50 100 150 200 250 300 KM
0 50 100 150 MILES

MAORI

Maoris make up 13 per cent of the population: the majority live in urban areas. Some, like those around Gisborne, continue their traditional way of life. Here a *haka*, or war dance, is performed.

Greenstone pendant, carved by a Maori artist.

Lemon · Apple · Kiwi fruit

FRUIT

New Zealand's mild climate is ideal for growing fruit. A lot of fruit is exported to countries in the northern hemisphere because the fruit season in New Zealand falls during the northern hemisphere's winter. Look for [mixed fruit symbol]

SHEEP

In New Zealand sheep have right of way on the roads and outnumber people 20-1. Sheep were first bred for their wool. But when refrigerated ships were developed, frozen lamb could be exported to Europe. Now exports go to the Middle East, Asia and the USA. Look for [sheep symbol]

MAP FEATURES

Timber: New Zealand has recently developed its timber industry and now exports wood pulp, chipboard and veneer. Look for [timber symbol]

Fishing: Fish, especially hoki and orange roughy, have become a major export. Shellfish farming is also being developed. Look for [fish symbol]

Cattle
Sheep

Mixed fruit
Wine

Hydro-electric power

Alternative power
Industrial centre

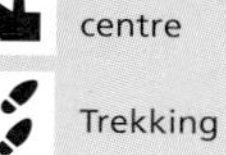

Trekking

GLOSSARY

This list provides clear and simple meanings for certain geographical and technical terms used in this atlas.

Acid rain Rain which has been made poisonous by industrial pollution.

AIDS (Acquired Immune Deficiency Syndrome). A fatal condition spread by infected blood and certain body fluids.

Alliance A union of nations, which has been agreed by treaty for economic, political or military purposes.

Alluvium Loose material, such as **silt**, sand and gravel, carried by rivers.

Alternative energy Sources of energy which can be renewed – such as solar or wind power. These forms of energy, unlike fossil fuel energy such as coal and oil, do not produce pollution.

Apartheid The policy, developed in South Africa, of separating peoples by race. Non-whites did not have the same democratic rights, and many public institutions were restricted to one race only.

Aquaculture Cultivation of fish and shellfish in lakes, **estuaries**, rivers or the sea.

Archipelago A group of islands.

Atoll A circular or horseshoe-shaped coral reef enclosing a shallow area of water.

Bilingual Speaking two languages.

Biotechnology The use of living organisms in the manufacture of food, drugs and other products. Yeast, for example, is used to make beer and bread.

Buddhism A religion that began in India in about 500 BC. It is based on the teachings of Buddha, who believed that good or evil deeds can be rewarded or punished in this life, or in other lives that will follow. Buddhists aim to achieve inner peace by living their lives according to the example set by Buddha.

Cash crop Agricultural produce grown for sale, often for foreign export, rather than to be consumed by the country or locality where it was grown.

Christianity A religion that began in the 1st century BC. Christians believe in one God and follow the teachings of Jesus Christ, whom they believe was the Son of God.

Civil war A war between rival groups of people who live in the same country.

Classical Art, architecture or literature which originated in the time of the ancient Greeks and Romans.

Colony A territory which belongs to another country. Also a group of people living separately within a country.

Communism An economic and political system of the 19th and 20th centuries in which farms, factories and the goods they produce are owned by the state.

Coniferous Trees or shrubs, like pine and fir, which have needles instead of leaves. Most are evergreen.

Conquistador The word is Spanish for "conqueror", and was applied to the Spanish explorers and invaders of Mexico and parts of South America in the 16th century.

Consumer goods Objects such as food, clothing, furniture, cars and televisions which are purchased by people for their personal and private use.

Continental plates The huge, interlocking plates which make up the Earth's surface. A plate margin is an area where two plates meet and is the point at which **earthquakes** occur most frequently.

Continental shelf The edge of a landmass which forms a shallow, raised shelf in the sea.

Cosmopolitan Influenced by foreign cultures.

Cottage industry The manufacture of products – often traditional ones like textiles or pottery – by people in their own homes.

Crude oil Oil in its original state, before chemicals and other oils have been removed by various processes in a refinery.

Crusades A series of wars from the 11th to 13th centuries when Christian European armies fought against non-Christian, often Islamic, armies for possession of the Holy Land, or Palestine.

Cultural heritage Anything handed down from a country's past, such as its traditions, art and architecture.

Currency The money of a particular country.

Deforestation The cutting of trees for timber or clearing of forest for farmland. The land is often left bare, leading to soil erosion and increasing the risk of flooding and landslides.

Democracy A political system in which everyone above a certain age has the right to vote for the election of his or her representative in the national and local government.

Desertification The creation of deserts either by changes in climate or by over-grazing, over-population, **deforestation** or over-cultivation.

Developing world Parts of the world which are still undergoing the process of industrialization.

Dictator A political leader who assumes absolute rule of a nation.

Earthquake A trembling or more violent movement of the ground caused by **seismic activity**. Earthquakes occur most frequently along **continental plate** margins.

Economy The organization of a country's finances, exports, imports, industry, agriculture and services.

Ecosystem A community of plants and animals dependent on each other and the habitat in which they live.

Electronics The use of electricity to produce signals that carry information and control devices, such as telephones or computers.

Emigrant A person who has moved from one country or region to settle in another country or region.

Empire A large group of countries ruled by one person – an emperor.

Equator An imaginary East-West line that circles the middle of the Earth at equal distance from the **Poles**. The Equator also marks the nearest point on the Earth's surface to the Sun, so it has a consistently hot climate.

Estuary The mouth of a river, where the saltwater of the tide meets the freshwater of the river.

Ethnic diversity People of several different cultures living in the same region.

Ethnic minority A group of people who share a culture, and are outnumbered by others living in the same region.

European Union (EU) (or European Community, EC) A group of European countries linked together by treaty to promote trade, industry and agriculture within a **free-market economy**.

Exports Goods produced in a country but sold abroad.

Fauna Animals of a region.

Flora Plants of a region.

Foreign debt The money owed by one country to the government, banks or institutions of one or more other countries.

Foreign exchange Money brought into a country from abroad, usually by the sale of **exports**, by **service industries** or by tourism.

Free-market economy An economy which is regulated by the price of goods bought and sold freely in national and international markets.

Geothermal energy Electricity produced from hot rocks under the Earth's surface which heat water and produce steam which can then be used to generate electricity.

Geyser A fountain of hot water or steam that erupts periodically as a result of underground streams coming into contact with hot rocks.

Greenhouse effect A rise in the global temperature caused as heat, reflected and radiated from the Earth's surface, is trapped in the atmosphere by a build up of "greenhouse" gases, such as carbon dioxide. Also called "global warming".

Habitat A place or region where a certain animal or plant usually lives.

Heavy industry Industry that uses large amounts of energy and raw materials to produce heavy goods, such as machinery, ships or locomotives.

Hunter-gatherers People who do not grow their food, but obtain it by hunting it and gathering it from their environment. There are few hunter-gatherer groups left in the world today.

Hydro-electric power (HEP) Electricity produced by harnessing the force of falling water.

ICBM (Inter-continental Ballistic Missile) A missile, usually with a nuclear warhead, that can be fired from one continent to land in another.

Immigrant A person who has come to live in a country from another country or region.

Incentives Something that arouses or encourages people to greater efforts.

Inflation The rate at which a country's prices increase.

Informal economy An economy in which people buy and sell from each other, not through shops or markets.

Infrastructure The buildings, transport and communication links that enable goods to be produced and then moved about within a country.

Irrigation A system of watering dry areas. Water is carried or pumped to the area through pipes or channels.

Islam A religion revealed to the prophet Mohammed in the 7th century AD in the Middle East. Its followers, called Muslims (or Moslems), believe in one God, called Allah. The rules and beliefs of Islam are contained in its holy book, the *Koran*.

Islamic fundamentalist A person who strictly follows the rules and beliefs of Islam contained in the holy book, the *Koran*. See **Islam**.

Isthmus A narrow piece of land, connecting two larger bodies of land, surrounded on two sides by water.

Labour intensive An activity which requires large amounts of work or large numbers of workers to accomplish it.

Lent A period of time lasting 40 days observed by Christians during which they fast and prepare for the festival of Easter.

Lignite Woody or brown coal.

Living standards The quality of life in a country, usually measured by income, material possessions, and levels of education and health care.

Malnutrition A prolonged lack of adequate food.

Market gardening Farms and **smallholdings** growing fruit and vegetables for sale.

Megalopolis A very large or continuous urban area in which several large towns or cities have joined as their urban areas have spread.

Metropolis A major city, often the capital.

Militarized zone An area occupied by armed military forces.

Multi-national company A company which has branches, or factories, in several countries.

Nationalists Groups of people united in their wish for independence from a government or from foreign rule.

Neutral country A country which refrains from taking part in international conflicts.

Nomad A person who does not settle in one place for any length of time, but moves in search of hunting or grazing land.

Oil shale Flaky rock containing oil.

Pastoralist A person who makes a living from grazing livestock.

Peat Decomposed vegetation found in bogs. It can be dried and used as fuel.

Peninsula A strip of land surrounded on three sides by water.

Permafrost Permanently frozen ground. The surface thaws in summer but water cannot drain away through the frozen subsurface. Typical of **subarctic** areas.

Pharmaceuticals The manufacture of medicinal drugs.

Plantation A large farm on which only one crop is usually grown.

Plate margin See **Continental plates**.

Polar regions The regions around the North and South Poles which are permanently frozen and where the temperature only rises above freezing point for a few months of the year.

Poles, the The term applied to the North and South Poles, the northernmost and southernmost points of the Earth's axis or rotation.

Prairie A Spanish/American term for a large area of grassland.

Privatization When state-owned activities and companies are taken over by private firms.

Protestant A member of one of the main Christian religions founded in the 16th century by those who did not agree with all aspects of the Roman Catholic Church. Protestantism became one of the main branches of **Christianity**.

Quota A maximum quantity imposed on the number of goods produced, imported or exported by a country.

Rainforest Dense forest found in hot and humid equatorial regions; often called tropical rainforest.

Raw materials Substances in a natural or unrefined state used in the manufacture of goods, like cotton for textiles and bauxite for aluminium.

Refugees People who flee their own country or region because of political, religious or racial persecution.

Republic The form of government in a country that has no monarch. The head of state is usually a president, like the President of the USA.

Reservation An area of land set aside for occupation by specific people, plants or animals.

Revenue Money paid to a government, like taxes.

Roman Catholic A Christian who accepts the Pope as his or her spiritual leader.

Rural In, or belonging to, the countryside.

Savannah Tropical grasslands where an annual dry season prevents the growth of most trees.

Seismic activity Tremors and shocks in the Earth's crust usually caused by the movement of plates along a fault.

Service industry An industry that supplies services, such as banking, rather than producing manufactured goods.

Shanty town An area in or around a city where people live in temporary shacks, usually without basic facilities such as running water.

Silt Small particles, finer than sand, often carried by water and deposited on river banks, at river mouths and harbours. See also **alluvium**.

Smallholding A plot of agricultural land smaller than a farm.

Socialism Political system whereby the economy is owned and controlled by the state and not by private companies or individuals.

Soviet bloc All those countries which were ruled directly or indirectly by the communist government of the former USSR.

Staple crop The main crop grown in a region.

Staple food The basic part of a diet, such as rice or bread.

Steppes An extensive, grass-covered and virtually treeless plain, such as those found in Siberia.

Stock Exchange A place where people buy and sell government bonds, **currency**, stocks and financial shares in large private companies.

Strategic Carefully planned or well placed from a military point of view.

Subarctic The climate in **polar** regions, characterized by extremely cold temperatures and long winters.

Technological The application of science through the use of machines.

Temperate The mild, variable climate found in areas between the **tropics** and cold **polar** regions.

Tropic of Cancer, Capricorn Two imaginary lines of latitude drawn on the Earth's surface above and below the **Equator**. The hottest parts of the world are between these two lines.

Tropics, the An area between the **Equator** and the **tropics of Cancer and Capricorn** that has heavy rainfall and high temperatures and lacks any clear seasonal variation.

Tundra Vegetation found in areas within the Arctic Circle, such as dwarf bushes, very short grasses, mosses and lichens.

United Nations (UN) An association of countries established to work together to prevent wars, and to supply aid, advice and research on an international basis.

Urban area Town, city or extensive built-up area.

West, the Those countries in Europe and North America with **free-market economies** and **democratic** governments.

Western The economic, cultural and political values shared by countries belonging to **the West**.

PICTURE CREDITS:

Bruce Coleman Ltd: back jacket tr. **Tony Stone Images:** back jacket tl. **3 J.R.Chapman:** bl. **7 Image Bank:** cml. **7 Science Photo Library:** David Parker cr; Martin Bas cmr. **7 Tony Waltham:** cl. **8 Robert Harding Picture Library:** tr, br, ctr. **8 Tony Stone Images:** cbr. **9 Robert Harding Picture Library:** tr. **9 Oxford Scientific Films:** br. **9 Tony Stone Images:** brc, trc. **10 FLPA - Images of nature:** tr. **10 Pictor International:** cr. **10 Tony Stone Images:** ct. **11 Bruce Coleman Ltd:** bl, blc. **11 Environmental Images:** tr. **11 Robert Harding Picture Library:** tr, clt. **11 Pictor International:** ctr. **11 Planet Earth Pictures:** tc. **11 Science Photo Library:** br. **12 Colorific!:** cl. **12 Robert Harding Picture Library:** cr. **12 Pictor International:** c. **12 Tony Stone Images:** b. **13 Colorific!:** tl. **13 Robert Harding Picture Library:** ct. **13 Image Bank:** bl. **13 Tony Stone Images:** bc. **17 FLPA - Images of nature:** Bruce Henry tr; Roger Wilmshurst bl. **17 Pictor International:** cr. **18 Camera Press:** tc. **18 Robert Harding Picture Library:** tr. **18 Pictor International:** cl. **19 Camera Press:** bl. **20 DK Picture Library:** Kim Sayer ct; Rob Reichenfeld br, lc. **20 Eye Ubiquitous:** D.Burrows cb; Paul Thompson lcb. **20 Robert Harding Picture Library:** tc; Christopher Nicholson bc; Roy Rainford bl. **20 Pictor International:** tr. **21 James Davis Travel Photography:** cl. **21 DK Picture Library:** tc, rc; Stephen Oliver rc. **21 Eye Ubiquitous:** Geoff Redmayne tr; Paul Bennett cr. **21 Robert Harding Picture Library:** bl; Rob Cousins tl. **22 DK Picture Library:** tc, c, ct. **22 Eye Ubiquitous:** Paul Thompson cbl. **22 Robert Harding Picture Library:** bl; David Hunter cb. **22 Panos Pictures:** Penny Tweedy rc. **22 Pictor International:** tr, bl. **23 DK Picture Library:** cr; Rob Reichenfeld tr. **23 Robert Harding Picture Library:** A.Williams bc; Rolf Richardson br; Roy Rainford rc. **23 N.H.P.A.:** Bill Coster cl. **23 Pictor International:** tl, bl, tcl, tcr. **24 Allsport:** Ben Radford br. **24 DK Picture Library:** cr; Joe Cornish tr. **24 Eye Ubiquitous:** A.J.G. Bell cl. **24 Robert Harding Picture Library:** lc; G.R. Richardson bl; Roy Rainford rt; Simon Harris tc. **24 Pictor International:** cb. **25 Collections:** Brian Shuel cb; Roger Scruton lc, rct. **25 DK Picture Library:** ct, rcb; Joe Cornish bl. **25 Robert Harding Picture Library:** Roy Rainford tl. **25 Panos Pictures:** Paulk Quayle c. **25 Pictor International:** tc, br. **25 Rex Features:** tr. **26 Allsport:** Andrew Redington tc. **26 Collections:** Collier's br. **26 James Davis Travel Photography:** lcb. **26 DK Picture Library:** cb. **26 Robert Harding Picture Library:** tr; Gavin Heller tr; R. Oulds crt. **26 N.H.P.A.:** Jane Gifford crb. **26 Panos Pictures:** Philip Welmuth bc. **26 Pictor International:** lc. **26 Rex Features:** Nils Jorgensen c. **27 DK Picture Library:** cb, bl. **27 Robert Harding Picture Library:** David Hunter tr; Duncan Maxwell rc. **27 N.H.P.A.:** Jane Gifford c. **27 Welsh Tourist Board:** br. **28 Collections:** Colin Inch rc. **28 James Davis Travel Photography:** c. **28 DK Picture Library:** ct, rct. **28 Eye Ubiquitous:** Marcus Stace bl. **28 Robert Harding Picture Library:** lc; Louise Murray tr. **28 N.H.P.A.:** Manfred Danegger cr; Roger Tidman tc. **29 Colorific!:** rc. **29 James Davis Travel Photography:** bc. **29 DK Picture Library:** Joe Cornish tl, clb. **29 Environmental Images:** Graham Burns lc. **29 N.H.P.A.:** Band C.Alexander tr. **29 Pictor International:** clt. **29 Telegraph Colour Library:** bl. **30 Collections:** Michael St Maur Shell ct. **30 James Davis Travel Photography:** trb. **30 DK Picture Library:** tr, lcb. **30 Eye Ubiquitous:** Tim Durham tc. **30 Robert Harding Picture Library:** c; Gavin Heller bc. **30 Hutchison Library:** lc. **30 Pictor International:** cb, crb. **31 Collections:** Michael Diggin bc. **31 James Davis Travel Photography:** tc. **31 DK Picture Library:** cb, bl, rcb; Alan Williams tr, rct; Tim Daly c. **31 Robert Harding Picture Library:** H.P.Merten br. **32 Hutchison Library:** bl. **32 FLPA - Images of Nature:** Terry Whittaker br. **32 N.H.P.A.:** Roger Tidman cr. **32 Planet Earth Pictures:** Margaret Welby cl. **32 Science Photo Library:** Simon Fraser tr. **35 Bruce Coleman Ltd:** tl, br, crc. **35 Planet Earth Pictures:** bl. **35 Tony Stone Images:** tc, cr, bc. **35 Zefa Picture Library:** clc. **36 Image Bank:** bc, ctr. **36 Magnum:** br. **36 Pictor International:** br. **36 Zefa Picture Library:** tr, cl. **37 Robert Estall Photo Library:** b. **37 Robert Harding Picture Library:** br. **37 Image Bank:** tl. **37 Pictor International:** tr. **38 Bryan And Cherry Alexander Photography:** tr. **38 James Davis Travel Photography:** b. **38 Paul Harris Photography:** bc. **38 Hutchison Library:** cl. **38 Tony Stone Images:** ca. **39 Bryan And Cherry Alexander Photography:** tr. **39 Still Pictures:** tc. **40 Bruce Coleman Ltd:** b. **40 Robert Harding Picture Library:** cr. **40 Magnum:** c. **41 Bruce Coleman Ltd:** tl, cr. **41 Robert Harding Picture Library:** tc, bl. **41 Zefa Picture Library:** bc. **42 Image Bank:** cl. **42 Images Colour Library:** bc. **42 Impact Photos:** bl. **42 Magnum:** br. **42 Pictor International:** ctc. **42 Tony Stone Images:** tr. **43 Robert Harding Picture Library:** bl. **43 Image Bank:** br. **43 Life File:** cl. **43 Tony Stone Images:** tr. **43 Zefa Picture Library:** cr. **44 Bruce Coleman Ltd:** cl. **44 Tony Stone Images:** cl, br, b. **45 The J. Allan Cash Photolibrary:** tr. **45 Image Bank:** bc. **45 Pictor International:** br. **45 Zefa Picture Library:** tl. **46 Bruce Coleman Ltd:** cl. **46 Colorific!:** c. **46 Pictor International:** br. **46 Tony Stone Images:** tr. **47 Colorific!:** c, cr. **47 Pictor International:** bl. **47 Tony Stone Images:** tl, tr. **48 Robert Harding Picture Library:** tr, br. **48 Image Bank:** cl. **48 Tony Stone Images:** c. **49 Bruce Coleman Ltd:** cr. **49 Robert Harding Picture Library:** cr. **49 Image Bank:** tr, bl. **50 The J. Allan Cash Photolibrary:** t. 50 Image Bank: cl. **50 Tony Stone Images:** cr, bl.

51 Image Bank: tr. **51 Tony Stone Images:** tl, tc, cl, bl. **52 The J. Allan Cash Photolibrary:** cr. **52 Bruce Coleman Ltd:** tc. **52 Still Pictures:** cb. **53 Robert Harding Picture Library:** cr, cb, bl, bc, tcr. **54 Bruce Coleman Ltd:** cl, crt. **54 Mountain Camera / John Cleare:** bl. **54 Oxford Scientific Films:** cr, crb. **54 Tony Stone Images:** tr, cb. **54 Alan Watson/forest Light:** ca. **54 World Wildlife Fund:** br. **55 Tony Stone Images:** bl. **56 The J. Allan Cash Photolibrary:** cl, bl. **56 Robert Harding Picture Library:** cr. **56 Hutchinson Library:** tr. **56 Image Bank:** br. **57 Robert Harding Picture Library:** tc, bl. **57 Hutchison Library:** cbr. **57 Image Bank:** tr, cr, cbl. **58 The J. Allan Cash Photolibrary:** b. **58 Hutchison Library:** tc. **58 Life File:** tl. **58 South American Pictures:** b. **59 Lynn Edelman:** bc. **59 Robert Harding Picture Library:** tc, cl. **59 Magnum:** tc. **59 Oxford Scientific Films:** clb. **59 Quadrant Picture Library:** tr. **59 South American Pictures:** bl. **60 James Davis Travel Photography:** b. **60 Robert Harding Picture Library:** tc, tr. **60 Panos Pictures:** c. **61 Robert Harding Picture Library:** tl, bl. **61 Image Bank:** tr. **61 Pictor International:** cr. **61 Tony Stone Images:** cr. **62 Life File:** l. **62 Lupe Cunha:** tc. **62 Pictor International:** tr. **63 Cephas Picture Library:** cl. **63 Anne Clarke:** bl. **63 Robert Harding Picture Library:** cr, br. **63 Hutchison Library:** tl. **63 Oxford Scientific Films:** bcr. **63 South American Pictures:** tr. **64 Bruce Coleman Ltd:** cl, cr, bl. **64 Image Bank:** tc. **64 Tony Stone Images:** br. **65 Bryan And Cherry Alexander Photography:** tr. **65 Bruce Coleman Ltd:** bc. **65 Robert Harding Picture Library:** br. **65 Image Bank:** cbl. **65 Tony Stone Images:** tcr. **65 Zefa Picture Library:** ct. **66 Robert Harding Picture Library:** cl. **66 Hutchison Library:** c. **66 Panos Pictures:** cr. **66 Tony Stone Images:** tc, tr. **67 James Davis Travel Photography:** cr, bl. **67 Robert Harding Picture Library:** bc. **67 Magnum:** tr. **67 Pirelli Cables:** br. **67 Tony Stone Images:** bcr. **69 Ecoscene:** tl. **69 Pictor International:** crc. **69 Science Photo Library:** tc, cr, bl. **69 Spectrum Colour Library:** tr, bc, clc. **69 Tony Stone Images:** cl, br. **70 The J. Allan Cash Photolibrary:** tl, bc. **70 Robert Harding Picture Library:** cl, c, tcl. **71 The J. Allan Cash Photolibrary:** bl, br, cbr. **71 Zefa Picture Library:** tr. **72 The J. Allan Cash Photolibrary:** tr. **72 DK Picture Library:** bc. **72 Frank Spooner Pictures:** Kelvin Boyes cl. **72 Tony Stone Images:** c. **73 Pictor International:** cl. **73 Tony Stone Images:** cr, bl, bc, br. **74 The J. Allan Cash Photolibrary:** bl. **74 Image Bank:** bc. **74 Life File:** tr. **74 Tim Motion:** c. **75 The J. Allan Cash Photolibrary:** c, bl, bc. **75 Images Colour Library:** cr, br. **76 The J. Allan Cash Photolibrary:** cr. **76 Robert Harding Picture Library:** c. **76 Tim Motion:** cr. **76 Panos Pictures:** br. **76 Tony Stone Images:** tc. **77 Max Alexander:** tr. **77 Robert Harding Picture Library:** c, cr, b. **78 Robert Harding Picture Library:** c. **78 Tony Stone Images:** b. **79 Bruce Coleman Ltd:** cl, br. **80 Robert Harding Picture Library:** tr, c. **80 Impact Photos:** tc. **80 Magnum:** cr. **81 Robert Harding Picture Library:** tl. **81 Image Bank:** br. **81 Tony Stone Images:** bl, bc. **82 The J. Allan Cash Photolibrary:** bl. **82 Robert Harding Picture Library:** tr, cl, c, cr. **83 James Davis Travel Photography:** bl. **83 Hutchison Library:** Crispin Hughes br. **83 Image Bank:** tc, bcl. **83 Tony Stone Images:** bc. **84 Impact Photos:** bl. **84 Panos Pictures:** ct. **84 Tony Stone Images:** c. **84 Zefa Picture Library:** tr. **85 The J. Allan Cash Photolibrary:** c. **85 Bruce Coleman Ltd:** bl. **85 Impact Photos:** tr. **85 Tony Stone Images:** bc, br. **85 Travel Photo International:** tc. **86 Comstock:** c. **86 Tony Stone Images:** tr. **86 Telegraph Colour Library:** bc. **87 Bruce Coleman Ltd:** cl. **87 Hutchison Library:** bl. **87 Tony Stone Images:** tc. **87 Zefa Picture Library:** br. **88 Bruce Coleman Ltd:** cl. **88 Colorific!:** cr. **88 Image Bank:** c. **88 Tony Stone Images:** bc, br. **89 Bruce Coleman Ltd:** br. **89 Colorific!:** bc. **89 Robert Harding Picture Library:** tc. **89 Image Bank:** c. **89 Frank Spooner Pictures:** Alain Buu-Noel Quidu tr. **90 The J. Allan Cash Photolibrary:** c, b. **90 Robert Harding Picture Library:** cr. **90 Jim Henderson:** cr. **91 Robin Hanbury Tennison:** cbr. **91 Robert Harding Picture Library:** tl, tc, clb. **91 Andrew J Lambert:** clb. **91 Pictor International:** br. **92 The J. Allan Cash Photolibrary:** bl. **92 Robert Harding Picture Library:** ct. **93 Robert Harding Picture Library:** tr, c, crb. **93 Hutchison Library:** clt. **93 Life File:** b. **93 Tony Stone Images:** cr. **94 Robert Harding Picture Library:** cr. **94 Panos Pictures:** Dermot Tatlow cl. **94 Zefa Picture Library:** c. **95 Hutchison Library:** cl, c. **95 John Massey Stewart:** tl. **95 Woodfall Wild Images:** b. **95 Zefa Picture Library:** tr. **96 Paul Harris Photography:** bl. **96 Tony Stone Images:** tc. **96 Survival Anglia Photo Library:** c. **97 Bruce Coleman Ltd:** tl. **97 Paul Harris Photography:** br. **97 Panos Pictures:** Tyrone Wheatcroft rc. **97 Zefa Picture Library:** tr. **98 Colorific!:** tl, c. **98 Zefa Picture Library:** bc. **99 Robert Harding Picture Library:** tr, brt. **99 Hutchison Library:** cr. **99 Image Bank:** bc. **99 Sygma:** cr. **100 Heather Angel:** ct. **100 Bruce Coleman Ltd:** ctr. **100 International Confederation for Conservation Education:** ctr. **100 N.H.P.A.:** bl. **100 Pictor International:** cb, br. **100 Tony Stone Images:** tr, cr. **101 Nature Photographers:** bl. **102 Image Bank:** tc. **102 J.R.Chapman:** br, btr. **102 Pippa Hurst:** cl. **102 Frank Spooner Pictures:** c. **103 Bruce Coleman Ltd:** tl. **103 James Davis Travel Photography:** ctr. **103 Robert Harding Picture Library:** tr, ct. **103 International Confederation for Conservation Education:** bl. **103 Anne Jousiffe:** br. **103 Magnum:** cb. **104 Chris Fairclough Colour Library:** ctr. **104 Robert Harding Picture Library:** br. **104 Magnum:** lb. **104 Pictor International:** tr. **104 Tony Stone Images:** ctl. **105 Robert Harding Picture Library:** bl. **105 Magnum:** tr, bl. **105 Zefa Picture Library:** bc. **106 The J. Allan Cash Photolibrary:** c. **106 Hutchison Library:** bc. **106 Magnum:** cl, br. **107 The J. Allan Cash Photolibrary:** br. **107 Bruce Coleman Ltd:** tc. **107 Robert Harding Picture Library:** bc. **107 Kaleidescope:** crb. **107 Mark Chapman:** tl. **107 Still Pictures:** tr. **107 World Wildlife Fund:** crt. **108 The J. Allan Cash Photolibrary:** cl. **108 Colorific!:** r. **108 Robert Harding Picture Library:** cr. **108 World Wildlife Fund:** bcl. **108 Zefa Picture Library:** br. **109 Bruce Coleman Ltd:** tl. **109 Robert Harding Picture Library:** ctl. **109 Hutchison Library:** cl. **109 Still Pictures:** c, bl, bl. **110 Impact Photos:** ctr. **110 J.R.Chapman:** tr. **110 Catherine Lucas:** cr. **110 Tony Stone Images:** cl. **110 Zefa Picture Library:** b. **111 Impact Photos:** tcr. **111 Nature Photographers:** tl. **111 Zefa Picture Library:** rcb. **112 Bruce Coleman Ltd:** cr. **112 Robert Harding Picture Library:** cb. **112 Magnum:** ct. **112 Nature Photographers:** cl. **112 Pictor International:** bc. **113 Bruce Coleman Ltd:** cb, b. **113 Colorific!:** c. **113 Steven J. Cooling:** ct. **113 Robert Harding Picture Library:** tl, crb. **113 Frank Spooner Pictures:** Paul Velasco rct. **113 Telegraph Colour Library:** tr. **114 The J. Allan Cash Photolibrary:** br. **114 Robert Harding Picture Library:** tc. **114 Hutchison Library:** cr. **114 Image Bank:** bl. **114 Tony Stone Images:** tr, tcr. **115 Bruce Coleman Ltd:** tl. **115 Hutchison Library:** tr. **115 Military and research services:** cl. **115 Pictor International:** bc. **115 Tony Stone Images:** br. **116 Colorific!:** ctl. **116 Environmental Images:** ctr. **116 Robert Harding Picture Library:** ct. **116 Hutchison Library:** br. **116 FLPA - Images of nature:** cbr. **116 Magnum:** bl, rcb. **116 Pictor International:** cbl. **116 Planet Earth Pictures:** tr. **117 Impact Photos:** bl. **117 Planet Earth Pictures:** tl. **118 The J. Allan Cash Photolibrary:** ct, lc. **118 Robert Harding Picture Library:** cb, brc. **118 Hutchison Library:** c, bl. **118 Tony Stone Images:** tr. **119 The J. Allan Cash Photolibrary:** br. **119 Robert Harding Picture Library:** c, bl. **119 Zefa Picture Library:** cr. **120 Stephanie Colasanti:** cr. **120 Chris Fairclough Colour Library:** c. **120 Zefa Picture Library:** tr. **121 James Davis Travel Photography:** c. **121 Sonia Halliday Photographs:** br. **121 Robert Harding Picture Library:** cr. **121 Hutchison Library:** bl. **121 Panos Pictures:** Morris Carpenter tl. **121 Survival Anglia Photo Library:** bc. **122 The J. Allan Cash Photolibrary:** bl, br. **122 Robert Harding Picture Library:** c. **122 Magnum:** tr. **122 Survival Anglia Photo Library:** cb. **122 Zefa Picture Library:** ct. **123 The J. Allan Cash Photolibrary:** tr, crb. **123 Magnum:** tc, bl. **123 Whitwell:** cra. **123 Zefa Picture Library:** bl. **124 The J. Allan Cash Photolibrary:** br. **124 Robert Harding Picture Library:** cl. **124 A. Hyman:** cr. **125 Robert Harding Picture Library:** b. **125 Image Bank:** crb. **125 John Pilkington:** cra. **125 Tony Stone Images:** tr, c. **126 Hutchison Library:** bl. **126 Life File:** tl. **126 Science Photo Library:** bl. **127 Paul Harris Photography:** tc, tr, br. **27 Hutchison Library:** rc. **127 Impact Photos:** bc. **128 The J. Allan Cash Photolibrary:** tr. **128 Bruce Coleman Ltd:** cl, bl, clt, ct. **128 Impact Photos:** br. **128 N.H.P.A.:** cr. **128 Tony Stone Images:** cla, c. **129 Robert Harding Picture Library:** tl. **130 Chris Fairclough Colour Library:** cl. **130 Ronald Grant Archive:** bc. **130 Robert Harding Picture Library:** bl, br, ct. **130 J.R.Chapman:** cr. **131 The J. Allan Cash Photolibrary:** cr. **131 Duncan Brown:** bl. **131 Chris Fairclough Colour Library:** c, tc. **131 J.R.Chapman:** tl. **132 Bruce Coleman Ltd:** br. **132 Paul Harris Photography:** tr. **132 Jimmy Holmes Himalayan Images:** cl, c. **133 Robert Harding Picture Library:** tl. **133 Paul Harris Photography:** cl. **133 Jimmy Holmes Himalayan Images:** cr. **133 Image Bank:** bl. **133 Magnum:** br. **133 Panos Pictures:** tr. **134 The J. Allan Cash Photolibrary:** crb. **134 Colorific!:** ct. **134 Image Bank:** tr, br. **134 Tony Stone Images:** bl. **134 Travel Photo International:** clb. **135 Bruce Coleman Ltd:** brb. **135 Robert Harding Picture Library:** cbl. **135 Hutchison Library:** cra. **135 Tony Stone Images:** tl, crb, b. **135 Telegraph Colour Library:** tr. **136 Bruce Coleman Ltd:** tr. **136 Eye Ubiquitous:** tl. **136 Paul Harris Photography:** c. **136 Image Bank:** cl. **136 Magnum:** bl. **136 Telegraph Colour Library:** cr. **137 The J. Allan Cash Photolibrary:** cb. **137 Jimmy Holmes Himalayan Images:** tl. **137 Image Bank:** tr. **137 Magnum:** cl. **137 Tony Stone Images:** b, ct. **138 Robert Harding Picture Library:** tc, cr. **138 Pictor International:** c. **138 Chris Whitwell:** tr. **139 Robert Harding Picture Library:** tl, c, bl, br, rct. **140 Bruce Coleman Ltd:** clb, b. **140 Robert Harding Picture Library:** tr, rtc. **140 Impact Photos:** c. **141 The J. Allan Cash Photolibrary:** tc. **141 Robert Harding Picture Library:** cr. **141 Images Colour Library:** cb. **142 Hutchison Library:** tl. **142 Images Colour Library:** cl, crc. **142 Pictor International:** bl. **142 Tony Stone Images:** tc, tr, cr, br, clc. **143 Tony Stone Images:** bl. **144 Bruce Coleman Ltd:** cb, lcb, rcb. **144 Image Bank:** ct. **144 N.H.P.A.:** tr. **144 Tony Stone Images:** b, rct. **145 Bruce Coleman Ltd:** crb. **145 Hutchison Library:** tc, tr. **145 Image Bank:** br. **145 Pictor International:** crt. **146 Tony Stone Images:** cl. **146 Sydney Freelance:** b. **147 Colorific!:** tl, tr, bl. **147 Robert Harding Picture Library:** ctr. **147 N.H.P.A.:** ca. **147 Tony Stone Images:** cb, cb. **148 Steven J. Cooling:** bl. **148 N.H.P.A.:** cla. **148 New Zealand Tourist Office:** rc. **148 Tony Stone Images.**

INDEX

Throughout the Atlas, population figures have been taken from the latest official estimates.

HOW TO USE THE GRID

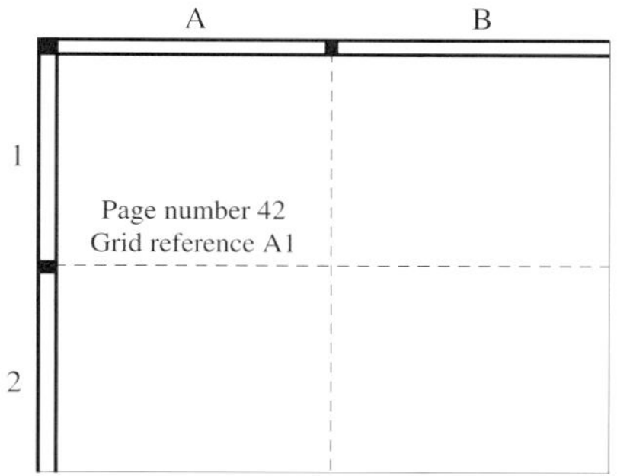
A
B
1
2
Page number 42
Grid reference A1

Grid references in the Index help you to find places on the map. For example, if you look up Nairobi in the Index, you will see the reference 111 O5. The first number, 111, is the page number of the map on which Nairobi appears. Find the letters and numbers which border the page, and trace a line across from the letter and down from the number. This directs you to the exact grid square in which Nairobi is located.
The numbers that appear after the names are the page numbers, followed by the grid references.
In the country factboxes throughout the index, many statistics are not yet available for the new states of the world. When we have been unable to find the correct figure, N/A is given, which stands for not available.

Population density
This is the total population divided by the land area of a country.

Average life expectancy
This is the average life expectancy at birth, barring war or natural disasters.

Literacy
This is the percentage of people over the age of 15 years who can read and write a simple sentence. Where figures for male (m) and female (f) have not been available, we have used an average (av.).

Death penalty
The countries with 'Yes' use the death penalty regularly. Some of the states with 'No' still have a law permitting the death penalty but do not use it.

Percentage of urban population
This is the percentage of the total population who live in towns or cities.

Calories consumed daily
The recommended daily number for a healthy life is about 2500 calories; the inhabitants of some countries consume far more than others.

The following abbreviations have been used in the index:

anc. = ancient name
Arch. = Archipelago
C. = Cape
E. = East
Ft. = Fort
I. = Island
Is. = Islands
L. = Lake
Mt. = Mountain
Mts. = Mountains
N. = North
N.P. = National Park
Pen. = Peninsula
prev. = previously
Pt. = Point
Res. = Reservoir
R. = River
S. = South
St. = Saint
var. = variant name
W. = West

A

A Coruña (Eng. Corunna) Spain 66 J8 74 G3
Aachen Germany 81 C11
Aalst Belgium 79 F14
Aarau Switzerland 82 F9
Aare *River* Switzerland 82 F9
Aba Nigeria 107 O13
Abadan Iran 123 L7
Abajo Mountains *Mountain range* Utah, USA 49 K5
Abakan Russian Federation 129 K11
Abashiri Japan 136 M3
Abéché Chad 108 K7
Abengourou Ivory Coast 107 K13
Åbenrå Denmark 70 H15
Abeokuta Nigeria 107 N12
Aberaeron Wales, United Kingdom 27 K9
Abercraf Wales, United Kingdom 27 M12
Aberdare Wales, United Kingdom 27 N13
Aberdare Range *Mountain range* Kenya 111 O5
Aberdaron Wales, United Kingdom 26 I5
Aberdeen Scotland, United Kingdom 28 N10
Aberdeen South Dakota, USA 47 N6
Aberdeen Washington, USA 50 G7
Aberdeen Scotland, United Kingdom 18 K7
Aberdeenshire Scotland, United Kingdom 18 J7
Aberdour *Beach* Scotland, United Kingdom 32 F7
Aberdyfi Wales, United Kingdom 27 L7
Aberfeldy Scotland, United Kingdom 29 K12
Abergavenny Wales, United Kingdom 27 O12
Aberkenfig Wales, United Kingdom 27 M14
Abersoch Wales, United Kingdom 26 J5
Abertillery Wales, United Kingdom 27 O13
Aberystwyth Wales, United Kingdom 27 L8
Abha Saudi Arabia 122 H13
Abidjan Ivory Coast 107 K13
Abilene Texas, USA 49 P10
Abingdon England, United Kingdom 21 N5
Abitibi, Lake *Lake* Ontario, Canada 39 K11
Abomey Benin 107 M12
Abu Dhabi United Arab Emirates 123 N11
Abu Simbel *Ancient monument* Egypt 104 F10
Abuja Nigeria 107 O11
Abydos *Archaeological site* Egypt 104 F8
Acapulco Mexico 52 M13
Accra Ghana 107 L13
Accrington England, United Kingdom 24 J14
Acheloos *River* Greece 92 H7
Achill Head *Headland* Republic of Ireland 30 H6
Achill Sound Republic of Ireland 30 I7
Achinsk Russian Federation 129 K10
Acklins Island *Island* Bahamas 57 M5
Aconcagua, Cerro *Mountain* Argentina 55
Ad Dafrah *Desert* United Arab Emirates 123 M11
Ad Dahna' Saudi Arabia 123 K9
Ad Dakhla Western Sahara 102 E9
Ad Damman Saudi Arabia 123 M9
Ad Diwaniyah Iraq 123 K5
Adak Island *Island* Alaska, USA 36 A6
Adamawa Highlands *Mountain range* Cameroon 101
Adana Turkey 119 M9
Adapazarı Turkey 118 J5
Adare, Cape *Cape* Antarctica 64 E12
Addis Ababa Ethiopia 105 J15
Adelaide South Australia, Australia 147 L13
Adelaide Island *Island* Antarctica 64 B8
Aden Yemen 122 I16 114 E7
Aden, Gulf of *Gulf* Indian Ocean 101 105 M14 114 E7 117 127
Adige *River* Italy 86 H7
Adiri Libya 103 O8
Adirondack Mountains *Mountain range* New York, USA 40 K8
Adıyaman Turkey 119 O8
Admiralty Islands *Island group* Papua New Guinea 147 N1
Adrar Algeria 102 J8
Adrian Michigan, USA 45 O10
Adrianople *see* Edirne
Adriatic Sea *Sea* Mediterranean Sea 68 86 I8 88 F5
Adwa Ethiopia 105 J13
Adycha *River* Russian Federation 129 O6
Aegean Sea *Sea* Mediterranean Sea 68 93 L5
Aeolian Islands *Island group* Italy 87 K16
Afghanistan *Country* C Asia 124 I12

Afghanistan 124-125

1919 • a Persian and Pashtu • Afghani • 34 • 45 • 13 • 31.5 • N/A • 7358 • Yes • 20 • 1523

Africa *Continent* 100-101
Africa, Horn of *Physical region* Ethiopia/Somalia 105 N14
African Plate *Tectonic plate* 34 55 68 101 117 127
Afrin Syria 121 N2
Afyon Turkey 118 J7
Agadez Niger 107 O7
Agadir Morocco 102 G6
Agartala India 131 P8
Agattu Island *Island* Alaska, USA 36 A4
Agen France 77 K13
Agios Efstratios *Island* Greece 93 M6
Agios Nikolaos Greece 93 N16
Agra India 131 K6
Ağrı Turkey 119 S6
Agri *River* Italy 87 M14
Agrigento Italy 87 J18
Aguarico, Río *River* Ecuador/Peru 58 D8
Aguascalientes Mexico 53 L10
Agulhas Basin *Undersea basin* Indian Ocean 101
Agulhas, Cape *Headland* South Africa 101 112 J16
Ahaggar *Plateau* Algeria 101 103 M10
Ahmadabad India 130 I7
Ahvaz Iran 123 M6
Aïr, Massif de l' *Mountain range* Niger 107 P7
Airdrie Scotland, United Kingdom 29 K14
Aire *River* England, United Kingdom 25 M14
Aix-en-Provence France 77 O13
Aizawl India 131 Q7
Ajaccio France 77 S16
Ajdabiya Libya 103 Q7
Ajmer India 130 J6
Akagera *National Park* Rwanda 111 L5
Akanthoú Cyprus 119
Akhisar Turkey 118 H7
Akita Japan 136 K7
Akola India 131 K9
Akron Ohio, USA 45 Q10
Aksai Chin *Disputed region* China/India 130 L1 132 E10
Aksaray Turkey 119 L8
Akseki Turkey 118 J9
Aksu China 132 F7
Aksum Ethiopia 105 J13
Aktau Kazakhstan 128 D10
Aktyubinsk Kazakhstan 128 F9
Al 'Amarah Iraq 123 L6
Al 'Aqabah Jordan 121 L14
Al Azraq al Janubi Jordan 121 N10
Al Bahah Saudi Arabia 122 H12
Al Bayda' Libya 103 R6
Al Bayda' Yemen 122 I16
Al Buraymi Oman 123 O11
Al Ghaydah Yemen 123 M16
Al Hasakah Syria 121 R5
Al Hillah Iraq 123 K5
Al-Hoceïma Morocco 102 J4
Al Hufuf Saudi Arabia 123 L10
Al Jaghbub Libya 103 S7
Al Jawf Saudi Arabia 122 I6
Al Jazirah *Physical region* Iraq/Syria 121 Q3
Al Jubayl Saudi Arabia 123 L9
Al Karak Jordan 121 M11
Al Khaburah Oman 123 O11
Al Khufrah Libya 103 R10
Al Khums Libya 103 O6
Al Kut Iraq 123 L5
Al Ladhiqiyah (Eng. Latakia) Syria 121 M4
Al Marj Libya 103 Q6
Al Matraq Jordan 121 N9
Al Mukalla Yemen 123 K16
Al Mukha (Eng. Mocha) Yemen 122 H16
Al Qunaytirah Syria 121 M8
Al Qurnah Iraq 123 L6
Alabama *State* USA 43 K7
Alajuela Costa Rica 56 E13
Alakol', Ozero *Lake* Kazakhstan 117
Alamogordo New Mexico, USA 49 M10
Aland Islands *Island group* Finland 71 M11
Alanya Turkey 119 K10
Alaska *State* USA 36 G6 65 O6
Alaska Peninsula *Peninsula* Alaska, USA 34
Alaska Range *Mountain range* Alaska, USA 34 36 G7
Alaska, Gulf of *Gulf* Pacific Ocean 34 36 G9 145 L3
Alassio Italy 86 C9
Alazani *River* Azerbaijan/Georgia 99 Q12
Alba Iulia Romania 90 I5
Albacete Spain 75 M10
Albania *Country* SE Europe 89 L13

Albania 89

1912 • a Albanian • Lek • 113 • 73 • 14 • 85 • 20 • 769 • Yes • 37 • 2605

Albany Western Australia, Australia 146 G13
Albany *River* Ontario, Canada 38 I9
Albany New York, USA 41 M9
Albany Oregon, USA 50 G9
Albert Canal *Canal* Belgium 79 I14
Albert Lea Minnesota, USA 44 H8
Albert Nile *River* Uganda 111 M3
Albert, Lake *Lake* Dem. Rep. Congo (Zaire)/Uganda 101 109 P11 111 L3
Alberta *Province* Canada 37 K13
Albi France 77 L13
Albina Surinam 58 O6
Ålborg Denmark 70 I14
Albuquerque New Mexico, USA 49 L8
Albury New South Wales, Australia 147 N13
Alcántara, Embalse de *Reservoir* Spain 74 H9
Aldabra Islands *Island Group* Seychelles 114 E9
Aldan *River* Russian Federation 129 O8
Alde *River* England, United Kingdom 23 S10
Aldeburgh England, United Kingdom 23 T11
Aldershot England, United Kingdom 21 O7
Aleg Mauritania 106 G7
Aleksinac Serbia, Yugoslavia 89 O7
Alençon France 76 J6
Aleppo Syria 121 O3
Alert Nunavut, Canada 65 O11
Alessandria Italy 86 D7
Ålesund Norway 66 K7 70 H8
Aleutian Basin *Undersea feature* Pacific Ocean 34 117
Aleutian Islands *Island group* Alaska, USA 36 A6 144 J4
Aleutian Trench *Undersea feature* Pacific Ocean 34 144 J4
Alexander Archipelago *Island group* Alaska, USA 36 H11
Alexandretta *see* Iskenderun
Alexandria Egypt 104 F6
Alexandria Romania 91 L10
Alexandria Louisiana, USA 42 H8
Alexandroupoli Greece 93 N3
Aleysk Russian Federation 128 I11
Alfreton England, United Kingdom 23 L6
Algeciras Spain 74 I15
Algeria *Country* NW Africa102 I8

Algeria 102-103

1962 • a Arabic • Algerian dinar • 13 • 69 • 15 • 60.3 • 25 • 1250 • Yes • 56 • 2897

Alghero Italy 87 C13
Algiers Algeria 66 K9 103 L4
Aliakmonas *River* Greece 92 I4
Alicante Spain 75 N11
Alice Springs Northern Territory, Australia 147 K9
Alicudi *Island* Italy 87 K16
Aligarh India 131 K5
Alkmaar Netherlands 78 H9
Allahabad India 131 M7
Allen, Lough *Lake* Republic of Ireland 31 L6
Allentown Pennsylvania, USA 41 K13
Allier *River* France 77 M11
Alloa Scotland, United Kingdom 29 K13
Alma-Ata (var. Almaty) Kazakhstan 128 H13
Almaty *see* Alma-Ata
Almelo Netherlands 78 M9
Almería Spain 75 L14
Alor, Pulau *Island* Indonesia 141 N15
Alor Setar Malaysia 139 I17
Alotau Papua New Guinea 147 O4
Alpena Michigan, USA 45 O6
Alphen aan den Rijn Netherlands 78 H10
Alps *Mountain range* C Europe 68 77 P11 82 G11 86 B7
Alsager England, United Kingdom 22 I6
Altai Mountains *Mountain range* C Asia 68 117 127 132 I4
Altamura Italy 87 K16
Altay China 132 I4
Altay Mongolia 133 K5
Altdorf Switzerland 82 G10
Altınkaya Barajı *Reservoir* Turkey 119 M4
Alton Illinois, USA 44 J14
Altoona Pennsylvania, USA 40 H13
Altun Ha *Ruins* Belize 56 C6
Altun Shan *Mountain range* China 127 132 G9
Alturas California, USA 51 I12
Alytus Lithuania 94 I10
Am Timan Chad 108 K8
Amakusa-nada *Gulf* Japan 137 A14
Amami-gunto *Island group* Japan 137 A19
Amami-O-shima *Island* Japan 137 B18
Amarapura Burma 139 F7
Amarillo Texas, USA 49 O8
Amasya Turkey 119 M5
Amazon *River* Brazil/Peru 55 58 G10 60 H7 67 F12
Amazon Basin *Basin* S America 55 60 D8
Ambarchik Russian Federation 129 P4
Ambato Ecuador 58 C9
Amble England, United Kingdom 25 L5
Ambon Indonesia 141 O13
Amboseli *National Park* Kenya 111 P6
Ambriz Angola 112 G4
Ameland *Island* Netherlands 78 K6
American Samoa *Dependent territory* Pacific Ocean 145 K9
Amersfoort Netherlands 78 J10
Amery Ice Shelf *Ice shelf* Antarctica 64 G8
Ames Iowa, USA 47 Q9
Amfissa Greece 92 I8
Amga *River* Russian Federation 129 O8
Amiens France 77 L3
Amirante Islands *Island group* Seychelles 114 F9
Amistad Reservoir *Reservoir* Mexico/USA 49 O13
Amlia Island *Island* Alaska, USA 36 B7
Amlwch Wales, United Kingdom 27 K1
Amman Jordan 121 M10
Ammanford Wales, United Kingdom 27 L13
Ammersee *Lake* Germany 81 J16
Amol Iran 123 O4
Amorgos *Island* Greece 93 O12
Amritsar India 130 J3
Amroth *Beach* Wales, United Kingdom 32 E12
Amstelveen Netherlands 78 I10
Amsterdam Netherlands 78 I9
Amsterdam New York, USA 41 L9
Amsterdam Island *Island* French Southern and Antarctic Territories 115 I13
Amstetten Austria 83 Q5
Amu Darya *River* C Asia 68 117 125 K8 127
Amundsen Gulf *Gulf* Northwest Territories, Canada 37 K6
Amundsen-Scott *US Research Station* Antarctic,
Amundsen Sea *Sea* Antarctica 64 B10
Amur *River* China/Russian Federation 117 129 P11 127 133 P1 135 O1
An Nabk Syria 122 H5
An Nafud *Desert* Saudi Arabia 117 122 H6
An Najaf Iraq 123 K5
An Nasiriyah Iraq 123 L6
Anabar *River* Russian Federation 129 M5
Anaconda Montana, USA 46 G6
Anadyr' Russian Federation 129 R3
Anambas, Kepulauan *Island group* Indonesia 140 F10
Anamur Turkey 119 K11
Anatolia *Physical region* Turkey 68 117 127
Anatolian Plate *Tectonic plate* 68 117
Anchorage Alaska, USA 36 G8
Ancona Italy 66 L8 86 J9
Andalucia *see* Andalusia
Andalusia (var. Andalucia) *Region* Spain 74 I13
Andaman Islands *Island group* India 114 K6 127
Andaman Sea *Sea* Indian Ocean 114 K6 117 127 139 E11
Anderson Indiana, USA 45 N12
Andes *Mountain range* South America 55 58 D8 62 H9
Andijon Uzbekistan 125 P7
Andorra *Country* W Europe 75 P4 77 L15

Andorra 77

1278 • a Catalan • French franc and Spanish peseta • 140 • 83 • 16 • 99 • 555 • No • 63 • 3708

Andorra la Vella Andorra 77 K16
Andover England, United Kingdom, N7
Andravida Greece 92 H9
Andros Greece 93 M9
Andros Island *Island* Bahamas 57 K3
Aneto *Mountain* Spain 68
Angara *River* Russian Federation 117 129 L9
Angarsk Russian Federation 129 L11
Ángel de la Guarda, Isla *Island* Mexico 52 G4
Angel Falls *Waterfall* Venezuela 55
Angeles Philippines 141 L4
Angermälven *River* Sweden 71 I8
Angers France 76 I7
Angkor Wat *Archaeological site* Cambodia 139 L13
Angle Wales, United Kingdom 26 H13
Anglesey *Cultural region* Wales, United Kingdom 26 J1
Anglesey *Island* Wales, United Kingdom 17 E11 26 J1 32 E10
Angol Chile 63 G12
Angola *Country* Southern Africa 112 H5

Angola 112

1975 • a Portuguese • Readjusted kwanza • 10 • 47 • 15 • 45 • 18 • 14300 • No • 32 • 1839

Angola Basin *Undersea basin* Atlantic Ocean 67 K13 101
Angoulême France 76 J10
Angren Uzbekistan 125 N6
Anguilla Anguilla 57 S9
Angus *Unitary authority* Scotland, United Kingdom 18 J8
Ankang China 135 K10
Ankara Turkey 119 K6
Ann Arbor Michigan, USA 45 O9
Annaba Algeria 103 M4
Annah Iraq 122 J4
Annalee *River* Republic of Ireland 31 M6
Annan Scotland, United Kingdom 29 L16
Annapolis Maryland, USA 43 S3
Annecy France 77 P9
Anshan China 135 O6
Antakya Turkey 119 N10
Antalya Turkey 118 J10

Date of independence • a Language (official or most commonly spoken) • Currency • Population density per square kilometre • Average life expectancy • School-leaving age • Literacy • Number of cars per 1,000 people • Number of people per doctor • Death penalty • Percentage of urban-based population • Average number of calories consumed daily per person

Antananarivo Madagascar 115 E11
Antarctic Circle *Line of latitude* Antarctica 55 143
Antarctic Plate *Tectonic plate* 55 101 143
Antarctica *Continent* Antarctica 55 G18 67 115 G17 145 143 M15
Anticosti, Île d' *Island* Quebec, Canada 39 Q9
Antigua *Island* Antigua and Barbuda 57 S11
Antigua and Barbuda *Country* W Indies 57 T10

Antigua and Barbuda 57

1981 • a English • Eastern Caribbean dollar • 156 • 75 • 16 • 95 • 1316 • Yes • 36 • 2458

Antipodes Islands *Island group* New Zealand 144 J13
Antofagasta Chile 62 G6 145 Q10
Antrim Northern Ireland, United Kingdom 31 O4
Antrim *District* Northern Ireland, United Kingdom 19 F11
Antrim Mountains *Mountain range* Northern Ireland, United Kingdom 31 O3
Antsirañana Madagascar 114 E10
Antwerp (var. Antwerpen) Belgium 79 G13
Antwerpen *see* Antwerp
Anzio Italy 87 I12
Aomori Japan 136 K6
Aosta Italy 86 B6
Aparri Philippines 141 L2
Apatin Serbia, Yugoslavia 89 L3
Apeldoorn Netherlands 78 L10
Apennines *Mountain range* Italy 68 86 E8
Aphrodisias *Archaeological site* Turkey 118 H9
Āpia Samoa 144 J9
Appalachian Mountains *Mountain range* USA 34 N5 40 H14
Appenzell Switzerland 82 H9
Appleton Wisconsin, USA 45 K7
Apure, Río *River* Venezuela 58 H5
Aqaba, Gulf of *Gulf* Red Sea 104 H7 121 L15 122 F6
Ar Ramadi Iraq 123 K4
Ar Raqqah Syria 121 Q3
Ar Rub'al Khali (Eng. Empty Quarter) *Desert* Saudi Arabia 117 122 J13
Ar Rustaq Oman 123 O12
Arabian Basin *Undersea basin* Indian Ocean 117 127
Arabian Peninsula *Peninsula* SW Asia 101 114 E5 117 127
Arabian Plate *Tectonic plate* 68 101 117 127
Arabian Sea *Sea* SW Asia 114 117 123 M16 127 131 H9
Aracaju Brazil 60 O10
Arad Romania 90 G5
Arafura Sea *Sea* Pacific Ocean 127 141 R13 144 F9 143 147 K4
Araguaia, Río *River* Brazil 55 60 I10
Arak Iran 123 M5
Aral Sea *Lake* Kazakhstan/Uzbekistan 68 117 124 I3 128 F11 127
Aran Island *Island* Republic of Ireland 31 K3
Aran Islands *Island group* Republic of Ireland 30 I10
Arandelovac Serbia, Yugoslavia 89 N6
Ar'ar Saudi Arabia 122 I5
Ararat, Mount *Mountain* Turkey 68
Aras *River* SW Asia 99 R14
Arauca Colombia 58 G6
Arauca, Río *River* Colombia/Venezuela 58 F6
Arbil Iraq 123 K3
Arbroath Scotland, United Kingdom 29 M12
Arcachon France 76 I12
Archangel Russian Federation 96 J7 128 G5
Arctic Circle *Line of latitude* 34 68
Arctic Ocean *Ocean* 34 36 F4 65 66 J2 68 71 N1 117 P9 127 G5 144
Arda *River* Bulgaria/Greece 91 K15
Ardabil Iran 123 M2
Ardee Republic of Ireland 31 O7
Ardennes *Physical region* Belgium/France 79 I18
Ardglass Northern Ireland, United Kingdom 31 P6
Ardnamurchan, Point of *Headland* Scotland, United Kingdom 29 F11
Ards *District* Northern Ireland, United Kingdom 19 G12
Arendal Norway 70 I12
Arequipa Peru 59 G15
Arezzo Italy 86 H9
Argentina *Country* S South America 63 I14

Argentina 63

1816 • a Spanish • Argentine peso • 13 • 73 • 14 • 96.5 • 127 • 370 • No • 88 • 2880

Argentine Basin *Undersea basin* Atlantic Ocean 55 67 G15
Argentino, Lago *Lake* Argentina 63 I18
Argeș *River* Romania 91 M9
Arghandab, Darya-ye *River* Afghanistan 125 L14
Argostoli Greece 92 F9
Argun (var. Ergun He) *River* China/Russian Federation 133 P2
Argyll and Bute *Unitary authority* Scotland, United Kingdom 18 F9
Århus Denmark 70 I15
Arica Chile 62 F3
Arizona *State* USA 48 H8
Arkansas City Kansas, USA 47 P13
Arkansas River *River* USA 34 42 I5 46 N13 49 N5
Arklow Republic of Ireland 31 O11
Arlberg Tunnel *Tunnel* Austria 82 I9
Arles France 77 N13
Arlon Belgium 79 K19
Armagh Northern Ireland, United Kingdom 31 O6
Armagh *District* Northern Ireland, United Kingdom 19 F12
Armenia Colombia 58 E6
Armenia *Country* SW Asia 99 Q14

Armenia 99

1991 • a Armenian • Dram • 117 • 71 • 17 • 98.8 • 0 • 298 • Yes • 69 •

Armidale New South Wales, Australia 147 O12
Arnhem Netherlands 79 K11
Arnhem Land *Physical region* Northern Territory, Australia 143 146 J5
Arnhem, Cape *Headland* Australia 147 L5
Arno *River* Italy 86 F9
Arnold England, United Kingdom 23 L7
Arran, Isle of *Island* Scotland, United Kingdom 17 E8 29 H15
Arras France 77 L2
Arta Greece 92 G6
Artesia New Mexico, USA 49 M10
Artigas Uruguay 62 N10
Artvin Turkey 119 R4
Aru, Kepulauan *Island group* Indonesia 141 R14
Arua Uganda 111 L2
Aruba *Dependent territory* W Indies 57 N13
Arun *River* Nepal 131 O6
Arusha Tanzania 111 O7
Aruwimi *River* Dem. Rep. Congo (Zaire) 109 M12
Arvayheer Mongolia 133 L5
Arviat Nunavut, Canada 37 O10
Arvidsjaur Sweden 71 M6
As Salt Jordan 121 M9
As Sulaymaniyah Iraq 123 L3
As Suwayda' Syria 121 N8
Asahikawa Japan 136 L3
Asansol India 131 O8
Ascension Island Atlantic Ocean 67 J12
Aseb Eritrea 105 L13
Asela Ethiopia 105 J15
Ash Shu'aybah Kuwait 123 L8
Ashbourne Republic of Ireland 31 O8
Ashburton River *River* Western Australia, Australia 146 F9
Ashby de la Zouch England, United Kingdom 23 K8
Asheville North Carolina, USA 43 O5
Ashford England, United Kingdom 21 R7
Ashgabat Turkmenistan 124 H9
Ashington England, United Kingdom 25 L6
Ashland Oregon, USA 51 H11
Ashmore and Cartier Islands *Dependent territory* Indian Ocean 114 N10
Ashtabula Ohio, USA 45 Q9
Asia *Continent* 116-117 126-127,138-139
Asir *Mountain range* Saudi Arabia 122 H12
Asmara Eritrea 105 J12
Aspen Colorado, USA 49 L4
Assad, Lake *Reservoir* Syria 121 P3
Assen Netherlands 78 M7
Assisi Italy 86 I10
Assynt-Coigach *Area of Outstanding Natural Beauty* Scotland, United Kingdom 32 E4
Astakos Greece 92 G8
Astana Kazakhstan 128 H10
Asti Italy 86 C7
Astoria Oregon, USA 50 G8
Astrakhan' Russian Federation 96 G15 128 D9
Astypalaia *Island* Greece 93 O13
Asunción Paraguay 62 N6
Aswan Egypt 104 G9
Aswan High Dam *Dam* Egypt 104 G9
Asyût Egypt 104 F8
At Țafilah Jordan 121 M11
Atacama Desert *Desert* Chile 55 62 F4
Atakpamé Togo 107 M12
Atar Mauritania 106 H5
Atatürk Barajı *Reservoir* Turkey 119 O9
Atbara Sudan 105 H11
Atbara *River* Eritrea/Sudan 105 H12
Ath Belgium 79 F15
Athabasca Alberta, Canada 37 L13
Athabasca *River* Alberta, Canada 37 M12
Athabasca, Lake *Lake* Alberta/Saskatchewan, Canada 34 37 L11
Athens Georgia, USA 43 N7
Athens (Gr. Athina) Greece 93 K9
Athina *see* Athens
Athlone Republic of Ireland 31 L8
Ati Chad 108 J7
Atka Island *Island* Alaska, USA 36 A7
Atlanta Georgia, USA 43 N7
Atlantic City New Jersey, USA 41 L15
Atlantic Ocean *Ocean* 66-67
Atlantic-Indian Basin *Undersea feature* 67 L16 115 D15
Atlantic-Indian Ridge *Undersea feature* 67 L16
Atlas Mountains *Mountain range* NW Africa 68 101 102 H6
Atlixco Mexico 53 N12
Attawapiskat Ontario, Canada 38 I8
Attawapiskat *River* Ontario, Canada 38 H9
Attersee *Lake* Austria 83 O6
Attu Island *Island* Alaska, USA 36 A4
Atyrau Kazakhstan 128 E9
Auburn New York, USA 40 J9
Auch France 77 K14
Auckland New Zealand 148 H4
Auckland Islands *Island group* New Zealand 144 I13
Augrabies Falls *National Park* South Africa 112 J13
Augsburg Germany 81 I15
Augusta Italy 87 L18
Augusta Western Australia, Australia 146 F13
Augusta Georgia, USA 43 O7
Augusta Maine, USA 41 P7
Aurillac France 77 L11
Aurora Colorado, USA 49 M4
Aurora Illinois, USA 45 L10
Austin Minnesota, USA 44 H8
Austin Texas, USA 49 Q12
Australasia *Geophysical region* 144-143
Australes, Îles *Island group* French Polynesia 145 L11
Australia *Country* Oceania 146 F9

Australia 146-147

1901 • a English • Australian dollar • 2 • 78 • 15 • 99 • 485 • 455 • No • 85 • 3179

Australian Alps *Mountain range* Australia 143 147 N14
Australian Capital Territory *Territory* Australia 147 O14
Austria *Country* C Europe 83 P6

Austria 82-83

1918 • a German • Schilling • 99 • 77 • 15 • 99 • 469 • 385 • No • 56 • 3497

Auxerre France 77 M7
Aveiro Portugal 74 F7
Aviemore Scotland, United Kingdom 29 K10
Avignon France 77 N13
Ávila Spain 74 J8
Avilés Spain 74 I3
Avon *River* England, United Kingdom 17 F13
Avon *River* England, United Kingdom 17 G12 21 K6 23 K11
Avonmouth England, United Kingdom 20 J6
Awasa Ethiopia 105 J16
Awash *River* Ethiopia 105 K14
Awash Ethiopia 105 K15
Awbar Libya 103 O9
Awe, Loch *Lake* Scotland, United Kingdom 17 E7
Axe *River* England, United Kingdom 20 J10
Axel Heiberg Island *Island* Northwest Territories, Canada 37 M3 65 O10
Ayacucho Peru 59 E13
Aydarkul *Lake* Uzbekistan 125 M6
Aydın Turkey 118 H8
Ayers Rock *see* Uluru
Aylesbury England, United Kingdom 21 N4
Ayon, Ostrov *Island* Russian Federation 129 P3
Ayr Scotland, United Kingdom 29 I15
Ayr *River* Scotland, United Kingdom 29 J15
Ayr, Point of *Headland* Wales, United Kingdom 27 N1
Ayre, Point of *Headland* Isle of Man 17 E9 24 G4
Ayutthaya Thailand 139 I12
Ayvalık Turkey 118 G7
Az Zarqa' Jordan 121 N9
Az Zubayr Iraq 123 L7
Azaouâd *Desert* Mali 107 K7
Azerbaijan *Country* SW Asia 99 R14

Azerbaijan 99

1991 • a Azerbaijani • Manat • 89 • 70 • 17 • 96.3 • 36 • 257 • No • 56 •

Azores *Island group* Portugal 34 66 I9
Azov, Sea of *Sea* Black Sea 68 96 C14 99 K9 128 C7
Azul Argentina 63 M11

B

Baabda Lebanon 121 M7
Baalbek Lebanon 121 N6
Baarle-Hertog *Physical region* Belgium 79 I13
Bab el Mandeb *Strait* Gulf of Aden/Red Sea 122 H16
Babahoyo Ecuador 58 C9
Babar, Pulau *Island* Indonesia 141 P15
Babruysk Belarus 95 M13
Babylon *Site of ancient city* Iraq 123 K5
Bacan, Pulau *Island* Indonesia 141 O11
Bacău Romania 91 M4
Bačka Topola Serbia, Yugoslavia 89 M3
Bacolod Philippines 141 M6
Bacton England, United Kingdom 23 S7
Bad Ischl Austria 83 O7
Badajoz Spain 74 H10
Badalona Spain 75 Q6
Baden Austria 83 S5
Badgastein Austria 83 N8
Badlands *Physical region* North Dakota, USA 47 L6
Bafatá Guinea-Bissau 106 G10
Baffin Bay *Sea* Atlantic Ocean 34 37 O3 65 M13 66 F6
Baffin Island *Island* Nunavut, Canada 34 37 P5 65 M12
Bafia Cameroon 108 F10
Bafoussam Cameroon 108 F10
Baghdad Iraq 123 K5
Baghlan Afghanistan 125 N10
Baguio Philippines 141 L3
Bahamas *Island group* Bahamas 55
Bahamas *Country* Bahamas 56 K3

Bahamas 57

1973 • a English • Bahamian dollar • 30 • 74 • 14 • 95.8 • 58 • 709 • Yes • 87 • 2624

Bahawalpur Pakistan 130 I4
Bahía Blanca Argentina 63 L12 67 F14
Bahir Dar Ethiopia 105 I14
Bahrain *Country* SW Asia 123 M9

Bahrain 123

1971 • a Arabic • Bahrain dinar • 891 • 73 • 15 • 86.3 • 174 • 9090 • Yes • 91 •

Baia Mare Romania 90 I2
Baidan Jaran Shamo *Desert* China 133 L8
Baikal, Lake *Lake* Russian Federation 117 129 M10 127
Băile Herculane Romania 90 H8
Bairiki Kiribati 144 J8
Baja Hungary 85 L15
Baker Oregon, USA 50 L9
Baker Island *Island* Baker and Howland Islands 144 J8
Bakewell England, United Kingdom 23 K5
Bakhtaran Iran 123 L4
Baku Azerbaijan 99 T13
Bala Wales, United Kingdom 27 M4
Balabac Strait *Strait* East South China Sea/ Sulu Sea 141 K7
Balakovo Russian Federation 96 H13 128 E8
Balaton, Lake *Lake* Hungary 68 85 K14
Balbina, Represa *Reservoir* Brazil 60 F7
Balbriggan Republic of Ireland 31 O9
Baleares, Islas *see* Balearic Islands
Balearic Islands (Sp. Baleares, Islas) *Island group* Spain 68 75 P10
Baleine, Grande Rivière de la *River* Quebec, Canada 39 L6
Bali *Island* Indonesia 127 143
Bali *Island* Indonesia 140 J15
Balıkesir Turkey 118 H6
Balikpapan Indonesia 141 K12
Balkan Mountains *Mountain range* Bulgaria/Yugoslavia 68 89 P10 90 I12
Balkhash Kazakhstan 128 H12
Balkhash, Lake (var. Ozero Balkhash) *Lake* Kazakhstan 117 128 H12 127
Balkhash, Ozero *see* Balkhash, Lake
Ballantrae Scotland, United Kingdom 29 I16
Ballarat Victoria, Australia 147 M14
Ballater Scotland, United Kingdom 29 L11
Balleny Islands *Island group* Antarctica 64 E12
Ballina Republic of Ireland 30 J6
Ballinskelligs Bay *Inlet* Republic of Ireland 30 G14
Ballybofey Republic of Ireland 31 L4
Ballycastle *Beach* Northern Ireland, United Kingdom 32 E8
Ballycroy Republic of Ireland 30 I6
Ballyhaunis Republic of Ireland 31 K7
Ballyhoura Mountains *Mountain range* Republic of Ireland 31 K12
Ballymena Northern Ireland, United Kingdom 31 O4
Ballymena *District* Northern Ireland, United Kingdom 19 F11
Ballymoe Republic of Ireland 31 K8
Ballymoney *District* Northern Ireland, United Kingdom 19 F11
Ballyquintin Point *Headland* Northern Ireland, United Kingdom 17 E9
Ballywalter Northern Ireland, United Kingdom 31 P5
Balsas, Río *River* Mexico 53 M12
Bălți Moldova 98 H7
Baltic Sea *Sea* Atlantic Ocean 66 68 71 M14 80 H5 84 I2 117 127 L8
Baltimore Maryland, USA 43 S2 66 D9
Baltinglass Republic of Ireland 31 N10
Baltiysk Russian Federation 94 E9
Balykchy Kyrgyzstan 125 Q5
Bamako Mali 106 I9
Bambari Central African Republic 108 K10
Bamberg Germany 81 I13
Bamburgh England, United Kingdom 25 L4
Bamenda Cameroon 108 E10
Bana, Wadi *Dry watercourse* Yemen 122 I16
Banbridge *District* Northern Ireland, United Kingdom 19 F12
Banbury England, United Kingdom 21 M4
Banchory Scotland, United Kingdom 29 M11
Banda, Kepulauan *Island group* Indonesia 141 P13
Banda Sea *Sea* Pacific Ocean 127 141 N13 144 F9
Bandaaceh Indonesia 140 B9
Bandar Seri Begawan Brunei 140 J9
Bandar-e 'Abbas Iran 123 O9
Bandarlampung Indonesia 140 F14
Bandırma Turkey 118 H5
Bandon Oregon, USA 50 F10
Bandon Republic of Ireland 30 J14
Bandundu Dem. Rep. Congo (Zaire) 109 I14
Bandung Indonesia 140 G15
Banff Scotland, United Kingdom 29 M9
Bangalore India 131 K13
Bangassou Central African Republic 108 L10
Banggai, Kepulauan *Island group* Indonesia 141 M12
Banggi, Pulau *Island* Borneo, Malaysia 141 K8
Bangka, Pulau *Island* Indonesia 140 G12
Bangkok Thailand 139 I13
Bangladesh *Country* S Asia 131 O7

Bangladesh 131

1971 • a Bengali • Taka • 948 • 58 • 10 • 39.9 • N/A • 5000 • Yes • 18 • 2019

Bangor Northern Ireland, United Kingdom 31 P4
Bangor Maine, USA 41 Q6
Bangor Wales, United Kingdom 27 K2
Bangui Central African Republic 108 J10
Bangweulu, Lake *Lake* Zambia 111 L12
Banhine *National Park* Mozambique 113 N10
Banja Luka Bosnia and Herzegovina 88 J5
Banjarmasin Indonesia 140 J13
Banjul Gambia 106 F9
Banks Island *Island* Northwest Territories, Canada 34 37 K5 65 N8
Banks Lake *Reservoir* Washington, USA 50 K6
Bann *River* Northern Ireland, United Kingdom 31 O3
Banská-Bystrica Slovakia 85 L11
Bantry Republic of Ireland 30 I15
Bantry Bay *Bay* Republic of Ireland 30 I15
Banyo Cameroon 108 F10
Banyuwangi Indonesia 140 J15
Baoji China 135 K9
Baotou China 133 N7
Bar Montenegro, Yugoslavia 89 L10
Bar-le-Duc France 77 N5
Barbados *Country* West Indies 55 57 T14

Barbados 57

1966 • a English • Barbados dollar • 626 • 76 • 16 • 97.6 • 44 • 885 • Yes • 48 • 3207

Barbuda *Island* Antigua and Barbuda 57 T10
Barcelona Spain 75 Q6
Barcelona Venezuela 58 J4
Bareilly India 131 L5
Barents Sea *Sea* Arctic Ocean 65 R12 68 96 K6 117 128 H4 127
Bari Italy 87 N13
Barinas Venezuela 58 G5
Barisan, Pegunungan *Mountain range* Indonesia 140 E12
Barito, Sungai *River* Indonesia 140 J12
Barking and Dagenham *London borough* England, United Kingdom 19 O19
Bârlad Romania 91 N5
Barlee, Lake *Lake* Western Australia, Australia 146 G11
Barmouth Wales, United Kingdom 27 L6
Barnard Castle England, United Kingdom 25 K9
Barnaul Russian Federation 128 J11
Barnet *London borough* England, United Kingdom 19 M19
Barnsley England, United Kingdom 25 L15
Barnsley *Unitary authority* England, United Kingdom 19 L13
Barnstaple England, United Kingdom 20 H8
Barnstaple Bay *Bay* England, United Kingdom 20 G8
Barquisimeto Venezuela 58 H4
Barra *Island* Scotland, United Kingdom 29 E11
Barra Head *Headland* Scotland, United Kingdom 17 C6
Barranquilla Colombia 58 E4
Barreiras Brazil 61 K11
Barreiro Portugal 74 F11
Barrie Ontario, Canada 39 K14
Barrow Alaska, USA 36 H4
Barrow *River* Republic of Ireland 17 D12
Barrow Island *Island* Western Australia, Australia 146 E8
Barrow-in-Furness England, United Kingdom 24 H12
Barry Wales, United Kingdom 27 N15
Bartang *River* Tajikistan 125 P9
Bartica Guyana 58 M6
Barton-upon-Humber England, United Kingdom 23 N3
Barychavichy Belarus 94 J12
Barysaw Belarus 95 L10
Basel (Eng. Basle) Switzerland 82 F8
Basilan *Island* Philippines 141 M8
Basildon England, United Kingdom 21 Q5
Basingstoke England, United Kingdom 21 N8
Basle *see* Basel
Basque Country, The *Region* Spain 75 L4
Basra Iraq 114 E4 123 L7

Bass Strait *Strait* Indian Ocean 143 147 M15
Basse-Terre Guadeloupe 57 S12
Basse Terre *Island* Guadeloupe 57 T12
Bassein Burma 138 E10
Bassenthwaite Lake *Lake* England, United Kingdom 24 H9
Basseterre Saint Kitts and Nevis 57 S11
Bastia France 77 S14
Bastogne Belgium 79 K18
Bata Equatorial Guinea 109 E12
Batangas Philippines 141 L4
Batavia *see* Jakarta
Batavia New York, USA 40 I9
Batdâmbâng Cambodia 139 K13
Bath England, United Kingdom 21 L6
Bath and North East Somerset *Unitary authority* England, United Kingdom 19 K17
Bathurst New Brunswick, Canada 39 P11
Bathurst Island *Island* Northern Territory, Australia 146 I4
Bathurst Island *Island* Nunavut, Canada 37 M4
Batman Turkey 119 Q8
Batna Algeria 102 M5
Baton Rouge Louisiana, USA 42 I9
Batticaloa Sri Lanka 131 L16
Battle Creek Michigan, USA 45 N9
Batu, Kepulauan *Island group* Indonesia 140 D11
Bat'umi Georgia 99 O13
Bauchi Nigeria 107 P11
Bautzen Germany 81 N11
Bavaria (Ger. Bayern) *Cultural region* Germany 81 I14
Bavarian Alps *Mountain range* Austria/Germany 81 J17
Bawean, Pulau *Island* Indonesia 140 I14
Bay City Michigan, USA 45 O8
Bayamo Cuba 57 K6
Bayan Har Shan *Mountain range* China 133 K10
Baydaratskaya Guba *Bay* Arctic Ocean 96 O6 128 I6
Baydhabo Somalia 105 M17
Bayern *see* Bavaria
Baykonur Kazakhstan 128 F11
Bayonne France 76 I14
Bayramaly Turkmenistan 124 J9
Bayreuth Germany 81 J13
Beachy Head *Headland* England, United Kingdom 17 H14 21 Q9
Beacon Hill *Hill* Wales, United Kingdom 27 N8
Beagle Channel *Channel* Atlantic Ocean 63 L20
Bear Lake *Lake* Idaho/Utah, USA 48 J1
Beaufort Sea *Sea* Alaska, Arctic Ocean 34 36 I5 65 N7
Beaufort West South Africa 112 J15
Beauly Scotland, United Kingdom 28 J9
Beaumont Texas, USA 49 S12
Beauvais France 77 L4
Beaver Island *Island* Michigan, USA 45 M5
Beccles England, United Kingdom 23 S9
Bečej Serbia, Yugoslavia 89 M3
Béchar Algeria 102 J6
Bedford England, United Kingdom 21 P3
Bedford Indiana, USA 45 M14
Bedford Level *Physical region* England, United Kingdom 23 O9
Bedfordshire *County* England, United Kingdom 19 M15
Bedworth England, United Kingdom 23 L9
Be'ér Sheva' Israel 121 L11
Beeston England, United Kingdom 23 L7
Bei'an China 135 O3
Beijing (Eng. Peking) China 135 M6
Beira Mozambique 113 O9 115 D11
Beirut (var. Beyrouth) Lebanon 121 M6
Beja Portugal 74 G12
Béjaïa Algeria 103 L4
Belarus (*var.* Belorussia) *Country* E Europe 94 J12

Belarus 94

1991 • Belorussian • Belarusian rouble • 50 • 68 • 15 • 99 • 110 • 244 • Yes • 71 • N/A

Belawan Indonesia 140 D9
Beledweyne Somalia 105 M16
Belém Brazil 60 J7
Belfast *Political division capital* Northern Ireland, United Kingdom 31 P5
Belfast City *District* Northern Ireland, United Kingdom 19 F11
Belfort France 77 P7
Belgaum India 130 I11
Belgium *Country* W Europe 79 E15

Belgium 79

1966 • English • Barbados dollar • 626 • 76 • 16 • 97.6 • 44 • 885 • Yes • 48 • 3207

Belgorod Russian Federation 96 E12
Belgrade Yugoslavia 89 N5
Belgrano II *Argentinian research station* Antarctica 64 D7
Belice *River* Italy 87 I18
Belitung, Pulau *Island* Indonesia 140 G13
Belize *Country* Central America 56 C7

Belize 56

1981 • English • Belizean dollar • 9 • 75 • 14 • 75 • 20 • 2128 • Yes • 47 • 2662

Belize *River* Belize/Guatemala 56 C6
Belize City Belize 56 C6
Bellavary Republic of Ireland 30 J7
Belle Fourche River *River* South Dakota/Wyoming, USA 47 K8
Belle Île *Island* France 76 G8
Belle Isle *Island* Newfoundland, Canada 39 R7
Belle Isle, Strait of *Strait* Atlantic Ocean 39 R8
Bellevue Washington, USA 50 H6
Bellingham Washington, USA 50 H5
Bellingshausen Plain *Undersea feature* Pacific Ocean 55
Bellingshausen Sea *Sea* Antarctica 64 B8
Bellinzona Switzerland 82 H12
Bello Colombia 58 E6
Belluno Italy 86 H6
Belmopan Belize 56 C6
Belmullet Republic of Ireland 30 I6
Belo Horizonte Brazil 61 L13
Beloit Wisconsin, USA 45 K9
Belorussia *see* Belarus
Belper England, United Kingdom 23 K7
Belyy, Ostrov *Island* Russian Federation 128 J5
Bemidji Minnesota, USA 44 G3
Ben Lawers *Mountain* Scotland, United Kingdom 29 J12
Ben Macdui *Mountain* Scotland, United Kingdom 29 K11
Ben Nevis *Mountain* Scotland, United Kingdom 17 E6 29 I12
Ben Nevis and Glen Coe *Area of Outstanding Natural Beauty* Scotland, United Kingdom 32 E6
Benbecula *Island* Scotland, United Kingdom 28 E10
Bend Oregon, USA 50 I9
Bendigo Victoria, Australia 147 M14
Benevento Italy 87 K13
Bengal, Bay of *Bay* Indian Ocean 114 J6 117 127 131 M12 138 D9
Benghazi Libya 103 Q6
Bengkulu Indonesia 140 E13
Benguela Angola 112 G6
Beni-Mellal Morocco 102 I6
Beni, Río *River* Bolivia 59 I13
Beni Suef Egypt 104 F7
Benidorm Spain 75 O11
Benin *Country* W Africa 107 M11

Benin 107

1960 • French • Franc de la Communauté financière africaine • 53 • 53 • 11 • 33.9 • 7 • 10000 • Yes • 31 • 2532

Benin City Nigeria 107 O13
Benin, Bight of *Gulf* Atlantic Ocean M13
Bennington Vermont, USA 41 M9
Benton Harbor Michigan, USA 45 M10
Benue *River* Cameroon/Nigeria 107 P12
Beppu Japan 137 D14
Berat Albania 89 M13
Berau, Teluk *Bay* Indonesia 141 Q12
Berbera Somalia 105 M14
Berbérati Central African Republic 109 H11
Berbice River *River* Guyana 58 M6
Berdyans'k Ukraine 99 L8
Berettyó *River* Hungary/Romania 85 N14
Bergamo Italy 86 E6
Bergen Norway 66 K7 70 H10
Bergen op Zoom Netherlands 79 G12
Bergisch Gladbach Germany 81 E11
Bering Sea *Sea* Pacific Ocean 34 36 B6 117 I3 129 R3 127 144
Bering Strait *Strait* Arctic Ocean/Pacific Ocean 34 36 E4 117 127 J2 144
Berkhamsted England, United Kingdom 21 O5
Berlin Germany 80 L9
Bermejo, Río *River* Argentina 62 K5
Bermuda *Dependent territory* Atlantic Ocean 66 E9
Bermuda Rise *Undersea rise* Atlantic Ocean 34
Bern Switzerland 82 E10
Berner Alpen (Eng. Bernese Oberland) *Mountain range* Switzerland 82 E12
Bernese Oberland *see* Berner Alpen
Berry Islands *Island group* Bahamas 57 K2
Bertoua Cameroon 108 G10
Beruniy Uzbekistan 124 J6
Berwick-upon-Tweed England, United Kingdom 25 K3
Besançon France 77 O7
Bethel Alaska, USA 36 E7
Bethlehem West Bank 121 M10
Betws-y-Coed Wales, United Kingdom 27 M3
Beulah Wales, United Kingdom 27 M10
Beverley England, United Kingdom 25 O13
Bexhill England, United Kingdom 21 R9
Bexley *London borough* England, United Kingdom 19 O19
Beykoz Turkey 118 I5
Beyrouth *see* Beirut
Beyşehir Turkey 118 J9
Beyşehir Gölü *Lake* Turkey 118 J8
Bhamo Burma 138 G6
Bhavnagar India 130 I8
Bhopal India 131 K8
Bhubaneshwar India 131 N9
Bhutan *Country* S Asia 131 P6

Bhutan 131

1656 • Dzongkha • Ngultrum • 45 • 61 • N/A • 44.2 • 10 • 5825 • No • 6 • 2553

Biak Indonesia 141 R11
Biak, Pulau *Island* Indonesia 141 R11
Biaiystok Poland 85 O4
Bianco, Monte *see* Blanc, Mont
Bicester England, United Kingdom 21 N4
Bicuari *National Park* Angola 112 G7
Biddeford Maine, USA 41 O8
Bideford England, United Kingdom 20 G8
Biel Switzerland 82 E9
Bielefeld Germany 80 F9
Bieler See *Lake* Switzerland 82 E10
Bielsko-Biała Poland 85 L9
Biên Hoa Vietnam 139 N14
Big Spring Texas, USA 49 O10
Bigbury Bay *Bay* England, United Kingdom 20 H11
Biggleswade England, United Kingdom 21 P3
Bighorn Mountains *Mountain range* Wyoming, USA 46 J7
Bighorn River *River* Montana/Wyoming, USA 46 J7
Bihac Bosnia and Herzegovina 88 H5
Bijagos Archipelago *Island group* Guinea-Bissau 106 F10
Bijelo Polje Montenegro, Yugoslavia 89 M8
Bikini *Atoll* Marshall Islands 144 I7
Bila Tserkva Ukraine 98 I5
Bilbao Spain 75 L3
Bilecik Turkey 118 I6
Bilhorod-Dnistrovs'kyy Ukraine 98 I8
Billingham England, United Kingdom 25 M9
Billings Montana, USA 46 J6
Biloxi Mississippi, USA 42 J9
Biltine Chad 108 K6
Bindura Zimbabwe 113 M8
Binghamton New York, USA 41 K10
Bingöl Turkey 119 Q7
Bintan, Pulau *Island* Indonesia 140 F11
Bío Bío, Río *River* Chile 63 H12
Bioko *Island* Equatorial Guinea 101
Birak Libya 103 O8
Birao Central African Republic 108 L8
Biratnagar Nepal 131 O6
Birganj Nepal 131 N6
Birkenhead England, United Kingdom 22 G5
Birmingham England, United Kingdom 22 J9
Birmingham Alabama, USA 43 L7
Birmingham *Unitary authority* England, United Kingdom 19 O12
Birnin Konni Niger 107 O9
Birr Republic of Ireland 31 L10
Biscay, Bay of *Bay* Atlantic Ocean 68 75 L3
Biscay Plain *Abyssal plain* Atlantic Ocean 68
Bishkek Kyrgyzstan 125 Q5
Bisho South Africa 113 L15
Bishop Auckland England, United Kingdom 25 L9
Biskra Algeria 103 M5
Bislig Philippines 141 N7
Bismarck North Dakota, USA 47 M5
Bismarck Archipelago *Island group* Papua New Guinea 147 O1
Bismarck Plate *Tectonic plate* 143
Bismarck Range *Mountain range* Papua New Guinea 143 147 M2
Bismarck Sea *Sea* Papua New Guinea 143 147 O1
Bissau Guinea-Bissau 106 F10
Bitrita Romania 90 J3
Bitrita *River* Romania 91 L3
Bitlis Turkey 119 R7
Bitola FYR Macedonia 89 O12
Bitterroot Range *Mountain range* Idaho/Montana, USA 46 F5
Biwa-ko *Lake* Japan 137 H11
Biysk Russian Federation 128 J11
Bizerte Tunisia 103 N4
Bjelovar Croatia 88 J2
Black Forest (Ger. Schwarzwald) *Mountain range* Germany 81 F15
Black Hills *Mountain range* South Dakota/Wyoming, USA 47 L8
Black Mountains *Mountain rangWales*, United Kingdom 27 O11
Black River *River* China/Vietnam 138 L8
Black River *River* Arkansas/Missouri, USA 42 I4
Black Rock Desert *Desert* Nevada, USA 48 F1
Black Sea *Sea* Asia/Europe 66 68 C15 90 O12 96 99 117 K10 119 L3 128 C8 127 N8
Black Volta *River* WAfrica 101 107 K11
Blackburn England, United Kingdom 24 J14
Blackburn *Unitary authority* England, United Kingdom 19 J13
Blackpool England, United Kingdom 24 H13
Blackpool *Unitary authority* England, United Kingdom 19 I13
Blackpool Sands *Beach* England, United Kingdom 32 F13
Blacksod Bay *Inlet* Republic of Ireland 30 I6
Blackwater *River* Northern Ireland, Republic of Ireland/United Kingdom 31 N6
Blackwater *River* Republic of Ireland 17 C12 31 L13
Blaenau Gwent *Unitary authority* Wales, United Kingdom 19 F17
Blagoveshchensk Russian Federation 129 P11
Blairgowrie Scotland, United Kingdom 29 K12
Blakeney Point *Headland* England, United Kingdom, 23 R6
Blanc, Mont (It. Monte Bianco) *Mountain* France/Italy 68
Blanca, Bahía *Bay* Atlantic Ocean 63 L13
Blanca, Costa *Physical region* Spain 75 N12
Blanco, Cape *Headland* Oregon, USA 50 F10
Blandford Forum England, United Kingdom 21 L9
Blanice *River* Czech Republic 84 H10
Blantyre Malawi 111 O15
Blenheim New Zealand 148 G8
Blida Algeria 103 L4
Bloemfontein South Africa 113 K13
Blois France 77 K7
Bloody Foreland *Headland* Republic of Ireland 17 C8 31 L2
Bloomington Minnesota, USA 44 H7
Bloomington Illinois, USA 45 K12
Bloomington Indiana, USA 45 M13
Blue Mesa Dam *Dam* Colorado, USA 49 L5
Blue Mountains *Mountain range* Oregon/Washington, USA 50 K10
Blue Nile *River* Ethiopia/Sudan 101 105 H13
Bluefields Nicaragua 56 E11
Blyth England, United Kingdom 25 M6
Bo Sierra Leone 106 H12
Bo Hai *Gulf* Yellow Sea 135 N7
Boa Vista Brazil 60 E6
Boaco Nicaragua 56 D11
Bobaomby, Tanjona *Headland* Madagascar 114 E10
Bobo-Dioulasso Burkina 107 K10
Bóbr *River* Poland 84 I6
Bocas del Toro Panama 56 F14
Bochum Germany 80 E10
Bodmin England, United Kingdom 20 F10
Bodmin *Area of Outstanding Natural Beauty* England, United Kingdom 32 E13
Bodmin Moor *Moorland* England, United Kingdom 17 E14 20 F10
Bodø Norway 71 L4
Bodrum Turkey 118 G9
Boende Dem. Rep. Congo (Zaire) 109 K12
Boggeragh Mountains *Mountain range* Republic of Ireland 17 B12 30 J13
Bognor Regis England, United Kingdom 21 P10
Bogor Indonesia 140 G15
Bogotá Colombia 58 E6
Bohemia *Region* Czech Republic 84 G10
Bohemian Forest *Mountain range* Austria/Czech Republic/Germany 81 L14
Bohol *Island* Philippines 141 M6
Boise Idaho, USA 46 F8
Bokaro India 131 N7
Boknafjorden *Fjord* Norway 70 G11
Bol Chad 108 H7
Bol'shevik, Ostrov *Island* Russian Federation 129 L4
Bolgatanga Ghana 107 L11
Bolivia *Country* C South America 59 H14

Bolivia 59

1825 • Spanish, Aymará and Quechua • Boliviano • 7 • 61 • 14 • 83.6 • 29 • 2500 • No • 61 • 2094

Bologna Italy 86 G8
Bolsena, Lago di *Lake* Italy 86 H11
Bolton *Unitary authority* England, United Kingdom 18 B9
Bolu Turkey 118 J5
Bolus Head *Headland* Republic of Ireland 30 H14
Bolvadin Turkey 118 J7
Bolzano Italy 86 G5
Boma Dem. Rep. Congo (Zaire) 109 G15
Bombay *see* Mumbai
Bomu *River* Central African Republic/Dem. Rep. Congo (Zaire) 109 L10
Bonaire *Island* Netherlands Antilles 57 O14
Bondo Dem. Rep. Congo (Zaire) 109 J11
Bone, Teluk *Bay* Indonesia 141 L13
Bonete, Cerro *Mountain* Argentina 55
Bongor Chad 108 H8
Bonifacio France 77 S16
Bonifacio, Strait of *Strait* Mediterranean Sea 87 D12
Bonn Germany 81 D11
Boosaaso Somalia 105 O14
Boothia, Gulf of *Gulf* Arctic Ocean 37 N6
Bootle England, United Kingdom 24 I15
Borås Sweden 70 J13
Bordeaux France 76 I12
Borger Texas, USA 49 O8
Borlänge Sweden 71 L11
Borneo *Island* SE Asia 114 M8 127 140 I11 143
Bornholm *Island* Denmark 71 K16
Borobudur Indonesia 140 H15
Borrisokane Republic of Ireland 31 L10
Borth Wales, United Kingdom 27 L7
Borujerd Iran 123 M5
Bosanska Gradiška Bosnia and Herzegovina 88 J4
Bosanska Krupa Bosnia and Herzegovina 88 I4
Bosna *River* Bosnia and Herzegovina 89 K6
Bosnia and Herzegovina *Country* SE Europe 88 I5

Bosnia and Herzegovina 88-89

1992 • Serbo-Croat • Marka • 74 • 63 • 15 • 92.7 • 43 • 1667 • No • 49 •

Bosobolo Dem. Rep. Congo (Zaire) 109 J11
Bosporus *Strait* Turkey 118 I5
Bossangoa Central African Republic 108 I10
Bosten Hu *Lake* China 132 H7
Boston Massachusetts, USA 41 O10
Boston England, United Kingdom 23 O7
Bothnia, Gulf of *Gulf* Baltic Sea 68 71 M9
Botoșani Romania 91 M2
Botswana *Country* Southern Africa 112 J10

Botswana 112-113

1966 • English • Pula • 3 • 47 • 74.4 • 15 • 5000 • Yes • 28 • 2266

Bouaké Ivory Coast 106 J12
Bouar Central African Republic 108 H10
Bougainville Island *Island* Papua New Guinea 147 P2
Bougouni Mali 106 I10
Boulder Colorado, USA 49 M4
Boulogne *see* Boulogne-sur-Mer
Boulogne-sur-Mer (var. Boulogne) France 66 K8 77 K2
Boumalne-Dad Ìes Morocco 102 I6
Bountiful Utah, USA 48 J2
Bounty Islands *Island group* New Zealand 144 J12
Bourge-en-Bresse France 77 O9
Bourges France 77 L8
Bourgogne *see* Burgundy
Bourke New South Wales, Australia 147 N11
Bournemouth England, United Kingdom 21 M10
Bournemouth *Unitary authority* England, United Kingdom 19 L18
Bournemouth *Beach* England, United Kingdom 32 G13
Bouvet Island *Dependent territory* Atlantic Ocean 67 K16
Bowland, Forest of *Forest* England, United Kingdom 24 J12
Bowling Green Kentucky, USA 43 M3
Boyle Republic of Ireland 31 L7
Boyoma Falls *Waterfall* Dem. Rep. Congo (Zaire) 109 M12
Bozeman Montana, USA 46 H6
Brac *Island* Croatia 88 I7
Bracciano, Lago di *Lake* Italy 87 H11
Bracknell Forest *Unitary authority* England, United Kingdom 19 M17
Bradano *River* Italy 87 M13
Bradford England, United Kingdom 25 L13
Bradford *Unitary authority* England, United Kingdom 19 K11
Brae Scotland, United Kingdom 28 O2
Braemar Scotland, United Kingdom 29 L11
Braga Portugal 74 F6
Bragança Portugal 75 H6
Brahmaputra *River* S Asia 127 131 Q6 132 G12
Braich y Pwll *Headland* Wales, United Kingdom 26 I5
Brăila Romania 91 O7
Brainerd Minnesota, USA 44 G5
Braintree England, United Kingdom 21 R4
Brampton England, United Kingdom 24 I7
Branco, Rio *River* Brazil 55
Brandenburg Germany 80 K9
Brandon Manitoba, Canada 37 O15
Brandon Mountain *Mountain* Republic of Ireland 30 H13
Brasília Brazil 61 K12
Brașov Romania 91 L6
Bratislava Slovakia 84 J12
Bratsk Russian Federation 129 L10
Brattleboro Vermont, USA 41 N9
Braunau am Inn Austria 83 N5
Braunschweig (Eng. Brunswick) Germany 80 I9
Brava, Costa *Region* Spain 75 R6
Bravo Del Norte, Río *River* Mexico/USA 53 K3
Brawley California, USA 51 N19
Brazil *Country* South America 60-61

Brazil 60-61

1822 • Portuguese • Real • 20 • 67 • 14 • 84 • 128 • 714 • No • 78 • 2824

Brazil Basin *Undersea basin* Atlantic Ocean 55 66 I12
Brazilian Highlands *Mountain range* Brazil 55 61 L12
Brazos River *River* Texas, USA 49 Q11
Brazzaville Congo 109 H14
Brechin Scotland, United Kingdom 29 M11
Brecon Wales, United Kingdom 27 N11
Brecon Beacons *Mountain rangWales*, United Kingdom 17 F13 27 M12
Brecon Beacons National Park *National Park* Wales, United Kingdom 32 F12
Breda Netherlands 79 H12
Bregalnica *River* FYR Macedonia 89 P10
Bregenz Austria 82 I8

Bremen Germany 80 G8
Bremerhaven Germany 66 L8 80 F7
Bremerton Washington, USA 50 I5
Brenig, Llyn *Lak*Wales, United Kingdom 27 N3
Brenner Pass *Pass* Austria/Italy 83 L9
Brent *London borough* England, United Kingdom 19 M19
Brentwood England, United Kingdom 21 Q5
Brescia Italy 86 F7
Breslau *see* Wrocπaw
Brest Belarus 94 H14
Brest France 76 F6
Bretagne *see* Brittany
Breton Sound *Sound* Louisiana, USA 42 I10
Bria Central African Republic 108 K10
Brianne Reservoir, Llyn *Reservoir* Wales, United Kingdom 27 L10
Bride Isle of Man 24 H5
Bridgend Wales, United Kingdom 27 M15
Bridgend *Unitary authority* Wales, United Kingdom 19 E17
Bridgeport Connecticut, USA 41 M12
Bridgetown Barbados 57 T14
Bridgwater England, United Kingdom 20 J8
Bridlington England, United Kingdom 25 P12
Bridlington Bay *Bay* England, United Kingdom 25 P12
Bridport England, United Kingdom 21 K9
Brienzer See *Lake* Switzerland 82 F11
Brig Switzerland 82 F12
Brigg England, United Kingdom 23 O4
Brigham City Utah, USA 48 J2
Bright Angel Point *Mountain* Arizona, USA 48 I7
Brighton England, United Kingdom 21 Q9
Brighton and Hove *Unitary authority* England, United Kingdom 19 N17
Brindisi Italy 87 P13
Brisbane Queensland, Australia 144 H11 147 P10
Bristol England, United Kingdom 21 K6
Bristol Bay *Bay* Bering Sea 36 E8
Bristol Channel *Inlet* United Kingdom 17 E13 20 H7 32 E12
Bristol, City of *Unitary authority* England, United Kingdom 19 J16
Britain *Island* United Kingdom 17 F11
British Columbia *Province* Canada 36 I13
British Indian Ocean Territory *Dependent territory* Indian Ocean 114 I9
British Isles *Island group* NW Europe
British Virgin Islands (var. Virgin Islands) *Dependent territory* West Indies 57 R9
Brittany (Fr. Bretagne) *Region* France 76 G6
Brno Czech Republic 84 J10
Broadford Scotland, United Kingdom 28 H10
Broads, The *Wetland* England, United Kingdom 17 I11 23 S8 32 I11
Broadstairs England, United Kingdom 21 T6
Brodick Scotland, United Kingdom 29 H14
Broken Arrow Oklahoma, USA 47 P14
Broken Hill New South Wales, Australia 147 M12
Broken Ridge *Undersea plateau* Indian Ocean 115 J12
Brokopondo Surinam 58 O6
Bromley England, United Kingdom 21 Q6
Bromley *London borough* England, United Kingdom 19 O20
Bromsgrove England, United Kingdom 22 J10
Brooks Range *Mountain range* Alaska, USA 34 36 H5
Broome Western Australia, Australia 146 G7
Brora Scotland, United Kingdom 28 K8
Brora *River* Scotland, United Kingdom 28 J8
Brough England, United Kingdom 25 K9
Brownsville Texas, USA 49 Q16
Bruges (var. Brugge) Belgium 79 D13
Brugge *see* Bruges
Brunei *Country* SE Asia 140 J9

Brunei 140

1984 • a Malay • Brunei dollar • 61 • 76 • 16 • 90.1 • 167 • 1133 • No • 70 • 2745

Brunswick Georgia, USA 43 O10
Brunswick *see* Braunschweig
Brunswick Maine, USA 41 P7
Brussel *see* Brussels
Brussels (var. Brussel, Bruxelles) Belgium 79 G15
Bruxelles *see* Brussels
Bryansk Russian Federation 96 E11 128 D6
Bryce Canyon *Canyon* Utah, USA 48 G5
Brynmawr Wales, United Kingdom 27 O12
Bubiyan, Jazirat *Island* Kuwait 123 L7
Bucaramanga Colombia 58 F5
Buchan Ness *Headland* Scotland, United Kingdom 17 G5 29 O10
Buchanan Liberia 106 H13
Bucharest (Rom. Bucureşti) Romania 91 L9
Buckie Scotland, United Kingdom 28 L9
Buckinghamshire *County* England, United Kingdom 19 M16
Buckley Wales, United Kingdom 27
Bucureşti *see* Bucharest
Budapest Hungary 85 L13
Bude England, United Kingdom 20 F9
Bude Bay *Bay* England, United Kingdom 20 F9
Buenaventura Colombia 58 D7 145 Q8
Buenos Aires Argentina 62 M10 67 F14
Buenos Aires, Lago *Lake* Argentina/Chile 63 I16
Buffalo New York, USA 40 H9
Bug (Eng. Western Bug) *River* E Europe 68 85 O4 94 H15
Builth Wells Wales, United Kingdom 27 N10
Bujumbura Burundi 111 L7
Bukavu Dem. Rep. Congo (Zaire) 109 O13
Bukhoro Uzbekistan 125 K7
Bukoba Tanzania 111 M5
Bulawayo Zimbabwe 113 L9
Bulgaria *Country* SE Europe 90 J12

Bulgaria 90-91

1908 • a Bulgarian • Lev • 75 • 71 • 16 • 98.2 • 208 • 303 • No • 71 • 2831

Bumba Dem. Rep. Congo (Zaire) 109 L11
Bunbury Western Australia, Australia 146 F13
Bundaberg Queensland, Australia 147 P9
Bunia Dem. Rep. Congo (Zaire) 108 P12
Buon Ma Thuot Vietnam 139 O13
Bûr Safâga Egypt 104 G8
Buraydah Saudi Arabia 122 J9
Burco Somalia 105 M14
Burdur Turkey 118 I9
Bure *River* England, United Kingdom 23 S8
Burgas Bulgaria 91 N13
Burgess Hill England, United Kingdom 21 P8
Burgos Spain 75 K5
Burgundy (Fr. Bourgogne) *Region* France 77 N8
Burkina *Country* W Africa 107 L9

Burkina 107

1960 • a French • Franc de la Communauté financière africaine • 42 • 44 • 14 • 20.7 • 4 • 57300 • Yes • 27 • 2387

Burlington Vermont, USA 41 M7
Burlington Iowa, USA 47 R10
Burma (var. Myanmar) *Country* SE Asia 138 D8

Burma 138-139

1948 • a Burmese • Kyat • 69 • 60 • 10 • 83.6 • 2.6 • 10000 • Yes • 26 • 2598

Burnham-on-Crouch England, United Kingdom 21 R5
Burnham-on-Sea England, United Kingdom 20 J7
Burnie Tasmania, Australia 147 M15
Burnley England, United Kingdom 25 K13
Burns Oregon, USA 50 K10
Burren *Physical region* Republic of Ireland 17 B11
Burren National Park *National park* Republic of Ireland 32 C10
Bursa Turkey 118 I6
Burtnieku Ezers *Lake* Latvia 94 I4
Burton upon Trent England, United Kingdom 23 K8
Buru, Pulau *Island* Indonesia 141 N12
Burundi *Country* C Africa 111 L7

Burundi 111

1962 • a French and Kirundi • Burundi franc • 257 • 42 • 13 • 44.6 • 3 • 3326 • Yes • 8 • 1941

Bury England, United Kingdom 25 K14
Bury *Unitary authority* England, United Kingdom 18 C9
Bury St Edmunds England, United Kingdom 23 Q10
Bushire Iran 123 M8
Buta Dem. Rep. Congo (Zaire) 109 M11
Butare Rwanda 111 L6
Bute, Island of *Island* Scotland, United Kingdom 29 H14
Butembo Dem. Rep. Congo (Zaire) 109 O12
Butler Pennsylvania, USA 40 G12
Buton, Pulau *Island* Indonesia 141 M13
Butte Montana, USA 46 H6
Butterworth , Malaysia 139 I17
Butuan Philippines 141 N7
Buxton England, United Kingdom 22 J5
Buyo, Lac de *Reservoir* Ivory Coast 106 J13
Buzau Romania 91 M7
Buzău *River* Romania 91 M7
Byaroza Belarus 94 I13
Bydgoszcz Poland 85 K4
Byerezino *River* Belarus 95 M11
Bykhaw Belarus 95 N12
Bylchau Wales, United Kingdom 27 N3
Bytantay *River* Russian Federation 129 N6
Bytom Poland 85 L8
Byuzmeyin Turkmenistan 124 H9

C

Caazapá Paraguay 62 N6
Caballo Reservoir *Reservoir* New Mexico, USA 49 L10
Cabanatuan Philippines 141 L4
Cabimas Venezuela 58 G4
Cabinda Angola 109 F14 112 F3
Cabinda *Province* Angola 112 F3
Cabora Bassa, Lake *Reservoir* Mozambique 113 M7
Cabot Strait *Strait* Newfoundland/Nova Scotia, Canada 39 R11
Cacak Serbia, Yugoslavia 89 N7
Cáceres Spain 74 H9
Cader Idris *Mountain* Wales, United Kingdom 27 L6
Cadiz Philippines 141 M6
Cádiz Spain 74 H14
Cadiz, Gulf of *Gulf* Spain 74 G13
Caen France 76 I4
Caergwrle Wales, United Kingdom 27 O3
Caernarfon Wales, United Kingdom 27 K3
Caernarfon Bay *Bay* NW Wales, United Kingdom 26 J3
Caerphilly Wales, United Kingdom 27 O14
Caerphilly *Unitary authority* Wales, United Kingdom 19 F17
Caersws Wales, United Kingdom 27 N7
Cagayan de Oro Philippines 141 N7
Cagliari Italy 87 D15
Cagliari, Golfo di *Gulf* Italy 87 D16
Caher Republic of Ireland 31 L12
Caherciveen Republic of Ireland 30 H14
Cahore Point *Headland* Republic of Ireland 31 O12
Cahors France 77 K12
Caicos Islands *Island group* Turks and Caicos Islands 55 57 N6
Cairngorm Mountains *Mountain range* Scotland, United Kingdom 17 F6 29 K10
Cairns Queensland, Australia 147 N6
Cairo Egypt 104 F6
Cajamarca Peru 59 C11
Cakovec Croatia 88 I2
Calabar Nigeria 107 P13
Calabria *Region* Italy 87 M16
Calais France 77 K1
Calais Maine, USA 41 R5
Calama Chile 62 G5
Călăraşi Romania 91 N9
Calbayog Philippines 141 N5
Calcutta India 114 J5 131 O8
Caldas da Rainha Portugal 74 F9
Calderdale *Unitary authority* England, United Kingdom 19 K13
Caldicot Wales, United Kingdom 27 P14
Caleta Olivia Argentina 63 J16
Calf of Man *Island* Isle of Man 17 E10 24 F7
Calgary Alberta, Canada 37 L14
Cali Colombia 58 D7
Calicut India 130 J14
California *State* USA 51 G13
California, Gulf of *Gulf* Pacific Ocean 34 52 H5 55 N6 145
Callander Scotland, United Kingdom 29 J13
Callao Peru 59 D13 145 Q9
Caltanissetta Italy 87 K18
Calvinia South Africa 112 I15
Cam *River* England, United Kingdom 21 P3 23 O11
Camagüey Cuba 56 J5
Cambay, Gulf of *see* Khambhat, Gulf of
Cambodia *Country* SE Asia 139 K13

Cambodia 139

1953 • a Khmer • Riel • 62 • 53 • 12 • 66 • 5 • 8120 • No • 21 • 2021

Cambrian Mountains *Mountain rang*Wales, United Kingdom 17 E12 27 L10 32 F11
Cambridge England, United Kingdom 23 P11
Cambridgeshire *County* England, United Kingdom 19 M15
Camden New Jersey, USA 41 K14
Camden *London borough* England, United Kingdom 19 N19
Cameia *National Park* Angola 112 J5
Cameron Highlands *Region* Malaysia 139 I18
Cameroon *Country* C Africa 108 E10

Cameroon 108-109

1960 • a English and French • Franc de la Coopération financière en Afrique central • 32 • 55 • 12 • 71.7 • 7 • 10000 • Yes • 45 • 1981

Campbell Island *Island* New Zealand 144 J13
Campbell Plateau *Undersea feature* Pacific Ocean 143
Campbell River British Columbia, Canada 36 I14
Campbeltown Scotland, United Kingdom 29 G15
Campeche Mexico 53 S11
Campeche, Bay of *Bay* Gulf of Mexico 53 P12
Campina Grande Brazil 60 O9
Campinas Brazil 61 J14
Campo Grande Brazil 61 H13
Campobasso Italy 87 K12
Cân Tho Vietnam 139 M15
Canada *Country* North America 36-39

Canada 36-39

1867 • a English and French • Canadian dollar • 3 • 79 • 16 • 99 • 441 • 455 • No • 77 • 3094

Canadian River *River* USA 47 Q15 49 N8
Canadian Shield *Physical region* Canada 34
Çanakkale Turkey 118 G6
Canary Islands *Island group* Spain 66 J10 101
Canberra Australian Capital Territory, Australia 147 O13
Cancer, Tropic of *Line of latitude* 34 55
Cancún Mexico 53 T10
Caniapiscau *River* Quebec, Canada 39 N6
Caniapiscau, Réservoir de *Reservoir* Quebec, Canada 39 M7
Çankırı Turkey 119 L5
Canna *Island* Scotland, United Kingdom 29 F11
Cannes France 77 Q13
Cannock England, United Kingdom 22 J8
Cannock Chase *Area of Outstanding Natural Beauty* England, United Kingdom 32 F11
Cantábrica, Cordillera *Mountain range* Spain 68 75 H4
Canterbury England, United Kingdom 21 S7
Canterbury Bight *Bight* Pacific Ocean 148 F10
Canton Illinois, USA 44 J12
Canton Ohio, USA 45 Q11
Canton *see* Guangzhou
Canyon de Chelly *Historic site* USA 49 K7
Canyon Ferry Lake *Lake* Montana, USA 46 H5
Cap-Haïtien Haiti 57 M7
Cape Basin *Undersea basin* Atlantic Ocean 67 K14 101
Cape Canaveral Florida, USA 43 O12
Cape Coast Ghana 107 L13
Cape Girardeau Missouri, USA 47 T12
Cape Town South Africa 67 M14 112 I16 114 B12
Cape Verde *Country* Atlantic Ocean 66 I10

Cape Verde 66

1975 • a Portuguese • Cape Verde escudo • 104 • 69 • 13 • 71 • 4 • 3448 • No • 56 • 2805

Cape Verde Basin *Undersea basin* Atlantic Ocean 67 H11
Cape Verde Islands *Island group* Cape Verde 101
Cape York Peninsula *Peninsula* Queensland, Australia 143 147 M5
Capitán Pablo Lagerenza Paraguay 62 K3
Cappadocia *Physical region* Turkey 119 M7
Capri *Island* Italy 87 K14
Capricorn, Tropic of *Line of latitude* 55 127 143
Caquetá, Río *River* Brazil/Colombia 58 F8
Caracas Venezuela 58 I4
Caratasca, Laguna de *Lagoon* Honduras 56 F9
Carbondale Illinois, USA 45 K15
Carcassonne France 77 L14
Cardiff *National region/* Wales, United Kingdom 27 O15
Cardiff *Unitary authority* Wales, United Kingdom 19 F18
Cardigan Wales, United Kingdom 26 J10
Cardigan Bay *Bay* United Kingdom 17 E12 26 J7 32 E11
Caribbean Plate *Tectonic plate* 34 55
Caribbean Sea *Sea* Atlantic Ocean 34 55 D10 56 58 I8 66 F3
Caribou Maine, USA 41 Q3
Carlisle England, United Kingdom 24 I8
Carlisle Pennsylvania, USA 40 I13
Carlow Republic of Ireland 31 N12
Carlow *County* Republic of Ireland 19 E15
Carloway Scotland, United Kingdom 28 F7
Carlsbad New Mexico, USA 49 M10
Carlsberg Ridge *Undersea ridge* Indian Ocean 114 G7
Carlyle Lake *Reservoir* Illinois, USA 45 K14
Carmarthen Wales, United Kingdom 27 K12
Carmarthen Bay *Inlet* Wales, United Kingdom 26 J13
Carmarthenshire *Unitary authority* Wales, United Kingdom 19 H16
Carmel Head *Headland* Wales, United Kingdom 26 J1
Carmen, Isla *Island* Mexico 52 H6
Carnarvon Western Australia, Australia 146 E10
Carnedd Llywelyn *Mountain* Wales, United Kingdom 27 L2
Carnegie, Lake *Salt lake* Western Australia, Australia 146 G10
Carnoustie Scotland, United Kingdom 29 M12
Carnsore Point *Headland* Republic of Ireland 17 D12
Carolina Brazil 60 K9
Caroline Islands *Island group* Micronesia 144 G8 143
Caroline Plate *Tectonic plate* 127 143
Caroline Ridge *Undersea feature* Pacific Ocean 143
Carpathian Mountains *Mountain range* E Europe 68 85 L10 91 K2 98 E5
Carpentaria, Gulf of *Gulf* Australia 143 147 L5
Carrauntoohil *Mountain* Republic of Ireland 17 B12 30 I13
Carrickfergus *District* Northern Ireland, United Kingdom 19 G11
Carrickmacross Republic of Ireland 31 N7
Carson City Nevada, USA 48 E3
Cartagena Colombia 58 E4 67 D11
Cartagena Spain 75 N12
Cartago Costa Rica 56 E13
Cartwright Newfoundland, Canada 39 R6
Casa Grande Arizona, USA 48 I9
Casablanca Morocco 66 K9 102 H5
Cascade Range *Mountain range* Oregon/Washington, USA 50 H10
Casey *Australian research station* Antarctica 64 G10
Cashel Republic of Ireland 31 L12
Casper Wyoming, USA 47 K9
Caspian Depression *Depression* Kazakhstan/Russian Federation 68
Caspian Sea *Inland sea* Asia/Europe 68 96 99 117 F17 123 N2 124 E5 128 D10 127 S12
Castelló de la Plana Spain 75 O9
Castelo Branco Portugal 74 G9
Castle Acre England, United Kingdom 23 Q8
Castle Douglas Scotland, United Kingdom 29 K16
Castlebar Republic of Ireland 30 J7
Castlebay Scotland, United Kingdom 29 D11
Castledawson Northern Ireland, United Kingdom 31 O4
Castleford England, United Kingdom 25 M14
Castleisland Republic of Ireland 30 I13
Castlereagh *District* Northern Ireland, United Kingdom 19 G12
Castletown Isle of Man 24 G6
Castries Saint Lucia 57 T13
Castro Chile 63 G15
Cat Island *Island* Bahamas 57 L3
Catalonia (Sp. Cataluña) Spain 75 P6
Cataluña *see* Catalonia
Catanduanes Island *Island* Philippines 141 M4
Catania Italy 87 L18
Catanzaro Italy 87 N16
Catskill Mountains *Mountain range* New York, USA 41 L10
Catterick England, United Kingdom 25 L10
Cauca, Río *River* Colombia 58 E5
Caucasus *Mountain range* Georgia/Russian Federation 68 96 99 D15 117 O11 128 C9 127
Cauquenes Chile 63 G12
Cavan Republic of Ireland 31 M7
Cavan *County* Republic of Ireland 19 E12
Cawnpore *see* Kanpur
Caxito Angola 112 G4
Cayenne French Guiana 58 P6 67 F11
Cayes Haiti 57 L8
Cayman Brac *Island* Cayman Islands 56 I6
Cayman Islands *Dependent territory* West Indies 56 H6
Ceará Plain *Undersea feature* Atlantic Ocean55
Cebu Philippines 141 M6
Cebu *Island* Philippines 141 M6
Cedar Rapids Iowa, USA 47 R9
Cedar River *River* Iowa/Minnesota, USA 47 Q8
Cedros, Isla *Island* Mexico 52 F4
Cefalù Italy 87 K17
Celaya Mexico 53 M11
Celebes (var. Sulawesi) *Island* Indonesia 127 141 L12
Celebes Sea *Sea* SE Asia 127 141 L10 144 143 F8
Celje Slovenia 83 R10
Celle Germany 80 H9
Celtic Sea *Sea* Republic of Ireland/United Kingdom 17 D13 31 M14 32 D12
Celtic Shelf *Undersea feature* Atlantic Ocean 68
Cemaes Wales, United Kingdom 26 J1
Cemaes Head *Headland* Wales, United Kingdom 26 I10
Central African Republic *Country* C Africa 108 J9

Central African Republic 108-109

1960 • a French • Franc de la Coopération financière en Afrique centrale • 6 • 45 • 14 • 42.4 • N/A • 5000 • No • 39 • 1690

Central America *Region* 54-55
Central Arizona Project *Irrigated agriculture* USA 49 I9
Central Makran Range *Mountain range* Pakistan 130 F5
Central Pacific Basin *Undersea feature* Pacific Ocean 143
Central Russian Upland *Mountain range* Russian Federation 68
Central Siberian Plateau *Mountain range* Russian Federation 117 129 K7 127
Centralia Illinois, USA 45 K14
Ceram *Island* Indonesia 127 143
Ceram Sea *Sea* Indonesia 141 O12
Ceredigion *Unitary authority* Wales, United Kingdom 19 I15
Cerralvo, Isla *Island* Mexico 52 H8
Cerro de Pasco Peru 59 D12
Cervia Italy 86 H8
Cesis Latvia 94 J5
Ceské Budějovice Czech Republic 84 H11
Cesma *River* Croatia 88 I3
Ceuta Spain 102 I4
Cévennes *Mountain range* France 77 M14
Ceyhan Turkey 119 N9
Ceylon Plain *Undersea feature* Indian Ocean 117 127

Chabahar Iran 114 G5 123 Q11
Chad *Country* C Africa 108 I6

Chad 108

1975 • Portuguese • Cape Verde escudo • 104 • 69 • 13 • 71 • 4 • 3448 • No • 56 • 2805

Chad, Lake *Lake* C Africa 101 107 R9 108 H7
Chagai Hills *Hill range* Pakistan 130 E4
Chagos-Laccadive Plateau *Undersea plateau* India 114 H9 117 I27
Chalbi Desert *Desert* Kenya 111 P3
Chalkida Greece 93 K8
Châlons-en-Champagne France 77 N5
Chambal *River* India 131 K6
Chambéry France 77 O10
Chambord France 77 K7
Champaign Illinois, USA 45 L12
Champasak Laos 139 M12
Champlain, Lake *Lake* Canada/USA 41 M6
Chañaral Chile 62 G7
Chandigarh India 131 K4
Changchun China 135 O4
Changsha China 135 L12
Changzhi China 135 L8
Chania Greece 93 L15
Channel Islands *Island group* W Europe 17 F16 32 F15
Channel, The *see* English Channel
Channel Tunnel *Tunnel* France/United Kingdom 21 T7
Channel-Port aux Basques Newfoundland, Canada 39 Q10
Chanthaburi Thailand 139 J13
Chapala, Lago de *Lake* Mexico 53 L11
Chard England, United Kingdom 20 J9
Chardzhev Turkmenistan 125 K8
Charente *River* France 76 I10
Chari *River* Central African Republic/Chad 108 H8
Chariton River *River* Missouri, USA 47 R10
Charleroi Belgium 79 H16
Charleston South Carolina, USA 43 P8
Charleston West Virginia, USA 43 P3
Charlestown Republic of Ireland 31 K7
Charleville Queensland, Australia 147 N10
Charleville-Mézières France 77 N3
Charlotte North Carolina, USA 43 P6
Charlotte Amalie Virgin Islands (US) 57 R9
Charlottesville Virginia, USA 43 Q3
Charlottetown Prince Edward Island, Canada 39 Q12
Chartres France 77 K6
Charus Nuur *Lake* Mongolia 133 N8
Chashma Barrage *Dam* Pakistan 130 I2
Châteauroux France 77 K8
Chatham England, United Kingdom 21 R6
Chatham Islands *Island group* New Zealand 144 J12
Chatham Rise *Undersea feature* Pacific Ocean 143
Chattanooga Tennessee, USA 43 M5
Chauk Burma 138 F8
Chaumont France 77 N6
Cheboksary Russian Federation 97 I11 128 F7
Cheboygan Michigan, USA 45 N5
Chechnya *Region* Russian Federation 96 E16
Cheju South Korea 135 P9
Chelan, Lake *Reservoir* Washington, USA 50 H6
Cheleken Turkmenistan 124 F7
Chełm Poland 85 P7
Chelmsford England, United Kingdom 21 Q5
Cheltenham England, United Kingdom 21 L4
Chelyabinsk Russian Federation 128 G9
Chelyuskin, Mys *Cape* Russian Federation 129 L4
Chemnitz Germany 81 M11
Chenab *River* Pakistan 130 I3
Chengdu China 134 J10
Chennai (prev. Madras) India 114 I7 131 L13
Chepstow Wales, United Kingdom 27 P16
Cherbourg France 76 H4
Cherepovets Russian Federation 96 G9 128 F5
Cherkasy Ukraine 98 J5
Cherkessk Russian Federation 97 D15 128 C9
Chernihiv Ukraine 98 I3
Chernivtsi Ukraine 98 F6
Chernobyl' Ukraine 98 I4
Chernyakhovsk Russian Federation 94 G10
Chesapeake Bay *Inlet* Virginia, USA 43 S3
Chesham England, United Kingdom 21 P5
Cheshire *County* England, United Kingdom 19 J14
Chester England, United Kingdom 22 H7
Chester-le-Street England, United Kingdom 25 L8
Chesterfield England, United Kingdom 23 K5
Chesterfield Inlet Nunavut, Canada 37 O9
Chesuncook Lake *Lake* Maine, USA 41 P4
Chetumal Mexico 53 T12
Chevaliers, Krak des *Castle* Syria 121 M5
Cheviot Hills *Hill range* England/Scotland, United Kingdom 17 F8 24 J6 29 M15
Cheviot, The *Mountain* England, United Kingdom 25 K4
Cheyenne Wyoming, USA 47 K10
Cheyenne River *River* South Dakota/Wyoming, USA 47 M7
Chiang Mai Thailand 138 H9
Chiang Rai Thailand 138 I9
Chiba Japan 137 L11
Chibougamau Quebec, Canada 39 M10
Chicago Illinois, USA 45 L10
Chichén-Itzá *Ruins* Mexico 53 T11
Chichester England, United Kingdom 21 O9
Chichester Harbour *Area of Outstanding Natural Beauty* England, United Kingdom 32 G13
Chiclayo Peru 59 C11
Chico California, USA 51 H13
Chicoutimi Quebec, Canada 39 N11
Chidley, Cape *Cape* Newfoundland, Canada 39 O3
Chiemsee *Lake* Germany 81 K16
Chifeng China 133 P6
Chihuahua Mexico 53 K5
Chile *Country* SW South America 62 G8

Chile 62-63

1818 • Spanish • Chilean peso • 20 • 75 • 13 • 95.2 • 71 • 909 • Yes • 84 • 2582

Chile Basin *Undersea feature* Pacific Ocean 55 145 P11
Chile Chico Chile 63 I16
Chillán Chile 63 G12
Chillicothe Ohio, USA 45 P13
Chiloé, Isla de *Island* Chile 55 63 G14 145 P12
Chilpancingo Mexico 53 N13
Chiltern Hills *Hill range* England, United Kingdom 17 G13 21 N5 32 G12
Chilung Taiwan 135 O13
Chimborazo *Volcano* Ecuador 55
Chimbote Peru 59 C12 145 Q9
Chimoio Mozambique 113 N9
Chin Hills *Mountain range* Burma 138 E7
China *Country* E Asia 132-135

China 132-135

1949 • Mandarin • Renminbi (People's Bank dollar), usually called the yuan • 136 • 70 • 15 • 83.9 • 3 • 629 • Yes • 30 • 2727

China Lake Naval Weapons Center *Military base* California, USA 51 L17
Chinandega Nicaragua 56 C10
Chindwin *River* Burma 138 F6
Chingola Zambia 111 K13
Chinhoyi Zimbabwe 113 M8
Chioggia Italy 86 H7
Chios Greece 93 O8
Chios *Island* Greece 93 O8
Chipata Zambia 111 M14
Chippenham England, United Kingdom 21 L6
Chippewa, Lake *Reservoir* Wisconsin, USA 44 J5
Chirchiq Uzbekistan 125 N6
Chiriquí Gulf *Gulf* Panama 56 E15
Chirk Wales, United Kingdom 27 O4
Chişinău Moldova 98 H8
Chita Russian Federation 129 N11
Chitré Panama 56 G15
Chittagong Bangladesh 131 P8
Chitungwiza Zimbabwe 113 M8
Chobe *National Park* Botswana 113 K8
Chobe *River* Botswana 113 K8
Chojnice Poland 85 K3
Cholula Mexico 53 N12
Choluteca Honduras 56 C10
Choma Zambia 110 J16
Chon Buri Thailand 139 J13
Ch'ŏngjin North Korea 135 Q5
Chongqing China 134 J11
Chorley England, United Kingdom 24 J14
Choybalsan Mongolia 133 O4
Christchurch New Zealand 148 F10
Christchurch England, United Kingdom 21 M9
Christiansted Virgin Islands (US) 57 R10
Christmas Island *Dependent territory* Indian Ocean 114 M9
Christmas Island *see* Kiritimati
Chu *River* Kazakhstan/Kyrgyzstan 128 G12
Chubut, Río *River* Argentina 63 I14
Chugoku-sanchi *Mountain range* Japan 137 D12
Chukchi Sea *Sea* Arctic Ocean 65 P5 129 Q2
Chumphon Thailand 139 H14
Chuquicamata Chile 62 G5
Chur Switzerland 82 I10
Church Stoke Wales, United Kingdom 27 O7
Church Stretton England, United Kingdom 22 H9
Churchill Manitoba, Canada 37 P11
Churchill *River* Manitoba/Saskatchewan, Canada 37 O11
Churchill Falls Newfoundland, Canada 39 P7
Cienfuegos Cuba 56 I4
Cincinnati Ohio, USA 45 O13
Ciovo *Island* Croatia 88 I7
Cirebon Indonesia 140 H15
Cirencester England, United Kingdom 21 M5
Ciudad Bolívar Venezuela 58 J5
Ciudad del Este Paraguay 62 O6
Ciudad Guayana Venezuela 58 K5
Ciudad Juárez Mexico 52 J3
Ciudad Madero Mexico 53 O10
Ciudad Obregón Mexico 52 I5
Ciudad Real Spain 75 K10
Ciudad Victoria Mexico 53 N9
Civitavecchia Italy 87 G11
Clackmannan *Unitary authority* Scotland, United Kingdom 18 N4
Clair Engle Lake *Reservoir* California, USA 51 G12
Clara Bog *Bog* Republic of Ireland 32 D10
Clare *County* Republic of Ireland 19 C14
Clare *River* Republic of Ireland 31 K9
Clare Island *Island* Republic of Ireland 30 I7
Clarecastle Republic of Ireland 30 J11
Claremont New Hampshire, USA 41 N8
Claremorris Republic of Ireland 30 J7
Clarence Strait *Strait* Australia 146 I5
Clarenville Newfoundland, Canada 39 S9
Clarion Fracture Zone *Undersea feature* Pacific Ocean 34 145 L7
Clarksville Tennessee, USA 43 L4
Clear Island *Island* Republic of Ireland 30 I16
Clearwater Florida, USA 43 N12
Cleethorpes England, United Kingdom 23 O4
Clermont Queensland, Australia 147 O8
Clermont-Ferrand France 77 M10
Clevedon England, United Kingdom 20 J6
Cleveland Ohio, USA 45 P10
Clew Bay *Inlet* Republic of Ireland 30 I7
Clifden Republic of Ireland 30 I8
Clipperton Fracture Zone *Fracture zone* 34 145 L8
Clipperton Island *Dependent territory* Pacific Ocean Clipperton Island 145 N7
Clitheroe England, United Kingdom 24 J13
Cloncurry Queensland, Australia 147 M8
Clondalkin Republic of Ireland 31 O9
Clonmel Republic of Ireland 31 M13
Clovelly England, United Kingdom 20 G8
Clovis New Mexico, USA 49 N9
Cluj-Napoca Romania 90 I4
Clwydian Range *Area of Outstanding Natural Beauty* Wales, United Kingdom 32 F10
Clwydian Range *Mountain range* Wales, United Kingdom 27 N2
Clydach Wales, United Kingdom 27 L13
Clydach Vale Wales, United Kingdom 27 M14
Clyde *River* Scotland, United Kingdom 17 E7 29 K14
Clyde, Firth of *Inlet* Scotland, United Kingdom 17 E7 29 I14
Clydebank Scotland, United Kingdom 29 J14
Clywedog, Llyn *Reservoir* Wales, United Kingdom 27 M7
Coast Ranges *Mountain range* California/Oregon/ Washington, USA 50 G10
Coatbridge Scotland, United Kingdom 29 K14
Coats Island *Island* Nunavut, Canada 37 P9
Coatzacoalcos Mexico 53 P13
Cobán Guatemala 56 B7
Cobija Bolivia 59 H13
Cochabamba Bolivia 59 I15
Cochin India 114 I7 130 J15
Cochrane Ontario, Canada 38 J11
Cochrane Chile 63 I17
Cockburn Sound *Sound* Australia 115 M12
Cockburn Town Turks and Caicos Islands 57 N6
Cockermouth England, United Kingdom 24 G9
Coco, Río *River* Honduras/Nicaragua 56 F9
Cocos Basin *Undersea feature* Indian Ocean 117 I27
Cocos Islands *Dependent territory* Indian Ocean 114 L10
Cocos Plate *Tectonic plate* 34 55
Cocos Ridge *Undersea feature* Indian Ocean 55 145 P8
Cod, Cape *Headland* Massachusetts, USA 34 41 P10
Cody Wyoming, USA 46 I7
Coeur d'Alene Idaho, USA 46 F4
Coiba, Isla de *Island* Panama 56 F15
Coihaique Chile 63 I16
Coimbatore India 130 J14
Coimbra Portugal 74 F8
Colchester England, United Kingdom 21 R4
Colditz *Castle* Germany 81 K11
Coldstream Scotland, United Kingdom 29 N14
Coleraine *District* Northern Ireland, United Kingdom 19 F11
Colhué Huapí, Lago *Lake* Argentina 63 J16
Colima Mexico 53 K12
Coll *Island* Scotland, United Kingdom 17 D6 29 F12
Collier Bay *Bay* Western Australia, Australia 146 H6
Collooney Republic of Ireland 31 K6
Colmar France 77 P6
Colne England, United Kingdom 25 K13
Cologne (Ger. Köln) Germany 81 D11
Colombia *Country* N South America 58 F9

Colombia 58

1819 • Spanish • Colombian peso • 40 • 70 • 12 • 90.6 • 19 • 1111 • No • 73 • 2677

Colombian Basin *Undersea feature* Caribbean Sea 55
Colombo Sri Lanka 114 I7 131 K16
Colón Panama 56 G14
Colón Argentina 62 N9
Colonia del Sacramento Uruguay 62 N10
Colonsay *Island* Scotland, United Kingdom 17 D7
Colorado *State* USA 34 49 L4
Colorado Plateau *Plateau* USA 48 I7
Colorado Project *Irrigated agriculture* USA 49 H9
Colorado River *River* Texas, USA 49 P11
Colorado River *River* Mexico/USA 49 K5 51 O19 52 G1 145 N5
Colorado Springs Colorado, USA 49 M5
Colorado, Río *River* Argentina 55 63 K12
Columbia Missouri, USA 47 R11
Columbia *River* Canada/USA 34 37 K14 50 K6 145 N4
Columbine, Cape *Headland* South Africa 112 I15
Columbus Georgia, USA 43 M8 47 F4
Columbus Indiana, USA 45 N13
Columbus Ohio, USA 45 P12
Colville River *River* Alaska, USA 36 H5
Colwyn Bay Wales, United Kingdom 27 M2
Comacchio, Valli di *Lagoon* Italy 86 H8
Comayagua Honduras 56 C9
Comeragh Mountains *Mountain range* Republic of Ireland 31 L13
Comilla Bangladesh 131 P8
Como, Lake *Lake* Italy 86 E6
Comodoro Rivadavia Argentina 63 J16
Comorin, Cape *Headland* India 114 I7 127
Comoro Islands *Island group* Comoros 101
Comoros *Country* Indian Ocean 114 E10

Comoros 114

1975 • Arabic and French • Comoros franc • 303 • 59 • 16 • 55.4 • 14 • 10000 • Yes • 31 • 1897

Conakry Guinea 106 G11
Concepción Chile 63 G12 145 Q12
Concepción Paraguay 62 M5
Conchos *River* Mexico 52 J5
Concord California, USA 51 H15
Concord New Hampshire, USA 41 O9
Concordia Argentina 62 N9
Congleton England, United Kingdom 22 I6
Congo *River* C Africa 67 L12 101 109 J12 112 F3
Congo *Country* C Africa 109 H13

Congo 109

1960 • French • Franc de la Coopération financière en Afrique • 8 • 49 • 16 • 76.9 • 14 • 3333 • No • 59 • 2296

Congo Basin *Drainage basin* C Africa 101
Congo (Zaire), Democratic Republic of *Country* C Africa 109 K13

Congo (Zaire), Dem. Rep. 108-109

1960 • French and English • Congolese franc • 22 • 51 • 77 • 17 • 10000 • Yes • 29 • 2060

Conn, Lough *Lake* Republic of Ireland 31 J6
Connecticut *State* USA 41 M11
Connecticut *River* Canada/USA 40 N8
Connemara *Physical region* Republic of Ireland 17 B10 30 I8
Connemara National Park *National Park* Republic of Ireland 32 C10
Consett England, United Kingdom 25 K8
Constance *see* Konstanz
Constance, Lake *Lake* C Europe 68 81 G17 82 H8
Constanţa Romania 91 P9
Constantine Algeria 103 M4
Contwoyto Lake *Lake* Nunavut, Canada 37 M8
Conwy Wales, United Kingdom 27 L2
Conwy *Unitary authority* Wales, United Kingdom 19 I14
Coober Pedy South Australia, Australia 147 K11
Cook Islands *Dependent territory* Pacific Ocean 145 K10
Cook Strait *Strait* New Zealand 144 I12 143 148 H7
Cook, Mount *Mountain* New Zealand 143
Cookstown Northern Ireland, United Kingdom 31 N4
Cookstown *District* Northern Ireland, United Kingdom 19 E11
Cooktown Queensland, Australia 147 N6
Cooper Creek *Seasonal river* Queensland/South Australia, Australia 147 L11
Coos Bay Oregon, USA 50 F10
Copán Honduras 56 C8
Copenhagen Denmark 70 J15
Copiapó Chile 62 G7
Coppermine *River* Northwest Territories/Nunavut, Canada 37 L8
Coppermine Nunavut, Canada 37 L8
Copşa Mică Romania 90 J5
Coquimbo Chile 62 G9
Corabia Romania 90 J10
Coral Sea *Sea* Pacific Ocean 144 H10 143 147 O4
Coral Sea Basin *Undersea feature* Pacific Ocean 143
Coral Sea Islands *Dependent territory* Pacific Ocean 144 H10
Corby England, United Kingdom 23 M9
Córdoba Argentina 62 J9
Córdoba (Eng. Cordova) Spain 74 J12
Cordova Alaska, USA 36 G9
Cordova *see* Córdoba
Corfu Greece 92 F5
Corfu (Gr. Kerkyra) *Island* Greece 92 F6
Corinth (Gr. Korinthos) Greece 92 J10
Corinth Canal *Canal* Greece 92 J9
Corinth, Gulf of *Gulf* Greece 92 I9
Corinto Nicaragua 56 C10
Cork Republic of Ireland 31 K14
Cork *County* Republic of Ireland 19 C16
Corner Brook Newfoundland, Canada 39 R9
Corning New York, USA 40 J10
Corno Grande *Mountain* Italy 68
Cornwall *County* England, United Kingdom 19 G18
Cornwall *Area of Outstanding Natural Beauty* England, United Kingdom 32 E14
Cornwallis Island *Island* Nunavut, Canada 37 N4
Coro Venezuela 58 H4
Coromandel New Zealand 148 I3
Coromandel Coast *Coast* India 131 L14
Coronel Chile 63 G12
Corpus Christi Texas, USA 49 R14
Corrib, Lough *Lake* Republic of Ireland 17 B11 31 J8
Corrientes Argentina 62 M7
Corris Wales, United Kingdom 27 L6
Corsica *Island* France 68 77 S14
Cortland New York, USA 41 K9
Çorum Turkey 119 M5
Corumbá Brazil 61 G13
Corunna *see* A Coruña
Corvallis Oregon, USA 50 G9
Corwen Wales, United Kingdom 27 N4
Cosenza Italy 87 N15
Costa Rica *Country* Central America 56 D12

Costa Rica 56

1838 • Spanish • Costa Rican colón • 76 • 76 • 18 • 95.1 • 85 • 1111 • No • 50 • 2883

Côte d'Azur *Physical region* France 77 Q14
Cotonou Benin 107 M13
Cotopaxi *Volcano* Ecuador 55
Cotswold Hills *Hill range* England, United Kingdom 17 F13 21 K5 32 G12
Cottbus Germany 80 M10
Council Bluffs Iowa, USA 47 P10
Courantyne River *River* Guyana/Surinam 58 N7
Courland Lagoon *Lagoon* Lithuania/Russian Federation 94 F9
Coventry England, United Kingdom 23 K10
Coventry *Unitary authority* England, United Kingdom 19 P12
Covilhã Portugal 74 G8
Cozumel, Isla *Island* Mexico 53 T11
Cracow *see* Kraków
Craigavon *District* Northern Ireland, United Kingdom 19 F12
Craiova Romania 90 J9
Cranborne Chase and West Wiltshire Downs *Area of Outstanding Natural Beauty* England, United Kingdom 32 G13
Craven Arms England, United Kingdom 22 H10
Crawley England, United Kingdom 21 P8
Cree Lake *Lake* Saskatchewan, Canada 37 M12
Cremona Italy 86 E7
Cres *Island* Croatia 88 G4
Crescent City California, USA 51 F11
Crete *Island* Greece 68 93 L15
Crete, Sea of *Sea* Mediterranean Sea 93 L15
Crewe England, United Kingdom 22 I6
Crickhowell Wales, United Kingdom 27 O12
Crieff Scotland, United Kingdom 29 K12
Crimea *Peninsula* Ukraine 68 98 J9
Crna Reka *River* FYR Macedonia 89 O12
Croatia *Country* SE Europe 88 I3

Croatia 88-89

1991 • Croatian • Kuna • 80 • 73 • 15 • 97.7 • 195 • 500 • No • 64 • N/A

Croker Island *Island* Northern Territory, Australia 146 J4
Cromarty Scotland, United Kingdom 28 J9
Cromer England, United Kingdom 23 R7
Cromer *Beach* England, United Kingdom 32 H10
Crooked Island *Island* Bahamas 57 M5
Crosby England, United Kingdom 24 H15
Cross Fell *Mountain* England, United Kingdom 24 J8
Cross Hands Wales, United Kingdom 27 L13
Crotone Italy 87 O15
Croydon England, United Kingdom 21 P7
Croydon *London borough* England, United Kingdom 19 N20
Crozet Basin *Undersea feature* Indian Ocean 115 G13
Crozet Islands *Island group* French Southern and Antarctic Territories 64 I5 115 F14
Cruzeiro do Sul Brazil 60 A9
Crymych Wales, United Kingdom 26 J11
Cuango *River* Angola/Dem. Rep. Congo (Zaire) 112 H3
Cuanza *River* Angola 112 G4
Cuba *Island* Cuba 55

Date of independence • Language (official or most commonly spoken) • Currency • Population density per square kilometre • Average life expectancy • School-leaving age • Literacy • Number of cars per 1,000 people • Number of people per doctor • Death penalty • Percentage of urban-based population • Average number of calories consumed daily per person

Cuba *Country* West Indies 56 I5

Cuba 56-57

1902 • a Spanish • Cuban peso • 101 • 76 • 16 • 95.9 • 16 • 278 • Yes • 76 • 2833

Cubango *River* Southern Africa 112 H7
Cúcuta Colombia 58 F5
Cuenca Ecuador 58 C9
Cueno Italy 86 B8
Cuernavaca Mexico 53 N12
Cuiabá Brazil 61 G11
Cuíto Cuanavale Angola 112 I7
Cuitzeo, Lago de *Lake* Mexico 53 M11
Culiacán Mexico 52 J4
Cumaná Venezuela 58 J4
Cumberland Plateau *Plateau* USA 43 M5
Cumberland Sound *Inlet* Nunavut, Canada 37 R6
Cumbernauld Scotland, United Kingdom 29 K14
Cumbria *County* England, United Kingdom 19 J11
Cumbrian Mountains *Mountain range* England, United Kingdom 17 F9 24 H9
Cumnock Scotland, United Kingdom 29 J15
Cunene *River* Angola/Namibia 112 G8
Cunnamulla Queensland, Australia 147 M10
Curaçao *Island* Netherlands Antilles 57 O14
Curicó Chile 63 G11
Curitiba Brazil 61 J15
Cusco Peru 59 F14
Cuttack India 131 N9
Cuxhaven Germany 80 G7
Cwmbran Wales, United Kingdom 27 O14
Cyclades (Gr. Kyklades) *Island group* Greece 93 M11
Cynwyl Elfed Wales, United Kingdom 27 K12
Cyprus *Country* SW Asia 119 L12

Cyprus 119

1960 • a Greek and Turkish • Cyprus pound (Turkish lira in TRNC) • 84 • 78 • 15 • 95.9 • 334 • 433 • No • 54 • 3779

Cyprus *Island* SW Asia 68
Cyrenaica *Region* Libya 103 Q7
Cyrene Libya 103 R6
Czech Republic *Country* C Europe 84 G9

Czech Republic 84-85

1993 • a Czech • Czech koruna • 131 • 74 • 15 • 99 • 344 • 345 • No • 65 • 3156

Częstochowa Poland 85 L8

D

Đa Lat Vietnam 139 O14
Da Nang Vietnam 139 O11
Da Qaidam China 132 J9
Dadu He *River* China 134 I9
Dagupan Philippines 141 L3
Dahlak Archipelago *Island group* Eritrea 105 K12
Dahuk Iraq 123 K2
Dakar Senegal 106 F8
Dalaman Turkey 118 H10
Dali China 134 H13
Dalian China 135 O7
Dalkeith Scotland, United Kingdom 29 L14
Dallas Texas, USA 49 R10
Dalmatia *Region* Croatia 88 H6
Daloa Ivory Coast 106 J12
Daman India 130 I9
Damar, Pulau *Island* Indonesia 141 O14
Damascus (var. Damashq) Syria 121 N7
Damashq *see* Damascus
Dampier Western Australia, Australia 146 F8
Danbury Connecticut, USA 41 M11
Danmark Havn Greenland 65 P13
Danube (Ger. Donau, Hung. Duna, Rom. Dun˘area) *River* Europe 68 81 K14 83 Q5 85 L14 89 L4 90 I10
Danube-Black Sea Canal *Canal* Romania 91 O9
Danube Delta *Delta* Romania 91 P7
Danville Illinois, USA 45 L12
Danville Virginia, USA 43 Q5
Danzig, Gulf of (var. Gulf of Gda´nsk) *Gulf* Poland/Russian Federation 85 L1
Dapaong Togo 107 M10
Dar'a Syria 121 N9
Dar es Salaam Tanzania 111 Q9 114 D9
Darhan Mongolia 133 M4
Darien, Gulf of *Gulf* Colombia/Panama 55 56 I15 58 D5
Darling River *River* New South Wales, Australia 143 147 M12
Darlington England, United Kingdom 25 L9
Darlington *Unitary authority* England, United Kingdom 18 M10
Darmstadt Germany 81 F13
Darnah Libya 103 R6
Darnley, Cape *Cape* Antarctica 64 G8
Dart *River* England, United Kingdom 20 H11
Dartmoor *Moorland* England, United Kingdom 17 E14 20 G10
Dartmoor National Park *National Park* England, United Kingdom 32 F13
Dartmouth England, United Kingdom 20 I11
Daru Papua New Guinea 147 M3
Darwin Northern Territory, Australia 146 J5
Dashkhovuz Turkmenistan 124 I5
Dasht-e Gowd-e-Zereh *Desert region* Afghanistan 124 J16
Dasht-e Lut *Desert* Iran 68 117 123 P7
Datong China 135 L6
Daugavpils Latvia 95 K7
Davangere India 130 J12
Davao Philippines 141 N7
Davenport Iowa, USA 47 S9
Daventry England, United Kingdom 23 L10
David Panama 56 F15
Davis Dam *Dam* USA 48 H7
Davis Mountains *Mountain range* Texas, USA 49 M12
Davis Sea *Sea* Antarctica 64 H9
Davis Strait *Strait* Atlantic Ocean 34 37 R5 65 M13 66 F7
Dawlish Warren *Beach* England, United Kingdom 32 F13
Dawros Head *Headland* Republic of Ireland 31 K4
Dawson Yukon Territory, Canada 36 I8
Dawson Creek British Columbia, Canada 37 K12
Daxue Shan *Mountain range* China 127
Dayr az Zawr Syria 121 R4
Dayton Ohio, USA 45 O12
Daytona Beach Florida, USA 43 O11
De Aar South Africa 113 K14
De Kalb Illinois, USA 45 K10
Dead Sea *Salt lake* Israel/Jordan 117 121 M10
Deal England, United Kingdom 21 T7
Dean, Forest of *Forest* England, United Kingdom 21 K5
Death Valley *Valley* California, USA 34
Debre Birhan Ethiopia 105 J15
Debre Mark'os Ethiopia 105 J14
Debrecen Hungary 85 N13
Decatur Illinois, USA 45 K12
Deccan *Plateau* India 117 127 130 J11
Dee *River* England/Wales, United Kingdom 27 P4
Dee *River* Scotland, United Kingdom 17 F6
Dee *River* Scotland, United Kingdom 17 E9 29 K16
Deeside and Lochnagar *Area of Outstanding Natural Beauty* Scotland, United Kingdom 32 F6
Dehra Dun India 131 K4
Del Rio Texas, USA 49 O13
Delaware *State* USA 41 K16
Delaware River *River* USA 41 K12
Delémont Switzerland 82 E9
Delft Netherlands 79 G11
Delfzijl Netherlands 78 N6
Delhi India 131 K5
Delhi China 133 K9
Delicias Mexico 53 K5
Delphi Greece 92 I8
Demchok *Disputed region* China/India 130 L3 132 F11
Demerara Plain *Undersea feature* Atlantic Ocean 55
Demirkopru Baraji *Dam* Turkey 118 H7
Den Helder Netherlands 78 H7
Denbigh Wales, United Kingdom 27 N2
Denbighshire *Unitary authority* Wales, United Kingdom 19 I13
Denizli Turkey 118 H8
Denmark *Country* N Europe 70 H13

Denmark 70-71

950 • a Danish • Danish krone • 125 • 76 • 16 • 99 • 331 • 345 • No • 85 • 3664

Denmark Strait *Strait* Atlantic Ocean 34 65 O15 66 I7
Denpasar Indonesia 140 J15
D'Entrecasteaux Islands *Island group* Papua New Guinea 147 P3
Denver Colorado, USA 49 M4
Dera Ghazi Khan Pakistan 130 I4
Dera Ismail Khan Pakistan 130 I3
Derby England, United Kingdom 23 K7
Derby, City of *Unitary authority* England, United Kingdom 19 L14
Derbyshire *County* England, United Kingdom 19 K14
Derg, Lough *Lake* Republic of Ireland 31 K10
Derry *see* Londonderry
Derwent *River* England, United Kingdom 17 G10 25 N11
Des Moines Iowa, USA 47 Q9
Des Moines River *River* USA 47 Q9
Dese Ethiopia 105 J14
Deseado, Río *River* Argentina 63 J16
Desna *River* Russian Federation/Ukraine 98 J3
Dessau Germany 80 K10
Detroit Michigan, USA 45 O9
Deva Romania 90 I6
Deventer Netherlands 78 L10
Deveron *River* Scotland, United Kingdom 29 M9
Devil's Bridge Wales, United Kingdom 27 L8
Devizes England, United Kingdom 21 L7
Devollit, Lumi i *River* Albania 89 M12
Devon *County* England, United Kingdom 19 I17
Devon Island *Island* Nunavut, Canada 34 37 N5 65 N11
Dewsbury England, United Kingdom 25 L14
Dezful Iran 123 M6
Dezhneva, Mys *Headland* Russian Federation 129 R1
Dhahran Saudi Arabia 123 M9
Dhaka Bangladesh 131 P8
Dhamar Yemen 122 I16
Dhanbad India 131 N7
Dharwad India 130 J11
Dhule India 130 J9
Diamantina River *River* Queensland/South Australia, Australia 147 M9
Dickinson North Dakota, USA 47 L5
Didcot England, United Kingdom 21 N6
Didyma *Archaeological site* Turkey 118 G9
Diego Garcia *Island* British Indian Ocean Territory 114 H9
Diekirch Luxembourg 79 L18
Dieppe France 77 K3
Diffa Niger 107 Q9
Digne France 77 P12
Digul, Sungai *River* Indonesia 141 T14
Dijon France 77 N7
Dikson Russian Federation 65 T11
Dili East Timor 141 N15
Dillon Montana, USA 46 H7
Dilolo Dem. Rep. Congo (Zaire) 109 L17
Dimbokro Ivory Coast 107 K13
Dinant Belgium 79 I17
Dinaric Alps *Mountain range* Bosnia and Herzegovina/Croatia 68 88 H5
Dingle Republic of Ireland 30 H13
Dingle Bay *Bay* Republic of Ireland 17 A12 30 H13
Dingwall Scotland, United Kingdom 28 J9
Diourbel Senegal 106 F8
Dipkarpaz Cyprus 119 L11
Dipolog Philippines 141 M7
Dire Dawa Ethiopia 105 L15
Dirk Hartog Island *Island* Western Australia, Australia 146 E10
Disappointment, Lake *Salt lake* Western Australia, Australia 146 H9
Disney World *Theme park* Florida, USA 43 N12
Dispur India 131 P6
Diss England, United Kingdom 23 R10
Divriği Turkey 119 O7
Diyarbakır Turkey 119 Q8
Djado, Plateau du *Mountain range* Niger 107 Q5
Djakarta *see* Jakarta
Djakovo Croatia 89 K4
Djambala Congo 109 H13
Djerba *Island* Tunisia 103 N5
Djibouti *Country* E Africa 105 K14

Djibouti 105

1977 • a Arabic and French • Djibouti franc • 27 • 50 • 12 • 48.6 • 11 • 5000 • No • 83 • 2338

Djibouti Djibouti 105 L14 114 E7
Dnieper *River* Belarus/Russian Federation/Ukraine 68 95 N15 96 E10 98 I5
Dniester *River* Moldova/Ukraine 68 98 F5
Dnipropetrovs'k Ukraine 99 K6
Dobele Latvia 94 H6
Doboj Bosnia and Herzegovina 89 K5
Dobrich Bulgaria 91 O11
Doctor Pedro P. Peña Paraguay 62 K5
Dodecanese *Island group* Greece 93 O11
Dodge City Kansas, USA 47 N13
Dodoma Tanzania 111 O9
Dogo *Island* Japan 137 E11
Doha Qatar 123 M10
Dolgellau Wales, United Kingdom 27 L6
Dolisie Congo 109 G14
Dolomites *Mountain range* Italy 86 G6
Dolores Argentina 63 N11
Dolwyddelan Wales, United Kingdom 27 L3
Dominica *Country* West Indies 57 T12

Dominica 57

1978 • a English • Eastern Caribbean dollar • 99 • 74 • 15 • 94 • N/A • 2174 • Yes • 69 •

Dominican Republic *Country* West Indies 57 N8

Dominican Republic 57

1865 • a Spanish • Dominican Republic peso • 174 • 71 • 14 • 82.6 • 28 • 909 • No • 65 • 2286

Don *River* Russian Federation 68 96 F13
Don *River* England, United Kingdom 17 G10 25 N14
Don *River* Scotland, United Kingdom 29 N10
Donaghadee Northern Ireland, United Kingdom 31 P4
Donau *see* Danube
Donawitz Austria 83 Q7
Donbass *Industrial region* Russian Federation/Ukraine 99 L6
Doncaster England, United Kingdom 25 N15
Doncaster *Unitary authority* England, United Kingdom 19 L13
Dondra Head *Headland* Sri Lanka 114 I7
Donegal Republic of Ireland 31 L4
Donegal *County* Republic of Ireland 19 D11
Donegal Bay *Bay* Republic of Ireland 17 C9 31 L5
Donets *River* Russian Federation/Ukraine 99 L5
Donets'k Ukraine 99 M7
Đông Hoi Vietnam 138 N10
Dongchuan China 134 I12
Dongguan China 135 M14
Dongsheng China 133 N8
Dongting Hu *Lake* China 135 L11
Dønna *Island* Norway 71 K5
Donostia-San Sebastián Spain 75 M3
Dorchester England, United Kingdom 20 K10
Dordogne *River* France 76 J12
Dordrecht Netherlands 79 H11
Dornbirn Austria 82 I8
Dornoch Scotland, United Kingdom 28 J8
Dornoch Firth *Inlet* Scotland, United Kingdom 32 F5
Dorset *County* England, United Kingdom 19 K17
Dorset *Area of Outstanding Natural Beauty* England, United Kingdom 32 F13
Dortmund Germany 80 E10
Dortmund-Ems-Canal *Canal* Germany 80 E9
Dosso Niger 107 N9
Dothan Alabama, USA 43 L9
Douala Cameroon 109 E11
Doubs *River* France/Switzerland 77 N8
Douglas Isle of Man 24 G6
Douglas Arizona, USA 48 J11
Douro *River* Portugal/Spain 68 74 H7
Dover Delaware, USA 41 K15
Dover England, United Kingdom 21 S7
Dover New Hampshire, USA 41 O8
Dover, Strait of *Strait* France/United Kingdom 17 I14 21 S9 32 H13
Down *District* Northern Ireland, United Kingdom 19 F12
Downham Market England, United Kingdom 23 P9
Downpatrick Northern Ireland, United Kingdom 31 P6
Dozen *Island* Japan 137 E11
Drachten Netherlands 78 L7
Drake Passage *Passage* Atlantic Ocean/Pacific Ocean 55 65 A6
Drakensberg *Mountain range* Lesotho/South Africa 101 113 K15
Drama Greece 93 L2
Drammen Norway 70 I11
Drau (Eng. Drave) *River* SE Europe 83 Q9 *see also* Drava
Drava (Eng. Drave) *River* SE Europe 83 R9 89 K3 *see also* Drau
Drave *see* Drau *and* Drava
Drawa *River* Poland 84 I4
Dresden Germany 81 M11
Driffield England, United Kingdom 25 O12
Drin, Gulf of *Gulf* Albania 89 L11
Drina *River* Bosnia and Herzegovina/Yugoslavia 68
Drinit, Lumi i *River* Albania 89 M10
Drobeta-Turnu Severin Romania 90 H8
Drogheda Republic of Ireland 31 O8
Droichead Nua Republic of Ireland 31 N10
Droitwich England, United Kingdom 22 J11
Dronfield England, United Kingdom 23 K5
Dronning Maud Land *Region* Antarctica 64 E6
Drumheller Alberta, Canada 37 L14
Drummondville Quebec, Canada 39 N13
Druridge Bay *Bay* England, United Kingdom 25 L6
Druskininkai Lithuania 94 H11
Dubai United Arab Emirates 123 O11
Dubăsari Moldova 98 H7
Dubawnt Lake *Lake* Nunavut, Canada 37 M9
Dubbo New South Wales, Australia 147 O12
Dublin Republic of Ireland 31 O9
Dublin *County* Republic of Ireland 19 F14
Dublin Bay *Bay* Republic of Ireland 17 D11
Dubrovnik Croatia 89 K9
Dubuque Iowa, USA 47 R8
Dudley England, United Kingdom 22 J10
Dudley *Unitary authority* England, United Kingdom 19 N12
Duero *River* Portugal/Spain 75 K6
Dugi Otok *Island* Croatia 88 G6
Duisburg Germany 80 D10
Dukhan Qatar 123 M10
Duluth Minnesota, USA 44 I4
Dumaguete Philippines 141 M6
Dumbarton Scotland, United Kingdom 29 J13
Dumfries Scotland, United Kingdom 29 K16
Dumfries and Galloway *Unitary authority* Scotland, United Kingdom 19 I11
Dumont d'Urville *French research station* Antarctica 64 F12
Dún Laoghaire Republic of Ireland 31 O9
Duna *see* Danube
Dunany Point *Headland* Republic of Ireland 31 O7
Dunărea *see* Danube
Duncansby Head *Headland* Scotland, United Kingdom 28 L6
Dundalk Republic of Ireland 31 O7
Dundalk Bay *Bay* Republic of Ireland 17 D10
Dundee Scotland, United Kingdom 29 M12
Dundee, City of *Unitary authority* Scotland, United Kingdom 19 J8
Dundrum Bay *Inlet* Northern Ireland, United Kingdom 31 P6
Dunedin New Zealand 148 E12
Dunfanaghy Republic of Ireland 31 L2
Dunfermline Scotland, United Kingdom 29 K13
Dungannon *District* Northern Ireland, United Kingdom 19 E12
Dungarvan Republic of Ireland 31 M13
Dungeness *Headland* England, United Kingdom 17 H14 21 S8
Dunglow Republic of Ireland 31 L3
Dungun Malaysia 139 K18
Dunkerque *see* Dunkirk
Dunkery Beacon *Mountain* England, United Kingdom 20 I8
Dunkirk *see* Dunkerque77 L1
Dunkirk New York, USA 40 H10
Dunnet Head *Headland* Scotland, United Kingdom 17 E4
Duns Scotland, United Kingdom 29 N14
Durance *River* France 77 P13
Durango Mexico 53 K8
Durango Colorado, USA 49 L6
Durazno Uruguay 62 N9
Durban South Africa 113 M14 115 C12
Durdle Door *Natural arch* England, United Kingdom 17 G14
Durham England, United Kingdom 25 L8
Durham North Carolina, USA 43 Q5
Durham *County* England, United Kingdom 19 K11
Durness Scotland, United Kingdom 28 I7
Durrës Albania 89 L11
Durrow Republic of Ireland 31 M11
Dursey Head *Headland* Republic of Ireland 30 H15
Dushanbe Tajikistan 125 N8
Düsseldorf Germany 81 D11
Dutch Harbor Alaska, USA 36 C8
Dutch New Guinea *see* Irian Jaya
Dutch West Indies *see* Netherlands Antilles
Dzhalal-Abad Kyrgyzstan 125 P6
Dzhugdzhur, Khrebet *Mountain range* Russian Federation 129 P9
Dzungaria *Physical region* China 117

E

Eagle Lake *Lake* California, USA 51 I12
Eagle Lake *Lake* Maine, USA 41 P3
Eagle Mountain Lake *Reservoir* Texas, USA 49 Q10
Eagle Pass Texas, USA 49 P14
Ealing *London borough* England, United Kingdom 19 M19
Earn *River* Scotland, United Kingdom 29 K13
Easkey Bog *Bog* Republic of Ireland 32 C9
Easky Republic of Ireland 31 K6
East Anglia *Physical region* England, United Kingdom 17 H12 22 Q9
East Ayrshire *Unitary authority* Scotland, United Kingdom 18 H10
East China Sea *Sea* Pacific Ocean 127 135 O12 137 A19 144 F5
East Dereham England, United Kingdom 23 R8
East Devon *Area of Outstanding Natural Beauty* England, United Kingdom 32 F13
East Dunbartonshire *Unitary authority* Scotland, United Kingdom 18 M4
East Frisian Islands *Island group* Germany 80 E7
East Grinstead England, United Kingdom 21 Q8
East Hampshire *Area of Outstanding Natural Beauty* England, United Kingdom 32 G13
East Indies *Island group* SE Asia 127 143
East Kilbride Scotland, United Kingdom 29 J14
East Liverpool Ohio, USA 45 Q11
East London South Africa 113 L15
East Lothian *Unitary authority* Scotland, United Kingdom 18 J9
East Mariana Basin *Undersea feature* Pacific Ocean 143
East Pacific Rise *Undersea feature* Pacific Ocean 55 145 N10
East Renfrewshire *Unitary authority* Scotland, United Kingdom 18 M5
East Riding of Yorkshire *Unitary authority* England, United Kingdom 19 M12
East Saint Louis Illinois, USA 44 J14
East Siberian Sea *Sea* Arctic Ocean 65 R6 117 129 O3 127
East Stewartry Coast *Area of Outstanding Natural Beauty* Scotland, United Kingdom 32 F8
East Sussex *County* England, United Kingdom 19 N17
East Timor *Disputed region* SE Asia 141 O15
Eastbourne England, United Kingdom 21 Q9
Easter Island *Island* Chile 145 N11
Eastern Euphrates *see* Murat Nehri
Eastern Ghats *Mountain range* India 131 K12
Eastern Sierra Madre *see* Madre Oriental, Sierra
Eastleigh England, United Kingdom 21 N8
Eastmain *River* Quebec, Canada 39 M9
Eastport Maine, USA 41 R6
Eau Claire Wisconsin, USA 44 I7
Ebbw Vale Wales, United Kingdom 27 O13
Ebolowa Cameroon 109 F11
Ebro *River* Spain 68 75 M5
Ecuador *Country* NW South America 58 D9

Ecuador 58

1830 • a Spanish • Sucre • 45 • 70 • 15 • 90.7 • 40 • 667 • No • 58 • 2583

Ed Damazin Sudan 105 H14
Ed Damer Sudan 105 H11
Ed Dueim Sudan 105 G13
Eday *Island* Scotland, United Kingdom 28 L5

Ede Netherlands 79 K11
Edea Cameroon 109 F11
Eden *River* England, United Kingdom 17 F9 24 I8
Eder *River* Germany 81 G11
Edessa Greece 92 I3
Edgeworthstown Republic of Ireland 31 M8
Edinburgh *National region* / Scotland, United Kingdom 29 L13
Edinburgh, City of *Unitary authority* Scotland, United Kingdom 18 O5
Edirne (Eng. Adrianople) Turkey 118 G4
Edmonds Washington, USA 50 H6
Edmonton Alberta, Canada 37 L13
Edward, Lake *Lake* Dem. Rep. Congo (Zaire)/Uganda 109 O12 111 L5
Edwards Air Base *Military base* California, USA 51 L18
Edwards Plateau *Plain* Texas, USA 49 O12
Eforie-Nord Romania 91 P9
Egadi *Island group* Italy 87 H17
Eglwyswrw Wales, United Kingdom 26 I11
Eğridir Gölü *Lake* Turkey 118 J8
Egypt *Country* NE Africa 104 D7

Egypt 104

1936 • Arabic • Egyptian pound • 68 • 66 • 14 • 52.7 • 23 • 556 • Yes • 45 • 33

Eiger *Mountain* Switzerland 82 F11
Eigg *Island* Scotland, United Kingdom 29 G11
Eilat *see* Elat
Eindhoven Netherlands 79 J13
Eisenstadt Austria 83 S5
Eivissa *see* Ibiza
El Calafate Argentina 63 I18
El Faiyum Egypt 104 F7
El Fasher Sudan 105 C13
El Giza (Eng. Gîza) Egypt 104 F7
El Manṣûra Egypt 105 F6
El Minya Egypt 104 F7
El Obeid Sudan 105 F13
El Oued Algeria 103 M6
El Paso Texas, USA 49 L11
El Salvador *Country* W Central America 56 B9

El Salvador 56

1841 • Spanish • Salvadorean colón • 299 • 69 • 14 • 77 • 30 • 1429 • No • 45 • 2663

El'brus *Mountain* Russian Federation 68
Elat (var. Eilat) Israel 121 L14
Elâzığ Turkey 119 P7
Elba *Island* Italy 86 F10
Elbasan Albania 89 M12
Elbe *River* Czech Republic/Germany 68 80 I8 84 H8
Elbert, Mount *Mountain* Colorado, USA 34
Elbląg Poland 85 L2
Elburz Mountains *Mountain range* Iran 123 M3
Elche (Sp. Elx) Spain 75 N11
Eldoret Kenya 111 O4
Elemi Triangle *Disputed region* Kenya/Sudan 105 H16 111 O1
Elephant Butte Reservoir *Reservoir* New Mexico, USA 49 L9
Elephant Island *Island* Antarctica 64 B6
Eleuthera Island *Island* Bahamas 57 L2
Elgin Scotland, United Kingdom 28 K9
Elista Russian Federation 96 F15 128 D9
Ełk Poland 85 N3
Elko Nevada, USA 48 H2
Ellensburg Washington, USA 50 J7
Ellesmere Island *Island* Nunavut, Canada 34 37 N1 65 O11
Ellesmere Port England, United Kingdom 22 H5
Ellon Scotland, United Kingdom 29 N10
Ellsworth Land *Physical region* Antarctica 64 C9
Elmira New York, USA 40 J10
Eltz *Castle* Germay 81 E12
Elwell, Lake *Reservoir* Montana, USA 46 H4
Elx *see* Elche
Ely England, United Kingdom 23 P10
Ely Wales, United Kingdom 27 O15
Ely Nevada, USA 48 H4
Elyria Ohio, USA 45 P10
Emba *River* Kazakhstan 128 E10
Emden Germany 80 E7
Emerson Barrage *Dam* Pakistan 130 I3
Emi Koussi *Mountain* Chad 101
Emmen Netherlands 78 N8
Emporia Kansas, USA 47 P12
Empty Quarter *see* Ar Rub 'al Khali
Ems *River* Germany 80 E8
En Nahud Sudan 105 E13
Encarnación Paraguay 62 O7
Endeh Indonesia 141 M15
Enderby Land *Physical region* Antarctica 64 F7
Enewetak Atoll *Atoll* Marshall Islands 144 H7
Enfield *London borough* England, United Kingdom 19 N18
Enggano, Pulau *Island* Indonesia 140 E14
England *National region* United Kingdom 19 K15 32 G11
English Channel *Channel* France/United Kingdom 17 G15 32 F14
Enguri *River* Georgia 99 O12
Enid Oklahoma, USA 47 O14
Enna Italy 87 K18
Ennis Republic of Ireland 30 J11
Enniscorthy Republic of Ireland 31 O12
Enniskillen Northern Ireland, United Kingdom 31 M5
Ennistimon Republic of Ireland 30 J10
Enns *River* Austria 83 O7
Enriquillo, Lago *Lake* Dominican Republic 57 N8
Enschede Netherlands 78 N10
Entebbe Uganda 111 M4
Enugu Nigeria 107 O13
Ephesus *Archaeological site* Turkey 118 G8
Epidaurus Greece 92 J10
Épinal France 77 P6
Epping England, United Kingdom 21 Q5
Equator *Line of latitude* 55 143
Equatorial Guinea *Country* C Africa 109 D11

Equatorial Guinea 109

1968 • Spanish • Franc de la Coopération financière en Afrique central • 16 • 50 • 11 • 79.9 • 2 • 4762 • Yes • 44 •

Er Roseires Dam *Dam* Sudan 105 H14
Er-Rachidia Morocco 102 I6
Erdenet Mongolia 133 L4
Ereğli Turkey 119 L9
Erenhot China 133 O6
Erfurt Germany 81 I11
Erg Chech *Desert Region* Mali 107 K4
Erguig, Bahr *River* Chad 108 H8
Ergun He *see* Argun
Ericht, Loch *Lake* Scotland, United Kingdom 17 E6
Erie Pennsylvania, USA 40 G10
Erie Canal *Canal* New York, USA 40 I8
Erie, Lake *Lake* Canada/USA 34 38 J15 45 P10
Eritrea *Country* E Africa 105 I12

Eritrea 105

1993 • Tigrinya • Nakfa • 31 • 51 • 13 • 25 • 2 • 5000 • Yes • 17 • 1610

Erlangen Germany 81 I13
Ermoupoli Greece 93 M11
Ernakulam India 130 J14
Erne *River* Republic of Ireland/United Kingdom 31 M7
Errigal Mountain *Mountain* Republic of Ireland 31 L3
Erris Head *Headland* Republic of Ireland 17 B9 30 I6
Erzincan Turkey 119 P6
Erzurum Turkey 119 Q6
Esbjerg Denmark 66 L7 70 H15
Escanaba Michigan, USA 45 L5
Esch-sur-Alzette Luxembourg 79 L19
Escuintla Guatemala 56 A8
Esk *River* England, United Kingdom 25 N10
Esk *River* England/Scotland, United Kingdom 17 F8 29 L15
Eskisehir Turkey 118 G7
Esla, Embalse de *Reservoir* Spain 74 I6
Esmeraldas Ecuador 58 C8
Esperance Western Australia, Australia 146 H13
Espinho Portugal 74 F7
Espíritu Santo, Isla del *Island* Mexico 52 H7
Esquel Argentina 63 H15
Essaouira Morocco 102 H6
Essen Germany 80 D10
Essequibo River *River* Guyana 58 M6
Essex *County* England, United Kingdom 19 N16
Estelí Nicaragua 56 D10
Estevan Saskatchewan, Canada 37 N15
Estonia *Country* NE Europe 94 I3

Estonia 94-95

1991 • Estonian • Kroon • 31 • 69 • 16 • 99 • 293 • 323 • No • 73 • N/A

Ethiopia *Country* E Africa 105 I15

Ethiopia 105

1896 • Amharic • Ethiopian birr • 67 • 42 • 13 • 35.4 • 1 • 25000 • Yes • 13 • 1610

Ethiopian Highlands *Plateau* Ethiopia 101 105 J14
Etna, Mount *Volcano* Italy 68
Etosha *National Park* Namibia 112 G9
Etosha Pan *Salt lake* Namibia 113 H9
Euboea (Gr. Evvoia) *Island* Greece 93 K7
Eugene Oregon, USA 50 G9
Eupen Belgium 79 L15
Euphrates *River* SW Asia 68 114 D4 117 119 P8 121 R4 123 K5 127
Eurasian Plate *Tectonic plate* 34 68 101 117 127 143
Eureka California, USA 51 F12
Europe *Continent* 68-69
Europoort Netherlands 79 G11
Evanston Illinois, USA 45 L10
Evansville Indiana, USA 45 L15
Everard, Lake *Salt lake* South Australia, Australia 147 K12
Everest, Mount *Mountain* China/Nepal 127 131 O5 132 H13
Everett Washington, USA 50 H6
Everglades, The *Wetland* Florida, USA 34 43 N14
Evesham England, United Kingdom 22 J12
Évora Portugal 74 G11
Évreux France 77 K5
Evvoia *see* Euboea
Exe *River* England, United Kingdom 17 F14 20 I8
Exeter England, United Kingdom 20 I10
Exmoor *Moorland* England, United Kingdom 17 F14 20 H8
Exmoor National Park *National Park* England, United Kingdom 32 F13
Exmouth England, United Kingdom 20 I10
Exmouth Plateau *Undersea feature* Pacific Ocean 143
Eyasi, Lake *Lake* Tanzania 111 O7
Eye Peninsula *Peninsula* Scotland, United Kingdom 28 G8
Eyemouth Scotland, United Kingdom 29 N14
Eyre, Lake *Salt lake* South Australia, Australia 143 147 K11

F

Fada-Ngourma Burkina 107 M10
Faeroe Islands *Dependent territory* Atlantic Ocean 66 I7
Faeroe Islands *Island group* Atlantic Ocean 68
Faguibine, Lac *Lake* Mali 107 K8
Fair Isle *Island* Scotland, United Kingdom 28 O4
Fairbanks Alaska, USA 36 H7
Fairmont Minnesota, USA 44 G8
Faisalabad Pakistan 130 J3
Fakenham England, United Kingdom 23 Q7
Falkirk Scotland, United Kingdom 29 K13
Falkirk *Unitary authority* Scotland, United Kingdom 18 M5
Falkland Escarpment *Undersea feature* Atlantic Ocean55
Falkland Islands *Dependent territory* Atlantic Ocean 67 F15
Falkland Islands *Island group* Atlantic Ocean 55
Fall River Massachusetts, USA 41 O11
Falmouth England, United Kingdom 20 F12
Falmouth Bay *Bay* England, United Kingdom 17 E15
Falun Sweden 71 L11
Famagusta Cyprus 119 L12
Faraday *UK research station* Antarctica 64 B7
Faradje Dem. Rep. Congo (Zaire) 109 O11
Farafangana Madagascar 115 E11
Fareham England, United Kingdom 21 N9
Farghona Uzbekistan 125 O7
Fargo North Dakota, USA 47 O5
Faribault Minnesota, USA 44 H7
Farmington New Mexico, USA 49 K6
Farnborough England, United Kingdom 21 O7
Farne Islands *Island group* England, United Kingdom 25 L3
Farnham England, United Kingdom 21 O7
Faro Yukon Territory, Canada 36 I9
Faro Portugal 74 G13
Fårö Sweden 71 M13
Farranfore Republic of Ireland 30 I13
Faversham England, United Kingdom 21 R6
Faya Chad 108 J5
Fayetteville Arkansas, USA 42 H3
Fayetteville North Carolina, USA 43 Q6
Fdérik Mauritania 106 H4
Fehmarn *Island* Germany 80 J6
Feira de Santana Brazil 61 M11
Felbertauern Tunnel *Tunnel* Austria 83 M8
Feldkirch Austria 82 I9
Felixstowe England, United Kingdom 23 S12
Femunden, Lake *Lake* Norway 70 J9
Fens, The *Wetland* England, United Kingdom 17 H12 23 P8
Feodosiya Ukraine 99 K10
Fergus Falls Minnesota, USA 44 F5
Fermanagh *District* Northern Ireland, United Kingdom 19 D12
Fermoy Republic of Ireland 31 L13
Fernando de Noronha *Island* Brazil 67 H12
Ferrara Italy 86 G8
Ferrol Spain 74 G3
Fethiye Turkey 118 H10
Fetlar *Island* Scotland, United Kingdom 28 P1
Feuilles, Rivière aux *River* Quebec, Canada 39 L5
Fez Morocco 102 I5
Fezzan *Region* Libya 103 Q9
Ffestiniog Wales, United Kingdom 27 L4
Fianarantsoa Madagascar 115 E11
Fier Albania 89 N13
Fife *Unitary authority* Scotland, United Kingdom 18 J9
Figueira da Foz Portugal 74 F8
Figuig Morocco 102 J6
Fiji *Country* Pacific Ocean 144 J10

Fiji 144

1970 • English • Fiji dollar • 44 • 73 • 15 • 91.8 • 59 • 1784 • No • 41 • 3089

Fiji *Island group* Pacific Ocean 143
Fiji Plate *Tectonic plate* 143
Filadelfia Paraguay 62 L4
Filchner Ice Shelf *Ice shelf* Antarctica 64 D8
Filey England, United Kingdom 25 P11
Filey Bay *Bay* England, United Kingdom 25 P11
Filicudi *Island* Italy 87 K16
Fimbul Ice Shelf *Ice shelf* Antarctica 64 E6
Findhorn *River* Scotland, United Kingdom 29 K10
Findlay Ohio, USA 45 O11
Finger Lakes *Lakes* New York, USA 40 J9
Finland *Country* N Europe 71 O9

Finland 71

1917 • Finnish and Swedish • Markka • 17 • 77 • 16 • 99 • 379 • 370 • No • 63 • 3018

Finland, Gulf of *Gulf* Baltic Sea 68 71 O12 96 E7
Firenze *see* Florence
Fishguard Wales, United Kingdom 26 H11
Fitzroy River *River* Western Australia, Australia 146 H7
Flagstaff Arizona, USA 48 I7
Flamborough Head *Headland* England, United Kingdom 17 H10 25 P11
Flaming Gorge Dam *Dam* USA 49 K3
Flaming Gorge Reservoir *Reservoir* Utah/Wyoming, USA 46 I10
Flathead Lake *Lake* Montana, USA 46 G4
Fleet Valley *Area of Outstanding Natural Beauty* Scotland, United Kingdom 32 E8
Fleetwood England, United Kingdom 24 H13
Flevoland *Province* Netherlands 78 J9
Flin Flon Manitoba, Canada 37 N13
Flinders *River* Queensland, Australia 143 147 M7
Flinders Island *Island* Tasmania, Australia 147 N15
Flinders Ranges *Mountain range* South Australia, Australia 143 147 L12
Flint Michigan, USA 45 O8
Flint Wales, United Kingdom 27 O2
Flintshire *Unitary authority* Wales, United Kingdom 19 J13
Flitwick England, United Kingdom 21 P4
Florence (It. Firenze) Italy 86 G9
Florence Alabama, USA 43 K5
Florence South Carolina, USA 43 P7
Florencia Colombia 58 E8
Flores Guatemala 56 B6
Flores *Island* Indonesia 141 L15 143
Flores Sea *Sea* Indonesia 127 141 K15
Florianópolis Brazil 61 J15
Florida Uruguay 62 O10
Florida Keys *Island group* Florida, USA 43 N16
Florida, Straits of *Strait* Atlantic Ocean 43 O15
Florina Greece 92 H3
Fly *River* Indonesia/Papua New Guinea 147 M3
Foča Bosnia and Herzegovina 89 L7
Focșani Romania 91 N6
Foggia Italy 87 M12
Föhr *Island* Germany 80 F5
Foix France 77 L15
Folkestone England, United Kingdom 21 S8
Fond du Lac Wisconsin, USA 45 K8
Fongafale Tuvalu 144 J9
Forest of Bowland *Area of Outstanding Natural Beauty* England, United Kingdom 32 F9
Forfar Scotland, United Kingdom 29 M12
Forlì Italy 86 H8
Formby England, United Kingdom 24 H15
Formentera *Island* Spain 75 P11
Formosa Argentina 62 M6
Formosa *see* Taiwan
Forres Scotland, United Kingdom 28 K9
Fort Augustus Scotland, United Kingdom 29 I10
Fort Bliss Military Reservation *Military base* New Mexico, USA 49 L10
Fort Collins Colorado, USA 49 M3
Fort-de-France Martinique 57 T13
Fort Dodge Iowa, USA 47 Q9
Fort Lauderdale Florida, USA 43 O14
Fort McMurray Alberta, Canada 37 L12
Fort McPherson Northwest Territories, Canada 36 J7
Fort Myers Florida, USA 43 N14
Fort Nelson British Columbia, Canada 36 J11
Fort Peck Lake *Reservoir* Montana, USA 46 J5
Fort Portal Uganda 111 L4
Fort Resolution Northwest Territories, Canada 37 L10
Fort-Shevchenko Kazakhstan 129 D10
Fort Simpson Northwest Territories, Canada 37 K10
Fort Smith Northwest Territories, Canada 37 L11
Fort Smith Arkansas, USA 42 H3
Fort St.John British Columbia, Canada 37 K12
Fort Vermilion Alberta, Canada 37 L11
Fort Wayne Indiana, USA 45 N11
Fort William Scotland, United Kingdom 29 H11
Fort Worth Texas, USA 49 Q10
Fortaleza Brazil 60 N8 67 H12
Forth Scotland, United Kingdom 29 K14
Forth *River* Scotland, United Kingdom 29 J13
Forth, Firth of *Estuary* Scotland, United Kingdom 17 F7 29 L13
Foula *Island* Scotland, United Kingdom 28 N2
Foveaux Strait *Strait* New Zealand 148 C13
Fowey *River* England, United Kingdom 20 F11
Foxe Basin *Sea* Nunavut, Canada 37 P7
Foxford Republic of Ireland 30 J6
Foyle *River* Republic of Ireland/United Kingdom 31 L3
Foyle, Lough *Inlet* Republic of Ireland/United Kingdom 31 N3
Foynes Republic of Ireland 30 J11
France *Country* W Europe 76-77

France 76-77

486 • French • French franc • 107 • 78 • 16 • 99 • 442 • 357 • No • 73 • 3633

Franceville Gabon 109 G13
Francis Case, Lake *Reservoir* South Dakota, USA 47 N8
Francistown Botswana 113 L10
Frankfort Indiana, USA 45 M12
Frankfort Kentucky, USA 43 N2
Frankfurt *see* Frankfurt am Main
Frankfurt am Main (var. Frankfurt) Germany 81 F12
Frankfurt an der Oder Germany 80 N9
Fränkische Alb *Mountain range* Germany 81 J14
Franz Josef Land *Island group* Russian Federation 65 R11 68 117 128 J3
Fraser *River* British Columbia, Canada 36 J13
Fraserburgh Scotland, United Kingdom 29 N9
Frauenfeld Switzerland 82 H8
Fray Bentos Uruguay 62 N9
Fredericton New Brunswick, Canada 39 P12
Frederikshavn Denmark 70 I13
Fredrikstad Norway 70 J12
Freeport Bahamas 56 J1
Freeport Illinois, USA 45 K10
Freeport Texas, USA 49 S13
Freetown Sierra Leone 106 G12
Freiburg im Breisgau Germany 81 E16
Freistadt Austria 83 P4
Fremantle Western Australia, Australia 115 M12 146 F12
French Guiana *Dependent territory* N South America 58 O7
French Polynesia *Dependent territory* Pacific Ocean 145 L9
French Southern and Antarctic Territories *Dependent territory* Indian Ocean 115 G14
Fresno California, USA 51 J16
Fria, Cape *Headland* Namibia 101 112 F9
Fribourg Switzerland 82 E10
Friedrichshafen Germany 81 G16
Frobisher Bay *Inlet* Northwest Territories, Canada 37 R7
Frobisher Lake *Lake* Saskatchewan, Canada 37 M12
Frome *River* England, United Kingdom 21 K9
Frome England, United Kingdom 21 K7
Frome, Lake *Salt lake* South Australia, Australia 147 L12
Frongoch Wales, United Kingdom 27 M4
Frontera Mexico 53 Q12
Frosinone Italy 87 J12
Fuenlabrada Spain 75 K8
Fuerte Olimpo Paraguay 62 M4
Fujairah United Arab Emirates 123 O11
Fuji, Mount *Mountain* Japan 127 137 J11
Fukui Japan 137 H11
Fukuoka Japan 137 C13
Fukushima Japan 136 K5
Fukushima Japan 136 K9
Fulda Germany 81 H12
Fulda *River* Germany 81 H11
Fundy, Bay of *Bay* Canada/USA 39 P13 66 F8
Furnas, Represa de *Reservoir* Brazil 61 K13
Fushun China 135 O5
Fuzhou China 135 N12
Fyn *Island* Denmark 70 I15
Fyne, Loch *Inlet* Scotland, United Kingdom 29 H13

Gaalkacyo Somalia 105 N16
Gabčíkovo Slovakia 85 K13
Gabès Tunisia 103 N5
Gabon *Country* C Africa 109 E12

Gabon 109

1960 • French • Franc de la Coopération financière en Afrique centrale • 5 • 52 • 16 • 66.2 • 22 • 2000 • Yes • 51 • 2500

Gaborone Botswana 113 K11
Gabrovo Bulgaria 91 L12
Gadsden Alabama, USA 43 L6
Gafsa Tunisia 103 N5
Gagnoa Ivory Coast 106 J13
Gagra Georgia 99 N11
Gainsborough England, United Kingdom 23 M5
Gairdner, Lake *Salt lake* South Australia, Australia 147 K12
Galapagos Islands *Island group* Ecuador 55 145 O8
Galashiels Scotland, United Kingdom 29 M14
Galați Romania 91 O7
Galesburg Illinois, USA 44 J11
Galicia *Cultural region* Spain 74 G3
Galilee, Sea of *see* Tiberias, Lake

Date of independence • Language (official or most commonly spoken) • Currency • Population density per square kilometre • Average life expectancy • School-leaving age • Literacy • Number of cars per 1,000 people • Number of people per doctor • Death penalty • Percentage of urban-based population • Average number of calories consumed daily per person

Galle Sri Lanka 131 K16
Gallego Rise *Undersea feature* Pacific Ocean 55
Gallipoli Italy 87 P14
Gallipoli Turkey 118 G5
Gällivare Sweden 71 N4
Galloway, Mull of *Headland* Scotland, United Kingdom 29 I17
Gallup New Mexico, USA 49 K7
Galty Mountains *Mountain range* Republic of Ireland 17 C12
Galveston Texas, USA 49 S13
Galway Republic of Ireland 30 J9
Galway *County* Republic of Ireland 19 C13
Galway Bay *Bay* Republic of Ireland 17 B11 30 I9
Gambia *Country* W Africa 106 F9

Gambia 106

1965 • English • Dalasi • 127 • 47 • 33.1 • 8 • 5000 • Yes • 30 • 2360

Gambier, Îles *Island group* French Polynesia 145 M10
Ganca Azerbaijan 99 R13
Gander Newfoundland and Labrador, Canada 39 S9
Gandi Reservoir *Reservoir* India 130 J7
Gangdisê Shan *Mountain range* China 132 F12
Ganges *River* Bangladesh/India 114 J5 117 127 131 L5
Ganges, Mouths of the *Delta* Bangladesh/India 117 127
Gangtok India 131 O6
Ganzhou China 135 M13
Gao Mali 107 L8
Gap France 77 P12
Gar China 132 F11
Garda, Lake *Lake* Italy 86 F6
Garden City Kansas, USA 47 M13
Garforth England, United Kingdom 25 M13
Garissa Kenya 111 Q5
Garmisch-Partenkirchen Germany 81 J17
Garonne *River* France 68 76 J12
Garoowe Somalia 105 O15
Garoua Cameroon 108 G9
Garron Point *Headland* Northern Ireland, United Kingdom 31 P3
Garry Lake *Lake* Nunavut, Canada 37 N8
Garth Scotland, United Kingdom 28 O2
Gary Indiana, USA 45 L10
Gaspé Quebec, Canada 39 P10
Gastonia North Carolina, USA 43 P6
Gateshead *Unitary authority* England, United Kingdom 18 N7
Gateshead England, United Kingdom 25 L7
Gatineau Quebec, Canada 39 L13
Gävle Sweden 71 L11
Gaya India 131 N7
Gaza Gaza Strip 121 L10
Gaza Strip *Disputed region* SW Asia 121 L10
Gaziantep Turkey 119 O9
Gbanga Liberia 106 I12
Gdańsk Poland 85 L2
Gdańsk, Gulf of *see* Danzig, Gulf of
Gdynia Poland 85 K2
Gedaref Sudan 105 H13
Geelong Victoria, Australia 147 M14
Gejiu China 134 I14
Gelsenkirchen Germany 80 D10
Gemena Dem. Rep. Congo (Zaire) 109 J11
Gemlik Turkey 118 I5
Gemsbok *National Park* Botswana 112 J12
Genale Wenz *River* Ethiopia 105 K16
General Eugenio A.Garay Paraguay 62 K4
General Santos Philippines 141 N8
Genesee River *River* New York/Pennsylvania, USA 40 I10
Geneva (Fr. Genève) Switzerland 82 C12
Geneva New York, USA 40 J9
Geneva, Lake *Lake* France/Switzerland 68 77 P9 82 D12
Genève *see* Geneva
Genk Belgium 79 K14
Genoa (It. Genova) Italy 86 D8
Genoa, Gulf of *Gulf* Mediterranean Sea 86 D8
Genova *see* Genoa
Gent *see* Ghent
Georg von Neumayer *German research station* Antarctica 64 D6
George Town Cayman Islands 56 H6
George Town Malaysia 114 L8 139 I17
Georgetown Gambia 106 G9
Georgetown Guyana 58 M6 67 F11
Georgetown Delaware, USA 41 K16
Georgia *Country* SW Asia 99 O12

Georgia 99

1991 • Georgian • Lari • 72 • 73 • 14 • 99 • 79 • 238 • No • 58 • N/A

Gera Germany 81 K11
Geraldton Western Australia, Australia 146 E11
Germany *Country* W Europe 80-81

Germany 80-81

1871 • German • Deutsche Mark • 235 • 77 • 18 • 99 • 500 • 303 • No • 87 • 3344

Getafe Spain 75 K8
Gettysburg Pennsylvania, USA 40 I14
Getz Ice Shelf *Ice shelf* Antarctica 64 C10
Ghadaf, Wadi al *Seasonal watercourse* Iraq 122 J5
Ghadamis Libya 103 N7
Ghana *Country* W Africa 107 L12

Ghana 107

1957 • English • Cedi • 86 • 60 • 14 • 66.4 • 5 • 25000 • Yes • 36 • 2199

Ghanzi Botswana 112 J10
Ghardaïa Algeria 103 L6
Gharyan Libya 103 O6
Ghat Libya 103 N10
Ghazni Afghanistan 125 N13
Ghent (var. Gent) Belgium 79 F14
Ghulam Muhammad Barrage *Dam* Pakistan 130 H6
Giant's Causeway *Lava flow* Northern Ireland, United Kingdom 31 O2
Gibraltar *Dependent territory* S Europe 74 I15
Gibraltar Gibraltar 66 K9 74 I15
Gibraltar, Strait of *Strait* Atlantic Ocean/Mediterranean Sea 68 74 I15 101 102 I4
Gibson Desert *Desert* Western Australia, Australia 143 146 H9
Giessen Germany 81 F12
Giffnock Scotland, United Kingdom 29 J14
Gifu Japan 137 H11
Giganta, Sierra de la *Mountain range* Mexico 52 G6
Gijón Spain 74 I3
Gila River *River* Arizona, USA 49 K10
Gillette Wyoming, USA 47 K8
Gillingham England, United Kingdom 21 R6
Giresun Turkey 119 O5
Girne Cyprus 119 L11
Girona Spain 75 Q5
Girre Cyprus 119 L11
Girvan Scotland, United Kingdom 29 I15
Gisborne New Zealand 148 J5
Giurgiu Romania 91 L10
Giza *see* El Giza
Gjøvik Norway 70 J10
Gladstone Queensland, Australia 147 O9
Glåma *River* Norway 70 J9
Glarus Switzerland 82 H10
Glasgow Montana, USA 47 K4
Glasgow Scotland, United Kingdom 29 J14
Glasgow, City of *Unitary authority* Scotland, United Kingdom 18 M5
Glastonbury England, United Kingdom 21 K8
Glen Affric *Area of Outstanding Natural Beauty* Scotland, United Kingdom 32 E5
Glen Canyon Dam *Dam* Arizona, USA 48 J6
Glen Coe *Valley* Scotland, United Kingdom 29 I12
Glen Mor *Valley* Scotland, United Kingdom 28 I10
Glendale California, USA 51 K18
Glendale Arizona, USA 48 I9
Glendive Montana, USA 47 K5
Gleneato Catchment *Bog* Republic of Ireland 32 D11
Glengad Head *Headland* Republic of Ireland 31 N2
Glengarriff Republic of Ireland 30 I14
Glenluce Scotland, United Kingdom 31 I16
Glenrothes Scotland, United Kingdom 29 L13
Glens Falls New York, USA 41 M8
Glenties Republic of Ireland 31 L4
Glenveagh National Park *National Park* Republic of Ireland 32 D8
Gliwice Poland 85 L8
Glossop England, United Kingdom 22 J4
Gloucester Massachusetts, USA 41 O9 66 E8
Gloucester England, United Kingdom 21 L4
Gloucestershire *County* England, United Kingdom 19 K16
Gmünd Austria 83 P3
Gmunden Austria 83 O6
Gnjilane Serbia, Yugoslavia 89 O9
Goba Ethiopia 105 K16
Gobabis Namibia 112 I10
Gobi *Desert* China/Mongolia 117 127 133 M7
Godavari *River* India 127 131 L10 131 L10
Godoy Cruz Argentina 62 H10
Goiânia Brazil 61 J12
Golan Heights *Mountain range* Syria 121 M8
Gold Coast *Cultural region* Queensland, Australia 147 P11
Golmud China 132 J10
Goma Dem. Rep. Congo (Zaire) 109 O13
Gómez Palacio Mexico 53 L7
Gonaïves Haiti 57 M7
Gonâve, Île de la *Island* Haiti 57 M8
Gonder Ethiopia 105 I13
Gonghe China 133 L10
Good Hope, Cape of *Cape* South Africa 67 M14 101 112 116 115 B12
Goodwick Wales, United Kingdom 26 H11
Goole England, United Kingdom 25 N14
Goondiwindi Queensland, Australia 147 N11
Goose Lake *Lake* California/Oregon, USA 51 I11
Gorakhpur India 131 M6
Gore Ethiopia 105 H15
Goré Chad 108 I9
Göreme Turkey 119 M7
Gorey Republic of Ireland 31 O11
Gorgan Iran 123 O3
Görlitz Germany 81 N11
Gorodets Russian Federation 96 H11
Goroka Papua New Guinea 147 N2
Gorongosa *National Park* Mozambique 113 N8
Gorontalo Indonesia 141 M11
Gort Republic of Ireland 31 K10
Gorzów Wielkopolski Poland 84 I4
Gosford New South Wales, Australia 147 O13
Gospić Croatia 88 H5
Gosport England, United Kingdom 21 N9
Gosselies Belgium 79 H16
Gostivar FYR Macedonia 89 N11
Gotha Germany 81 I11
Gothenburg Sweden 70 J13
Gotland *Island* Sweden 71 L14
Goto-retto *Island group* Japan 137 A14
Göttingen Germany 81 H10
Gouda Netherlands 79 H11
Gough Island *Island* Tristan da Cunha 67 J15
Gouin, Réservoir *Reservoir* Quebec, Canada 39 L11
Goulburn New South Wales, Australia 147 O13
Govind Ballabh Pant Reservoir *Reservoir* India 131 M7
Gower *Area of Outstanding Natural Beauty* Wales, United Kingdom 32 F12
Gower *Peninsula* Wales, United Kingdom 17 E13 27 K14
Gozo *Island* Malta 87 K20
Gračanica Bosnia and Herzegovina 89 K5
Grafton New South Wales, Australia 147 P11
Grahamstown South Africa 113 L15
Grampian Mountains *Mountain range* Scotland, United Kingdom 17 E6 29 I12
Gran Chaco *Lowland plain* C South America 55 62 J7
Granada Nicaragua 56 D11
Granada Spain 75 K13
Grand Bahama Island *Island* Bahamas 57 K1
Grand Banks *Undersea feature* Atlantic Ocean 39 T10 66 F8
Grand Canal *Canal* China 135 N9
Grand Canal *Canal* Republic of Ireland 31 N9
Grand Canyon *Canyon* Arizona, USA 34 48 H7
Grand Cayman *Island* Cayman Islands 56 H6
Grand Erg Occidental *Desert* Algeria 103 K7
Grand Erg Oriental *Desert* Algeria/Tunisia 103 L7
Grand Falls New Brunswick, Canada 39 O12
Grand Falls Newfoundland, Canada 39 S9
Grand Forks North Dakota, USA 47 O4
Grand Island Nebraska, USA 47 O10
Grand Junction Colorado, USA 49 K4
Grand Rapids Michigan, USA 45 M9
Grand Teton Mountains *Mountain range* Wyoming, USA 46 H8
Grande Comore *Island* Comoros 114 E10
Grande de Matagalpa, Río *River* Nicaragua 56 E10
Grande de Santiago, Río *River* Mexico 53 K10
Grande Prairie Alberta, Canada 37 K13
Grande Terre *Island* Guadeloupe 57 T11
Grande, Bahía *Bay* Argentina 63 J18
Grande, Rio *River* Mexico/USA 53 N6
Grandes, Salinas *Salt lake* Argentina 55
Grangemouth Scotland, United Kingdom 29 K13
Grantham England, United Kingdom 23 N7
Grantown-on-Spey Scotland, United Kingdom 29 K10
Grants Pass Oregon, USA 51 G11
Grasse France 77 Q13
Gravesend England, United Kingdom 21 Q6
Graz Austria 83 R8
Great Abaco *Island* Bahamas 57 K1
Great Artesian Basin *Lowlands* Queensland, Australia 143
Great Australian Bight *Bight* Indian Ocean 143 146 I13
Great Barrier Reef *Reef* Pacific Ocean 144 H10 143 147 N5 148 I3
Great Basin *Basin* Nevada, USA 34 48 G2
Great Bear Lake *Lake* Northwest Territories, Canada 34 37 K8
Great Bend Kansas, USA 47 O12
Great Britain *see* Britain and United Kingdom
Great Dividing Range *Mountain range* Australia 143 147 M7
Great Exhibition Bay *Inlet* New Zealand 148 G1
Great Exuma Island *Island* Bahamas 57 L4
Great Falls Montana, USA 46 H5
Great Hungarian Plain *Plain* C Europe 68 85 L15
Great Inagua *Island* Bahamas 57 M6
Great Khingan Range *Mountain range* China 127 133 P5
Great Lakes *Lakes* Canada/USA 34
Great Malvern England, United Kingdom 22 I11
Great Ormes Head *Headland* Wales, United Kingdom 27 L1
Great Ouse *River* England, United Kingdom 17 H12 23 P8
Great Plain of China *Plain* China 117 127
Great Plains *Plains* Canada/USA 34 46 J6
Great Rift Valley *Depression* Africa/Asia 101 111 O7
Great Ruaha *River* Tanzania 111 N10
Great Salt Desert *see* Kavir, Dasht-e
Great Salt Lake *Salt lake* Utah, USA 34 48 I2
Great Salt Lake Desert *Plain* Utah, USA 48 I3
Great Sandy Desert *Desert* Western Australia, Australia 143 146 G8
Great Slave Lake *Lake* Northwest Territories, Canada 34 37 L10
Great St. Bernard Tunnel *Tunnel* Switzerland 82 E13
Great Torrington England, United Kingdom 20 G9
Great Victoria Desert *Desert* South Australia/Western Australia, Australia 143 146 H10
Great Wall of China *Ancient monument* China 133 P7 134 I7
Great Yarmouth England, United Kingdom 23 T8
Greater Antarctica *Physical region* Antarctica 64 F9
Greater Antilles *Island group* West Indies 34 55 56 H5
Gredos, Sierra de *Mountain range* Spain 74 I8
Greece *Country* SE Europe 92-93

Greece 92-93

1829 • Greek • Drachma • 81 • 78 • 15 • 96.6 • 223 • 250 • No • 65 • 3815

Greeley Colorado, USA 49 N3
Green Bay Wisconsin, USA 45 L7
Green River *River* Kentucky, USA 43 M3
Green River *River* USA 46 I9 49 K3
Greenfield Massachusetts, USA 41 N10
Greenland *Dependent territory* North America 34 65 N13
Greenland *Island* Greenland 66 G6 117
Greenland Sea *Sea* Atlantic Ocean 65 P14 66 J6 68
Greenock Scotland, United Kingdom 29 I13
Greensboro North Carolina, USA 43 P5
Greenville South Carolina, USA 43 O6
Greenville Liberia 106 I13
Greenwich *London borough* England, United Kingdom 19 O19
Greifswald Germany 80 L6
Grenada *Country* West Indies 57 S15

Grenada 57

1974 • English • Eastern Caribbean dollar • 290 • 72 • 16 • 96 • N/A • 2000 • Yes • 37 • 2402

Grenadines, The *Island group* Grenada/St Vincent and the Grenadines 57 S14
Grenoble France 77 O11
Gretna Scotland, United Kingdom 29 L16
Grevena Greece 92 H4
Greymouth New Zealand 148 E9
Grimsby England, United Kingdom, 23 O3
Groningen Netherlands 78 M7
Groote Eylandt *Island* Northern Territory, Australia 147 L5
Grootfontein Namibia 112 I9
Grosseto Italy 86 G10
Groznyy Russian Federation 97 F16 128 D9
Grudziądz Poland 85 L3
Gstaad Switzerland 82 E11
Guacanayabo, Golfo de *Gulf* Cuba 56 J6
Guadalajara Mexico 53 L11
Guadalajara Spain 75 L8
Guadalcanal *Island* Solomon Islands 144 I9
Guadalquivir *River* Spain 68 74 I12
Guadalupe Mexico 53 L9
Guadarrama, Sierra de *Mountain range* Spain 75 K7
Guadeloupe *Dependent territory* West Indies 57 S11
Guadiana *River* Portugal/Spain 74 G11
Gualeguaychú Argentina 62 M9
Guam *Dependent territory* Pacific Ocean 144 G7
Guanare Venezuela 58 H5
Guangxi Zhuangzu Zizhiqu *Region* China 135 K13
Guangzhou (Eng. Canton) China 135 L14
Guantánamo Cuba 57 L7
Guarda Portugal 74 H8
Guatemala *Country* NW Central America 56 A7

Guatemala 56

1838 • Spanish • Quetzal • 102 • 64 • 14 • 66.6 • 10 • 3333 • Yes • 41 • 2255

Guatemala Basin *Undersea feature* Pacific Ocean 55
Guatemala City Guatemala 56 B8
Guaviare, Río *River* Colombia 58 F7
Guayaquil Ecuador 58 C9 145 Q8
Guayaquil, Gulf of *Gulf* Pacific Ocean 58 B9
Guaymas Mexico 52 H5
Guddu Barrage *Dam* Pakistan 130 H4
Guernsey *Island* NW Europe 17 F16
Guernsey *Dependent territory* NW Europe 19 J19
Guiana Highlands *Mountain range* N South America 34 55
Guider Cameroon 108 G8
Guildford England, United Kingdom 21 P7
Guilin China 135 K13
Guinea *Country* W Africa 106 G10

Guinea 106

1958 • French • Franc guinéen (Guinea franc) • 30 • 47 • 13 • 37.9 • 2 • 5000 • No • 30 • 2389

Guinea Basin *Undersea basin* Atlantic Ocean 67 K12 101
Guinea, Gulf of *Gulf* Atlantic Ocean 67 K11 101 109 D11
Guinea-Bissau *Country* W Africa 106 F10

Guinea-Bissau 106

1974 • Portuguese • Guinea peso • 43 • 45 • 13 • 33.6 • 6 • 5556 • No • 22 • 2556

Guiyang China 134 J12
Gujranwala Pakistan 130 J3
Gujrat Pakistan 130 J2
Gulf, The (var. Persian Gulf) *Gulf* Indian Ocean 68 101 114 F5 117 123 M8 127
Gulfport Mississippi, USA 42 J9
Gulu Uganda 111 M3
Gümüshane Turkey 119 P5
Guri, Embalse de *Reservoir* Venezuela 58 K5
Gusau Nigeria 107 O10
Gusev Russian Federation 94 G10
Gushgy Turkmenistan 124 J11
Guwahati India 131 P6
Guyana *Country* N South America 58 L6

Guyana 58

1966 • English • Guyana dollar • 4 • 64 • 14 • 98.1 • N/A •

Gwalior India 131 K6
Gweedore Republic of Ireland 31 L3
Gweru Zimbabwe 113 M9
Gwynedd *Unitary authority* Wales, United Kingdom 19 I14
Gwytherin Wales, United Kingdom 27 M3
Gyangzê China 132 I13
Gydanskiy Poluostrov *Peninsula* Russian Federation 128 J6
Győr Hungary 85 K13
Gytheio Greece 92 I12
Gyumri Armenia 99 P13
Gyzylarbat Turkmenistan 124 G8
Gzhel' Russian Federation 96 G10

H

Ha Giang Vietnam 138 M7
Haapsalu Estonia 94 I2
Haarlem Netherlands 78 H9
Habomai Islands *Island group* Japan 136 O3
Hachinohe Japan 136 L6
Hachioji Japan 137 K11
Hackney *London borough* England, United Kingdom 19 O18
Hadd, Ra's al *Headland* Oman 114 G5
Haddington Scotland, United Kingdom 29 M13
Hadejia *River* Nigeria 107 P10
Hadhramaut *Mountain range* Yemen 122 J16
Hadleigh England, United Kingdom 21 R6
Hadrian's Wall *Ancient wall* England, United Kingdom 24 J7
Haeju North Korea 135 P7
Hafen Pwhelli *Beach* Wales, United Kingdom 32 E11
Hag's Head *Headland* Republic of Ireland 30 I10
Hagen Germany 81 E11
Hagi Japan 137 D13
Hai Phong Vietnam 138 N8
Haifa Israel 121 L8
Ha'il Saudi Arabia 122 I8
Haikou China 135 K15
Hailar China 133 P3
Hailsham England, United Kingdom 21 Q9
Hainan *Province* China 127
Hainan Dao *Island* China 135 K16
Hainburg Austria 83 T4
Haines Alaska, USA 36 I10
Haines Junction Yukon Territory, Canada 36 H9
Haiti *Country* West Indies 57 M8

Haiti 57

1804 • French and French Creole • Gourde • 294 • 54 • 12 • 45.8 • 4 • 10000 • No • 32 • 1706

Hajir, Wadi *Dry watercourse* Yemen 123 J16
Hajjah Yemen 122 I15
Hakkâri Turkey 119 S8
Hakodate Japan 136 K5 144 G5
Halden Norway 70 J12
Halicarnassus Turkey 118 G9
Halifax Nova Scotia, Canada 39 P13 66 F8
Halifax England, United Kingdom 25 L14
Halkirk Scotland, United Kingdom 28 K7
Halladale *River* Scotland, United Kingdom 28 K7
Halle Germany 80 J10
Hallein Austria 83 N7
Halley *UK research station* Antarctica 64 D7
Halls Creek Western Australia, Australia 146 I7
Halmahera, Pulau *Island* Indonesia 127 141 O10
Halmstad Sweden 70 J14
Halton *Unitary authority* England, United Kingdom 19 K14
Haltwhistle England, United Kingdom 24 J7
Hamada Japan 137 D12
Hamadan Iran 123 M4

Hamah Syria 121 N4
Hamamatsu Japan 137 J12
Hamar Norway 70 J10
Hamburg Germany 80 H7
Hämeenlinna Finland 71 O10
Hamersley Range *Mountain range* Western Australia, Australia 143 146 F8
Hamhŭng North Korea 135 P6
Hami China 132 J7
Hamilton Ontario, Canada 39 K14
Hamilton New Zealand 148 H4
Hamilton Scotland, United Kingdom 29 J14
Hamm Germany 80 E10
Hammar, Hawr al *Lake* Iraq 123 L6
Hammerfest Norway 71 O1
Hammersmith and Fulham *London borough* England, United Kingdom 19 O19
Hampshire *County* England, United Kingdom 19 L17
Hamun-e-Saberi *Salt pan* Afghanistan 124 I14
Handan China 135 M8
Hangayn Nuruu *Mountain range* Mongolia 133 K4
Hangzhou China 135 O11
Hanley England, United Kingdom 22 J6
Hannover *see* Hanover
Hanoi Vietnam 138 M8
Hanover (Ger. Hannover) Germany 80 H9
Happy Valley-Goose Bay Newfoundland, Canada 39 Q7
Harad Saudi Arabia 123 L10
Harare Zimbabwe 113 M8
Harbin China 135 P4
Hardangerfjorden *Fjord* Norway 70 H10
Harderwijk Netherlands 78 K9
Harer Ethiopia 105 L15
Hargeysa Somalia 105 M15
Hari, Batang *River* Indonesia 140 E12
Haringey *London borough* England, United Kingdom 19 N19
Harirud *River* Afghanistan 125 K12
Harlan County Lake *Reservoir* Nebraska, USA 47 N11
Harlech Wales, United Kingdom 27 L5
Harlingen Netherlands 78 J7
Harlow England, United Kingdom 21 Q5
Harney Lake *Lake* Oregon, USA 50 K10
Härnösand Sweden 71 M9
Harpenden England, United Kingdom 21 P4
Harper Liberia 106 I14
Harris *Physical region* Scotland, United Kingdom 17 D5 28 F8
Harris, Sound of *Strait* Scotland, United Kingdom 28 E9
Harrisburg Pennsylvania, USA 40 J13
Harrogate England, United Kingdom 25 M12
Harrow England, United Kingdom 21 P5
Harrow *London borough* England, United Kingdom 19 M19
Harry S. Truman Reservoir *Reservoir* Missouri, USA 47 Q12
Harstad Norway 71 M3
Hartford Connecticut, USA 41 M11
Hartland Point *Headland* England, United Kingdom 17 E14 20 F8
Hartlepool *Unitary authority* England, United Kingdom 18 O9
Hartlepool England, United Kingdom 25 M8
Harwich England, United Kingdom 21 S4
Haslemere England, United Kingdom 21 O8
Hasselt Belgium 79 J14
Hastings New Zealand 148 I6
Hastings Nebraska, USA 47 O11
Hastings England, United Kingdom 21 R9
Hat Yai Thailand 139 I17
Hatfield England, United Kingdom 21 P5
Hatteras Plain *Undersea feature* Atlantic Ocean 34
Hatteras, Cape *Headland* North Carolina, USA 34 43 S6
Hattiesburg Mississippi, USA 42 J8
Haugesund Norway 66 K7 70 H11
Havana Cuba 56 H3
Havant England, United Kingdom 21 O9
Haverfordwest Wales, United Kingdom 26 H12
Haverhill England, United Kingdom 23 Q11
Havering *London borough* England, United Kingdom 19 O19
Havre Montana, USA 46 J6
Havre-St-Pierre Quebec, Canada 39 O9
Hawaii *State* USA 145 L7
Hawes England, United Kingdom 25 K11
Hawick Scotland, United Kingdom 29 M15
Hawke Bay *Bay* New Zealand 148 I6
Haworth England, United Kingdom 25 K13
Hawran, Wadi *Dry watercourse* Iraq 122 I4
Hay River Northwest Territories, Canada 37 K10
Hay-on-Wye Wales, United Kingdom 27 O11
Hayes *River* Manitoba, Canada 37 P12
Hays Kansas, USA 47 H12
Haywards Heath England, United Kingdom 21 Q8
Hazleton Pennsylvania, USA 41 K12
Heard and McDonald Islands *Dependent territory* Indian Ocean 115 H15
Heard Island *Island* Indian Ocean 64 I7
Hebrides, Sea of the *Sea* Scotland, United Kingdom 17 D5 28 F10
Heerenveen Netherlands 78 K7
Heerlen Netherlands 79 L15
Hefei China 135 N10
Heidelberg Germany 81 F14
Heilbronn Germany 81 G14
Heilong Jiang *River* China/Russian Federation 135 O1
Hejaz *Physical region* Saudi Arabia 122 G7
Helena Montana, USA 46 H5
Helensburgh Scotland, United Kingdom 29 I13
Helgoland Bay *Bay* Germany 80 F6
Helmand, Darya-ye *River* Afghanistan 125 L13
Helmond Netherlands 79 K13
Helmsdale Scotland, United Kingdom 28 K8
Helmsley England, United Kingdom 25 M11
Helsingborg Sweden 70 J15
Helsingør Denmark 70 J15
Helsinki Finland 71 O11
Helston England, United Kingdom 20 E12
Helvellyn *Mountain* England, United Kingdom 24 I9
Helwan Egypt 104 F7
Henderson Nevada, USA 48 H6
Hengelo Netherlands 79 N10
Henley-on-Thames England, United Kingdom 21 N6
Henzada Burma 138 F10
Herat Afghanistan 124 J12
Hereford England, United Kingdom 22 H12
Herefordshire *Unitary authority* England, United Kingdom 19 J15
Herisau Switzerland 82 H9
Herma Ness *Headland* Scotland, United Kingdom 17 G1 28 O1
Hermansverk Norway 70 H9
Hermit Islands *Island group* Papua New Guinea 147 N1
Hermosillo Mexico 52 H4
Herrenchiemsee *Castle* Germany 81 K16
Herstal Belgium 79 K15
Hertfordshire *County* England, United Kingdom 19 M16
Hessle England, United Kingdom 25 O14
Hexham England, United Kingdom 24 K7
Hialeah Florida, USA 43 O15
Hibbing Minnesota, USA 44 H3
Hida-sanmyaku *Mountain range* Japan 137 H11
Hidaka-sanmyaku *Mountain range* Japan 136 L4
Hidalgo del Parral Mexico 53 K6
High Atlas *Mountain range* Morocco 68
High Weald *Area of Outstanding Natural Beauty* England, United Kingdom 32 H13
High Willhays *Mountain* England, United Kingdom 20 H10
High Wycombe England, United Kingdom 21 O5
Highland *Unitary authority* Scotland, United Kingdom 18 F7
Hiiumaa *Island* Estonia 94 H2
Hildesheim Germany 80 H9
Hillingdon *London borough* England, United Kingdom 19 M19
Hillsboro Oregon, USA 50 H8
Hillsborough Northern Ireland, United Kingdom 31 P5
Hilversum Netherlands 78 J10
Himalayas *Mountain range* S Asia 68 114 J5 117 127 131 K3 132 F12
Hims Syria 121 N5
Hindu Kush *Mountain range* Afghanistan/Pakistan 117 125 N11 127
Hinnøya *Island* Norway 71 L3
Hirakud Reservoir *Reservoir* India 131 M8
Hirfanlı Barajı *Reservoir* Turkey 119 L7
Hiroshima Japan 137 E13
Hispaniola *Island* Dominican Republic/Haiti 34 55
Hit Iraq 122 J4
Hitachi Japan 136 L10
Hitra *Island* Norway 70 I7
Hjørring Denmark 70 I13
Hlybokaye Belarus 95 L9
Hô Chi Minh (var. Ho Chi Minh City; prev. Saigon) Vietnam 139 N14
Ho Chi Minh City *see* Hô Chi Minh
Hobart Tasmania, Australia 147 N16
Hobbs New Mexico, USA 49 N10
Hodeida Yemen 122 H15
Hoek van Holland (Eng. Hook of Holland) Netherlands 79 G11
Hof Germany 81 K12
Hohe Tauern *Mountain range* Austria 83 N8
Hohenschwangau *Castle* Germany 81 I17
Hohhot China 133 O7
Hokkaido *Island* Japan 127 136 K3
Holguín Cuba 57 K6
Holland Michigan, USA 45 M9
Hollywood California, USA 51 K18
Hollywood Florida, USA 43 O15
Holon Israel 121 L10
Holstebro Denmark 70 H14
Holt England, United Kingdom 23 R7
Holt Wales, United Kingdom 27 P3
Holy Island England, United Kingdom 25 L3
Holy Island *Island* England, United Kingdom 17 G8
Holy Island *Island* Wales, United Kingdom 17 E11 26 J2
Holyhead Wales, United Kingdom 26 J1
Holyhead Bay *Bay* Wales, United Kingdom 26 J1
Homer Alaska, USA 36 F8
Homyel' Belarus 95 O14
Honduras *Country* Central America 56 C8

Honduras 56

1838 • Spanish • Lempira • 56 • 69 • 12 • 70.7 • 13 • 2500 • No • 44 • 2305

Honduras, Gulf of *Gulf* Caribbean Sea 56 C7
Hønefoss Norway 70 J11
Hông Gai Vietnam 138 N8
Hong Kong China 135 M14 144 E7
Hongshui He *River* China 134 J13
Hongze Hu *Lake* China 135 N9
Honiara Solomon Islands 144 I9
Honiton England, United Kingdom 20 I9
Honolulu Hawaii, USA 145 K6
Honshu *Island* Japan 127 136 J9
Hoogeveen Netherlands 78 M8
Hook of Holland *see* Hoek van Holland
Hoorn Netherlands 78 I8
Hoover Dam *Dam* Arizona/Nevada, USA 48 H7
Hopa Turkey 119 Q4
Hopedale Newfoundland, Canada 39 P6
Hopkinsville Kentucky, USA 43 L3
Horki Belarus 95 O11
Horley England, United Kingdom 21 P7
Horlivka Ukraine 99 M6
Hormuz, Strait of *Strait* Gulf of Oman/The Gulf 123 O10
Horn, Cape *Headland* Chile 55 63 L20 66 E16 145 Q13
Horncastle England, United Kingdom 23 O5
Hornsea England, United Kingdom 25 P13
Horsens Denmark 70 I15
Horsham England, United Kingdom 21 P8
Hot Springs Arkansas, USA 42 H5
Hotan China 132 F9
Houayxay Laos 138 I9
Houlton Maine, USA 41 Q4
Hounslow *London borough* England, United Kingdom 19 M19
Houston Texas, USA 49 S13
Hovd Mongolia 132 I4
Hove England, United Kingdom 21 P9
Hovsgol Nuur *Lake* Mongolia 133 K3
Howardian Hills *Area of Outstanding Natural Beauty* England, United Kingdom 32 G9
Howland Island *Island* Baker and Howland Islands 144 J8
Hoy *Island* Scotland, United Kingdom 17 F3 28 K6
Hoy and West Mainland *Area of Outstanding Natural Beauty* Scotland, United Kingdom 32 F4
Hradec Králové Czech Republic 84 I9
Hrodna Belarus 94 H11
Hron *River* Slovakia 85 L12
Huainan China 135 N10
Huambo Angola 112 H6
Huancayo Peru 59 E13
Huánuco Peru 59 D12
Huascarán, Nevado *Mountain* Peru 55
Hubli India 130 J12
Hucknall England, United Kingdom 23 L6
Huddersfield England, United Kingdom 25 L14
Huddinge Sweden 71 L12
Hudiksvall Sweden 71 L10
Hudson Bay *Bay* Canada 34 37 P10 38 I5 66 D7
Hudson River *River* New Jersey/New York, USA 41 M10
Hudson Strait *Strait* Nunavut/Quebec, Canada 34 37 R8 39 L2
Hudson-Mohawk Gap *Gap* New York, USA 41 M9
Huê Vietnam 139 N11
Huehuetenango Guatemala 56 A7
Huelva Spain 74 H13
Huesca Spain 75 N5
Hugh Town England, United Kingdom 20 E14
Hughenden Queensland, Australia 147 N8
Hull *see* Kingston upon Hull
Hull *River* England, United Kingdom 25 O12
Hulun Nur *Lake* China 133 P3
Humber *Estuary* England, United Kingdom 17 H10 23 O3 25 P14
Humboldt River *River* Nevada, USA 48 H2
Hun Libya 103 P8
Hungary *Country* C Europe 84 J13

Hungary 84-85

1918 • Hungarian • Forint • 109 • 71 • 16 • 99 • 226 • 278 • No • 65 • 3503

Hunstanton England, United Kingdom 23 P7
Huntingdon England, United Kingdom 23 O10
Huntington West Virginia, USA 43 P3
Huntington Beach California, USA 51 L19
Huntly Scotland, United Kingdom 29 M10
Huntsville Alabama, USA 43 L5
Huron South Dakota, USA 45 P10
Huron, Lake *Lake* Michigan/Ontario, Canada/USA 34 38 I13 45 O5
Hurunui *River* New Zealand 148 F9
Husum Germany 80 G6
Hutchinson Kansas, USA 47 O13
Huy Belgium 79 J16
Hvar *Island* Croatia 88 I8
Hwange *National Park* Zimbabwe 113 L9
Hwange Zimbabwe 113 L8
Hyargas Nuur *Lake* Mongolia 133 J4
Hyderabad Pakistan 130 H6
Hyderabad India 131 K11
Hyères, Îles d' *Island group* France 77 P14
Hythe England, United Kingdom 21 S8
Hyvinkää Finland 71 O11

I

Ialomiţa *River* Romania 91 N9
Iaşi Romania 91 N3
Ibadan Nigeria 107 N12
Ibagué Colombia 58 E7
Ibar *River* Serbia, Yugoslavia 89 N8
Ibarra Ecuador 58 C8
Ibb Yemen 122 I16
Iberian Peninsula *Physical region* Portugal/Spain 68
Ibiza (Sp. Eivissa) *Island* Spain 75 P10
Ibotirama Brazil 61 L11
Ibri Oman 123 O12
Ica Peru 59 E14
Iceland *Country* NW Europe 65 O16 66 I7

Iceland 66

1944 • Icelandic • Icelandic króna • 3 • 79 • 16 • 99 • 142 • 333 • No • 92 • 3058

Iceland *Island* Atlantic Ocean 68
Iceland Plateau *Undersea feature* Atlantic Ocean 68
Idaho *State* USA 46 F7
Idaho Falls Idaho, USA 46 H8
Idfu Egypt 104 G8
Ieper (Fr. Ypres) Belgium 79 C15
Ifôghas, Adrar des *Mountain range* Mali 107 M6
Iglesias Italy 87 C15
Igoumenitsa Greece 92 F6
Iguaçu Falls *Waterfall* Brazil 61 H14
Iguaçu, Rio *River* Argentina/Brazil 61 H15
Iisalmi Finland 71 P8
IJmuiden Netherlands 78 H9
IJssel *River* Netherlands 78 K9
IJsselmeer *Lake* Netherlands 78 J8
Ijzer *River* Belgium 79 C14
Ikaria *Island* Greece 93 O10
Iki *Island* Japan 137 B13
Ilagan Philippines 141 L3
Ilam Iran 123 L5
Ilebo Dem. Rep. Congo (Zaire) 109 K14
Ilford England, United Kingdom 21 Q6
Ilfracombe England, United Kingdom 20 G7
Ilgaz Dağları *Mountain range* Turkey 119 L5
Ili *River* Kazakhstan 117 128 H12
Iliamna Lake *Lake* Alaska, USA 36 F8
Iligan Philippines 141 N7
Ilkeston England, United Kingdom 23 L7
Ilkley England, United Kingdom 25 L13
Illapel Chile 62 G10
Illinois *State* USA 44 J12
Illinois River *River* Illinois, USA 44 J13
Illizi Algeria 103 L11
Ilo Peru 145 R10
Iloilo Philippines 141 M6
Ilorin Nigeria 107 N12
Imandra, Ozero *Lake* Russian Federation 96 I5
Imatra Finland 71 Q10
Imperial Dam *Dam* California, USA 48 H9
Impfondo Congo 109 I12
Imphal India 131 Q7
Inarijärvi *Lake* Finland 71 P2
Inch'ŏn South Korea 135 P7 144 F5
Independence Missouri, USA 47 Q12
India *Country* S Asia 130 I7

India 130-131

1947 • Hindi and English • Indian rupee • 336 • 63 • 14 • 53.5 • 4 • 2500 • Yes • 27 • 2395

Indian Ocean *Ocean* 114-115
Indiana Pennsylvania, USA 40 H12
Indiana *State* USA 45 L11
Indianapolis Indiana, USA 45 M12
Indigirka *River* Russian Federation 129 O5
Indo-Australian Plate *Tectonic plate* 68 117 127 143
Indonesia *Country* SE Asia 140 H13

Indonesia 140-141

1949 • Bahasa Indonesia • Rupiah • 116 • 65 • 15 • 85 • 13 • 6423 • Yes • 35 • 2752

Indore India 130 J8
Indus *River* S Asia 114 H5 117 127 130 G5
Ingleborough *Mountain* England, United Kingdom 24 J11
Ingolstadt Germany 81 J15
Inhambane Mozambique 113 O11
Inishannon Republic of Ireland 31 K14
Inishbofin *Island* Republic of Ireland 30 H8
Inishmore *Island* Republic of Ireland 30 I9
Inishtrahull *Island* Republic of Ireland 31 N1
Inishturk *Island* Republic of Ireland 30 I8
Inland Sea *Sea* Japan 137 E13
Inle, Lake *Lake* Burma 138 G8
Inn *River* C Europe 81 L15 83 K8
Inner Hebrides *Island group* Scotland, United Kingdom 17 D6 28 E12
Inner Mongolia *Region* China 133 P5
Innsbruck Austria 83 L8
Inongo Dem. Rep. Congo (Zaire) 109 J13
Insein Burma 138 F10
Interlaken Switzerland 82 F11
Inukjuak Quebec, Canada 39 K4
Inuvik Northwest Territories, Canada 36 J7
Inveraray Scotland, United Kingdom 29 H13
Inverbervie Scotland, United Kingdom 29 N11
Invercargill New Zealand 148 C12
Inverclyde *Unitary authority* Scotland, United Kingdom 18 K5
Invergordon Scotland, United Kingdom 28 J9
Inverness Scotland, United Kingdom 28 J9
Inverurie Scotland, United Kingdom 29 M10
Investigator Strait *Strait* South Australia, Australia 147 K13
Ioannina Greece 92 G5
Iona *National Park* Angola 112 F8
Iona *Island* Scotland, United Kingdom 29 F12
Ionian Islands *Island group* Greece 92 F9
Ionian Sea *Sea* Mediterranean Sea 68 87 N17 92 F7
Ios *Island* Greece 93 N12
Iowa *State* USA 47 P9
Iowa City Iowa, USA 47 R9
Ipel' *River* Hungary/Slovakia 85 L12
Ipoh Malaysia 139 I18
Ipswich Queensland, Australia 147 P10
Ipswich England, United Kingdom 23 R11
Iqaluit Nunavut, Canada 37 R7
Iquique Chile 62 F4
Iquitos Peru 58 F10
Iracoubo French Guiana 58 P6
Irakleio Greece 93 M16
Iran *Country* SW Asia 123 M3

Iran 123

1502 • Farsi (Persian) • Iranian rial • 41 • 69 • 11 • 73.3 • 30 • 3333 • Yes • 59 • 286

Iranian Plate *Tectonic plate* 68 101 117 127
Iranian Plateau *Plateau* Iran 68 117
Irapuato Mexico 53 M11
Iraq *Country* SW Asia 122 J5

Iraq 122-123

1932 • Arabic • Iraqi dinar • 51 • 62 • 12 • 58 • 36 • 1667 • Yes • 75 • 2121

Irbid Jordan 121 M9
Ireland *Island* Republic of Ireland/United Kingdom 17 C10
Ireland, Republic of *Country* NW Europe 19 C13 31 K8 32 C10

Ireland, Republic of 30-31

1922 • Irish and English • Punt • 54 • 76 • 15 • 99 • 272 • 500 • No • 58 • 3847

Irian Jaya (prev. Dutch New Guinea) *Province* Indonesia 141 R12
Iringa Tanzania 111 O10
Irish Sea *Sea* Atlantic Ocean 17 E10 32 E10
Irkutsk Russian Federation 129 L11
Ironbridge England, United Kingdom 22 I9
Irrawaddy *River* Burma 114 K6 117 127 138 G7
Irtysh *River* N Asia 68 117 128 H8 127 132 H4
Irvine USA 29 I14
Irvinestown Northern Ireland, United Kingdom 31 M5
Ischia, Isola d' *Island* Italy 87 J13
Iseo, L. d' *Lake* Italy 86 E6
Isfahan Iran 123 N6
Ishikari-gawa *River* Japan 136 K4
Ishikari-wan *Bay* Japan 136 K4
Ishim *River* Kazakhstan/Russian Federation 128 G10
Isiro Dem. Rep. Congo (Zaire) 109 N11
İskenderun (Eng. Alexandretta) Turkey 119 N10
Iskŭr *River* Bulgaria 90 J11
Iskŭr, Yazovir *Reservoir* Bulgaria 90 I13
Islam Barrage *Dam* 130 I4
Islamabad Pakistan 130 J2
Islay *Island* Scotland, United Kingdom 17 D7 29 G14
Isle of Anglesey *Unitary authority* Wales, United Kingdom 19 H13
Isle of Man *Dependent territory* NW Europe 19 H12 24 H5
Isle of Wight *Unitary authority* England, United Kingdom 19 L18 21 N10
Isle of Wight *Area of Outstanding Natural Beauty* England, United Kingdom 32 G13
Isles of Scilly *Unitary authority* England, United Kingdom 19 F19 20 D14
Islington *London borough* England, United Kingdom 19 O20
Isma'iliya Egypt 104 G6
İsparta Turkey 119 J9

Date of independence • Language (official or most commonly spoken) • Currency • Population density per square kilometre • Average life expectancy • School-leaving age • Literacy • Number of cars per 1,000 people • Number of people per doctor • Death penalty • Percentage of urban-based population • Average number of calories consumed daily per person

Israel *Country* SW Asia 121 L9

Israel 121

1948 • Hebrew and Arabic • New Israeli shekel • 300 • 78 • 15 • 95.4 • 213 • 350 • No • 91 • 3050

Issyk-Kul', Ozero *Lake* Kyrgyzstan 125 R5
Istanbul Turkey 118 H5
Itaipú Dam *Dam* Brazil/Paraguay 62 O6
Itaipú, Represa de *Reservoir* Brazil/Paraguay 55 61 H14
Italy *Country* S Europe 86-87

Italy 86-87

1870 • Italian • Italian lira • 195 • 78 • 14 • 98.3 • 533 • 588 • No • 67 • 3561

Itanagar India 131 Q6
Itea Greece 92 I8
Ithaca New York, USA 40 J10
Ittoqqortoormiit (Eng. Scoresby Sound) Greenland 65 O15
Iturup, Ostrov *Island* Russian Federation 136 P1
Ivalo Finland 71 P3
Ivangrad Yugoslavia 89 M9
Ivano-Frankivs'k Ukraine 98 F5
Ivanovo Russian Federation 96 H10 128 F6
Ivory Coast *Country* W Africa 106 J12

Ivory Coast 106-107

1960 • French • Franc de la Communauté financière africaine • 46 • 47 • 13 • 42.6 • 21 • 10000 • No • 44 • 2491

Iwaki Japan 136 L9
Izabal, Lago de *Lake* Guatemala 56 B8
Izhevsk Russian Federation 97 K11 128 F7
Izhma *River* Russian Federation 96 L8
İzmir Turkey 118 G8
İzmit Turkey 118 I5
İznik Turkey 118 I5
Iztaccíhuatl, Volcán *Volcano* Mexico 53 N12
Izu-shoto *Island group* Japan 136 K12

J

Jabalpur India 131 L8
Jackson Michigan, USA 45 N9
Jackson Mississippi, USA 42 J7
Jackson Lake *Lake* Wyoming, USA 46 H8
Jacksonville Florida, USA 43 O10
Jacksonville Illinois, USA 44 J13
Jacmel Haiti 57 M8
Jaén Spain 75 K12
Jaffna Sri Lanka 131 L15
Jaipur India 130 J6
Jaisalmer India 130 I5
Jajce Bosnia and Herzegovina 88 J6
Jakarta (prev. Djakarta, Dut. Batavia) Indonesia 140 G14
Jakobstad Finland 71 N8
Jalalabad Afghanistan 125 O12
Jalandhar India 131 J3
Jalapa Mexico 53 O12
Jamaica *Country* West Indies 56 J8

Jamaica 56-57

1962 • English • Jamaican dollar • 240 • 75 • 12 • 85.5 • 41 • 2000 • Yes • 54 • 2607

Jamaica *Island* West Indies 55
Jamalpur Bangladesh 131 P7
Jambi Indonesia 140 F12
James Bay *Bay* Ontario/Quebec, Canada 38 J7
James River *River* North Dakota/South Dakota, USA 47 O7
Jamestown New York, USA 40 H10
Jamestown North Dakota, USA 47 N5
Jamnagar India 130 H8
Jamshedpur India 131 N8
Jan Mayen *Dependent territory* Atlantic Ocean 65 P15
Jan Mayen *Island* Atlantic Ocean 68
Janakpur Nepal 131 N6
Janesville Wisconsin, USA 45 K9
Japan *Country* E Asia 136-137

Japan 136-137

1600 • Japanese • Yen • 336 • 80 • 15 • 99 • 373 • 556 • Yes • 78 • 2903

Japan Trench *Undersea feature* Pacific Ocean 127 144 G6
Japan, Sea of *Sea* Pacific Ocean 129 Q12 127 G5 133 T5 136 H10 144
Jardines de la Reina, Archipiélago de los *Island group* Cuba 56 I5
Jari, Rio *River* Brazil 60 H6
Järvenpää Finland 71 O11
Jask Iran 123 P10
Jasper Alberta, Canada 37 K13
Java *Island* Indonesia 114 M9 127 140 H15 143
Java Sea *Sea* SE Asia 114 M9 127 140 G13 143
Java Trench *Trench* Indonesia 114 L9 127 143
Jaya, Puncak *Mountain* Indonesia 127
Jayapura Indonesia 141 T12
Jaz Murian, Hamun-e *Lake* Iran 123 P10
Jazirat Masirah Oman 114 G6
Jebel Aulia Dam *Dam* Sudan 105 G13
Jedburgh Scotland, United Kingdom 29 M15
Jedda Saudi Arabia 122 G11
Jefferson City Missouri, USA 47 R12
Jēkabpils Latvia 94 J7
Jelgava Latvia 94 I6
Jember Indonesia 140 J15
Jena Germany 81 J11
Jenbach Austria 83 L8
Jendouba Tunisia 103 N4
Jérémie Haiti 57 L8
Jeréz de la Frontera Spain 74 I14
Jericho West Bank 121 M10
Jerid, Chott el *Salt lake* Tunisia 101 103 M5
Jersey *Dependent territory* NW Europe 19 K20
Jersey *Island* Jersey 17 G16
Jerusalem Israel 121 M10
Jesenice Slovenia 83 P10
Jessore Bangladesh 131 O8
Jeziorak, Jezioro *Lake* Poland 85 L3
Jhelum Pakistan 130 J2
Jiamusi China 135 Q3
Jihlava Czech Republic 84 I10
Jihlava *River* Czech Republic 84 I10
Jijiga Ethiopia 105 L15
Jilib Somalia 105 L18
Jilin China 135 P4
Jima Ethiopia 105 I15
Jinan China 135 M8
Jingdezhen China 135 N11
Jingmen China 135 L10
Jining China 133 O7
Jinja Uganda 111 N4
Jinnah Barrage *Dam* Pakistan 130 I2
Jinotega Nicaragua 56 D10
Jinsha Jiang *River* China 134 H11
Jiu *River* Romania 90 J10
Jixi China 135 Q4
Jizan Saudi Arabia 122 H14
Jizzakh Uzbekistan 125 M7
João Pessoa Brazil 60 P9
Jodhpur India 130 I6
Joensuu Finland 71 Q9
Johannesburg South Africa 113 L12
John Day River *River* Oregon, USA 50 J9
John o'Groats Scotland, United Kingdom 28 K6
Johnson City Tennessee, USA 43 O5
Johnston Wales, United Kingdom 26 H13
Johnston Atoll *Dependent territory* Pacific Ocean 145 K7
Johnstown Pennsylvania, USA 40 H13
Johor Bahru Malaysia 139 K20
Joinville Brazil 61 J15
Jokkmokk Sweden 71 M5
Joliet Illinois, USA 45 L10
Jolo Philippines 141 L8
Jolo *Island* Philippines 141 L8
Jonglei Canal *Canal* Sudan 105 F16
Joniškis Lithuania 94 H7
Jönköping Sweden 71 K13
Jonquière Quebec, Canada 39 N11
Joplin Missouri, USA 47 Q13
Jordan *Country* SW Asia 121 N12

Jordan 121

1946 • Arabic • Jordanian dinar • 73 • 70 • 15 • 87.2 • 50 • 625 • Yes • 71 • 3022

Jordan *River* SW Asia 121 M9
Jos Nigeria 107 P11
Jos Plateau *Plateau* Nigeria 107 P11
Joseph Bonaparte Gulf *Gulf* Australia 146 I5
Juan de Fuca Plate *Tectonic plate* 34
Juan de Fuca, Strait of *Strait* Pacific Ocean 50 F5
Juan Fernández, Islas *Island group* Chile 145 P11
Juazeiro Brazil 60 N10
Juba Sudan 105 F17
Juba *River* Ethiopia/Somalia 105 L18
Júcar *River* Spain 75 M10
Judenburg Austria 83 Q8
Juigalpa Nicaragua 56 D11
Juiz de Fora Brazil 61 L14
Juliaca Peru 59 G14
Juneau Alaska, USA 36 H10
Jungfrau *Mountain* Switzerland 82 F11
Junín Argentina 62 O9
Jura (var. Jura Mountains) *Mountain range* France/Switzerland 77 O9 82 D10
Jura *Island* Scotland, United Kingdom 17 D7 29 G14
Jura Mountains *see* Jura
Jura, Sound of *Strait* Scotland, United Kingdom 29 G14
Jurbarkas Lithuania 94 H9
Juruá, Rio *River* Brazil/Peru 55 60 B9
Juticalpa Honduras 56 D9
Jutland *Island* Denmark 70 H14
Jutland *see* Jylland
Juventud, Isla de la *Island* Cuba 56 G4
Jwaneng Botswana 113 K11
Jylland (Eng. Jutland) *Peninsula* Denmark 68
Jyväskylä Finland 71 O9

K

K2 *Mountain* China/Pakistan 127
Kabaena, Pulau *Island* Indonesia 141 M14
Kabalega Falls *Waterfall* Uganda 111 M3
Kabalo Dem. Rep. Congo (Zaire) 109 N15
Kabia, Palau *Island* Indonesia 141 L14
Kabul *River* Afghanistan/Pakistan 125 N12
Kabwe Zambia 111 K14
Kachchh, Gulf of *Gulf* India 130 G7
Kachchh, Rann of (var. Rann of Kutch) *Salt marsh* India/Pakistan 127 130 H7
Kadugli Sudan 105 F14
Kaduna Nigeria 107 O11
Kaédi Mauritania 106 G8
Kaesŏng North Korea 135 P7
Kafue Zambia 111 K15
Kafue *National park* Zambia 110 J14
Kafue *River* Zambia 110 J14
Kafue Flats *Plain* Zambia 110 J15
Kaga Bandoro Central African Republic 108 J10
Kagoshima Japan 137 C15
Kahmard, Darya-ye *River* Afghanistan 125 M11
Kahramanmaraş Turkey 119 N9
Kai, Kepulauan *Island group* Indonesia 141 Q13
Kaikoura New Zealand 148 G9
Kainji Reservoir *Reservoir* Nigeria 107 N11
Kaipara Harbour *Harbour* New Zealand 148 G3
Kairouan Tunisia 103 N5
Kaiserslautern Germany 81 E14
Kajaani Finland 71 P7
Kakamega Kenya 111 N4
Kakhovka Reservoir *Reservoir* Ukraine 99 K7
Kalahari Desert *Desert* Southern Africa 101 112 J11
Kalahari Gemsbok *National Park* South Africa 112 J12
Kalamata Greece 92 I12
Kalamazoo Michigan, USA 45 M9
Kalamits'ka Zatoka *Gulf* Ukraine 98 J10
Kalemie Dem. Rep. Congo (Zaire) 109 O15
Kalgoorlie Western Australia, Australia 146 H12
Kaliningrad Russian Federation 94 F9
Kalispell Montana, USA 46 G4
Kalisz Poland 85 K6
Kalmar Sweden 71 L14
Kaluga Russian Federation 96 F10 128 E6
Kalyenkavichy Belarus 95 M15
Kama *River* Russian Federation 96 L10 128 G7
Kamaran *Island* Yemen 122 H15
Kamchatka *Peninsula* Russian Federation 117 129 R6 144 H4
Kamchatka *River* Russian Federation 34
Kamchiya *River* Bulgaria 91 N12
Kamenjak, Rt *Headland* Croatia 88 F5
Kamina Dem. Rep. Congo (Zaire) 109 M16
Kamloops British Columbia, Canada 37 K15
Kampala Uganda 111 M4
Kampong Cham Cambodia 139 M14
Kampong Chhnang Cambodia 139 L14
Kampong Saom Cambodia 139 K14
Kampong Thum Cambodia 139 L13
Kampot Cambodia 139 L14
Kamskoye Vodokhranilishche *Reservoir* Russian Federation 96 L11
Kam"yanets'-Podil's'kyy Ukraine 98 G6
Kananga Dem. Rep. Congo (Zaire) 109 L15
Kanazawa Japan 136 H10
Kanchanaburi Thailand 139 I12
Kandahar Afghanistan 125 L14
Kandi Benin 107 N10
Kandla India 130 H7
Kandy Sri Lanka 131 L16
Kangaroo Island *Island* South Australia, Australia 147 L14
Kangchenjunga *Mountain* India 127
Kangean, Pulau *Island* Indonesia 140 J15
Kanggye North Korea 135 P6
Kangnŭng South Korea 135 Q7
Kanjiža Serbia, Yugoslavia 89 M2
Kankakee Illinois, USA 45 L11
Kankan Guinea 106 I11
Kano Nigeria 107 P10
Kanpur (Eng. Cawnpore) India 131 L6
Kansas *State* USA 47 N12
Kansas City Kansas, USA 47 Q12
Kansk Russian Federation 129 K10
Kaohsiung Taiwan 135 O14
Kaolack Senegal 106 F9
Kapchagay Kazakhstan 128 H13
Kapfenberg Austria 83 Q7
Kapuas, Sungai *River* Indonesia 140 H11
Kara Togo 107 M11
Kara Kum *Desert* Turkmenistan 68 I17
Kara Kum Canal *Canal* Turkmenistan 125 K9
Kara Sea (Rus. Karskoye More) *Sea* Arctic Ocean 65 68 96 N5 117 S11 128 I5 127
Kara-Balta Kyrgyzstan 125 P5
Kara-Bogaz-Gol, Zaliv *Bay* Turkmenistan 124 F6
Karabük Turkey 119 K5
Karachi Pakistan 114 H5 130 G6
Karaganda Kazakhstan 128 H11
Karaginskiy, Ostrov *Island* Russian Federation 129 R5
Karaj Iran 123 N4
Karakaya Barajı *Reservoir* Turkey 119 O7
Karakol Kyrgyzstan 125 S5
Karakoram Range *Mountain range* S Asia 132 E9
Karaman Turkey 119 L9
Karamay China 132 H5
Karasburg Namibia 112 I13
Karasjok Norway 71 O2
Karbala' Iraq 123 K5
Karditsa Greece 92 I6
Kärdla Estonia 94 H2
Kariba Dam *Dam* Zimbabwe 111 K15
Kariba, Lake *Reservoir* Zambia/Zimbabwe 101 111 K16 113 L8
Karimata, Kepulauan *Island group* Indonesia 140 H12
Karkinits'ka Zatoka *Gulf* Ukraine 98 J9
Karlovac Croatia 88 H3
Karlovy Vary Czech Republic 84 G8
Karlskrona Sweden 71 K15
Karlsruhe Germany 81 F14
Karlstad Sweden 71 K12
Karpathos *Island* Greece 93 Q15
Kars Turkey 119 R5
Karskoye More *see* Kara Sea
Karystos Greece 93 L9
Kasai *River* Angola/Dem. Rep. Congo (Zaire) 109 J14
Kasama Zambia 111 M11
Kasese Uganda 111 L4
Kashan Iran 123 N5
Kashi China 132 E8
Kashmir *Region* 131 K1
Kaskaskia River *River* Illinois, USA 45 K14
Kasongo Dem. Rep. Congo (Zaire) 109 N14
Kassala Sudan 105 I12
Kassandra, Gulf of *Gulf* Greece 93 K4
Kassel Germany 81 G11
Kastamonu Turkey 119 L4
Kastoria Greece 92 H3
Kastoria, Limni *Lake* Greece 92 H3
Kasumiga-ura *Lake* Japan 136 L10
Kasungu *National Park* Malawi 111 N13
Kasur Pakistan 130 J3
Katakolo Greece 92 H10
Katavi *National Park* Tanzania 111 L9
Katerini Greece 92 J4
Katha Burma 138 G6
Kathmandu Nepal 131 N5
Katowice Poland 85 L9
Katsberg Tunnel *Tunnel* Austria 83 O9
Katsina Nigeria 107 O9
Kattegat *Strait* Denmark 70 I14
Kaub *Castle* Germany 81 E12
Kaunas Lithuania 94 I9
Kavadarci FYR Macedonia 89 O11
Kavala Greece 93 L2
Kavir, Dasht-e (var. Great Salt Desert) *Salt pan* Iran 68 123 N5
Kawa *Archaeological site* Sudan 105 F11
Kawasaki Japan 137 K11
Kayan Burma 141 K10
Kayes Mali 106 H9
Kayseri Turkey 119 M7
Kazakh Uplands *Plateau* Kazakhstan 128 H11
Kazakhstan *Country* C Asia 128 E10

Kazakhstan 126

1991 • Kazakh • Tenge • 6 • 68 • 17 • 99 • 62 • 265 • No • 60 • N/A

Kazan' Russian Federation 96 I11 128 F7
Kazanlŭk Bulgaria 91 L13
Kea *Island* Greece 93 L10
Keban Barajı *Dam* Turkey 119 O7
Kebnekaise *Mountain* Sweden 68
Kecskemét Hungary 85 M14
Kediri Indonesia 140 I15
Keetmanshoop Namibia 112 I12
Kefalonia *Island* Greece 92 G9
Kelkit Çayı *River* Turkey 119 O6
Kells Republic of Ireland 31 N8
Kelmé Lithuania 94 H8
Kelso Scotland, United Kingdom 29 M14
Kem' Russian Federation 96 H7 128 G4
Kemerovo Russian Federation 128 J10
Kemi Finland 71 O6
Kemijärvi Finland 71 P5
Kemijoki *River* Finland 71 O5
Kenai Alaska, USA 36 G8
Kendal England, United Kingdom 24 I10
Kendari Indonesia 141 M13
Kenema Sierra Leone 106 H12
Kenge Dem. Rep. Congo (Zaire) 109 I14
Kenilworth England, United Kingdom 23 K10
Kénitra Morocco 102 I5
Kenmare Republic of Ireland 30 I14
Kennebec River *River* Maine, USA 40 P5
Kennedy Space Center Florida, USA 43 O12
Kennet *River* England, United Kingdom 17 G13
Kennewick Washington, USA 50 K8
Kenora Ontario, Canada 38 E9
Kenosha Wisconsin, USA 45 L9
Kensington and Chelsea *London borough* England, United Kingdom 19 O20
Kent *County* England, United Kingdom 19 N17
Kent Downs *Area of Outstanding Natural Beauty* England, United Kingdom 32 H12
Kentucky *State* USA 43 L3
Kenya *Country* E Africa 111 O4

Kenya 111

1963 • Swahili and English • Kenya shilling • 52 • 52 • 14 • 79.3 • 10 • 6667 • Yes • 28 • 2075

Kenya, Mount *see* Kirinyaga
Kerch Ukraine 99 L9
Kerch Strait *Strait* Russian Federation/Ukraine 68 96 C14 99 L9
Kerguelen *Island* French Southern and Antarctic Territories 64 I7 115 H14
Kerguelen Plateau *Undersea feature* Indian Ocean 115 H14
Kerkyra *see* Corfu
Kermadec Islands *Island group* Pacific Ocean 144 J11
Kermadec Ridge *Undersea feature* Pacific Ocean 143
Kermadec Trench *Undersea feature* Pacific Ocean 144 J11 143
Kerman Iran 123 P8
Kerry *County* Republic of Ireland 19 B15
Kerry Head *Headland* Republic of Ireland 30 I12
Kerulen *River* China/Mongolia 117 127 133 N4
Keswick England, United Kingdom 24 H9
Ket' *River* Russian Federation 128 J9
Ketchikan Alaska, USA 36 I12
Kettering England, United Kingdom 23 M10
Kewanee Illinois, USA 44 J11
Keweenaw Bay *Lake* Michigan, USA 45 K4
Key West Florida, USA 43 N16
Keynsham England, United Kingdom 21 K7
Khabarovsk Russian Federation 129 Q11
Khambhat, Gulf of (Eng. Gulf of Cambay) *Gulf* India 130 I9
Khamis Mushayt Saudi Arabia 122 I13
Khan Yunis Gaza Strip 121 L11
Khanaqin Iraq 123 L4
Khanka, Lake *Lake* China/Russian Federation 127
Khanthabouli Laos 139 L11
Kharkiv Ukraine 99 L5
Khartoum Sudan 105 G12
Khartoum North Sudan 105 G12
Khasab Oman 123 O10
Khashm el 'Girba Dam *Dam* Sudan 105 I12
Khaskovo Bulgaria 91 L14
Khatanga *River* Russian Federation 129 K6
Kherson Ukraine 98 J8
Khmel 'nyts'kyy Ukraine 98 G5
Khon Kaen Thailand 139 K11
Khorramshahr Iran 123 L7
Khorugh Tajikistan 125 O9
Khouribga Morocco 102 I5
Khujand Tajikistan 125 N7
Khujayli Uzbekistan 124 I5
Khulna Bangladesh 131 O8
Khyber Pass *Pass* Afghanistan/Pakistan 125 O12
Kičevo FYR Macedonia 89 N11
Kidderminster England, United Kingdom 22 J10
Kidepo *National Park* Uganda 111 N2
Kidlington England, United Kingdom 21 N4
Kidwelly Wales, United Kingdom 27 K13
Kiel Germany 80 H6
Kiel Canal *Canal* Germany 80 H6
Kielce Poland 85 M8
Kielder Water *Lake* England, United Kingdom 24 J6
Kieta Papua New Guinea 147 Q2
Kiev (Ukr. Kyyiv) Ukraine 98 I4
Kiev Reservoir *Reservoir* Ukraine 98 I4
Kiffa Mauritania 106 H7
Kigali Rwanda 111 L6
Kigoma Tanzania 111 L8
Kikwit Dem. Rep. Congo (Zaire) 109 J14
Kilbeggan Republic of Ireland 31 M9
Kilcolgan Republic of Ireland 31 K9
Kildare *County* Republic of Ireland 19 E14
Kilgetty Wales, United Kingdom 26 I13
Kilimanjaro *Volcano* Tanzania 101 111 P6
Kilis Turkey 119 N10
Kilkee Republic of Ireland 30 I11
Kilkeel Northern Ireland, United Kingdom 31 P6
Kilkelly Republic of Ireland 31 K7
Kilkenny Republic of Ireland 31 M11

Kilkenny *County* Republic of Ireland 19 E15
Kilkis Greece 92 J2
Killarney Republic of Ireland 30 I13
Killarney National Park *National Park* Republic of Ireland 32 C11
Killeen Northern Ireland, United Kingdom 31 O6
Killimer Republic of Ireland 30 J11
Killybegs Republic of Ireland 31 K4
Kilmaine Republic of Ireland 30 J8
Kilmarnock Scotland, United Kingdom 29 J14
Kilrush Republic of Ireland 30 I11
Kilwa Masoko Tanzania 111 Q10
Kimberley South Africa 113 K13
Kimberley Plateau *Plateau* Western Australia, Australia 143 146 H6
Kimito *Island* Finland 71 N11
Kinbrace Scotland, United Kingdom 28 K7
Kinder Scout *Mountain* England, United Kingdom 22 J4
Kindia Guinea 106 G11
Kindu Dem. Rep. Congo (Zaire) 109 M13
King Island *Island* Tasmania, Australia 147 M15
King Leopold Ranges *Mountain range* Western Australia, Australia 146 H6
King William Island *Island* Nunavut, Canada 37 N7
King's Lynn England, United Kingdom 23 P8
Kingman Reef *Dependent territory* Pacific Ocean 145 K8
Kingston Jamaica 57 K8
Kingston Ontario, Canada 39 L14
Kingston New York, USA 41 L11
Kingston upon Hull England, United Kingdom 25 P13
Kingston upon Hull, City of *Unitary authority* England, United Kingdom 19 M13
Kingston upon Thames England, United Kingdom 21 P7
Kingston upon Thames *London borough* England, United Kingdom 19 M20
Kingstown Saint Vincent and the Grenadines 57 S14
Kinnegad Republic of Ireland 31 N8
Kinross Scotland, United Kingdom 29 K13
Kinshasa Dem. Rep. Congo (Zaire) 109 H14
Kintyre *Peninsula* Scotland, United Kingdom 17 D8 29 H14
Kintyre, Mull of *Headland* Scotland, United Kingdom 29 G16
Kirghiz Range *Mountain range* Kazakhstan/Kyrgyzstan 125 P5
Kirghiz Steppe *Grassland* Kazakhstan 68 117 128 F10
Kiribati *Country* Pacific Ocean 144 J8

Kiribati 144

1979 • English • Australian dollar • 110 • 60 • 15 • 98 • N/A • 1939 • No • 36 • 2651

Kırıkkale Turkey 119 L6
Kirinyaga (var. Mount Kenya) *Volcano* Kenya 101 111 P5
Kiritimati (prev. Christmas Island) *Atoll* Kiribati 145 K8
Kiriwina Islands *Island group* Papua New Guinea 147 P3
Kirkby England, United Kingdom 24 I15
Kirkby Stephen England, United Kingdom 25 K10
Kirkcaldy Scotland, United Kingdom 29 L13
Kirkcudbright Scotland, United Kingdom 29 J16
Kirkenes Norway 71 P2
Kırklareli Turkey 118 G4
Kirklees *Unitary authority* England, United Kingdom 19 K13
Kirksville Missouri, USA 47 R10
Kirkuk Iraq 123 K3
Kirkwall Scotland, United Kingdom 28 L5
Kirov Russian Federation 96 J10 128 F7
Kirovohrad Ukraine 98 J6
Kirriemuir Scotland, United Kingdom 29 L12
Kirsehir Turkey 119 L7
Kiruna Sweden 71 N4
Kisangani Dem. Rep. Congo (Zaire) 109 M12
Kiska Island *Island* Alaska, USA 36 A5
Kismaayo Somalia 105 L18
Kisumu Kenya 111 N4
Kitakyushu Japan 137 C13
Kitale Kenya 111 O4
Kitami Japan 136 M3
Kitchener Ontario, Canada 38 J14
Kitimat British Columbia, Canada 36 I12
Kitwe Zambia 111 K13
Kitzbühel Austria 83 M8
Kiunga Marine Reserve *National Park* Tanzania/Kenya 111 R6
Kivu, Lake *Lake* Dem. Rep. Congo (Zaire)/Rwanda 109 O13 111 K6
Kızıl Irmak *River* Turkey 119 L5
Kizyl-Atrek Turkmenistan 124 F9
Klagenfurt Austria 83 P10
Klaipėda Lithuania 94 G8
Klamath Falls Oregon, USA 51 H11
Klang Malaysia 139 I19
Klerksdorp South Africa 113 L12
Ključ Bosnia and Herzegovina 88 I5
Klosterneuburg Austria 83 S4
Kluane Lake *Lake* Yukon Territory, Canada 36 H9
Klyuchevskaya Sopka, Vulkan *Volcano* Russian Federation 117
Knapdale *Area of Outstanding Natural Beauty* Scotland, United Kingdom 32 E7
Knaresborough England, United Kingdom 25 M12
Knighton Wales, United Kingdom 27 O9
Knin Croatia 88 I6
Knittelfeld Austria 83 Q8
Knockmoyle/Shesin *Bog* Republic of Ireland 32 D11
Knocktopher Republic of Ireland 31 M12
Knossos *Prehistoric site* Greece 93 M16
Knowle England, United Kingdom 23 K10
Knowsley *Unitary authority* England, United Kingdom 18 B10
Knoxville Tennessee, USA 43 N5
Knud Rasmussen Land *Physical region* Greenland 65 O12
Kobe Japan 137 G12 144 F5
Koblenz Germany 81 E12
Kobryn Belarus 94 I14
Kočani FYR Macedonia 89 P11
Kočevje Slovenia 83 Q12
Kochi Japan 137 F13
Kodiak Alaska, USA 36 F9
Kodiak Island *Island* Alaska, USA 36 F9
Kofarnihon Tajikistan 125 N9
Kohima India 131 Q6
Kohtla-Järve Estonia 95 K1
Kokkola Finland 71 N8
Kokomo Indiana, USA 45 M12
Kokshaal-Tau *Mountain range* China/Kyrgyzstan 125 R6
Kokshetau Kazakhstan 128 H10
Kola Peninsula *Peninsula* Russian Federation 68 96 J6 128 G4
Kolda Senegal 106 G9
Kölen *Mountain range* Norway/Sweden 68
Kolguyev, Ostrov *Island* Russian Federation 112 L6 142 H5
Kolka Latvia 94 H4
Köln *see* Cologne
Kolubara *River* Serbia, Yugoslavia 89 M6
Kolwezi Dem. Rep. Congo (Zaire) 109 M17
Kolyma *River* Russian Federation 129 P5
Kolyma Range *Mountain range* Russian Federation 129 Q6
Kôm Ombo Egypt 104 G9
Komoé *River* Ivory Coast 107 K11
Komoran, Pulau *Island* Indonesia 141 S14
Komotini Greece 93 N2
Komsomolets, Ostrov *Island* Russian Federation 129 K3
Komsomol'sk-na-Amure Russian Federation 129 Q10
Kongolo Dem. Rep. Congo (Zaire) 109 N14
Kongsberg Norway 70 I11
Konjic Bosnia and Herzegovina 89 K7
Konstanz (Eng. Constance) Germany 81 G16
Konya Turkey 119 K8
Kopaonik *Mountain range* Serbia, Yugoslavia 89 N8
Koper Slovenia 83 P13
Koprivnica Croatia 88 I2
Korçë Albania 89 N13
Korčula *Island* Croatia 88 I8
Korčulanski Kanal *Channel* Croatia 88 I8
Korea Bay *Bay* China/North Korea 135 O7
Korea Strait *Channel* Japan/South Korea 127 135 P9 137 A13
Korhogo Ivory Coast 106 J11
Korinthos *see* Corinth
Koriyama Japan 136 K9
Korla China 132 H7
Kornat *Island* Croatia 88 H6
Körös *River* Hungary 85 M14
Kortrijk Belgium 79 D15
Koryak Range *Mountain range* Russian Federation 129 R3
Kos Greece 92 Q12
Kos *Island* Greece 93 Q12
Kosciusko, Mount *Mountain* New South Wales, Australia 143
Ko9sice Poland 85 N11
Kosovo *Cultural region* Serbia, Yugoslavia 89 N10
Kosovska Mitrovica Serbia, Yugoslavia 89 N8
Kossou, Lac de *Lake* Ivory Coast 106 J12
Kosti Sudan 105 G13
Kostroma Russian Federation 96 H10
Koszalin Poland 84 J2
Kota India 130 J6
Kota Bharu Malaysia 139 J17
Kota Kinabalu Borneo, Malaysia 140 J8
Kotka Finland 71 P11
Kotlas Russian Federation 96 J9 128 G6
Kotto *River* Central African Republic/Dem. Rep. Congo (Zaire) 109 L10
Kotzebue Alaska, USA 36 G5
Kotzebue Sound *Inlet* Alaska, USA 36 F4
Koudougou Burkina 107 K10
Kourou French Guiana 58 P6
Kouvola Finland 71 P10
Kozani Greece 92 H4
Kozina Slovenia 83 P12
Kra, Isthmus of *Isthmus* Malaysia/Thailand 127 139 H15
Kracheh Cambodia 139 M13
Kragujevac Serbia, Yugoslavia 89 N7
Kraków (Eng. Cracow) Poland 85 M9
Kralendijk Netherlands Antilles 57 O14
Kraljevo Serbia, Yugoslavia 89 N7
Kramators'k Ukraine 99 L6
Kranj Slovenia 83 P11
Krāslava Latvia 95 K8
Krasnodar Russian Federation 96 D14 128 C8
Krasnoyarsk Russian Federation 129 K10
Krefeld Germany 81 D11
Kremenchuk Ukraine 98 J6
Kremenchuk Reservoir *Reservoir* Ukraine 98 J5
Krems an der Donau Austria 83 R4
Kretinga Lithuania 94 G7
Kribi Cameroon 109 E11
Krishna *River* India 127 130 J11
Kristiansand Norway 70 H12
Kristianstad Sweden 71 K15
Kristiansund Norway 66 L7
Krk *Island* Croatia 88 G4
Krka *River* Slovenia 88 H6
Krong Kaoh Kong Cambodia 139 K14
Krško Slovenia 83 R11
Kruger National Park *National Park* South Africa 113 M11
Kruševac Serbia, Yugoslavia 89 O7
Krychaw Belarus 95 O11
Kryvyy Rih Ukraine 98 J7
Kuala Belait Brunei 140 J9
Kuala Lumpur Malaysia 139 J19
Kuala Terengganu Malaysia 139 K18
Kualakapuas Indonesia 140 J13
Kuantan Malaysia 139 K19
Kuban' *River* Russian Federation 96 D15
Kuching Borneo, Malaysia 140 H10
Kudat Borneo, Malaysia 141 K8
Kufstein Austria 83 M7
Kuito Angola 112 H6
Kujawy Poland 85 K4
Kuldīga Latvia 94 G5
Kulob Tajikistan 125 N9
Kuma *River* Russian Federation 96 F15
Kumamoto Japan 137 C14
Kumanovo FYR Macedonia 89 O10
Kumasi Ghana 107 L13
Kumon Range *Mountain range* Burma 138 G5
Kunashir, Ostrov *Island* Russian Federation 136 O2
Kunduz Afghanistan 125 N10
Kunlun Mountains *Mountain range* China 127 132 F10
Kunming China 134 I13
Kuopio Finland 71 P8
Kupa *River* Croatia/Slovenia 88 I3
Kupang Indonesia 141 N16
Kupiano Papua New Guinea 147 N4
Kura *River* SW Asia 99 P13
Kurashiki Japan 137 F12
Kuressaare Estonia 94 H3
Kurgan Russian Federation 128 H9
Kuria Muria Islands *see* =Hal¯an¯iy¯at, Juzur al123 N15
Kurile Islands *Island Group* Japan 129 127 H4 136 O2 144 S10
Kurile Trench *Trench* Alaska, USA 127 144 H4
Kursk Russian Federation 96 E11 128 D6
Kusadası Turkey 119 G8
Kushiro Japan 136 N4 144 G5
Kustanay Kazakhstan 128 G9
Kütahya Turkey 119 I7
K'ut'aisi Georgia 99 P12
Kutch, Rann of *see* Kachchh, Rann of
Kuujjuaq Quebec, Canada 39 M4
Kuujjuarapik Quebec, Canada 39 K7
Kuusamo Finland 71 P5
Kuusankoski Finland 71 P10
Kuwait *Country* SW Asia 123 L7

Kuwait 123

1961 • Arabic • Kuwaiti dinar • 107 • 76 • 14 • 80.4 • 317 • 5000 • Yes • 97 • 2523

Kuwait Kuwait 114 E5 123 L7
Kuytun China 132 H6
Kvarner *Gulf* Croatia 88 F4
Kvarnerićka Vrata *Channel* Croatia 88 G4
Kwa *River* Dem. Rep. Congo (Zaire) 109 I13
Kwangju South Korea 135 P8
Kwango *River* Angola/Dem. Rep. Congo (Zaire) 109 I15
Kwilu *River* Dem. Rep. Congo (Zaire) 109 I15
Kyaikkami Burma 139 G11
Kyklades *see* Cyclades
Kyle of Lochalsh Scotland, United Kingdom 28 H10
Kyllini Greece 92 G9
Kymi Greece 93 L8
Kyoga, Lake *Lake* Uganda 111 M4
Kyoto Japan 137 H12
Kyrgyzstan *Country* C Asia 125 P6

Kyrgyzstan 125

1991 • Kyrgyz and Russian • Som • 24 • 68 • 16 • 97 • 32 • 291 • No • 39 • N/A

Kythira *Island* Greece 92 J13
Kythnos *Island* Greece 93 L11
Kyushu *Island* Japan 137 C14
Kyushu-Palau Ridge *Undersea feature* Pacific Ocean 144 G7
Kyyiv *see* Kiev
Kyzyl Russian Federation 129 K11
Kyzyl Kum *Desert* Kazakhstan/Uzbekistan 117
Kyzyl-Kiya Kyrgyzstan 125 O7
Kzyl-Orda Kazakhstan 128 F11

L

La Asunción Venezuela 58 J4
La Ceiba Honduras 56 D8
La Chaux-de-Fonds Switzerland 82 D10
La Crosse Wisconsin, USA 44 J8
La Esperanza Honduras 56 C9
La Grande Oregon, USA 50 K8
La Grande Rivière *River* Quebec, Canada 39 K7
La Grande Rivière HEP Project *Dam* Canada 39 L8
La Guaira Venezuela 58 I4 67 E11
La Libertad El Salvador 56 B9
La Ligua Chile 62 G10
La Louvière Belgium 79 G16
La Martre, Lac *Lake* Northwest Territories, Canada 37 K9
La Oroya Peru 59 E13
La Palma Panama 56 H15
La Paz Bolivia 59 H15
La Perouse Strait *Strait* Japan/Russian Federation 136 K1
La Plata Argentina 62 N10
La Rance *Power station* France 66 K8
La Rioja Argentina 62 I8
la Roche-sur-Yon France 76 I9
la Rochelle France 76 I10
La Romana Dominican Republic 57 O9
La Salle Illinois, USA 45 K11
La Serena Chile 62 G9
La Spezia Italy 86 E9
La Tuque Quebec, Canada 39 M12
Laâyoune Western Sahara 102 F7
Labé Guinea 106 H10
Laborec *River* Slovakia 85 N10
Labrador *Cultural region* Newfoundland, Canada 34 39 O7
Labrador City Newfoundland, Canada 39 N8
Labrador Sea *Sea* Atlantic Ocean 34 39 O3 66 F7
Laccadive Islands *Island group* India 114 H7 127
Laconia New Hampshire, USA 41 O8
Ladoga, Lake *Lake* Russian Federation 68 96 G7 128 F4
Lae Papua New Guinea 147 N2
Lafayette Louisiana, USA 42 H9
Lagdo, Lac de *Lake* Cameroon 108 G9
Lågen *River* Norway 70 J9
Laghouat Algeria 103 M5
Lagos Nigeria 67 L11 107 N13
Lagos Portugal 74 F13
Lagos de Moreno Mexico 53 L10
Lagouira Western Sahara 102 D10
Lahad Datu Borneo, Malaysia 141 K9
Lahij Yemen 122 I16
Lahore Pakistan 130 J3
Laï Chad 108 I9
Lairg Scotland, United Kingdom 28 J8
Lake District *Physical region* England, United Kingdom 17 F9 24 H10
Lake District National Park *National Park* England, United Kingdom 32 F9
Lakewood Colorado, USA 49 M4
Lakonikos Kolpos *Gulf* Greece 92 J13
Lambaréné Gabon 109 F13
Lambert Glacier *Glacier* Antarctica 64 G8
Lambeth *London borough* England, United Kingdom 19 N19
Lamia Greece 92 I7
Lampang Thailand 138 I10
Lampedusa *Island* Italy 87 I20
Lampeter Wales, United Kingdom 27 L10
Lanao, Lake *Lake* Philippines 141 N7
Lanark Scotland, United Kingdom 29 K14
Lancashire *County* England, United Kingdom 19 J13
Lancaster England, United Kingdom 24 I12
Lancaster New Hampshire, USA 41 N6
Lancaster Ohio, USA 45 P12
Lancaster Pennsylvania, USA 40 J13
Lancaster Sound *Sound* Nunavut, Canada 37 O4
Land's End *Headland* England, United Kingdom 17 D15 20 D12
Landeck Austria 82 J9
Landshut Germany 81 K15
Lang Son Vietnam 138 N8
Langholm Scotland, United Kingdom 29 L16
Langkawi, Pulau *Island* Malaysia 139 H17
Länkäran Azerbaijan 99 S15
Lansing Michigan, USA 45 N9
Lanzhou China 134 J8
Laoag Philippines 141 L2
Laois *County* Republic of Ireland 19 E14
Laon France 77 M4
Laos *Country* SE Asia 138 J8

Laos 138-139

1991 • Kyrgyz and Russian • Som • 24 • 68 • 16 • 97 • 32 • 291 • No • 39 • N/A

Lapland *Cultural region* N Europe 71 M4
Lappeenranta Finland 71 P10
Laptev Sea *Sea* Arctic Ocean 65 S7 68 117 129 M4 127
L'Aquila Italy 87 J11
Laramie Wyoming, USA 47 K10
Laramie River *River* Wyoming, USA 47 K10
Laredo Texas, USA 49 P15
Largs Scotland, United Kingdom 29 I14
Larisa Greece 92 I5
Lark *River* England, United Kingdom 23 P10
Larkana Pakistan 130 H5
Larnaca Cyprus 119 L12
Larne Northern Ireland, United Kingdom 31 P4
Larne *District* Northern Ireland, United Kingdom 19 G11
Larsen Ice Shelf *Ice shelf* Antarctica 64 B7
Las Cruces New Mexico, USA 49 L10
Las Tablas Panama 56 G16
Las Tunas Cuba 57 K6
Las Vegas Nevada, USA 48 G6
Lashio Burma 138 H7
Lastovo *Island* Croatia 88 I9
Lastovski Kanal *Channel* Croatia 88 I8
Latacunga Ecuador 58 C9
Latvia *Country* NE Europe 94 G6

Latvia 94-95

1991 • Latvian • Lat • 37 • 68 • 15 • 99 • 175 • 333 • No • 73 • N/A

Lau Basin *Undersea feature* Pacific Ocean 143
Launceston Tasmania, Australia 147 N16
Launceston England, United Kingdom 20 G10
Laurentian Mountains *Plateau* Canada/USA 34
Lausanne Switzerland 82 D11
Laval France 76 I6
Laval Quebec, Canada 39 M13
Lavenham England, United Kingdom 23 Q11
Lavon, Lake *Lake* USA 49 R10
Lavrio Greece 93 L10
Lawrence Massachusetts, USA 41 O9
Lawton Oklahoma, USA 47 O16
Lázaro Cárdenas Mexico 53 L13
le Havre France 76 J4
le Mans France 76 J6
Le Port Réunion 115 F11
le Puy France 77 N11
Lebanon New Hampshire, USA 41 N8
Lebanon *Country* SW Asia 121 M7

Lebanon 121

1944 • Arabic • Lebanese pound • 313 • 70 • 84.4 • 299 • 526 • Yes • 87 • 3317

Lebu Chile 63 G12
Lecce Italy 87 P14
Leduc Alberta, Canada 37 L13
Leech Lake *Lake* Minnesota, USA 44 G4
Leeds England, United Kingdom 25 M13
Leeds *Unitary authority* England, United Kingdom 19 L13
Leek England, United Kingdom 22 J6
Leeuwarden Netherlands 78 K7
Leeuwin, Cape *Headland* Western Australia, Australia 115 M12 146 F13
Leeward Islands *Island group* West Indies 55 57 R9
Lefkada Greece 92 G7
Lefkada *Island* Greece 92 G7
Legaspi Philippines 141 M5
Leghorn *see* Livorno
Legnica Poland 84 J7
Leicester England, United Kingdom 23 L9
Leicester, City of *Unitary authority* England, United Kingdom 19 L15
Leicestershire *County* England, United Kingdom 19 L14
Leiden Netherlands 78 H10
Leighton Buzzard England, United Kingdom 21 O4
Leipzig Germany 81 K11
Leiria Portugal 74 F9
Leitrim *County* Republic of Ireland 19 D12
Leixlip Republic of Ireland 31 O9
Leizhou Peninsula *Peninsula* China 135 K15
Lek *River* Netherlands 79 I11
Lelystad Netherlands 78 J9
Lena *River* Russian Federation 117 129 N6 127
Lenghu China 132 J9
Lenin Peak *Mountain* Kyrgyzstan/Tajikistan 117
Leningradskaya *Russian research station* Antarctica 64 F12
Leoben Austria 83 Q7
Leominster England, United Kingdom 22 H11
León Spain 74 I4
León Nicaragua 56 C10
León Mexico 53 L10
Leonido Greece 92 J11
Lepontine Alps *Mountain range* Italy/Switzerland 82 G11
Leptis Magna Libya 103 O6
Lérida *see* Lleida
Lerwick Scotland, United Kingdom 28 O2
les Sables-d'Olonne France 76 H9
Lesbos *Island* Greece 93 O7
Leshan China 134 I11
Leskovac Serbia, Yugoslavia 89 O8
Lesotho *Country* Southern Africa 113 L13

Lesotho 113

1966 • English and Sesotho • Loti • 69 • 56 • 13 • 82.3 • 6 • 20000 • Yes • 23 • 2201

Date of independence • Language (official or most commonly spoken) • Currency • Population density per square kilometre • Average life expectancy • School-leaving age • Literacy • Number of cars per 1,000 people • Number of people per doctor • Death penalty • Percentage of urban-based population • Average number of calories consumed daily per person

Lesse *River* Belgium 79 J17
Lesser Antarctica *Physical region* Antarctica 64 D9
Lesser Antilles *Island group* West Indies 34 55 57 Q10
Lesser Slave Lake *Lake* Alberta, Canada 37 L12
Lesser Sunda Islands *Island group* Indonesia 141 K16
Leszno Poland 84 J6
Letchworth England, United Kingdom 21 P4
Lethbridge Alberta, Canada 37 L15
Lethem Guyana 58 L7
Leti, Kepulauan *Island group* Indonesia 141 O15
Leticia Peru 58 G10
Letterkenny Republic of Ireland 31 M3
Letterston Wales, United Kingdom 26 H12
Leuven Belgium 79 H15
Lévêque, Cape *Cape* Western Australia, Australia 146 G6
Leverkusen Germany 81 D11
Levin New Zealand 148 H7
Levittown Pennsylvania, USA 41 L13
Lewes England, United Kingdom 21 Q9
Lewis, Butt of *Headland* Scotland, United Kingdom 17 D4 28 F7
Lewis, Isle of *Island* Scotland, United Kingdom 17 D4 28 F8
Lewisham *London borough* England, United Kingdom 19 N19
Lewiston Idaho, USA 46 F5
Lewiston Maine, USA 41 O7
Lewistown Pennsylvania, USA 40 I13
Lexington Kentucky, USA 43 N3
Leyland England, United Kingdom 24 I14
Leyte *Island* Philippines 141 N6
Lhasa China 132 I13
Lianyungang China 135 N9
Liaoyuan China 135 O5
Liberal Kansas, USA 47 M14
Liberec Czech Republic 84 I8
Liberia Costa Rica 56 D12
Liberia *Country* W Africa 106 H13

Liberia 106

1847 • a English • Liberian dollar • 30 • 47 • 16 • 38.3 • 41 • 9350 • Yes • 45 • 1640

Libreville Gabon 67 L12 109 E12
Libya *Country* N Africa 103 O8

Libya 103

1951 • a Arabic • Libyan dinar • 3 • 70 • 15 • 76.5 • 159 • 909 • Yes • 86 • 3308

Libyan Desert *Desert* N Africa 101
Lichfield England, United Kingdom 23 K9
Lida Belarus 94 J11
Liechtenstein *Country* C Europe 82 I9

Liechtenstein 82

1719 • a German • Swiss franc • 196 • 78 • 16 • 99 • 948 • No • 21 • N/A

Liège Belgium 79 K15
Lienz Austria 83 N9
Liepāja Latvia 66 M7 94 F6
Liestal Switzerland 82 F8
Liezen Austria 83 P7
Liffey *River* Republic of Ireland 17 D11 31 N10
Liffey Head *Bog* Republic of Ireland 32 D10
Lifford Republic of Ireland 31 M4
Ligger Bay *Bay* England, United Kingdom 20 E11
Ligurian Sea *Sea* Mediterranean Sea 86 D9
Likasi Dem. Rep. Congo (Zaire) 109 N17
Lille France 77 L2
Lillehammer Norway 70 J10
Lilongwe Malawi 111 N14
Lima Peru 59 D13
Lima Ohio, USA 45 O11
Limassol Cyprus 119 K12
Limavady *District* Northern Ireland, United Kingdom 19 E11
Limavady Northern Ireland, United Kingdom 31 N3
Limbe Cameroon 109 E11
Limerick Republic of Ireland 31 K11
Limerick *County* Republic of Ireland 19 C15
Limnos *Island* Greece 93 M5
Limoges France 77 K10
Limón Costa Rica 56 E13
Limpopo *River* Botswana/Mozambique/South Africa/Zimbabwe 101 113 L11 115 C11
Linares Chile 63 G11
Lincoln Nebraska, USA 47 O10
Lincoln England, United Kingdom 23 N5
Lincoln Edge *Ridge* England, United Kingdom 23 N5
Lincolnshire *County* England, United Kingdom 19 M14 23 N5
Lincolnshire Wolds *Area of Outstanding Natural Beauty* England, United Kingdom 32 G10
Linderhof *Castle* Germany 81 I17
Lindi Tanzania 111 Q11
Lindisfarne *Abbey* England, United Kingdom 25 L3
Line Islands *Island group* Kiribati 145 K8
Lingga, Pulau *Island* Indonesia 140 F11
Linhe China 133 N7
Linköping Sweden 71 K13
Linnhe, Loch *Inlet* Scotland, United Kingdom 29 H12
Linosa *Island* Italy 87 I20
Linth Walensee *Lake* Switzerland 82 H9
Linz Austria 83 P5
Lion, Gulf of *Gulf* France 68
Lipari *Island* Italy 87 L16
Lipetsk Russian Federation 96 F12 128 E7
Lisboa *see* Lisbon
Lisbon (Port. Lisboa) Portugal 74 F10
Lisburn Northern Ireland, United Kingdom 31 O5
Lisburn *District* Northern Ireland, United Kingdom 19 F12
Liscannor Bay *Inlet* Republic of Ireland 17 B11
Listowel Republic of Ireland 30 I12
Litang China 134 H11
Lithuania *Country* NE Europe 94 G8

Lithuania 94-95

1991 • a Lithuanian • Litas • 57 • 70 • 15 • 99 • 238 • 250 • No • 72 • N/A

Little Abaco *Island* Bahamas 57 K1
Little Cayman *Island* Cayman Islands 56 I6
Little Minch, The *Strait* Scotland, United Kingdom 17 D5 28 F9
Little Missouri River *River* USA 47 L6
Little Ouse *River* England, United Kingdom 23 Q9
Little Rock Arkansas, USA 42 I4
Littlehampton England, United Kingdom 21 P9
Liuwa Plain *Plain* Zambia 110 H14
Liuzhou China 135 K13
Liverpool Nova Scotia, Canada 39 P13
Liverpool England, United Kingdom 24 I15
Liverpool *Unitary authority* England, United Kingdom 18 B10
Liverpool Bay *Bay* England/Wales, United Kingdom 17 F11
Livingston Scotland, United Kingdom 29 K14
Livingston, Lake *Reservoir* Texas, USA 49 S12
Livingstone Zambia 110 J16
Livno Bosnia and Herzegovina 88 J7
Livorno (Eng. Leghorn) Italy 66 L8 86 F9
Liwonde *National Park* Malawi 111 O14
Lixouri Greece 92 F9
Lizard Point *Headland* England, United Kingdom 17 E15 20 E13
Ljubljana Slovenia 83 Q11
Ljusnan *River* Sweden 71 L9
Llanaelhaearn Wales, United Kingdom 26 J4
Llanbedr Wales, United Kingdom 27 L5
Llanbrynmair Wales, United Kingdom 27 M7
Llandeilo Wales, United Kingdom 27 L12
Llandovery Wales, United Kingdom 27 M11
Llandrindod Wells Wales, United Kingdom 27 N9
Llandudno Wales, United Kingdom 27 L1
Llanelli Wales, United Kingdom 27 K13
Llanfaelog Wales, United Kingdom 26 J2
Llanfair Caereinion Wales, United Kingdom 27 N6
Llanfair Talhaiarn Wales, United Kingdom 27 M2
Llanfihangel-nant-Melan Wales, United Kingdom 27 O10
Llangurig Wales, United Kingdom 27 M8
Llanidloes Wales, United Kingdom 27 N8
Llanllyfni Wales, United Kingdom 27 K3
Llanos *Physical region* Colombia/Venezuela 55
Llanrhaeadr-ym-Mochnant Wales, United Kingdom 27 N5
Llanrhidian Wales, United Kingdom 27 K14
Llanrwst Wales, United Kingdom 27 M3
Llansteffan Wales, United Kingdom 26 J13
Llantwit Major Wales, United Kingdom 27 N15
Llanuwchllyn Wales, United Kingdom 27 M5
Llanwrda Wales, United Kingdom 27 L11
Llanwrtyd Wells Wales, United Kingdom 27 M10
Lleida (Sp. Lérida) Spain 75 O6
Lleyn Peninsula *Peninsula* Wales, United Kingdom 26 J5
Lloydminster Alberta/Saskatchewan, Canada 37 M13
Llyswen Wales, United Kingdom 27 N11
Lobatse Botswana 113 K12
Lobito Angola 112 G6
Locarno Switzerland 82 H12
Loch Lomond *Area of Outstanding Natural Beauty* Scotland, United Kingdom 32 E7
Loch na Keal *Area of Outstanding Natural Beauty* Scotland, United Kingdom 32 E6
Loch Shiel *Area of Outstanding Natural Beauty* Scotland, United Kingdom 32 E6
Loch Tummel *Area of Outstanding Natural Beauty* Scotland, United Kingdom 32 F6
Lochboisdale Scotland, United Kingdom 28 E10
Lochdon Scotland, United Kingdom 29 H12
Lochgilphead Scotland, United Kingdom 29 H13
Lochinver Scotland, United Kingdom 28 H8
Lochmaddy Scotland, United Kingdom 28 E9
Lochy, Loch *Lake* Scotland, United Kingdom 29 I11
Loch Rannoch and Glen Lyon *Area of Outstanding Natural Beauty* Scotland, United Kingdom 32 E6
Lockerbie Scotland, United Kingdom 29 L16
Lockport New York, USA 40 H8
Lodja Dem. Rep. Congo (Zaire) 109 L14
Łódź Poland 85 L6
Loei Thailand 138 J10
Lofoten *Island group* Norway 71 L3
Logan Utah, USA 48 J2
Logansport Indiana, USA 45 M11
Logroño Spain 75 L5
Loire *River* France 68 76 J8
Loja Ecuador 58 C10
Lokichokio Kenya 111 N2
Lokoja Nigeria 107 O12
Loksa Estonia 94 J1
Lomami *River* Dem. Rep. Congo (Zaire) 109 M13
Lombardy *Cultural region* Italy 86 E7
Lombok, Pulau *Island* Indonesia 141 K15
Lomé Togo 107 M13
Lomond, Loch *Lake* Scotland, United Kingdom 17 E7 29 J13
London Ontario, Canada 38 J15
London England, United Kingdom 21 P6
London, City of *London borough* England, United Kingdom 19 O20
Londonderry *District* Northern Ireland, United Kingdom 19 E11
Londonderry Northern Ireland, United Kingdom 31 M3
Londonderry, Cape *Cape* Western Australia, Australia 146 H5
Londrina Brazil 61 I14
Long Beach California, USA 51 K19 145 M5
Long Branch New Jersey, USA 41 L13
Long Eaton England, United Kingdom 23 L7
Long Island *Island* Bahamas 57 L4
Long Island *Island* New York, USA 41 N12
Long Xuyên Vietnam 139 M15
Longford Republic of Ireland 31 M7
Longford *County* Republic of Ireland 19 D13
Longmont Colorado, USA 49 M3
Longreach Queensland, Australia 147 N9
Longview Washington, USA 50 H8
Longyearbyen Svalbard 65 R13
Loop Head *Promontory* Republic of Ireland 17 B12
Lop Nur *Seasonal lake* China 127 132 I8
Lopatka, Mys *Headland* Russian Federation 129 S8
Lord Howe Island *Island* Australia 144 I11
Lord Howe Rise *Undersea feature* Pacific Ocean 144 I11 143
Lord Howe Seamounts *Undersea feature* Pacific Ocean 143
Lorengau Papua New Guinea 147 O1
Lorient France 66 K8 76 G7
Lorn, Firth of *Inlet* Scotland, United Kingdom 17 D7 29 H13
Los Alamos New Mexico, USA 49 L7
Los Ángeles Chile 63 G12
Los Angeles California, USA 51 K18
Los Mochis Mexico 52 I7
Lošinj *Island* Croatia 88 G5
Lossiemouth Scotland, United Kingdom 28 L9
Lot *River* France 77 K12
Lötschbergtunnel *Tunnel* Switzerland 82 F11
Louangnamtha Laos 138 J8
Louangphabang Laos 138 K9
Louga Senegal 106 F8
Loughborough England, United Kingdom 23 L8
Loughrea Republic of Ireland 31 K9
Louisiade Archipelago *Island group* Papua New Guinea 147 Q4
Louisiana *State* USA 42 G7
Louisville Kentucky, USA 43 M2
Louisville Ridge *Undersea feature* Pacific Ocean 143
Louth England, United Kingdom 23 O5
Louth *County* Republic of Irel 19 F13
Loutra Aidipsou Greece 92 J7
Lovech Bulgaria 91 K12
Lowell Massachusetts, USA 41 O9
Lower California *Peninsula* Mexico 34 52 P3
Lower Lough Erne *Lake* Northern Ireland, United Kingdom 17 C9 31 M5
Lower Red Lake *Lake* Minnesota, USA 44 G3
Lower Tunguska *River* Russian Federation 129 M8
Lower Zambezi *National Park* Zambia 111 L15
Lowestoft England, United Kingdom 23 T9
Loznica Serbia, Yugoslavia 89 L5
Lučenec Poland 85 M12
Lučnice *River* Czech Republic 84 H10
Lualaba *River* Dem. Rep. Congo (Zaire) 109 M13
Luanda Angola 112 G4
Luang, Thale *Lagoon* Thailand 139 I16
Luangwa *River* Mozambique/Zambia 111 M12
Luanshya Zambia 111 K13
Lubango Angola 112 G7
Lubāns *Lake* Latvia 95 K6
Lubbock Texas, USA 49 O9
Lübeck Germany 80 I7
Lubin Poland 85 O7
Lubumbashi Dem. Rep. Congo (Zaire) 109 N17
Lucapa Angola 112 J4
Lucca Italy 86 F9
Luce Bay *Inlet* Scotland, United Kingdom 31 I16
Lucena Philippines 141 L4
Lucknow India 131 L6
Lüderitz Namibia 66 M14 112 H12
Ludhiana India 131 K3
Ludlow England, United Kingdom 22 H10
Ludza Latvia 95 L6
Luena Angola 112 I5
Lugano Switzerland 82 H12
Lugano, Lago di *Lake* Switzerland 82 H13
Lugenda, Rio *River* Mozambique 113 O6
Lugnaquillia Mountain *Mountain* Republic of Ireland 31 O10
Lugo Spain 74 G4
Luhans'k Ukraine 99 M6
Luke Air Force Range *Military base* USA 48 H10
Lukusuzi *National Park* Zambia 111 M13
Luleå Sweden 71 N6
Luleälven *River* Sweden 71 M4
Lulua *River* Dem. Rep. Congo (Zaire) 109 L16
Lumbala N'Guimbo Angola 112 J6
Lumphat Cambodia 139 N13
Lundazi Zambia 111 N13
Lundy *Island* England, United Kingdom 17 E14 20 F7
Lüneburg Germany 80 I8
Luninyets Belarus 95 K14
Luoyang China 135 L9
Lusaka Zambia 111 K15
Lusambo Dem. Rep. Congo (Zaire) 109 L14
Luton England, United Kingdom 21 P4
Luton *Unitary authority* England, United Kingdom 19 M16
Luts'k Ukraine 98 F4
Lutzow-Holm Bay *Bay* Antarctica 64 F6
Luxembourg Luxembourg 79 L19
Luxembourg *Country* NW Europe 79 K18

Luxembourg 79

1867 • a French, German and Letzebuergisch • Luxembourg franc. The Belgian franc is also legal tender • 165 • 77 • 15 • 99 • 248 • 476 • No • 90 • 3681

Luxor Egypt 104 G8
Luzern Switzerland 82 G10
Lužnice *River* Czech Republic 84 H10
Luzon *Island* Philippines 141 L3
Luzon Strait *Strait* Philippines/Taiwan 141 L1
L'viv Ukraine 98 F4
Lydstep *Beach* Wales, United Kingdom 32 E12
Lyepyel' Belarus 95 M9
Lyme Bay *Bay* England, United Kingdom 17 F14 20 J10
Lyme Regis England, United Kingdom 20 J10
Lymington England, United Kingdom 21 N9
Lynn Massachusetts, USA 41 O10
Lynn Lake Manitoba, Canada 37 N12
Lynton England, United Kingdom 20 H7
Lyon (Eng. Lyons) France 77 N10
Lyons *see* Lyon
Lytham St Anne's England, United Kingdom 24 I14

M

Ma'an Jordan 121 M13
Maas *River* W Europe 79 L12
Maastricht Netherlands 79 H14
Mablethorpe England, United Kingdom 23 P5
Macao China 135 M14
Macapá Brazil 60 J7
Macclesfield England, United Kingdom 22 J5
Macdonnell Ranges *Mountain range* Northern Territory, Australia 143 146 I9
Macduff Scotland, United Kingdom 29 M9
Macedonia *Country* SE Europe 89 N11

Macedonia 89

1991 • a Macedonian • Macedonian denar • 78 • 73 • 15 • 94 • 141 • 435 • No • 6 • N/A

Maceió Brazil 60 O10
Machakos Kenya 111 P6
Machala Ecuador 58 C10
Machupicchu Peru 59 F13
Machynlleth Wales, United Kingdom 27 L7
Mackay Queensland, Australia 147 O8
Mackay, Lake *Salt lake* Northern Territory/Western Australia, Australia 143 146 J8
Mackenzie *River* Northwest Territories, Canada 37 K9
Mackenzie Bay *Bay* Antarctica 64 G8
Mackenzie Bay *Bay* Yukon Territory, Canada 36 J6
Mackenzie Mountains *Mountain range* Northwest Territories, Canada 36 J8
Mackinac, Straits of *Lake* Michigan, USA 45 M5
Macleod, Lake *Lake* Western Australia, Australia 146 E9
Macomb Illinois, USA 44 J12
Mâcon France 77 N9
Macon Georgia, USA 43 N8
Macquarie Island *Island* New Zealand 144 I13
Macquarie Ridge *Undersea feature* Pacific Ocean144 I13 143
Macroom Republic of Ireland 30 J14
Madagascar *Country* Indian Ocean 114 F10

Madagascar 114

1960 • a French and Malagasy • Franc malagache (Malagasy franc) • 27 • 58 • 13 • 47 • 5 • 10000 • No • 27 • 2135

Madagascar *Island* Indian Ocean 101 127
Madagascar Basin *Undersea basin* 101 115 F11
Madagascar Plateau *Undersea plateau* 115 E12
Madang Papua New Guinea 147 N2
Madeira *Island* Portugal 66 J9 101
Madeira Ridge *Undersea feature* Atlantic Ocean 101
Madeira, Rio *River* Bolivia/Brazil 55 60 F8
Madeleine, Îles de la *Island group* Quebec, Canada 39 Q11
Madison Wisconsin, USA 45 K9
Madona Latvia 95 K6
Madras *see* Chennai
Madre de Dios, Río *River* Bolivia/Peru 59 H13
Madre del Sur, Sierra *Mountain range* Mexico 53 M13
Madre Occidental, Sierra (var. Western Sierra Madre) *Mountain range* Mexico 34 52 I5
Madre Oriental, Sierra (var. Eastern Sierra Madre) *Mountain range* Mexico 34 53 M7
Madre, Sierra *Mountain range* Guatemala/Mexico 55
Madrid Spain 75 K8
Madura, Pulau *Island* Indonesia 140 I15
Madurai India 131 K15
Mae Nam Mun *River* Thailand 139 K12
Mae Nam Ping *River* Thailand 139 I11
Maebashi Japan 136 J10
Maentwrog Wales, United Kingdom 27 L4
Maesteg Wales, United Kingdom 27 M14
Mafeteng Lesotho 113 L14
Mafia *Island* Tanzania 111 Q10
Magadan Russian Federation 129 Q7
Magdalena, Río *River* Colombia 55 58 E5
Magdeburg Germany 80 J9
Magee, Island *Island* Northern Ireland, United Kingdom 31 P4
Magellan, Strait of *Strait* Argentina/Chile 55 63 J19
Magerøya *Island* Norway 71 O1
Maggiore, Lake *Lake* Italy/Switzerland 82 G12 86 D6
Maghera Northern Ireland, United Kingdom 31 N4
Magherafelt *District* Northern Ireland, United Kingdom 19 F11
Magnitogorsk Russian Federation 128 G9
Mahajanga Madagascar 114 E10
Mahalapye Botswana 113 L11
Mahanadi *River* India 131 N9
Mahé *Island* Seychelles 114 F9
Mahilyow Belarus 95 N11
Mahón Spain 75 S8
Mai-Ndombe, Lake *Lake* Congo (Zaire) 109 J13
Maidenhead England, United Kingdom 21 O6
Maidstone England, United Kingdom 21 R7
Maiduguri Nigeria 107 R10
Main *River* Germany 81 G13
Maine *State* USA 41 P4
Mainland *Island* Scotland, United Kingdom 17 F3 28 L5
Mainland *Island* Scotland, United Kingdom 17 G1 28 O2
Mainz Germany 81 F13
Maitland New South Wales, Australia 147 O12
Majorca (Sp. Mallorca) *Island* Spain 75 R9
Majuro Atoll *Atoll* Marshall Islands 144 J8
Makassar Strait *Strait* Indonesia 141 K13
Makeni Sierra Leone 106 H11
Makhachkala Russian Federation 96 F17 129 D10
Makiyivka Ukraine 99 M7
Makkovik Newfoundland, Canada 39 Q6
Makokou Gabon 109 G12
Makurdi Nigeria 107 P12
Malabar Coast *Coast* India 130 I13
Malabo Equatorial Guinea 109 F11
Malacca *see* Melaka
Malacca, Strait of *Strait* Indonesia/Malaysia 114 K7 127 139 H18
Maladzyechna Belarus 95 K10
Málaga Spain 74 J14
Malahide Republic of Ireland 31 O9
Malakal Sudan 105 G15
Malang Indonesia 140 I15
Malanje Angola 112 H4
Malatya Turkey 119 O8
Malawi *Country* S Africa 111 N13

Malawi 111

1964 • a English • Malawi kwacha • 113 • 39 • 14 • 57.7 • 3 • 50000 • No • 14 • 1825

Malay Peninsula *Peninsula* Malaysia/Thailand 127
Malaysia *Country* SE Asia 139 J18 140 H10

Malaysia 125, 126

1963 • a English and Bahara Malay • Ringgit (Malaysian dollar) • 66 • 72 • 16 • 85.7 • 154 • 2076 • Yes • 54 • 2888

Maldives *Country* Indian Ocean 114 H8

Maldives 114-115

1965 • a Dhivehi (Maldivian) • Rufiyaa (Maldivian rupee) • 927 • 65 • 95.7 • 2 • 1955 • No • 27 • 2580

Male Maldives 114 H8

Malheur Lake *Lake* Oregon, USA 50 K10
Mali *Country* W Africa 106 K7

Mali 106-107

1960 • French • Franc de la Communauté financière africaine • 9 • 53 • 16 • 35.5 • 3 • 10000 • Yes • 27 • 2278

Malin Republic of Ireland 31 O2
Malin Head *Headland* Republic of Ireland 17 C8 31 M2
Malindi Kenya 111 Q7
Mallaig Scotland, United Kingdom 29 G11
Mallorca *see* Majorca
Mallow Republic of Ireland 31 K13
Mallwyd Wales, United Kingdom 27 M6
Malmédy Belgium 79 L16
Malmö Sweden 70 J15
Malopolska *Plateau* Poland 85 M9
Malta *Country* S Europe 87 K20

Malta 87

1964 • English and Maltese • Maltese lira • 1206 • 77 • 16 • 91.1 • 406 • No • 89 • 3486

Maltahöhe Namibia 112 H11
Malton England, United Kingdom 25 N11
Malvern Hills *Area of Outstanding Natural Beauty* England, United Kingdom 32 F11
Malvern Hills *Hill range* England, United Kingdom 17 F12 22 I11
Mamallapuram India 131 L13
Mamberamo, Sungai *River* Indonesia 141 S11
Mamoré, Rio *River* Bolivia/Brazil 59 J13
Mamry, Jezioro *Lake* Poland 85 N2
Man Ivory Coast 106 I12
Man, Isle of *Island* NW Europe 17 E10 32 E9
Mana Pools *National Park* Zimbabwe 113 M7
Manado Indonesia 141 N10
Managua Nicaragua 56 D11
Managua, Lake *Lake* Nicaragua 56 D11
Manama Bahrain 114 F5 123 M10
Manaslu *Mountain* Nepal 127
Manaus Brazil 60 F8
Manchester England, United Kingdom 25 K15
Manchester New Hampshire, USA 41 O9
Manchester *Unitary authority* England, United Kingdom 18 C10
Manchuria *Cultural region* China 135 O4
Manchurian Plain *Plain* China 117 I27
Mandalay Burma 138 G7
Mandera Kenya 111 R2
Manfredonia Italy 87 M12
Mangalia Romania 91 O10
Mangalore India 130 J13
Mangerton *Bog* Republic of Ireland 32 C11
Mangla Reservoir *Reservoir* Pakistan 130 J2
Mangueni, Plateau du *Mountain range* Niger 107 Q4
Manhattan Kansas, USA 47 P12
Manicouagan, Réservoir *Lake* Quebec, Canada 39 N9
Manila Philippines 141 L4 144 F7
Manisa Turkey 118 G7
Manistee Michigan, USA 45 M7
Manistee River *River* Michigan, USA 45 M7
Manitoba *Province* Canada 37 N12
Manitoba, Lake *Lake* Manitoba, Canada 34
Manitowoc Wisconsin, USA 45 L7
Manizales Colombia 58 E6
Mankato Minnesota, USA 44 H7
Mannar Sri Lanka 131 K15
Mannheim Germany 81 F14
Mannu *River* Italy 87 D15
Manokwari Indonesia 141 Q11
Manono Dem. Rep. Congo (Zaire) 109 N15
Mansa Zambia 111 K12
Mansfield England, United Kingdom 23 L6
Mansfield Ohio, USA 45 P11
Manta Ecuador 58 B9
Mantova Italy 86 F7
Manyara, Lake *Lake* Tanzania 111 O7
Manzanillo Mexico 53 K12
Manzhouli China 133 O3
Manzini Swaziland 113 M12
Mao Chad 108 H7
Maoke, Pegunungan *Mountain range* Indonesia 141 R12
Maputo Mozambique 113 N12
Mar Chiquita, Laguna *Lake* Argentina 62 K8
Mar del Plata Argentina 63 N12 67 F14
Mar'ib Yemen 122 I15
Maracaibo Venezuela 58 G4
Maracaibo, Lake *Inlet* Venezuela 55 58 G5
Maracay Venezuela 58 I4
Maradi Niger 107 I9
Marambio *Argentinian research station* Antarctica 64 B7
Maranhão, Barragem do *Reservoir* Portugal 74 G10
Marañón, Río *River* Peru 55 58 D10
Marathon Greece 93 L9
Marbella Spain 74 J14
March England, United Kingdom 23 O9
Marche-en-Famenne Belgium 79 J17
Mardan Pakistan 130 I2
Mardin Turkey 119 Q9
Maree, Loch *Lake* Scotland, United Kingdom 28 H9
Margarita, Isla de *Island* Venezuela 58 J4
Margate England, United Kingdom 21 T6
Margherita, Lake *Lake* Ethiopia 105 I16
Mariana Trench *Undersea feature* Pacific Ocean144 G6 143
Maribor Slovenia 83 R9
Marie Byrd Land *Physical region* Antarctica 64 C9
Marie-Galante *Island* Guadeloupe 57 T12
Mariehamn Finland 71 M11
Mariental Namibia 112 I11
Mariestad Sweden 71 K12
Marijampolė Lithuania 94 H10
Marinette Wisconsin, USA 45 L6
Marion Indiana, USA 45 N11
Marion Ohio, USA 45 O11
Maritsa *River* Bulgaria/Greece/Turkey 91 L14
Mariupol' Ukraine 99 L8
Marka Somalia 105 M18
Market Harborough England, United Kingdom 23 M9
Marmara, Sea of *Sea* Turkey 118 H5
Marmaris Turkey 118 H10
Marne *River* France 77 M4
Maroni River *River* French Guiana/Surinam 58 O7
Maroua Cameroon 108 H8
Marquesas Islands *Island group* French Polynesia 145 M9
Marquette Michigan, USA 45 L4
Marrakech (Eng. Marrakesh) Morocco 102 H6
Marrakesh *see* Marrakech
Marsá al Burayqah Libya 103 Q7
Marsabit *National Park* Kenya 111 P3
Marseille (Eng. Marseilles) France 66 L8 77 O14
Marseilles *see* Marseille
Marsh Island *Island* Louisiana, USA 42 H9
Marshall Islands *Country* Pacific Ocean 144 I7

Marshall Islands 144

1986 • Marshallese and English • United States dollar • 327 • 64 • 14 • 91 • 3294 • No • 69 •

Marshall Islands *Island group* Pacific Ocean 143
Marshall Seamounts *Undersea feature* Pacific Ocean 143
Marshfield Wisconsin, USA 44 J7
Martaban, Gulf of *Gulf* Indian Ocean 139 F11
Martha's Vineyard *Island* Massachusetts, USA 41 O11
Martigny Switzerland 82 E12
Martin Slovakia 85 L11
Martinique *Dependent territory* West Indies 57 T13
Mary Turkmenistan 124 J9
Maryland *State* USA 43 R3
Maryville Missouri, USA 47 P10
Masai Mara *National Park* Kenya 111 N5
Masai Steppe *Grassland* Tanzania 111 O8
Masaka Uganda 111 M5
Masbate *Island* Philippines 141 M5
Masbate Philippines 141 M5
Mascarene Plain *Undersea feature* Indian Ocean 127
Mascarene Plateau *Undersea feature* Indian Ocean 114 G9
Maseru Lesotho 113 L14
Mashhad Iran 123 Q4
Masinloc Philippines 141 L3
Masira, Gulf of *Gulf* Indian Ocean 123 P14
Masirah, Jasirat *Island Group* Oman 123 P14
Mask, Lough *Lake* Republic of Ireland 17 B10 31 J8
Masqat *see* Muscat
Massachusetts *State* USA 41 N10
Massada Israel 121 L11
Massawa Eritrea 105 J12
Massena New York, USA 41 L6
Massif Central *Plateau* France 68 77 L10
Massillon Ohio, USA 45 Q11
Masterton New Zealand 148 H7
Masvingo Zimbabwe 113 M9
Matadi Dem. Rep. Congo (Zaire) 109 G15
Matagalpa Nicaragua 56 D10
Matam Senegal 106 G8
Matamoros Mexico 53 O7
Matanzas Cuba 56 H3
Matara Sri Lanka 131 L16
Matlock England, United Kingdom 23 K6
Mato Grosso, Planalto de *Plateau* Brazil 60 G10
Matruh Egypt 104 D6
Matsue Japan 137 E11
Matsuyama Japan 137 E13
Matterhorn *Mountain* Italy/Switzerland 82 F13
Mattoon Illinois, USA 45 L13
Maturín Venezuela 58 K4
Maumee River *River* Indiana/Ohio, USA 45 N11
Maun Botswana 113 K9
Mauritania *Country* W Africa 106 G6

Mauritania 106

1960 • Arabic and French • Ouguiya • 3 • 54 • 12 • 38.4 • 8 • 10000 • Yes • 54 • 2685

Mauritius *Country* E Africa 115 F11

Mauritius 115

1968 • English • Mauritian rupee • 645 • 71 • 12 • 83 • 64 • 1250 • No • 41 • 2690

Mawson *Australian research station* Antarctica 64 G7
Maya *River* Russian Federation 129 O8
Mayaguana *Island* Bahamas 57 M5
Mayagüez Puerto Rico 57 P9
Maybole Scotland, United Kingdom 29 I15
Mayo *County* Republic of Ireland 19 C13
Mayotte *Dependent territory* Indian Ocean 114 E10
Mazar-e Sharif Afghanistan 125 M10
Mazaruni River *River* Guyana 58 L6
Mazatenango Guatemala 56 A8
Mazatlán Mexico 52 J4
Mažeikiai Lithuania 94 G7
Mazyr Belarus 95 M15
Mbabane Swaziland 113 M12
Mbaïki Central African Republic 109 I11
Mbala Zambia 111 M10
Mbale Uganda 111 N4
Mbalmayo Cameroon 109 F11
Mbandaka Dem. Rep. Congo (Zaire) 109 J12
Mbarara Uganda 111 L5
Mbeya Tanzania 111 N10
Mbuji-Mayi Dem. Rep. Congo (Zaire) 109 L15
McAllen Texas, USA 49 Q16
McClellan Air Base *Military base* California, USA 51 I14
McClintock Channel *Channel* Nunavut, Canada 37 M6
McClure Strait *Strait* Northwest Territories, Canada 37 K5
McKinley, Mount *Mountain* Alaska, USA 34
McMillan, Lake *Reservoir* New Mexico, USA 49 M10
Mead, Lake *Reservoir* Arizona/Nevada, USA 48 H6
Meadville Pennsylvania, USA 40 G11
Meath *County* Republic of Ireland 19 F13
Mecca Saudi Arabia 122 H11
Mechelen Belgium 79 H14
Mecklenburger Bucht *Bay* Germany 80 J6
Medan Indonesia 140 D10
Medellín Colombia 58 E6
Médenine Tunisia 103 N6
Medford Oregon, USA 51 H11
Medicine Hat Alberta, Canada 37 L15
Medina Saudi Arabia 122 H9
Medina Lake *Lake* USA 49 P13
Mediterranean Sea *Sea* Africa/Asia/Europe 66 68 75 N13 77 M15 93 K16 101 102 J4 117 121 L6 127 K9
Medvezh'i, Ostrova *Island group* Russian Federation 129 P4
Medway *River* England, United Kingdom 21 Q6
Meekatharra Western Australia, Australia 146 F10
Meerut India 131 K4
Mek'ele Ethiopia 105 J13
Meknès Morocco 102 I5
Mekong *River* SE Asia 114 L5 117 127 133 K12 134 H14 138 I8
Mekong, Mouths of the *Delta* Vietnam 127
Melaka (var. Malacca) Malaysia 114 L8 139 J20
Melanesia *Island group* Pacific Ocean 144 H8 143
Melanesian Basin *Undersea feature* Pacific Ocean143
Melbourne Victoria, Australia 144 G12 147 N14
Melbourne Florida, USA 43 O12
Melghir, Chott *Salt lake* Algeria 103 M5
Melilla *Spanish enclave* NW Africa 102 J4
Melitopol' Ukraine 99 K8
Melk Austria 83 Q5
Melo Uruguay 62 P9
Melton Mowbray England, United Kingdom 23 M8
Melun France 77 L5
Melville Saskatchewan, Canada 37 N14
Melville Island *Island* Northern Territory, Australia 146 J4
Melville Island *Island* Northwest Territories/Nunavut, Canada 37 L4 65 N9
Memphis Tennessee, USA 42 J4
Menai Bridge Wales, United Kingdom 27 K2
Menai Strait *Strait* Wales, United Kingdom 26 K3
Mendawai, Sungai *River* Indonesia 140 I12
Mende France 77 M12
Mendi Papua New Guinea 147 M2
Mendip Hills *Area of Outstanding Natural Beauty* England, United Kingdom 32 F12
Mendip Hills *Hill range* England, United Kingdom 17 F13 20 J7
Mendocino Fracture Zone *Undersea feature* Pacific Ocean 34 145 L5
Mendoza Argentina 62 H10
Menongue Angola 112 H7
Menorca *see* Minorca
Meppel Netherlands 78 L8
Mequinenza, Embalse de *Reservoir* Spain 75 O6
Merced California, USA 51 I15
Mercedes Argentina 62 J10
Mercedes Uruguay 62 N9
Mergui Burma 139 H13
Mergui Archipelago *Island group* Burma 139 G14
Mérida Mexico 53 S11
Mérida Spain 74 H10
Mérida Venezuela 58 G5
Meridian Mississippi, USA 42 J7
Meroe *Archaeological site* Sudan 105 G11
Mersey *River* England, United Kingdom 17 F11 22 H6
Mersin Turkey 119 M10
Merthyr Tydfil Wales, United Kingdom 27 N13
Merthyr Tydfil *Unitary authority* Wales, United Kingdom 19 E17
Merton *London borough* England, United Kingdom 19 N20
Meru Kenya 111 P4
Mesa Arizona, USA 48 I9
Mesolongi Greece 92 H8
Messenia, Gulf of *Gulf* Greece 92 I12
Messina Italy 87 M17
Messina, Strait of *Strait* Italy 68 87 M17
Mestre Italy 86 H7
Meta, Río *River* Colombia/Venezuela 58 G6
Metković Croatia 88 J8
Metz France 77 O4
Meuse *River* W Europe 68 77 N4 79 I16
Mexborough England, United Kingdom 25 M15
Mexico *Country* Central America 52-53

Mexico 52-53

1836 • Spanish • Mexican peso • 51 • 72 • 14 • 90.1 • 93 • 769 • No • 75 • 3146

Mexico Basin *Undersea feature* Gulf of Mexico 34 55
Mexico City Mexico 53 N12
Mexico, Gulf of *Gulf* Atlantic Ocean 34 43 K10 49 R15 55 66 C10
Meymaneh Afghanistan 125 L11
Mezen' *River* Russian Federation 96 K7 128 G5
Miami Florida, USA 43 O15
Mianyang China 134 J10
Michigan *State* USA 45 K5
Michigan City Indiana, USA 45 M10
Michigan, Lake *Lake* Indiana/Michigan/Wisconsin, USA 34 45 L7
Micronesia *Country* Pacific Ocean 144 H7

Micronesia 144

1986 • English • United States dollar • 156 • 67 • 14 • 89 • N/A • 2311 • No • 28 •

Micronesia *Island group* Pacific Ocean 144 G8 143
Mid-Atlantic Ridge *Undersea feature* Atlantic Ocean 34 55 66 G10 101
Mid-Indian Basin *Undersea feature* Indian Ocean 127
Mid-Indian Ridge *Undersea feature* Indian Ocean 114 G8 127
Mid-Pacific Mountains *Undersea feature* Pacific Ocean144 I6
Middelburg Netherlands 79 E12
Middle America Trench *Undersea feature* Pacific Ocean 55
Middle Atlas *Mountain range* Morocco 68
Middle Loup River *River* Nebraska, USA 47 M9
Middlesbrough England, United Kingdom 25 M9
Middlesbrough *Unitary authority* England, United Kingdom 18 O10
Middletown Wales, United Kingdom 27 O6
Middletown New York, USA 41 L11
Middlewich England, United Kingdom 22 I6
Midland Texas, USA 49 O11
Midland Michigan, USA 45 N8
Midleton Republic of Ireland 31 L14
Midlothian *Unitary authority* Scotland, United Kingdom 18 P5
Midway Islands *Dependent territory* Pacific Ocean 144 J6
Mikkeli Finland 71 P10
Mikumi *National Park* Tanzania 111 P9
Milagro Ecuador 58 C9
Milan (It. Milano) Italy 86 D7
Milano *see* Milan
Milas Turkey 118 G9
Mildenhall England, United Kingdom 23 Q10
Mildura Victoria, Australia 147 M13
Miles City Montana, USA 47 K6
Miletus *Archaeological site* Turkey 118 G9
Milford Delaware, USA 41 K15
Milford Haven Wales, United Kingdom 26 H13
Milford Sound New Zealand 148 C11
Mille Lacs Lake *Lake* Minnesota, USA 44 H5
Millisle Lagoon *Beach* Northern Ireland, United Kingdom 32 E8
Millstätter See *Lake* Austria 83 O9
Milos *Island* Greece 93 L12
Milton Keynes England, United Kingdom 21 O4
Milton Keynes *Unitary authority* England, United Kingdom 19 M15
Milwaukee Wisconsin, USA 45 L9
Minatitlán Mexico 53 P13
Minbu Burma 138 F8
Minch, The *Strait* Scotland, United Kingdom 17 D5 28 G7
Mindanao *Island* Philippines 141 N8
Minden Germany 80 G9
Mindoro *Island* Philippines 141 L5
Mindoro Strait *Strait* Philippines 141 L5
Minehead England, United Kingdom 20 I7
Mingäçevir Su Anbarı *Reservoir* Azerbaijan 99 R13
Minna Nigeria 107 O11
Minneapolis Minnesota, USA 44 H6
Minnesota *State* USA 44 F3
Miño Spain 74 G4
Minorca (Sp. Menorca) *Island* Spain 75 S8
Minot North Dakota, USA 47 M4
Minsk Belarus 95 L11
Miri Borneo, Malaysia 140 J9
Mirim Lagoon *Lagoon* Brazil/Uruguay 55 61 I17 62 P9
Mirimar Naval Air Station *Military base* California, USA 51 L19
Mirny *Russian research station* Antarctica 64 G9
Mirpur Khas Pakistan 130 H6
Miskolc Hungary 85 M12
Misool, Pulau *Island* Indonesia 141 P12
Misratah Libya 103 P6
Mississippi *State* USA 42 I8
Mississippi Delta *Delta* Louisiana, USA 34 42 I10
Mississippi River *River* USA 34 42 H8 45 K15 47 R10 66 C9
Missoula Montana, USA 46 G5
Missouri *State* USA 34 47
Missouri River *River* USA 46 I4
Mistassini, Lac *Lake* Quebec, Canada 39 L9
Mitchell South Dakota, USA 47 O8
Mitchell River *River* Queensland, Australia 147 M6
Mito Japan 136 L10
Mittelland Canal *Canal* Germany 80 J9
Mittersill Austria 83 M8
Mitú Colombia 58 G8
Mitumba Range *Mountain range* Dem. Rep. Congo (Zaire) 109 O15
Miyazaki Japan 137 D15
Mizen Head *Headland* Republic of Ireland 17 A13 30 I15
Mjøsa *Lake* Norway 70 J10
Mljet *Island* Croatia 88 J9
Mmabatho South Africa 113 K12
Mo i Rana Norway 71 L5
Moate Republic of Ireland 31 M9
Mobile Alabama, USA 43 K9
Moçambique Mozambique 113 Q7
Mocha *see* Al Mukha
Mocímboa da Praia Mozambique 113 Q5
Mocoa Colombia 58 D8
Modena Italy 86 F8
Modesto California, USA 51 I15
Mödling Austria 83 S5
Modriča Bosnia and Herzegovina 89 K4
Moelfre Wales, United Kingdom 27 K1
Moffat Scotland, United Kingdom 29 L15
Mogadishu (var. Muqdisho) Somalia 105 M15
Mohawk River *River* New York, USA 41 L9
Mojave California, USA 51 K17
Mojave Desert *Plain* California, USA 34 51 L18
Molde Norway 70 I8
Moldova *Former province* Romania 98 G7
Moldova *Country* SE Europe 98 G7

Moldova 98

1991 • Romanian • Leu • 131 • 68 • 17 • 98.3 • 39 • 278 • No • 52 • N/A

Mollendo Peru 59 F15
Molodezhnaya *Russian research station* Antarctica 64 G7
Molokai Fracture Zone *Undersea feature* Pacific Ocean 34
Molucca Sea *Sea* Indonesia 141 N11
Moluccas *Island group* Indonesia 127 141 O11 143
Mombasa Kenya 111 Q7 114 D9
Mona Passage *Channel* Dominican Republic/Puerto Rico 57 O9
Monaco Monaco 77 Q13
Monaco *Country* W Europe 77 Q13

Monaco 77

1861 • French • French franc • 16410 • 78 • 16 • 99 • 373 • No • 100 • N/A

Monaghan Republic of Ireland 31 N6
Monaghan *County* Republic of Ireland 19 E12
Monastir Tunisia 103 N5
Mönchengladbach Germany 81 D11
Monclova Mexico 53 M6
Moncton New Brunswick, Canada 39 P12
Monessen Pennsylvania, USA 40 G13
Moneymore Northern Ireland, United Kingdom 31 N4
Mongo Chad 108 J7
Mongolia *Country* E Asia 133 K6

Mongolia 133

1924 • Khalka Mongol • Tugrik (togrog) • 2 • 66 • 16 • 84 • 14 • 370 • Yes • 61 • 1899

Mongu Zambia 110 H15
Monmouth Wales, United Kingdom 27 P12
Monmouthshire *Unitary authority* Wales, United Kingdom 19 J16
Mono Lake *Lake* California, USA 51 K15
Monolithos Greece 93 Q14
Monroe Louisiana, USA 42 H7
Monroe Michigan, USA 45 O10
Monrovia Liberia 106 H13

Date of independence • Language (official or most commonly spoken) • Currency • Population density per square kilometre • Average life expectancy • School-leaving age • Literacy • Number of cars per 1,000 people • Number of people per doctor • Death penalty • Percentage of urban-based population • Average number of calories consumed daily per person

Mons Belgium 79 F16
Mont-de-Marsan France 76 I13
Montana Bulgaria 90 I11
Montana *State* USA 46 H5
Montauban France 77 K13
Monte Albán *Ruins* Mexico 53 O13
Monte Bello Islands *Island group* Australia 146 E8
Monte Cristi Dominican Republic 57 N7
Montego Bay Jamaica 56 J7
Montenegro *Region* Yugoslavia 89 L8
Monterey California, USA 51 H16 145 N5
Montería Colombia 58 D5
Monterrey Mexico 53 M7
Montevideo Uruguay 62 O10
Montgomery Alabama, USA 43 L8
Montpelier Vermont, USA 41 N7
Montpellier France 77 N13
Montréal (Eng. Montreal) Quebec, Canada 39 M13
Montreux Switzerland 82 E11
Montrose Scotland, United Kingdom 29 M11
Montserrat *Dependent territory* West Indies 57 S11
Monument Valley *Valley* Arizona/Utah, USA 48 J6
Monywa Burma 138 F7
Monza Italy 86 D6
Moore, Lake *Lake* Western Australia, Australia 146 F11
Moorhead Minnesota, USA 44 F4
Moose Jaw Saskatchewan, Canada 37 N15
Moosehead Lake *Lake* Maine, USA 41 P4
Moosonee Ontario, Canada 38 J9
Mopti Mali 107 K9
Mora Sweden 71 K10
Moradabad India 131 L5
Morar, Loch *Lake* Scotland, United Kingdom 20 H11
Morava *River* C Europe 85 K11
Moravia *Cultural region* Czech Republic 84 J11
Moray *Unitary authority* Scotland, United Kingdom 18 I7
Moray Firth *Inlet* Scotland, United Kingdom 17 E5 28 K9
Moreau River *River* South Dakota, USA 47 L7
Morecambe England, United Kingdom 24 I12
Morecambe Bay *Inlet* England, United Kingdom 17 F10 24 H12
Moree New South Wales, Australia 147 O11
Morehead City North Carolina, USA 43 R7
Morelia Mexico 53 M11
Morena, Sierra *Mountain range* Spain 74 H12
Morghab, Darya-ye *River* Afghanistan 125 K11
Morioka Japan 136 L7
Mornington Abyssal Plain *Undersea feature* Pacific Ocean 55
Morocco *Country* N Africa 102 H5

Morocco 102-103

1956 • Arabic • Moroccan dirham • 63 • 67 • 16 • 45.9 • 38 • 2500 • Yes • 48 • 2984

Morogoro Tanzania 111 P9
Mörön Mongolia 133 K4
Moroni Comoros 114 E10
Morotai, Pulau *Island* Indonesia 141 O10
Moroto Uganda 111 N3
Morpeth England, United Kingdom 25 L6
Moscow (Rus. Moskva) Russian Federation 96 F10 128 E6
Moscow-Volga Canal *Canal* Russian Federation 96 G10
Mosel (Fr. Moselle) *River* France/Germany/Luxembourg 81 E13 *see also* Moselle
Moselle (Ger. Mosel) *River* France/Germany/Luxembourg 77 O5 79 M19 *see also* Mosel
Moses Lake *Lake* Washington, USA 50 K7
Moshi Tanzania 111 P7
Moskva *see* Moscow
Mosquito Gulf *Gulf* Caribbean Sea 56 F14
Moss Norway 70 J11
Mossendjo Congo 109 G13
Mossoró Brazil 60 O9
Mostaganem Algeria 103 K4
Mostar Bosnia and Herzegovina 89 K8
Móstoles Spain 75 K8
Mosul Iraq 123 K3
Motala Sweden 71 K12
Motherwell Scotland, United Kingdom 29 K14
Motril Spain 75 K14
Mouila Gabon 109 F13
Mould Bay Northwest Territories, Canada 65 O9
Moulins France 77 M9
Moulmein Burma 139 G11
Moundou Chad 108 H9
Mount Brandon *Bog* Republic of Ireland 32 D11
Mount Gambier South Australia, Australia 147 L14
Mount Hagen Papua New Guinea 147 M2
Mount Magnet Western Australia, Australia 146 F11
Mount Pleasant Michigan, USA 45 N8
Mount Vernon Illinois, USA 45 K14
Mount's Bay *Inlet* England, United Kingdom 20 E12
Mourne Mountains *Mountain range* Northern Ireland, United Kingdom 17 D10 31 O6
Mouscron Belgium 79 D15
Moyale Ethiopia 105 J17
Moyle *District* Northern Ireland, United Kingdom 19 F11
Mozambique *Country* Southern Africa 113 N11

Mozambique 113

1975 • Portuguese • Metical • 25 • 45 • 14 • 40.5 • 0 • 50000 • No • 34 • 1680

Mozambique Channel *Strait* Indian Ocean 113 Q8
Mpika Zambia 111 M12
Mtwara Tanzania 111 Q11
Muang Khong Laos 139 M12
Muchinga Escarpment *Escarpment* Zambia 111 L14
Muck *Island* Scotland, United Kingdom 29 F11
Mufulira Zambia 111 K13
Muğla Turkey 118 H9
Mühlhausen Germany 81 I11
Mulhouse France 77 P6
Mull, Isle of *Island* Scotland, United Kingdom 17 D7 29 G12
Muller, Pegunungan *Mountain range* Indonesia 140 I11
Mullingar Republic of Ireland 31 M8
Multan Pakistan 130 I4
Mumbai (prev. Bombay) India 114 H6 130 I10
Muna, Pulau *Island* Indonesia 141 M13
München *see* Munich
Muncie Indiana, USA 45 N12
Mundesley *Beach* England, United Kingdom 32 H10
Munich (Ger. München) Germany 81 J16
Münster Germany 81 E10
Muonioälv *River* Finland/Sweden 71 N3
Mupa *National Park* Angola 112 H7
Muqdisho *see* Mogadishu
Mur *River* C Europe 83 P8 *see also* Mura
Mura *River* C Europe 83 S9 *see also* Mur
Murat Nehri (var. Eastern Euphrates) *River* Turkey 119 Q7
Murchison River *River* Western Australia, Australia 146 F10
Murcia Spain 75 N12
Mureș *River* Hungary/Romania 90 H6
Murfreesboro Tennessee, USA 43 L4
Murgab *River* Afghanistan/Turkmenistan 125 K11
Müritz *Lake* Germany 80 K7
Murmansk Russian Federation 66 M7 96 I5 128 G3
Murmansk Rise *Undersea feature* Arctic Ocean 68
Murray Fracture Zone *Undersea feature* Pacific Ocean34 145 L5
Murray River *River* New South Wales/South Australia/Victoria, Australia 143 147 L13
Murrumbidgee River *River* New South Wales, Australia 147 M13
Murska Sobota Slovenia 83 S9
Murzuq Libya 103 O9
Mus Turkey 119 R7
Muscat (var. Masqat) Oman 123 P12
Muskegon Michigan, USA 45 M8
Muskegon River *River* Michigan, USA 45 M7
Muskogee Oklahoma, USA 47 Q14
Musoma Tanzania 111 N6
Mussau Island *Island* Papua New Guinea 147 O1
Mutare Zimbabwe 113 N9
Muynoq Uzbekistan 124 I4
Muztag Feng *Mountain* China 127
Mwanza Tanzania 111 M6
Mweelrea *Mountain* Republic of Ireland 30 I8
Mwene-Ditu Dem. Rep. Congo (Zaire) 109 L15
Mweru Wantipa *National Park* Zambia 111 K10
Mweru, Lake *Lake* Dem. Rep. Congo (Zaire)/Zambia 101 109 O16 111 K10
Myanmar *see* Burma
Mycenae Greece 92 J10
Myingyan Burma 138 F8
Myitkyina Burma 138 H5
Mykolayiv Ukraine 98 J8
Mykonos *Island* Greece 93 N11
Mymensingh Bangladesh 131 P7
Mysore India 130 J13
Mytilini Greece 93 O7
Mzuzu Malawi 111 N12

N

Naas Republic of Ireland 31 N10
Naberezhnyye Chelny Russian Federation 97 J12 128 F8
Nacala Mozambique 113 Q7
Naestved Denmark 70 I16
Nafplio Greece 92 J10
Naga Philippines 141 M4
Nagano Japan 136 J10
Nagarjuna Reservoir *Reservoir* India 131 K11
Nagasaki Japan 137 B14 144 F6
Nagercoil India 130 J15
Nagles Mountains *Mountain range* Republic of Ireland 31 K13
Nagornyy Karabakh *Region* Azerbaijan 99 R14
Nagoya Japan 137 I11
Nagpur India 131 K9
Nagqu China 132 I12
Nagykanizsa Hungary 84 J15
Naha Japan 137 A20
Nahuel Huapí, Lago *Lake* Argentina 63 H14
Nain Newfoundland, Canada 39 O5
Nairn Scotland, United Kingdom 28 K9
Nairobi Kenya 111 P5
Naissaar *Island* Estonia 94 I1
Najran Saudi Arabia 122 I14
Nakamura Japan 137 E14
Nakhodka Russian Federation 128 J6
Nakhon Ratchasima Thailand 139 J12
Nakhon Sawan Thailand 139 I11
Nakhon Si Thammarat Thailand 139 I16
Nakskov Denmark 70 I16
Nakuru Kenya 111 O5
Nam Co *Lake* China 132 I12
Nam Đinh Vietnam 139 M9
Nam Ngum Dam *Dam* Laos 138 K10
Nam Ou *River* Laos 138 K8
Nam Theun *River* Laos 138 L10
Namakzar *Marsh* Afghanistan/Iran 124 I12
Namangan Uzbekistan 125 O6
Namib Desert *Desert* Namibia 101 112 G9
Namib Naukuuft *National Park* Namibia 112 H12
Namibe Angola 112 F7
Namibia *Country* Southern Africa 112 H10

Namibia 112

1990 • English • Namibian dollar at par with South African rand • 2 • 52 • 16 • 79.8 • 47 • 5000 • No • 37 • 2134

Namjagbarwa Feng *Mountain* China 127
Nampa Idaho, USA 46 F8
Namp'o North Korea 135 P7
Nampula Mozambique 113 P7
Namur Belgium 79 I16
Nan Thailand 138 J9
Nan Ling *Mountain range* China 127
Nanchang China 135 M11
Nancy France 77 O5
Nanded India 131 K9
Nanjing China 135 N10
Nanning China 135 K14
Nanping China 135 N12
Nantes France 76 H8
Nantucket Massachusetts, USA 41 P12
Nantwich England, United Kingdom 22 I6
Napa Valley *Valley* California, USA 51 H15
Napier New Zealand 148 I6
Naples (It. Napoli) Italy 66 L9 87 K13
Naples, Gulf of *Gulf* Italy 87 K13
Napo, Río *River* Ecuador/Peru 58 E9
Napoli *see* Naples
Narach, Vozyera *Lake* Belarus 95 K10
Narathiwat Thailand 139 J17
Narberth Wales, United Kingdom 26 I12
Nares Plain *Undersea feature* Atlantic Ocean 34 55
Nares Strait *Strait* Canada/Greenland 37 N1
Narew *River* Poland 85 N4
Narmada *River* India 127 130 I8
Narodnaya, Gora *Mountain* Russian Federation 68 I17
Narsarsuaq Greenland 65 M15
Narva Estonia 95 L1
Narva *River* Estonia/Russian Federation 95 L2
Narvik Norway 71 M3
Naryn Kyrgyzstan 125 Q6
Naryn *River* Kyrgyzstan/Uzbekistan 125 Q6
Nashik India 130 I9
Nashua New Hampshire, USA 41 O9
Nashville Tennessee, USA 43 L4
Nassau Bahamas 57 K2
Nasser, Lake *Lake* Egypt/Sudan 101 104 G9
Natal Brazil 60 P9
Natal Basin *Undersea feature* Pacific Ocean 101
Natitingou Benin 107 M11
Natuna Besar, Pulau *Island* Indonesia 140 G9
Natuna, Kepulauan *Island group* Indonesia 140 G9
Naturaliste, Cape *Headland* Australia 146 F13
Nauru *Country* Pacific Ocean 144 I9

Nauru 144

1968 • Nauruan • Australian dollar • 514 • 67 • 16 • 99 • 700 • No • 100 • N/A

Navajo Dam *Dam* New Mexico, USA 49 L6
Navajo Indian Reservation *Reservation* New Mexico, USA 49 K7
Navan Republic of Ireland 31 N8
Navapolatsk Belarus 95 L8
Navarin, Mys *Cape* Russian Federation 129 R3
Nawabshah Pakistan 130 H6
Nawoiy Uzbekistan 125 L7
Naxçıvan Azerbaijan 99 Q15
Naxos *Island* Greece 93 N12
Nazareth Israel 121 M8
Nazca Peru 59 E14
Nazca Plate *Tectonic plate* 55
Nazca Ridge *Undersea feature* Pacific Ocean 55
Nazilli Turkey 118 H8
N'Dalatando Angola 112 G4
Ndélé Central African Republic 108 K9
Ndjamena Chad 108 H7
Ndola Zambia 111 K13
Neagh, Lough *Lake* Northern Ireland, United Kingdom 17 D9 31 O5
Neapoli Greece 92 J13
Neath Wales, United Kingdom 27 M14
Neath Port Talbot *Unitary authority* Wales, United Kingdom 19 D17
Nebitdag Turkmenistan 124 F7
Nebraska *State* USA 47 L10
Nechako *River* British Columbia, Canada 36 I13
Neches River *River* Texas, USA 49 S11
Neckar *River* Germany 81 G15
Necochea Argentina 63 N13
Nefyn Wales, United Kingdom 26 J4
Negev *Desert* Israel 121 L12
Negrais, Cape *Headland* Burma 139 E11
Negro, Río *River* Argentina 63 K13
Negro, Río *River* Brazil/Uruguay 62 O9
Negro, Rio *River* N South America 55 60 D7
Negro, Río *see* Chixoy, Río 55
Negros *Island* Philippines 141 M6
Neiva Colombia 58 E7
Nejd *Cultural region* Saudi Arabia 122 I9
Nek'emte Ethiopia 105 I15
Nellis Air Force Range *Military base* Nevada, USA 48 G5
Nellore India 131 L12
Nelson *River* Manitoba, Canada 37 O12
Nelson New Zealand 148 G7
Nelson England, United Kingdom 25 K13
Néma Mauritania 106 J8
Neman *River* E Europe 94 I12
Nemuro Japan 136 O3
Nenagh Republic of Ireland 31 L11
Nene *River* England, United Kingdom 17 G12 23 O8
Neosho River *River* Kansas/Oklahoma, USA 47 P12
Nepal *Country* S Asia 131 L4

Nepal 131

1769 • Nepali • Nepalese rupee • 171 • 57 • 11 • 38.1 • 1 • 12500 • No • 14 • 1957

Nepalganj Nepal 131 M5
Nephin *Mountain* Republic of Ireland 30 J7
Neretva *River* Bosnia and Herzegovina/Croatia 89 K7
Neris *River* Belarus/Lithuania 94 I9
Nesebŭr Bulgaria 91 O12
Ness, Loch *Lake* Scotland, United Kingdom 17 E5 28 J10
Netherlands *Country* NW Europe 79 G12

Netherlands 78-79

1815 • Dutch • Netherlands gulden (guilder) or florin • 463 • 78 • 18 • 99 • 372 • 400 • No • 89 • 3222

Netherlands Antilles (prev. Dutch West Indies) *Dependent territory* West Indies 57 N14
Neubrandenburg Germany 80 L7
Neuchâtel Switzerland 82 E10
Neuchâtel, Lac de *Lake* Switzerland 82 D10
Neufchâteau Belgium 79 J18
Neukirchen Austria 83 S6
Neumünster Germany 80 H6
Neuquén Argentina 63 I13
Neuschwanstein *Castle* Germany 81 I16
Neusiedler See *Lake* Austria/Hungary 83 S5
Nevada *State* USA 48 F3
Nevada Test Site *Military base* Nevada, USA 48 G6
Nevada, Sierra *Mountain range* Spain 75 K14
Nevada, Sierra *Mountain range* California, USA 34 51 I13
Nevel' Russian Federation 96 E9 128 E5
Nevers France 77 M8
Nevsehir Turkey 119 M8
New Albany Indiana, USA 45 N14
New Amsterdam Guyana 58 M6
New Bedford Massachusetts, USA 41 O11
New Britain *Island* Papua New Guinea 143 147 P2
New Brunswick *Province* Canada 39 P11
New Brunswick New Jersey, USA 41 L13
New Caledonia *Dependent territory* Pacific Ocean 144 H10
New Caledonia *Island* Pacific Ocean 143
New Caledonia Basin *Undersea feature* Pacific Ocean 143
New Castle Pennsylvania, USA 40 G12
New Delhi India 131 K5
New England *Cultural region* USA 41 N8
New Forest *Physical region* England, United Kingdom 17 G14 21 M9 32 G13
New Guinea *Island* Indonesia/Papua New Guinea 127 144 G9 143 147 M2
New Hampshire *State* USA 41 N9
New Hanover *Island* Papua New Guinea 147 O1
New Haven Connecticut, USA 41 M12
New Hebrides Trench *Undersea feature* Pacific Ocean 143
New Ireland *Island* Papua New Guinea 143 147 P1
New Jersey *State* USA 41 L14
New Lanark Scotland, United Kingdom 29 K14
New London Connecticut, USA 41 N12
New Mexico *State* USA 49 K8
New Orleans Louisiana, USA 43 I9 66 C9
New Plymouth New Zealand 148 G5
New Providence *Island* Bahamas 57 K2
New Quay Wales, United Kingdom 27 K10
New Quay *Beach* Wales, United Kingdom 32 E11
New River *River* West Virginia, USA 43 P3
New Ross Republic of Ireland 31 N12
New Siberian Islands *Island group* Russian Federation 65 R7 117 129 N4
New South Wales *State* Australia 147 N12
New Ulm Minnesota, USA 44 G7
New York New York, USA 41 L12 66 E9
New York *State* USA 40 I10
New Zealand *Country* Pacific Ocean 148

New Zealand 148

1926 • English and Maori • New Zealand dollar • 14 • 77 • 16 • 99 • 451 • 476 • No • 86 • 3669

New Zealand *Island group* Pacific Ocean 143
Newark Delaware, USA 41 K14
Newark New Jersey, USA 41 L13
Newark Ohio, USA 45 P12
Newark-on-Trent England, United Kingdom 23 M6
Newborough Wales, United Kingdom 27 K2
Newborough *Beach* Wales, United Kingdom 32 E10
Newbridge Wales, United Kingdom 27 O13
Newbridge on Wye Wales, United Kingdom 27 N10
Newburgh New York, USA 41 L11
Newbury England, United Kingdom 21 M7
Newbury *Unitary authority* England, United Kingdom 19 L16
Newcastle New South Wales, Australia 147 O12
Newcastle Northern Ireland, United Kingdom 31 P6
Newcastle *see* Newcastle upon Tyne
Newcastle Emlyn Wales, United Kingdom 26 J11
Newcastle-under-Lyme England, United Kingdom 22 I7
Newcastle upon Tyne England, United Kingdom 25 K7
Newcastle upon Tyne *Unitary authority* England, United Kingdom 18 N7
Newfoundland *Province* Canada 39 P6
Newfoundland *Island* Canada 34 39 R9 66 F8
Newfoundland Basin *Undersea feature* Atlantic Ocean 66 G9
Newham *London borough* England, United Kingdom 19 O19
Newhaven England, United Kingdom 21 Q9
Newmarket England, United Kingdom 23 P10
Newport Oregon, USA 50 G9
Newport Rhode Island, USA 41 O11
Newport Wales, United Kingdom 26 I11
Newport *Unitary authority* Wales, United Kingdom 19 F17
Newport Wales, United Kingdom 27 P14
Newport England, United Kingdom 21 N10
Newport News Virginia, USA 43 S5
Newport Pagnell England, United Kingdom 21 O3
Newquay England, United Kingdom 20 E11
Newry Northern Ireland, United Kingdom 31 O6
Newry and Mourne *District* Northern Ireland, United Kingdom 19 F12
Newton Abbot England, United Kingdom 20 I10
Newton Stewart Scotland, United Kingdom 29 J16
Newtown Wales, United Kingdom 27 N7
Newtown St Boswells Scotland, United Kingdom 29 M14
Newtownabbey Northern Ireland, United Kingdom 31 P
Newtownabbey *District* Northern Ireland, United Kingdom 19 G11
Newtownstewart Northern Ireland, United Kingdom 31 M4
Neyshabur Iran 123 Q4
Ngaoundéré Cameroon 108 G9
Ngauruhoe, Mount *Mountain* New Zealand 148 H5
N'Giva Angola 112 H8
Ngorongoro Crater *Crater* Tanzania 101
Nguigmi Niger 107 R9
Nguru Nigeria 107 P9
Nha Trang Vietnam 139 O14
Niagara Falls *Waterfall* Canada/USA 34
Niagara Falls New York, USA 40 H9
Niagara Falls Ontario, Canada 39 K15
Niagara Peninsula *Peninsula* Ontario, Canada 39 K15
Niamey Niger 107 M9
Niangay, Lac *Lake* Mali 107 K8
Nias, Pulau *Island* Indonesia 140 C11
Nicaragua *Country* Central America 56 D10

Nicaragua 56

1838 • Spanish • Córdoba oro • 41 • 68 • 12 • 63.4 • 16 • 1429 • No • 63 • 2293

Nicaragua, Lake *Lake* Nicaragua 55 56 D11
Nice France 77 Q14
Nicobar Islands *Island group* India 114 K7 127
Nicosia Cyprus 119 L12
Nicoya, Golfo de *Gulf* Costa Rica 56 D13
Niedere Tauern *Mountain range* Austria 83 O8
Nifa Italy 87 I12
Niğde Turkey 119 M8
Niger *River* W Africa 67 K11 101 107 L7
Niger *Country* W Africa 107 O8

Niger 107

1960 • French • Franc de la Communauté financière africaine • 8 • 49 • 15 • 14.3 • 4 • 33333 • No • 17 • 2257

Niger Delta *Delta* Nigeria 101
Niger, Mouths of the *Delta* Nigeria 107 O14

Nigeria *Country* W Africa 107 N10

Nigeria 107

1960 • a English • Naira • 120 • 50 • 12 • 59.5 • 7 • 5000 • Yes • 39 • 2124

Niigata Japan 136 J9
Nijmegen Netherlands 79 K11
Nikopol' Ukraine 99 K7
Nikšić Montenegro, Yugoslavia 89 L9
Nile *River* NE Africa 66 N10 101 104 F8 114 C5
Nile Delta *Delta* Egypt 101
Niles Michigan, USA 45 M10
Nîmes France 77 N13
Ninetyeast Ridge *Undersea feature* Indian Ocean 114 J10 117 127
Nineveh Iraq 123 K2
Ningbo China 135 O11 144 F6
Ningxia *Region* China 134 J8
Ninigo Group *Island group* Papua New Guinea 147 M1
Niobrara River *River* Nebraska/Wyoming, USA 47 L9
Nioro Mali 106 I8
Nipigon, Lake *Lake* Ontario, Canada 38 G10
Niš Serbia, Yugoslavia 89 O8
Nissan Island *Island* Papua New Guinea 147 Q2
Nith *River* Scotland, United Kingdom 29 K15
Nith Estuary *Area of Outstanding Natural Beauty* Scotland, United Kingdom 32 F8
Nitra Slovakia 85 K12
Niue *Dependent territory* Pacific Ocean 145 K10
Nivelles Belgium 79 G16
Nizhnevartovsk Russian Federation 128 I8
Nizhniy Novgorod Russian Federation 97 H11 128 F7
Nizhniy Tagil Russian Federation 128 G8
Nizwa Oman 123 O12
Njombe Tanzania 111 N11
Nkhotakota Malawi 111 N13
Nkongsamba Cameroon 108 E10
Nobeoka Japan 137 D14
Nogales Mexico 52 H3
Nome Alaska, USA 36 F5
Nonacho Lake *Lake* Northwest Territories, Canada 37 M10
Nord Greenland 65 P12
Nordfjord *Fjord* Norway 70 H8
Nordhausen Germany 80 I10
Nordstrand *Island* Germany 80 G6
Nore *River* Republic of Ireland 17 C12 31 M11
Norfolk Nebraska, USA 47 O9
Norfolk Virginia, USA 43 S5
Norfolk *County* England, United Kingdom 19 N14
Norfolk Coast *Area of Outstanding Natural Beauty* England, United Kingdom 32 H10
Norfolk Island *Dependent territory* Pacific Ocean 144 H11
Noril'sk Russian Federation 129 K6
Norman Oklahoma, USA 47 O15
Norman Wells Northwest Territories, Canada 36 J8
Normandie *see* Normandy
Normandy (Fr. Normandie) *Cultural region* France 76 I5
Norrköping Sweden 71 L12
Norrtälje Sweden 71 M12
North America *Continent* 34-35
North American Plate *Tectonic plate* 55 68 117 127
North Arran *Area of Outstanding Natural Beauty* Scotland, United Kingdom 32 E7
North Australian Basin *Undersea feature* Indian Ocean 143
North Ayrshire *Unitary authority* Scotland, United Kingdom 18 G10
North Battleford Saskatchewan, Canada 37 M14
North Bay Ontario, Canada 39 K13
North Berwick Scotland, United Kingdom 29 M13
North Cape *Headland* Norway 70 O1
North Carolina *State* USA 43 Q6
North Channel *Strait* Northern Ireland/Scotland, United Kingdom 17 D8
North Dakota *State* USA 47 L5
North Devon *Area of Outstanding Natural Beauty* England, United Kingdom 32 E13
North Down *District* Northern Ireland, United Kingdom 19 G11
North Downs *Hill range* England, United Kingdom 17 H13 21 Q7
North East Lincolnshire *Unitary authority* England, United Kingdom 19 N13
North Esk *River* Scotland, United Kingdom 29 M11
North European Plain *Plain* N Europe 68
North Fiji Basin *Undersea feature* Pacific Ocean 143
North Foreland *Headland* England, United Kingdom 17 I13
North Frisian Islands *Island group* Germany 80 F5
North Island *Island* New Zealand 143 148 G4
North Korea *Country* E Asia 135 P6

North Korea 135

1948 • a Korean • North Korean won • 197 • 63 • 15 • 95 • 370 • Yes • 61 • 2833

North Lanarkshire *Unitary authority* Scotland, United Kingdom 18 N5
North Las Vegas Nevada, USA 48 H6
North Lincolnshire *Unitary authority* England, United Kingdom 19 M13
North Luangwa *National Park* Zambia 111 M12
North Pennines *Area of Outstanding Natural Beauty* England, United Kingdom 32 F8
North Platte Nebraska, USA 47 M10
North Pole *Pole* 34 65 Q10 68 117 127
North Sea *Sea* Atlantic Ocean 2 N8
North Sound, The *Sound* Scotland, United Kingdom 28 M5
North Tyne *River* England, United Kingdom 24 J6
North Tyneside *Unitary authority* England, United Kingdom 18 N6
North Uist *Island* Scotland, United Kingdom 17 C5 28 E9
North Wessex Downs *Area of Outstanding Natural Beauty* England, United Kingdom 32 G12
North West Cape *Cape* Western Australia, Australia 115 M11 146 E8
North West Highlands *Mountain range* Scotland, United Kingdom 17 E6 28 H10 32 E6
North West Somerset *Unitary authority* England, United Kingdom 19 J17
North York Moors *Moorland* England, United Kingdom 17 G9 25 N10
North York Moors National Park *National Park* England, United Kingdom 32 G9
North Yorkshire *County* England, United Kingdom 19 K12
Northallerton England, United Kingdom 25 M10
Northampton England, United Kingdom 23 M11
Northampton Massachusetts, USA 41 M10
Northamptonshire *County* England, United Kingdom 19 L15
Northern Dvina *River* Russian Federation 68 96 J8
Northern Ireland *Political division* United Kingdom 19 G12 31 M4 32 D8
Northern Mariana Islands *Dependent territory* Pacific Ocean 144 H7
Northern Sporades *Island group* Greece 93 L7
Northern Territory *Territory* Australia 146 J7
Northumberland *County* England, United Kingdom 18 K10
Northumberland Coast *Area of Outstanding Natural Beauty* England, United Kingdom 32 G7
Northumberland National Park *National park* England, United Kingdom 32 F8
Northwest Territories *Territory* Canada 37 K9
Northwich England, United Kingdom 22 I6
Norton Sound *Inlet* Alaska, USA 36 F6
Norway *Country* NW Europe 70 I9

Norway 70-71

1905 • a Norwegian • Norwegian krone • 14 • 78 • 15 • 99 • 399 • 303 • No • 73 • 3244

Norwegian Basin *Undersea feature* Atlantic Ocean 68
Norwegian Sea *Sea* Atlantic Ocean 34 68 71 K5 117 127
Norwich England, United Kingdom 23 S8
Noteć *River* Poland 85 K4
Nottingham England, United Kingdom 23 L7
Nottingham, City of *Unitary authority* England, United Kingdom 19 K14
Nottinghamshire *County* England, United Kingdom 19 L14
Nouâdhibou Mauritania 106 F5
Nouâdhibou, Râs *Headland* Mauritania 106 F5
Nouakchott Mauritania 106 F7
Nouméa New Caledonia 144 I10
Nova Gorica Slovenia 83 O12
Nova Gradiška Croatia 88 J4
Nova Kakhovka Ukraine 98 J8
Nova Scotia *Province* Canada 39 P12
Nova Scotia *Physical region* Canada 34
Novara Italy 86 D7
Novato California, USA 51 G15
Novaya Zemlya *Island group* Russian Federation 68 96 M5 117 128 I4
Novgorod Russian Federation 96 F8 128 E5
Novi Pazar Serbia, Yugoslavia 89 N8
Novi Sad Serbia, Yugoslavia 89 M4
Novo Mesto Slovenia 83 R12
Novokuznetsk Russian Federation 128 J11
Novolazarevskaya *Russian research station* Antarctica 64 E6
Novosibirsk Russian Federation 128 J10
Nsanje Malawi 111 O16
Ntomba, Lake *Lake* Dem. Rep. Congo (Zaire) 109 I13
Nubian Desert *Desert* Sudan 101 105 G10
Nuevo Laredo Mexico 53 N6
Nuku'alofa Tonga 144 J10
Nukus Uzbekistan 124 I5
Nullarbor Plain *Plain* South Australia/Western Australia, Australia 143 146 H12
Nunap Isua *Headland* Greenland 65 M16
Nunavut *Territory* Canada 37 N7
Nuneaton England, United Kingdom 23 L9
Nunivak Island *Island* Alaska, USA 36 D6
Nuoro Italy 87 D14
Nuremberg (Ger. Nürnberg) Germany 81 I14
Nuri *Archaeological site* Sudan 105 G11
Nürnberg *see* Nuremberg
Nuuk Greenland 65 M14
Nxai Pan *National Park* Botswana 113 K9
Nyala Sudan 105 C14
Nyalam China 132 G13
Nyasa, Lake *Lake* Southern Africa 101 111 N13 113 O6
Nyeri Kenya 111 P5
Nyika *National Park* Malawi 111 N11
Nyingchi China 132 J13
Nyíregyháza Hungary 85 N12
Nykøbing Denmark 70 I16
Nyköping Sweden 71 L12
Nzérékoré Guinea 106 I12

Oa, Mull of *Headland* Scotland, United Kingdom 29 F14
Oakham England, United Kingdom 23 M8
Oakland California, USA 50 H15
Oakley Kansas, USA 47 M12
Oaxaca Mexico 53 O13
Ob' *River* Russian Federation 68 117 128 127 I7
Ob', Gulf of *Gulf* Arctic Ocean 128 I7
Oban Scotland, United Kingdom 29 H12
Obertshausen Germany 80 D10
Obi, Pulau *Island* Indonesia 141 O12
Obihiro Japan 136 M4
Obo Central African Republic 108 N10
Oceanside California, USA 51 L19
Och'amch'ire Georgia 99 O12
Ocotlán Mexico 53 L11
October Revolution Island *Island* Russian Federation 129 K4
Odense Denmark 70 I15
Oder *River* C Europe 68 80 M8 84 H4
Odesa Ukraine 98 I8
Odessa Texas, USA 49 O11
Odienné Ivory Coast 106 I11
Ofanto *River* Italy 87 M13
Offaly *County* Republic of Ireland 19 D14
Offenbach Germany 81 G13
Ogallala Nebraska, USA 47 M10
Ogbomosho Nigeria 107 N12
Ogden Utah, USA 48 J2
Ogdensburg New York, USA 41 K6
Ogooué *River* Congo/Gabon 109 E13
Ogre Latvia 94 I6
Ogulin Croatia 88 H4
Ohio *State* USA 45 O11
Ohio River *River* USA 43 O5 45 O13
Ohre *River* Czech Republic/Germany 84 G8
Ohrid FYR Macedonia 89 N12
Ohrid, Lake *Lake* Albania/FYR Macedonia 89 N12
Oil City Pennsylvania, USA 40 G11
Oita Japan 137 D14
Ojos del Salado, Cerro *Mountain* Argentina 55
Oka *River* Russian Federation 129 L11
Okahandja Namibia 112 H10
Okara Pakistan 130 J3
Okavango *River* Southern Africa 101
Okavango Delta *Wetland* Botswana 101 112 J9
Okayama Japan 137 F12
Okazaki Japan 137 I12
Okeechobee, Lake *Lake* Florida, USA 34 43 O1
Okefenokee Swamp *Wetland* Georgia, USA 34 43 N10
Okehampton England, United Kingdom 20 H9
Okhotsk Russian Federation 129 P7
Okhotsk, Sea of *Sea* Pacific Ocean 34 117 129 Q8 127 G4 136 M2 144
Oki-shoto *Island group* Japan 137 E11
Okinawa *Island* Japan 137 A20
Okinawa-shoto *Island group* Japan 137 A20
Okinoerabu-jima *Island* Japan 137 A19
Oklahoma *State* USA 47 N14
Oklahoma City Oklahoma, USA 47 O15
Oktyabr'skiy Bol'sheretsk Russian Federation 129 R7
Okushiri-to *Island* Japan 136 J5
Öland *Island* Sweden 71 L14
Olavarria Argentina 63 M11
Olbia Italy 87 E13
Old Crow Yukon Territory, Canada 36 I7
Old Head of Kinsale *Headland* Republic of Ireland 17 C13 30 K15
Oldenburg Germany 81 F8
Oldham England, United Kingdom 25 K15
Oldham *Unitary authority* England, United Kingdom 18 C9
Olean New York, USA 40 I10
Olëkma *River* Russian Federation 129 N9
Olenëk Russian Federation 129 M7
Olenëk *River* Russian Federation 129 M5
Olenëkskiy Zaliv *Bay* Russian Federation 129 M5
Olga, Mount *Mountain* Northern Territory, Australia 143
Olgiy Mongolia 132 I4
Ollantaytambo *Archaeological site* Peru 59 G13
Olmaliq Uzbekistan 125 N7
Olomouc Czech Republic 84 J10
Olovyannaya Russian Federation 129 N11
Olsztyn Poland 85 M3
Olt *River* Romania 91 K10
Olten Switzerland 82 F9
Ölüdeniz Turkey 118 H10
Olympia Greece 92 H10
Olympia Washington, USA 50 H7
Olympic National Park *National Park* Washington, USA 50 G6
Olympus, Mount *Mountain* Greece 309
Olyutorskiy, Mys *Headland* Russian Federation 129 R4
Omagh Northern Ireland, United Kingdom 31 M4
Omagh *District* Northern Ireland, United Kingdom 19 E11
Omaha Nebraska, USA 47 P10
Oman *Country* SW Asia 123 N14

Oman 123

1951 • a Arabic • Omani rial • 12 • 71 • N/A • 67.1 • 97 • 1111 • Yes • 13 • 3013

Oman, Gulf of *Gulf* Indian Ocean 114 G5 117 123 P11 127
Omdurman Sudan 105 G12
Omo *River* Ethiopia/Kenya 105 I16
Omsk Russian Federation 128 H10
Ondangwa Namibia 112 H8
Ondava *River* Slovakia 85 N10
Ondorhaan Mongolia 133 N4
Onega *River* Russian Federation 96 I8
Onega, Lake *Lake* Russian Federation 68 96 H8 128 F5
Ongole India 131 L12
Onitsha Nigeria 107 O13
Onon Gol *River* Mongolia 133 N4
Ontario *Province* Canada 38 F9
Ontario, Lake *Lake* Canada/USA 34 39 L14
Oostende *see* Ostend
Oosterschelde *Inlet* Netherlands 79 D12
Opole Poland 85 K8
Oporto (Port. Porto) Portugal 66 J9
Oradea Romania 90 G3
Oran Algeria 103 K4
Orange New South Wales, Australia 147 N12
Orange River *River* Southern Africa 101 112 I13
Oranjestad Aruba 57 N13
Orapa Botswana 113 K10
Ord River *River* Australia 146 I6
Ordos Desert *Desert* China 133 N8
Ordu Turkey 119 O5
Ore Mountains *Mountain range* Czech Republic/Germany 81 K12
Örebro Sweden 71 K12
Oregon *State* USA 50 G9
Orël Russian Federation 96 E11 128 D6
Orellana, Embalse de *Reservoir* Spain 74 I10
Orem Utah, USA 48 J3
Orenburg Russian Federation 96 K14 128 F9
Oreor Palau 144 G8
Orford Ness *Headland* England, United Kingdom 23 T11
Orinoco, Río *River* Colombia/Venezuela 34 55 58 K5
Oristano Italy 87 C14
Orivesi, Lake *Lake* Finland 71 Q9
Orizaba Mexico 53 O12
Orizaba, Volcán Pico de *Mountain* Mexico 34
Orkney Islands *Unitary authority* Scotland, United Kingdom 18 I4
Orkney Islands *Island group* Scotland, United Kingdom 17 E3 28 K6 32 F3
Orlando Florida, USA 43 O12
Orléans France 77 K6
Ormskirk England, United Kingdom 24 I15
Örnsköldsvik Sweden 71 M8
Orontes *River* SW Asia 121 N4
Orsha Belarus 95 N10
Orsk Russian Federation 96 L14
Orumiyeh Iran 123 L2
Oruro Bolivia 59 I15
Orwell *River* England, United Kingdom 23 R11
Osaka Japan 137 G12
Osh Kyrgyzstan 125 P7
Oshkosh Wisconsin, USA 45 K7
Oshogbo Nigeria 107 N12
Osijek Croatia 89 L3
Oskarshamn Sweden 71 L14
Oslo (prev. Christiania, Kristiania) Norway 70 J11
Oslofjorden *Fjord* Norway 70 I12
Osmaniye Turkey 119 N9
Osnabrück Germany 80 F9
Osorno Chile 63 G14
Oss Netherlands 79 J12
Ossora Russian Federation 129 R5
Ostend (var. Oostende) Belgium 79 C13
Östersund Sweden 71 L8
Ostia Italy 87 H12
Ostrava Czech Republic 85 K9
Ostrołęka Poland 85 N4
Osumi-kaikyo *Strait* Japan 137 C16
Osumi-shoto *Island group* Japan 137 C16
Osumit, Lumi i *River* Albania 89 M13
Oswego New York, USA 40 J8
Oswestry England, United Kingdom 22 H8
Otaru Japan 136 K4
Otjiwarongo Namibia 112 H9
Otley England, United Kingdom 25 L13
Otra *River* Norway 70 H12
Otranto Italy 87 P14
Otranto, Strait of *Strait* Mediterranean Sea 68 89 L13
Ottawa Kansas, USA 47 P12
Ottawa Illinois, USA 45 K11
Ottawa Ontario, Canada 39 L13
Ottawa *River* Ontario/Quebec, Canada 39 K12
Otterburn England, United Kingdom 25 K6
Ötztaler Alpen *Mountain range* Austria 83 K10
Ou-sanmyaku *Mountain range* Japan 136 K7
Ouachita River *River* Arkansas/Louisiana, USA 42 H5
Ouagadougou Burkina 107 L10
Ouahigouya Burkina 107 L9
Ouargla Algeria 103 L6
Oudtshoorn South Africa 112 J15
Ouémé *River* Benin 107 M11
Ouessant, Île d' *Island* France 76 E6
Ouésso Congo 109 H12
Oughterard Republic of Ireland 30 J8
Oujda Morocco 102 J5
Oulu *River* Finland 71 P7
Oulu Finland 71 M6
Oulujärvi *Lake* Finland 71 P7
Ounasjoki *River* Finland 71 O3
Ourense Spain 74 G5
Ouro Preto Brazil 61 L13
Ourthe *River* Belgium 79 J16
Ouse *River* England, United Kingdom 17 G10 25 N14
Outer Hebrides *Island group* Scotland, United Kingdom 17 C6 28 E7 32 D6
Ovalle Chile 62 G9
Overflakkee *Island* Netherlands 79 G12
Overton Wales, United Kingdom 27 P4
Oviedo Spain 74 I3
Owando Congo 109 H12
Owatonna Minnesota, USA 44 H7
Owen Sound Ontario, Canada 38 J13
Owen Stanley Range *Mountain range* Papua New Guinea 143 147 N3
Owenduff *Bog* Republic of Ireland 32 C9
Owerri Nigeria 107 O13
Owosso Michigan, USA 45 N8
Owyhee River *River* Idaho/Oregon, USA 50 L10
Oxford England, United Kingdom 21 N5
Oxfordshire *County* England, United Kingdom 19 L16
Oxnard California, USA 51 J18
Oyem Gabon 109 F12
Ozark Plateau *Plain* Arkansas/Missouri, USA 47 R13
Ozarks, Lake of the *Reservoir* Missouri, USA 47 R12

P

Paamiut Greenland 65 M15
Pa-an Burma 139 G11
Pabna Bangladesh 131 O7
Pachuca Mexico 53 N11
Pacific Ocean *Ocean* 144-145
Pacific Plate *Tectonic plate* 34 55 127 143
Pacific-Antarctic Ridge *Undersea feature* Pacific Ocean 144 J14 143
Padang Indonesia 140 D12
Paderborn Germany 80 G10
Padova *see* Padua
Padua (It. Padova) Italy 86 H7
Paducah Kentucky, USA 43 K3
Páfos Cyprus 119 K12
Pag *Island* Croatia 88 G5
Pagai Selatan, Pulau *Island* Indonesia 140 D13
Pagai Utara, Pulau *Island* Indonesia 140 D13
Pagan *Archaeological site* Burma 138 F8
Pahang, Sungai *River* Malaysia 139 J18
Paide Estonia 94 J2
Paignton England, United Kingdom 20 I11
Painted Desert *Desert* Arizona, USA 48 J6
Paisley Scotland, United Kingdom 29 I14
Pakistan *Country* S Asia 130 F4

Pakistan 130

1947 • a Urdu • Pakistani rupee • 198 • 64 • • 40.9 • 5 • 1915 • Yes • 35 • 2315

Pakokku Burma 138 F8
Pakwach Uganda 111 M3
Pakxan Laos 138 L10
Pakxe Laos 139 M12
Palau *Country* Pacific Ocean 144 G8

Palau 144-145

1994 • a Belauan and English • United States dollar • 36 • 71 • 14 • 92 • • 83 • No • 29 • N/A

Palawan *Island* Philippines 141 K6
Paldiski Estonia 94 I1
Palembang Indonesia 140 F13
Palencia Spain 74 J5
Palenque *Ruins* Mexico 53 R13
Palermo Italy 87 J17
Palikir Micronesia 144 H8
Palk Strait *Strait* India/Sri Lanka 127
Palm Springs California, USA 51 M19
Palma de Mallorca Spain 75 R9
Palmas do Tocantins Brazil 60 K10
Palmer Alaska, USA 36 G8
Palmer Land *Physical region* Antarctica 64 C8
Palmerston North New Zealand 148 H7
Palmira Colombia 58 D7
Palmyra Atoll *Dependent territory* Pacific Ocean 145 K8
Palu Indonesia 141 L12
Pamir *River* Afghanistan/Tajikistan 125 P10
Pamirs *Mountain range* C Asia 117 125 O10 127
Pampa Texas, USA 49 O8
Pampas *Plain* Argentina 55 63 J12
Pamplona Spain 75 M4
Pamukkale Turkey 118 H8
Pan-American Highway *Road* Chile 62 G8
Panaji India 130 I11

Date of independence • a Language (official or most commonly spoken) • Currency • Population density per square kilometre • Average life expectancy • School-leaving age • Literacy • Number of cars per 1,000 people • Number of people per doctor • Death penalty • Percentage of urban-based population • Average number of calories consumed daily per person

Panama *Country* Central America 56 F15

Panama 56

1903 • a Spanish • Balboa • 37 • 74 • 15 • 91.1 • 76 • 556 • No • 53 • 2242

Panama Canal *Canal* Panama 56 G14
Panama City Panama 56 G15 67 D11 145 Q7
Panama City Florida, USA 43 L10
Panama, Gulf of *Gulf* Panama 55 56 G15
Panama, Isthmus of *Isthmus* Panama 55
Panay Island *Island* Philippines 141 M5
Pančevo Serbia, Yugoslavia 89 N5
Panevėžys Lithuania 94 I8
Pangani Tanzania 111 Q8
Pangani *River* Tanzania 111 P7
Pangkalpinang Indonesia 140 G12
Pangnirtung Nunavut, Canada 37 R6 65 M13
Panj *River* Afghanistan/Tajikistan 125 N10
Pantanal *Swamp* Brazil 61 G12
Pantelleria Italy 87 H19
Pánuco, Río *River* Mexico 53 N10
Panzhihua China 134 I12
Papeete French Polynesia 145 L10
Papua New Guinea *Country* Pacific Ocean 147 O2

Papua New Guinea 147

1975 • a English • Kina • 10 • 58 • N/A • 73.7 • 7 • 10000

Papua, Gulf of *Gulf* Papua New Guinea 147 N3
Paraguarí Paraguay 62 N6
Paraguay *Country* C South America 62 K5

Paraguay 62

1811 • a Spanish • Guaraní • 14 • 70 • 12 • 92.4 • 14 • 3333 • No • 53 • 2670

Paraguay *River* South America 55 61 G13 62 M5
Parakou Benin 107 N11
Paramaribo Surinam 58 O6
Paramushir, Ostrov *Island* Russian Federation 129 S8
Paraná Argentina 62 L9
Paraná *River* South America 55 61 H14 62 N7
Paranaíba, Rio *River* Brazil 60 K9
Pardubice Czech Republic 84 I9
Parecis, Chapada dos *Mountain range* Brazil 60 E10
Parepare Indonesia 141 L13
Paris France 77 L5
Parker Dam *Dam* USA 48 H8
Parma Italy 86 F8
Parnaíba Brazil 60 M8
Parnaíba, Rio *River* Brazil 55
Pärnu Estonia 94 I3
Pärnu *River* Estonia 94 J3
Paros *Island* Greece 93 M12
Parrett *River* England, United Kingdom 20 J8
Parry Islands *Island group* Northwest Territories/Nunavut, Canada 37 M4
Partney England, United Kingdom 23 O5
Partry Mountains *Mountain range* Republic of Ireland 30 J8
Pasadena California, USA 51 L18
Pasadena Texas, USA 49 S13
Pasargadae *Site of ancient city* Iran 123 N7
Pasley, Cape *Headland* Australia 146 H13
Passau Germany 81 M15
Passo Fundo Brazil 61 H15
Pasto Colombia 58 D8
Patagonia *Semi arid region* Argentina/Chile 55 63 J18
Paterson New Jersey, USA 41 L12
Pathfinder Reservoir *Reservoir* Wyoming, USA 46 J9
Patna India 131 N7
Patos, Lagoa dos *Lagoon* Brazil 61 I16
Patra Greece 92 H9
Patra, Gulf of *Gulf* Greece 92 G9
Patrickswell Republic of Ireland 31 K12
Pattani Thailand 139 J17
Pattaya Thailand 139 J13
Patuca, Río *River* Honduras 56 E9
Pátzcuaro, Lago de *Lake* Mexico 53 L12
Pau France 76 J14
Pavlodar Kazakhstan 128 I11
Paysandú Uruguay 62 N9
Pazardzhik Bulgaria 90 J14
Peak District *Physical region* England, United Kingdom 17 F11 23 K6
Peak District National Park *National Park* England, United Kingdom 32 F10
Pearl Harbor *Inlet* Hawaii, USA 145 K7
Pearl River *River* Louisiana/Mississippi, USA 42 J8
Peć Serbia, Yugoslavia 89 M9
Pechora *River* Russian Federation 68 96 L8 128 H6
Pecos Texas, USA 49 N11
Pecos River *River* New Mexico/Texas, USA 49 M9
Pécs Hungary 85 K15
Pedro Juan Caballero Paraguay 62 N4
Peebles Scotland, United Kingdom 29 L14
Peel Isle of Man 24 G5
Pegasus Bay *Bay* New Zealand 148 F9
Pegu Burma 138 F10
Peipus, Lake *Lake* Estonia/Russian Federation 95 L2
Pekanbaru Indonesia 140 E11
Peking *see* Beijing
Pelagie, Isole *Island group* Italy 87 I20
Pelée, Montagne *Mountain* Martinique 55
Pelješac *Peninsula* Croatia 88 J8
Peloponnese *Region* Greece 92 H9
Pelotas Brazil 61 I16
Pematangsiantar Indonesia 140 D10
Pemba Mozambique 113 Q6
Pemba *Island* Tanzania 111 Q8
Pembrey Wales, United Kingdom 27 K13
Pembroke Wales, United Kingdom 26 I13
Pembroke Dock Wales, United Kingdom 26 I13
Pembrokeshire *Unitary authority* Wales, United Kingdom 19 G16
Pembrokeshire Coast National Park *National park* Wales, United Kingdom 32 E12
Pen y Fan *Mountain* Wales, United Kingdom 27 N12
Pen-y-ghent *Mountain* England, United Kingdom 24 K12
Penarth Wales, United Kingdom 27 O15
Pendleton Oregon, USA 50 K8
Pennine Alps *Mountain range* Italy/Switzerland 82 E13
Pennines *Mountain range* England, United Kingdom 17 F8 24 J8 32 F8
Pennsylvania *State* USA 40 H12
Penobscot River *River* Maine, USA 41 Q5
Penonomé Panama 56 G15
Penrith England, United Kingdom 24 I9
Pensacola Florida, USA 43 K9
Penticton British Columbia, Canada 37 K15
Pentland Firth *Strait* Scotland, United Kingdom 17 F4 28 L6
Pentland Hills *Hill range* Scotland, United Kingdom 29 L14
Pentraeth Wales, United Kingdom 27 K2
Pentrefoelas Wales, United Kingdom 27 M3
Penybont Wales, United Kingdom 27 N9
Penza Russian Federation 96 H12 128 E7
Penzance England, United Kingdom 20 D12
Peoria Illinois, USA 45 K11
Pereira Colombia 58 E6
Pergamon *Archaeological site* Turkey 118 G7
Perge *Archaeological site* Turkey 118 J9
Périgueux France 77 K11
Perito Moreno Argentina 63 I16
Perm' Russian Federation 96 L11 128 G8
Pernik Bulgaria 90 I13
Perpignan France 77 M15
Persepolis *Site of ancient city* Iran 123 N7
Persian Gulf *see* Gulf, The
Perth Western Australia, Australia 146 F12
Perth Scotland, United Kingdom 29 K12
Perth and Kinross *Unitary authority* Scotland, United Kingdom 18 I8
Perth Basin *Undersea feature* Indian Ocean 143
Peru *Country* W South America 59 E11

Peru 59

1824 • a Spanish and Quechua • Nuevo sol (new sol) • 20 • 68 • 12 • 88.7 • 59 • 1000 • No • 72 • N/A •

Peru Basin *Undersea feature* Pacific Ocean 55
Peru-Chile Trench *Undersea feature* Pacific Ocean 55 145 Q9
Perućko Jezero *Lake* Croatia 88 I6
Perugia Italy 86 H10
Pesaro Italy 86 I9
Pescara Italy 87 K11
Peshawar Pakistan 130 I2
Petah Tiqwa Israel 121 L9
Petaluma California, USA 51 G15
Peter I Island *Dependent territory* Antarctica 64 B9
Peterborough Ontario, Canada 39 K14
Peterborough England, United Kingdom 23 O9
Peterborough *Unitary authority* England, United Kingdom 19 M15
Peterhead Scotland, United Kingdom 29 O9
Peterlee England, United Kingdom 25 M8
Petersburg Alaska, USA 36 I11
Petra *Archaeological site* Jordan 121 M12
Petropavlovsk Kazakhstan 129 H9
Petropavlovsk-Kamchatskiy Russian Federation 129 S7
Petrozavodsk Russian Federation 96 G8 128 F5
Pevek Russian Federation 65 Q5 129 P3
Pforzheim Germany 81 F14
Phangan, Ko *Island* Thailand 139 I15
Phetchabun Thailand 139 J11
Phetchaburi Thailand 139 I13
Philadelphia Pennsylvania, USA 41 K14
Philae *Archaeological site* Egypt 104 G9
Philippeville Belgium 79 H17
Philippine Basin *Undersea feature* Pacific Ocean 127 143
Philippine Plate *Tectonic plate* 127 143
Philippine Sea *Sea* Pacific Ocean 127 141 M3 143
Philippine Trench *Undersea feature* Pacific Ocean 127 143
Philippines *Island group* Pacific Ocean 127 143
Philippines *Country* SE Asia 141 K7

Philippines 141

1946 • a English and Filipino • Philippine peso • 250 • 68 • 12 • 94.6 • 10 • 10000 • Yes • 54 • 2257

Phitsanulok Thailand 139 I11
Phnom Penh Cambodia 139 L14
Phoenix Arizona, USA 48 I9
Phoenix Islands *Island group* Kiribati 144 J8 143
Phofung *Mountain* Lesotho 101
Phôngsali Laos 138 K8
Phuket Thailand 139 G16
Phuket, Ko *Island* Thailand 139 G16
Phumĭ Sâmraông Cambodia 139 K12
Piacenza Italy 86 E7
Piţra-Neam@t Romania 91 M3
Piave *River* Italy 86 H6
Pichilemu Chile 63 G11
Pickering England, United Kingdom 25 N11
Picos Brazil 60 M9
Picton New Zealand 148 G7
Piedras Negras Mexico 53 M5
Pielinen *Lake* Finland 71 P8
Pierre South Dakota, USA 47 N7
Pietermaritzburg South Africa 113 M14
Pietersburg South Africa 113 M11
Pilar Paraguay 62 M6
Pilcomayo *River* C South America 62 M5
Pinar del Río Cuba 56 G3
Pinatubo, Mount *Volcano* Philippines 127
Pindus Mountains *Mountain range* Greece 68 92 G5
Pine Bluff Arkansas, USA 42 I5
Pinega *River* Russian Federation 96 J8
Pineios *River* Greece 92 I5
Pingxiang China 134 J14
Pingxiang China 134 M12
Pini, Pulau *Island* Indonesia 140 D11
Pinsk Belarus 94 J15
Pioneer Fracture Zone *Undersea feature* Pacific Ocean 34
Piotrków Trybunalski Poland 85 L7
Piqua Ohio, USA 45 O12
Piraeus Greece 93 K9
Pisa Italy 86 F9
Pisac Peru 59 G13
Pistoia Italy 86 F9
Pita Guinea 84 J4
Pitcairn Islands *Dependent territory* Pacific Ocean 145 N10
Piteå Sweden 71 N6
Piteälven *River* Sweden 71 M5
Piteşti Romania 91 K8
Pitlochry Scotland, United Kingdom 29 K11
Pittsburg Kansas, USA 47 Q13
Pittsburgh Pennsylvania, USA 40 G13
Pittsfield Massachusetts, USA 41 M10
Piura Peru 58 B10
Pivdennyy Buh *River* Ukraine 98 I6
Placentia Bay *Inlet* Newfoundland, Canada 39 S10
Plainview Texas, USA 49 O9
Plata, Río de la *Estuary* Argentina/Uruguay 55
Plate *River* Argentina/Uruguay 63 N10
Platte River *River* Nebraska, USA 34 47 N10
Plattsburgh New York, USA 41 M6
Plauen Germany 81 K12
Plenty, Bay of *Bay* New Zealand 148 I4
Pleven Bulgaria 91 K11
Płock Poland 85 L5
Ploieşti Romania 91 L8
Płońsk Poland 85 M5
Plovdiv Bulgaria 91 K14
Plungė Lithuania 94 G7
Plymouth Montserrat 57 S11
Plymouth England, United Kingdom 20 H11
Plymouth *Unitary authority* England, United Kingdom 19 I18
Plzeň Czech Republic 84 G9
Po *River* Italy 68 86 C7
Pobedy, Pik *Mountain* China/Kyrgyzstan 117 127
Pocatello Idaho, USA 46 H9
Podgorica Montenegro, Yugoslavia 89 L9
Podlasie Poland 85 O5
Poinsett, Cape *Cape* Antarctica 64 G10
Pointe-à-Pitre Guadeloupe 57 T12
Pointe-Noire Congo 109 F14
Poitiers France 76 J9
Pol-e Khomri Afghanistan 125 N11
Poland *Country* C Europe 84 J5

Poland 84-85

1918 • a Polish • Zloty • 127 • 73 • 15 • 99 • 221 • 435 • No • 65 • 3301

Polatsk Belarus 95 M8
Pólis Cyprus 119 K12
Poltava Ukraine 99 K5
Polygyros Greece 93 K4
Polynesia *Island group* Pacific Ocean 144 J12
Pomerania *Cultural region* Germany/Poland 84 H3
Pomeranian Bay *Bay* Baltic Sea 84 H2
Pompei Italy 87 K13
Ponca City Oklahoma, USA 47 P14
Ponce Puerto Rico 57 Q9
Pondicherry India 131 K14
Pontardawe Wales, United Kingdom 27 L13
Pontardulais Wales, United Kingdom 27 L13
Pontchartrain, Lake *Lake* Louisiana, USA 42 I5
Pontevedra Spain 74 F4
Pontiac Michigan, USA 45 O9
Pontianak Indonesia 140 H11
Pontypool Wales, United Kingdom 27 O13
Pontypridd Wales, United Kingdom 27 N14
Ponziane *Island* Italy 87 I13
Poole England, United Kingdom 21 L10 32 G13
Poole *Unitary authority* England, United Kingdom 19 K18
Poole *Beach* England, United Kingdom 32 G13
Poole Bay *Bay* England, United Kingdom 21 M10
Poopó, Lago *Lake* Bolivia 59 I15
Popayán Colombia 58 D7
Poplar Bluff Missouri, USA 47 S13
Popocatépetl *Volcano* Mexico 34 53 N12
Popondetta Papua New Guinea 147 O3
Poprad Slovakia 85 M10
Porbandar India 130 H8
Porcupine River *River* Canada/USA 36 H6
Pori Finland 71 N10
Poronaysk Russian Federation 129 R10
Porpoise Bay *Bay* Antarctica 64 G11
Porsangen *Fjord* Norway 71 O1
Porsgrunn Norway 70 I12
Port Angeles Washington, USA 50 G6
Port Antonio Jamaica 57 K8
Port Arthur Texas, USA 49 T13
Port Askaig Scotland, United Kingdom 29 G14
Port Augusta South Australia, Australia 147 L12
Port Dickson Malaysia 139 J19
Port Elizabeth South Africa 113 K16
Port Ellen Scotland, United Kingdom 29 G14
Port Erin Isle of Man 24 F6
Port Eynon *Beach* Wales, United Kingdom 32 E12
Port Harcourt Nigeria 107 O13
Port Hardy British Columbia, Canada 36 I14
Port Hedland Western Australia, Australia 146 G8
Port Hope Simpson Newfoundland, Canada 39 R7
Port Huron Michigan, USA 45 P8
Port Isaac Bay *Bay* England, United Kingdom 20 F10
Port Lincoln South Australia, Australia 147 K13
Port Louis Mauritius 115 F11
Port Moresby Papua New Guinea 147 N3
Port Nolloth South Africa 67 M14
Port of Ness Scotland, United Kingdom 28 G7
Port Said Egypt 66 N9 104 G6 114 D4
Port Sudan Sudan 105 I11
Port Talbot Wales, United Kingdom 27 M14
Port-au-Prince Haiti 57 M8
Port-de-Paix Haiti 57 M7
Port-Eynon Wales, United Kingdom 27 K14 32 E12
Port-Gentil Gabon 109 E13
Port-of-Spain Trinidad and Tobago 57 S16
Port-Vila Vanuatu 144 I10
Portadown Northern Ireland, United Kingdom 31 O5
Portaferry Northern Ireland, United Kingdom 31 P5
Portalegre Portugal 74 G10
Portales New Mexico, USA 49 N9
Porthcawl *Beach* Wales, United Kingdom 32 F13
Porthcawl Wales, United Kingdom 27 M15
Portimão Portugal 74 F13
Portishead England, United Kingdom 20 J6
Portland Maine, USA 41 O8 66 E8
Portland Oregon, USA 50 H8
Portland Bill *Headland* England, United Kingdom 17 F14 21 K10
Portland, Isle of *Island* England, United Kingdom 21 K10
Portlaoise Republic of Ireland 31 M10
Porto *see* Oporto
Porto Alegre Brazil 61 I16
Porto Velho Brazil 60 E9
Porto-Novo Benin 107 M13
Portoviejo Ecuador 58 B9
Portree Scotland, United Kingdom 28 G10
Portrush *Beach* Northern Ireland, United Kingdom 32 D8
Portskerra Scotland, United Kingdom 28 K7
Portsmouth England, United Kingdom 21 O9
Portsmouth New Hampshire, USA 41 O9
Portsmouth Ohio, USA 45 P13
Portsmouth, City of *Unitary authority* England, United Kingdom 19 M18
Portugal *Country* SW Europe 74 G12

Portugal 74

1640 • a Portuguese • Portuguese escudo • 108 • 75 • 15 • 90.8 • 288 • 345 • No • 36 • 3634

Porvenir Chile 63 J19
Posadas Argentina 62 O7
Postojna Slovenia 83 P12
Potenza Italy 87 M13
Potenza *River* Italy 86 I10
P'ot'i Georgia 99 O12
Potosí Bolivia 59 I16
Potsdam Germany 80 L9
Poughkeepsie New York, USA 41 L11
Poulton-le-Fylde England, United Kingdom 24 I13
Poŭthĭsăt Cambodia 139 L13
Powder River *River* Montana/Wyoming, USA 47 K7
Powell, Lake *Lake* Utah, USA 48 J5
Powys *Unitary authority* Wales, United Kingdom 19 I15
Poyang Hu *Lake* China 127 135 M11
Poza Rica Mexico 53 O11
Požarevac Serbia, Yugoslavia 89 N5
Poznań Poland 84 J5
Pozo Colorado Paraguay 62 M5
Prachin Buri Thailand 139 J12
Prachuap Khiri Khan Thailand 139 I14
Prague Czech Republic 84 H9
Praia Cape Verde 66 I10
Prato Italy 86 G9
Pratt Kansas, USA 47 O13
Pravets Bulgaria 90 J12
Prešov Poland 85 N11
Prescott Arizona, USA 48 I8
Preseli, Mynydd *Mountain rangWales*, United Kingdom 26 I11
Prespa, Limni *Lake* SE Europe 89 N12 92 G
Presque Isle Maine, USA 41 Q3
Prestatyn Wales, United Kingdom 27 N1
Preston England, United Kingdom 24 I13
Prestwick Scotland, United Kingdom 29 I15
Pretoria South Africa 112 L12
Preveza Greece 92 G7
Priboj Serbia, Yugoslavia 89 M7
Priene *Archaeological site* Turkey 118 G8
Prijedor Bosnia and Herzegovina 88 I4
Prilep FYR Macedonia 89 O12
Prince Albert Saskatchewan, Canada 37 N14
Prince Charles Island *Island* Northwest Territories, Canada 37 Q6
Prince Edward Island *Province* Canada 39 Q11
Prince Edward Islands *Island group* South Africa 115 E14
Prince George British Columbia, Canada 36 J13
Prince of Wales Island *Island* Queensland, Australia 147 L4
Prince of Wales Island *Island* Nunavut, Canada 37 M6
Prince Patrick Island *Island* Northwest Territories/Nunavut, Canada 37 L4 65 O9
Prince Rupert British Columbia, Canada 36 I12 145 M3
Princess Charlotte Bay *Bay* Queensland, Australia 147 N5
Princeton New Jersey, USA 41 L13
Príncipe *Island* Sao Tome and Principe 67 L12 101 109 D12
Pripet *River* Belarus/Ukraine 95 L14
Priština Serbia, Yugoslavia 89 N9
Prizren Serbia, Yugoslavia 89 N10
Progreso Mexico 53 S10
Prome Burma 138 F9
Prosna *River* Poland 85 K6
Provence *Cultural region* France 77 O13
Providence Rhode Island, USA 41 O11
Provideniya Russian Federation 129 R2
Provo Utah, USA 48 J3
Prudhoe Bay Alaska, USA 36 I5
Prudhoe Bay *Bay* Alaska, USA 65 O6
Prut *River* SE Europe 91 O5
Pruzhany Belarus 94 I13
Prydz Bay *Bay* Antarctica 64 G8
Pskov Russian Federation 96 E8 128 E4
Ptsich *River* Belarus 95 M13
Ptuj Slovenia 83 S10
Pucallpa Peru 59 E12
Puebla Mexico 53 N12
Pueblo Colorado, USA 49 N5
Puerto Aisén Chile 63 H16
Puerto Ayacucho Venezuela 58 I6
Puerto Barrios Guatemala 56 C8
Puerto Cabello Venezuela 58 H4
Puerto Cabezas Nicaragua 56 F10
Puerto Carreño Colombia 58 I6
Puerto Cortés Honduras 56 C8
Puerto Deseado Argentina 63 K17
Puerto Inírida Colombia 58 H7
Puerto Madryn Argentina 63 K14
Puerto Montt Chile 63 H14
Puerto Natales Chile 63 I19
Puerto Plata Dominican Republic 57 N7
Puerto Princesa Philippines 141 K6
Puerto Rico *Dependent territory* West Indies 57 Q10
Puerto Rico Trench *Undersea feature* Atlantic Ocean 55
Puerto Santa Cruz Argentina 63 J18
Puerto Vallarta Mexico 53 K11
Pula Croatia 88 F4
Pumsaint Wales, United Kingdom 27 L11
Punakha Bhutan 131 P5
Pune India 130 I10
Puno Peru 59 G14
Punta Arenas Chile 63 J19
Puntarenas Costa Rica 56 D13
Pur *River* Russian Federation 128 J7
Purgatoire River *River* Colorado, USA 49 N6
Purmerend Netherlands 78 I9
Purus, Rio *River* Brazil/Peru 55 60 D9
Pusan South Korea 135 Q8 144 F5
Putorana Mountains *Mountain range* Russian Federation 129 K6
Putumayo, Río *River* South America 55 58 F9
Puyo South Korea 135 P8
Pwllheli Wales, United Kingdom 26 J4
Pyaozero, Ozero *Lake* Russian Federation 96 H6 128 G4
Pyapon Burma 139 F11

Pyasina *River* Russian Federation 129 K6
Pyinmana Burma 138 F9
Pylos Greece 92 H12
Pyongyang North Korea 135 P7
Pyramid Lake *Lake* Nevada, USA 48 F2
Pyrenees *Mountain range* SW Europe 68 75 M4 76 I14
Pyrgos Greece 92 H10

Qaanaaq Greenland 65 O11
Qaidam Pendi *Basin* China 127
Qamdo China 133 K12
Qaqortoq Greenland 65 M15
Qarshi Uzbekistan 125 L8
Qatar *Country* SW Asia 213 M10

Qatar 123

1971 • a Arabic • Qatar riyal • 54 • 72 • 80 • 190 • 699 • No • 92 • N/A •

Qattara Depression *Desert* Egypt 101 104 E6
Qazvin Iran 123 N3
Qena Egypt 104 G8
Qeqertarsuaq Greenland 65 N13
Qeshm Island *Island* Iran 123 O10
Qilian Shan *Mountain range* China 127
Qin Ling *Mountain range* China 127 135 K9
Qingdao China 135 N8 144 E6
Qinghai *Province* China 133 K9
Qinghai Hu *Lake* China 127 133 L9
Qinhuangdao China 135 N6
Qiqihar China 135 O3
Qom Iran 123 N4
Quang Ngai Vietnam 139 O12
Quantock Hills and Blackdown Hills *Area of Outstanding Natural Beauty* England, United Kingdom 32 F13
Quba Azerbaijan 99 S12
Québec (var. Quebec) Quebec, Canada 39 M12
Quebec *Province* Canada 39 L10
Queen Charlotte Islands *Island group* British Columbia, Canada 36 H12
Queen Charlotte Sound *Sound* Pacific Ocean 36 H13
Queen Elizabeth Islands *Island group* Northwest Territories/Nunavut, Canada 37 L3 65 N10
Queensferry Wales, United Kingdom 27 O3
Queensland *State* Australia 147 L9
Queenstown New Zealand 148 D11
Quelimane Mozambique 113 O8
Querétaro Mexico 53 M11
Quetta Pakistan 130 G3
Quezaltenango Guatemala 56 A8
Quibdó Colombia 58 D6
Quicama *National Park* Angola 112 G5
Quillota Chile 62 G10
Quimper France 76 F6
Quincy Illinois, USA 44 I12
Quito Ecuador 58 C8
Quqon Uzbekistan 125 O7
Qurghonteppa Tajikistan 125 N9
Quy Nhơn Vietnam 139 O13

R

Raasay *Island* Scotland, United Kingdom 28 G9
Raba Indonesia 141 L15
Rába *River* Austria/Hungary 84 J14
Rabat Morocco 102 I5
Rabaul Papua New Guinea 147 P2
Race, Cape *Cape* Newfoundland, Canada 34 39 T10
Rach Gia Vietnam 139 L15
Racine Wisconsin, USA 45 L9
Radom Poland 85 N7
Radstadt Austria 83 O8
Rafah Gaza Strip 121 L11
Raglan Wales, United Kingdom 27 P13
Ragusa Italy 87 L19
Rahimyar Khan Pakistan 130 H5
Rainier, Mount *Volcano* Washington, USA 34 50 I7
Raipur India 131 L9
Rajahmundry India 131 L11
Rajang, Batang *River* Borneo, Malaysia 140 I10
Rajkot India 130 H8
Rajshahi Bangladesh 131 O7
Rakaia *River* New Zealand 148 E10
Rakvere Estonia 95 K1
Raleigh North Carolina, USA 43 Q5
Ramla Israel 121 L10
Râmnicu Vâlcea Romania 90 J7
Ramree Island *Island* Burma 138 E9
Ramsey Isle of Man 24 G5
Ramsgate England, United Kingdom 21 T6
Ramsgate *Beach* England, United Kingdom 32 I12
Ranau Borneo, Malaysia 141 K8
Rancagua Chile 63 H11
Ranchi India 131 N8
Randers Denmark 70 I14
Rangoon Burma 114 K6 138 F10
Rangpur Bangladesh 131 O6
Rankin Inlet Nunavut, Canada 37 O9
Rantoul Illinois, USA 45 L12
Rapid City South Dakota, USA 47 L8
Ras al Khaymah United Arab Emirates 123 O10
Râs Ghârib Egypt 104 G7
Rasht Iran 123 N3
Ratchaburi Thailand 139 I13
Rathburn Lake *Lake* Iowa, USA 47 Q10
Rathkeale Republic of Ireland 30 J12
Rathlin Island *Island* Northern Ireland, United Kingdom 31 O2
Ratisbon *see* Regensburg
Rauma Finland 71 N10
Raurkela India 131 N8
Ravenglass England, United Kingdom 24 G11
Ravenna Italy 86 H8
Rawalpindi Pakistan 130 J2
Rawlins Wyoming, USA 46 J10
Rawson Argentina 63 K14
Rayong Thailand 139 J13
Raysut Oman 123 M15
Razgrad Bulgaria 91 M11
Razim, Lacul *Lagoon* Romania 91 P8
Reading England, United Kingdom 21 N6
Reading Pennsylvania, USA 41 K13
Reading *Unitary authority* England, United Kingdom 19 M16
Rebun-to *Island* Japan 136 K2
Rechytsa Belarus 95 N14
Recife Brazil 60 P9 67 H12
Recklinghausen Germany 80 E10
Red Bluff Lake *Lake* USA 49 M11
Red Deer Alberta, Canada 37 K14
Red Lake River *River* Minnesota, USA 44 F3
Red River *River* China/Vietnam 138 L7
Red River *River* USA 34 47 O16 49 R9
Red River *River* Louisiana, USA 42 G6
Red Sea *Sea* Indian Ocean 101 104 H8 114 D5 117 122 G10 127
Red Volta *River* Burkina/Ghana 107 L10
Red Wharf Bay *Bay* Wales, United Kingdom 27 K1
Red Wing Minnesota, USA 44 I7
Redbridge *London borough* England, United Kingdom 19 O19
Redcar England, United Kingdom 25 N9
Redcar and Cleveland *Unitary authority* England, United Kingdom 18 O9
Redding California, USA 51 H13
Redditch England, United Kingdom 22 J10
Redhill England, United Kingdom 21 P7
Redruth England, United Kingdom 20 E12
Ree, Lough *Lake* Republic of Ireland 17 C11 31 L8
Rega *River* Poland 84 I3
Regensburg (Eng. Ratisbon) Germany 81 K14
Reggio di Calabria Italy 87 M17
Reggio nell' Emilia Italy 86 F8
Regina Saskatchewan, Canada 37 N15
Rehoboth Namibia 112 H11
Reims (Eng. Rheims) France 77 M4
Reindeer Lake *Lake* Manitoba/Saskatchewan, Canada 34 37 M12
Remscheid Germany 81 E11
Rend Lake *Reservoir* Illinois, USA 45 K15
Renfrewshire *Unitary authority* Scotland, United Kingdom 18 L5
Reni Ukraine 98 H9
Rennes France 76 H6
Reno *River* Italy 86 G8
Reno Nevada, USA 48 E3
Republican River *River* Kansas/Nebraska, USA 47 N11
Resistencia Argentina 62 M7
Reşiţa Romania 90 G7
Resolute Nunavut, Canada 37 N5 65 N10
Resolven Wales, United Kingdom 27 M13
Rethymno Greece 93 L16
Réunion *Dependent territory* Indian Ocean 115 F11
Reus Spain 75 P7
Revillagigedo Islands *Island group* Mexico 145 N7
Rey, Isla del *Island* Panama 56 H15
Reykjavík Iceland 66 I7
Reynosa Mexico 53 N7
Rhaetian Alps *Mountain range* Austria/Itlay/Switzerland 82 I12
Rhayader Wales, United Kingdom 27 N9
Rheims *see* Reims
Rhein *see* Rhine
Rheinfels *Castle* Germany 81 E12
Rhine (var. Rhein) *River* W Europe 68 77 Q4 79 L11 81 E15 82 H10
Rhode Island *State* USA 41 N11
Rhodes *see* Rodos
Rhodope Mountains *Mountain range* Bulgaria/Greece 68 90 I14
Rhondda Wales, United Kingdom 27 N14
Rhondda Cynon Taff *Unitary authority* Wales, United Kingdom 19 E17
Rhône *River* France/Switzerland 68 77 N12 82 E12
Rhos Wales, United Kingdom 27 K11
Rhossili Wales, United Kingdom 27 K14
Rhum *Island* Scotland, United Kingdom 17 D6 29 F11
Rhyl Wales, United Kingdom 27 N1
Rhymney Wales, United Kingdom 27 N13
Ribble *River* England, United Kingdom 17 F10 24 J13
Ribe Denmark 70 H15
Ribeirão Preto Brazil 61 J13
Riccione Italy 86 I9
Richland Washington, USA 50 K8
Richmond Indiana, USA 45 N12
Richmond England, United Kingdom 25 K10
Richmond upon Thames *London borough* England, United Kingdom 19 M20
Ricobayo, Embalse de *Reservoir* Spain 74 I6
Ridsdale England, United Kingdom 25 K6
Riesa Germany 81 L11
Riffe Lake *Lake* Washington, USA 50 H7
Rīga Latvia 94 I6
Riga, Gulf of *Gulf* Estonia/Latvia 94 I4
Riihimäki Finland 71 O11
Riiser-Larsen Ice Shelf *Ice shelf* Antarctica 64 D6
Rijeka Croatia 88 G4
Rila *Mountain range* Bulgaria 90 I14
Rimini Italy 86 H8
Ringkøbing Denmark 70 H14
Ringvassøy *Island* Norway 71 M2
Ringwood England, United Kingdom 21 M9
Rio Branco Brazil 60 B10
Río Cuarto Argentina 62 K10
Rio de Janeiro Brazil 61 L14 66 G13
Río Gallegos Argentina 63 J19
Río Grande Argentina 63 K19
Rio Grande Brazil 61 I17
Rio Grande *River* Texas, USA 34 49 M6
Rio Grande Rise *Undersea feature* Atlantic Ocean 55
Riobamba Ecuador 58 C9
Ríohacha Colombia 58 F4
Ripon England, United Kingdom 25 L12
Rishiri-to *Island* Japan 136 K2
Rivas Nicaragua 56 D11
Rivera Uruguay 62 O8
Riverside California, USA 51 L18
Rivne Ukraine 98 G4
Riyadh Saudi Arabia 123 K10
Rize Turkey 119 Q5
Rizhao China 135 N8
Rkîz, Lac *Lake* Mauritania 106 G7
Road Town British Virgin Islands 57 R9
Roanoke Virginia, USA 43 Q4
Roanoke River *River* North Carolina/Virginia, USA 43 R5
Robertsport Liberia 106 H12
Robin Hood's Bay England, United Kingdom 25 O10
Rocha Uruguay 62 P10
Rochdale England, United Kingdom 25 K14
Rochdale *Unitary authority* England, United Kingdom 18 C9
Rochester Minnesota, USA 44 I8
Rochester New Hampshire, USA 41 O8
Rochester New York, USA 40 I9
Rock Island Illinois, USA 44 J11
Rock Springs Wyoming, USA 46 I10
Rockford Illinois, USA 45 K10
Rockhampton Queensland, Australia 147 P9
Rockies *see* Rocky Mountains
Rockingham Western Australia, Australia 146 F13
Rockwood Maine, USA 41 P5
Rocky Mountains (var. Rockies) *Mountain range* Canada/USA 34 36 I10 46 G4 49 L3
Rodez France 77 L12
Rodos (Eng. Rhodes) Greece 93 R13
Rodos (Eng. Rhodes) *Island* Greece 93 R14
Roermond Netherlands 79 L14
Roeselare Belgium 79 D14
Roggeveen Basin *Undersea feature* Pacific Ocean 55
Roma Queensland, Australia 147 N10
Roma *see* Rome
Romania *Country* SE Europe 90 H5

Romania 90-91

1878 • a Romanian • Leu • 97 • 70 • 15 • 97.8 • 107 • 556 • No • 55 • 3051

Romanovka Russian Federation 129 M11
Rome (It. Roma) Italy 87 H12
Rome Georgia, USA 43 M6
Rome New York, USA 41 K9
Romsey England, United Kingdom 21 M8
Roncador, Serra do *Mountain range* Brazil 61 I11
Rønne Denmark 71 K16
Ronne Ice Shelf *Ice shelf* Antarctica 64 C8
Ronse Belgium 79 E15
Roosendaal Netherlands 79 H12
Roraima, Mount *Mountain* South America 55
Røros Norway 70 J8
Rosario Argentina 62 L9
Roscommon Republic of Ireland 31 L8
Roscommon *County* Republic of Ireland 19 D13
Roscrea Republic of Ireland 31 L10
Roseau Dominica 57 T12
Roseburg Oregon, USA 50 G10
Rosenheim Germany 81 K16
Roses Spain 75 R5
Ross Carbery Republic of Ireland 30 J15
Ross Ice Shelf *Ice shelf* Antarctica 64 D10
Ross Lake *Lake* Washington, USA 50 I5
Ross Sea *Sea* Antarctica 64 D11 143
Ross-on-Wye England, United Kingdom 22 I12
Rossel Island *Island* Papua New Guinea 147 Q4
Rössing Namibia 112 H10
Rosslare Republic of Ireland 31 O13
Rosslare Harbour Republic of Ireland 31
Rosso Mauritania 106 F7
Rostock Germany 80 K6
Rostov-na-Donu (Eng. Rostov-on-Don) Russian Federation 96 D14 128 D8
Rostov-on-Don *see* Rostov-na-Donu
Roswell New Mexico, USA 49 M9
Rother *River* England, United Kingdom 21 O8
Rotherham England, United Kingdom 25 M15
Rotherham *Unitary authority* England, United Kingdom 19 L13
Rothesay Scotland, United Kingdom 29 H14
Roti, Pulau *Island* Indonesia 141 M16
Rotorua New Zealand 148 I5
Rotterdam Netherlands 66 K8 79 H11
Rouen France 77 K4
Rousay *Island* Scotland, United Kingdom 28 L5
Rovaniemi Finland 71 O5
Rovuma *River* Mozambique 113 O5
Roxas City Philippines 141 M5
Royal Leamington Spa England, United Kingdom 23 K10
Royal Tunbridge Wells England, United Kingdom 21 Q7
Royale, Isle *Island* Michigan, USA 45 K3
Royston England, United Kingdom 21 P3
Ruabon Wales, United Kingdom 27 O4
Ruaha *National Park* Tanzania 111 N9
Ruapehu, Mount *Volcano* New Zealand 143
Rudolf, Lake *Lake* Kenya 101 105 I17 110 O2
Rufiji *River* Tanzania 111 P10
Rugby England, United Kingdom 23 L10
Rugeley England, United Kingdom 22 J8
Rügen *Cape* Germany 80 L6
Ruhr *River* Germany 81 F11
Rukwa, Lake *Lake* Tanzania 101 111 M10
Rum Cay *Island* Bahamas 57 L4
Rum, Wadi *Seasonal watercourse* Jordan 121 M13
Rumbek Sudan 105 F16
Rumford Maine, USA 41 O6
Rumney Wales, United Kingdom 27 O15
Runcorn England, United Kingdom 22 H6
Rundu Namibia 112 I8
Rupert, Rivière de *River* Quebec, Canada 39 K9
Ruse Bulgaria 91 L10
Rushden England, United Kingdom 23 N10
Rushmore, Mount *Mountain* South Dakota, USA 47 L8
Russian Federation *Country* Asia/Europe 94 96 128-129

Russian Federation 94, 96-97, 126-127

1991 • a Russian • Rouble • 9 • 67 • 15 • 99 • 120 • 219 • No • 76 • N/A

Rust'avi Georgia 99 Q13
Ruthin Wales, United Kingdom 27 N3
Rutland Vermont, USA 41 M8
Rutland *Unitary authority* England, United Kingdom 19 M14
Rutland Water *Lake* England, United Kingdom 17 G12 23 N8
Ruvuma *River* Mozambique/Tanzania 111 P12
Ruwenzori *Mountain range* Dem. Rep. Congo (Zaire)/Uganda 111 L4
Ruwenzori *National Park* Uganda 111 L5
Rwanda *Country* C Africa 111 L6

Rwanda 111

1962 • a French and Rwandan • Franc Rwandais (Rwanda franc) • 289 • 41 • 13 • 63 • 2 • 40600 • Yes • 6 • 1821

Ryazan' Russian Federation 96 G11 128 E6
Rybnik Poland 85 K9
Rye England, United Kingdom 21 R8
Rye *River* England, United Kingdom 25 N11
Rye Patch Reservoir *Reservoir* Nevada, USA 48 F2
Ryukyu Islands *Island group* Japan 127 137 B20
Rzeszów Poland 85 N9

S

Saale *River* Germany 80 J10
Saarbrücken Germany 81 D14
Saaremaa *Island* Estonia 94 H2
Šabac Serbia, Yugoslavia 89 M5
Sabadell Spain 75 Q6
Sabah *Region* Malaysia 141 K9
Sabaki *River* Kenya 111 Q7
Sab'atayn, Ramlat as *Desert* Yemen 122 J15
Sabha Libya 103 O9
Sabine River *River* Louisiana/Texas, USA 49 S10
Sable, Cape *Cape* Newfoundland, Canada 39 P14
Sabzevar Iran 123 Q4
Sachsen *see* Saxony
Sacramento California, USA 51 I14
Sa'dah Yemen 122 I14
Sado *Island* Japan 136 I9
Saffron Walden England, United Kingdom 21 Q3
Safi Morocco 66 J9 102 H5
Saga Japan 137 C14
Sagaing Burma 138 F7
Sagami-nada *Inlet* Japan 137 K11
Saginaw Michigan, USA 45 O8
Saginaw Bay *Lake bay* Michigan, USA 45 O7
Sahara *Desert* N Africa 101 102 J10 106 H6
Saharan Atlas *Mountain range* Algeria/Morocco 68
Sahel *Physical region* W Africa 101 106 I9
Saïda Lebanon 121 M7
Saidpur Bangladesh 131 O7
Saigon *see* Hô Chi Minh
Saimaa *Lake* Finland 71 P10
St Abb's Head *Headland* Scotland, United Kingdom 17 G7
St Alban's Head *Headland* England, United Kingdom 21 M10
St Albans England, United Kingdom 21 P5
St Andrews Scotland, United Kingdom 29 M12
St Anton Austria 82 J9
St Austell England, United Kingdom 20 F11
St Austell Bay *Bay* England, United Kingdom 20 F11
St Bees Head *Headland* England, United Kingdom 17 E9 24 G10
St Brides Bay *Inlet* Wales, United Kingdom 26 H13
St-Brieuc France 76 G6
St Catherine's Point *Headland* England, United Kingdom 21 N10
Saint Charles Missouri, USA 47 S11
Saint Clair Shores Michigan, USA 45 O9
St Clears Wales, United Kingdom 26 J12
Saint Cloud Minnesota, USA 44 G6
St Croix *Island* Virgin Islands (US) 57 R10
St David's Wales, United Kingdom 26 G12
St David's *Beach* Wales, United Kingdom 32 E12
St-Étienne France 77 N10
Saint Eustatius *Island* Netherlands Antilles 57 S10
St.George's Grenada 57 S15
St George's Channel *Channel* Republic of Ireland/United Kingdom 17 D13 31 O14
St.Gotthard Tunnel *Tunnel* Switzerland 82 G11
Saint Helena *Dependent territory* Atlantic Ocean 67 K13
Saint Helens, Mount *Volcano* Washington, USA 34
St Ives England, United Kingdom 20 D12
St Ives *Beach* England, United Kingdom 32 E14
St-Jean, Lac *Lake* Quebec, Canada 39 M11
St John's Antigua and Barbuda 57 S11
St.John New Brunswick, Canada 39 O13 66 E8
St.John's Newfoundland, Canada 39 S9 66 G8
St John's Point *Headland* Republic of Ireland 31 K4
Saint Joseph Missouri, USA 47 Q11
Saint Kitts and Nevis *Country* West Indies 57 S11

St Kitts and Nevis 57

1983 • a English • Eastern Caribbean dollar • 114 • 70 • 17 • 90 • N/A 1124 • Yes • 34 • 2419

St-Laurent-du-Maroni French Guiana 58 O6
St.Lawrence, Gulf of *Gulf* Canada 39 P10
Saint Lawrence Island *Island* Alaska, USA 36 E5
Saint Lawrence River *River* Canada/USA 34 66 E8
St.Lawrence Seaway *Seaway* Canada 39 N10
St-Lô France 76 I5
Saint Louis Senegal 106 F8
Saint Louis Missouri, USA 47 S11
Saint Lucia *Country* West Indies 57 T13

St. Lucia 57

1979 • a English • Eastern Caribbean dollar • 249 • 70 • 15 • 82 • 16 • 2857 • Yes • 38 • 2588

St Magnus Bay *Bay* Scotland, United Kingdom 28 O2
St-Malo France 76 H5
St Margaret's Hope Scotland, United Kingdom 28 L6
St.Martin *Island* Guadeloupe/Netherlands Antilles 57 S10
Saint Matthew Island *Island* Alaska, USA 36 D5
St.Moritz Switzerland 82 I11
St-Nazaire France 76 H8
St Neots England, United Kingdom 23 O11
Saint Paul Minnesota, USA 44 H6
St. Paul Island *Island* French Southern and Antarctic Territories 115 I13
Saint Petersburg (Rus. Sankt-Petersburg) Russian Federation 96 F8 128 E4
Saint Petersburg Florida, USA 43 N13
Saint-Pierre Saint Pierre and Miquelon 39 R10
Saint Pierre and Miquelon *Dependent territory* North America 39 R10
St-Quentin France 77 M3
Saint Vincent *Island* Saint Vincent and the Grenadines 57 S14
Saint Vincent and the Grenadines *Country* West Indies 57 T14

St Vincent and the Grenadines 57

1979 • a English • Eastern Caribbean dollar • 327 • 73 • 15 • 82 • N/A • 2174 • Yes • 50 • 2347

Date of independence • a Language (official or most commonly spoken) • Currency • Population density per square kilometre • Average life expectancy • School-leaving age • Literacy • Number of cars per 1,000 people • Number of people per doctor • Death penalty • Percentage of urban-based population • Average number of calories consumed daily per person

Saintes France 76 I10
Sajama, Nevado *Mountain* Bolivia 55
Sakakah Saudi Arabia 122 I6
Sakakawea, Lake *Reservoir* North Dakota, USA 47 M5
Sakarya *River* Turkey 118 I6
Sakhalin *Island* Russian Federation 117 129 R10 127 144 G4
Sala y Gomez Ridge *Undersea feature* Pacific Ocean 55
Salado, Río *River* Argentina 55 62 K7
Salalah Oman 114 F6 123 N15
Salamanca Spain 74 I7
Salamat, Bahr *River* Chad 108 J8
Salamis *Archaeological site* Cyprus 119 L11
Salavan Laos 139 N11
Salcombe England, United Kingdom 20 H12
Saldanha South Africa 112 I15
Saldus Latvia 94 G6
Sale Victoria, Australia 147 N14
Salekhard Russian Federation 128 I6
Salem India 131 K14
Salem Oregon, USA 50 H9
Salerno Italy 87 K13
Salerno, Gulf of *Gulf* Italy 87 K14
Salford England, United Kingdom 25 K15
Salford *Unitary authority* England, United Kingdom 18 B10
Salihorsk Belarus 95 L13
Salima Malawi 111 N14
Salina Kansas, USA 47 O12
Salina Utah, USA 48 J4
Salina *Island* Italy 87 L16
Salinas Mexico 53 P12
Salinas California, USA 51 H16
Salisbury England, United Kingdom 21 M8
Salisbury Plain *Plain* England, United Kingdom 17 G13 21 L7
Salmon River *River* Idaho, USA 46 F6
Salo Finland 71 O11
Salonica (Gr. Thessaloníki) Greece 92 J3
Salso *River* Italy 87 J18
Salt Lake City Utah, USA 48 J3
Salt River *River* Arizona, USA 48 J9
Salta Argentina 62 I6
Saltash England, United Kingdom 20 G11
Saltillo Mexico 53 M7
Salto Argentina 62 N9
Salto del Guairá Paraguay 62 O5
Salton Sea *Lake* California, USA 51 M19
Salvador Brazil 61 N11 67 H13
Salween *River* SE Asia 132 J12 134 H13 138 H9
Salzburg Austria 83 N7
Salzgitter Germany 80 H9
Sama'il Oman 123 P12
Samakhixai Laos 139 N12
Samaná Dominican Republic 57 O8
Samar *Island* Philippines 141 N5
Samara Russian Federation 96 I13 128 F8
Samarinda Indonesia 141 K11
Samarqand Uzbekistan 125 M8
Samarra' Iraq 123 K4
Sambre *River* Belgium/France 79 G17
Samoa *Country* Pacific Ocean 144 J9

Samoa 144

1962 • English and Samoan • Tala • 63 • 71 • N/A • 98 • N/A • 2632 • No • 22 • 2828

Samoa Basin *Undersea feature* Pacific Ocean 143
Samobor Croatia 88 H2
Samos Greece 93 P10
Samos *Island* Greece 93 P10
Samothraki *Island* Greece 93 N3
Samsun Turkey 119 N4
Samui, Ko *Island* Thailand 139 I15
San *River* Cambodia 139 N13
San *River* Poland 85 O8
San Ambrosio, Isla *Island* Chile 145 P11
San Andreas Fault *Fault* USA 34
San Andrés Colombia 58 F6
San Andres Mountains *Mountain range* New Mexico, USA 49 L10
San Angelo Texas, USA 49 P11
San Antioco, Isola di *Island* Italy 87 C16
San Antonio Chile 62 G10
San Antonio Texas, USA 49 Q13
San Antonio Oeste Argentina 63 K13
San Antonio River *River* Texas, USA 49 Q13
San Benedetto del Tronto Italy 86 J10
San Bernardino California, USA 51 L18
San Bernardino Tunnel *Tunnel* Switzerland 82 H11
San Bernardo Chile 62 H10
San Carlos Nicaragua 56 E12
San Carlos Venezuela 58 H4
San Carlos de Bariloche Argentina 63 H14
San Clemente California, USA 51 L19
San Cristóbal Venezuela 58 F5
San Diego California, USA 51 L20 145 N5
San Felipe Chile 62 G10
San Felipe Venezuela 58 H4
San Félix, Isla *Island* Chile 145 P10
San Fernando Philippines 141 L3
San Fernando Spain 74 H14
San Fernando Trinidad and Tobago 57 S16
San Fernando Venezuela 58 I5
San Fernando del Valle de Catamarca Argentina 62 I8
San Francisco California, USA 51 H15 145 N5
San Francisco de Macorís Dominican Republic 57 O8
San Gorgonio Pass *Pass* California, USA 51 L18
San Ignacio Belize 56 C6
San Joaquin River *River* California, USA 51 I15
San Jorge, Gulf of *Gulf* Argentina 63 K16
San José Costa Rica 56 E13
San Jose California, USA 51 H15
San José del Guaviare Colombia 58 F7
San José, Isla *Island* Mexico 52 H7
San José, Isla *Island* Panama 56 H15
San Juan Puerto Rico 57 Q9
San Juan Argentina 62 H9
San Juan Peru 59 E14
San Juan Mountains *Mountain range* Colorado, USA 49 L5
San Juan Bautista Paraguay 62 N6
San Juan de los Morros Venezuela 58 H4
San Juan Islands *Island group* Washington, USA 50 H5
San Juan River *River* Colorado/Utah, USA 49 K6
San Juan, Río *River* Costa Rica/Nicaragua 56 E12
San Lorenzo Honduras 56 C10
San Luis Argentina 62 J10
San Luis Obispo California, USA 51 I17
San Luis Potosí Mexico 53 M10
San Marino *Country* S Europe 86 H9

San Marino 86

301 • Italian • Lira • 431 • 81 • 14 • 96.1 • N/A • 375 • No • 94 • 3561

San Marino San Marino 86 H9
San Martín Argentina 64 B8
San Martín, Lago *Lake* Argentina 63 I18
San Matías, Gulf of *Gulf* Argentina 63 K14
San Miguel El Salvador 56 C9
San Miguel de Tucumán Argentina 62 J7
San Miguel, Río *River* Bolivia 59 K14
San Nicolás de los Arroyos Argentina 62 M10
San Pedro Paraguay 62 N5
San Pedro Sula Honduras 56 C8
San Pietro, Isola di *Island* Italy 87 C15
San Rafael Argentina 63 I11
San Remo Italy 86 B9
San Salvador El Salvador 56 B9
San Salvador *Island* Bahamas 57 M3
San Salvador de Jujuy Argentina 62 I6
Sana Yemen 123 I15
Sanaga *River* Cameroon 108 F10
Sanandaj Iran 123 L4
Sandakan Borneo, Malaysia 141 K8
Sandanski Bulgaria 90 I15
Sanday *Island* Scotland, United Kingdom 17 F3 28 M5
Sandbach England, United Kingdom 22 I6
Sandnes Norway 70 H11
Sandoway Burma 138 E9
Sandown England, United Kingdom 21 N10
Sandviken Sweden 71 L11
Sandwell *Unitary authority* England, United Kingdom 19 N12
Sanford Maine, USA 41 O8
Sangatte France 21 T8
Sângeorz-Băi Romania 90 J3
Sangha *River* Central African Republic/Congo 109 I12
Sangihe, Pulau *Island* Indonesia 141 N9
Sangir, Kepulauan *Island group* Indonesia 141 N10
Sangre de Cristo Mountains *Mountain range* Colorado/New Mexico, USA 49 M7
Sangro *River* Italy 87 K12
Sankt Gallen Switzerland 82 H8
Sankt Pölten Austria 83 R5
Sankt Veit an der Glan Austria 83 P9
Sankt-Peterburg *see* Saint Petersburg
Sankt-Vith Belgium 79 L17
Şanlıurfa Turkey 119 P9
Sant Jordi, Golf de *Gulf* Spain 75 P7
Santa Ana El Salvador 56 B9
Santa Ana California, USA 51 L19
Santa Barbara California, USA 51 J18
Santa Catalina, Isla *Island* Mexico 52 H7
Santa Clara Cuba 56 I4
Santa Clara Valley *Valley* California, USA 51 H15
Santa Cruz Bolivia 59 K15
Santa Cruz California, USA 51 H16
Santa Cruz River *River* Arizona, USA 48 I11
Santa Elena de Uairén Venezuela 58 L6
Santa Fe Argentina 62 L9
Santa Fe New Mexico, USA 49 M7
Santa Maria Brazil 61 H16
Santa Maria California, USA 51 I18
Santa Marta Colombia 58 E4
Santa Rosa Argentina 63 K11
Santa Rosa California, USA 51 G14
Santa Rosalía Mexico 52 H5
Santander Spain 75 K3
Santarém Brazil 60 H7
Santarém Portugal 74 F10
Santiago Chile 62 H10
Santiago Dominican Republic 57 N8
Santiago Panama 56 F15
Santiago Spain 74 F4
Santiago de Cuba Cuba 57 K6
Santiago del Estero Argentina 62 J7
Santo Domingo Dominican Republic 57 O9
Santo Domingo de los Colorados Ecuador 58 C9
Santos Brazil 61 K14
Santos Plateau *Undersea feature* Atlantic Ocean 55
Sanya China 135 K16
São Francisco, Rio *River* Brazil 61 L12
São Jose dos Campos Brazil 61 K14
São Luís Brazil 60 L7
São Manuel, Rio *River* Brazil 60 G9
São Paulo Brazil 61 J14
São Roque, Cabo de *Headland* Brazil 55 60 P8
São Tomé Sao Tome and Principe 109 D12
São Tomé *Island* Sao Tome and Principe 67 L12 101
Sao Tome and Principe *Country* Atlantic Ocean 109 D12

Sao Tome and Principe 109

1975 • Portuguese • Dobra • 140 • 64 • 14 • 75 • 6 • 3125 • No • 44 • 2129

São Tomé, Cabo de *Headland* Brazil 61 M14
São Vicente, Cabo de *Cape* Portugal 74 F13
Saône *River* France 77 O7
Sapporo Japan 136 K4
Sapri Italy 87 M14
Saqqara *Archaeological site* Egypt 104 F7
Sara Buri Thailand 139 J12
Saragossa *see* Zaragoza
Sarajevo Bosnia and Herzegovina 89 K6
Saransk Russian Federation 96 H12 128 E7
Saratoga Springs New York, USA 41 L9
Saratov Russian Federation 96 H13 128 E8
Sarawak *Region* Malaysia 140 I10
Sardegna *see* Sardinia
Sardinia (It. Sardegna) *Island* Italy 68 87 C14
Sargasso Sea *Sea* Atlantic Ocean 66 E9
Sargodha Pakistan 130 I3
Sarh Chad 108 J9
Sari Iran 123 O4
Sarikei Malaysia 140 I10
Sarıyer Turkey 118 I5
Sarnen Switzerland 82 G10
Sarnia Ontario, Canada 38 I15
Sarroch Italy 87 D16
Sartang *River* Russian Federation 129 N6
Sarykamyshkoye Ozero *Salt lake* Kazakhstan/Uzbekistan 124 H5
Sasebo Japan 137 B14
Saskatchewan *Province* Canada 37 M13
Saskatchewan *River* Manitoba/Saskatchewan, Canada 37 N13
Saskatoon Saskatchewan, Canada 37 M14
Sassari Italy 87 C13
Satu Mare Romania 90 I2
Saudi Arabia *Country* SW Asia 122 I11

Saudi Arabia 122-123

1932 • Arabic • Saudi riyal • 10 • 71 • N/A • 73.4 • 90 • 769 • Yes • 80 • 2735

Sault Sainte Marie Michigan, USA 45 N4
Sault Ste.Marie Ontario, Canada 38 I12
Saundersfoot Wales, United Kingdom 26 I13
Saundersfoot *Beach* Wales, United Kingdom 32 E12
Saurimo Angola 112 I4
Sava (Eng. Save) *River* SE Europe 83 R11 88 J4 89 L4
Savanna-La-Mar Jamaica 56 J8
Savannah Georgia, USA 43 O9
Save *River* Mozambique/Zimbabwe 113 N10
Save *see* Sava
Savona Italy 86 C8
Savonlinna Finland 71 Q9
Saxony (Ger. Sachsen) *Cultural region* Germany 80 H8
Saynshand Mongolia 133 N5
Scafell Pike *Mountain* England, United Kingdom 17 F9 24 H10
Scandinavia *Geophysical region* N Europe 68
Scapa Flow *Sea basin* North Sea 28 L6
Scarborough Trinidad and Tobago 57 T16
Scarborough England, United Kingdom 25 O11
Scarborough *Beach* England, United Kingdom 32 G9
Schaffhausen Switzerland 82 G8
Schärding Austria 83 N5
Schefferville Quebec, Canada 39 N6
Scheldt *River* NW Europe 79 F14
Schenectady New York, USA 41 L9
Schiermonnikoog *Island* Netherlands 78 L6
Schleswig Germany 80 H6
Schouten Islands *Island group* Papua New Guinea 147 N1
Schwäbische Alb *Mountain range* Germany 81 G16
Schwaner, Pegunungan *Mountain range* Indonesia 140 I12
Schwarzwald *see* Black Forest
Schweinfurt Germany 81 H13
Schwerin Germany 80 J7
Schweriner See *Lake* Germany 80 J7
Schwyz Switzerland 82 G10
Scilly, Isles of *Island group* England, United Kingdom 17 D15 32 D14
Scioto River *River* Ohio, USA 45 O11
Scoresby Sound *see* Ittoqqortoormiit
Scotch Corner England, United Kingdom 25 L10
Scotia Plate *Tectonic plate* 55
Scotia Sea *Sea* Atlantic Ocean 64 C6 67 F16
Scotland *National region* United Kingdom 18 G8 32 E6
Scott Base *New Zealand research station* Antarctica 64 E11
Scottsbluff Nebraska, USA 47 L10
Scottsdale Arizona, USA 48 I9
Scousburgh Scotland, United Kingdom 28 O3
Scranton Pennsylvania, USA 41 K11
Scunthorpe England, United Kingdom 23 M3
Scutari, Lake *Lake* Albania/Yugoslavia 68 89 L10
Seaford England, United Kingdom 21 Q9
Seaford Delaware, USA 41 K16
Seal *River* Manitoba, Canada 37 O11
Seascale England, United Kingdom 24 G10
Seattle Washington, USA 50 H6 145 M4
Sebastopol *see* Sevastopol'
Sefton *Unitary authority* England, United Kingdom 18 A9
Segovia Spain 75 K7
Segura Portugal 75 L11
Segura, Sierra de *Mountain range* Spain 75 L12
Seikan Tunnel *Tunnel* Japan 136 K6
Seinäjoki Finland 71 N9
Seine *River* France 68 77 K4
Sekondi-Takoradi Ghana 107 L13
Selby England, United Kingdom 25 M13
Selebi Phikwe Botswana 113 L10
Selenga *River* Mongolia/Russian Federation 133 L3
Selkirk Manitoba, Canada 37 P14
Selkirk Scotland, United Kingdom 29 M15
Sellafield England, United Kingdom 24 H10
Selma Alabama, USA 43 K8
Selous *National Park* Tanzania 111 P10
Selvas *Physical region* Colombia/Venezuela 55
Semarang Indonesia 140 H15
Semipalatinsk Kazakhstan 128 I11
Semnan Iran 123 O4
Sen *River* Cambodia 139 L13
Sendai Japan 136 L8 144 G5
Senegal *Country* W Africa 106 F8

Senegal 106

1960 • French • Franc de la Communauté financière africaine • 48 • 52 • 13 • 34.6 • 10 • 10000 • No • 42 • 2262

Senegal *River* W Africa 101 106 G7
Senja *Island* Norway 71 M2
Sennar Dam *Dam* Sudan 105 H13
Sennen Cove *Beach* England, United Kingdom 32 D14
Sennybridge Wales, United Kingdom 27 M12
Senta Serbia, Yugoslavia 89 M3
Seoul South Korea 135 P7
Sept-Îles Quebec, Canada 39 O9
Seraing Belgium 79 J16
Seram, Pulau *Island* Indonesia 141 O12
Serbia *Republic* Yugoslavia 89 M6
Serbia (Ger. Serbien, Serb. Srbija) *Republic* Serbia, Yugoslavia
Seremban Malaysia 139 J19
Serengeti *National Park* Tanzania 111 N6
Serengeti Plain *Plain* Tanzania 101
Serifos *Island* Greece 93 L11
Serov Russian Federation 128 H8
Serowe Botswana 113 L10
Serra Pelada Brazil 60 J8
Serres Greece 93 K2
Sétif Algeria 103 L4
Settle England, United Kingdom 24 K12
Setúbal Portugal 74 F11
Seul, Lac *Lake* Ontario, Canada 38 G9
Sevan, Lake *Lake* Armenia 99 Q14
Sevan-Hrazdan *Dam* Armenia 99 Q13
Sevastopol' (Eng. Sebastopol) Ukraine 98 J10
Sevenoaks England, United Kingdom 21 Q7
Severn *River* Ontario, Canada 38 H7
Severn *River* England/Wales, United Kingdom 17 F13 21 K5 22 I10 27 N8
Severn Bridge *Bridge* England/Wales, United Kingdom 27 Q14
Severn, Mouth of the *Estuary* England/Wales, United Kingdom 27 P15
Severnaya Zemlya *Island group* Russian Federation 65 S10 117 129 L3
Severskiy Donets *River* Russian Federation/Ukraine 96 D14
Sevier Lake *Lake* Utah, USA 48 I4
Sevilla *see* Seville
Seville (Sp. Sevilla) Spain 74 I13
Seward Alaska, USA 36 G8
Seychelles *Country* Indian Ocean 114 F9

Seychelles 114

1976 • Seselwa (French Creole) • Seychelles rupee • 279 • 71 • 16 • 84 • 9 • 962 • No • 55 • 2287

Seyhan Turkey 119 M9
Sfântu Gheorghe Romania 91 L6
Sfax Tunisia 66 L9 103 N5
s-Gravenhage *see* The Hague
Shache China 132 E8
Shackleton Ice Shelf *Ice shelf* Antarctica 64 H9
Shadehill Reservoir *Reservoir* South Dakota, USA 47 M6
Shaftesbury England, United Kingdom 21 L8
Shahjahanpur India 131 L5
Shahr-e Kord Iran 123 N6
Shandong Peninsula *Peninsula* China 135 O8
Shanghai China 135 O10 144 E6
Shannon Republic of Ireland 30 J11
Shannon *River* Republic of Ireland 17 C10 30 J11
Shannon Erne Waterway *Canal* Republic of Ireland 31 L6
Shannon, Mouth of the *Estuary* Republic of Ireland 30 I12
Shantou China 135 N14
Shaoguan China 135 M13
Shaoxing China 135 O11
Shaoyang China 135 L12
Shapinsay *Island* Scotland, United Kingdom 28 L5
Sharjah United Arab Emirates 123 O10
Shark Bay *Bay* Western Australia, Australia 146 E10
Shasta Lake *Reservoir* California, USA 51 H12
Shebeli *River* Ethiopia/Somalia 101 105 M16
Sheboygan Wisconsin, USA 45 L8
Sheelin, Lough *Lake* Republic of Ireland 31 M7
Sheerness England, United Kingdom 21 R6
Sheerness *Beach* England, United Kingdom 32 H12
Sheffield England, United Kingdom 25 M15
Sheffield *Unitary authority* England, United Kingdom 19 K13
Shelby Montana, USA 46 H4
Shelikof Strait *Strait* Alaska, USA 36 E9
Shenyang China 135 O5
Sheppey, Isle of *Island* England, United Kingdom 17 H13 21 R6
Shepton Mallet England, United Kingdom 21 L8
Sherbrooke Quebec, Canada 39 N13
Sheridan Wyoming, USA 46 J7
Sheringham *Beach* England, United Kingdom 32 H10
s-Hertogenbosch Netherlands 79 J12
Shetland Islands *Unitary authority* Scotland, United Kingdom 18 L2
Shetland Islands *Island group* Scotland, United Kingdom 17 G1 28 O1 32 G2
Shihezi China 132 H6
Shijiazhuang China 135 M7
Shikarpur Pakistan 130 H5
Shikoku *Island* Japan 127 137 E13
Shikotan, Ostrov *Island* Russian Federation 136 P2
Shildon England, United Kingdom 25 L9
Shilka *River* Russian Federation 129 N11
Shillong India 131 P7
Shimla India 131 K3
Shimo-jima *Island* Japan 137 B15
Shimonoseki Japan 137 C13
Shin, Loch *Lake* Scotland, United Kingdom 28 I8
Shinano-gawa *River* Japan 136 J10
Shingu Japan 137 H13
Shinyanga Tanzania 111 N7
Shiraz Iran 123 N8
Shizuoka Japan 137 J12
Shkodër Albania 89 M10
Shkumbin *River* Albania 89 L12
Shoreham-by-Sea England, United Kingdom 21 P9
Shreveport Louisiana, USA 42 G6
Shrewsbury England, United Kingdom 22 H8
Shropshire *County* England, United Kingdom 19 J15
Shropshire Hills *Area of Outstanding Natural Beauty* England, United Kingdom 32 F11
Shumen Bulgaria 91 N11
Shwebo Burma 138 F7
Shymkent Kazakhstan 128 G13
Šiauliai Lithuania 94 H7
Šibenik Croatia 88 H7
Siberia *Physical region* Russian Federation 129 L7
Siberut, Pulau *Island* Indonesia 140 D12
Sibiloi *National Park* Kenya 111 O2
Sibiti Congo 109 G14
Sibiu Romania 90 J6
Sibolga Indonesia 140 D10
Sibu Borneo, Malaysia 140 I10
Sibut Central African Republic 108 J10
Sichuan Pendi *Basin* China 127
Sicilia *see* Sicily
Sicily (It. Sicilia) *Island* Italy 68 87 I17
Side *Archaeological site* Turkey 118 J10
Sidi Bel Abbès Algeria 103 K5
Sidlaw Hills *Mountain range* Scotland, United Kingdom 29 L12
Sidmouth England, United Kingdom 20 J10
Siegen Germany 81 F11
Siena Italy 86 G10
Sierra Leone *Country* W Africa 106 H11

Sierra Leone 106

1961 • English • Leone • 66 • 37 • N/A • 33.3 • 4 • 14300 • Yes • 36 • 1694

Sierre Switzerland 82 F12
Sifnos *Island* Greece 93 M12
Siirt Turkey 119 R8
Sikasso Mali 106 J10
Silesia *Physical region* Poland 84 I7
Silifke Turkey 119 L10
Siling Co *Lake* China 132 H12

Simeulue, Pulau *Island* Indonesia 140 C10
Simferopol' Ukraine 99 K10
Simon's Town South Africa 115 B12
Simplon Pass *Pass* Switzerland 82 F12
Simplon Tunnel *Tunnel* Italy/Switzerland 82 G12
Simpson Desert *Desert* Northern Territory/South Australia, Australia 143 147 K10
Sinai *Physical region* Egypt 104 G7 117 120 J13
Sincelejo Colombia 58 E5
Sines Portugal 74 F12
Singapore *Country* SE Asia 139 K20

Singapore 139

1965 • Malay, English, Mandarin Chinese and Tamil • Singapore dollar • 5738 • 77 • N/A • 91.4 • 4 • 664 • Yes • 100 • 3128

Singapore Singapore 114 L8
Singapore Strait *Strait* South China Sea 139 K20 140 E11
Singida Tanzania 111 N8
Singitic Gulf *Gulf* Greece 93 K4
Singkep, Pulau *Island* Indonesia 140 F12
Sinoie, Lacul *Lagoon* Romania 91 P8
Sinop Turkey 119 M4
Sint-Niklaas Belgium 79 G14
Sinŭiju North Korea 135 O6
Sioma Zambia 110 I16
Sion Switzerland 82 E12
Sioux City Iowa, USA 47 P9
Sioux Falls South Dakota, USA 47 O8
Sipura, Pulau *Island* Indonesia 140 D12
Sir Edward Pellew Group *Island group* Northern Territory, Australia 147 L6
Siracusa (Eng. Syracuse) Italy 87 L18
Siret *River* Romania/Ukraine 91 M2
Sirikit Reservoir *Lake* Thailand 138 I10
Sirte, Gulf of *Gulf* Libya 101 103 P6
Sirwan Nahr Diyala *River* Iraq 123 K4
Sisak Croatia 88 I3
Sitka Alaska, USA 36 H11
Sittang *River* Burma 138 G9
Sittwe Burma 138 D8
Sivas Turkey 119 N6
Sivuchiy, Mys *Cape* Russian Federation 129 R6
Skagen Denmark 66 L7
Skagerrak *Channel* North Sea 68 71 H13
Skagway Alaska, USA 36 H10
Skegness England, United Kingdom 23 P6
Skegness *Beach* England, United Kingdom 32 H10
Skeleton Coast *National Park* Namibia 112 G9
Skellefteå Sweden 71 N7
Skiathos Greece 92 K7
Skiddaw *Mountain* England, United Kingdom 24 I9
Skikda Algeria 103 M4
Skipton England, United Kingdom 25 K13
Skomer Island *Island* Wales, United Kingdom 26 G13
Skopje FYR Macedonia 89 O10
Skövde Sweden 71 K13
Skovorodino Russian Federation 129 O10
Skye, Isle of *Island* Scotland, United Kingdom 17 D5 28 G10
Skyros *Island* Greece 92 M7
Slagelse Denmark 70 I15
Slane Republic of Ireland 31 O8
Slaney *River* Republic of Ireland 31 N12
Slatina Romania 90 J9
Slavonski Brod Croatia 89 K4
Sleaford England, United Kingdom 23 N7
Sleat, Sound of *Strait* Scotland, United Kingdom 29 G11
Slieve Bloom Mountains *Bog* Republic of Ireland 32 C10
Slieve Gamph *Mountain range* Republic of Ireland 31 K6
Slieve Mish Mountains *Mountain range* Republic of Ireland 30 H13
Sligo Republic of Ireland 31 L6
Sligo *County* Republic of Ireland 19 C12
Sligo Bay *Inlet* Republic of Ireland 31 K6
Sliven Bulgaria 91 M13
Slobozia Romania 91 N8
Slonim Belarus 94 J12
Slough England, United Kingdom 21 P6
Slough *Unitary authority* England, United Kingdom 19 M16
Slovakia *Country* C Europe 85 L11

Slovakia 84-85

1993 • Slovak • Koruna • 110 • 73 • 15 • 99 • 211 • 357 • No • 59 • 3156

Slovenia *Country* C Europe 83 P11

Slovenia 83

1991 • Slovene • Tolar (from October 1991) • 99 • 74 • 15 • 99 • 385 • 455 • No • 64 • N/A

Sluch *River* Ukraine 98 G4
Słupsk Poland 84 J2
Slutsk Belarus 95 L13
Slyne Head *Headland* Republic of Ireland 17 A10 30 H9
Smallwood Reservoir *Lake* Newfoundland, Canada 39 O7
Smara Western Sahara 102 G8
Smarhon' Belarus 95 K10
Smederevo Serbia, Yugoslavia 89 N5
Smoky Hill River *River* Kansas, USA 47 M12
Smoky Hills *Hill range* Kansas, USA 47 N12
Smøla *Island* Norway 70 I7
Smolensk Russian Federation 96 E10 128 E5
Snaefell *Mountain* Isle of Man 24 G5
Snake River *River* USA 34 46 F8 50 K7
Śniardwy, Jezioro *Lake* Poland 85 N3
Snohomish Washington, USA 50 H6
Snowdon *Mountain* Wales, United Kingdom 17 E11 27 L3
Snowdonia *Mountain rangWales*, United Kingdom 17 E11 27 L3
Snowdonia National Park *National Park* Wales, United Kingdom 32 F10
Snyder Texas, USA 49 P10
Sobradinho, Represa de *Reservoir* Brazil 55 60 L10
Sochi Russian Federation 96 D15 128 C8
Society Islands *Island group* French Polynesia 145 L10
Socotra *Island* Yemen 101 114 F7 117
Sodankylä Finland 71 O4
Sofia (var. Sofiya) Bulgaria 90 I13
Sofiya *see* Sofia
Sognefjord *Fjord* Norway 70 H9
Sohâg Egypt 104 F8
Soignies Belgium 79 G16
Sokhumi Georgia 99 O11
Sokodé Togo 107 M11
Sokoto Nigeria 107 N9
Sokoto *River* Nigeria 107 O9
Sol, Costa del *Coastal region* Spain 74 J14
Solapur India 130 J10
Solihull England, United Kingdom 23 K10
Solihull *Unitary authority* England, United Kingdom 19 O12
Solińskie, Jezioro *Lake* Poland 85 O10
Sololá Guatemala 56 A8
Solomon Islands *Country* Pacific Ocean 144 H9

Solomon Islands 144

1978 • English • Solomon Islands dollar • 15 • 72 • N/A • 62 • N/A • 8719 • No • 18 • 2173

Solomon Islands *Island group* Pacific Ocean 143
Solomon Plate *Tectonic plate* 143
Solomon Sea *Sea* Pacific Ocean 143 147 P2
Solothurn Switzerland 82 F9
Šolta *Island* Croatia 88 I7
Solway Coast *Area of Outstanding Natural Beauty* Scotland, United Kingdom 32 F8
Solway Firth *Inlet* England/Scotland, United Kingdom 17 F9 24 G8 29 K16
Solwezi Zambia 110 J13
Somali Basin *Undersea feature* Indian Ocean 101 114 E8 127
Somalia *Country* E Africa 105 L17

Somalia 105

1960 • Arabic and Somali • Somali shilling • 15 • 47 • 14 • 24.1 • N/A • 14300 • Yes • 26 •

Sombor Serbia, Yugoslavia 89 L3
Somerset *County* England, United Kingdom 19 J17
Somerset Island *Island* Nunavut, Canada 37 N5
Somes *River* Hungary/Romania 90 I3
Somme *River* France 77 K3
Somoto Nicaragua 56 D10
Son *River* India 131 M7
Sơn La Vietnam 138 L8
Sønderborg Denmark 70 I16
Søndre Strømfjord Greenland 65 M14
Songea Tanzania 111 O12
Songkhla Thailand 139 I16
Sonoran Desert *Desert* Mexico/USA 34 48 G9 51 M20
Soria Spain 75 L6
Sorong Indonesia 141 P11
Sørøya *Island* Norway 71 N1
Sorrento Italy 87 K13
Sosnowiec Poland 85 L8
Soûr Lebanon 121 M7
Souris River *River* Canada/USA 47 M4
Sousse Tunisia 103 N4
South Africa *Country* Southern Africa 112 I13

South Africa 112-113

1934 • Afrikaans and English • Rand • 33 • 55 • 16 • 84 • 100 • 1695 • No • 51 • 2695

South America *Continent* 54-55
South American Plate *Tectonic plate* 34 55 101
South Australia *State* Australia 147 K10
South Australian Basin *Undersea feature* Indian Ocean 143
South Ayrshire *Unitary authority* Scotland, United Kingdom 18 H10
South Bend Indiana, USA 45 M10
South Carolina *State* USA 43 O6
South China Basin *Undersea feature* Pacific Ocean 127
South China Sea *Sea* Pacific Ocean 114 M7 127 E7 135 L16 139 M16 140 144 143
South Dakota *State* USA 47 L7
South Downs *Hill range* England, United Kingdom 17 H14 21 O8
South East Cape *Headland* Tasmania, Australia 147 N16
South Esk *River* Scotland, United Kingdom 29 M12
South Fiji Basin *Undersea feature* Pacific Ocean 143
South Georgia *Island* South Georgia and the South Sandwich Islands 55 66 H16
South Gloucestershire *Unitary authority* England, United Kingdom 19 K16
South Indian Basin *Undersea feature* Indian Ocean 115 K15 143
South Island *Island* New Zealand 143 148 B12
South Korea *Country* E Asia 135 P8

South Korea 135

1948 • Korean • South Korean won • 471 • 72 • 15 • 97.2 • 165 • 784 • Yes • 81 • 3285

South Lanarkshire *Unitary authority* Scotland, United Kingdom 18 I10
South Lewis, Harris and North Uist *Area of Outstanding Natural Beauty* Scotland, United Kingdom 32 D5
South Luangwa *National Park* Zambia 111 M13
South Molton England, United Kingdom 20 I8
South Orkney Islands *Island group* Antarctica 64 B6 67 G16
South Platte River *River* Colorado/Nebraska, USA 49 N3
South Pole *Pole* Antarctica 64 E9
South Ronaldsay *Island* Scotland, United Kingdom 28 L6
South Sandwich Islands *Island group* South Georgia and the South Sandwich Islands 67 I16
South Sandwich Trench *Undersea feature* Atlantic Ocean 55
South Shetland Islands *Island group* Antarctica 64 B7 67 F16
South Shields England, United Kingdom 25 M7
South Tyne *River* England, United Kingdom 24 J8
South Tyneside *Unitary authority* England, United Kingdom 18 O7
South Uist *Island* Scotland, United Kingdom 17 C6 28 E10
South West Mainland *Area of Outstanding Natural Beauty* Scotland, United Kingdom 32 F2
Southampton England, United Kingdom 21 N8
Southampton, City of *Unitary authority* England, United Kingdom 19 L17
Southampton Island *Island* Nunavut, Canada 34 37 P8
Southeast Indian Ridge *Undersea feature* Indian Ocean 115 K14
Southeast Pacific Basin *Undersea feature* Pacific Ocean 145 N14
Southend-on-Sea England, United Kingdom 21 R6
Southend-on-Sea *Unitary authority* England, United Kingdom 19 O16
Southern Alps *Mountain range* New Zealand 143 148 D11
Southern Ocean *Ocean* 144 114 143
Southern Uplands *Mountain range* Scotland, United Kingdom 17 E8 29 J15 32 E8
Southport England, United Kingdom 24 H14
Southwark *London borough* England, United Kingdom 19 O20
Southwest Indian Ridge *Undersea feature* Indian Ocean 101 115 D14
Southwest Pacific Basin *Undersea feature* Pacific Ocean 145 K12
Southwold England, United Kingdom 23 T10
Sovetsk Russian Federation 94 G9
Sovetskaya Gavan' Russian Federation 129 Q10 144 G4
Soweto South Africa 113 L12
Sozopol Bulgaria 91 O13
Spain *Country* SW Europe 74 J7

Spain 74-77

1492 • Spanish, Galician, Basque and Catalan • Spanish peseta • 79 • 78 • 16 • 97.2 • 389 • 244 • No • 76 • 3708

Spalding England, United Kingdom 23 O8
Spanish Town Jamaica 56 J8
Sparks Nevada, USA 48 E3
Spartanburg South Carolina, USA 43 O6
Sparti Greece 92 I12
Spartivento, Capo *Headland* Italy 87 D16
Spencer Iowa, USA 47 P8
Spencer Gulf *Gulf* South Australia, Australia 147 K13
Spennymoor England, United Kingdom 25 L8
Sperrin Mountains *Mountain range* Northern Ireland, United Kingdom 17 D9
Spitsbergen *Island* Svalbard 65 R13 68
Spittal Austria 83 O9
Split Croatia 88 I7
Spokane Washington, USA 50 L6
Springfield Illinois, USA 45 K13
Springfield Massachusetts, USA 41 N10
Springfield Missouri, USA 47 R13
Springfield Ohio, USA 45 O12
Springfield Oregon, USA 50 H9
Spurn Head *Headland* England, United Kingdom 17 H10 23 O3 25 Q14
Squamish British Columbia, Canada 36 J15
Squillace, Golfo di *Gulf* Italy 87 N16
Srebrenica Bosnia and Herzegovina 89 L6
Sri Lanka *Country* S Asia 131 L15

Sri Lanka 131

1948 • Sinhala, Tamil and English • Sri Lanka rupee • 287 • 73 • 15 • 90.7 • 6 • 10000 • Yes • 22 • 2273

Sri Lanka *Island* S Asia 114 I7 117 127
Srinagar Pakistan 130 J2
Srinagarind Reservoir *Lake* Thailand 139 H12
Stafford England, United Kingdom 22 J8
Staffordshire *County* England, United Kingdom 19 K14
Staines England, United Kingdom 21 O6
Staithes England, United Kingdom 25 O9
Stalingrad *see* Volgograd
Stamford England, United Kingdom 23 N8
Stanhope England, United Kingdom 25 K8
Stanley England, United Kingdom 25 L8
Stanovoy Khrebet *Mountain range* Russian Federation 117 129 M10
Stans Switzerland 82 G10
Stara Zagora Bulgaria 91 L13
Starnberger See *Lake* Germany 81 J16
Start Bay *Bay* England, United Kingdom 20 I12
Start Point *Headland* England, United Kingdom 17 F15 20 I12
State College Pennsylvania, USA 40 I12
Stavanger Norway 66 K7 70 H11
Stavropol' Russian Federation 96 E15 128 D8
Steinkjer Norway 70 J7
Stendal Germany 80 J9
Sterling Colorado, USA 49 N3
Sterling Illinois, USA 45 K10
Sterling Heights Michigan, USA 45 O9
Steubenville Ohio, USA 45 Q11
Stevenage England, United Kingdom 21 P4
Stevens Point Wisconsin, USA 45 K7
Stewart Island *Island* New Zealand 148 C13
Steyr Austria 83 P6
Stickford England, United Kingdom 23 O6
Stillwater Minnesota, USA 44 H6
Štip FYR Macedonia 89 O11
Stirling *Unitary authority* Scotland, United Kingdom 18 H9
Stirling Scotland, United Kingdom 29 J13
Stockerau Austria 83 R4
Stockholm Sweden 71 L12
Stockport England, United Kingdom 25 K15
Stockport *Unitary authority* England, United Kingdom 18 C10
Stockton California, USA 51 I15
Stockton-on-Tees England, United Kingdom 25 L9
Stockton-on-Tees *Unitary authority* England, United Kingdom 18 N9
Stœng Trêng Cambodia 139 M13
Stoke *see* Stoke-on-Trent
Stoke-on-Trent England, United Kingdom 22 J7
Stoke-on-Trent, City of *Unitary authority* England, United Kingdom 19 K14
Stone England, United Kingdom 22 J7
Stonehaven Scotland, United Kingdom 29 N11
Stonehenge *Ancient monument* England, United Kingdom 21 L7
Stony Tunguska *River* Russian Federation 129 K9
Stornoway Scotland, United Kingdom 28 F7
Storsjön *Lake* Sweden 71 K8
Storuman Sweden 71 M6
Stour *River* England, United Kingdom 21 K8
Stourport-on-Severn England, United Kingdom 22 I10
Stowmarket England, United Kingdom 23 R11
Strabane Northern Ireland, United Kingdom 31 M4
Strabane *District* Northern Ireland, United Kingdom 19 E11
Stralsund Germany 80 L6
Strangford Lough *Inlet* Northern Ireland, United Kingdom 31 P5
Stranraer Scotland, United Kingdom 29 I16
Strasbourg France 77 Q5
Stratford *see* Stratford-upon-Avon
Stratford-upon-Avon England, United Kingdom 23 K11
Stromboli *Volcano* Italy 87 L16
Stromeferry Scotland, United Kingdom 28 H10
Stromness Scotland, United Kingdom 28 K6
Stronsay *Island* Scotland, United Kingdom 17 F3 28 M5
Stroud England, United Kingdom 21 L5
Struma *River* Bulgaria/Greece 90 H13
Strumble Head *Headland* Wales, United Kingdom 26 H11
Strumica FYR Macedonia 89 P12
Strymonas *River* Bulgaria/Greece 93 K2
Stupia *River* Poland 85 K2
Stuttgart Germany 81 G15
Stylida Greece 92 J7
Styr *River* Belarus/Ukraine 98 G3
Suakin Sudan 105 I11
Subotica Serbia, Yugoslavia 89 M2
Suck *River* Republic of Ireland 31 L8
Sucre Bolivia 59 J16
Sudan *Country* NE Africa 105 D11

Sudan 104-105

1956 • Arabic • Sudanese pound or dinar • 12 • 55 • 13 • 53.3 • 10 • 10000 • Yes • 25 • 2202

Sudbury Ontario, Canada 38 J12
Sudbury England, United Kingdom, S8 Q11
Sudd *Swamp region* Sudan 101 105 E15
Sudeten *Mountain range* Czech Republic/Poland 84 I8
Suez Egypt 114 D4
Suez Canal *Canal* Egypt 104 G6 114 D4
Suez, Gulf of *Gulf* Red Sea 104 G7 120 I13
Suffolk *County* England, United Kingdom 19 O15
Suffolk Coast and Heaths *Area of Outstanding Natural Beauty* England, United Kingdom 32 H11
Suhar Oman 123 O11
Sühbaatar Mongolia 133 M3
Suhl Germany 81 I12
Suir *River* Republic of Ireland 17 C12 31 L13
Sukabumi Indonesia 140 G15
Sukkur Pakistan 130 H5
Sula *River* Ukraine 98 J5
Sula, Kepulauan *Island group* Indonesia 141 N12
Sulaimān Range *Mountain range* Pakistan 127
Sulawesi *see* Celebes
Sulb Temple *Archaeological site* Sudan 104 F10
Sullana Peru 58 B10
Sulu Archipelago *Island group* Philippines 141 L9
Sulu Sea *Sea* Pacific Ocean 127 141 K8
Sumatra *Island* Indonesia 114 L8 127 140 D11 143
Sumba *Island* Indonesia 141 L16
Sumbawa *Island* Indonesia 141 K16
Sumbawabesar Indonesia 141 K15
Sumbawanga Tanzania 111 M10
Sumbe Angola 112 G5
Sumbu *National Park* Zambia 111 L10
Sumburgh Scotland, United Kingdom 28 O3
Sumburgh Head *Headland* Scotland, United Kingdom 17 G2 28 O3
Summer Lake *Lake* Oregon, USA 50 I10
Sumqayıt Azerbaijan 99 T13
Sumy Ukraine 99 K4
Sun City South Africa 113 L12
Sunbury Pennsylvania, USA 40 J12
Sunda Shelf *Undersea feature* Indian Ocean/Pacific Ocean 127 143
Sunderland *Unitary authority* England, United Kingdom 18 O7
Sunderland England, United Kingdom 25 M7
Sundsvall Sweden 71 L9
Suntar Russian Federation 129 M8
Sunyani Ghana 107 L12
Superior Wisconsin, USA 44 I4
Superior, Lake *Lake* Canada/USA 34 38 G11 45 K3
Sur Oman 123 P12
Surabaya Indonesia 140 I15
Surat India 130 I8
Surat Thani Thailand 139 H15
Sûre *River* NW Europe 79 L18
Surigao Philippines 141 N6
Surinam *Country* N South America 58 N7

Surinam 58

1975 • Dutch • Surinam gulden (guilder) or florin • 3 • 70 • 12 • 93.5 • 59 • 2500 • No • 50 • 2547

Surkhob *River* Tajikistan 125 O8
Surrey *County* England, United Kingdom 19 L17
Surrey Hills *Area of Outstanding Natural Beauty* England, United Kingdom 32 H12
Surt Libya 103 P7
Susquehanna River *River* New York/Pennsylvania, USA 40 J10
Sussex Downs *Area of Outstanding Natural Beauty* England, United Kingdom 32 H13
Sutton England, United Kingdom 21 P7
Sutton *London borough* England, United Kingdom 19 N20
Sutton Coldfield England, United Kingdom 23 K9
Sutton-on-Sea *Beach* England, United Kingdom 32 H10
Suva Fiji 144 J10
Suwałki Poland 85 O2
Svalbard *Dependent territory* Arctic Ocean 65 R12
Svay Riĕng Cambodia 139 M14
Svobodnyy Russian Federation 129 O10
Svyetlahorsk Belarus 95 M13
Swakopmund Namibia 112 G11
Swale *River* England, United Kingdom 17 G9 25 L10
Swanage *Beach* England, United Kingdom 32 G13

Date of independence • Language (official or most commonly spoken) • Currency • Population density per square kilometre • Average life expectancy • School-leaving age • Literacy • Number of cars per 1,000 people • Number of people per doctor • Death penalty • Percentage of urban-based population • Average number of calories consumed daily per person

Swanage England, United Kingdom 21 M10
Swansea Wales, United Kingdom 27 L14
Swansea *Unitary authority* Wales, United Kingdom 19 C17
Swansea Bay *Bay* Wales, United Kingdom 27 L14
Swaziland *Country* Southern Africa 113 M12

Swaziland 113

1968 • English and Swazi • Lilangeni • 57 • 60 • 13 • 77.5 • 61 • 18800 • Yes • 32 • 2706

Sweden *Country* N Europe 71 K11

Sweden 70-71

1809 • Swedish • Swedish krona • 22 • 79 • 15 • 99 • 418 • 333 • No • 83 • 2972

Sweetwater Texas, USA 49 P10
Swift Current Saskatchewan, Canada 37 M14
Swindon England, United Kingdom 21 L6
Swindon *Unitary authority* England, United Kingdom 19 K16
Swinford Republic of Ireland 30 J7
Switzerland *Country* W Europe 82 E10

Switzerland 82

1291 • French, German and Italian • Swiss franc • 184 • 79 • 16 • 99 • 469 • 323 • No • 61 • 3379

Sydney New South Wales, Australia 144 H12 147 O13
Sydney Nova Scotia, Canada 39 R11
Syktyvkar Russian Federation 96 K9 128 G6
Sylhet Bangladesh 131 P7
Sylt *Island* Germany 80 F5
Syowa *Japanese research station* Antarctica 64 F6
Syr Darya *River* C Asia 68 117 128 F13 127
Syracuse New York, USA 41 K9
Syracuse *see* Siracusa
Syria *Country* SW Asia121 N5

Syria 121

1946 • Arabic • Syrian pound • 85 • 69 • 12 • 71.6 • 10 • 1250 • Yes • 52 • 3175

Syrian Desert *Desert* SW Asia 68 117 121 O9 122 I5
Syros *Island* Greece 93 M11
Szczecin Poland 84 H3
Szeged Hungary 85 M15
Székesfehérvár Hungary 85 K14
Szekszárd Hungary 85 M15
Szolnok Hungary 85 M14
Szombathely Hungary 84 J14

T

Tabar Islands *Island group* Papua New Guinea 147 P1
Tabasco Mexico 53 L10
Table Bay *Bay* South Africa 112 I16
Table Mountain *Mountain* South Africa 112 I16
Tábor Czech Republic 84 H10
Tabora Tanzania 111 M8
Tabriz Iran 123 L2
Tabuk Philippines 122 G6
Tacloban Philippines 141 N5
Tacna Peru 59 G15
Tacoma Washington, USA 50 H7
Tacuarembó Uruguay 62 O9
Taegu South Korea 135 Q8
Taejŏn South Korea 135 P8
Tagula Island *Island* Papua New Guinea 147 P4
Tagus *River* Portugal/Spain 68 74 G9
Tahat *Mountain* Algeria 101
Tahiti *Island* French Polynesia 145 L10
Tahoe, Lake *Lake* California/Nevada, USA 48 E3 51 J14
Tahoua Niger 107 N8
Tai'an China 135 N8
Taieri *River* New Zealand 148 D11
Ta'if Saudi Arabia 122 H11
Tain Scotland, United Kingdom 28 J9
Taipei Taiwan 135 O13
Taiping Malaysia 139 I18
Taiping Ling *Mountain* China 127
Taiwan *Country* E Asia 135 O13

Taiwan 135

1949 • Mandarin Chinese • Taiwan dollar • 673 • 77 • 15 • 94 • 203 • 894 • Yes • 69 • N/A

Taiwan (var. Formosa) *Island* Taiwan 127
Taiwan Strait *Strait* China/Taiwan 127 135 N14
Taiyuan China 135 L7
Ta'izz Yemen 122 I16
Tajikistan *Country* C Asia 125 N8

Tajikistan 125

1991 • Tajik • Tajik rouble • 43 • 67 • 17 • 98.9 • 0 • 476 • Yes • 32 • N/A

Tak Thailand 139 H11
Takamatsu Japan 137 F12
Takev Cambodia 139 L14
Takla Makan Desert *Desert* China 117 127 132 F8
Talak *Desert Region* Niger 107 N7
Talas Kyrgyzstan 125 O5
Talaud, Kepulauan *Island group* Indonesia 141 O9
Talca Chile 63 G11
Talcahuano Chile 63 G12
Taldykorgan Kazakhstan 128 H13
Talgarth Wales, United Kingdom 27 O11
Tallahassee Florida, USA 43 M10
Tallinn Estonia 66 M7 94 J1
Tallow Republic of Ireland 31 L13
Talsi Latvia 94 H5
Tamabo, Banjaran *Mountain range* Borneo, Malaysia 140 J10
Tamale Ghana 107 L11
Tamanrasset Algeria 103 L11
Tamar *River* England, United Kingdom 20 G9
Tambacounda Senegal 106 G9
Tambov Russian Federation 96 G12 128 E7
Tameside *Unitary authority* England, United Kingdom 18 C10
Tampa Florida, USA 43 N12
Tampere Finland 71 O10
Tampico Mexico 53 O10
Tamworth New South Wales, Australia 147 O12
Tamworth England, United Kingdom 23 K9
Tan-Tan Morocco 102 G7
Tana Norway 71 O3
Tana, Lake *Lake* Ethiopia 101 105 I14
Tanami Desert *Desert* Northern Territory, Australia 143
Tanana River *River* Alaska, USA 36 H7
Tanega-shima *Island* Japan 137 D16
Tanga Tanzania 111 Q8
Tanganyika, Lake *Lake* E Africa 101 109 O14 111 L9
Tanggula Shan *Mountain range* China 132 I11
Tangier Morocco 102 I4
Tangra Yumco *Lake* China 132 I13
Tangshan China 135 N7
Tanimbar, Kepulauan *Island group* Indonesia 141 Q14
Tanjungpinang Indonesia 140 F11
Tanta Egypt 104 F6
Tanzam Railway *Railway* Tanzania 111 N10
Tanzania *Country* E Africa 111 L8

Tanzania 111

1961 • English and Swahili • Tanzanian shilling • 37 • 48 • 14 • 71.6 • 1 • 25000 • Yes • 24 • 2018

Taormina Italy 87 L17
Taos New Mexico, USA 49 M7
Tapachula Mexico 53 R15
Tapajós, Rio *River* Brazil 55 60 G8
Tapti *River* India 130 J8
Taranto Italy 87 O14
Taranto, Golfo di (Eng. Gulf of Taranto) *Gulf* Italy 87 N14
Taranto, Gulf of *see* Taranto, Golfo di
Tarawa *Atoll* Kiribati 144 J8
Tarbat Ness *Headland* Scotland, United Kingdom 28 K9
Tarbela Dam *Dam* Pakistan 130 J2
Tarbela Reservoir *Reservoir* Pakistan 130 J1
Tarbert Scotland, United Kingdom 28 F8
Tarbert Scotland, United Kingdom 29 H14
Tarbes France 76 J14
Taree New South Wales, Australia 147 O12
Târgovişte Romania 91 L8
Târgu Jiu Romania 90 I8
Târgu Mureş Romania 91 K4
Tarija Bolivia 59 J17
Tarim Basin *Basin* China 132 F8
Tarim He *River* China 132 G7
Tarn *River* France 77 L13
Tarnów Poland 85 N9
Tarragona Spain 75 P7
Tarsus Turkey 119 M10
Tartu Estonia 95 K3
Tartus Syria 121 M5
Tashkent Uzbekistan 125 N6
Tasiilaq Greenland 65 N15
Tasman Bay *Inlet* New Zealand 148 G7
Tasman Plateau *Undersea feature* Pacific Ocean 143
Tasman Sea *Sea* Pacific Ocean 144 H12 143 147 O15 148 C10
Tasmania *State* Australia 147 M16
Tasmania *Island* Australia 143
Tassili-n-Ajjer *Plateau* Algeria 101 103 M9
Tatlısu Cyprus 119 L11
Tatvan Turkey 119 R7
Tauern Tunnel *Tunnel* Austria 83 N9
Taunggyi Burma 138 G8
Taunton England, United Kingdom 20 J8
Taupo New Zealand 148 I5
Taupo, Lake *Lake* New Zealand 148 H5
Tauragė Lithuania 94 G8
Tauranga New Zealand 148 I4
Taurus Mountains *Mountain range* Turkey 68
Tavoy Burma 139 H12
Taw *River* England, United Kingdom 20 H8
Tawakoni, Lake *Reservoir* Texas, USA 49 R10
Tawau Borneo, Malaysia 141 K9
Tawitawi *Island* Philippines 141 L8
Taxco Mexico 53 N12
Tay *River* Scotland, United Kingdom 17 F7 29 K12
Tây Ninh Vietnam 139 M14
Tay, Firth of *Inlet* Scotland, United Kingdom 17 F7
Tay, Loch *Lake* Scotland, United Kingdom 17 E7
Taymyr, Ozero *Lake* Russian Federation 129 L5
Taymyr, Poluostrov *Peninsula* Russian Federation 65 T9 117 129 K5
Taz *River* Russian Federation 128 J7
Tbilisi Georgia 99 Q12
Tchibanga Gabon 109 F13
Te Anau, Lake *Lake* New Zealand 148 C11
Tébessa Algeria 103 M5
Tedzhen Turkmenistan 124 I9
Tedzhen *River* Afghanistan/Iran 124 J10
Tees *River* England, United Kingdom 17 G9 25 K9
Tegucigalpa Honduras 56 D9
Tehran Iran 123 N4
Tehuantepec Mexico 53 P14
Tehuantepec, Gulf of *Gulf* Caribbean Sea 53 P15
Teifi *River* Wales, United Kingdom 26 J11
Teignmouth England, United Kingdom 20 I10
Tekirdağ Turkey 118 G5
Tel Aviv-Yafo Israel 121 L9
Telford England, United Kingdom 22 I8
Telluride Colorado, USA 49 L5
Teluk Intan Malaysia 139 I18
Temuco Chile 63 G13
Tenby Wales, United Kingdom 26 I13
Tenby *Beach* Wales, United Kingdom 32 E12
Ténéré *Physical region* Niger 107 Q6
Tengiz, Ozero *Salt lake* Kazakhstan 128 G10
Tennessee *State* USA 34 43 K5
Tennessee River *River* USA 43 K4
Teotihuacán *Ruins* Mexico 53 N11
Tepic Mexico 53 K10
Tequila Mexico 53 K10
Teresina Brazil 60 L8
Termiz Uzbekistan 125 M10
Terneuzen Netherlands 79 F13
Terni Italy 87 I11
Ternopil' Ukraine 98 F5
Terrassa Spain 75 Q6
Terre Haute Indiana, USA 45 L13
Terschelling *Island* Netherlands 78 J6
Teruel Spain 75 N8
Test *River* England, United Kingdom 21 M8
Tete Mozambique 113 N7
Tétouan Morocco 102 I4
Tetovo FYR Macedonia 89 N10
Tevere *see* Tiber
Teviot *River* Scotland, United Kingdom 29 L15
Texas *State* USA 49 O11
Texas City Texas, USA 49 S13
Texel *Island* Netherlands 78 H7
Thac Ba, Lake *Lake* Vietnam 138 M8
Thai Nguyên Vietnam 138 M8
Thailand *Country* SE Asia 139 I11

Thailand 138-139

1782 • Thai • Baht • 119 • 69 • 15 • 94.7 • 28 • 4180 • Yes • 20 • 2432

Thailand, Gulf of *Gulf* South China Sea 114 L7 117 127 139 I14
Thakhèk Laos 138 L10
Thame England, United Kingdom 21 N5
Thames New Zealand 148 H4
Thames *River* England, United Kingdom 17 H13 21 P6
Thane India 130 I9
Thanh Hoa Vietnam 138 M9
Thar Desert *Desert* India/Pakistan 68 117 127 130 H5
Tharthar, Buhayrat ath *Lake* Iraq 123 K4
Thasos *Island* Greece 93 M3
Thatcham England, United Kingdom 21 N7
Thaton Burma 138 G10
Thayetmyo Burma 138 F9
The Borders *Unitary authority* Scotland, United Kingdom 18 J10
The Cairngorm Mountains *Area of Outstanding Natural Beauty* Scotland, United Kingdom 32 F6
The Cuillin Hills *Area of Outstanding Natural Beauty* Scotland, United Kingdom 32 D6
The Dalles Oregon, USA 50 I8
The Hague (Dut. 's-Gravenhage) Netherlands 78 G10
The Medway Towns *Unitary authority* England, United Kingdom 19 O16
The Pas Manitoba, Canada 37 N13
The Small Isles *Area of Outstanding Natural Beauty* Scotland, United Kingdom 32 D6
The Vale of Glamorgan *Unitary authority* Wales, United Kingdom 19 E18 27 N15
The Valley Anguilla 57 S10
The Wrekin *Unitary authority* England, United Kingdom 19 K14
Thebes *Archaeological site* Egypt 104 G8
Theodore Roosevelt Lake *Reservoir* Arizona, USA 48 J9
Thermaic Gulf *Gulf* Greece 92 J4
Thessaloniki *see* Salonica
Thetford England, United Kingdom 23 Q9
Thienen Belgium 79 I15
Thika Kenya 111 P5
Thimphu Bhutan 131 P6
Thionville France 77 O4
Thira *Island* Greece 93 N13
Thirsk England, United Kingdom 25 M11
Thohoyandou South Africa 113 M11
Thompson Manitoba, Canada 37 O12
Thornbury England, United Kingdom 21 K6
Thornhill Scotland, United Kingdom 29 K15
Thrace Greece 93 N2
Thun Switzerland 82 F10
Thunder Bay Ontario, Canada 38 G11
Thuner See *Lake* Switzerland 82 F11
Thuringia *Cultural region* Germany 81 I12
Thuringian Forest *Mountain range* Germany 81 I11
Thurles Republic of Ireland 31 L12
Thurrock *Unitary authority* England, United Kingdom 19 N16
Thurso Scotland, United Kingdom 28 K7
Tianjin China 135 M7 144 E5
Tiaret Algeria 103 K5
Tiber (It. Tevere) *River* Italy 68 87 H11
Tiberias, Lake (var. Sea of Galilee) *Lake* Israel 121 M8
Tibesti *Mountain range* N Africa 101 109 I4
Tibet *Cultural region* China 132 H12
Tibet, Plateau of *Plateau* E Asia 117 127
Tiburón, Isla *Island* Mexico 52 G4
Tidjikja Mauritania 106 H6
Tien Shan *Mountain range* C Asia 68 117 125 Q6 127 132 F7
Tierra del Fuego *Island* Argentina/Chile 55 63 J20
Tighina Moldova 98 H8
Tigris *River* Iraq/Turkey 68 114 E4 117 119 Q8 121 T1 123 K3 127
Tikal *Archaeological site* Guatemala 56 C6
Tikrit Iraq 123 K4
Tiksi Russian Federation 65 T7 129 N5
Tilburg Netherlands 79 I12
Tillabéri Niger 107 M9
Timaru New Zealand 148 E11
Timbuktu Mali 107 K8
Timgad Algeria 103 M5
Timirist, Râs *Headland* Mauritania 106 F6
Timiş *River* Romania 90 H6
Timişoara Romania 90 G6
Timmins Ontario, Canada 38 J11
Timor *Island* Indonesia 127 141 N16 143
Timor Sea *Sea* Indian Ocean 141 N16 143 146 H5
Tindouf Algeria 102 H8
Tinos *Island* Greece 93 M10
Tipperary Republic of Ireland 31 L13
Tirana Albania 89 M12
Tiraspol Moldova 98 H8
Tiree *Island* Scotland, United Kingdom 17 D7 29 F12
Tirso *River* Italy 87 D14
Tiruchchirappalli India 131 K14
Tisza *River* C Europe 68 85 N12
Titicaca, Lake *Lake* Bolivia/Peru 55 59 H14
Tiverton England, United Kingdom 20 I9
Tiznit Morocco 102 G7
Tlaxcala Mexico 53 N12
Tlemcen Algeria 102 J5
Toamasina Madagascar 114 E10
Toba Kakar Range *Mountain range* Pakistan 130 G3
Toba, Danau *Lake* Indonesia 140 D10
Tobago *Island* Trinidad and Tobago 34 55 57 T16
Tobermory Scotland, United Kingdom 29 G12
Tobruk Libya 103 R6
Tocantins, Rio *River* Brazil 55 60 J10
Tocopilla Chile 62 F5
Togian, Kepulauan *Island group* Indonesia 141 M11
Togo *Country* W Africa 107 M12

Togo 107

1960 • French • Franc de la Communauté financière africaine • 83 • 49 • 12 • 53.2 • 19 • 10000 • No • 31 • 2242

Tokara-retto *Island Group* Japan 137 B17
Tokat Turkey 119 N6
Tokelau *Dependent territory* Pacific Ocean 144 J9
Tokmak Kyrgyzstan 125 Q5
Tokuno-shima *Island* Japan 137 B19
Tokushima Japan 137 G13
Tokyo Japan 137 K11
Toledo Spain 75 K9
Toledo Ohio, USA 45 O10
Toledo Bend Reservoir *Reservoir* Louisiana/Texas, USA 49 T11
Toliara Madagascar 115 E11
Tolmin Slovenia 83 O11
Tol'yatti Russian Federation 97 I12 128 F8
Tomakomai Japan 136 L4
Tomé Chile 63 G12
Tomini, Gulf of *Bay* Indonesia 141 L11
Tomintoul Scotland, United Kingdom 29 L10
Tomsk Russian Federation 128 J10
Tonga *Country* Pacific Ocean 144 J10

Tonga 144

1970 • English and Tongan • Pa'anga (Tongan dollar) • 135 • 70 • 14 • 99 • 2 • 2176 • No • 42 • 2946

Tonga *Island group* Pacific Ocean 143
Tonga Trench *Undersea feature* Pacific Ocean 143
Tongking, Gulf of *Gulf* South China Sea 127 135 K15 138 N9
Tongliao China 133 Q5
Tongtian He *River* China 132 J11
Tongue Scotland, United Kingdom 28 J7
Tonle Sap *Lake* Cambodia 139 L13
Tooele Utah, USA 48 J3
Toowoomba Queensland, Australia 147 O10
Topeka Kansas, USA 47 P12
Tor Bay *Bay* England, United Kingdom 17 F14 20 I11
Torbay *Unitary authority* England, United Kingdom 19 I18
Torbay *Beach* England, United Kingdom 32 F13
Torfaen *Unitary authority* Wales, United Kingdom 19 F17
Torhout Belgium 79 D14
Torino *see* Turin
Torkestan Mountains *Mountain range* Afghanistan 125 K11
Torneälven *River* Finland/Sweden 71 N4
Torneträsk *Lake* Sweden 71 N3
Tornio Finland 71 O6
Toronto Ontario, Canada 39 K14
Torquay England, United Kingdom 20 I10
Torremolinos Spain 74 J14
Torrens, Lake *Salt lake* South Australia, Australia 143 147 K11
Torreón Mexico 53 L7
Torres del Paine *National Park* Chile 63 I19
Torres Strait *Strait* Australia/Papua New Guinea 143 147 M4
Torridge *River* England, United Kingdom 20 H9
Torridon, Loch *Inlet* Scotland, United Kingdom 28 G9
Torrington Wyoming, USA 47 P9
Toruń Poland 85 L4
Tory Island *Island* Republic of Ireland 31 L2
Tory Sound *Sound* Republic of Ireland 31 L2
Toscano, Arcipelago (Eng. Tuscan Archipelago) *Island group* Italy 87 E11
Totternish *Area of Outstanding Natural Beauty* Scotland, United Kingdom 32 D5
Tottori Japan 137 F11
Toubkal, Jbel *Mountain* Morocco 101
Touggourt Algeria 103 M6
Toulon France 77 P14
Toulouse France 77 K14
Toungoo Burma 138 G9
Tournai Belgium 79 E16
Tours France 76 J7
Towcester England, United Kingdom 23 M11
Tower Hamlets *London borough* England, United Kingdom 19 O20
Townsville Queensland, Australia 147 N7
Towuti, Danau *Lake* Indonesia 141 M12
Toyama Japan 136 I10
Toyama-wan *Bay* Japan 136 I10
Tozeur Tunisia 103 M5
Trabzon (Eng. Trebizond) Turkey 119 P5
Trafford *Unitary authority* England, United Kingdom 18 C10
Tralee Republic of Ireland 30 I12
Tralee Bay *Bay* Republic of Ireland 30 H12
Trang Thailand 139 H16
Trans-Canada Highway *Road* Canada 36 I15
Transantarctic Mountains *Mountain range* Antarctica 64 D8
Transylvania *Cultural region* Romania 90 H5
Transylvanian Alps *Mountain range* Romania 68 90 H7
Trapani Italy 87 I17
Trasimeno, Lago *Lake* Italy 86 H10
Traun Austria 83 P5
Traun, Lake *Lake* Austria 83 O6
Traverse City Michigan, USA 45 M6
Travis, Lake *Reservoir* Texas, USA 49 Q12
Trawsfynydd Wales, United Kingdom 27 L4
Trbovlje Slovenia 83 R11
Trearddur Bay *Beach* Wales, United Kingdom 32 E10
Trebinje Bosnia and Herzegovina 89 K9
Trebizond *see* Trabzon
Treffgarne Wales, United Kingdom 26 H12
Tregaron Wales, United Kingdom 27 L9
Treinta y Tres Uruguay 62 P9
Trelew Argentina 63 K14
Tremadog Bay *Bay* Wales, United Kingdom 27 K5

Tremiti, Isole *Island group* Italy 87 L11
Trenčín Slovakia 85 K11
Trent *River* England, United Kingdom 17 G11 23 M3
Trento Italy 86 G6
Trenton New Jersey, USA 41 L13
Treorchy Wales, United Kingdom 27 N13
Tres Arroyos Argentina 63 M12
Tres Marías, Islas *Island group* Mexico 52 J10
Tretower Wales, United Kingdom 27 O12
Treviso Italy 86 H6
Trichonis, Limni *Lake* Greece 92 H8
Trier Germany 81 D13
Trieste Italy 86 J6
Trikala Greece 92 H6
Trincomalee Sri Lanka 114 I7 131 L15
Trindade, Ilha da *Island* Brazil 67 I13
Trinidad Bolivia 59 J14
Trinidad *Island* Trinidad and Tobago 34 55 57 S16
Trinidad and Tobago *Country* West Indies 57 S16

Trinidad and Tobago 57

1962 • a English • Trinidad and Tobago dollar • 253 • 74 • 12 • 97.8 • 94 • 1429 • Yes • 72 • 2585

Trinity River *River* Texas, USA 49 R11
Tripoli Greece 92 I10
Tripoli Lebanon 121 M6
Tripoli Libya 103 O6
Tripolitania Libya 103 N7
Tristan da Cunha *Dependent territory* Atlantic Ocean 67 J14
Trivandrum India 130 J15
Trnava Slovakia 85 K12
Trois-Rivières Quebec, Canada 39 M12
Trollhättan Sweden 70 J13
Tromsø Norway 71 M2
Trondheim Norway 70 J8
Troon Scotland, United Kingdom 29 I14
Trowbridge England, United Kingdom 21 L7
Troy *Archaeological site* Turkey 118 G6
Troyes France 77 M6
Trujillo Honduras 56 E8
Trujillo Peru 59 C11
Trujillo Venezuela 58 G5
Truro Nova Scotia, Canada 39 Q12
Truro England, United Kingdom 20 F11
Trwyn Cilan *Headland* Wales, United Kingdom 26 J5
Tsaritsyn *see* Volgograd
Tsavo Kenya 111 P6
Tsetserleg Mongolia 133 L5
Tshikapa Dem. Rep. Congo (Zaire) 109 K15
Tshuapa *River* Dem. Rep. Congo (Zaire) 109 K12
Tsimlyanskoye Vodokhranilishche *Reservoir* Russian Federation 96 F14
Tsugaru-kaikyo *Strait* Japan 136 K5
Tsumeb Namibia 112 H9
Tsushima *Island group* Japan 137 B13
Tuam Republic of Ireland 31 K8
Tuamotu Islands *Island group* French Polynesia 145 M10
Tübingen Germany 81 G15
Tucson Arizona, USA 48 J10
Tucupita Venezuela 58 K5
Tucuruí, Represa de *Reservoir* Brazil 60 J8
Tudmur Syria 121 N5
Tugela *River* South Africa 113 M13
Tuguegarao Philippines 141 L2
Tukangbesi, Kepulauan *Island group* Indonesia 141 N14
Tuktoyaktuk Northwest Territories, Canada 36 J6
Tula Russian Federation 96 F11 128 E6
Tulcea Romania 91 P7
Tullamore Republic of Ireland 31 M9
Tullow Republic of Ireland 31 N11
Tulsa Oklahoma, USA 47 P14
Tulsk Republic of Ireland 31 L7
Tummel *River* Scotland, United Kingdom 29 K11
Tunceli Turkey 119 P7
Tundzha *River* Bulgaria/Turkey 91 M14
Tungaru *Island group* Kiribati 144 J9 143
Tunis Tunisia 103 N4
Tunisia *Country* N Africa 103 N6

Tunisia 103

1956 • a Arabic • Tunisian dinar • 61 • 70 • 16 • 67 • 30 • 1667 • Yes • 57 • 3330

Tunja Colombia 58 F6
Tupungato, Volcán *Volcano* Argentina 55
Turan Lowland *Plain* C Asia 124 I6
Turin (It. Torino) Italy 86 B7
Turkey *Country* SW Asia 118 I7

Turkey 118-119

1923 • a Turkish • Turkish lira • 85 • 69 • 14 • 83.2 • 59 • 909 • Yes • 69 • 3429

Turkmenbashi Turkmenistan 124 F6
Turkmenistan *Country* C Asia 124 G7

Turkmenistan 124-125

1991 • a Turkmen • Manat • 9 • 65 • 17 • 98 • N/A • 313

Turks and Caicos Islands *Dependent territory* West Indies 57 N6
Turks Islands *Island group* Turks and Caicos Islands 55 57 N6
Turku Finland 71 N11
Turnhout Belgium 79 I13
Turpan China 132 I7
Turpan Pendi *Depression* China 127
Tursunzoda Tajikistan 125 M9
Turtkul Uzbekistan 124 J6
Tuscan Archipelago *see* Toscana, Archipelago
Tuscany *Cultural region* Italy 86 F9
Tuvalu *Country* Pacific Ocean 144 J9

Tuvalu 144

1978 • a English • Australian dollar and Tuvaluan dollar • 377 • 64 • 14 • 95 • N/A • 2767 • No • 40 • N/A

Tuxpán Mexico 53 O11
Tuxtla Mexico 53 Q14
Tuz, Lake *Lake* Turkey 68 119 L7
Tuzla Bosnia and Herzegovina 89 L5
Tver' Russian Federation 96 F10 128 E6
Tweed *River* England/Scotland, United Kingdom 17 F8 25 K3 29 L14
Tweedmouth England, United Kingdom 25 K13
Twin Falls Idaho, USA 46 G9
Tyler Texas, USA 49 S10
Tyne *River* England, United Kingdom 17 G9
Tynemouth England, United Kingdom 25 M7
Tyrella *Beach* Northern Ireland, United Kingdom 32 E9
Tyrrhenian Sea *Sea* Mediterranean Sea 68 87 F13
Tyumen' Russian Federation 128 H9
Tywi *River* Wales, United Kingdom 27 L12
Tywyn Wales, United Kingdom 27 L7

Ubangi *River* C Africa 101 109 J10
Uberlândia Brazil 61 K13
Ubon Ratchathani Thailand 139 L12
Ucayali, Río *River* Peru 55 59 E11
Uchiura-wan *Bay* Japan 136 K5
Uchquduq Uzbekistan 125 K5
Uckfield England, United Kingdom 21 Q8
Uddevalla Sweden 70 J13
Uddjaur *Lake* Sweden 71 M5
Udine Italy 86 I6
Udon Thani Thailand 138 K10
Uele *River* Dem. Rep. Congo (Zaire) 109 M11
Ufa Russian Federation 96 K13 128 G8
Uganda *Country* E Africa 111 M4

Uganda 111

1962 • a English and Swahili • New Uganda shilling • 106 • 40 • N/A • 64 • 2 • 25000 • Yes • 13 • 2159

Úhlava *River* Czech Republic 84 G10
Uig Scotland, United Kingdom 28 F9
Uíge Angola 112 G3
Ujungpandang Indonesia 141 L14
Ukmergė Lithuania 94 I9
Ukraine *Country* E Europe 98 H6

Ukraine 98-99

1991 • a Ukrainian • Hryvnia • 84 • 69 • 15 • 99 • 96 • 227 • Yes • 70 • N/A

Ulaangom Mongolia 132 J4
Ulan Bator Mongolia 133 M4
Ulan-Ude Russian Federation 129 M11
Ulanhot China 133 Q4
Uldz *River* Mongolia 133 O3
Uliastay Mongolia 133 K5
Ullapool Scotland, United Kingdom 28 I8
Ullswater *Lake* England, United Kingdom 24 I9
Ulm Germany 81 H15
Uluru (var. Ayers Rock) *Rocky outcrop* Northern Territory, Australia 143 146 J10
Ulverston England, United Kingdom 24 H11
Ul'yanovsk Russian Federation 97 I12 128 F7
Umeå Sweden 71 M8
Umeälven *River* Sweden 71 M7
Umnak Island *Island* Alaska, USA 36 B8
Umtata South Africa 113 L15
Una *River* Bosnia and Herzegovina/Croatia 88 H4
Unalaska Island *Island* Alaska, USA 36 C8
Ungava Bay *Bay* Quebec, Canada 39 N4
Unimak Island *Island* Alaska, USA 36 C8
Uniontown Pennsylvania, USA 40 G14
United Arab Emirates *Country* SW Asia 123 M11

United Arab Emirates 123

1971 • a Arabic • UAE dirham • 29 • 75 • 12 • 74.8 • 82 • 1250 • Yes • 84 • 3384

United Kingdom *Country* NW Europe 19 H11

United Kingdom 17-32

1707 • a English, Welsh (in Wales) • Pound sterling • 243 • 77 • 16 • 99 • 371 • 667 • No • 89 • 3317

United States of America (var. USA) *Country* North America 40-51

United States of America 40-51

1776 • a English • United States dollar • 30 • 77 • 16 • 99 • 489 • 400 • Yes • 76 • 3732

Unst *Island* Scotland, United Kingdom 17 G1 28 P1
Ünye Turkey 119 N5
Upernavik Greenland 65 N13
Upington South Africa 112 J13
Upper Klamath Lake *Lake* Oregon, USA 51 H11
Upper Lough Erne *Lake* Republic of Ireland/United Kingdom 17 C10 31 M6
Upper Red Lake *Lake* Minnesota, USA 44 G3
Upper Tweeddale *Area of Outstanding Natural Beauty* Scotland, United Kingdom 32 F7
Uppsala Sweden 71 L11
Ur *Site of ancient city* Iraq 123 K6
Ural *River* Kazakhstan/Russian Federation 68 128 E9
Ural Mountains *Mountain range* Kazakhstan/Russian Federation 68 96 L13 117 128 F9 127
Ural'sk Kazakhstan 128 F9
Uranium City Saskatchewan, Canada 37 M11
Urawa Japan 137 K11
Ure *River* England, United Kingdom 25 L11
Urgench Uzbekistan 124 J6
Urmia, Lake *Lake* Iran 68 123 L2
Uroševac Serbia, Yugoslavia 89 N10
Uroteppa Tajikistan 125 N7
Uruapan Mexico 53 L12
Uruguay *Country* E South America 62 N9

Uruguay 62

1828 • a Spanish • Uruguayan peso • 19 • 74 • 14 • 97.5 • 158 • 313 • No • 90 • 2750

Uruguay *River* South America 55 61 H15 62 N8
Urumqi China 132 H6
USA *see* United States of America
Usa *River* Russian Federation 96 M8
Usak Turkey 118 I7
Ushuaia Argentina 63 K20
Usk Wales, United Kingdom 27 P13
Usk *River* Wales, United Kingdom 27 P14
Ussuri *River* China/Russian Federation 129 Q11
Ust'-Chaun Russian Federation 129 P3
Ust'-Ilimsk Russian Federation 129 L10
Ust'-Kamchatsk Russian Federation 129 R6
Ust'-Kamenogorsk Kazakhstan 129 I11
Ustica Italy 87 I16
Ústínad Labem Czech Republic 84 H8
Ustyurt Plateau *Plateau* Kazakhstan/Uzbekistan 68 124 H3
Utah *State* USA 48 I4
Utah Lake *Lake* Utah, USA 48 J3
Utena Lithuania 94 J8
Utica New York, USA 41 K9
Utrecht Netherlands 78 I10
Utsunomiya Japan 136 K10
Uttaradit Thailand 138 I10
Uttoxeter England, United Kingdom 22 J7
Uura *Area of Outstanding Natural Beauty* Scotland, United Kingdom 32 E7
Uvira Dem. Rep. Congo (Zaire) 109 O14
Uvs Nuur *Lake* Mongolia/Russian Federation 132 J3
Uwajima Japan 137 E14
Uxmal *Ruins* Mexico 53 S11
Uyuni Bolivia 59 I16
Uzbekistan *Country* C Asia 124 J5

Uzbekistan 124-125

1991 • a Uzbek • Som • 53 • 68 • 17 • 99 • N/A 301 • Yes • 41 • N/A

Uzgen Kyrgyzstan 125 P7
Uzhhorod Ukraine 98 E6

V

Vaal *River* South Africa 113 K13
Vaasa Finland 71 N8
Vacaville California, USA 51 H14
Vadodara India 130 I8
Vadsø Norway 71 P1
Vaduz Liechtenstein 82 I9
Váh *River* Slovakia 85 L10
Vail Colorado, USA 49 M4
Vakh *River* Russian Federation 128 J8
Val-d'Or Quebec, Canada 39 K11
Valdés, Península *Peninsula* Argentina 63 K14
Valdez Alaska, USA 36 G8
Valdosta Georgia, USA 43 N10
Valence France 77 O11
Valencia Spain 75 N9
Valencia Venezuela 58 H4
Valencia *Region* Spain 75 M10
Valencia Island *Island* Republic of Ireland 30 H14
Valenciennes France 77 M2
Valentine Nebraska, USA 47 M9
Valga Estonia 95 K4
Valjevo Serbia, Yugoslavia 89 M6
Valkeakoski Finland 71 O10
Valladolid Spain 74 J6
Valledupar Colombia 58 F4
Vallenar Chile 62 G8
Valletta Malta 87 K20
Valley of the Kings *Ancient monument* Egypt 104 G8
Valmiera Latvia 94 J4
Valparaíso Chile 62 G10 145 Q11
Van Turkey 119 S7
Van, Lake *Salt lake* Turkey 68 119 R7
Vanadzor Armenia 99 Q13
Vancouver British Columbia, Canada 36 J15 145 M4
Vancouver Washington, USA 50 H8
Vancouver Island *Island* British Columbia, Canada 34 36 I14
Vandenburg Air Force Base *Military base* California, USA 51 I18
Vänern *Lake* Sweden 68 71 K12
Vanimo Papua New Guinea 147 M1
Vannes France 76 G7
Vanuatu *Country* Pacific Ocean 144 I10

Vanuatu 144

1980 • a Bislama, English and French • Vatu • 16 • 67 • 12 • 64 • 6 • 14100 • No • 19 • 2739

Vanuatu *Island group* Pacific Ocean 143
Varanasi India 131 M7
Varangerfjorden *Fjord* Norway 71 Q1
Varano, Lago di *Lake* Italy 87 M12
Varaždin Croatia 88 I2
Varberg Sweden 70 J14
Vardar *River* FYR Macedonia/Greece 89 P12 92 J2
Vardø Norway 71 P1
Varkaus Finland 71 P9
Varna Bulgaria 91 O11
Vaslui Romania 91 N4
Västerås Sweden 71 L12
Västervik Sweden 71 L13
Vatican City *Country* S Europe 87 H12

Vatican City 87

1929 • a Italian and Latin • Lira and Italian lira • 2273 • 78 • N/A 99 • N/A • No • 100 • 3561

Vättern *Lake* Sweden 68 71 K13
Vawkavysk Belarus 94 I12
Växjö Sweden 71 K14
Vaygach, Ostrov *Island* Russian Federation 96 N6
Vega *Island* Norway 71 K5
Vegoritis, Limni *Lake* Greece 92 I3
Vejle Denmark 70 I15
Velenje Slovenia 83 R10
Veles FYR Macedonia 89 O11
Velika Plana Serbia, Yugoslavia 89 N6
Velingrad Bulgaria 90 J14
Velsen-Noord Netherlands 78 H9
Venezia *see* Venice
Venezuela *Country* N South America 58 H6

Venezuela S America 58

1821 • a Spanish and Amerindian languages • Bolívar • 27 • 72 • 15 • 92 • 68 • 625 • No • 93 • 2618

Venezuela, Gulf of *Gulf* Venezuela 58 G4
Venezuelan Basin *Undersea feature* Caribbean Sea 55
Venice (It. Venezia) Italy 86 H7
Venice, Gulf of *Gulf* Mediterranean Sea 86 I7
Venlo Netherlands 79 L13
Ventspils Latvia 94 G5
Ventura California, USA 51 J18
Vera Argentina 62 L8
Veracruz Mexico 53 O12
Verde, Cape *Headland* Bahamas 67 I11
Verdun France 77 N4
Vereeniging South Africa 113 L12
Verkhoyanskiy Khrebet *Mountain range* Russian Federation 117 129 N6
Vermont *State* USA 41 M8
Vernon British Columbia, Canada 37 K15
Vernon Texas, USA 49 P9
Veroia Greece 92 I3
Verona Italy 86 G7
Versailles France 77 L5
Verviers Belgium 79 K16
Vesoul France 77 O7
Vesterålen *Island group* Norway 71 L3
Vestfjorden *Fjord* Norway 71 L3
Veszprém Hungary 85 K14
Vetluga *River* Russian Federation 96 O10
Veurne Belgium 79 C14
Viana do Castelo Portugal 74 F6
Vianden Luxembourg 79 L18
Viareggio Italy 86 F9
Vicenza Italy 86 G7
Vichy France 77 M9
Victoria British Columbia, Canada 36 J15
Victoria Seychelles 114 F9
Victoria *River* Northern Territory, Australia 143
Victoria *State* Australia 147 M14
Victoria Falls Zimbabwe 113 K8
Victoria Falls *Waterfall* Zambia/Zimbabwe 101 110 J16
Victoria Island *Island* Northwest Territories/Nunavut, Canada 34 36 L6
Victoria Land *Physical region* Antarctica 64 E11
Victoria Nile *River* Uganda 111 M3
Victoria River *River* Northern Territory, Australia 146 J6
Victoria, Lake *Lake* E Africa 101 111 M5
Vidin Bulgaria 90 H10
Viedma Argentina 63 L13
Viedma, Lago *Lake* Argentina 63 I18
Vienna (Ger. Wien) Austria 83 S4
Vientiane Laos 138 K10
Vierwaldstätter See *Lake* Switzerland 82 G10
Viêt Tri Vietnam 138 M8
Vietnam *Country* SE Asia 138 M9

Vietnam 138-139

1954 • a Vietnamese • Dông • 242 • 67 • 11 • 91.9 • N/A • 2417 • Yes • 21 • 2250

Vigan Philippines 141 L3
Vigo Spain 74 F5
Vijayawada India 131 L11
Vijosës, Lumi i *River* Albania/Greece 89 M14
Vikna *Island* Norway 70 J6
Viljandi Estonia 94 J3
Villa María Argentina 62 K9
Villach Austria 83 O10
Villahermosa Mexico 53 Q13
Villarrica Paraguay 62 N6
Villarrica, Volcán *Volcano* Chile 55
Villavicencio Colombia 58 F7
Vilnius Lithuania 94 J10
Vilyuy *River* Russian Federation 129 N7
Viña del Mar Chile 62 G10
Vincennes Indiana, USA 45 L14
Vincennes Bay *Bay* Antarctica 64 G10
Vinderälven *River* Sweden 71 M6
Vineland New Jersey, USA 41 K14
Vinh Vietnam 138 M10
Vinnytsya Ukraine 98 H5
Virgin Islands (US) *Dependent territory* West Indies (US) 57 R9
Virgin Islands *see* British Virgin Islands
Virginia Minnesota, USA 44 I3
Virginia *State* USA 43 Q4
Virovitica Croatia 88 J3
Virtsu Estonia 94 I3
Vis *Island* Croatia 88 I8

Date of independence • a Language (official or most commonly spoken) • Currency • Population density per square kilometre • Average life expectancy • School-leaving age • Literacy • Number of cars per 1,000 people • Number of people per doctor • Death penalty • Percentage of urban-based population • Average number of calories consumed daily per person

Visakhapatnam India 114 J6 131 M11
Visayan Sea *Sea* Philippines 141 M5
Visby Sweden 71 L14
Viscount Melville Sound *Sound* Northwest Territories/Nunavut, Canada 37 L5
Viseu Portugal 74 G7
Visoko Bosnia and Herzegovina 89 K6
Vistula (Pol. Wisła) *River* Poland 68 85 L2
Vitim *River* Russian Federation 129 M9
Vitória Brazil 61 M13
Vitoria-Gasteiz Spain 75 L4
Vitsyebsk Belarus 95 N9
Vladikavkaz Russian Federation 96 E16 128 C9
Vladimir Russian Federation 96 G10 128 E6
Vladivostok Russian Federation 129 Q12 144 F5
Vlieland *Island* Netherlands 78 I6
Vlissingen Netherlands 79 E13
Vlorë Albania 89 L13
Vöcklabruck Austria 83 O6
Vohimena, Tanjona *Headland* Madagascar 115 E11
Voinjama Liberia 106 I12
Volga *River* Russian Federation 68 97 G14 127
Volgograd (prev. Stalingrad, Tsaritsyn) Russian Federation 97 F14 128 D8
Vologda Russian Federation 96 H9 128 F6
Volos Greece 92 J6
Volta, Lake *Reservoir* Ghana 101 107 L12
Voring Plateau *Undersea feature* Atlantic Ocean 68
Vorkuta Russian Federation 96 O7 128 I6
Vormsi *Island* Estonia 94 H2
Voronezh Russian Federation 97 F12 128 D7
Võrtsjärv *Lake* Estonia 95 K3
Võru Estonia 95 K4
Vosges *Mountain range* France 77 P6
Vostochnyy Russian Federation 129 Q9
Vostok *Russian research station* Antarctica 64 F9
Vratsa Bulgaria 90 I12
Vrbas *River* Bosnia and Herzegovina 88 J4
Vršac Serbia, Yugoslavia 89 O4
Vryburg South Africa 113 K12
Vukovar Croatia 89 L4
Vulcano *Island* Italy 87 L17
Vulci Italy 87 G11
Vyatka *River* Russian Federation 96 J11

Wa Ghana 107 K11
Waal *River* Netherlands 78 J11
Waalwijk Netherlands 79 I12
Wabash River *River* USA 45 L12
Waco Texas, USA 49 R11
Wad Medani Sudan 105 G13
Waddenzee *Sea* Netherlands 78 I7
Wadebridge England, United Kingdom 20 F10
Wadi Halfa Sudan 104 F10
Wagga Wagga New South Wales, Australia 147 N13
Waigeo, Pulau *Island* Indonesia 141 P11
Waipapakauri New Zealand 148 G2
Wairau *River* New Zealand 148 G8
Waitaki *River* New Zealand 148 E11
Wajir Kenya 111 Q3
Wakasa-wan *Bay* Japan 137 G11
Wakatipu, Lake *Lake* New Zealand 148 C11
Wakayama Japan 137 G12
Wake Island *Dependent territory* Pacific Ocean 144 I7
Wakefield England, United Kingdom 25 M14
Wakefield *Unitary authority* England, United Kingdom 19 L13
Wakkanai Japan 136 K2
Wałbrzych Poland 84 J8
Wales *National region* United Kingdom 19 I15 32 F11
Walker Lake *Lake* Nevada, USA 48 F4
Walla Walla Washington, USA 50 K8
Wallasey England, United Kingdom 22 G5
Wallis and Futuna *Dependent territory* Pacific Ocean 144 I9
Walney, Isle of *Island* England, United Kingdom 24 H12
Walsall England, United Kingdom 22 J9
Walsall *Unitary authority* England, United Kingdom 19 O11
Waltham Forest *London borough* England, United Kingdom 19 O18
Walvis Bay Namibia 112 G11
Walvis Bay *Bay* Namibia 67 M13
Walvis Ridge *Undersea feature* Atlantic Ocean 67 K14 101
Wandsworth *London borough* England, United Kingdom 19 O20
Wanganui New Zealand 148 H6
Wanxian China 135 K10
Warminster England, United Kingdom 21 L7
Warrington England, United Kingdom 22 H5
Warrington *Unitary authority* England, United Kingdom 19 K13
Warrnambool Victoria, Australia 147 L15
Warsaw (Pol. Warszawa) Poland 85 N5
Warszawa *see* Warsaw
Warta *River* Poland 84 I5
Wartburg Germay 81 H11
Warwick England, United Kingdom 23 K11
Warwickshire *County* England, United Kingdom 19 L15
Wash, The *Inlet* England, United Kingdom 17 H11 23 P7
Washington England, United Kingdom 25 L7
Washington Pennsylvania, USA 40 G13
Washington *State* USA 50 H7
Waterbury Connecticut, USA 41 M11
Waterford Republic of Ireland 31 N13
Waterford *County* Republic of Ireland 19 D15
Waterloo Iowa, USA 47 R8
Watertown New York, USA 41 K7
Watertown South Dakota, USA 47 O7
Waterville Maine, USA 41 P6
Waterville Republic of Ireland 30 H14
Watford England, United Kingdom 21 P5
Watson Lake Yukon Territory, Canada 36 J10
Wau Sudan 105 E15
Waukegan Illinois, USA 45 L9
Wausau Wisconsin, USA 45 K6
Wauwatosa Wisconsin, USA 45 L8
Waveney *River* England, United Kingdom 23 S9
Wawa Ontario, Canada 38 I11
Wda *River* Poland 85 K3
Weald, The *Lowlands* England, United Kingdom 17 H14 21 Q8
Wear *River* England, United Kingdom 17 G9 25 K8
Weda, Teluk *Bay* Indonesia 141 O11
Weddell Sea *Sea* Antarctica 64 C7 67 G17
Weed California, USA 51 H12
Weert Netherlands 79 K13
Welland *River* England, United Kingdom 23 O8
Wellesley Islands *Island group* Queensland, Australia 147 L6
Wellingborough England, United Kingdom 23 M10
Wellington New Zealand 144 J12 148 H8
Wellington England, United Kingdom 20 J8
Wells, Lake *Lake* Western Australia, Australia 146 H10
Wells-next-the-Sea England, United Kingdom 23 Q7
Wels Austria 83 O5
Welshpool Wales, United Kingdom 27 O6
Wembere *River* Tanzania 111 N8
Wenzhou China 135 O12
Weser *River* Germany 80 G9
Wessel Islands *Island group* Northern Territory, Australia 147 K4
West Bank *Disputed region* SW Asia 121 M9
West Bromwich England, United Kingdom 22 J9
West Dunbartonshire *Unitary authority* Scotland, United Kingdom 18 L4
West Frisian Islands *Island group* Netherlands 78 I6
West Grand Lake *Lake* Maine, USA 41 Q5
West Ice Shelf *Ice shelf* Antarctica 64 H9
West Indies *Island group* North America 34 66 E10
West Lothian *Unitary authority* Scotland, United Kingdom 18 O5
West Lunga *River* Zambia 110 I13
West Mariana Basin *Undersea feature* Pacific Ocean 143
West Palm Beach Florida, USA 43 O14
West Siberian Plain *Plain* Russian Federation 68 128 I7
West Sussex *County* England, United Kingdom 19 M17
West Virginia *State* USA 43 P2
West Wittering *Beach* England, United Kingdom 32 H13
Wester Ross *Area of Outstanding Natural Beauty* Scotland, United Kingdom 32 E5
Western Australia *State* Australia 146 F9
Western Bug *see* Bug
Western Dvina *River* E Europe 68 95 M9
Western Ghats *Mountain range* India 130 I11
Western Isles *see* Outer Hebrides
Western Isles *Unitary authority* Scotland, United Kingdom 18 E6
Western Sahara *Disputed territory* NW Africa 102 E9
Western Sierra Madre *see* Madre Occidental, Sierra
Westerschelde *Inlet* Netherlands 79 F13
Westmeath *County* Republic of Ireland 19 D13
Westminster, City of *London borough* England, United Kingdom 19 O20
Weston-super-Mare England, United Kingdom 20 J7
Westport New Zealand 148 E8
Westport Republic of Ireland 30 I7
Westray *Island* Scotland, United Kingdom 17 F3 28 L5
Wetar, Pulau *Island* Indonesia 141 N15
Wetaskiwin Alberta, Canada 37 K14
Wetherby England, United Kingdom 25 L13
Wewak Papua New Guinea 147 M1
Wexford Republic of Ireland 31 O13
Wexford *County* Republic of Ireland 19 E15
Weyburn Saskatchewan, Canada 37 N15
Weymouth England, United Kingdom 21 L10
Whalsay *Island* Scotland, United Kingdom 28 P2
Whangarei New Zealand 148 G2
Wharfe *River* England, United Kingdom 17 G10 25 K11
Whernside *Mountain* England, United Kingdom 24 J11
Whitby England, United Kingdom 25 O9
Whitchurch England, United Kingdom 22 H7
White Mountains *Mountain range* Maine/New Hampshire, USA 41 N8
White Nile *River* Sudan 101 105 G14
White Plains New York, USA 41 M12
White River South Dakota, USA 47 M8
White River *River* Arkansas, USA 42 I3
White River *River* Colorado/Utah, USA 49 L3
White River *River* Indiana, USA 45 M14
White River *River* South Dakota, USA 47 M8
White Sands Missile Range *Military base* New Mexico, USA 49 L10
White Sea *Sea* Russian Federation 96 I7 128 G4
White Volta *River* Burkina/Ghana 107 L11
Whitehaven England, United Kingdom 24 G9
Whitehead Northern Ireland, United Kingdom 31 P4
Whitehorse Yukon Territory, Canada 36 I9
Whithorn Scotland, United Kingdom 29 J17
Whitland Wales, United Kingdom 26 J12
Whitley Bay England, United Kingdom 25 M7
Whitney, Mount *Mountain* California, USA 34
Whitstable England, United Kingdom 21 S6
Whyalla South Australia, Australia 147 K13
Wichita Kansas, USA 47 O13
Wichita Falls Texas, USA 49 Q9
Wick Scotland, United Kingdom 28 L7
Wicklow Republic of Ireland 31 O10
Wicklow *County* Republic of Ireland 19 F14
Wicklow Head *Headland* Republic of Ireland 17 D11
Wicklow Mountains *Mountain range* Republic of Ireland 17 D11 31 O10
Wicklow Mountains National Park *National park* Republic of Ireland 32 D10
Widnes England, United Kingdom 22 H5
Wien *see* Vienna
Wiener Neustadt Austria 83 S6
Wiesbaden Germany 81 F13
Wigan England, United Kingdom 24 J17
Wigan *Unitary authority* England, United Kingdom 18 B9
Wight, Isle of *Island* England, United Kingdom 17 G14
Wigston England, United Kingdom 23 M9
Wigton England, United Kingdom 24 H8
Wigtown Scotland, United Kingdom 29 J16
Wigtown Bay *Bay* Scotland, United Kingdom 29 J17
Wilhelm, Mount *Mountain* Papua New Guinea 143
Wilhelmshaven Germany 80 F7
Wilkes Barre Pennsylvania, USA 41 K12
Wilkes Land *Physical region* Antarctica 64 G10
Willemstad Netherlands Antilles 57 O14
Williamsport Pennsylvania, USA 40 J12
Williston North Dakota, USA 47 L4
Willmar Minnesota, USA 44 G6
Wilmington Delaware, USA 41 K14
Wilmington North Carolina, USA 43 Q7
Wilmslow England, United Kingdom 22 I5
Wilson North Carolina, USA 43 R6
Wiltshire *County* England, United Kingdom 19 K17
Winchester England, United Kingdom 21 M8
Wind River *River* Wyoming, USA 46 I8
Wind River Range *Mountain range* Wyoming, USA 46 I8
Windermere *Lake* England, United Kingdom 17 F9 24 H11
Windhoek Namibia 112 H11
Windsor Ontario, Canada 38 I15
Windsor England, United Kingdom 21 O6
Windsor and Maidenhead *Unitary authority* England, United Kingdom 19 L16
Windward Islands *Island group* West Indies 55 57 S12
Windward Passage *Channel* Cuba/Haiti 57 L7
Winisk *River* Ontario, Canada 38 I7
Winnebago, Lake *Lake* Wisconsin, USA 45 K8
Winnemucca Nevada, USA 48 G2
Winnipeg Manitoba, Canada 37 P14
Winnipeg, Lake *Lake* Manitoba, Canada 34 37 O13
Winnipegosis, Lake *Lake* Manitoba, Canada 37 N14
Winona Minnesota, USA 44 I8
Winschoten Netherlands 78 N7
Winston-Salem North Carolina, USA 43 P5
Winterthur Switzerland 82 G8
Wirral *Unitary authority* England, United Kingdom 18 A10
Wisbech England, United Kingdom 23 P8
Wisconsin *State* USA 44 I6
Wisconsin Rapids Wisconsin, USA 44 J7
Wisconsin River *River* Wisconsin, USA 44 J9
Wisłoka *River* Poland 85 N9
Wismar Germany 80 J7
Wista *see* Vistula
Witham England, United Kingdom 21 R4
Witham *River* England, United Kingdom 17 H11 23 O6
Withernsea England, United Kingdom 25 Q14
Witney England, United Kingdom 21 M5
Wittenberg Germany 80 K10
Włocławek Poland 85 L5
Włocławskie, Jezioro *Lake* Poland 85 L5
Wodonga Victoria, Australia 147 N14
Woking England, United Kingdom 21 O7
Wokingham England, United Kingdom 21 N6
Wokingham *Unitary authority* England, United Kingdom 19 L17
Wolds, The *Hill range* England, United Kingdom 17 H10 23 O5
Wolds, The *Hill range* England, United Kingdom 25 N12
Wolf River *River* Wisconsin, USA 45 K6
Wolfsberg Austria 83 Q9
Wolfsburg Germany 80 I9
Wollaston Lake *Lake* Saskatchewan, Canada 37 M11
Wollongong New South Wales, Australia 147 O13
Wolverhampton England, United Kingdom 22 J9
Wolverhampton *Unitary authority* England, United Kingdom 19 N11
Wŏnsan North Korea 135 P6
Woodlark Island *Island* Papua New Guinea 147 P3
Woods, Lake of the *Lake* Manitoba/Ontario/Minnesota, Canada/USA 34 38 F10 44 G2
Woolacombe *Beach* England, United Kingdom 32 E13
Wooler England, United Kingdom 25 K4
Worcester England, United Kingdom 22 J11
Worcester Massachusetts, USA 41 N10
Worcestershire *County* England, United Kingdom 19 K15
Workington England, United Kingdom 24 G9
Worksop England, United Kingdom 23 L5
Worland Wyoming, USA 46 J8
Wörther See *Lake* Austria 83 P9
Worthing England, United Kingdom 21 P9
Wowoni, Pulau *Island* Indonesia 141 M13
Wragby England, United Kingdom 23 N5
Wrangel Island *Island* Russian Federation 65 Q6 129 P2
Wrangell Alaska, USA 36 I11
Wrath, Cape *Headland* Scotland, United Kingdom 17 E4 28 I7
Wrexham Wales, United Kingdom 27 O3
Wrexham *Unitary authority* Wales, United Kingdom 19 J14
Wrocław (Eng. Breslau) Poland 84 J7
Wuhai China 133 M8
Wuhan China 135 M11
Wuppertal Germany 81 E11
Würzburg Germany 81 H13
Wuwei China 134 I7
Wuxi China 135 O10
Wuzhou China 135 L14
Wye *River* England/Wales, United Kingdom 17 F12 22 H12
Wye Valley *Area of Outstanding Natural Beauty* England, United Kingdom 32 F12
Wyndham Western Australia, Australia 146 I6
Wyoming *State* USA 46 I9
Wyre *River* England, United Kingdom 24 I13

Xaafuun, Raas *Cape* Somalia 114 F7
Xai-Xai Mozambique 113 N12
Xaignabouli Laos 138 J9
Xam Nua Laos 138 L9
Xankändi Azerbaijan 99 R14
Xanthi Greece 93 M2
Xi'an China 135 K9
Xiamen China 135 N13
Xiangfan China 135 L10
Xiangkhoang Laos 138 K9
Xiao Hinggan Ling *Mountain range* China 135 N1
Xichang China 134 I12
Xigazê China 132 H13
Xilinhot China 133 P6
Xingu, Rio *River* Brazil 55 60 I8
Xining China 133 L9
Xinjiang Uygur *Region* China 132 G6
Xinyang China 135 M10
Xuwen China 135 K15
Xuzhou China 135 N9

Yafran Libya 103 O6
Yakeshi China 133 P3
Yakima Washington, USA 50 J7
Yakima River *River* Washington, USA 50 J7
Yaku-shima *Island* Japan 137 C16
Yakutsk Russian Federation 129 O8
Yala Thailand 139 I17
Yalong Jiang *River* China 134 H9
Yalta Ukraine 99 K10
Yamagata Japan 136 K8
Yamaguchi Japan 137 D13
Yamal, Poluostrov *Peninsula* Russian Federation 117 128 I6
Yambol Bulgaria 91 M13
Yamoussoukro Ivory Coast 106 J13
Yampa River *River* Colorado, USA 49 L3
Yamuna *River* India 131 L6
Yamzho Yumco *Lake* China 132 I13
Yana *River* Russian Federation 129 N5
Yanbu 'al Bahr Saudi Arabia 122 G9
Yangtze *River* China 117 127 135 K10
Yankton South Dakota, USA 47 O9
Yantai China 135 O7
Yaoundé Cameroon 109 F11
Yap Trench *Undersea feature* Pacific Ocean 143
Yapen, Pulau *Island* Indonesia 141 R11
Yare *River* England, United Kingdom 8 S8 17 I12
Yarmouth Nova Scotia, Canada 39 P13
Yaroslavl' Russian Federation 96 G10 128 F6
Yasothon Thailand 139 L11
Yasuj Iran 123 N7
Yazd Iran 123 O6
Ye Burma 139 G11
Yekaterinburg Russian Federation 128 G8
Yelizavety, Mys *Cape* Russian Federation 129 Q8
Yell *Island* Scotland, United Kingdom 17 G1 28 O1
Yell Sound *Strait* Scotland, United Kingdom 28 O1
Yellow River *River* China 117 127 133 O8 135 L7
Yellow Sea *Sea* Pacific Ocean 127 133 Q7 135 O8
Yellowknife Northwest Territories, Canada 37 L10
Yellowstone Lake *Lake* Wyoming, USA 46 I7
Yellowstone River *River* Montana/Wyoming, USA 46 I6
Yemen *Country* SW Asia 122 J15

Yemen 122-123

1990 • a Arabic • Rial (North Yemen) and dinar (South Yemen) are both legal tender throughout Yemen • 33 • 58 • 15 • 42.5 • 15 • 10000 • Yes • 34 • 2203

Yenisey *River* Mongolia/Russian Federation 68 117 129 K8 127
Yeovil England, United Kingdom 21 K8
Yerevan Armenia 99 Q14
Yeşilırmak *River* Turkey 119 N5
Yevpatoriya Ukraine 98 J9
Yichang China 135 L11
Yichun China 135 P3
Yinchuan China 134 J7
Yining China 132 G6
Yogyakarta Indonesia 140 H15
Yokohama Japan 137 K11 145 G5
Yokosuka Japan 137 K11
Yola Nigeria 107 Q11
Yopal Colombia 58 F6
York England, United Kingdom 25 N12
York Pennsylvania, USA 40 J14
York *Unitary authority* England, United Kingdom 19 L12
York, Cape *Headland* Queensland, Australia 144 G9 143 147 M4
Yorkshire Dales *Physical region* England, United Kingdom 17 G10 25 K10
Yorkshire Dales National Park *National Park* England, United Kingdom 32 F9
Yorkton Saskatchewan, Canada 37 N14
Yos Sudarso, Pulau *Island* Indonesia 141 S14
Yosemite National Park *National Park* California, USA 51 J15
Youghal Republic of Ireland 31 L14
Youngstown Ohio, USA 45 Q10
Yozgat Turkey 119 M6
Ypres *see* Ieper
Ystad Sweden 70 J15
Ystrad Aeron Wales, United Kingdom 27 K10
Ystrad Mynach Wales, United Kingdom 27 O14
Ythan *River* Scotland, United Kingdom 29 N10
Yuan Jiang *River* China 135 K12
Yucatan Basin *Undersea feature* Caribbean Sea 34 55
Yucatan Peninsula *Peninsula* Guatemala/Mexico 55
Yueyang China 135 L11
Yugoslavia *Country* SE Europe 89 M8

Yugoslavia 89

1992 • a Serbo-croat • Yugoslav dinar • 104 • 72 • 15 • 93.3 • 173 • 500 • Yes • 57 • N/A

Yukon *River* Canada/USA 36 F6 145 K3
Yukon Territory *Territory* Canada 36 I8
Yuma Arizona, USA 48 G9
Yumen China 134 H6
Yungay Peru 59 D12
Yushu China 133 K11
Yuzhno-Sakhalinsk Russian Federation 129 R10
Yverdon Switzerland 82 D11

Z

Zaanstad Netherlands 78 I9
Zacapa Guatemala 56 B8
Zacatecas Mexico 53 L9
Zadar Croatia 88 H6
Zagreb Croatia 88 I2
Zagros Mountains *Mountain range* Iran 68 117 123 M6 127
Zahedan Iran 123 Q8
Zahlé Lebanon 121 M6
Zaječar Serbia, Yugoslavia 89 P7
Zakynthos Greece 92 G10
Zakynthos *Island* Greece 92 G10
Zala *River* Hungary 84 J14
Zalaegerszeg Hungary 84 J14
Zalantun China 133 Q3
Zambezi Zambia 110 H13
Zambezi *River* Southern Africa 101 110 I15 113 M7 114 C10
Zambia *Country* Southern Africa 110 I14

Zambia 110-111

1964 • a English • Zambian kwacha • 12 • 40 • 14 • 75.1 • 17 • 10000 • Yes • 43 • 1931

Zamboanga Philippines 141 M8
Zamora Spain 74 I6
Zamora de Hidalgo Mexico 53 L11
Zanesville Ohio, USA 45 P12
Zanjan Iran 123 M3
Zanzibar Tanzania 111 Q9
Zanzibar *Island* Tanzania 101 111 Q8
Zaozhuang China 135 N9
Zapala Argentina 63 H13
Zaporizhzhya Ukraine 99 K7
Zarafshon Uzbekistan 125 K6
Zaragoza (Eng. Saragossa) Spain 75 N6
Zaria Nigeria 107 O10
Zaysan, Ozero *Lake* Kazakhstan 128 I12
Zealand *Island* Denmark 70 J16
Zeebrugge Belgium 79 D13
Zell am See Austria 83 N8
Zenica Bosnia and Herzegovina 89 K6
Zeravshan *River* Tajikistan/Uzbekistan 125 L7
Zeya Reservoir *Reservoir* Russian Federation 129 O10
Zhambyl Kazakhstan 128 G13
Zhanjiang China 135 L15
Zhengzhou China 135 M9

Zhezkazgan Kazakhstan 128 G11
Zhlobin Belarus 95 N13
Zhodzina Belarus 95 L11
Zhongshan *Chinese research station* Antarctica 64 G8
Zhytomyr Ukraine 98 H4
Zibo China 135 N8
Zielona Góra Poland 84 I6
Zigong China 134 J11
Ziguinchor Senegal 106 F9
Žilina Slovakia 85 L10
Zillertaler Alpen *Mountain range* Austria/Italy 83 L9
Zimbabwe *Country* Southern Africa 113 L9

Zimbabwe 113

1980 • a English • Zimbabwe dollar • 30 • 44 • 15 • 90.9 • 29 • 10000 • Yes • 32 • 1985

Zinave *National Park* Mozambique 113 N10
Zinder Niger 107 P9
Zinjibar Yemen 122 I16
Žirje *Island* Croatia 88 H7
Zlatni Pyasŭtsi Bulgaria 91 O11
Zoetermeer Netherlands 78 H10
Zomba Malawi 111 O15
Zonguldak Turkey 119 K4
Zouérat Mauritania 106 H4
Zrenjanin Serbia, Yugoslavia 89 N4
Zug Switzerland 82 G9
Zunyi China 134 J12
Zürich (Eng. Zurich) Switzerland 82 G9
Zurich, Lake *Lake* Switzerland 82 G9
Zutphen Netherlands 78 L10
Zvornik Bosnia and Herzegovina 89 L6
Zwedru Liberia 106 I13
Zwickau Germany 81 K12
Zwolle Netherlands 78 L9

NORTH AMERICA

CANADA
PAGES 36-39

UNITED STATES OF AMERICA
PAGES 40-51

MEXICO
PAGES 52-53

CENTRAL AND SOUTH AMERICA

ANTIGUA & BARBUDA
PAGES 56-57

BAHAMAS
PAGES 56-57

BARBADOS
PAGES 56-57

BELIZE
PAGES 56-57

COSTA RICA
PAGES 56-57

JAMAICA
PAGES 56-57

NICARAGUA
PAGES 56-57

PANAMA
PAGES 56-57

ST. KITTS & NEVIS
PAGES 56-57

ST. LUCIA
PAGES 56-57

ST. VINCENT & THE GRENADINES
PAGES 56-57

TRINIDAD & TOBAGO
PAGES 56-57

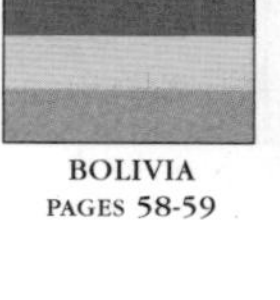
BOLIVIA
PAGES 58-59

CHILE
PAGES 62-63

PARAGUAY
PAGES 62-63

URUGUAY
PAGES 62-63

THE ATLANTIC OCEAN

CAPE VERDE
PAGES 66-67

ICELAND
PAGES 66-67

EUROPE

DENMARK
PAGES 70-71

FINLAND
PAGES 70-71

NORWAY
PAGES 70-71

BELGIUM
PAGES 78-79

LUXEMBOURG
PAGES 78-79

NETHERLANDS
PAGES 78-79

GERMANY
PAGES 80-81

AUSTRIA
PAGES 82-83

LIECHTENSTEIN
PAGES 82-83

SLOVENIA
PAGES 82-83

SWITZERLAND
PAGES 82-83

ALBANIA
PAGES 88-89

BOSNIA & HERZEGOVINA
PAGES 88-89

CROATIA
PAGES 88-89

MACEDONIA
PAGES 88-89

YUGOSLAVIA
PAGES 88-89

BULGARIA
PAGES 90-91

ROMANIA
PAGES 90-91

GREECE
PAGES 92-93

MOLDOVA
PAGES 98-99

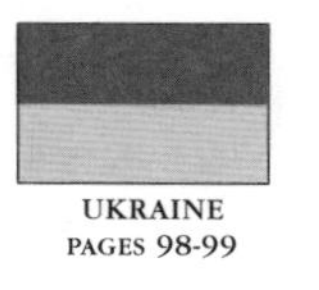
UKRAINE
PAGES 98-99

AFRICA

ALGERIA
PAGES 102-103

LIBYA
PAGES 102-103

MOROCCO
PAGES 102-103

TUNISIA
PAGES 102-103

WESTERN SAHARA
PAGES 102-103

DJIBOUTI
PAGES 104-105

GHANA
PAGES 106-107

GUINEA
PAGES 106-107

GUINEA-BISSAU
PAGES 106-107

IVORY COAST
PAGES 106-107

LIBERIA
PAGES 106-107

MALI
PAGES 106-107

MAURITANIA
PAGES 106-107

NIGER
PAGES 106-107

DEM. REP. CONGO (ZAIRE)
PAGES 108-109

EQUATORIAL GUINEA
PAGES 108-109

GABON
PAGES 108-109

SAO TOME & PRINCIPE
PAGES 108-109

BURUNDI
PAGES 110-111

KENYA
PAGES 110-111

MALAWI
PAGES 110-111

RWANDA
PAGES 110-111

SOUTH AFRICA
PAGES 112-113

SWAZILAND
PAGES 112-113

ZIMBABWE
PAGES 112-113

THE INDIAN OCEAN

COMOROS
PAGES 114-115

MADAGASCAR
PAGES 114-115

MALDIVES
PAGES 114-115

MAURITIUS
PAGES 114-115

SEYCHELLES
PAGES 114-115

IRAN
PAGES 122-123

KUWAIT
PAGES 122-123

OMAN
PAGES 122-123

QATAR
PAGES 122-123

SAUDI ARABIA
PAGES 122-123

UNITED ARAB EMIRATES
PAGES 122-123

YEMEN
PAGES 122-123

AFGHANISTAN
PAGES 124-125

PAKISTAN
PAGES 130-131

NEPAL
PAGES 130-131

SRI LANKA
PAGES 130-131

CHINA
PAGES 132-135

MONGOLIA
PAGES 132-133

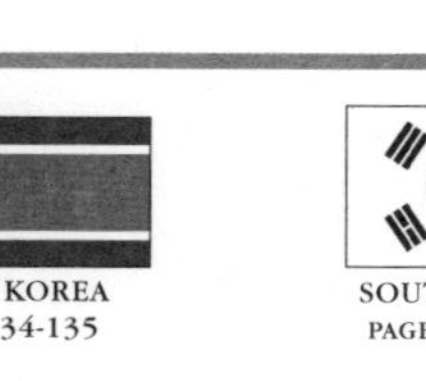
NORTH KOREA
PAGES 134-135

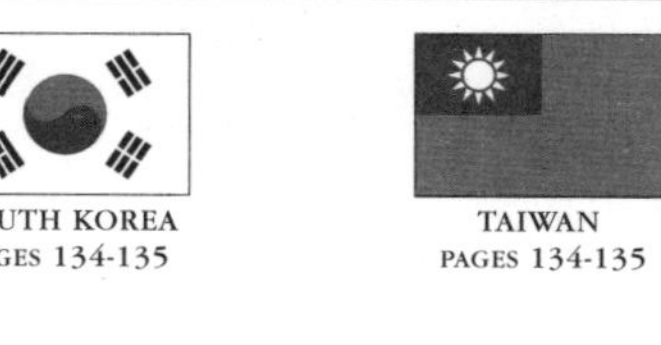
SOUTH KOREA
PAGES 134-135

TAIWAN
PAGES 134-135

BRUNEI
PAGES 140-141

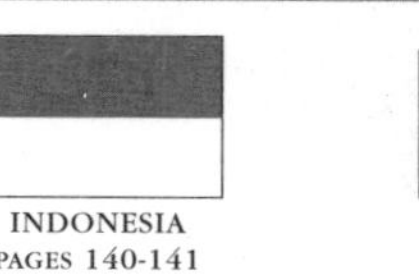
INDONESIA
PAGES 140-141

PHILIPPINES
PAGES 140-141

AUSTRALASIA AND OCEANIA

FIJI
PAGES 144-145

KIRIBATI
PAGES 144-145

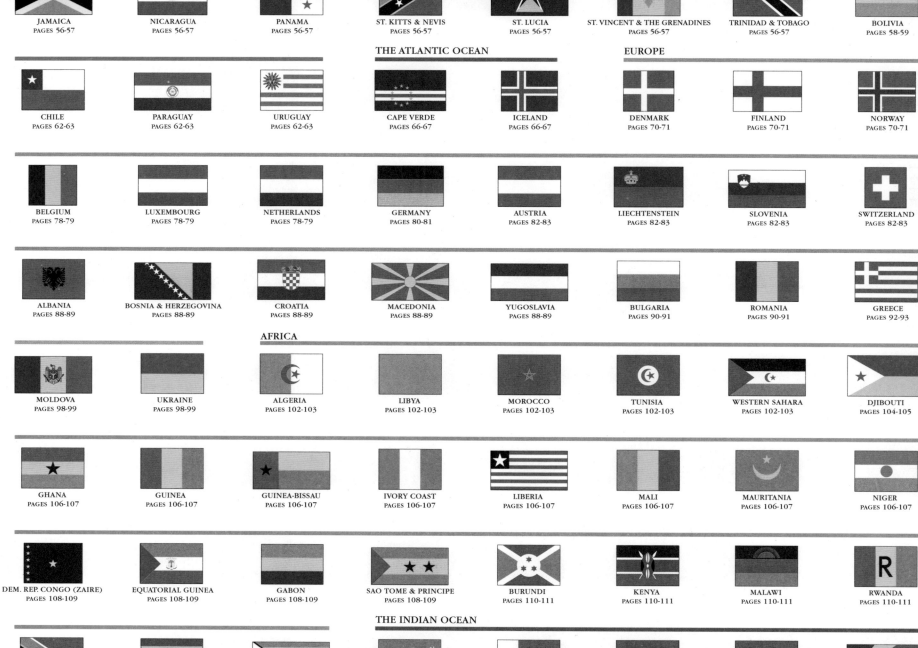

MARSHALL ISLANDS
PAGES 144-145

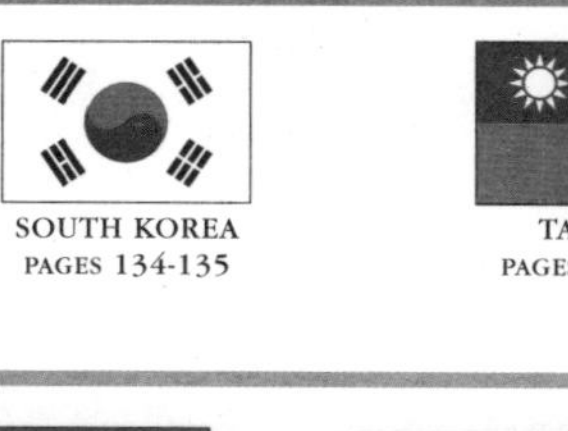
MICRONESIA
PAGES 144-145

NAURU
PAGES 144-145

Notes